AF701477

International Humanitarian Action

Hans-Joachim Heintze • Pierre Thielbörger
Editors

International Humanitarian Action

NOHA Textbook

Assisted by Robin Ramsahye

Springer

Editors
Hans-Joachim Heintze
Institute for International Law of Peace and Armed Conflict
Ruhr-University Bochum
Bochum, Germany

Pierre Thielbörger
Institute for International Law of Peace and Armed Conflict
Ruhr-University Bochum
Bochum, Germany

ISBN 978-3-319-14453-5 ISBN 978-3-319-14454-2 (eBook)
DOI 10.1007/978-3-319-14454-2

Library of Congress Control Number: 2017954402

© Springer International Publishing AG 2018
This work is subject to copyright. All rights are reserved by the Publisher, whether the whole or part of the material is concerned, specifically the rights of translation, reprinting, reuse of illustrations, recitation, broadcasting, reproduction on microfilms or in any other physical way, and transmission or information storage and retrieval, electronic adaptation, computer software, or by similar or dissimilar methodology now known or hereafter developed.
The use of general descriptive names, registered names, trademarks, service marks, etc. in this publication does not imply, even in the absence of a specific statement, that such names are exempt from the relevant protective laws and regulations and therefore free for general use.
The publisher, the authors and the editors are safe to assume that the advice and information in this book are believed to be true and accurate at the date of publication. Neither the publisher nor the authors or the editors give a warranty, express or implied, with respect to the material contained herein or for any errors or omissions that may have been made. The publisher remains neutral with regard to jurisdictional claims in published maps and institutional affiliations.

Printed on acid-free paper

This Springer imprint is published by Springer Nature
The registered company is Springer International Publishing AG
The registered company address is: Gewerbestrasse 11, 6330 Cham, Switzerland

Preface

NOHA (The Network on Humanitarian Action) is an international association of 12 European universities and five global partner universities. The aim of NOHA is to enhance professionalism in the humanitarian sector through education and training, research and publications, and a variety of other projects. The NOHA Joint Master's Programme in International Humanitarian Action lies at the centre of NOHA's activities. It is managed and executed by more than 150 academics from a range of disciplines. The process involves anthropologists, lawyers, logisticians, managers, medical experts, political scientists and sociologists coordinating and constantly refining a unique programme on humanitarian action, a subject that has not been taught at universities for all too long. Central to NOHA's growth and evolution is a core set of principles, shared by universities and humanitarian organisations the world over. It includes values such as academic rigour, shared learning, respect for peer institutions and humility, serving as the base of a cohesive and coherent network with common principles and values. Founded in 1993, NOHA today brings together over 3000 graduates working all around the world. It publishes the International Journal of International Humanitarian Action (JIHA) and organises international conferences with renowned academics and practitioners. The NOHA programme's first semester comprises the same five modules in all NOHA universities currently offering this degree. An equal level of knowledge after the first term is a precondition for the exchange of students among the NOHA universities in the second term. With this new textbook, we aim to strengthen the coherence of our first semester curriculum and to provide all students with a solid base of knowledge from the core modules of anthropology, law, management, public health and world politics. We believe that only a solid understanding of these five disciplines, and related fields, will enable our graduates to advance in their studies and eventually become professional humanitarian aid workers.

First, students must seek to understand in which governance structures the different humanitarian actors operate and what interests motivate their actions. This involves embedding the humanitarian education in international relations theory and also understanding the changing nature of conflicts, the basic structures of aid governance, as well as acquiring knowledge of humanitarian principles and the need for humanitarian professionalism (Part I: World Politics).

Second, students must understand the different legal frameworks in which States and humanitarian organisations operate. A solid legal education is key for work at humanitarian organisations both at headquarters and in the field. Students must be familiar with the applicable law, in particular public international law, international humanitarian law, international criminal law, human rights law, disaster response law, as well as migration and refugee law (Part II: International Law).

The third element of the NOHA education in the first term is public health. Divided into a larger number of chapters in order to address the variety of relevant questions individually, the authors discuss a variety of specific health-related elements of humanitarian action.

This includes basic demographic and epidemiological concepts, the coordination of medical aid, the recognition of diseases and injuries and a basic introduction to their treatment.

The part then turns to specific issues of particular relevance for the humanitarian sector, such as HIV/Aids, water and sanitation, as well as mental health problems (Part III: Public Health).

Fourth, students are introduced to a variety of different anthropological and ethnological perspectives on and within humanitarian action. They learn about the anthropology of war and look into different current humanitarian issues (such as forced migration and refugee settings) from an anthropological point of view (Part IV: Anthropology).

Finally, the fifth part addresses questions surrounding the management of humanitarian action. Students are introduced to concepts of project management and programming, logistics, security management, human resource management, as well as financial management in the humanitarian sector (Part V: Management).

Editing a textbook like this one, with chapters from more than 20 different authors, is a challenging exercise. We are very thankful to every author who has contributed to it. We are also very thankful to Robin Ramsahye and Maximilian Bertamini for their relentless efforts and their hard work. We hope that this book, uniting a large number of NOHA scholars and practitioners, will be highly useful to all students of our Joint Master's Programme and to anyone with an interest in understanding the numerous and interlinked facets of humanitarian action.

Bochum, Germany — Hans-Joachim Heintze
Bochum, Germany — Pierre Thielbörger
May 2017

Contents

Part I
World Politics

The Changing Context of Humanitarian Action: Key Challenges and Issues

Cristina Churruca-Muguruza

1 Introduction

Peace, stability and sustainable economic growth seem unachievable goals in many places of the world today. As the United Nations (UN) Secretary General acknowledges in his landmark report 'One Humanity: Shared Responsibility' for the World Humanitarian Summit (WHS), we are approaching a point in history in which there is a need 'to agree that we can and must do better to end conflict, alleviate suffering and reduce risk and vulnerability'.[1]

The inability to resolve protracted crises and intractable conflicts and the convergence of global trends such as climate change, migration and population growth, urbanisation, growing inequalities and resource scarcity are exacerbating people's vulnerability. At the same time, the international aid system has not kept pace with the impact of these challenges on the caseloads of humanitarian agencies and their operational environments. The recognition of the need to adapt to a changing humanitarian context and make humanitarian action more effective and inclusive to respond to the needs of people in crises led UN Secretary General Ban Ki-Moon in 2013 to convene the first ever WHS in Istanbul in May 2016.[2]

[1]UN General Assembly (2016a).

[2]UN Secretary General Ban Ki-Moon took stock of these changes in his address to the 66th General Assembly, '*We the Peoples*', on 21 September 2011. One of the actions foreseen for building a safer and more secure world was to build a more global, accountable and robust humanitarian system by, among other specific measures, '*convening a world humanitarian summit to help share knowledge and establish common best practices among the wide spectrum of organisations involved in humanitarian action*' (UNSG 2011, p. 8).

C. Churruca-Muguruza (✉)
University of Deusto, Bilbao, Spain
e-mail: cristina.churruca@deusto.es

© Springer International Publishing AG 2018
H.-J. Heintze, P. Thielbörger (eds.), *International Humanitarian Action*,
DOI 10.1007/978-3-319-14454-2_1

In this context, the aim of this chapter is to provide an overview of the main external (global trends and current armed violence and conflict) and internal challenges facing humanitarian action and the key issues in its agenda. Most have been the subject of broad discussion under the four themes that were selected for the regional and expert consultations, which preceded the humanitarian summit (humanitarian effectiveness, reducing vulnerability and managing risk, transformation through innovation and serving the needs of people in conflict). Others unfolded over the years in the process of policy discussions, regarding the meaning and understanding of humanitarian action and its limits and links with development and peacebuilding.[3]

2 The Confluence of Global Trends

Several reports, studies and policy papers have acknowledged the currents of change that are transforming the foundations of the humanitarian domain, and the world, in unprecedented ways. Different global issues whose effects have not been sufficiently studied contribute to the risk of major large-scale and complex crises that will increase the suffering of vulnerable populations. Humanitarian stakeholders are greatly concerned about the impact that these issues may have on the caseloads of humanitarian agencies and their operational environments.[4] The following long-term problems should be mentioned:

- *Climate change, environmental degradation and fragility*: climate change results in more frequent and extreme-weather events, such as floods, tropical storms and droughts with devastating impacts in areas with fragile ecological systems and large population concentrations.
- *Population growth and migration*: the global population is estimated to grow to over 8 billion by 2025, and migration is and will continue to be one of the biggest challenges both within and across borders.
- *Rapid and unplanned urbanisation, rising youth population and social discontent*: the urban population is expected to double in Asia and increase by 150% in Africa from today to 2050. The large degree of urbanisation will fuel massive social inequities and break up the social fabric, especially in times of conflict.

[3]This chapter draws on research conducted for a study commissioned to the author by the European Union Directorate-General for External Policies of the Union at the request of the European Parliament's Committee on Development (DEVE) to prepare a common European position for the World Humanitarian summit: Churruca Muguruza (2015), http://www.europarl.europa.eu/thinktank/en/document.html?reference=EXPO_STU(2015)549048.

[4]See: Borton (2009); Cairns (2012); CaLP (2013); EUPRHA (2013), http://www.euprha.org/library; Gelsdorf (2010); Global Humanitarian Assistance (2014), available (together with older as well as the most recent reports) at: www.globalhumanitarianassistance.org/reports/; OCHA (2014).

- *Extreme poverty and inequality*: these ongoing issues leave whole communities and households in an almost irreversibly devastating state of vulnerability and need.
- *Increased resource scarcity and food crises*: water scarcity and energy demand represent major threats, both from a humanitarian and a geopolitical point of view.
- *Health pandemics and infectious diseases*: the impacts of health disasters amplify the pressures on weak and fragile States.

Recurring disasters often lead to chronic poverty. Disasters destroy material goods (homes, schools, infrastructure, livestock and seeds) and negatively impact social capital (for example, by decreasing access to education, eroding social norms and values and contributing to incentives for longer-term migration). As a result, a vicious cycle ensues: chronic poverty makes it difficult to take measures necessary to mitigate effects of disasters. Where such disasters occur, they may cripple resources and increase poverty. The financial and economic crisis that began in 2007, for example, has lowered the standards of living of many and curtailed critical safety nets. In addition, austerity measures and shrinking foreign aid budgets in the developed world have reduced overall humanitarian resources required to cope with the increasing needs of ever more vulnerable populations.

Moreover, the confluence of several of the above-mentioned problematic global trends exacerbates existing problems. For example, climate change may have implications for energy, food and water shortages and increase what Betts has referred to as the number of so-called survival migrants.[5] Other issues exacerbate the vulnerability of people, scupper years of development cooperation and peacebuilding and can increase the risk of major conflict.[6] Such difficulties include growing migration, increasing inequality, social and demographic changes (ageing population in Western countries and exponential growth of the younger population in developing countries with unmet demands), rapid urbanisation and ensuing lack of access to service, as well as crime and disease, which are especially prone to occur in urban settlements.

3 Change and Continuity in Armed Conflict and Other Forms of Violence

The last three decades have witnessed both continuity and change in global dynamics of conflict and armed violence. One in every four people on the planet, a total of more than 1.5 billion people, lives in fragile areas affected by conflict or

[5]Betts (2010), pp. 361–382.

[6]OECD (2015).

high levels of organised crime and (urban) violence.[7] Current international conflictivity includes various forms of violence that often coexist and feed each other, challenging compartmentalised approaches to armed violence. Despite a downward trend in the number of conflicts and violent deaths, conflict has not disappeared.

Although the era of interstate armed conflict seems to have come to an end, internal conflicts persist. After declining for much of the late 1990s and early 2000s, the number of civil wars or internal conflicts of high intensity almost tripled, from 4 in 2007 to 11 in 2014.[8] New forms of violence, committed by international terrorist networks and transnational criminal organisations, further complicate the situation, challenging States, especially fragile ones, and systems of global governance.[9]

Most violent deaths occur in States suffering from endemic and prolonged violence concentrated in the more densely populated urban areas and among the poorest, most marginalised and vulnerable social groups, particularly young people. Studies indicate that it is the aggregation of risk that enhances the likelihood and intensity of urban violence. Some predictions show how risks are aggravated by the socio-spatial characteristics of cities such as their heterogeneity, inability to absorb surplus low-skill labour, uneven provision of services and deep inequalities.[10] Savage and Muggha note that 'the degradation of complex systems of service delivery and taxation due to rapid urban expansion leads to what are often referred to as "cascading" problems that over-ride municipal capacities'.[11]

Some cities (Ciudad Juárez, Mexico; Medellin, Colombia; Rio de Janeiro, Brazil; Karachi, Pakistan; and Tegucigalpa, Honduras, among others) are experiencing levels of bloodshed and disturbances that have been termed 'other situations of violence'[12] (OSV), which, by the high numbers of casualties and wounded and the enormity of displaced refugee populations, share many of the characteristics of conventional armed conflict.[13] This kind of urban violence is present all over the world from Latin America to sub-Saharan Africa, Asia and the Middle East.

Civilians, either as targeted or as accidental victims of the use of force, make up the largest number of casualties of conflict. Most of these conflicts are characterised by *shocking levels of brutality and gross disregard for human life and dignity*.[14] Armed conflict has devastating effects on civilians, whether as the direct victims of

---

[7]World Bank (2011), p. 2.

[8]See, von Seidel et al. (2014).

[9]Ibáñez Muñoz and Sánchez Aviles (2015); Stepanova (2010), http://www.sipri.org/yearbook/2010/02. World Bank (2011), p. 2.

[10]Muggha (2012).

[11]Savage and Muggah (2012), http://sites.tufts.edu/jha/archives/1524.

[12]*Ibid.*

[13]*Ibid.*

[14]See, UN Security Council (2015).

death, torture, kidnapping, physical injury, sexual violence, forced displacement and separation of families and damage of property or, as indirect victims, through conflict-induced increases in disease, hunger and malnutrition. Control over the civilian population is often one of the things at stake in a conflict.[15]

Direct and deliberate attacks on schools, hospitals and humanitarian workers, as well as the failure to comply with the most elementary norms of international humanitarian law, (IHL) are still the norm. Forced displacement has reached the highest level since World War II, causing an unprecedented migration crisis. It is estimated that by the end of 2015, 61 million people worldwide had been forcibly displaced as a result of persecution, conflict, generalised violence or human rights violations: more specifically, these 61 million consist of 20.2 million refugees displaced outside the borders of their home States, 40.8 million internally displaced people (IDPs) and 1.8 million asylum seekers, half of whom are women.[16]

Most of today's conflicts take on an international dimension linked to factors such as population displacements due to violence, trafficking in weapons and resources, support from neighbouring countries for one of the belligerents or participation of foreign fighters. Regionalisation, internationalisation and transnationalisation tend to make conflicts more lethal and long-lasting. This is one, but not the only, reason for the increasing complexity and fragmentation of contemporary conflicts. The increasing presence of violent extremist groups in conflict areas, with little or no interest in reaching political agreements, drives up the presence of organised crime and terrorist groups with transnational connections. Organised crime depends on ongoing conflict to continue extracting profit from operations in illegal markets. Criminals have thus no interest in contributing to ending conflict. Mark Duffield believes that these new forms of autonomy, resistance and organised violence, composed of non-State actors and private actors, are the expression of a new security scenario defined by what he calls 'network war'.[17] The multitude of actors with a stake in the violent clashes reflects that armed conflict has ceased to solely be a State activity.

As a consequence of these trends, the international community is in constant crisis management. Almost two-thirds of United Nations peacekeepers and almost 90% of personnel in United Nations special political missions are working in or on countries experiencing high-intensity conflict.[18] During the last decade, over 80% of humanitarian funding has gone towards saving lives in conflict settings.[19] The 2011 World Development Report highlighted to what degree violence has become a

[15] *Ibid.*

[16] UN General Assembly (2016c).

[17] Duffield (2002), pp. 153–166.

[18] UN General Assembly (2016a).

[19] At the end of 2015, each of the 10 largest consolidated humanitarian appeals involved situations of armed conflict. At the beginning of 2016, and throughout that year, the world had to deal with four L3 (level 3) disasters, the highest UN categorisation of crises: South Sudan, Syria, Iraq and Yemen.

development problem. The report noted the changing patterns of violence, which is becoming less structured around notions of civil war and conflict and more focused around criminal violence, terrorism and civil unrest. New poverty data reveals that poverty is declining in many parts of the world, whereas countries affected by violence are lagging behind in this regard. No conflict-affected State has achieved a single Millennium Development Goal as of yet.[20] The Global Peace Index estimates the economic impact of containing or dealing with the consequences of violence and conflict in 2015 to stand at $13.6 trillion, or 13.3% of the global economy.[21] This is equivalent to the combined economies of Brazil, Canada, France, Germany, Spain and the United Kingdom.

4 Protection at the Centre of Humanitarian Action

The increasing scale and severity of human suffering in some regions and the insufficient funds available to counter it (6% including relief coordination and support services with the majority of funds benefiting coordination and support services) make a case for according protection a higher priority in humanitarian action.[22] In this vein, the Inter-Agency Standing Committee Principals adopted a statement on 17 December 2013, which affirms that

> protection of all persons affected and at risk must inform humanitarian decision-making and response, including engagement with States and non-state parties to conflict. It must be central to our preparedness efforts, as part of immediate and life-saving activities, and throughout the duration of humanitarian response and beyond.[23]

The statement complements and reinforces the Rights Up Front initiative, which aims to strengthen United Nations action in protecting people from serious violations of international human rights law (HRL) and IHL.

A central component of protection is to understand the different rights and needs of specific vulnerable groups (such as women, children, displaced persons, migrants, refugees and those with disabilities). These groups are often neglected in the assessment, preparedness, design and delivery of humanitarian relief, making them *invisible* to relief operations. With the adoption of the 2030 Agenda for Sustainable Development, member States committed to leaving no one behind, including vulnerable people, such as IDPs and refugees, and those living in areas affected by complex humanitarian emergencies.[24] Protection and assistance of IDPs

[20] World Bank (2011), p. 4.

[21] Institute for Economics and Peace (2016), p. 3.

[22] European Parliament Directorate-General for External Policies, Policy Department (2015), p. 21.

[23] Inter-Agency Standing Committee Principals, The Centrality of Protection in Humanitarian Action, 17 December 2013, http://interagencystandingcommittee.org/sites/default/files/centrality_of_protection_in_humanitarian_action_statement_by_iasc_princi.pdf.

[24] UN General Assembly (2015).

is a matter of growing concern. In the absence of solutions to their plight, their number keeps rising. Women and girls are also disproportionately affected by crisis and exposed to gendered risks and vulnerabilities. Gender-based violence in some crisis settings affects more than 70% of women. It is a human rights, protection and health issue, which is exacerbated in times of conflict, disaster and displacement.

Obtaining and maintaining humanitarian access to populations affected by conflict has been a constant challenge since the birth of modern humanitarianism. Access plays a key role in the protection of civilians and is a litmus test for effective humanitarian operations. Yet, in today's reality, many humanitarian organisations struggle daily to gain access to people in need. In Syria, the combination of extraordinary levels of displacement, both as a survival strategy and as a tool of sectarian cleansing with the high levels of deliberate siege or protracted entrapment of civilians, have posed a strategic test to effective humanitarian operations.[25]

The increasing scale and severity of attacks against civilians in current conflicts also calls for greater respect of international laws that govern the protection of civilians. As the International Committee of the Red Cross (ICRC) recognises, 'the general lack of protection in crises affecting civilians caught up in armed conflict and other situations of violence is due, not to an inadequate legal framework, but to poor compliance'.[26] Parties to a conflict bear the primary responsibility for the safety and well-being of people in areas under their control. Their compliance with their obligations under IHL and HRL is paramount to ensuring the protection of people affected by conflict.

5 Humanitarian Implications of Migration Flows

Large movements of refugees and migrants are not a new phenomenon, but the current scale of forced displacement is different from earlier crises. Some countries have seemed ill-prepared and unwilling to receive large movements of people, causing internal tensions, stringent border restrictions and limited access to asylum. People remain displaced for ever longer periods of time in the absence of solutions, yet the response to the refugee crisis focuses almost exclusively on providing humanitarian assistance. This has put an enormous strain on not only the people displaced but also the countries and communities receiving them.[27]

According to the United Nations Population Division, the number of international migrants has soared from 173 million to 244 million over the past 15 years.[28] This figure is likely to continue to rise.

[25]Slim and Trombetta (2014), p. 45.

[26]ICRC (2012), p. 7.

[27]UN General Assembly (2016b).

[28]UN Department of Economic and Social Affairs, Population Division (2015).

Beyond numbers, displacement and migration patterns have changed significantly in recent years. Increasing numbers of migrants are crossing international borders in search of protection and a better life. Following the Arab Spring, the Mediterranean region has been the theatre where irregular migration has gained the largest visibility due to the ever more dangerous trajectories used and the high number of migrant deaths.[29] Between 1998 and 2015, more than 22,000 persons are documented to have died in attempting to migrate to the European Union. The conditions leading to this death toll have become an issue of humanitarian concern.[30] Furthermore, even before crossing the European border, whether by sea or by land, migrants are often exposed to serious risks of abuse and exploitation en route, including by smugglers. This is particularly true for women and girls who are often stranded in transit countries where they may face sexually based violence.

The challenges regarding border management and irregular migration are neither new nor unique to the European Union. However, the trend in the number of migrants coming to the region continues to increase and reaches far beyond the numbers of refugees and asylum seekers. Migrant flows are mixed, meaning economic migrants travel the same routes as asylum seekers and refugees. The humanitarian implications of these mixed flows include the need to decrease or prevent deaths of migrants on their way to Europe, help families to know the fate of missing relatives and identify and process asylum seekers in order to protect refugees and their rights.[31] Other concerns are the mistreatment of migrants at the borders, including practices that infringe their liberty and security, and detention regimes on both sides of the European Union borders that fail to adequately respect minimum human rights standards.

6 Demanding a Paradigm Shift: From Managing Crisis to Managing Risk

Humanitarian organisations are more and more frequently faced with situations where populations come under different layers of pressure due to a combination of trends and factors (demographic, economic, environmental degradation, climate change, violence, chronic poverty), which increase their vulnerability. Humanitarian needs are on the rise because of an increase in the incidence of natural disasters and the inability to resolve protracted crises and complex political emergencies

[29]The majority of these migrants set sail from Libya and are either Syrians or Sub-Saharan Africans, especially from Eritrea, Somalia and Ethiopia. See, MHub (2015), http://www.mixedmigrationhub.org/wp-content/uploads/2015/11/Conditions-and-Risks-in-Mixed-Migration-in-North-East-Africa.pdf.

[30]International Organization for Migration (IOM) (2015), http://missingmigrants.iom.int/latest-global-figures; Brian and Laczko (2014).

[31]The Overseas Development Institute (ODI) (2015), p. 15.

caused by armed conflict. In turn, disasters and conflict are entwined in different ways. Violent conflict causes and aggravates social vulnerability and conflict, and complex political emergencies continue to exacerbate natural disasters. There is a wide recognition that the humanitarian system is not currently optimally set up to help people and governments manage current global trends in order to limit unnecessary loss of life and suffering, better protect livelihoods and in the long term reduce the need for humanitarian assistance.[32]

Unresolved protracted political emergencies and chronic vulnerability make it difficult to take appropriate measures to mitigate disaster effects and therefore heighten the possibility of new disasters happening. It is a vicious cycle, which demands that disaster risk reduction and disaster risk management are mainstreamed not only in the humanitarian but also in the development sectors. In addition, chronic vulnerability challenges the humanitarian system in a critical way, whereby a humanitarian crisis context becomes indistinguishable from a transitional period or a development era. It fact, it is not the context but the actors' approach that differs. Understanding chronic vulnerability and preventing slow-onset emergencies requires humanitarian and development actors to work together more collaboratively.[33] A recurrent example is the response of the international community and affected countries to the crises in the Horn of Africa and the Sahel since 2011, which has brought significant progress to both regions. Solutions to other chronic problems remain elusive. For example, expanding slum populations have raised concerns about the abilities of cities to cope with and adapt to further population influx.

The primordial importance of prevention (preventing a crisis from breaking out) and preparedness (ensuring that an individual, a household, a country or a region is ready to manage the effects of such crisis) has shifted to the centre of discussions at the 2016 WHS. Humanitarian actors stand at the crossroads of a policy shift from a culture of reaction to a culture of prevention through disaster risk reduction and disaster risk management. This policy shift, underlying the WHS initiative, came together in the Hyogo Framework for Action 2005–2015. The United Nations Office for the Coordination of Humanitarian Affairs' (OCHA's) flagship report Saving Lives Today and Tomorrow: Managing the Risk of Humanitarian Crises, which was launched in New York on 31 March 2014, calls for a fundamental shift in the way that humanitarian and development actors operate. It suggests that aid groups and donors begin to shift from responding to crises in a purely reactive manner and instead adopt an approach that proactively anticipates and prevents crises through effective risk management. Such an approach is urgently needed in a context of a chronically underfunded global humanitarian budget.

---

[32]There is evidence of the rising impact disasters have had over the past 30 years: over 3.3 million people killed; 50% of deaths occurred in poverty-stricken countries, but they accounted for only 9% of disasters. The economic cost of disasters has tripled. Disasters also push people into poverty. Poverty levels after the Haiti 2010 earthquake and Djibouti 2011 drought returned to early 2001–2003 levels. See, OCHA (2014).

[33]Rubin (2006).

7 A Common Understanding of Humanitarian Action and Its Limits?

Humanitarian aid is by definition a response to man-made crises and natural disasters, a fundamental expression of the universal value of solidarity between people. Working towards solidarity is, in theory, the core function of humanitarians.

What differentiates humanitarian aid from any other type of aid is that it is provided according to the humanitarian principles of humanity, neutrality, impartiality and independence, although organisations understand their mission differently depending on their mandate and the context in which they operate. On one end of the spectrum, we find the ICRC *whose exclusively humanitarian mission is to protect the lives and dignity of victims of armed conflict and other situations of violence and to provide them with assistance.*[34] On the other, many organisations, such as Save the Children, are inspired by the idea that *integrated interventions can achieve much more than saving lives by promoting overall regional stability,*[35] for which the humanitarian system should *place emphasis on seeking opportunities to transform and rebuild communities, using their own capacity and based on their own priorities and aspirations.*[36]

The main conceptual challenge for humanitarian actors is to clarify the different types of humanitarian action and decide to which extent aid can and should be principled on the strategic objective to transform communities and societies for the better. It might be advisable to differentiate between a humanitarian action based on humanitarian principles in situations of armed conflict and other situations of violence and humanitarian action as emergency relief or early recovery assistance, aiming at *supporting communities to overcome crises and protect and promote human rights.*[37] In this vein, humanitarian actors must examine what results humanitarians can deliver, in which capacities the sector should invest and which responsibilities they should hand over to other actors.

The humanitarian sector must be realistic as to what it can achieve and its added value. Issues of resilience, disaster risk reduction, preparedness, prevention and risk management are not the core task of humanitarians alone, although humanitarians are more and more called upon to shoulder the lion's share of responsibility. Neither can humanitarians address root causes of poverty and vulnerability. Therefore, collaboration with development actors is a must. On the other hand, there is an underlying tension between needs-based and rights-based approaches to humanitarian action. The incorporation of protection of vulnerable populations into humanitarian action resembles a human rights approach, which some humanitarians

---

[34]ICRC (2014), p. 5.

[35]Save the Children (2014), p. 15.

[36]*Ibid.*

[37]*Id.*, p. 1.

still consider a political issue, distinct from humanitarian action. Yet more and more affected populations are seeking the implementation of HRL, IHL and an end to impunity of those violating these frameworks.

Humanitarian actors should accept that they have to apply not only *a framework of context* and *risk analysis, needs assessments*[38] but also *a rights-based approach that helps to identify threats and vulnerabilities and their causes as well as violations of international human rights and humanitarian law, and to establish appropriate responses.*[39] Yet reports suggest that protection issues are still not systematically identified and addressed in humanitarian response and advocacy.[40] This underlines the need for enhanced collaboration between humanitarian and human rights actors.

8 A Call for a More Inclusive Humanitarian System

Discussions on humanitarian effectiveness start with the question of how to meet the humanitarian needs of all people with timely and appropriate aid that is delivered in a collaborative and sustainable manner. This involves gaining a better understanding of what aid vulnerable people and communities require and what they are currently doing to meet their own needs. In this regard, the main challenge lies in how to respond to the demands of developing countries, which seek support to create resilient national and local capacities to sustainably end the underlying conditions that create humanitarian crises. However, this is not a simple and straightforward process. There are a number of underlying tensions that should be taken into consideration.

Host States are becoming increasingly reluctant to get involved in what they perceive as *humanitarian interventionism* at the expense of their national prerogatives. This reluctance is asserted in two different ways. On the one hand, certain host States are developing disaster management systems, which are both willing and able to act as *host coordinators*, as well as *implementers* of disaster responses during crisis. In this vein, many States have increased the capacities of their national disaster management authorities and improved local efforts to prepare

[38]Office of the UN High Commissioner for Human Rights (OHCHR) and Office of the UN High Commissioner for Refugees (UNHCR) Inter Agency Standing Committee Principals (2013), p. 5, http://www.globalprotectioncluster.org/_assets/files/tools_and_guidance/human_rights_protection/OHCHR-UNHCR%20Joint%20Paper_EN.pdf.

[39]*Ibid.*

[40]There is a lot of confusion about the meaning of protection. Protection can be understood in three ways: as an objective, as a legal responsibility and as an activity. Protection is an objective that requires equal respect for the rights of all individuals, without discrimination, in accordance with national and international law. Protection is also a legal responsibility, mainly of the State and its agents. Protection of civilians is a legal concept based on IHL, human rights and refugee law. It refers to the protection of civilians in armed conflict according to IHL and human rights law.

for and respond to humanitarian crises.[41] On the other hand, authoritarian States are prepared to contain or keep a close eye on humanitarian interventions, hindering humanitarians' access to people in need. Host governments are not always capable or willing to respond to the needs of affected people, notably in the case of IDPs and refugees.

As the current armed conflict in Syria and the expulsion of aid agencies from Sudan in 2009 clearly highlight, providing humanitarian assistance depends on a certain amount of State consent. The experiences of the last years in Syria and other States in crisis need to be evaluated to find the most creative ways of working in States *where humanitarian action is firmly nationalised and leaves little room for a diverse array*.[42]

Humanitarian nationalism, as it appeared in Sri Lanka, Sudan or Myanmar, is likely to be increasingly common. The need to support more localised humanitarian responses, particularly by directly funding local actors, faces several challenges besides differing from international humanitarian financing practice based on appeals. These challenges include fiduciary risks, aid diversion and corruption at a time where there is a growing request for greater accountability and transparency in developed countries. In some contexts, a local-level response is not the most effective, and working with local actors may lead to mixed results, as in the case of *aid gatekeepers*, experienced by IDPs in Mogadishu, Somalia.[43] Last but not least, there is the resistance of international NGOs that are increasingly competing for funds in a humanitarian landscape dominated by five international *mega* NGOs.[44]

Tensions also exist between western-based humanitarian agencies and emerging humanitarian institutions from other regions, which may have different codes of conduct and work outside the multilateral framework. For example, the humanitarian role of the Organisation of Islamic Cooperation (OIC), and the NGOs working under its umbrella, is based on the Islamic principles of charity (*Zakat*) and a shared religious community among Muslims (*Ummah*), which clashes with traditional humanitarian principles of universality and neutrality.[45] This raises concerns but also emphasises the need to include a variety of actors in the current humanitarian system.

Besides increasing capacities and expertise of national authorities and local responders, many new actors have also begun to engage in humanitarian action. They include militaries, national and international businesses, *digital humanitarians* and diaspora groups, among others. The question remains how all the major actors involved in humanitarian action can better *inter-operate* with each other.

---

[41]Harvey (2009).

[42]Slim and Trombetta (2014), p. 61.

[43]Drumtra (2014).

[44]Médecins Sans Frontières (MSF), Catholic Relief Services (CRS), Oxfam International, the International Save the Children Alliance and World Vision International (ALNAP, 2015).

[45]Svoboda et al. (2015).

Depending on the context, one must determine which actors are best placed to respond, who should lead or coordinate humanitarian responses and what goals need to be met. International humanitarian aid now involves a multitude of actors, including regional organisations, which are developing their own coordination mechanisms and member States with their own capabilities and structures. An array of non-core humanitarian actors works in parallel and often in coordination with the rest of the humanitarian system, working towards different goals and approaches that need to be considered. These include militaries, private-sector entities, including commercial contractors, religious institutions and diaspora groups, together with formal and informal private givers. Despite the differences between these actors, it is less important who is delivering the assistance than how well the needs of people are met.

9 Conclusion

The WHS process was a unique opportunity to address the external and internal challenges facing global humanitarian action today. The need for enhanced investment in risk mitigation and risk management, which existing structures are not equipped to provide, is real, but it should not overshadow the more important problem: humanitarianism has become a global big leaf to avoid addressing the causes of disasters.

Preventing or reducing the risk of disaster is only one part of dealing with long-term consequences of humanitarian crises. The underlying processes of chronic poverty, environmental degradation, global climate change and political marginalisation are the true issues to address. Shifting the focus from curing maladies to preventing them presents challenges at multiple levels, for the humanitarian community and, even more so, for governments and development actors. The latter dispose of adequate tools to address underlying causes (livelihood diversification, resource conservation, practices and political participation). Finding solutions to protracted crises is fundamentally a political issue that requires the full extent of political will, capacity and resources of donor governments and affected States. Access to people in need and compliance with IHL are not limited to but depend mainly on commitment from governments.

Humanitarian aid continues to be used to address gaps where political and development solutions have failed. This leads the humanitarian system to overstretch, so that it can no longer meet increasing needs. As Sadako Ogata, long-term humanitarian civil servant, wrote in her autobiography on her experiences during a decade serving as the UN High Commissioner for Refugees: 'There are no humanitarian solutions to humanitarian problems.'[46]

[46]Ogata (2005).

References

Betts A (2010) Survival migration: a new protection framework. Glob Gov 16:361–382

Borton J (2009) Future of the humanitarian system: impact of internal changes. Feinstein International Center, Medford

Brian T, Laczko F (eds) (2014) Fatal journeys: tracking lives lost during migration. IOM, Geneva

Cairns E (2012) Crises in a new world order: challenging the humanitarian project, Oxfam Briefing Papers 158. Oxfam International

CaLP (2013) Drivers of change, adapted from the Cash Transfer Programming Trends Analysis Meeting, June

Churruca Muguruza C (2015) Towards more effective global humanitarian action: how the EU can contribute, EP/EXPO/B/DEVEFWC/08/, PE 549048 at http://www.europarl.europa.eu/thinktank/en/document.html?reference=EXPO_STU(2015)549048

Drumtra J (2014) Internal displacement in Somalia, Brooking-LSE Project on internal displacement. Brookings Institution, Washington

Duffield M (2002) War as a network enterprise. The new security terrain and its implications. Cult Values J Cult Res 6(1&2):153–166

EUPRHA (2013) State of the art in humanitarian action. EUPRHA Report at http://www.eupr ha.org/library

European Parliament Directorate-General for External Policies, Policy Department (2015) Towards more effective global humanitarian action: how the EU can contribute

Gelsdorf K (2010) Global challenges and their impact on international humanitarian action, OCHA Occasional Policy Briefing Series, No. 1

Global Humanitarian Assistance (2014) Global Humanitarian Assistance Report 2014. Development Initiatives, London at www.globalhumanitarianassistance.org

Harvey P (2009) Towards good humanitarian government, the role of the affected state in disaster response. HPG Report 29. ODI, London

Ibáñez Muñoz J, Sánchez Aviles C (Dir.) (2015) Mercados ilegales y violencia armada. Los vínculos entre la criminalidad organizada y la conflictividad internacional. Tecnos, Madrid

ICRC (2012) Enhancing protection for civilians in armed conflict and other situations of violence. ICRC, Geneva

ICRC (2014) ICRC strategy 2015–2018 adopted by the ICRC assembly on 18 June 2014. ICRC, Geneva

Institute for Economics and Peace (2016) The global peace index, p 3

International Organization for Migration (IOM) (2015) Missing Migrants Project database, "Latest global figures, 2015". Available from http://missingmigrants.iom.int/latest-global-figures

MHub (2015) Conditions and risks of mixed migration in North East Africa Study 2, November, http://www.mixedmigrationhub.org/wp-content/uploads/2015/11/Conditions-and-Risks-in-Mixed-Migration-in-North-East-Africa.pdf

Muggha R (2012) Researching the urban dilemma: urbanization, poverty and violence. International Development Research Centre (IDRC) and the United Kingdom's Department for International Development (DFID), Ottawa

OCHA (2014) Saving lives today and tomorrow: managing the risk of humanitarian crises. OCHA, New York

ODI (2015) Humanitarian trends and trajectories to 2030: Europe and others group. ODI, London, p 15

OECD (2015) States of fragility 2015. OECD, Washington

Ogata S (2005) The turbulent decade: confronting the refugee crisis in the 1990s. W.W. Norton, New York

ONCHR, UNHCR IASC Principals. The protection of human rights in humanitarian crises, a joint background paper, 8 May 2013., http://www.globalprotectioncluster.org/_assets/files/tools_and_guidance/human_rights_protection/OHCHR-UNHCR%20Joint%20Paper_EN.pdf

Rubin V (2006) The humanitarian-development debate and chronic vulnerability: lessons from Niger. Humanitarian Exchange, no 33, March

Savage K, Muggah R (2012) Urban violence and humanitarian action: engaging the fragile city. J Humanit Assist 1, at http://sites.tufts.edu/jha/archives/1524

Save the Children (2014) Education in emergencies: a community's need, a child's right. World Humanitarian Summit – Regional Consultation: East and Southern Africa Engagement, London

Slim HL, Trombetta L (2014) Syria crisis common context analysis. Report commissioned by the IASC Inter-Agency Humanitarian Evaluations Steering Group as part of the Syria Co-ordinated Accountability and Lessons Learning (CALL) Initiative. IASC Inter-Agency Humanitarian Evaluations Steering Group, New York, May

Stepanova E (2010) Armed conflict, crime and criminal violence, Chapter 2, SIPRI Yearbook 2010. SIPRI, http://www.sipri.org/yearbook/2010/02

Svoboda E, Zyck SA, Osman D, Hashi A (2015) Islamic humanitarianism? The evolving role of the Organisation for Islamic Cooperation in Somalia and beyond. Humanitarian Policy Group, February, p 5

UN Secretary General Ban Ki-Moon (2011) We the Peoples, 21 September 2011. UNSG, p 8

United Nations, Department of Economic and Social Affairs, Population Division, Trends in international migration, 2015, Population Facts, No. 2015/4, December 2015

United Nations-General Assembly, Transforming our world: the 2030 Agenda for Sustainable Development, A/RES/70/1, 21 October 2015

United Nations-General Assembly, One humanity: shared responsibility. Report of the Secretary General for the World Humanitarian Summit, A/70/709, 2 February 2016a

United Nations-General Assembly, In safety and dignity: addressing large movements of refugees and migrants. Report of the Secretary-General, A/70/59, 21 April 2016b

United Nations–General Assembly, Economic and Social Council, Strengthening of the coordination of humanitarian and disaster relief assistance of the United Nations, including special economic assistance, A/71/82–E/2016/60, 26 April 2016c

United Nations–Security Council, Report of the Secretary General on the protection of civilians in armed conflicts, S/2015/243, 18 June 2015

von Seidel S et al (2014) Major recent trends in violent conflict, Occasional Paper 1. University Centre for Policy Research, Tokyo

World Bank (2011) World Development Report 2011. Conflict, security, and development. The World Bank, Washington, p 2

Further Readings

Armstrong J (2013) The future of humanitarian security in fragile contexts. European Interagency Security Forum

Austin B, Fisher RJ, Giessmann HJ (eds) (2011) Advancing conflict transformation. The Berghof Handbook II. Barbara Budrich Publishers, Pladen/Framington Hills. Online at www.berghof-handbook.net

Barnett M, Weiss TG (eds) (2011) Humanitarianism contested. Cornell University, Ithaca and London

Donini A (ed) (2012) The golden fleece. Manipulation and independence in humanitarian action. Kumarian Press, Sterling

Duffield M (2007) Security, development and unending wars. Polity, London

Gibbons P, Heintze H-J (2015) The humanitarian challenge. 20 years European Network on Humanitarian Action (NOHA). Springer, Berlin

Mac Ginty R, Peterson JH (2016) The Routledge companion to humanitarian action. Routledge, London

Walker P, Maxwell D (2009) Shaping the humanitarian world. Routledge, London and New York

Cristina Churruca-Muguruza is Associate Professor of International Relations and Coordinator of the World Politics and Humanitarian Action Module of the NOHA Joint Master's Programme in International Humanitarian Action at the Institute of Human Rights of the University of Deusto, Spain.

Humanitarian Action in International Relations: Power and Politics

Anna Khakee

1 Introduction

Traditionally, humanitarians have often thought of themselves as shielding away from politics: neutral, independent and impartial in the delivery of the essentials to ensure the dignified survival of disaster victims. Power politics, many of those who set out to work in the humanitarian sector believe, is a dirty business—in contrast to the purer and nobler humanitarianism. Remaining outside politics, both at the national and international levels, is also, and crucially, a way for humanitarian organisations to ensure access to victims and to gain the respect and cooperation of different powerful groups and States. Consequently, for United Nations (UN) agencies and the International Committee of the Red Cross (ICRC), for instance, taking sides politically goes against their mandates.

This anti-politics philosophy has been further reinforced by the fact that many humanitarian emergencies, such as interstate and intrastate conflict, famines and large-scale industrial disasters, are caused by politics, or political, economic and societal failures. Many other calamities result from a mix of natural and man-made causes, where, again, the inadequate use of power and a lack of political leadership are key explanatory factors. Thus, earthquakes, landslides, floods, tsunamis and volcanic activity are made worse by the pattern and quality of human settlements—the 2011 Fukushima nuclear disaster is a case in point. Likewise, anthropogenic climate change causes more extreme temperatures and meteorological conditions: droughts, wildfires, cyclones and hurricanes.

Hence, humanitarians have often tried to eschew the politics and power plays that create or sustain so much human misery for higher grounds, or what Michael

A. Khakee (✉)
University of Malta, Msida, Malta
e-mail: anna.khakee@um.edu.mt

© Springer International Publishing AG 2018
H.-J. Heintze, P. Thielbörger (eds.), *International Humanitarian Action*,
DOI 10.1007/978-3-319-14454-2_2

Barnett calls 'a place of purity'.[1] Humanitarians are often seen as relatively powerless: traditionally entering scenes of conflict unarmed, they are at the mercy of government and non-State armed forces of various stripes. The only protection they rely on has traditionally been their reputation as protectors of human life and dignity, symbolised by their emblems and their status as organisations with a purely humanitarian mandate in accordance with international law. There are many poignant examples that seem to illustrate the point that humanitarians are at the mercy of—violent—State and non-State actors: humanitarian workers operating under fire for victims of violence and persecution with their only shield being the Red Cross or Red Crescent, the sky-blue UN family logos or the red-and-white emblem of Médecins Sans Frontières.

To any aspiring humanitarian wishing to work along these premises, the words of Sadako Ogata, long-term humanitarian civil servant and head of the United Nations High Commissioner for Refugees (UNHCR), will appear unsettling. Implicit in her assertion that there are 'no humanitarian solutions to humanitarian problems'[2] is that, instead, humanitarian crises require political or perhaps economic or even military responses and are hence part and parcel of power politics.

This chapter aims to place humanitarian action in the context of international politics and to discuss the relationship between humanitarianism and international power structures. It addresses questions such as: are humanitarians powerless? Or do humanitarian agencies wield independent power in international relations? If so, what kind of power? How do they relate to other powerful actors in international politics? The chapter examines how humanitarianism can be, and has been, discussed in relation to political, economic and military power.

Many argue that such questions have taken on a new importance since the end of the Cold War and in the post-9/11 period as humanitarianism—or 'the new humanitarianism' as it has sometimes been labelled—has become increasingly central to power politics.[3] In this context, many humanitarian organisations working in the so-called Wilsonian tradition—i.e., humanitarian non-governmental organisations (NGOs) cooperating with governments that they see as pursuing compatible goals—have also become more implicated in wider human rights and peacebuilding political agendas in the last decades. Of course, this is a wide and complex question: the notion of power is one of the most debated in the social sciences generally and in international relations particularly. Scholars have been analysing various elements of power in relation to humanitarianism for decades. The aim of this chapter is thus much more modest: to briefly introduce to the student some of the main parameters of the discussion on humanitarianism and power.

---

[1] Barnett (2011), p. 237.

[2] Cited in Walker and Maxwell (2009), p. xiii.

[3] See for example Kent et al. (2013); Rieff (2002); Duffield et al. (2001), pp. 269–274.

2 Humanitarians as Subject to State Power

One long-dominant way of analysing humanitarian aid has been in terms of the interests and pursuits of powerful States. Here, humanitarian and development assistance is perceived as yet another tool that States can potentially use to gain influence and build alliances internationally. In this tradition, the debate is often not about whether humanitarian aid is subservient to State interests—which is taken for granted—but how useful a tool of statecraft it is, for instance in reinforcing alliances or buttressing military campaigns.[4] In this conception of humanitarian aid, it is thus States that are powerful, not humanitarian multilateral agencies or NGOs.

States, it is pointed out, are the primary financial sponsors of multilateral and non-governmental humanitarian action, as well as principal donors of bilateral humanitarian and development aid, going directly to recipient State coffers. As a consequence, it is primarily States that determine the size and scope of humanitarian efforts in various parts of the globe based on their strategic and wider political interests.[5] Humanitarian organisations, in this view, have relatively little independent agency. They are part and parcel of State power politics: powerless pawns of all-powerful States. When Colin Powell, United States (US) Secretary of State under President George W Bush, (in-)famously referred to humanitarian NGOs as 'force multipliers', an appendix to US fighting forces in Afghanistan, he gave expression to this view of humanitarianism as a supplementary means of projecting State power.[6]

The debate on the role and importance of political and strategic interests in humanitarian aid is ongoing. For instance, in an analysis of US disaster assistance data over three decades, A. Cooper Drury, Richard Stuart Olson and Douglas A. Van Belle conclude that 'our results paint a picture of high U.S. foreign policy decision makers as realists at heart, seeing disasters as opportunities to enhance [national] security'.[7] In a study covering the wider global response in the wake of 270 natural disasters—which, at first glance, should be less likely candidates for politicisation than man-made armed conflicts—Günther Fink and Silvia Redaelli come to a similar conclusion: on average, 'donor governments provide aid more frequently to oil exporting countries, and give disproportionately more to geographically closer and politically less affine countries [as a means to create alliances], as well as to their former colonies'.[8] Conclusions such as these are in line with the long-noted problem of forgotten emergencies—emergencies in States that mostly are of little strategic interest to donor States, and which, as a result, receive a much smaller share of emergency assistance.

[4]See for example Morgenthau (1962), pp. 301–309.

[5]Minear (2012).

[6]Cited in Kenyon Lischer (2007), p. 99.

[7]Cooper et al. (2005), p. 470.

[8]Fink and Redaelli (2011), p. 742. See also Rye Olsen et al. (2003), pp. 109–126.

This equation of humanitarianism with State action—particularly action by the most powerful States—is reflected in the interest generated by the concepts of 'humanitarian intervention' and the 'responsibility to protect' (R2P), i.e. entering into armed conflict with the purported aim to prevent or stop war crimes, ethnic cleansing, crimes against humanity or genocide committed by a State against (part of) its people. Although much less common than non-military humanitarian action, humanitarian intervention arguably receives the bulk of the interest in humanitarianism in the current literature on international relations.[9] Given the preponderant role of armed forces in such interventions, powerful States are, again, the main players with humanitarian agencies relegated to mere side shows. In this vein, humanitarianism is primarily an instrument in the hands of the great powers.

Others have noted that recipient States and non-State armed actors also can and do instrumentalise humanitarian agencies: they are able to determine which organisations receive access to specific populations in need or to particular areas of the respective State and under what conditions they may do so. Thus, recipient States and non-State armed groups, as well as donor States, use humanitarian organisations and the aid they provide for their own purposes: for instance, to punish or reward segments of the population in accordance with their degree of loyalty, to induce population movements and to nourish and arm their soldiers (through taxation of humanitarian agencies). Many examples have been used to illustrate how humanitarian organisations are subject to the power of recipient States and non-State armed groups, from Cambodia in the late 1970s,[10] Ethiopia in the 1980s[11] and North Korea in the 1990s[12] to Somalia over the last decade.[13] In cases where few other resources are available to belligerents, humanitarian assets become particularly valuable to gain a military advantage, and their misuse becomes particularly salient.[14]

To summarise, analyses based on Realpolitik or Realist thinking in international relations stress how humanitarian action regularly becomes part and parcel of a State's foreign and security policy, a—more or less useful—tool of statecraft available to States and, in many cases, non-State armed groups. It can be used in tandem with, in lieu or independently of, military action to achieve political goals.

[9]For a variety of perspectives on the responsibility to protect doctrine, see for example Chomsky (2011), Evans (2009) and Pommier (2011).

[10]Terry (2002).

[11]de Waal (1997).

[12]Flake and Snyder (eds) (2003).

[13]Jackson and Aynte (2013).

[14]Terry (2002) and Maxwell (2012).

3 Humanitarianism as Part of Western Hegemony

A second way of analysing humanitarian action in international relations also stresses the relative powerlessness of humanitarian actors, but this time in relation to a North-South politico-economic system that leaves relatively little room for humanitarians to act autonomously. That today's international humanitarian order has its roots in the Western hemisphere is not controversial among those that have attempted to trace its emergence and evolution.[15] The towering historical figures of humanitarian action—Henri Dunant, Florence Nightingale, Eglantyne Jebb, Fridtjof Nansen, Herbert Hoover, Folke Bernadotte, Mother Theresa, Bernard Kouchner—while very different in character, nevertheless have one thing in common: they are all of European or North American origin. More importantly, Western States, which dominated the international system after World War I and World War II, set up the intergovernmental institutions forming the basis of the present-day humanitarian system. The key international NGOs in the sector, such as Médecins Sans Frontières (MSF), Oxfam, Save the Children, and World Vision International, also mostly originate in Europe and North America.

While the Western origins of the current humanitarian system are hardly disputed, the consequences of this historical development are. Traditionally, it has been argued that the origins of humanitarian organisations matter little since the UN system is now global in reach and humanitarian action is firmly linked to universally accepted humanitarian and human rights law. Moreover, it is argued, while the foundations may be Western, humanitarian ethics and impulses are universal, found for example in all major religions.

For other analysts, these origins have a much stronger—and more problematic—bearing on how the international humanitarian system functions. They see traces of previous colonial and post-colonial practices reflected in current humanitarian action. In particular, they perceive the broader peacebuilding agenda within which a number of humanitarian agencies operate as a modern-day variant of colonial paternalism or *mission civilisatrice*. For instance, according to Roland Paris, '[w]ithout exception, peacebuilding missions in the post-Cold War period have attempted to "transplant" the values and institutions of the liberal democratic core into the domestic affairs of peripheral host states'.[16] This has been the case most conspicuously in, but not restricted to, Kosovo and East Timor, where the UN has taken on proxy governance functions in the absence of local authorities in the aftermath of humanitarian interventions. While authors such as Paris are ambivalent vis-à-vis this agenda, perceiving its intentions as mainly benevolent, others are more critical.

Thus, authors such as Antonio Donini perceive the Northern/Western 'dominant, multi-billion dollar, visible face of humanitarianism'[17] as part and parcel of

[15]See for example Davey et al. (2013), Walker and Maxwell (2009) and Barnett (2011).

[16]Paris (2002), p. 638.

[17]Donini (2010), pp. S220–S237.

globalised power structures dominated by the global North. According to Donini, 'humanitarianism in its Northern and Western incarnations is increasingly consubstantial with and functional to processes of economic, social and cultural globalisation, and, more often than not, to world ordering and securitisation agendas'.[18] In other words, even if individual humanitarian organisations strive to oppose an unjust global order, they in reality help perpetuate it, or as Roberto Belloni puts it, 'humanitarianism is at best ineffective and at worst counterproductive'.[19]

The reason is that humanitarians cannot escape a system in which humanitarian assistance is distorting the realities of unequal North–South relations, so that the humanitarian management of crises across the globe captures attention and resources while the long-term, structural inequalities and the realities of violent conflict persist without serious questioning or action. Moreover, humanitarian actors, by taking over State functions, weaken States in the global South and hence serve privatisation and wider liberal economic agendas emanating from the North/West.

The headquarters of the largest international NGOs and humanitarian agencies in global centres such as New York and Geneva reflect their considerable—and growing—financial resources as compared to, for instance, small developing countries: the largest of the humanitarian NGOs report yearly expenditures larger than the yearly gross national income of States such as Gambia, Guinea Bissau, Djibouti and Guatemala. From this point of view, humanitarian aid is mainly about control and containment.[20] Just as (limited) humanitarian aid and public works programmes were used in the colonial period—for example, in British-ruled India—to prevent mass uprisings of colonial subjects during periods of extreme food scarcity, so humanitarian aid in today's world is about securitisation or containment of peripheral areas and peoples of the globe.

To summarise, to those that perceive humanitarian action as part and parcel of Western hegemony and fundamentally unequal North–South relations, humanitarianism is powerful—but vis-à-vis those at the receiving end only (individuals and States in the global South). In contrast, humanitarians hardly ever manage to change the way that an unjust international system, of which humanitarian crises are a recurrent feature, operates. Instead, they in fact assist in perpetuating it.

4 Humanitarianism Wielding Normative Power

More recently, international relations scholars of the so-called Liberal school have become interested in how principled actors, i.e. non-governmental actors basing their agenda on normative concerns—and, in this case, primarily humanitarian

[18]*Ibid.*, p. 223; see also Duffield (2007).

[19]Belloni (2007), p. 454.

[20]For a discussion of the '*three Cs*' of humanitarianism: compassion, change and containment, see Walker and Maxwell (2009), p. 21.

organisations—have wielded power over States. In so doing, such scholars argue, advocacy-oriented organisations have shaped the evolution of international politics in a positive direction.[21] Such principled actors base their advocacy on ideas of a common humanity and the inherent and equal worth of every human being. An additional—and arguably equally important—basis, particularly in the case of humanitarian action, is the human impulse of assisting those in extreme need, coupled with a growing sense of obligation, of both individuals and States, towards distant strangers beyond their borders.[22] In pushing governments towards a more moral and human-centred approach, advocates of humanitarian and human rights principles make use of the fact that people generally wish the foreign policy of their country to be based not only on self-interest but also on some form of ethical standards and values.[23] The lobbying of such principled actors has resulted in norms and institutions that restrict States' behaviour and ability to project power in various ways.

Humanitarian actors, especially those striving to remain independent of States—for example, the Red Cross movement and several international NGOs—are acutely aware of the political power field in which they are operating and have attempted to resist and reshape it at various levels through advocacy. One of Henri Dunant's main actions was to (successfully) lobby for the First Geneva Convention of 1864. In so doing, he advocated in favour of respect for what in today's vocabulary would be labelled a 'humanitarian space', a space that makes it possible to resist the power of States and operate in accordance with the humanitarian principles of humanity, neutrality, impartiality and independence.[24] Such lobbying for normative change enabling humanitarian actors to operate more freely of State power has continued ever since.

Hence, if we look back at the evolution of humanitarian action, we see, in parallel to the humanitarian activities on the ground, the evolution of an international legal and normative framework establishing humanitarian principles and rules (the relevant humanitarian, human rights and refugee law are described elsewhere in this volume). Not least through the successful persuasion efforts of humanitarian actors or norm entrepreneurs, this framework has been strengthened over time, often in response to particularly blatant failures of the international community to prevent or alleviate large-scale human tragedies. For example, the Genocide Convention followed the horrors of the concentration camps targeting Jews, Roma and other 'undesirable' groups during World War II, and the Sphere standards and other quality and accountability codes were developed after the Rwandan genocide of 1994.

The extent to which such normative developments have changed international relations is still debated. One of the main criticisms levelled against this approach is

---

[21] See for example Keck and Sikkink (1998).

[22] Barnett (2011).

[23] Barnett (2012) and Walker and Maxwell (2009).

[24] For a discussion of humanitarian space see for example Collinson and Elhawary (2012).

that it has focused mostly on formal norms, procedures and institutions but has failed to properly examine how and to what extent these actually affect State policy and action. Another point of criticism advanced against humanitarian actors rather than the liberal theoretical framework is that humanitarians have been reluctant to take on the responsibilities that come with the new-found normative power. As noted by David Kennedy:

> Humanitarians have come into rulership. They have become, in a word, political. Yet modern humanitarianism remains a Gordian knot of participation and denial, willful blindness posing as strategic insight. Just when we have gotten in the door and found them speaking our language, we turn back. Drop this bomb, here? Kill those people, there? No, we prefer to think of ourselves as outside power, judging the powerful, opposing government, speaking to it with the truth of law or ethics.[25]

To summarise, in this liberal line of thought, humanitarian actors are far from powerless. In fact, through their successful, piecemeal advocacy, they have over centuries managed to change the normative environment in which States operate, so that States now have to take international laws and norms into account and must contend with moral arguments when deciding on their line of action in the global sphere.

5 Humanitarians and Power

The theories analysed so far—boiled down to their essential parameters in the preceding paragraphs—try to situate humanitarian action in the broader matrix of international politics and form part and parcel of three of the main broad schools of thought in international relations: realism, dependency perspectives and liberalism. A number of analysts have either contested the conclusions arrived at or focused more squarely on the relationship between humanitarian actors and the particular settings in which they work.

This section very briefly reviews a couple of conclusions that such analysts have drawn regarding the relationship between humanitarianism and power. It has no pretence of completeness and merely aims to illustrate that the relationship between humanitarianism and political power is even more complex than the previous paragraphs, with their focus on international relations, were able to demonstrate.

A growing body of literature on humanitarian action focuses on the relationships between humanitarians and beneficiaries in the field. It explores the reluctance of humanitarians to assume that this is indeed an unequal relationship and that they have power over individuals in extreme need. Several authors have stressed that humanitarian actors are more comfortable discussing the power that other actors—States, non-State armed groups, corporations—wield over them than their own power vis-à-vis vulnerable populations. Yet the discrepancy in power is obviously wide. Humanitarians retort that they base their action on selfless values and on the

[25] Kennedy (2005).

stated goals of humanitarianism. However, as noted by Michael Barnett, '[a]ny "-ism" that arrives with promises of progress must be closely watched for signs of domination over those whose lives are supposed to be bettered'.[26]

Another, by now classical, analysis examining the relationship between humanitarian actors, local populations and governments focuses on humanitarianism and the particular problem of famine prevention, a core humanitarian concern over the centuries. In *Famine Crimes*, Alex de Waal's assertion (itself based on Amartya Sen's classic work on the causes of famine and famine prevention) is that famine is best prevented through a political contract between the government and the population. Such a political contract is a 'result of a popular movement successfully articulating a new right [not to have to suffer from famine]'.[27] However, because it weakens political accountability, humanitarian aid can counter the emergence of such a contract between rulers and ruled. Famines become a technical, professional, institutional issue rather than a political one, and thus the power of those suffering from famine is eroded. De Waal's conclusions are severe: 'the intractability of famine is the price that is paid for the ascendancy of humanitarianism'.[28] According to De Waal, the solution, echoing Ogata's statement cited at the outset of this chapter, is that 'non-humanitarian means are needed to meet humanitarian goals'.[29]

To summarise, a focus on international politics and power dynamics can easily obfuscate the more national and local power dynamics involved in the delivery of humanitarian aid. It is thus important to complement general theories with theories more grounded in the various individual contexts.

6 Conclusion

This chapter set out to review how the relationship between humanitarianism and power is discussed in international relations. Although humanitarianism has never been a core concern of any of the three main schools of thought within this discipline (and sometimes sits rather uncomfortably with the main assumptions of each school—a discussion that is beyond the scope of this chapter), all three manage to throw a different light on the aspects of the humanitarian system and its workings. Does that mean that they are sufficient to elucidate humanitarian action? Those devoting their careers to the study of humanitarian action would mostly argue that they are not, as they fail to discuss, for instance, the complex power relationship between those individuals and groups affected by disasters and the humanitarian actors or how State–society relations are affected by humanitarian aid. With their focus on the level of the international system, they clarify some issues while obfuscating others.

[26]Barnett (2011), p. 13.

[27]de Waal (1997), p. 11.

[28]*Id.*, p. 5.

[29]*Ibid.*

References

Barnett M (2011) Empire of humanity: a history of humanitarianism. Cornell University Press, Ithaca

Barnett M (2012) "Duties Beyond Borders". In: Smith S, Hadfield A, Dunne T (eds) Foreign policy: theories, actors, cases. Oxford University Press, Oxford, pp 221–239

Belloni R (2007) The trouble with humanitarianism. Rev Int Stud 33:451–474

Chomsky N (2011) A new generation draws the line: Kosovo, East Timor, and the responsibility to protect today. Paradigm Publishers, Boulder

Collinson S, Elhawary S (2012) Humanitarian space: a review of trends and issues. HPG Report 32, London

Cooper D, Stuart Olson R, Van Belle DA (2005) The politics of humanitarian aid: U.S. foreign disaster assistance, 1964–1995. J Polit 67(2):454–473

Davey E, Borton J, Foley M (2013) A history of the humanitarian system: western origins and foundations. HPG Working Paper, London

de Waal A (1997) Famine crimes: politics and the disaster relief industry in Africa. African Rights & the International African Institute

Donini A (2010) The far side: the meta-functions of humanitarianism in a globalized world. Disasters 34(s2):220–237

Duffield M (2007) Development, security and unending war: governing the world of peoples. Polity Press, Cambridge

Duffield M, Macrae J, Curtis D (2001) Editorial: politics and humanitarian aid. Disasters 25 (4):269–274

Evans G (2009) The responsibility to protect: ending mass atrocity crimes once and for all. Brookings Institution Press, Washington

Fink G, Redaelli S (2011) Determinants of international emergency aid—humanitarian need only? World Dev 39(5):741–757

Flake GL, Snyder S (2003) Paved with good intentions: the NGO experience in North Korea. Praeger, London

Jackson A, Aynte A (2013) Talking to the other side: humanitarian negotiations with Al-Shabaab in Somalia. Overseas Development Institute, London

Keck M, Sikkink K (1998) Activists beyond borders. Cornell University Press, Ithaca

Kennedy D (2005) The dark sides of virtue: reassessing international humanitarianism. Princeton University Press, Princeton

Kent R, Armstrong J, Obrecht A (2013) The future of non-governmental organisations in the humanitarian sector: global transformations and their consequences. Humanitarian Futures Programme, King's College, London

Kenyon Lischer S (2007) Military intervention and the humanitarian "Force Multiplier". Glob Gov 13(1):99–118

Maxwell D (2012) "Those With Guns Never Go Hungry": the instrumental use of humanitarian food assistance in conflict. In: Donini A (ed) The Golden Fleece: manipulation and independence in humanitarian action. Kumarian Press, Boulder

Minear L (2012) Humanitarian action and politicization: a review of experience since World War II. In: Donini A (ed) The Golden Fleece: manipulation and independence in humanitarian action. Kumarian Press, Boulder

Morgenthau H (1962) A political theory of foreign aid. Am Polit Sci Rev 55:301–309

Paris R (2002) International peacebuilding and the 'mission civilisatrice'. Rev Int Stud 28 (4):637–656

Pommier B (2011) The use of force to protect civilians and humanitarian action: the case of Libya and beyond. Int Rev Red Cross 884

Rieff D (2002) A bed for the night: humanitarianism in crisis. Simon & Schuster, New York

Rye Olsen G, Carstensen N, Høyen K (2003) Humanitarian crises: what determines the level of emergency assistance? Media coverage, donor interests and the aid business. Disasters 27 (1):109–126

Terry F (2002) Condemned to repeat? The paradox of humanitarian action. Cornell University Press, Ithaca

Walker P, Maxwell D (2009) Shaping the humanitarian world. Routledge, Abingdon/New York

Further Reading

Barnett M (2011) Empire of humanity: a history of humanitarianism. Cornell University Press, Ithaca

de Waal A (1997) Famine crimes: politics and the disaster relief industry in Africa. African Rights & the International African Institute

Donini A (2010) The far side: the meta-functions of humanitarianism in a globalized world. Disasters 220–237

Terry F (2002) Condemned to repeat? The paradox of humanitarian action. Cornell University Press

Anna Khakee is Senior Lecturer, Head of Department and Director of the NOHA Joint Master's Programme in International Humanitarian Action at the Department of International Relations of the University of Malta.

World Politics and Humanitarian Action: Mutual Influences

Marie-Josée Domestici-Met

1 Introduction

Is there a relationship between world politics and humanitarian action, and if so, what does it look like? Whereas humanitarian action is a tool for protection and assistance, the term world politics relates to the behaviour of international political actors in a global setting, encompassing human and economic as well as physical and territorial aspects.

World politics is the academic discipline that analyses the actions of international players. In this vein, the chapter explores the relationship between humanity, impartiality, neutrality and independence—the fundamental principles of humanitarian action—and politics. Are they antinomic? Or could humanitarian action be a way of alleviating the suffering that all too often results from geopolitical power politics?

The NOHA curriculum has always accorded importance to the study of world politics because geopolitical relations have to be well identified by the actors responsible for implementing humanitarian projects and policies. This chapter will analyse two trends: on the one hand, the phenomenon of world politics permeating humanitarian action throughout almost the entire process of its application and, on the other hand, the role of world politics as an important facet of international relations.

M.-J. Domestici-Met (✉)
Aix-Marseille University, Aix-en-Provence, France
e-mail: marie.domesticimet@univ-amu.fr

© Springer International Publishing AG 2018
H.-J. Heintze, P. Thielbörger (eds.), *International Humanitarian Action*,
DOI 10.1007/978-3-319-14454-2_3

2 World Politics and Lawmaking

2.1 *The Influence of World Politics on Humanitarian Norms*

World politics has strongly shaped the genealogy of international humanitarian law (IHL). After all, it was witnessing the horrors of the battle of Solferino, which impelled a Geneva citizen to act. When he stood close to the battlefield in 1859, Henry Dunant was following an important geopolitical event: the strife of the King of Piémont against the Habsburg Empire in view of unifying all Italians (Dunant 1862). What was at stake was the possibility of an Italian nation State, in the broader context of a common trend among European peoples, to rise up and call for statehood. The presence of French Emperor Louis-Napoleon, Napoleon III (whom Dunant had hoped to meet on the battlefield), was also tightly linked to world politics. France had been struggling for centuries against the Roman Germanic Empire and the Habsburg dynasty. Louis-Napoleon himself, as a young man, had been strongly advocating and struggling for the concept of the nation State. Would Napoleon III have taken part in the battle if the stakes had been lower? And would Henry Dunant, eagerly looking for an occasion to meet him, have otherwise witnessed the horrific slaughter that prompted him to begin advocating for a treaty on armed conflict? The convergence of several geopolitical events thus led to the birth of IHL or the law of armed conflict with the adoption of the First Geneva Convention (GC) for the Amelioration of the Condition of the Wounded in Armies in the Field in 1864.

An expansion of the beneficiaries of the initial Geneva law was induced by other conflicts, geopolitical events as well. The famous naval battle of Tsushima, which saw the first victory of a non-European State's army (the Japanese) over a European one (that of Russia), paved the way for the 1906 adoption of a new Convention: the GC for the Amelioration of the Condition of Wounded, Sick and Shipwrecked Members of Armed Forces at Sea. World War I shed light upon the condition of detained soldiers from enemy troops, which paved the way for the 1929 Convention relative to the Treatment of Prisoners of War, introducing the latter term. Two European tragedies of the twentieth century, brought about by totalitarian ideologies—the Spanish civil war and the Shoah—led to significant developments in IHL: the establishment of a minimum yardstick for the protection of persons taking no active part in hostilities and the wounded and sick in non-international armed conflict (NIAC), Common Article 3 GCs of 1949, and of civilians (GC IV of 1949).

The content of IHL is linked to international relations since the applicability of its conventions and rules depends upon whether a conflict is classified as an international armed conflict (IAC), fought between States, or NIAC, opposing State and armed non-State actors. For example, in NIACs, Additional Protocol (AP) II to the Geneva Conventions, which regulates the rules applicable in NIACs, applies only if a rebel group holds territory, is able to conduct concerted hostilities and ensures that IHL is respected (Article 2) within the territory under its control. If the situation does not reach this level, only Common Article 3 GCs applies.

2.2 *The Example of Refugee Law*

World politics has also heavily influenced the framework of refugee law. To be accorded refugee status, a human being must, among others, find himself or herself outside the territory of the country of which he or she holds the nationality.

The first international attempt of the twentieth century to establish protection for refugees—the Nansen Passport—followed the Bolshevik revolution and the outflow of the so-called "White" Russians, in comparison to the "Red" -or Bolshevik-ones into Western Europe. The adoption of the 1951 Refugee Convention, which was intended to address the European post-war situation, was linked to the establishment of the communist system in Eastern European and Asian countries, followed by major waves of exiled persons leaving the Communist bloc. In 1967, an Additional Protocol enlarged the scope of the Refugee Convention, making it universally applicable.

The 1969 Organization of African Unity Convention Governing the Specific Aspects of Refugee Problems in Africa (Addis Ababa Convention) was openly designed to address several African specificities concerning refugee flows. Its creation coincided with both the final phase of the decolonisation period,[1] marked by the apartheid policy of South Africa and other States,[2] and post-decolonisation disturbances linked to secession attempts of several regions from newly independent African States. As a result of such conflict, large numbers of people fled, often on foot, in the simple hope of finding a place to survive in the neighbouring States of *White Africa*. Having crossed the border and reached safety, they depended on the non-refoulement rule—the primordial rule of refugee law—to avoid deportation to their home States, remaining in their new homes. Hence, the Addis Ababa Convention, going back to the 1951 Refugee Convention's criteria for refugee status, accords this status to *every person who, owing to external aggression, occupation, foreign domination or events seriously disturbing public order in his country of origin or nationality, is compelled to leave his place of habitual residence.*[3]

3 World Politics and Humanitarian Needs

Humanitarian action is based upon the needs of vulnerable populations. One very explicit expression of this conception of humanitarian action is included in the *Humanitarian Consensus* reached by the European Union (EU) in 2007; a similar

---

[1]Decolonisation reached its peak in the 1950s and 1960s, with a large number of States gaining independence.

[2]Southern Rhodesia, having self-proclaimed independence from the UK, with a system closely resembling apartheid, as well as Angola and Mozambique, still Portuguese colonies at the time.

[3]Art. 1(2) Addis Ababa Convention.

approach can be found in the Geneva Conventions and Protocols under Articles 23 GC IV, 70 API and 18 APII.

A needs-based approach to humanitarian action offers a guarantee for impartiality in the treatment of victims of armed conflict: impartial humanitarian actors grant them protection in the sole consideration of their needs, irrespective of who they are and which belligerent party they fought for. However, the history of humanitarian action shows that elements of a geopolitical nature may influence the assessment of victims' needs, which a thorough knowledge of world politics may further help analyse.

3.1 Geopolitical Games Induce Humanitarian Needs

The term 'game' echoes historical realities, such as the events during the nineteenth century that have come to be known as the *big game*, denoting the struggle between the British Indian Empire and the Russian Empire for influence and territory in Central Asia and the Greater Middle East. Such geopolitical games inevitably result in conflict, the alleviation of which requires needs-based humanitarian action, as evidenced by the following examples.

Mitigating the impacts of conflict is the classical and most important domain of humanitarian action. The law of armed conflict provides that, once *hors de combat*, members of enemy forces are to be treated with humanity and without any adverse discrimination. IHL, essentially originating from a geopolitical event, the Solférino battle, offers the clearest example of what humanity in armed conflict means.

World politics also influences humanitarian needs in the context of natural disasters. In the first row, purely geographic—and sometimes geologic—factors are responsible causes of disasters. However, these factors may remain under control if properly addressed by national authorities. The severity of damage and the number of victims caused by disasters thus strongly depend on geopolitical factors.

Where low levels of development persist, they may hinder the successful management of disasters: common difficulties include a lack of civil protection services, medical networks to receive victims and insufficient road networks allowing access to victims. Attempts to mitigate disasters may also be hindered by bad governance, be it governance subverted by corruption or mismanagement of diversity, as reflected in the 2008 Myanmar case. The constitution of Myanmar, formerly Burma, recognises seven ethnic *national* States,[4] the inhabitants of which

[4]Kachin, Chin, Arakan, Shan, Kayan, Kayin, Mon. However, there is another minority within these larger groups of minorities, whose unclear status derives from an issue of contested boundaries: the Rohingyas. Originating from the western side of the Burmese border—today's Bangladesh, formerly part of the British Empire—they were first brought to Burma under British rule. When Burma was granted independence, Rohingya on Burmese territory were separated from their brethren in Bangladesh, then Eastern Pakistan, and became a Muslim minority within Buddhist dominated Burma, mostly concentrated in the Arakan/Rakhine State.

hold a status different from the ethnic Burmese majority. A 1962 military coup brought to power an authoritarian regime, which promoted the *Burmese way to socialism*. On 2 May 2008, Myanmar was struck by Hurricane Nargis. The disaster badly affected *national* populations, but Myanmar's authoritarian government was reluctant to let external actors witness what was happening inside the country and refused them access.

3.2 Understanding World Politics Helps Tackle Humanitarian Needs

Studying world politics helps foresee crises since it identifies fault lines, which are often underlying factors of conflict. Given fault lines can be reinforced by others, which we will name *potentialising* factors; the actual outburst of conflict is usually sparked by a *triggering* factor. Geopolitical awareness contributes to keeping track of these factors and events in order to provide efficient responses.

3.2.1 Conflict Triggers: Lack of National Sentiment

States without any national sentiment are extremely vulnerable to political infighting and eventually even disintegration.

The history of the Balkans, which is essentially a history of fault lines, serves as an apt example. Different populations arrived in the Balkan region in several waves. Slavic tribes first settled in the area after the division of the Roman Empire; from the beginning, their conversion to Christianity was impacted by the differences between Western and Eastern rites within the Christianity belief.

Since the *Great Schism* of 1054, Slavs belonged to either one of two Confessions: the Roman Catholic or the Orthodox Church. Different Kingdoms were created, either Catholic—Carantania (future Slovenia), Croatia and Bosnia, or Orthodox dominated—Serbia and Bulgaria.

In the wake of the Ottoman Empire's victory over the Serbs at the Kosovo Polje battle of 1389, a second fault line developed: Croats and Slovenes became subjects of the Habsburg Emperor; Serbs, together with Bulgarians, Albanians and with the population of Bosnia were ruled by the Ottoman Sultan.

During the twentieth century, in the wake of World War I, the Yugoslav State was created, first as a Kingdom, then a Socialist Republic, consisting of areas that had been part of the former Habsburg and Ottoman Empires. Yugoslavia was reformed after World War II, at the end of a terrible struggle of resistance against Nazi Germany, which had prompted infighting between two different movements—communists and royalists. Existing fault lines were thus carried over into the new nation State.

During the 1980s, the last years of socialism in Yugoslavia, the State was made up of six federated republics, each of them encompassing several different population groups. The ethnic and religious heterogeneity was supposed to have been transcended by a common socialist ideology, promulgated by Josip Broz Tito, who had ruled Yugoslavia since the end of World War II. However, after Tito's death in 1980, and with the demise of the socialist world, the ideological cement in Yugoslavia receded in the face of nationalist ideologies. Slobodan Milosevic highlighted the Serb heritage with a huge celebration of the Kosovo Polje battle, on its 600th anniversary, in 1989. With Croats reaffirming the Croatian national tradition and political leaders in Bosnia propagating the belonging of Muslim Bosniaks to the Umma,[5] Yugoslavia fell apart. Yet each of the six Republics was to a certain—and varying—degree home to a mixed population. Tragically, the breakup of Yugoslavia was to be characterised by ethnic cleansing, the rationale of which is to compel minority groups to leave a given territory, turning it into an ethnically *pure* area, i.e. homogeneous in its population.

In Bosnia-Herzegovina, the claim of Serbian and Croat populations for independence from the Sarajevan Muslim-led government, together with attempts to unite Bosnian Serbs with Serbia and Bosnian Croats with Croatia, resulted in severe campaigns of ethnic cleansing. Different means were used: spreading fear among minority groups or threatening, raping or killing members of such groups in their strongholds. This ethnic component of the crisis, crossed with several purely geographic features of the country,[6] and the high level of armament, gave way to one of the most devastating conflicts of the last decades. In Kosovo, once the cradle of the Serb Kingdom, the Ottoman presence, ensuing revolts and repression had led, over centuries, to a replacement of Serbs with an overwhelming majority of ethnic Albanians. Such was the situation when Milosevic began to suppress Kosovo's autonomy.

3.2.2 Conflict Triggers: Regional Turbulences and Other External Factors

World politics also offers examples of events reinforcing underlying factors of crises, such as conflict in a neighbouring country with the same ethnic groups, often inducing a flux of refugees or an economic crisis resulting in reduced livelihoods.

The case of Lebanon demonstrates how events in the neighbourhood may increase the severity of underlying crisis factors. A major feature of the Lebanese political system is its recognition of different religious confessions as distinct

[5]Alija Izetbegovic was the President of Bosnia-Herzegovina during the wars of independence that led to Yugoslavia's end as a unified State. In the 1980s, he had promised to make Bosnia an Islamic Republic.

[6]A large number of valleys, and the location of the biggest cities in valleys alongside the rivers, enabled Bosnian Serb troops to surround Sarajevo, the Bosnian capital and Gorazde and expose them to heavy shelling from the slopes of these valleys.

elements of the population, a remnant of the system established by the Ottoman Empire: non-Muslim monotheists were allowed to practise their religion, subject to payment of specific taxes. Births, marriages and deaths were registered only within religious communities. Later, in the Lebanese national covenant of 1943, political functions were distributed according to religious affiliation. The President was to be a Maronite Christian, the Prime Minister a Sunni Muslim and the Speaker of the Chamber of Deputies a Shia Muslim. Seats in Parliament were distributed pursuant to a ratio that was also extended to other public offices. The 1932 census was used to establish these ratios. With the creation of Israel in 1948 and the 1967 *Six–Day War*, influxes of Muslim Palestinian refugees put an end to the religious balance. Conflict erupted in 1975, leading to full-scale civil war and only ended in 1989 with the Taef agreement, which increased the ratio of Muslims in Parliament. Today, with the imbalance between the number of Lebanese citizens and refugees due to the large number of the latter from war-torn Syria, there is a danger of renewed conflict.

Another example for underlying crisis factors reinforced by external factors, in this case impoverishment and climate change, is Darfur. In this western part of Sudan, no underlying religious factor to precipitate crisis existed—all inhabitants of the region were Muslim. However, economic and social fault lines developed, pitting nomadic pastoralists against sedentary farmers. This is certainly a universal factor of conflict; however, it may remain an underlying issue, as long as the respective *system*, in which the fault line is present, functions on the basis of trade and peaceful coexistence between the groups. In Darfur, an increase in droughts and ensuing desertification reinforced this crisis factor, possibly for the worst. The pressure mounted and finally became unbearable, with another triggering factor amplifying the danger: Sudan's North–South divide. The triggering factor for the outbreak of violent conflict in Darfur was a peace agreement between the Sudanese regime and the SPLM/SPLA[7] dating back to 2002. The Khartoum government, located in the North, utilised demobilised Darfuri horsemen originating from Northern Darfur, which became known as *Janjaweed*, to return to Darfur to carry out its repressive policy in the South. These semi-nomadic tribes terrorised and murdered scores of sub-Saharan Southern Darfuri peasants.

3.2.3 Conflict Triggers: Absence of Democratic Structures

Another type of event that is well known for triggering open crises is democratic or supposedly democratic elections in democratically unstable States. Instead of representing the will of the people, such elections often only serve to highlight

[7]The SPL with its armed branch, the SPLA, was the main movement representing the South Sudanese. It struggled for years to put an end to the domination of the Khartum government. This decade-long conflict raged independently of the situation in Darfur, except for the utilisation of Northern Darfuri semi Nomads by the central government.

and crystallise the respective strength of different population groups. Whenever elections occur in a context of ethnic divide with mono-ethnic or quasi mono-ethnic political parties, the eventual outcome of an election may often be clear before the results are even announced, from simply analysing the demographic balance. Irrespective of the demographic context, where the democratic tradition of a State is a short one, the defeated party or politician is likely either to invoke cheating and refuse to accept the result or—even worse—to proclaim him-, her- or itself elected. Examples of such cases are extremely numerous on the African continent, but they also frequently occur in other regions.

A striking example of a contested election as a kick-starting factor of crisis is Kenya. The country had long been one of the most stable ones in Eastern Africa, and its diversity of population did not seem to be a crisis factor. The Kikuyu tribe, which had waged a liberation war against the British, had given the country many Presidents. However, in late 2007, a crisis burst out when a Kikuyu President—Mwai Kibaki—tried to extend his mandate for another term, his main challenger, Raïla Odinga, being a member of the Luo ethnic group. The results were contested. Finally, the political contestation gave way to ethnic violence, when adherents of the two candidates began turning on each other along ethnic lines.

The 2010 Ivory Coast electoral crisis was different. A lack of national sentiment[8] had for decades been masked by a charismatic leader, Felix Houphoët-Boigny, and solid economic development following independence in 1960. However, Houphoët's death brought to light tensions similarly existing in other parts of Western Africa: between a northern Muslim area and a southern Christian one. In the Ivory Coast, these tensions had already manifested themselves violently for a decade before the 2010 election. When, after years of postponing, the elections finally took place, incumbent President Laurent Gbagbo entered the final stages of his political career. Refusing to accept defeat to opposition candidate Alassane Ouattara, a Muslim northerner, the situation worsened and violence erupted, which led to a French military intervention. Laurent Gbagbo was later transferred to The Hague to stand trial before the International Criminal Court (ICC).

Closely monitoring developments in world politics is currently gaining more and more importance in the field of humanitarian action. Humanitarian agencies today dedicate specific units to such activities, the role of which is not only to predict potential crises but also to immediately take notice of any surge of violence in ongoing crises. The continuously turbulent situation in the eastern part of the Democratic Republic of Congo (DRC) is a fitting example of a protracted crisis. Whenever new armed groups appear in this region, a sustained geopolitical watch allows for a timely and fitting humanitarian response.

[8]The Ivory Coast, a former French colony, was one of the most successful post-colonial States in Africa, under the Presidency of Felix Houphoët-Boigny. After his death, no successor was able to muster the same charisma or to hold the State together the way he did; Konan Bédié even made use of the concept of '*ivoirité*', which could have been used in order to overcome the divides between the Muslim North and the Christian South. Instead, it was used to disenfranchise the northern population.

3.3 *World Politics Influences Awareness of Humanitarian Crises*

World politics may influence the evaluation of humanitarian needs. Among a wealth of dire situations, only some are considered emergency priorities, whereas others remain ignored by donors.

Priority is often accorded for geographic reasons, as illustrated, once again, by the end of Yugoslavia. Situated between Austria and Greece, Yugoslavia was a potential future Member State of the European Union at the time some of its federate Republics began proclaiming their independence. Proximity to Europe was one of the main factors leading to robust crisis management from external actors. The United Nations also saw stability in Europe as of utmost importance and dedicated substantial manpower to dealing with Yugoslavia.

Similarly, geopolitically important States, such as Kenya—a rear basis for humanitarian operations in Eastern Africa—usually receive support much faster than strategically less important States would in times of crisis. The same applies to emergencies that strike global tourist destinations, as was the case with Thailand during the 2004 Indian Ocean Tsunami. Lastly, disasters occurring in developed States, where images of disasters are rare and thus unusual, will be perceived as more severe than similar disasters might in a *less developed country*, where the lack of human security is permanent.

In the same vein, certain peoples in need seem to be forgotten or overlooked. For example, when Iraqi Kurds in 1991 fled Saddam Hussein's persecutions and were saved by the intervention of American troops, nobody took notice of the Assyrian and Chaldean Christians who were in a similar situation in the vicinity. Even worse, some people seem to be considered as morally deprived of their right to protection. Such was the atmosphere concerning the Rwandese Hutus in the Goma, Bukavu and Uvira camps in the eastern DRC, when these camps were attacked in 1996 by the Rwandan government, since they were arbitrarily deemed to harbour only perpetrators of the 1994 Rwandan genocide. Similarly, when Muammar Gaddafi was brutally killed in 2013, few denounced the fact he had been denied his right to a fair trial.

The European Union Humanitarian and Civil Protection Office (ECHO) pledges to devote itself to the response to crises that make headlines, as well as to forgotten crises by setting up specific indicators.

4 World Politics and Humanitarian Responses

At first glance, the humanitarian response to crises is independent of world politics. At least, that is the way it should be. However, exceptions abound. Thus, in the last third of the twentieth century, new types of conflicts not only triggered rescue missions on a new scale but also led to the development of a new approach to humanitarian action.

When programming humanitarian action, the exact beneficiaries of aid must be determined, and world politics sometimes comes to play a role in this process.

4.1 World Politics and Beneficiaries of Humanitarian Action

In 1859, the day following the battle of Solferino, Henry Dunant experienced first hand the selective treatment applied to potential beneficiaries of humanitarian action, when he witnessed severely wounded soldiers being transferred to a hospital (Dunant 1862). The countrywomen present opposed selecting wounded soldiers on the sole basis of their needs and the degree of their wounds. They argued that it made no sense to medically treat the *German* enemies—i.e., the Austrian empire's soldiers. Medical facilities were to be used only by *Italians* and their allies.

Today, with a growing number of civilians entitled to aid as victims of conflict, helping members of one specific group may be considered a hostile activity by other groups, specifically within ethnic conflicts that induce one belligerent to consider the very population that the opposing party belongs to as the enemy.

Such was the case during the Biafra conflict in the late 1960s. Following Nigeria's independence, the Igbos, inhabitants of Southeastern Nigeria, were providing the newly independent State with a good number of civil servants.[9] However, the Muslim Haussas did not accept non-Muslim rule over Nigeria. This triggered an anti-Igbo pogrom campaign in the North, a Haussa stronghold. The Igbos fled the northern States, mainly heading towards their birthplaces in the southeast, which they proclaimed as an independent State under the name of Biafra. The Nigerian government decided to put down the secession. During the ensuing conflict, the Nigerian army also lashed out against civilians, as well as against humanitarian workers and medical facilities, as if helping sick and wounded Igbos to survive were akin to engaging in warfare against the Nigerian State. The government assumed that humanitarian actors had chosen to take sides, and attacking them was therefore not off-limits anymore.

4.2 The Influence of World Politics on Protection

4.2.1 World Politics Shapes Assistance and Protection Needs

The means of humanitarian action vary, depending on emergencies and needs. For example, the United Nations High Commissioner for Refugees (UNHCR) was

[9]This was in large part due to their superior knowledge of English, whereas the Northern Haussas had for the most part only attended coranic schools.

created with a protective mandate, which it was supposed to implement through advocacy work with States. The latter remained free in their determination of people as refugees.

However, in 1971, with the secession of East Pakistan, today Bangladesh, UNHCR for the first time faced the challenge of directly providing assistance to refugees.[10] The organisation subsequently carried out assistance activities towards Vietnamese and Cambodian refugees who had fled their countries after the establishment of communist governments in both States in 1975 and whose plight peaked with the Boat People crisis in 1979 and 1980.[11] At the same time, UNHCR also had to deal with the Afghan refugee crisis, with five million Afghans—one-third of the country's entire population—displaced outside the country.[12]

It was not only events such as these that prompted UNHCR to expand its scope of activity, the development of numerous and large refugee camps also brought a new geopolitical element to the forefront. The camps established at borders were often used as *sanctuaries* by armed groups. For example, *white* and *pink* Cambodian camps in Thailand were used by opposition forces for their combat against the Khmer Rouge regime of Pol Pot in Cambodia. This, in turn, created a risk for camps and refugees since they functioned not exactly as they were supposed to, namely as civilian premises.

In Bosnia-Herzegovina, humanitarian action had to adapt to specific features of the Yugoslav wars to be effective. The geographic distribution of populations shaped the type of attacks they were subjected to, which in turn shaped humanitarian responses to the violence. In many places, urban Bosniak[13] Muslims were surrounded and besieged by Serb fighters from rural areas firing at them from surrounding hills, with guns and sometimes tanks. Ethnic cleansing directly targeted civilians, who were forcibly displaced and sometimes even killed. Humanitarian assistance for besieged cities was often blocked by militia-held checkpoints. The response that humanitarian actors developed was to proclaim certain places *safe areas* or *safe havens*, where civilians were to be protected by peacekeeping forces.

[10]UN General Assembly Resolution 2790 (XXVI), 6 December 1971 states: '*considering that the international community, [...] has seldom been confronted with a refugee problem of such enormous dimensions as that of the refugees from East Pakistan in India; Endorses the designation by the Secretary-General of the United Nations High Commissioner for Refugees to be the focal point for the co-ordination of assistance to East Pakistan refugees in India, from and through the United Nations system*'.

[11]It is estimated that between 1975 and 2000, three million people fled from Cambodia and Vietnam.

[12]During this crisis, approximately three million Afghans fled to Pakistan and two million to Iran.

[13]'*Bosniak*' is a term used for Bosnian Muslims. '*Bosnian*' is used to refer to any Bosnian.

4.2.2 Safe Havens

IHL as well as refugee law provide for the protection of a range of beneficiaries: civilians, wounded soldiers, prisoners of war and those entitled to refugee status. However, belligerents do not always accord them this protection. Gathering these people in specific secure places may provide them safety. This concept of *safe havens* or security zones for civilians is enshrined in Articles 14 and 15 GC IV; GC III provides for immunity of prisoner-of-war camps.

However, the Bosnian war has shown that implementation of these novel concepts was flawed. On 19 March 1993, French General Morillon, commander of the second United Nations Protection Force (UNPROFOR), promised the besieged population of Srebrenica that he would not abandon the town and its inhabitants. A new concept was born: the UN could declare besieged cities *security zones* to safeguard their populations. In Bosnia, the six selected cities/security zones were also of strategic importance for the belligerents.[14] Most of them—especially Srebrenica—were host to the Bosnian and Herzegovinian Army, which reinforced their strategic value. For these reasons, the United Nations Security Council (UNSC) resolution according these places safe area status was not sufficient to guarantee any effective protection.

In Srebrenica, the robust mandate set up by UNSC Resolution 836 of 6 June 1993 did not translate to decisive action by the international community. The Dutch *blue helmets* were outnumbered by Bosnian Serb forces besieging the city, the safety zone was not precisely delimited and Bosniak forces left the city despite the increasing danger of Bosnian Serb forces approaching.

GA Resolution 45/100 (1990) created a second new concept under the label ‘humanitarian corridors’. However, such corridors cannot be created without a certain amount of goodwill on the side of the belligerent parties.[15] As such, by the second half of the 1990s, the safe areas created for physical humanitarian protection had been disqualified.

The events, which occurred in late 1996 in eastern Zaïre (today’s Democratic Republic of Congo), were no less dramatic than those in Yugoslavia since they saw incursions of armed forces onto the grounds of refugee camps. By late June and early July, some ethnic Tutsi Rwandese citizens had been protected in southwest Rwanda by a military multinational operation[16] and then settled in Goma, a Congolese city close to the Rwandan border. Ethnic Tutsi represented the bulk of

[14]Sarajevoe, as the capital, was of particular importance. In the Drina Valley, the cities of Zepa, Gorazde and Srebrenica were highly contested due to the historic importance given to this valley by the Bosnian Serb population and militia. Tuzla and Bihac were Muslim strongholds surrounded by Serb strongholds which reinforced their value as stake in the war.

[15]This approach, often put forward as a possible alleviation measure for the human suffering in Syria, is not favoured by most humanitarian actors. See for example IRIN, Why humanitarians wary of ‘humanitarian corridors’, 19 March 2012.

[16]The latter was overwhelmingly French. ‘*Operation Turquoise*’, the mission to protect the refugees who fled to eastern Congo, had been mandated by the UNSC.

victims of the genocide that Hutu extremists carried out in the spring of 1994. However, the Rwandan Patriotic Front, which finally overthrew the extremists, was largely made up of Tutsis. In mid-August 1994, some two million Rwandans fled to eastern Congo/Zaïre, where they settled in camps. The new Rwandan Tutsi authorities claimed that the camps harboured the perpetrators of the genocide. The camps also came under attack from Zairian Tutsis supported by Rwandan forces, without receiving any support from the international community. Thus, Hutu refugees in Goma, Bukavu and Uvira were attacked, wounded and even killed and compelled to flee into the surrounding jungle.

5 Humanitarian Action as a Facet of World Politics

5.1 Humanitarian Action as a Substitute for Political Measures

Humanitarian action in conflict can be a means to demonstrate solidarity with and even support for a particular party to a conflict.

An interesting example relates to humanitarian action as a substitute for State recognition, during the Biafra conflict in 1960s Nigeria. France—then led by Charles de Gaulle—would have preferred recognising the Igbo State of Biafra, in the name of the right to self-determination of peoples, but de Gaulle knew that it would have been politically dangerous. Thus, for the first time in its history, France sent its National Society of the Red Cross abroad and seconded staff to the ICRC. The French aid workers thus acted as a humanitarian substitute for the political support that the French withheld from the Biafra rebels.

Humanitarian support is often offered by diaspora groups to co-nationals residing in their country of origin. The aid efforts of the Haitian diaspora in the wake of the earthquake that struck the country in 2010 are a good example of an important, though not overly coordinated, humanitarian diaspora effort. Diasporas are vigilant towards the situation of co-nationals in their countries of origin, especially where minority issues are at stake. This was also the case for the Armenian diaspora during the time Armenia was a Federated Republic of the Union of Soviet Socialist Republics (USSR). When an earthquake struck Armenia in 1988, it was the diaspora's perception that the USSR would refuse any external aid to Armenians.[17] However, this assumption proved to be untrue, and the international community's surprise was so enormous that Moscow's acceptance was attributed to UN General Assembly (UNGA) Resolution 43/131, which had just been passed.[18]

[17]Compare concerts organised in the name of the diaspora by Charles Aznavour: 'Arménie, tu vivras'.

[18]Compare with Sect. 6.1 below.

There are numerous examples of disaster-stricken minorities, whose governments are reluctant to welcome humanitarian action, sometimes for reasons such as ethnic cleansing, if not genocide, perpetrated or tolerated by the regimes in power. In such extreme cases, refusing humanitarian assistance is a cynical way of dealing with minorities. However, such circumstances can also be an opportunity for the international community to boost support for vulnerable minorities.

5.2 Humanitarian Action as a Provisional Measure

Political actors occasionally use humanitarian action as a substitute for political decisions during crisis management.

The UNSC is entrusted with keeping the peace and ensuring collective security. To this end, Chapter VII of the UN Charter enables the UNSC to adopt coercive measures, including the use of force (Article 42), or measures not involving armed force (Article 41) and also provisional measures (Article 40). During the Cold War, it was usually not possible to invoke Chapter VII due to frequent blockades of the Council. However, since the end of the Cold War, the Security Council has achieved several breakthroughs regarding humanitarian action. It progressively began to focus more on human than on collective security. Although the Security Council has often failed to bring an end to crises, it has successively begun ordering States to take measures in favour of vulnerable populations.

In Bosnia-Herzegovina, decisive humanitarian action helped 2.7 million people to survive. The particular way that humanitarian aid was delivered played a dramatically important role in the survival of besieged Bosnian cities. European States dedicated two-thirds of their total amount of humanitarian assistance to the former Yugoslavia. The six security zones created in the most besieged cities by the UN Security Council drew their relative efficiency from, both, European funding for a large amount of assistance—led in the field by the UNHCR but implemented by European NGOs—and the military protection of populations delivered by European soldiers of the United Nations Protection Force (UNPROFOR) mission.[19] The logistically most difficult action and strong point of the security zone campaign was the Sarajevo airlift—the longest in history—which kept a city with several hundreds of thousands of inhabitants alive for 46 months.

Nevertheless, offering humanitarian assistance instead of armed protective action was criticised. The Bosnian—Bosniak-led—government, together with the US and the Organisation of Islamic Cooperation, organised a campaign against creating *well fed dead*.

[19]It was created in February 1992 to supervise the cease-fire in Croatia and, then, reinforced for Bosnia-Herzegovina in August September 1993. All battalions were seconded by European countries, namely France, Germany, Italy, the Netherlands, Spain and the UK, and American troops guarded the strategic bridge of Bosanski Brod.

Is this criticism justified? One must keep in mind that humanitarian action does not aim at resolving crises, which is essentially the task of political actors and stakeholders involved. The role of humanitarians is nevertheless crucial: ensuring people's survival. It should be assessed accordingly. In Yugoslavia, due to the combination of the armed protection of humanitarian assistance convoys, the four security zones that remained untouched, the robust mandate of UNPROFOR II[20] and the presence of NATO,[21] both humanitarian assistance and physical protection were to a large degree successful. They assured that, in the theatre of the worst outbreak of armed conflict on European soil since World War II, neither famine nor epidemics occurred and ensured most victims affected by the conflict survived.

5.3 Humanitarian Action Supporting Special Status for Conflict Areas

In 1991, Operation Provide Comfort established that, for 3 months, no Iraqi public authority was accepted on the soil of Iraqi Kurdistan. The Peshmerga—the armed wing of the Kurdish political parties—enjoyed full freedom of movement. Public sanitary services were provided by the foreign armies, as well as civil engineers—causing the government in Bagdad to disappear from the landscape. Saddam Hussein's armed forces were never again in a position to seriously threaten the Iraqi Kurds. Today, some 25 years later, the Iraqi Kurds carry a part of the hopes of other local populations and interact with the newly formed Iraqi army in the battle against the Islamic State (IS). Without Operation Provide Comfort, the political situation in Iraq would have developed in a very different direction.

In Kosovo, the international community's humanitarian responses eventually led to Kosovo's declaration of independence. The air strike campaign launched by NATO on the—weak—legal basis of UNSC Resolution 1199[22] ended on 9 June 1999 with the Kumanovo Agreement. Soon after, the UNSC established the United Nations Mission to Kosovo (UNMIK), an integrated mission, devoted to providing humanitarian assistance, especially to enable the return of displaced people to Kosovo,[23] as well as to temporarily administer its territory and support its justice

[20]UNPROFOR II was not the inactive force that some observers made it out to be; it was active for example in Gorazde to resist an attack against the Security zone, in cooperation with the NATO air strikes.

[21]NATO imposed a no-fly zone over the conflict area, issued an ultimatum to the Serb militias in Sarajevo (1994) to hand over their weapons, and, finally, enforced the end of the Sarajevo siege (1995).

[22]Adopted in September 1998, the resolution welcomed a cease fire between the Serb army and the Kosovar Liberation army, creating a monitoring mechanism (the OSCE-led Kosovo Verification Mission), allowing for stronger measures to be taken. Yet, this resolution could not prevent the slaughter that was to take place and eventually gave rise to a NATO intervention.

[23]Nearly one million ethnic Albanians from Kosovo had fled to Albania and Macedonia at the beginning of the NATO air strikes.

system. After a government for Kosovo had been established, a power sharing agreement split authority over the country's affairs between international and local officials. During the mid-2000s, the EU developed a new legal framework,[24] which culminated in the creation of the European Union Rule of Law Mission in Kosovo (EULEX), tasked with offering guidance to Kosovo's authorities. This was done in spite of the wording of UNSC Resolution 1244, which had called for *autonomy* for Kosovo. The way towards a declaration of independence was open, and Kosovo's parliament made use of this occasion on 17 February 2008.

5.4 Humanitarian Action as a Complement to Stabilisation Policies

The concept of stabilisation was first used in Bosnia-Herzegovina. After the wars of the 1990s in Bosnia were ended by the Dayton Peace Accords, the international community faced the task of implementing the agreement. This encompassed, first, ending the sieges around the security zones that were still ongoing, especially in the hills around Sarajevo; second, organising the return of all displaced people; and, third, setting up two political entities—Republika Srpska, as an autonomous Serb region within Bosnia, as well as a Croat-Muslim Federation. After severe campaigns of ethnic cleansing, and ongoing tensions between different ethnic and religious communities in many places, it was decided to militarily monitor all steps necessary to implement the agreement. Hence, the Implementation Force (IFOR), led by NATO, was created in November 1995 and carried out its tasks for one year. In December 1996, a follow-up group, the Stabilisation Force (SFOR), came into existence.

The stabilisation approach applies both to military forces overseeing order in the region as well as to UN integrated missions[25] and was used in other countries too. The first integrated missions were established in 1999 for Kosovo and East Timor. Integrated missions also include humanitarian action departments.[26] The work of these departments and of humanitarian action more broadly contributes to the daily survival of people who may no longer live in fear of persecution but who have to

---

[24] Kai Eid Report (2005), followed by Ahtisaari Proposal (2007).

[25] Examples of such missions include the United Nations Stabilisation Mission in Haiti (MINUSTAH), Mission de l'Organisation des Nations Unies pour la Stabilisation en RD Congo (MONUSCO) and the United Nations Multidimensional Integrated Stabilisation Mission in the Central African Republic (MINUSCA).

[26] These constructs have been disputed in the humanitarian community. Humanitarian workers have been mostly hostile to integrated missions, fearing for their independence. When humanitarian action becomes part of an inherently political mission, it may become more difficult for humanitarians to be accepted on the ground. Consider the example of Bosnia Herzegovina: even though the creation of Republika Srpska was meant to provide Bosnian Serbs with an autonomous region within Bosnia, Serbs remained hostile towards the UN and the international community.

rebuild their lives, often from scratch. Without access to food, medical facilities and economic security for livelihoods, these vulnerable populations still depend upon assistance.

Protection remains relevant as well since, even in the aftermath of conflict, adverse groups may punctually strike at (parts of) the population or external actors present in the country. This is especially the case where members of a population group that have been in a minority position earlier return to a territory that they have been ethnically cleansed from before. Since hostile acts are likely to occur in these and comparable cases and given that IHL is no longer applicable in this constellation,[27] a vigilant monitoring of human rights with a protection component is necessary.

5.5 *Humanitarian Action as a Tool Against Ethnic Cleansing*

During the infamous Ethiopian famine between 1983 and 1985, the Ethiopian government, through mismanagement of assistance, was able to accelerate the forced displacement of peasants. Conversely, in Bosnia, humanitarian assistance helped put a halt to ethnic cleansing. From September 1992 onwards, the course of the Bosnian war changed: the front line mostly remained in place between areas dominated by the respective belligerents, and no major forced displacement occurred. Most of the besieged people in the security zones were saved, except for one major and dreadful exception: the fall of Srebrenica and the ensuing slaughter of thousands of men and boys. This tragedy was caused by very specific failures regarding the concept[28] and working mechanism[29] of the security zone.

Hence, despite these horrific events, one may conclude that, during the conflict, humanitarian action was used not only to alleviate suffering but also as a crisis management tool, with positive results, for example in combating forced migration. The events following the 1995 Dayton peace agreement confirm and complement this first assessment. The new State of Bosnia-Herzegovina was built on the idea of ethnic reconciliation. Yet, at the same time, the international community by way of using humanitarian action measures set to reverse the impacts of ethnic cleansing. In each of the areas concerned, ECHO funding for reconstruction purposes primarily aimed at enabling displaced ethnic or religious minorities to return to their

[27]IHL remains applicable in post-conflict situations involving occupation and the continuous holding of prisoners of war.

[28]Security zones, according to IHL (Arts. 14 and 15 GC IV), should be established in areas without any stake in the conflict. However, the Bosniak army used Srebrenica as a rear basis for its troops. The Bosniak retreat from the city must have seemed to the Bosnian Serb militias to be a welcome opportunity to go on the attack.

[29]The safety zone of Srebrenica was created without precisely defining its topographic specificities and geographic extension, which made it impossible to identify the zone's exact borders to determine where infringement by troops outside the zone began.

former territories, instead of only grouping people of the same ethnicity or religion together. Thus, humanitarian action became part of post-conflict management.

The above-envisaged five functions that humanitarian action is likely to have in crisis management raise questions: how and up to what point can humanitarian action and assistance to vulnerable populations be a substitute for political action, such as recognising a given State's independence, and why should humanitarian measures be integrated into the process of rebuilding peace and reconstructing a nation?

The answers to these questions relate to the type of security that the UNSC aims to achieve: human security within States, rather than interstate collective security, characterised by the mere absence of interstate conflicts. Humanitarian action is thus a benchmark for the changing international community that emerged from the Cold War and is steadily being further constructed. Humanism has become the new UN ideology, and humanitarian concerns have become central to peacekeeping, as a major facet of soft power. One may even be tempted to claim that the place humanitarian action is accorded in any given society today is a mirror of its ideology.

6 Humanitarian Action as a Mirror of the International Community?

Even though keeping within its mandate and mission—the protection of vulnerable populations—the humanitarian measures deployed in Bosnia-Herzegovina went in fact beyond this goal and had a political impact as well. Humanitarian action is thus likely to have a second, underlying objective, more linked to *jus contra bellum*, the law regulating under what circumstances armed force may be used, than to *jus in bello*, the law of armed conflict. Could this be due to a specific contemporary approach of the international community? This conclusion seems obvious looking at the diachronic dimension of humanitarian action: in each era of international relations, the features of humanitarian action were different. The same holds true for the synchronic dimension: approaches to humanitarian action are not the same in all areas of the world.

6.1 Era-Specific Features of Humanitarian Action

During the times of chivalry in the Middle Ages, Europe developed a particular humanitarian culture, consisting of concepts such as truces, immunities and assistance to vulnerable people.

Peoples in other regions of the world had also developed similar approaches, all of which make up the *first, pre-modern, era of humanitarianism.*

The second era of humanitarianism was the so-called *Dunantian* one, during which humanitarian activities were for the first time carried out independently of religious consigns. Soon after, the humanitarian imperative was enshrined in the secular First Geneva Convention for the Amelioration of the Condition of the Wounded in Armies in the Field of 1864. However, at this time, the very idea of secularism continued to be an affront to some States.[30] As we shall see, this led to a certain degree of regionalism in humanitarian matters.

The Dunantian era is marked by the creation of the International Committee of the Red Cross (ICRC), a neutral and impartial intermediary, implementing protection measures through discrete interventions with the belligerents expected to comply with IHL. It is true that, after World War II, the strong weight of ideologies challenged the idea of neutrality on many occasions. During the war, criticism was raised against the ICRC's principle of confidentiality, an operational facet of neutrality, which many equated with a lack of action against the Third Reich's atrocities. The same criticism was put forward against the ICRC after the Biafran conflict of Nigeria. In a now famous press conference held in Paris in 1970, Bernard Kouchner, at the time employed by the French Red Cross, who had been sent to the ICRC mission in Biafra, described his harrowing experiences of the conflict. He had witnessed the shelling of field hospitals and the bombing of airstrips both on the territories of Biafra and neighbouring Cameroon (which invoked neutrality in order not to have to guarantee safe passage for aid workers and refugees). Bernard Kouchner and some of his colleagues invoked the Hippocratic Oath, usually taken by physicians, which prohibits absenting from helping victims, no matter who they are. Kouchner thus equated the ICRC's traditionally cautious approach towards stakeholders with cowardice towards the victims of armed conflict.

The third era of humanitarianism came about as a response to such criticism. It was marked not only by the creation of Médecins Sans Frontiéres/Doctors Without Borders (MSF), as well as the birth and growth of many other NGOs, but also by a relative setback of humanitarian protection efforts. Assistance in kind was no longer a minor aspect of IHL but had become a facet of international relations *per se*, the most visible aspect of humanitarianism.

This development was prompted by the massive displacement of people in a number of crisis areas. It was also a product of evolving relations between the Eastern and Western blocks and of the developing civil society in Western countries after the 1968 student movements. During the last years of the Cold War, the Soviet–Afghan Conflict (1979–1989) marked a turning point in the history of humanitarian action. During the ensuing refugee crisis, the presence of Afghan warriors in Pakistani refugee camps and unrestricted freedom of movement in Pakistan's so-called *tribal areas* bordering Afghanistan, allowed humanitarian

---

[30]Such discontent is exemplified by the origin of the Red Crescent Society. In the late nineteenth century, when the Bosnian Serbs—at the time making up the majority of Bosnia's population—and the Bulgarians rose against the Ottoman Empire, the ICRC asked the Ottomans to allow them to establish a National Society for rescuing the sick and wounded. The Ottoman Empire refused to host an official Red Cross society, creating a Red Crescent Society instead.

workers to enter Afghanistan without visas issued by the pro-Soviet government in Kabul. They instead relied on the help of the armed groups battling Russia's Red Army. These *mujjahiddin*, celebrated as *freedom fighters* by the *free world* and supported by the US with Stinger missiles, helped bring the *French Doctors* across the border from Pakistan to Afghanistan and expected from them humanitarian support for their own troops. Once again, world politics shaped the way humanitarian action was exercised.

The NGOs' conduct in Afghanistan amounted to an approach that only provided partial aid to certain stakeholders in the war. Underpinning these actions were the feelings among humanitarians of engaging in an epic adventure and acting for a *just cause*. The Western world welcomed, bypassing the Soviet-controlled Afghan State. The NGOs involved were celebrated due to their perceived support for the Afghan people's right to self-determination and resistance to Soviet oppression.

This created the illusion of a *post-state centric* situation, with civil society capable of imposing its moral values on States: as per this concept, human life and humanitarian access to victims trump State sovereignty. This doctrine eventually came to be termed as 'humanitarian intervention'. However, UNGA Resolution 43/131 (1988) on humanitarian assistance to victims of natural disasters and similar emergency situations did not mention this concept. It was, nevertheless, considered a big step forward, in as much as it referred to NGOs as full-fledged actors in the domain of humanitarian action, and highlighted States' responsibilities towards victims by providing for them and cooperating with intergovernmental and non-governmental humanitarian organisations in coordinating relief efforts.[31]

The fourth era of humanitarianism began with the fall of the Berlin Wall. The feeling of a Western victory over the Communist system gave way to a blossoming of Western civil society as a symbol of a free and democratic system. NGOs received strong support from Western States, particularly from the EU.

In the meantime, confrontations between ethnic groups became the predominant model of conflict, blurring the lines of soldiers and civilians, due to the often-strong attachment of civilians to a particular warring party, on ethnic or related grounds.

In the face of this new challenge, international politics seemed to shift from hard power approaches to a more human-centred way of crisis management. A first step was made during the Iraqi–Kurdish conflict (see Sect. 5.3), which happened to be both the climax of the so-called *interventionist* approach and the beginning of a new era of humanitarian assistance schemes drawn up by the UN Security Council. The Kurdish Iraqi minority, which had suffered under Saddam Hussein's regime, opposed him during the 1991 Gulf war. Although Saddam had been defeated, this did not amount to the end of his regime. The Kurds, fearing reprisals, fled their cities in great number and headed to the Turkish and Iranian borders. In early April 1991, more than one million Kurds were living in the mountainous border regions, exhausted and exposed to cold and hunger. The following American-led intervention was an armed operation, not comparable to the illegal cross-border

[31] Art. 1 of UNGA Resolution 43/131 provides for the '*primary responsibility*' of the local State.

humanitarian activities carried out by small groups of physicians in Afghanistan in the 1980s.

For the first time, an intervention aimed at providing humanitarian assistance echoed a UNSC resolution, although not mandated by it. This turning point was marked by UNSC Resolution 688, which the UNSC adopted in the face of atrocities committed by Saddam's regime both in southern Iraq (against the Shia majority) and in the North (against the Kurdish minority). For the first time, the UNSC recognised a situation as a 'threat to the peace' under Article 39 UN Charter that involved a State abusing the human rights of its own population.[32] However, the UNSC did not order precise measures aimed at restoring internal order. Without a UNSC mandate, the intervention, termed 'Operation Provide Comfort', brought together a coalition of States, including France, the Netherlands, Spain, the UK and the USA, upon a French initiative. It was up to the main States of the victorious coalition to take a strong attitude: without proper Iraqi authorisation, having only notified an Iraqi General, several coalition battalions entered the Iraqi Kurdish region via Turkey. Staying for some three months, they re-established security and supported the Kurds' return to their cities by means of roads specially constructed for this purpose, the so-called *blue roads*. The UNSC did not go any further than qualifying the situation and calling upon the Iraqi State to cooperate in order to improve the populations' situation.

From an international legal point of view, the intervention was an unauthorised interference in Iraq's internal affairs, although aimed at providing *comfort* to the distressed population. This was the archetype of the *ingérence* concept, a marked difference to the nineteenth century *intervention d'humanité*.[33] Humanitarian intervention is active upon the consequences of the slaughter, which is to be stopped, while *intervention d'humanité* works upstream, upon the causes of suffering. In the case of Iraq, the involved troops, each in their area of responsibility, acted more as a sort of police force with added medical and logistical assets. They provided services—among them, security—independent of the military situation.

Over the following months and years, the UNSC raised great hopes every time it characterised a situation as a 'threat to the peace', especially where the actions in question directly targeted civilian populations or hindered the delivery of vital humanitarian assistance to vulnerable populations. Soon, however, hope turned into disappointment in the face of complex crises, which the UNSC was unable

[32]UN Security Council Resolution 688, para.1: '*Condemns the repression of the Iraqi civilian population in many parts of Iraq, including most recently in Kurdish-populated areas, the consequences of which threaten international peace and security.*'

[33]In the nineteenth and early twentieth century, the term was used to describe a short military operation aimed at saving people whose lives were immediately threatened. On this basis, a sort of legal regime built on practice emerged, a customary exception to the major rule of sovereignty. It encompassed a collective approach—authorisation or ratification of the '*Concert des Nations*'—proportionality, prohibition of using intervening for any other reasons than to save lives. This customary exception to the major rule of sovereignty has been theorised in the last years of the period (Rougier 1910).

to remedy due to disagreements among its members. The decision to rely upon peacekeeping forces, even entrusting them with the mandate to defend besieged cities qualified as *security zones*, proved insufficient to avoid tragedies such as the Rwandan genocide and the slaughter in Srebrenica. Disillusioned with this state of affairs, most States consequently applauded an operation undertaken under the aegis of protection of populations bypassing both State sovereignty and the UNSC: the NATO air strikes on Kosovo and Serbia.

The desire to improve respect for international law led to the development of the *responsibility to protect* (R2P) doctrine, although limited to four specific situations[34] and not appropriate to ameliorate the daily humanitarian needs of populations in crisis zones.

6.2 Regional Specificities of Humanitarian Action

The humanitarian chronology shows that a Western ideology was universalised through the U.N., as proven by two different examples. From the perspective of States in the global south, this approach, centred on enforcing the individual well-being of oppressed citizens in third countries, did not necessarily represent progress. At least, it was not in line with the strong role that many of them attached to the principle of State sovereignty.

Some cultural areas have expressed reluctance towards certain aspects of global humanitarianism in diverse ways. One historic example, briefly evoked above, is the Turk Ottoman Empire. When called upon by the ICRC to create its national society for rescue to the sick and wounded, it decided to instead establish the Red Crescent society. Acting in this way, it expressed the conviction that humanitarian action had to reflect a religious imperative, together with the proclamation of the belonging of Turkey to Dar-Al-Islam.

Much more recently, several North African States have expressed hostility towards humanitarian action. Faced with ethnic cleansing and massacres in Darfur, the UNSC had decided to provide military protection to endangered Darfuri through a Hybrid Afro-UN force, the United Nations Mission in Darfur (UNMID).[35] Its creation was postponed for months due to Sudan's hostility towards the operation. Likewise, the government of Chad managed to delay the arrival of the EUFOR mission to Chad. This European force—authorised with the mandate of supporting UNMID with Darfuri refugees[36]—was regarded with little enthusiasm by Chad as the mission was supposed to be based in that State. Taking advantage of the mistake of a French NGO,[37] Chad tried to outright discredit humanitarian

---

[34]Genocide, Crimes against Humanity, War Crimes, Aggression.

[35]UN Security Council Resolution 1769 (2007).

[36]UN Security Council Resolution 1778 (2007).

[37]'*L'Arche de Zoe*', which had organised the transfer of a group of '*Darfuri orphans*' who proved to be neither Darfuri, nor orphaned, but a Chadian citizen.

action, as well as Western military protection. Finally, in 2009, Sudan expelled dozens of Western NGOs as a reaction to the arrest warrant against President Omar Al Bashir, issued by the ICC.

Similar events took place in Asia. As one of the most evident phenomena, one may note a certain humanitarian *isolationism* in some States. After the December 2004 tsunami devastated parts of South and Southeast Asia, the Association of Southeast Asian Nations (ASEAN) created its own disaster response mechanism, demonstrating that ASEAN member States are not willing to depend on Western humanitarian interventions to safeguard their populations. After Hurricane Nargis struck Myanmar in 2008, the country's military dictatorship refused Western and UN aid workers' entry to Myanmar. However, the authorities accepted 160 Asian humanitarian workers from Bangladesh, China, India and Thailand, although even those humanitarians were not granted free access to victims. Almost every element of assistance had to be delivered to the Myanmar army, which then distributed it to the population. The Karen national minority in the Arakan State was especially affected by a lack of help. Despite calls by some, especially Bernard Kouchner, then French Minister for Foreign Affairs, to apply the R2P, they were dismissed by UN Secretary General Ban Ki Moon. The concept was not to be applied in case of natural disaster.

7 Conclusion

The years 2007, 2008 and 2009 witnessed a decline in international humanitarian rescue missions, especially in Africa and Asia with hurricane Nargis in Myanmar or the end of the Sri Lankan civil war, which became a largely forgotten crisis, in spite of decades of horrific violence. During the last decade, some obvious changes have occurred in the humanitarian action landscape regarding the main stakeholders, operators and donors. Companies, the activities of which often seem driven by economic interest, have entered the humanitarian stage and are called upon to provide funding, or free services, for example as regards water supply.

Newly independent and certain developing States tend to organise the protection of their population in a pragmatic way, making use of all forces at their disposal. They may even involve their military and other public services, an approach that differs from the one taken by Western countries.

Several of the Gulf States have emerged as new donors. Some actors are faith-based and pander towards specific religious communities. Such approaches are unusual in the eyes of Western humanitarian workers, who usually consider them a danger to the principle of impartiality. Time will tell whether the various currently existing approaches can be reconciled or whether they will progress independently of each other.

What does the future of humanitarian action hold in an ever more globalised world? The current crises, especially the Syrian civil war and the conflict in Yemen, have seen a waning of respect for humanitarian aid workers and institutions, such as medical aid services. Humanitarian access to the most strongly affected regions has become even more difficult. Despite setbacks and the danger that many humanitarian workers operate under, the value of humanitarian action is today undisputed within the international community.

Former UN Secretary General Ban Ki-Moon has made a lot of effort to reinforce humanitarian protection.[38] The UNSC, through Resolutions 2165 and 2175, has made it clear that in times of conflict, belligerent parties are expected to respect humanitarian action and humanitarian actors who are setting up a robust regime for cross-border activities in Syria. If nothing else, it may contribute to alleviate the suffering of the Syrian people to a certain degree and encourage humanitarians to intensify their important efforts to alleviate the suffering of vulnerable populations all over the world.

References

Dunant H (1862) A Memory of Solferino. Geneva

Organization of African Unity Convention Governing the Specific Aspects of Refugee Problems in Africa (Addis Ababa Convention). http://www.achpr.org/files/instruments/refugee-convention/achpr_instr_conv_refug_eng.pdf

Rougier A (1910) L'intervention d'humanité. Revue Générale de Droit International Public, Paris

United Nations General Assembly Resolution 2790, 6 December 1971. http://www.un.org/en/ga/search/view_doc.asp?symbol=A/RES/2790%28XXVI%29

Further Reading

Domestici-Met M-J, Frognier A-P, Nordquist K-Å, Roosens C, Runblom H, Swain A, Wallensteen P, Öberg M (1998) NOHA volume 3, Geopolitics in humanitarian assistance. EU bookshop

Donini A (2010) The far side: the "meta functions" of humanitarisms in a globalized world. Disasters 34-s2(12)

Drapac V (2010) Constructing Yugoslavia. A transnational history European studies series. Palgrave Macmillan, Basingstoke

Flin C (2011) Introduction to geopolitics. Routledge

Ismail O, Sköns E (2014) The security activities of external actors in Africa, SIPRI monographs. Oxford University Press, New York

Lowe V, Roberts A, Welsh J, Zaum D (2010) The United Nations Security Council and War the evolution of thought and practice since 1945. Oxford University Press, New York

[38] In light of the violence committed in Jaffna (Sri Lanka) in 2009 by government troops, Ban Ki-Moon launched an inquiry and created the initiative 'Rights Upfront', with the aim of improving the sensitivity of UN staff towards human rights violations. In December 2012, he launched the World Humanitarian Summit process, which concluded with the Istanbul summit of May 2016.

Malone D (2007) The international struggle over Iraq. Politics in the UN Security Council 1980–2005. Oxford University Press, New York
Mazower M (2002) The Balkans. A short history. Modern Library, New York
Sempa FP (2002) Geopolitics: from the cold war to the 21st century. Transaction Publishers
Seybolt TB (2008) Humanitarian military intervention. The conditions for success and failure, SIPRI monographs. Oxford University Press, New York
Tuathail GÓ, Dalby S, Routledge P (2006) The geopolitics reader, 2nd edn. Routledge
United Nations Security Council Resolution XXXX

Marie-Josée Domestici-Met is Professor Emeritus Dr Hab. at Aix-Marseille University, France, where she holds the Jean Monnet Chair ad personam. Between 2004 and 2016, she acted as Director of the Institute for International Humanitarian Studies. She is also a member of the French Commission for the Implementation of Humanitarian Law.

The Changing Nature of Conflict: The Need for a Conflict-Sensitive Approach

Sulagna Maitra

1 Introduction

Conflicts and complex emergencies provide the most pervasive context for contemporary humanitarian action as they drive more than 80% of current humanitarian need.[1] Conflicts are a universal feature of society, although every conflict is unique in terms of its actors, causes, consequences and dynamics. For humanitarian organisations

> the word 'conflict' is usually used with reference to countries where there is politically motivated violence, internally or internationally, and where several parties (e.g. states, communities, political parties or groups) are involved in acting out their disagreement using violence.[2]

It is imperative for humanitarian actors to understand the dynamics of conflict contexts as they seek to bring relief and protection to vulnerable populations caught up in complex emergencies. A 2011 study by Zicherman et al.[3] found that 85% of humanitarian practitioners surveyed had witnessed aid inadvertently causing or exacerbating an existing conflict. The respondents agreed that *understanding the context*[4] was one of the top challenges for any aid worker. The instrumentalisation

---

[1]Global Peace Index (2016), http://economicsandpeace.org/wp-content/uploads/2016/06/GPI-2016-Report_2.pdf; UN WHS Secretariat (2015).

[2]Trocaire (2011), p. 6, http://www.trocaire.org/resources/policyandadvocacy/conflict-sensitivity-toolkit.

[3]Zicherman et al. (2011), p. 6. This study surveyed five members of the Conflict Sensitivity Consortium, ActionAid International, CAFOD, CARE International, Plan International and World Vision International.

[4]*Id.*, p. 9.

S. Maitra (✉)
University College Dublin, Dublin, Ireland
e-mail: sulagna.maitra@ucd.ie

© Springer International Publishing AG 2018

H.-J. Heintze, P. Thielbörger (eds.), *International Humanitarian Action*,
DOI 10.1007/978-3-319-14454-2_4

of humanitarian aid in the complex emergencies of the early 1990s led to the realisation that *when international assistance is given in the context of a violent conflict, it becomes a part of that context and thus also of the conflict.*[5]

Awareness, both of self and of the context one operates in, is critical to gaining access to vulnerable populations, negotiating with social gatekeepers, maintaining security of humanitarian personnel, remaining neutral in a politically charged and polarised environment, coordinating with peacekeeping and development actors and minimising the inadvertent harmful impact of humanitarian aid.[6]

The changing character and protracted nature of contemporary conflicts have also forced the humanitarian community to re-evaluate its response to violent crises and demand greater political leadership in preventing and ending violent conflicts. The international organisation Médecins Sans Frontières/Doctors Without Borders (MSF) while explaining its decision to pull out of the World Humanitarian Summit (WHS) of 2016 said that a 'fig-leaf of good intentions'[7] was no longer acceptable as a sop for failure of States to fulfil international humanitarian commitments and their obligations to uphold humanitarian and refugee law.

The deliberate targeting of aid workers and humanitarian establishments,[8] the widening gap between humanitarian needs and available funding, the blatant violation of international humanitarian and human rights law, unprecedented levels of mass displacement and the lack of protection for at-risk populations point to the need for a seismic shift in humanitarian response to contemporary crises.[9] The recently concluded WHS identified political leadership to prevent and end conflicts as Core Responsibility #1 in its Agenda for Humanity.[10] Other shared responsibilities include upholding the norms that safeguard humanity, protecting at-risk populations, shifting focus of aid from delivering relief to ending need and, finally, investing in capacity building.[11]

While the modern humanitarian profession is said to have originated from the battlefields of Solferino in 1859, systematic analysis of conflicts and the call to mainstream conflict-sensitive humanitarian responses to complex emergencies is a relatively recent phenomenon. Conflict analysis as a field of study progressed during the Cold War years primarily to handle the tensions between the American and Soviet power blocs.[12] Using tools such as system analysis and game theory, analysts tried to understand the dynamics of conflict in terms of changing relations

[5]Anderson (1999).

[6]Loane (2011).

[7]Médecins Sans Frontières (2016, May 5), http://www.msf.org.uk/article/msf-to-pull-out-of-world-humanitarian-summit; UN Secretary-General (2016).

[8]In 2015, 75 hospitals managed or supported by Médecins Sans Frontières/Doctors Without Borders (MSF) were bombed.

[9]MSF (2016, May 5) and UN Secretary-General (2016).

[10]UN Secretary General, *ibid*.

[11]World Humanitarian Summit (2016).

[12]Wallensteen (2007).

between conflict parties,[13] assessing the risks of a global conflict in a nuclear world and strategic analysis.[14] The 1960s and 1970s saw a broadening of conflict analysis to study needs, greed and grievances to understand intrastate, local, societal conflicts that were plaguing nations, especially the United States.[15] Peace research expanded the meaning of violence to incorporate cultural and structural violence, and analysts differentiated between negative peace, i.e. absence of physical violence, and positive peace, i.e. a condition characterised by cooperation, freedom from fear and want, absence of exploitation, freedom of action and prevalence of economic development, pluralism, justice, equality and dynamism.[16]

With the thaw in the Cold War and the scaling down of some regional and interstate conflicts, the 1980s and 1990s saw a renewed interest in conflict resolution.[17] Simultaneously, for humanitarian practitioners, conflict of the early 1990s, especially the Rwandan genocide, resulted in the Do No Harm doctrine and the rise of a conflict-sensitive approach to humanitarian action.[18] Since 2001, after 9/11 and the subsequent *War on Terror*, however, conflict analysis again became preoccupied with strategic analysis, especially in conflicts relating to terrorism.[19]

While tools for conflict analysis continue to evolve and become more sophisticated, applying the conflict-sensitive approach to humanitarian action remains problematic.[20] The divergent origins of conflict analysis have led to a multitude of frameworks, all of which must be understood to comprehensively analyse conflicts.[21] However, the complexity of contexts in which humanitarian actors operate, lack of access to information and the speed at which humanitarian professionals are required to respond leave little scope for sophisticated analysis and data collection.[22] Thus, conflict analysis in humanitarian practice is a constant trade-off between the desirable level of analysis and what is feasible within a given context.

[13]The Cold War demonstrated how allies such as the US, UK and USSR who fought a major war together can get locked into a dangerous conflagration within a matter of few years. At the same time, the coming together of two former enemies, Germany and France, under the same bloc showed a potential for reversing the conflict dynamics (Wallensteen 2007).

[14]Wallensteen (2007) and Ramsbotham et al. (2011).

[15]Wallensteen (2007).

[16]Galtung (1967), http://www.transcend.org/files/Galtung_Book_unpub_Theories_of_Peace_-_A_Synthetic_Approach_to_Peace_Thinking_1967.pdf; Galtung (1969), pp. 167–191.

[17]Wallensteen (2007).

[18]Conflict Sensitivity Consortium (Undated), http://www.conflictsensitivity.org/do-no-harm-local-capacities-for-peace-project; Zicherman et al. (2011).

[19]Wallensteen (2007).

[20]Zicherman et al. (2011).

[21]Wallensteen (2007).

[22]Zicherman et al. (2011).

2 Definition and Types of Conflict

There is no one universally accepted definition of conflict or a theoretical framework that presents a typology of conflict in terms of its scale, intensity and consequences. However, according to the following definition, which is widely accepted and considered to be comprehensive, conflict is a *social situation in which a minimum of two actors (parties) strive to acquire at the same moment in time an available set of scarce resources.*[23] International humanitarian law identifies two main types of armed conflicts during which it is applicable[24]:

- *international armed conflict* between two or more opposing States;
- *non-international armed conflict* between governmental forces and non-governmental armed groups or, in certain cases, between such groups only.

The category of 'other situations of violence' is frequently used by humanitarian actors, especially the International Committee of the Red Cross (ICRC) to describe situations of violence that do not fall under either of the two above-mentioned legal categories.[25] The challenges to classify situations of violence due to imprecise criteria of conflict categories in legal texts are recognised and accepted.[26]

The classification of armed conflicts is often linked to political considerations as parties involved tend to interpret facts in accordance with interest.[27] Commenting on water conflicts, Kalpakian opines that 'serious conflict means war, tense diplomatic standoffs, insurgencies and openly hostile diplomatic relations. Water disputes can and often do occur between states that have no serious conflicts with each other'.[28] Other scholars, such as Zeitoun, however, disagree[29]:

> We need to make a distinction between violent conflict and conflict itself... Absence of war does not mean absence of conflict...In Chad, in Western Darfur, you have different tribes, sometimes members of the same tribe fighting over limited resources of water.[30]

Various efforts have been made to systematically analyse conflicts and categorise them to identify trends, triggers and impacts. The categories and criteria for inclusion of conflicts vary between databases and are constantly evolving with the changing nature of conflict.

---

[23]Wallensteen (2007).

[24]ICRC (2008), http://www.icrc.org/eng/assets/files/other/opinion-paper-armed-conflict.pdf.

[25]Lawand (2012), http://www.icrc.org/eng/resources/documents/interview/2012/12-10-niac-non-international-armed-conflict.htm.

[26]Vite (2009), pp. 70–94; Human Security Report Project (2013).

[27]For example, sometimes States tend to play down the intensity of a situation of violence and claim to undertake actions in the name of maintaining public order, see Vite, *ibid.*

[28]Kalpakian (2004), p. 193.

[29]Zeitoun and Mirumachi (2008), pp. 297–316.

[30]Inter Press Service News Agency, Wars, No, Conflicts, Yes, 2007, http://www.globalpolicy.org/component/content/article/198/40379.html.

The Uppsala Conflict Data Program (UCDP) deems a conflict to be active if *there are at least 25 battle-related deaths per calendar year in one of the conflict's dyads*.[31] In the case of one-sided violence, an actor is considered active if *an organised group incurs at least 25 deliberate killings of civilians in a year*.[32]

The Correlates of War Project (COW), one of the first initiatives to systematically analyse war, stipulated that the threshold for war is 1000 battle-related deaths in a year to distinguish it from other situations of violence.[33] Prior to the end of the Cold War, the COW project categorised conflicts into international wars and civil wars depending on whether military action was taking place within or beyond the State's territory.[34] However, critics point out that stringent data coding rules regarding the *number of battle-related deaths* mean that a large percentage of the deaths that result from organised criminal violence or as an indirect result of the conflict (such as epidemics, forced displacement) cannot be coded and therefore do not get recorded.[35]

The UCDP currently classifies conflicts into four main categories in terms of actors and their location. These are extrasystemic armed conflict, interstate armed conflict, internal armed conflict and internationalised internal armed conflict.[36]

The Heidelberg Conflict Barometer (HIIK)[37] measures conflict intensity on a five-point scale of dispute, non-violent crisis, violent crisis, limited war and war. It determines the intensity of a conflict by collating points along five parameters: weapons (type and usage), personnel (total number of conflict actors), casualties (number of direct conflict-related deaths), refugees and IDPs, and destruction (or threat to existence).[38] Thus, the Conflict Barometer takes into account the means as well as the consequences of violent conflict in order to determine its intensity. While HIIK's parameters are comprehensive enough to capture conflicts of varying intensity, they are also subjective. Hence, it is important to keep in mind that the methodology for calculating the number of conflicts, its actors and the number of people affected by it is constantly evolving and trying to keep up with the changing nature of conflict. Conflicts may also be categorised by the level at which

---

[31]UCDP, Definitions, http://www.pcr.uu.se/research/ucdp/definitions/.

[32]*Ibid.*

[33]Sarkees (2011), http://cow.la.psu.edu/COW2%20Data/WarData_NEW/COW%20Website%20-%20Typology%20of%20war.pdf.

[34]Sarkees and Schafer (2000), pp. 123–144.

[35]Human Security Report Project (2013).

[36]UCDP, Definitions, http://www.pcr.uu.se/research/ucdp/definitions/, extrasystemic conflicts refer to colonial wars or wars of independence, which occur between governments and non-state groups located outside a State's own territory. Interstate armed conflicts involve two or more States. Internal armed conflicts are those that take place between the government and non-state groups located within the State or between two non-state actors within one State. It does not involve outside actors. Internationalised internal conflict however, is an internal conflict with intervention from external actors on one or both sides.

[37]HIIK (2015), http://www.hiik.de/en/konfliktbarometer/pdf/ConflictBarometer_2015.pdf.

[38]*Ibid.*

Table 1 Examples of conflict at different levels (developed from Ramsbotham, O; Woodhouse, T; Miall, H; Contemporary Conflict Resolution, 2011)

Level	Example of conflict
Global	Geopolitical transition, North–South economic divide, weapons proliferation, ideological contestations
Regional	Outwards (spillover, contagion, diffusion), inwards (influence, interference, intervention)
State	Contextual and structural
- Social	Weak social institutions: ethnic, class stratifications
- Economic	Weak economy: poor resource base, relative deprivation (uneven development)
- Political	Weak polity: partisan government, regime illegitimacy
Conflict Party	Relational—group mobilisation, intergroup dynamics
Elite/ Individual	Exclusionist policy, factional interest, belligerent leadership

they occur. Table 1 lists examples of conflicts at various levels and their possible causes.

While conflict often involves personal loss and societal destruction, not all conflicts are characterised by physical violence and devastation.[39]

Galtung suggests that conflict be viewed as a triangle with three vertices or key aspects[40]: attitude (A), behaviour (B) and contradiction (C). To characterise a situation as a full-blown conflict, all three elements (A, B, C) need to be present. A conflict without physical violence or conflict behaviour (B) is known as a latent conflict, as well as negative or unstable peace. It denotes a situation where individuals, groups, communities or countries have differences and a negative attitude towards each other but neither party attacks the opposite side. Unequal distribution of power, marginalisation, contest over resources, differing interests or values all have the potential to spark conflict if a triggering event occurs.[41]

Paul Wehr observes that 'social life is above all a struggle for power and status regardless of the type of structure. An inevitable power differential between groups, and between individuals, produces latent conflict in all social relations'.[42] The post-Cold War era particularly saw a proliferation of so-called protracted complex emergencies, which may be described as follows:

> [They] tend to have multiple causes, but are essentially political in nature and entail violent conflict. They typically include a breakdown of legitimate institutions and governance, widespread suffering and massive population displacements, and they often involve and require a range of responses from the international community, including intense diplomacy and conflict resolution efforts, UN policing actions, and the provision of multilateral and bilateral humanitarian assistance by official and private agencies. A complex

---

[39]Jeong (2008).

[40]Galtung (1967, 1969).

[41]Brahm (2003), http://www.beyondintractability.org/essay/latent-conflict.

[42]*Ibid*, citing Wehr, P., Conflict Emergence, http://www.colorado.edu/conflict/peace/problem/cemerge.htm.

> emergency tends to be very dynamic, characterized by rapid changes that are difficult to predict. Thus, complex issues are raised regarding the timing, nature and scale of response.[43]

At this stage, it is useful to note the characteristics of intractable conflicts as distinguished from manageable ones. Deutsch and Coleman have summarised the key features of an intractable conflict as follows[44]:

- *Time and intensity*: intractable conflicts tend to persist and cycle over time, with sporadic increases in intensity and occasional outbreaks of violence. These protracted social conflicts typically last at least a generation, often many generations. At times, they may go underground and appear to be resolved, but if their root causes are not addressed they tend to resurface and intensify when external circumstances permit or encourage their expression.
- *Issue centrality*: intractable conflict tends to involve needs or values that the disputants experience as critical to their own (or their group's) survival. Often these concerns are unrelated to the issues that initially trigger the conflict, but as the conflict escalates the issues are often transformed and ultimately take on a basic and threatening character. Deutsch offered the label 'malignant social process'[45] to characterise this stage of intense, conflict-filled relationship that is 'increasingly dangerous and costly and from which the participants see no way of extricating themselves without becoming vulnerable to an unacceptable loss in a value central to their self-identifies or self-esteem'.[46]
- *Conflict pervasiveness*: the experience of threat associated with such conflict is often so central and basic to the human experience that the effects of the conflict spread and become pervasive, affecting most aspects of a person's or a community's social and political life. Cultural, religious, educational, public and political institutions become involved with the conflict, as do many of the community's scholars and leaders.
- *Hopelessness*: typically, the disputants in an intractable conflict reach a point where they feel hopeless about the potential for constructive resolution. The conflict is usually experienced as a lose–lose situation.
- *Motivation to harm*: at this stage of intensity, the motivations of the disputants are typically at a point where their primary objective is to physically and psychologically harm one another.
- *Resistance to resolution*: finally, intractable conflicts are resistant to repeated and concerted attempts to resolve them. Traditional approaches such as diplomacy, negotiation, mediation and unilateral use of threats or force by either side often fail to bring about conflict de-escalation or resolution. Intractable conflicts require development of extraordinary alternatives to be resolved.

---

[43]Joint Evaluation of Emergency Assistance to Rwanda (1996), p. 3, http://www.oecd.org/derec/sweden/50189495.pdf.

[44]Deutsch and Coleman (2000), pp. 428–450.

[45]Deutsch (1983).

[46]*Id.*, p. 4.

Humanitarian actors acknowledge that, in recent decades, horrific bloodshed has been the outcome of diverse situations of violence in rural and urban spaces, which did not necessarily meet the criteria of armed conflict or reach the threshold of battle-related deaths stipulated by various databases and therefore did not constitute a humanitarian crisis in the conventional sense.[47] In this vein, a recent ICRC policy document states that

> sometimes chronic situations of violence, whether spawned by social or political upheaval, identity-related tension and/or repressive or discriminatory State policies, or criminal acts, create dramatic humanitarian situations with consequences that are as, or even more far-reaching than those of armed conflicts. They have emerged against the backdrop of globalization, which in some cases has worsened inequalities within societies, hastened the privatization of violence in the absence of State services in certain contexts or encouraged 'identitarianism' or political or social contestation. Phenomena such as easily accessible weapons, climate change, urbanization, migration and the development of communication technologies have accelerated the emergence of violence and play in favour of certain perpetrators. The violence may also be the work of the State, which, through its use of law enforcement, arrests and detentions, etc., itself becomes a perpetrator of the violence.[48]

3 Contemporary Conflict Trends and Humanitarian Response

There are several organisations and projects that systematically map situations of violence on a yearly basis, making it possible to assess the changing nature of conflict over time.

Frequently used databases that provide a comprehensive overview of conflicts at various levels include the following:

- Uppsala Conflict Data Program (UCDP),
- Heidelberg Conflict Barometer,
- Global Peace Index,
- ECHO Forgotten Crisis Assessment,
- OECD States of Fragility Report,
- Human Security Report Project.

The Correlations of War project was established in 1963 by J. David Singer as one of the earliest initiatives in this field. The Uppsala Conflict Data Program and Heidelberg Conflict Barometer are frequently used to analyse global conflict trends. Other reports such as the Global Peace Index, the OECD States of Fragility Report and the Human Security Report are not strictly speaking conflict databases. They go beyond the stringent definitions of conflict events to analyse violence from a societal perspective. However, these reports help to assess the impact of conflict

[47]Human Security Report Project (2013).

[48]ICRC (2014), p. 277.

on global peace, human security and fragility of States. DG ECHO's Forgotten Crisis Assessment (FCA)

> identifies serious humanitarian crisis situations where the affected populations do not receive enough international aid or even none at all. These crises are characterised by low media coverage, a lack of donor interest (as measured through aid per capita) and a weak political commitment to solve the crisis, resulting in an insufficient presence of humanitarian actors.[49]

Estimates of the total number of conflicts and casualties worldwide vary. It is reported that the total number of active conflicts has remained stable at 31–37 over the last decade.[50] However, if we broaden the criteria of conflict, it is estimated that there were 409 active political conflicts in 2015, including 43 highly violent conflicts.[51]

Table 2 provides an overview of conflicts (2010–2015) and their geographical breakdown over the last 5 years, based on data from the Heidelberg Conflict Barometer. The figures in brackets indicate the number of highly violent conflicts recorded in the region. From the table it is clear that there has been an increase in the overall number of political conflicts, though there are slight variations every year. The greatest proportion of conflict events (almost one-third) was recorded in Asia. However, sub-Saharan Africa has been afflicted by the largest number of highly violent conflicts over the years. The Middle East has seen an increase in the number of political conflicts and a marginal increase in the number of violent conflicts. The data also shows that more political conflicts have been recorded in Europe compared to the Americas over the last 5 years. Nevertheless, Europe is clearly the most peaceful region in this estimation with the lowest number of highly violent conflicts.

Table 2 2010–2015 conflict overview

	2015	2014	2013	2012	2011	2010
Asia and Oceania	126 (6)	127 (6)	129 (8)	128 (10)	124 (8)	114 (9)
Sub-Saharan Africa	97 (20)	104 (18)	97 (18)	90 (19)	91 (12)	85 (6)
Middle East	71 (10)	74 (14)	71 (12)	69 (9)	62 (13)	55 (9)
Europe	62 (1)	67 (3)	63 (1)	58 (1)	65 (1)	64 (2)
Americas	53 (6)	52 (5)	54 (6)	51 (3)	46 (4)	45 (2)
Total	409 (43)	424 (46)	414 (45)	396 (42)	388 (38)	363 (28)

Developed by the author, Sulagna Maitra, compiled from data belonging to the Heidelberg Conflict Barometer 2010–2015. Data used by kind permission of the publisher, Heidelberg Institute for International Conflict Research (HIIK 2015), http://hiik.de/en/konfliktbarometer/ (accessed on 14 April 2017)

[49] DG ECHO (2015), http://ec.europa.eu/echo/what/humanitarian-aid/needs-assessments_en.

[50] Global Peace Index (2016) and United Nations WHS Secretariat (2015).

[51] HIIK (2015).

Approximately 1.5 billion people live in States affected by repeated cycles of violent conflict.[52] The economic impact of violence was estimated to have attained $13.6 trillion in 2015 (13% of the global economy) with losses of up to $2.5 trillion and $742 billion from crime and/or interpersonal violence and conflict respectively. A total of 76% of the world's poor live in countries that are environmentally vulnerable or politically fragile or both.[53] The Global Peace Index 2016 states that

> overall global levels of peace continue to deteriorate while the gap between the most and least peaceful countries continues to widen…So intense is the violence and conflict in the Middle-East and North Africa (MENA) region that, when looking at the rest of the world, the average levels of peacefulness in fact increased.[54]

Along with the internationalisation of the MENA conflicts, the report also noted an increase in efforts by States over the last 10 years to fund UN peacekeeping operations and a decrease in global military spending over the last 3 years.[55] A worrying trend is that 91% of official humanitarian assistance in 2014 went to long- and medium-term recipients, including regions facing long-term and protracted crises.[56]

In terms of causes, terrorism and political instability have emerged as the two main factors destabilising global peace.[57] Terrorism-related deaths increased by 80% between 2014 and 2015, and the number of *battle-related deaths* are the highest in 25 years.[58] While there is currently no way of assessing the total number of people affected by conflict and the severity of their needs, reports show that the number of people displaced by conflict doubled between 2007 and 2015, reaching a total of 65.3 million people.[59]

In terms of long-term trends in conflict, the Global Peace Index[60] collates information from the UCDP to report the following findings:

- Over the last 50 years, the number of countries involved in internal conflicts has overtaken the number of countries involved in external conflicts. Since the end of World War II, three-quarters of all conflicts have been intrastate conflicts.[61] While the rate of *civil-war onset* was stable during the Cold War, the end of that period saw a dramatic rise in intrastate conflicts.[62]

---

[52]United Nations WHS Secretariat (2015).

[53]Global Humanitarian Assistance (GHA) Report (2016).

[54]Global Peace Index (2016), http://economicsandpeace.org/wp-content/uploads/2016/06/GPI-2016-Report_2.pdf.

[55]*Ibid.*

[56]*Ibid.*

[57]*Ibid.*

[58]*Ibid.*

[59]GHA Report (2016).

[60]Global Peace Index (2016), http://economicsandpeace.org/wp-content/uploads/2016/06/GPI-2016-Report_2.pdf.

[61]PRIO (2015), http://www.prio.org/Projects/Extensions/ConflictTrends/Graphs/, accessed on 06 December, 2016.

[62]Uppsala Conflict Data Program (2016a, b, c).

- The last decade has seen an increase in the number of internationalised internal conflicts. They constituted only 3% of total conflicts in 1991 but made up for 32.5% of the total number of conflicts in 2014.
- Up to 2,023,283 million people (1989–2015) have died as a direct result of violence in State-based, non-State-based and one-sided conflicts since the end of the Cold War.[63] The number of battle-related deaths reached a 25-year high in 2014 due to the conflict in Syria. The number of deaths from one-sided violence has also increased in the last decade. Six episodes of genocidal violence, resulting in the deaths of more than 256,000 people, have been recorded since 1965.

Overall, there is a strong consensus that, even though the world has become less violent since the end of World War II, the last decade has seen an increase in conflict and violence.[64] Going forward, analysts caution against a high risk of internationalisation of internal armed conflicts in the next 10 years, given the interconnectedness of global politics and trends in mass migration.[65] Due to the complex and protracted nature of contemporary conflicts, humanitarian interventions in most crises last for more than 5 years.[66] The humanitarian response to conflicts also operates in a constant state of scarcity.

Needs of vulnerable populations as a result of political and environmental crises are higher than ever before. There was a 45% recorded shortfall in meeting humanitarian needs in 2015, even though the total amount of international aid reached an all-time high of US$ 28 billion.[67] Humanitarian professionals are thus increasingly required to serve people in a politically charged, polarised and highly volatile environment. The constant shortfall in aid implies that humanitarian relief needs to be efficient and effective in order to succeed in an environment of scarcity.

Furthermore, contemporary humanitarian workers are required to operate as part of joint integrated missions involving a host of other actors and local stakeholders, such as UN peacekeeping forces, development organisations, private for-profit actors, local governments, regional and local political, social and economic power brokers and gatekeepers. The plethora of actors operating in a humanitarian context does not necessarily share a commitment to the humanitarian principles, which in turn directly affects the humanitarian space available in a complex emergency.

---

[63] *Ibid.*

[64] Global Peace Index (2016), http://economicsandpeace.org/wp-content/uploads/2016/06/GPI-2016-Report_2.pdf.

[65] United Nations WHS Secretariat (2015).

[66] *Ibid.*

[67] GHA Report (2016).

4 Conflict Analysis Frameworks and Tools

The analytical framework for conflict can be broadly classified into three categories, depending on their focus: conflict dynamics, causes of conflict (basic needs) and rational calculations (game theory). Based on these theoretical frameworks, several tools have been developed to map conflicts.

Galtung's Conflict Triangle (1969) is one of the influential models in contemporary conflict resolution.[68] While Galtung revised and clarified his analysis in his subsequent publications,[69] the ABCs of conflict dynamics remain key analytical categories in conflict research today. Galtung is joined by several other scholars, such as Kriesberg, Mitchell, Pruitt and Rubin and Wiberg, in attempting to present a dynamic perspective of conflict analysis paralleling advances in game theory.[70] Figure 1 represents a diagrammatic presentation of the ABC triangle.

Galtung postulated that conflict moves among the triangle's three corners where corner A refers to conflict attitudes, B to conflict behaviour and C to the conflict or contradiction itself. Conflict resolution or conflict transformation is therefore a *never-ending* process and a solution in the *sense of a steady-state, durable formation is at best a temporary goal.*[71]

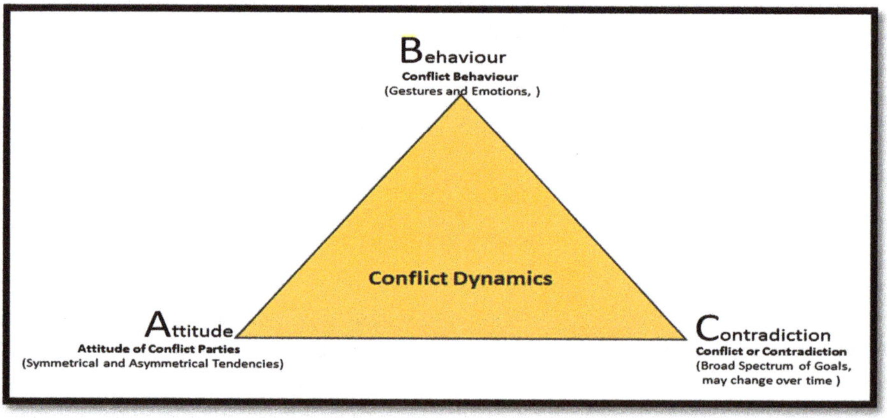

Fig. 1 Galtung's conflict triangle. Reproduced and adapted by kind permission of the publisher from Oliver Ramsbotham, Tom Woodhouse & Hugh Miall Alexander, Contemporary Conflict Resolution, Figure 1.1, p. 12 (Polity Press, 4th Edition, 2016)

---

[68]Ramsbotham et al. (2011).

[69]See www.transcend.org for a comprehensive bibliography of Galtung's publications on peace and conflict research.

[70]Wallensteen (2007).

[71]*Ibid.*

All conflicts usually involve some sort of behaviour or action.[72] It is important to note that conflict does not always involve inflicting physical harm as action or behaviour. It may also include coercion, verbal abuse and other types of hostile behaviour.[73] An end to hostile behaviour or physical violence, however, rarely means an end to conflict.[74] The underlying *issues* referred to or the contradictions that motivate their behaviour need to be resolved to truly end conflict.[75] A full-blown conflict encompasses all three characteristics, i.e., contradictions, negative attitude and coercive or violent behaviour.

It is interesting to note that Galtung in his conceptualisation of the conflict triangle acknowledged the existence of *secondary* conflicts, i.e. those that emerge as the *core* conflict spreads and deepens, *sucking in* other issues and actors.[76] This observation does not feature explicitly in his discussion on institutionalised conflict resolution and thus creates problems in understanding how the conflict resolution mechanisms deal with these *secondary* conflicts. However, at this stage, it is important to point out that while the category of *secondary* conflicts may exist conceptually or in the eye of the respective conflict resolution mechanism, it may not be regarded as such by the parties to the conflict. Hence, they might want to deal with the core and the *secondary* conflicts simultaneously. This will create a challenge (or *stress* in terms of systems analysis) on the conflict resolution mechanism.

Another limitation of the conflict dynamics framework concerns its ability to analyse the start of a conflict within its broader context, i.e. the reasons for the contradictions and the negative attitudes to emerge.[77] Here, alternative frameworks focusing on basic needs, position, interest and power provide helpful insights. Scholars such as Coser and subsequently Azar argued that the basis of a conflict is the denial of others' needs, and therefore any conflict resolution process must identify those needs and find ways to respond to them.[78] Other scholars posit that there is a difference between the needs or interests of conflict parties and the positions they assume. For example, in negotiations between Egypt and Israel over Sinai, even though both parties position their claims around national sovereignty, Egypt's main interest was national territorial integrity, while Israel's primary concern was security.[79] Thus, while both parties' positions were incompatible, discussions on their respective interests yielded in the Camp David settlements.

---

[72] *Ibid.*

[73] Galtung (1971), pp. 173–206.

[74] Wallensteen (2007).

[75] *Ibid.*; Galtung (1971).

[76] Ramsbotham et al. (2011).

[77] Wallensteen (2007).

[78] *Ibid.*; Ramsbotham et al. (2011).

[79] Ramsbotham et al. (2011).

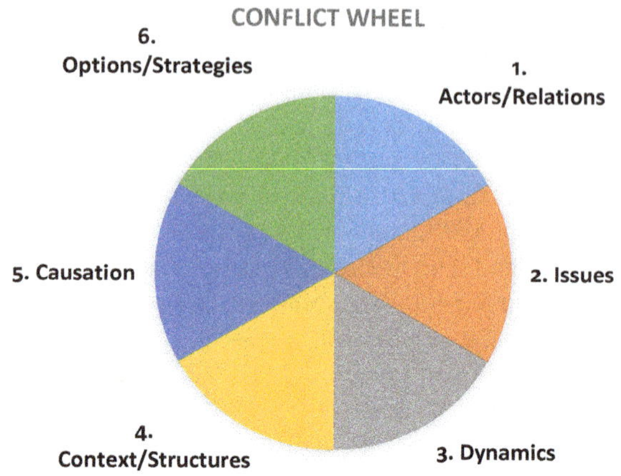

Fig. 2 Conflict wheel. Reproduced and adapted by kind permission of the publisher from Swiss Agency of Development and Cooperation (SDC), Conflict Analysis Tools, Tool 1, p. 3 (SDC 2005), http://www.files.ethz.ch/isn/15416/CSPM%20Tipp%20Conflict%206.3.pdf (accessed on 14 April 2017)

At this point, it is useful to briefly summarise the conflict tools available to analyse conflicts. The following summary of frameworks has been collated from The Centre for Security Studies' Conflict Analysis Tip Sheet,[80] Trocaire's Conflict Sensitivity Toolkit (2011),[81] OECD's Conflict Analysis and its use in Evaluation (2012)[82] and Ramsbotham et al. (2011).[83]

The Conflict Wheel The conflict wheel is a meta conflict analysis tool. The *wheel* is divided into six parts: actors/relations, issues, dynamics, context or structures, causation, and options or strategies (see Fig. 2). Each of these sections needs to be further analysed with the help of relevant tools discussed below. The main purpose of the conflict wheel is to help organise the various conflict analysis tools focusing on a specific part/section of the conflict (for example, actors, issues, etc.) and provide an overview of the conflict. The wheel symbolises wholeness and movement.

The Conflict Tree The *conflict tree* (Fig. 3) is a visualising and sorting tool. This influential framework model was developed and applied in the Responding to Conflict Programme at Birmingham.[84] The tree helps to visualise the interaction between the root causes or structural factors, core problems or issues and its multiple effects. It also helps to differentiate the time horizons of various conflict transformation approaches.

Conflict Map A conflict map simplifies the conflict and attempts to visualise the actors and their powers or influence on the conflict, their mutual relationship and the

---

[80]SDC (2005), http://www.css.ethz.ch/content/dam/ethz/special-interest/gess/cis/center-for-securities-studies/pdfs/Conflict-Analysis-Tools.pdf.

[81]Trocaire (2011).

[82]OECD (2012).

[83]Ramsbotham et al. (2011).

[84]*Ibid.*

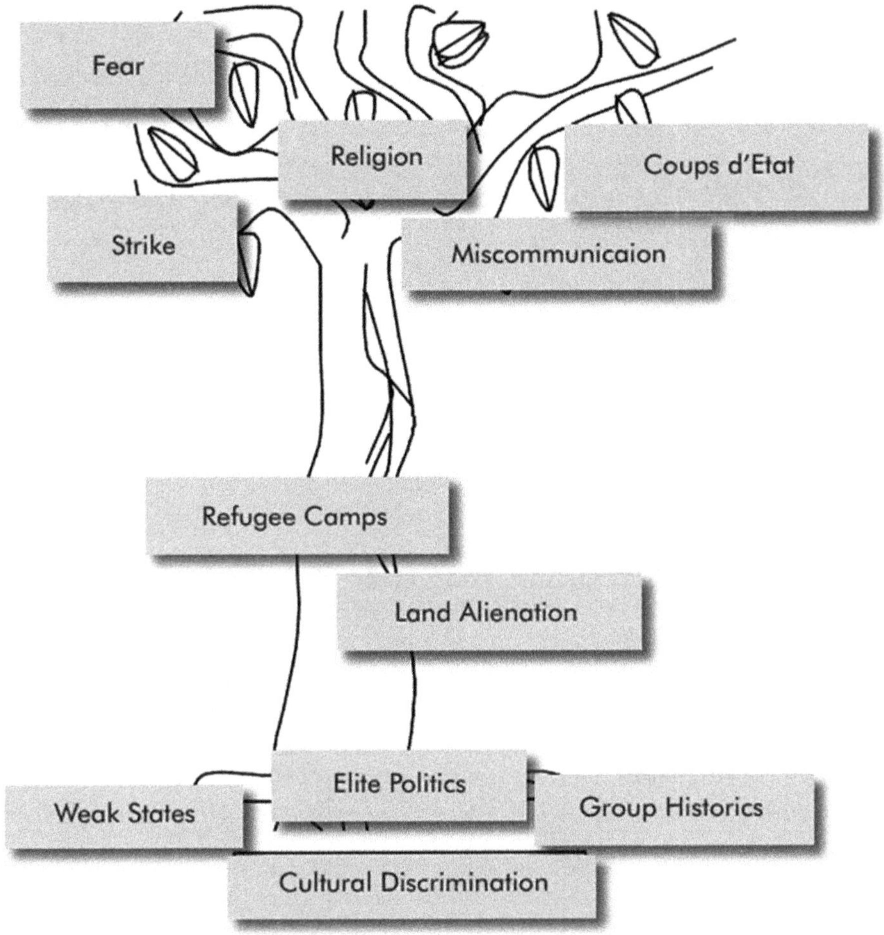

Fig. 3 Conflict tree. Reproduced by kind permission of the publisher from Swiss Agency of Development and Cooperation (SDC), Conflict Analysis Tools, Tool 2, p. 4 (SDC 2005), http://www.files.ethz.ch/isn/15416/CSPM%20Tipp%20Conflict%206.3.pdf (accessed on 14 April 2017)

conflict issues at hand. Unlike the other conflict analysis tools, this framework represents the specific viewpoint of a conflict actor (individual or group), of a specific conflict situation (in a simplified manner) at a specific moment in time. Thus, similar to a geographical map, it presents a static image of the conflict terrain. Figure 4 provides a basic template for conflict mapping. In the figure, different symbols are used to denote the respective type of actor, its allies and enemies, the power/influence it exerts and its direction.

Conflict Escalation Model The purpose of this tool (see Fig. 5) is to examine the level of escalation of conflict. The form and force of any conflict intervention must

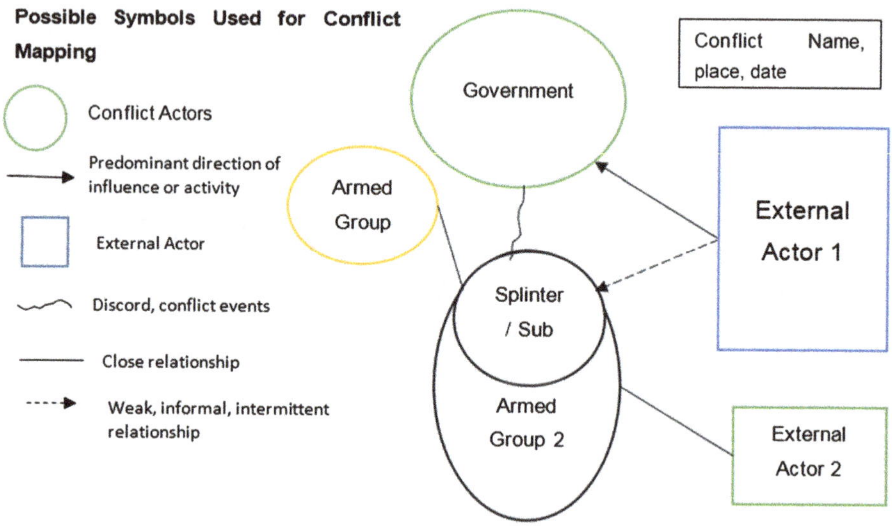

Fig. 4 Conflict map. Reproduced and adapted by kind permission of the publisher from Swiss Agency of Development and Cooperation (SDC), Conflict Analysis Tools, Tool 3, p. 5 (SDC 2005), http://www.files.ethz.ch/isn/15416/CSPM%20Tipp%20Conflict%206.3.pdf (accessed on 14 April 2017)

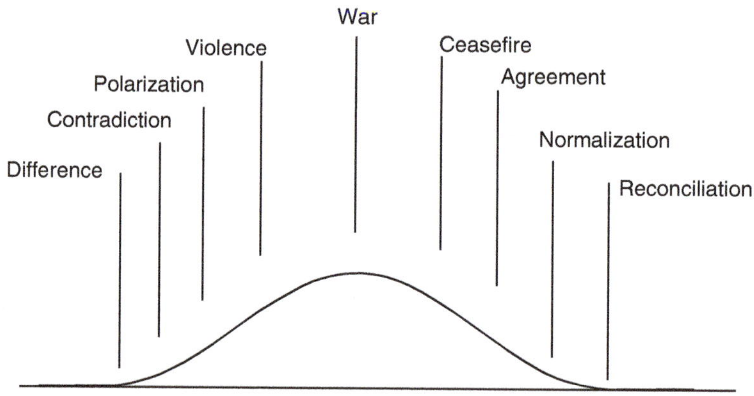

Fig. 5 Conflict escalation and de-escalation model. Reproduced by kind permission of the publisher from Oliver Ramsbotham, Tom Woodhouse & Hugh Miall Alexander, Contemporary Conflict Resolution, Figure 1.3, p. 16 (Polity Press, 4th Edition, 2016)

be appropriate to this level. Escalation refers to an increase in tension in a conflict. The process of conflict escalation is complex and unpredictable. Glasl presents a nine-tier model of escalation where the conflict parties increasingly get sucked into the conflict dynamics.[85] The model thus chooses a downward movement to denote

[85]*Ibid.*

Table 3 Needs-fears mapping framework

Actors	Issues	Interests/Needs	Fears	Means	Options
A1					
A2					

Reproduced and adapted by kind permission of the publisher from Swiss Agency of Development and Cooperation (SDC), Conflict Analysis Tools, Tool 6, p. 10 (SDC 2005), http://www.files.ethz.ch/isn/15416/CSPM%20Tipp%20Conflict%206.3.pdf (accessed on 14 April 2017)

the downward spiral. The progressive levels of escalation, according to Glasl, are (1) hardening of attitudes; (2) debates, polemics, (3) actions instead of words; (4) images, coalitions; (5) loss of face; (6) strategies of threats; (7) limited destructive blows; (8) fragmentation of the enemy; (9) together into the abyss. Conflict levels 1–3 may be managed or transformed through self-help and moderation. Levels 4–7 need various forms of third party mediation. Level 8 needs arbitration to transform the conflict. Finally, at level 9, conflict may be resolved only through power interventions. The stronger a conflict escalates, the more forceful the intervention needs to be. At the initial levels, conflict escalation parties may accept external intervention out of trust. As the conflict escalates into war, intervention may require a substantial use of force, even submission of conflict parties. Thus, the potential for self-help or de-escalation of conflict through self-regulation is higher at relatively lower levels of the tier.

Needs-Fears Mapping This tool seeks to clarify in a comparable format the various actors' attributes in terms of their needs and fears and possible options to deal with these. It is useful to understand mutual perceptions and stimulate discussion. Table 3 presents a simplified template for Needs-Fears Mapping.

For each actor, the issues, interests/expectations/needs, fears, means and options are listed in a comparative table.

Multi-Causal Role Model This tool (see Fig. 6) may be used to trace causal mechanisms, patterns, to distinguish between the different quality and role of the various factors that lead to conflicts.

TWINS Matrix of Conflict and Cooperation The Transboundary Waters Interaction Nexus (TWINS) framework borrows from and builds on Craig's (1993) analysis of transboundary river water conflict and cooperation, Arnstein's ladder of participation (1969), the EU Water Framework Directive of risk-taking projects and the securitisation theory of the Copenhagen School to develop the scales of cooperation and conflict. This framework is especially useful to map environmental and social conflicts that simmer below active conflict threshold levels and oscillate between cooperation and confrontation. The matrix allows to prepare for different levels of cooperation (for example, ad hoc measures or risk-taking measures) based on intent and action, as well as different levels of conflict from the perspective of the State

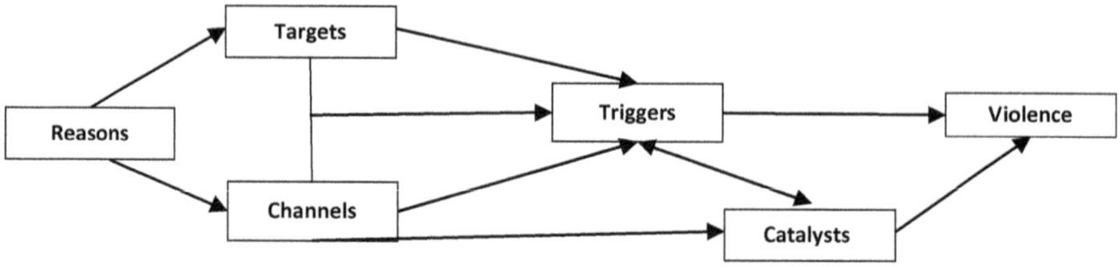

Fig. 6 Multi-causal role model. Reproduced by kind permission of the publisher from: Swiss Agency of Development and Cooperation (SDC), Conflict Analysis Tool 7, p. 11 (SDC 2005), http://www.files.ethz.ch/isn/15416/CSPM%20Tipp%20Conflict%206.3.pdf (accessed on 14 April 2017)

(non-politicised where the issue is off the radar to politicised where measures of warfare are taken).[86]

5 Challenges of Conflict Analysis in Humanitarian Action

Since its advent in the early 1990s, most humanitarian organisations working in conflict incorporate a conflict-sensitive approach into their operations:

> A conflict sensitive approach involves gaining a sound understanding of the two-way interaction between activities and context and acting to minimise negative impacts and maximise positive impacts of intervention on conflict, within an organisation's given priorities/objectives (mandate).[87]

Some of the prominent conflict sensitive analysis toolkits are listed below.[88] Further, humanitarian charters and standards such as SPHERE, while not explicitly mentioning conflict-sensitive approach, incorporate measures to minimise the negative impacts of aid:

- Conflict Assessment Framework—United States Agency for International Development (USAID);
- Conflict-Related Development Analysis—United Nations Development Programme (UNDP);
- Manual of Conflict Analysis—Swedish International Development Cooperation Agency (SIDA);
- Aid for Peace—Paffenholz and Reychler (2007);
- Making Sense of Turbulent Contexts: Analysis Tools for Humanitarian Actors—World Vision;

86 Zeitoun and Mirumachi (2008).

87 Conflict Sensitivity Consortium, Introduction, http://www.conflictsensitivity.org/an-introduction-to-conflict-sensitivity-3/.

88 OECD (2012).

- Conflict Prognosis: A Conflict and Policy Assessment Framework—Goor and Verstegen (2000), Clingendael Institute;
- Conflict Sensitivity Toolkit: A Resource for Trocaire Staff—Trocaire;
- Participatory Conflict Vulnerability Analysis (PCVA) Framework—Action Aid;
- Benefits-Harm Analysis—CARE International;
- Quick Guide to Good Enough Conflict Analysis—CARE International;
- Local Capacities for Peace—World Vision.

These resources provide detailed and step-by-step instructions on how to evaluate conflict context during all the different stages of a project cycle. Good practice warrants that conflict analysis should ideally take place during the design and implementation period and mainstreamed at all stages of the project cycle to incorporate conflict risk reduction within the programme.

However, Zicherman et al. have revealed several challenges in operationalising a conflict-sensitive approach to humanitarian action.[89]

First, it was found that *questions on conflict tend to be included mostly as part of the recovery phase (generally at least four weeks from the beginning of the emergency) rather than as part of the initial assessment,*[90] where it could help to figure out possible ways in which negative impact of aid may be eliminated or at least minimised.

Second, the capacity of staff to carry out systematic data collection is key to the success of the analysis as the frameworks are multi-layered and the context quite volatile and subjective. In spite of the availability of operational checklists to implement conflict-sensitive approaches, the process remains a challenge for untrained staff, especially surge capacity staff employed during large-scale emergencies. Human Resources and Logistics/Procurement staff thus need exposure and training in these approaches.

Third, humanitarian protection and the language of human rights are not a perfect match for a conflict-sensitive approach. Protection- and human-rights-focused programmes generally tend to assign blame and categorise actors as either victims or perpetrators of human rights abuses. This language can pose challenges for conflict analysis if not handled carefully within a volatile context.

The study further found that organisations usually employ *good-enough approaches* to conflict analysis in the immediate aftermath of crisis and undertook a more detailed analysis in weeks 6–12, i.e. during the so-called *re-design* phase. Ad hoc measures without a conflict sensitivity tag were undertaken by organisations to minimise the harmful impacts of aid and improve its effectiveness. These included inviting headquarter staff with specific regional and sectoral knowledge to country offices for expert consultations, initiating detailed discussions about

[89]Zicherman et al. (2011).

[90]*Id.*, p. 3.

staff's ethnic identities and related risks involved in working on sensitive programmes, developing inter-agency codes of conduct and advocacy with donors to widen the beneficiary population in order to avoid causing conflict.

6 Conclusion

A review of existing frameworks and tools reveals that conflict analysis is playing constant catch-up with the changing nature of conflict. Significant progress has been made in developing sophisticated frameworks for an in-depth analysis of conflicts. However, applying them on a regular basis in humanitarian contexts still remains a massive challenge.

Meanwhile, humanitarian actors continue to struggle to cope with the increasing needs of vulnerable populations caught in protracted crisis. Humanitarianism is not a tool to end war or to create peace,[91] but it must constantly deal with the consequences of conflict. Throughout history, the nature of conflict has significantly shaped humanitarian action. Death, destruction, disease and displacement caused by conflicts mobilised civilians to instinctively organise rescue and relief efforts for vulnerable populations struck by political crisis and institutional failure. However, today's humanitarian system is on the brink of a breakdown baulking at the widening gap between needs and available resources. The global political system needs to generate the necessary political will to end and prevent violent conflicts and deliver on its commitments to uphold international humanitarian frameworks and standards.

References

Anderson MB (1999) Do no harm: how aid can support peace-or war. Lynne Rienner Publishers Inc., London

Brahm E (2003) Latent conflict stage. Retrieved from Beyond Intractability: http://www.beyondintractability.org/essay/latent-conflict

Conflict Sensitivity Consortium (Undated) Do no harm. Retrieved from Conflict Sensitivity Consortium: http://www.conflictsensitivity.org/do-no-harm-local-capacities-for-peace-project/

Conflict Sensitivity Consortium (Undated) Introduction. Retrieved from Conflict Sensitive Consortium: http://www.conflictsensitivity.org/an-introduction-to-conflict-sensitivity-3/

Deutsch M (1983) The prevention of World War III: a psychological perspective. Polit Psychol 4 (1):3–31, p 6, 24 and others

Deutsch M, Coleman P (2000) The handbook of conflict resolution: theory and practice. Jossey-Bass Publishers, San Francisco, pp 428–450

[91]Orbinski (1999), http://www.nobelprize.org/nobel_prizes/peace/laureates/1999/msf-lecture.html.

DG ECHO (2015, February 2) Assessing needs vulnerability and risk. Retrieved from European Commission Humanitarian Aid and Civil Protection: http://ec.europa.eu/echo/what/humanitarian-aid/needs-assessments_en

Galtung J (1967) Theories of peace: a synthetic approach to peace thinking. Unpublished, Oslo. Retrieved from http://www.transcend.org/files/Galtung_Book_unpub_Theories_of_Peace_-_A_Synthetic_Approach_to_Peace_Thinking_1967.pdf

Galtung J (1969) Violence, peace, and peace research. J Peace Res (3):167–191

Galtung J (1971) The Middle East and the theory of conflict. J Peace Res 8(3/4):173–206

GHA Report (2016) Global humanitarian assistance report. Global Humanitarian Assistance, New York

Global Peace Index (2016) Global Peace Index 2016. Institute for Economics and Peace, Brussels

HIIK (2015) Conflict Barometer 2015. The Heidelberg Institute for International Conflict Research, Heidelberg. Retrieved from http://www.hiik.de/en/konfliktbarometer/pdf/ConflictBarometer_2015.pdf

Human Security Report Project (2013) Human Security Report 2013. Human Security Research Group, Vancouver

ICRC (2008) How is the term "Armed Conflict" defined in International Humanitarian Law? - Opinion paper. ICRC, Geneva. Retrieved from http://www.icrc.org/eng/assets/files/other/opinion-paper-armed-conflict.pdf

ICRC (2014) The International Committee of the Red Cross's (ICRC's) role in situations of violence below the threshold of armed conflict- Policy Document. Int Rev Red Cross 275–304

Jeong H-W (2008) Understanding conflict and conflict analysis. Sage Publications Limited, London

Joint Evaluation of Emergency Assistance to Rwanda (1996) The international response to conflict and genocide: lessons from the Rwanda experience: synthesis report. Retrieved from http://www.oecd.org/derec/sweden/50189495.pdf

Kalpakian J (2004) Identity, conflict and cooperation in international river systems. Ashgate, Morocco

Lawand K (2012, December 10) Internal conflicts or other situations of violence – what is the difference for victims? Retrieved from International Committee of the Red Cross: http://www.icrc.org/eng/resources/documents/interview/2012/12-10-niac-non-international-armed-conflict.htm

Loane G (2011) Applying Conflict Sensitivity in Emergency Response (Questions and Discussion). Applying conflict sensitivity in emergency response: current practice and ways forward (Conference Paper, p. 70). Overseas Development Institute, London

Médecins Sans Frontières (2016, May 5) MSF to pull out of World Humanitarian Summit. Retrieved from MSF UK: http://www.msf.org.uk/article/msf-to-pull-out-of-world-humanitarian-summit

OECD (2012) Conflict analysis and its use in evaluation. In: OECD (ed) Evaluating peacebuilding activities in settings of conflict and fragility: improving learnings for results. OECD

Orbinski J (1999) Nobel Lecture. Retrieved July 2016, from http://www.nobelprize.org/nobel_prizes/peace/laureates/1999/msf-lecture.html

PRIO (2015) Graphs. PRIO Conflict Trends Project. Retrieved from http://www.prio.org/Projects/Extensions/ConflictTrends/Graphs/

Ramsbotham O, Woodhouse T, Miall H (2011) Contemporary conflict resolution. Polity Press, Cambridge

Sarkees RM (2011) The COW typology of war: defining and categorizing wars (version 4 of the data). The Correlates of War Project. Retrieved from http://cow.la.psu.edu/COW2%20Data/WarData_NEW/COW%20Website%20-%20Typology%20of%20war.pdf

Sarkees MR, Schafer P (2000) The correlates of war data on war: an update to 1997. Conflict Manag Peace Sci 18:123–144

SDC (2005) Conflict analysis tools -tip sheet. Retrieved from http://www.css.ethz.ch/content/dam/ethz/special-interest/gess/cis/center-for-securities-studies/pdfs/Conflict-Analysis-Tools.pdf
The Global Peace Index (2016) Global cost of conflict reaches $14.3tn, says report. Institute for Economics and Peace, Brussels
Trocaire (2011) Conflict sensitivity toolkit. Trocaire, Dublin. http://www.trocaire.org/resources/policyandadvocacy/conflict-sensitivity-toolkit
UCDP (2016a) Definitions. Retrieved from Uppsala Conflict Data Program: http://www.pcr.uu.se/research/ucdp/definitions/#dyad
UCDP (2016b) Fatalities view. Retrieved from Uppsala Conflict Data Program: http://ucdp.uu.se/#/exploratory
UCDP (2016c) Uppsala conflict data program. Uppsala University, Uppsala. Retrieved from http://ucdp.uu.se/#/encyclopedia
UN Secretary-General (2016) World Humanitarian Summit- chair's summary. The United Nations, Istanbul
Vite S (2009) Typology of armed conflicts in international humanitarian law: legal concepts and actual situations. Int Rev Red Cross 873:70–94
Wallensteen P (2007) Understanding conflict resolution: war peace and the global system. Sage Publications, Sweden
WHS (2016) One humanity shared responsibility. The United Nations, New York
WHS Secretariat (2015) Restoring humanity: systhesis of the consultation process for the World Humanitarian Summit. United Nations, New York
Zeitoun M, Mirumachi N (2008) Transboundary water interaction I: reconsidering conflict and cooperation. Int Environ Agreements 297–316
Zicherman N, Khan A, Street A, Heyer H, Chevreau O (2011) Applying conflict sensitivity in emergency response: current practice and ways forward. Humanitarian Practice Network, London

Further Reading

Ramsbotham O, Woodhouse T, Miall H (2011) Contemporary conflict resolution. Polity Press, Cambridge
Trocaire (2011) Conflict sensitivity toolkit. Trocaire, Dublin. http://www.trocaire.org/resources/policyandadvocacy/conflict-sensitivity-toolkit
Wallensteen P (2007) Understanding conflict resolution: war peace and the global system. Sage Publications, Sweden

Sulagna Maitra is a Lecturer at the Centre for Humanitarian Action of University College Dublin, Ireland, and Director of the NOHA Joint Master's Programme in International Humanitarian Action at University College Dublin.

The Governance of Humanitarian Action in World Politics

Uwe Andersen and Katharina Behmer

1 Introduction

In May 2016, the World Humanitarian Summit took place in Istanbul. It was the first global consultation process on the international humanitarian system launched by the United Nations Secretariat. As a result, researchers, practitioners and policy makers have unanimously reaffirmed the necessity to foster cooperation, coordination and quality assurance in humanitarian affairs.

Within the wider framework of world politics, the humanitarian ecosystem[1] is a weakly institutionalised system with an increasing number of diverse actors, which partly cooperate but also compete because of different perspectives and interests and for scarce resources.[2] Grasping the interaction of these actors in the context of the complex international political and economic system is a prerequisite for understanding why humanitarian action succeeds or fails and how to improve it.

This chapter introduces a multilevel governance approach to adequately depict the humanitarian system and its actors. This angle of analysis is the most suitable way to understand how the current international humanitarian system operates in the context of international politics. After a brief introduction to humanitarian governance and its principles and actors, the chapter explores the international political environment in which humanitarian action takes place. It goes on to discuss the humanitarian architecture, with its different types of actors, based on the conditions that motivate, enable and limit their actions against the aforementioned parameters.

[1]Dallaire Ferland, http://blogs.icrc.org/law-and-policy/2016/05/26/istanbul-dispatch/.

[2]Dijkzeul and Lieser (2013).

U. Andersen • K. Behmer (✉)
Ruhr University Bochum, Bochum, Germany
e-mail: uwe.andersen@rub.de; katharina.behmer@rub.de

© Springer International Publishing AG 2018

H.-J. Heintze, P. Thielbörger (eds.), *International Humanitarian Action*,
DOI 10.1007/978-3-319-14454-2_5

2 Humanitarian Governance: Principles and Actors

The debate on global (or regional) governance tries to outline how governance can be achieved without a government.[3] Global governance, or *collective problem-solving arrangements*,[4] becomes visible in the increase and prominence of non-State organisations and institutions, as well as through the growing influence of global norms and international legal arrangements. The term 'global governance' thus encompasses an analytical perspective to understand world politics and the transformation of the international system. Moreover, it also refers to a global policy that addresses world problems, such as global health, migration and refugees, climate change and terrorism. Barnett defines humanitarian governance as 'the increasingly organized and internationalized attempt to save lives, enhance the welfare, and reduce the suffering of the world's most vulnerable populations'.[5]

Three central observations are made regarding the international political environment of humanitarian action (see Fig. 1).

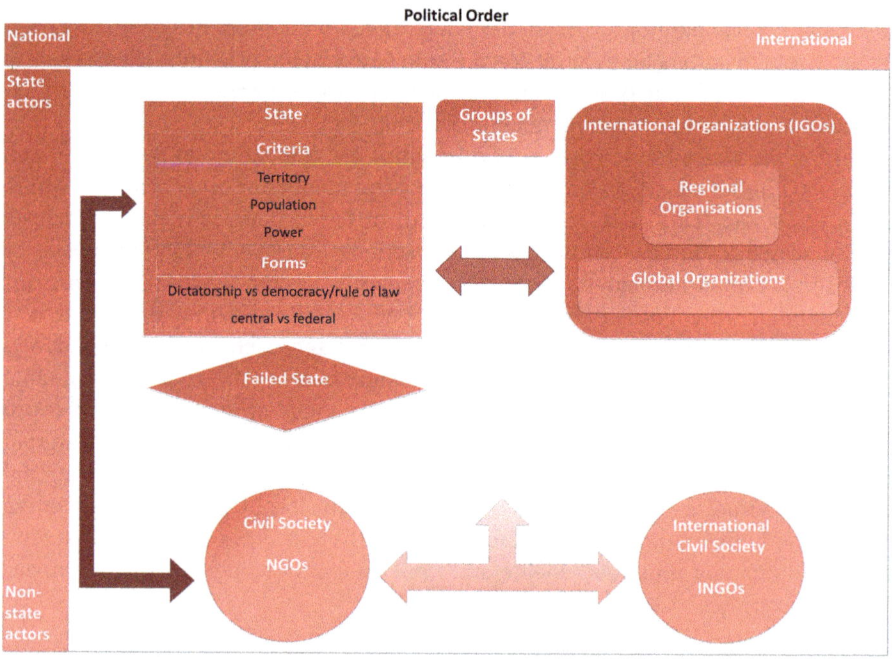

Fig. 1 Political order. Developed by the authors, Katharina Behmer and Uwe Andersen

[3]Rosenau and Czempiel (1992).

[4]Thakur and Weiss (2009), p. 25.

[5]Barnett (2013), p. 379.

First, sovereignty and traditional authority of nation States are increasingly limited. In accordance with most global governance approaches, we assume that actors beyond the traditional nation State increasingly influence international politics. This is because of two core problems that weaken State sovereignty. On the national stage, depending on the form of the State, civil society increasingly demands transparency, accountability and participation in decision- and policy-making processes, which effect society as a whole. At the same time, on the international stage, States are forced to cooperate on issues exceeding individual State capacities.

Second, the variety of actors parallels an increase of norms and policies, mostly of a self-binding nature, to coordinate action and facilitate cooperation.[6] However, norm interpretation and compliance differ immensely, and norms are frequently contested.

Third, we recognise two conflictive tendencies: on the one hand, civil society actors and international norms exert a growing influence on governance, which can be interpreted as a pluralisation or even a *democratisation*[7] of international politics with the inclination to find common problem-solving and decision-making mechanisms. On the other hand, a reinforcement of traditional power politics is visibly backed by the reappearance of nationalism and ideology. In other words, many powerful actors pursue their interests by all means, drawing heavily on traditional sources of power such as military as well as economic capabilities.

These principal parameters determine the framework in which humanitarian action operates and are at least partly responsible for the major challenges in the humanitarian system, namely the politics, paternalism and insufficiency of humanitarian action, which will be shortly addressed in the final section of the text.

The humanitarian principles, humanity, impartiality, neutrality and independence,[8] are the glue of the humanitarian system, despite the fact that not all actors involved in the humanitarian (eco-)system uphold these principles at all times. The principles aim to provide for a non-political so-called *humanitarian space*. However, they are subject to controversial discussion by scholars of humanitarian studies. The assumption underlying these principles is that (safe) access to suffering populations for relief operations requires the consent of all parties to the conflict and can only be guaranteed when the aid provided is neutral, impartial and independent. The norms shaping the international humanitarian system are mainly rooted in international law, particularly in international humanitarian law. Increasingly, humanitarian action is also influenced by international human rights law,

---

[6]The increase of norms in international politics is often discussed within the debate on '*Verrechtlichung*' or judicialisation (cf. Zürn and Zangl 2004).

[7]This term is heavily employed in the political debate although its use is problematic with reference to States (instead of individual citizens).

[8]Humanity—alleviate human suffering wherever it may be found; Impartiality—deliver assistance on the basis of need, with no discrimination on the basis of race, religion, class, gender or other; Neutrality—not taking sides on political grounds of a conflict; Independence—capacity of holding and publicly expressing views that are different from that of the donor, host State or conflict party.

international disaster response law and international criminal law. While only a few legal norms are binding on the actors involved, many different groups of actors have started to create joint rules and regulations based on the evolving international legal framework.[9]

Apart from expressing rules, the humanitarian principles define humanitarian action by explaining how it ought to function, especially in contrast to other forms of international interventions, such as military interventions and development, peace- and State-building approaches. For example, the predominantly short-term-oriented neutral humanitarian action is often differentiated from long-term-oriented development approaches that follow specific political agendas. However, in the practice of humanitarian crises, the lines between short-term humanitarian assistance and long-term development cooperation are blurred and require coordinated and complementary approaches. At the same time, the political context of humanitarian crises often leads to an unsolved dilemma.[10] *Humanitarian Action per se does not challenge the status quo, nor should it, many of its proponents would argue.*[11] However, if the suffering of entire populations is demonstrably induced by ruthless power politics, moral and ethical imperatives may at times impede a neutral position, as well as aid, which unintentionally reinforces such unjust systems and may even provide for a valuable resource in war economies.

The multiple actors in the humanitarian system are described by Pfanner as

> actors with different objectives, principles and modi operandi, [which] intervene in situations of armed conflict and internal violence in order to alleviate the plight of the victims of those situations: governmental and nongovernmental organizations (NGOS), international organizations, national Red Cross and Red Crescent societies, private companies and even the armed forces.[12]

Every humanitarian crisis, that is to say, every operational context, has distinctive characteristics and is shaped by political, socio-economic, religious and cultural factors. Hence, no humanitarian actor can meet all needs in emergency situations—diversity is therefore an asset and a liability, as well as a challenge for the humanitarian community.

The governments of affected States still retain the primary responsibility for the well-being of their citizens. States as donors or providers of technical assistance provide the majority of humanitarian financing. States' armed forces may also form part of humanitarian responses, partly under the flag of the United Nations (UN), for example, in peace enforcement, peacekeeping or peacebuilding missions. Military

[9]See for instance the 'The Code of Conduct for the International Red Cross and Red Crescent Movement and NGOs in Disaster Relief' or the Spehre Project on the 'Humanitarian Charter and Minimum Standards in Humanitarian Response' as the most prominent ones. Many more exist regarding specific issue areas such as for instance gender in humanitarian action.

[10]Slim (1997), pp. 244–257.

[11]Donini (2010), http://villierspark.org.uk/wp-content/uploads/2014/09/0061-Donini-2010-Meta-level-humanitarianism.pdf.

[12]Pfanner (2007), http://www.icrc.org/eng/resources/documents/article/review/review-865-p5.htm.

and civil actors often share the operational space notwithstanding the fact that their mission and motives differ.

Non-State armed forces, such as rebels, militias or criminal organisations, which operate in or control certain areas in which humanitarian emergencies occur, often increase the complexity of humanitarian crises, limiting access to victims and threatening the humanitarian space. Both citizens of affected areas and the general public increasingly hold governments and the international community accountable. In addition, the authority and sovereignty of States, particularly failing or failed States, is also limited through international organisations, taking over traditional State functions in humanitarian emergencies. Moreover, international organisations are increasingly gaining influence in international humanitarian affairs as coordinators and providers of multilateral international relief operations. Finally, the humanitarian world is predominantly shaped and operated by a multitude of different local, national and international non-governmental organisations (NGOs), which often act as transnational agents implementing humanitarian assistance at the local level, as well as advocating for the victims of armed conflict and disaster in the national or global sphere. In this context, the Red Cross and Red Crescent Movement enjoy a special role, with a distinctive mandate and the most advanced humanitarian network.

In addition, new actors such as multinational companies, foundations, as well as faith-based and migrant organisations increasingly engage in humanitarian activities. However, ultimately, immediate first aid, protection and support are mostly given by those closest to the centre of the emergency, such as the affected persons themselves, neighbours and local communities. To strengthen the capacities, the empowerment and the representation of these local actors and engagement in meaningful partnerships with them have been a key claim of the above-mentioned World Humanitarian Summit 2016.

3 Setting the Stage

3.1 The Role of the State

At least since the peace of Westphalia in 1648, States have been accepted as the dominant actors in the international system. They are traditionally defined by three elements: territory, population and power. Today, these elements have become increasingly unclear: territorial borders are perforated by cross-border migration of people and almost unlimited economic exchange. The conceptualisation of a defined population as a homogenous unity has always been debatable due to socio-economic stratification, cultural and religious differences, ethnic minorities, migrants and refugees. However, today, in an increasingly globalised world, the mobility of persons has reached new dimensions. Finally, civil society actors have challenged the power and authority of the State by claiming greater participation in decision- and policy-making processes.

The central idea of power with a focus on legitimate use of force is emphasised by political scientist Max Weber, who defines a State as '[...] the form of human community that (successfully) lays claim to the monopoly of legitimate physical violence within a particular territory [...]'.[13] Likewise, power is the prerequisite for the fulfilment of key functions of the State: providing physical security and a minimum of material well-being for its citizens (as well as for people under its authority).

This, however, depends on the form of government of States, which are located between two parameters: democracies with a pluralistic setting, division of power and the rule of law on the one hand and dictatorships on the other hand. While institutionalised participation is a key element of democracy, participation in dictatorships, where it occurs at all, is generally limited and strictly controlled. However, in between highly participatory democracies and strict dictatorships we find very different forms of more or less authoritarian governments allowing for varying degrees of participation. Another distinction needs to be made between centralised States and federal States, the latter characterised by a vertical division of power.

These different forms of government are a key factor shaping the political space and structure of NGOs. For example, federal States often encourage the establishment of NGOs with federal structures. In reality, the majority of international humanitarian action is delivered to failing or failed States, which usually are not able or only partly able to carry out basic State tasks, namely ensuring the physical security and material well-being of its citizens. For instance, according to the Global Humanitarian Assistance Report 2015, 93% of people in need of assistance live in politically fragile and/or environmentally vulnerable countries.[14] In the context of civil wars, the affected governments are often party to the conflict, opposed by armed groups struggling for control over resources and territory. In this context, the access for humanitarian action is much more complex and as mentioned before subject to permission from all parties controlling certain conflict areas.

3.2 *The State vs. Civil Society: From Government to Governance*

The State as a special part of society is responsible for security, material well-being and participatory rule within its borders.

However, society also acts beyond the State level. NGOs play a crucial role in modern civil society. The term NGO stresses the self-prescribed function of many

---

[13]Owen and Strong (2004), p. 33.

[14]Swithern et al. (2015), Global Humanitarian Assistance—A Development Initiative, 2015, www.globalhumanitarianassistance.org/reports/.

NGOs as a counterpart towards the State, which they see as part of their identity. However, civil society organisations or civic organisations would be a more adequate term. Their independence or rather degree of independence from governmental control is reflected by their financing, personnel and field of activities.

The political space for organised civil society varies depending on the type of government and political culture of the State it is embedded in. For instance, Americans are traditionally very sceptical towards State actions and interventions in all aspects of social life. Social problems are expected to be solved by society itself, for example, by NGOs. In contrast, Germans generally see social welfare to be the duty of the State. More generally, NGOs have gained in importance in diverse political and social spaces.

The political power of the State based on hierarchical authority is weakened by the influence of alternative actors. This development is often termed 'governance' in contrast to 'government'. The term government in this regard refers to an actor that is able to set rules and ideally has the means to enforce rule compliance. Conversely, *governance* is defined by the more pluralistic, conflictive process of norm negotiation and norm enforcement, instead of enforcement through formal authority or institutionalised hierarchy as displayed in the modern nation State.

The relationship between State and non-State actors, such as NGOs, is highly ambivalent as the State can determine and control the framework of action for non-State actors. At the same time, especially in the context of fragile states, NGOs may also partly take over State functions or hold governments accountable. While the majority of NGOs reject influence and control by the State, a dysfunctional development can be observed in 'Quasi-Non-Governmental-Organisations' (QUANGOs) or 'Government-Organised Non-Governmental Organisations' (GONGOs), where the State exercises full control. Whereas NGOs are usually not-for-profit organisations, business-oriented NGOs, which aim to increase profit mainly for the benefit of a small number of leaders, have also sprung up. As mentioned above, the key channels for influencing the decisions within NGOs are finance and personnel recruitment. Furthermore, the sources of NGO funding are mainly membership fees, donations and State subsidies. Where State subsidies provide for the largest share of the financial income of an NGO, independence is questionable. This is of utmost importance in the humanitarian context, in which dependence on State funding often means having to work in close accordance with foreign policies of donor States, which compromises the ideal of independent humanitarian action.

As in other fields of action, the NGO landscape in the humanitarian context is very diverse but can be categorised according to certain indicators. Political scientists normally classify NGOs according to their size, level of activity (local, regional or national), mandate (single vs. multi-mandated), as well as religious or secular mission. Given that organisations specialising in international humanitarian assistance from the Global North mostly develop projects abroad, the boundaries between national and international humanitarian organisations are blurred. Further specific features applying to the humanitarian context will be discussed in the following section on international organisations and the humanitarian architecture.

3.3 International Organisations

States enjoy equal sovereignty within the international community of States. Together with the principle of non-intervention,[15] this bedrock principle of the international order is enshrined in the UN Charter, which aims to protect the world from conflict and ensure peace, cooperation and prosperity. Globalisation, coupled with an increase in problems that exceed national capacities, has made cooperation between States necessary and thus also resulted in States losing aspects of their formal sovereignty.

In the absence of a global government, new forms of global governance have become necessary and visible. For instance, international governmental organisations (IGOs)[16] have emerged as bridges between sovereign States and the necessity of solving international problems. They are recognised as subjects of international law. IGOs, under most definitions, consist of at least three States with their members held together by formal intergovernmental agreements and organisational structures. Some IGOs are established with one specific mandate (for example, specific organisations within the UN, such as the World Food Programme); others perform a broad range of tasks (for example, the UN).[17]

Among IGOs, the UN enjoys a special role as it is the largest and the only all-encompassing international organisation. It is also the most complex, comprised of sometimes competing organisations, reflecting the different interests of and power struggles between various member groups. This makes the coordinating body, the Economic and Social Council (ECOSOC), particularly important. However, ECOSOC has so far failed to fulfil its task effectively, which has provoked calls for urgent reform of the UN system over the last few decades, including of its five main organs[18]: the General Assembly, the Security Council, the Secretariat headed by the Secretary General, the Economic and Social Council and the International Court of Justice.

From an international relations perspective, the assumptions about the role and power of international organisations in world politics are shaped by the underlying theoretical approach.[19] (Neo-)realists would assume that States create international organisations to enhance their legitimacy and image of good statehood. States are

[15]Exceptions to this rule can only be made in the case of self-defense or if the UN Security Council defines a situation as a threat to international peace and mandates an international response.

[16]One must distinguish international organisations from international institutions, which can be defined as '*the collective forms or basic structures of social organization as established by law or by human tradition*' such as for example human rights.

[17]Karns and Mingst (2004), p. 7.

[18]The Trusteeship Council, as the sixth principal UN organ, which was concerned with colonial territories, became defunct following successful de-colonisation.

[19]For a short overview of relevant international relations theories see, for instance, Slaughter 2011; for more details on each approach, see Baylis and Smith (2006); for an overview on how the different international relations perspectives play out regarding international organisations, see, for instance, Oestreich (2011).

still perceived as the main decision-makers within international organisations. (Neo-)liberals would assert that IGOs exist to facilitate coordination and joint action, which creates benefits for the member States. IGOs are conceptualised as independent actors. Constructivists would argue that IGOs influence world politics as they advocate for norms and principles and thus shape the perspective and behaviour of the decision- and policy-making individuals in governments. According to Marxists, choosing Wallerstein's world system theory as an example, the emergence of IGOs is a response to increasing interdependence between States. However, this interdependence, as well as the structure and role of IGOs, is still dominated by economic power stratification and class conflict.

In addition, the degree to which IGOs enjoy independence from the national interests of their member States, associated with the debate on the 'principle-agent-problem', also differs according to the respective schools of thought. While realists would perceive independent action as a problem, liberals would consider limited independence as an advantage for enhancing cooperation. Constructivists would assume that independent international organisations can act as drivers of international political change to the benefit of international peace and security. Lastly, Marxists would state that IGOs reflect the economic imbalance in the international system, according to the interests of different classes.

International organisations have always been established in response to international challenges, particularly crises and catastrophes. For example, in the direct aftermath of World War I, the international community made its first attempt to create an IGO, the League of Nations, in the most sensitive realm of security. However, the League of Nations failed to secure peace, partly because influential States, such as the US, did not join. After World War II, the second attempt resulted in the successful establishment of the United Nations in 1945.[20]

How to cope with the differing size and power of member States is a problem affecting the role and the decision-making of IGOs such as the UN. While all states are formally sovereign and equal, major differences in power between smaller States, such as Luxembourg or Barbados, and bigger States, such as China or the US, persist. Still, in most IGOs, the formal principle 'one State = one vote' prevails. While developing States dominate many IGOs in terms of their number, a real power asymmetry nevertheless remains in current world politics, with a limited number of powerful (mostly industrialised, western) States usually making major decisions. For example, developing States hold the majority of votes in the UN General Assembly (UNGA), but this organ's formal decisions are not binding on UN member States. Consider UNGA Resolution 46/182 (1991) on Humanitarian Assistance, which we will discuss in the following paragraph on access to the victims of humanitarian crises.

[20] As a reflection of the political reality at the time of its foundation, the UN first excluded the Axis powers Germany, Japan and Italy.

In order for IGOs to be influential actors as opposed to paper tigers, they must reflect the basic distribution of power among their member States in their specific field of action. Currently, two possible solutions exist.

One way is weighted voting, as practised by the World Bank, the International Monetary Fund and the European Union. However, it is difficult to reach a common agreement on criteria to weigh the importance of different member States in various fields and the voting power that should accrue as a result of such criteria.

A second way is the formation of powerful groups or clubs with limited membership. The most prominent examples of a formally privileged group within an IGO are the five permanent members wielding veto power within the UN Security Council (UNSC),[21] which in contrast to the UNGA can take binding decisions. A more recent phenomenon that is now frequently encountered in international politics is the formation of clubs comprising specific groups of States. Important examples are the G7/8,[22] G20[23] or BRICS.[24] The G7/8 and G20 were the first fora where heads of States directly engaged in, for the most part, annual meetings to solve common problems. The creation of these fora was prompted, once again, by crisis, this time the so-called petrol crisis in the 1970s, which led to the creation of the G7 in 1975. To combat the global economic crisis of 2008–2010, the G7 responded to the shift in economic power by calling for more participation of *emerging markets*, eventually creating the G20 as a new forum. Critics, especially from smaller States, argue that notwithstanding the fact that the G20 is much more representative of the world in terms of population, economic weight and regional balance than the G7, informal decisions in this restricted G20 club forecast the formal decisions later taken by IGOs, bypassing the latters' general fora for all member States. The same issue arises in the case of major international decisions on humanitarian assistance.

Apart from the formal decision-making process in international organisations expressed through voting, power is also exercised via finances and human resources. This is reflected by the recruitment process for influential positions, which is directly related to the financial contribution of member States. Hence, although international bureaucrats should act on behalf of their organisations, a certain degree of national loyalty often reinforces the given distribution of power within IGOs.

International conferences are a further temporary setting for political summits or, increasingly, consultation processes in view of precipitating changes in

[21]China, Russia, France, United Kingdom, United States.

[22]Canada, France, Germany, Italy, Japan, the United Kingdom, and the United States; Russia was invited to the head of State meetings of the G7. The enlarged group was then referred to as G8, but Russia was suspended in 2014 with the outbreak of the conflict in Ukraine and the Russian annexation of Crimea.

[23]Argentina, Australia, Brazil, Canada, China, France, Germany, India, Indonesia, Italy, Japan, South Korea, Mexico, Russia, Saudi Arabia, South Africa, Turkey, the United Kingdom, the United States and the European Union.

[24]Brazil, Russia, India, China, South Africa.

governance. This holds especially true for reform processes, or the launch and promotion of new topics on the international agenda. The 1992 UN Conference on Environment and Development (UNCED), also known as the Rio de Janeiro Earth Summit, and the 2015 follow-up conference in Paris are today considered milestones in the development of a global policy on climate change. Moreover, two special sessions of the UNGA were seminal in advancing the Agenda of International Development Policy: in 2000, the Millennium Development Goals (MDGs) were adopted, followed in 2015 by their successors, the Sustainable Development Goals. Similarly, the Fourth UN World Conference on Women of 1995 in Beijing triggered major developments in the area of gender mainstreaming, among others. These UN-led global events have also been increasingly characterised by the participation of diverse actors, such as international and local NGOs, research institutes, as well as private actors and enterprises. While the outcome of the World Humanitarian Summit 2016 is thus far perceived to be rather disillusioning, only the future will show if it may nevertheless have initiated a meaningful and sustainable reform process in international humanitarian affairs.

While some of the current international challenges, such as natural disasters, the impact of climate change, migration or terrorism, require truly global solutions, others concern specific regions of the world or groups of States, for example, questions of water governance or regional migration.

We must thus differentiate between global and regional governance approaches. Both have advantages and disadvantages: while cultural similarities may ease cooperation within regional arrangements, such relations are often also marked by complex historical conflicts and competition. Regional organisations may be rooted in common economic or security-related interests or in solidarity between countries sharing the same history, culture, religion or the same allies and enemies (for example, European Union, Organization of Islamic States, ASEAN, OAS, Arab League or African Union, etc.).[25]

One key issue in this regard is the degree to which States are willing to defer parts of their sovereignty to regional supranational bodies in the name of integration. Moreover, the relationship between regional and global organisations is determined by the two concepts of *subsidiarity* and *supremacy*. Subsidiarity is rooted in the assumption that States are more committed to regional arrangements and that responses to regional problems by regional arrangements are culturally more appropriate, more informed and thus more effective. Based on the principle of supremacy, higher-level organisations may in theory step in when regional organisations lack the will or capacity to adequately respond to problems. Ideally, global and regional governance systems complement each other in a way similar to a federal system. However, there is also a danger of conflictive competition between regional and global or different regional organisations.

[25]Zyck (2013).

3.4 International Non-governmental Organisations

A large number of NGOs have an international dimension that manifests itself either in their membership or their activities. This is particularly the case for humanitarian organisations, which often operate in emergencies occurring outside their home States.

Many large international NGOs are described as 'transnational federations' with formal long-term links to national groups or subsidiaries, for example the International Federation of the Red Cross and Red Crescent Societies, Oxfam, CARE, Médecins Sans Frontières (MSF), Save the Children and many more. We differentiate regional organisations, transnational organisations[26] and international organisations with federal structures.[27]

While some NGOs engage in advocacy work, including through cooperation with IGOs, other NGOs concentrate on the implementation of practical projects. International NGOs and transnational networks are playing an ever-increasing role in global political affairs and thus influence global policies.[28]

4 Humanitarian Architecture

4.1 Victims, Beneficiaries and Stakeholders

In times of armed conflict or disaster, the first people to come to the rescue of victims are usually neighbours, family, friends, local organisations, networks or communities and local and/or regional State institutions. However, the lack of international media coverage of this dimension of humanitarianism has often led to the perception of local populations and communities as passive victims and beneficiaries of aid.

This is partly because the international public is eager to see *their* organisation helping the victims of disasters and armed conflict and further because organisations use media coverage to generate donations or because governments wish to show their citizens the results of taxpayer money spent on international aid.[29] Despite these tendencies, beneficiaries of aid must be perceived as stakeholders by the humanitarian actors implementing humanitarian action projects.

In this regard, it is important that the public hold their governments accountable for foreign policies in general and humanitarian donor policies in particular.

[26]According to Pries, the transnationalisation dynamic stands for '*different forms re-arrangements geographical-social spaces beyond, alongside and above the formerly dominant national society paradigm*' (Pries 2008).

[27]Karns and Mingst (2004), p. 12.

[28]For an overview see, for instance DeMars and Dijkzeul; Keck and Sikkink (1998).

[29]For further discussion see, for instance Robinson (2015), pp. 254–266.

Moreover, as Valerie Amos, former head of the UN Humanitarian Affairs Department, said, people tend to believe that disasters are great equalisers, that in time of emergencies society suffers as a whole. The opposite is true. How we are affected by conflict and disaster, as well as the capabilities and recourses we have to recover, depends on who we are and how the group we are identified with is valued and represented in society. Indicators such as gender and age, as well as socio-economic status and ethnic background, can tell a lot about who is affected by humanitarian crises and in what way. Humanitarian responses that take this (local) knowledge into account are better suited to meet the needs of the people they aim to serve.

4.2 *Access, Safety and Security*

States differ significantly in the way they prepare for, and respond to, emergencies. So-called *disaster preparedness* depends on States' respective systems of governance and their previous experience in handling natural disasters. State sovereignty implies that the State holds the primary responsibility for the well-being of its citizens. The UNGA re-emphasised in Resolution 46/182 that

> [e]ach State has the responsibility first and foremost to take care of the victims of natural disasters and other emergencies occurring on its territory. Hence, the affected State has the primary role in the initiation, organization, coordination, and implementation of humanitarian assistance within its territory.[30]

Ideally, a State will only ever briefly be unable to alleviate the suffering of its population due to a humanitarian crisis. In such a situation, it would issue a call for international humanitarian action, coordinated through international organisations, such as the UN and implemented by its sub-organisations and/or international NGOs. The State itself would then engage in coordinating the funnelling of international humanitarian action to the right channels, facilitate aid workers' movements, support and protect them.

Humanitarian action implemented on the territory of a State requires that State's consent. While the international community has not yet agreed to recognise a right to access to a State for third actors in humanitarian crises, it is commonly understood that a State's arbitrary rejection of humanitarian action is unacceptable.[31] Moreover, non-State armed groups, such as rebels and warlords, which control certain conflict areas, might also restrict access to populations in need. Experience shows that, in this context, aid is often used as a weapon, causing a dilemma for humanitarian organisations and heightening concerns for the security of their personnel.

The ICRC with its specific mandate in international law enjoys a unique position in the negotiation of access to crisis regions. The ICRC's policy on neutrality has

[30]UNGAA/RES/46/182: 1991.

[31]For further discussion, see for instance Heintze (2015), pp. 149–167.

been shaped by a long history and was subject to controversial discussions, such as the organisation's position during World War II in Germany. Unlike States, non-State actors are only bound by international law in particular contexts (see the chapter on IHL). Hence, the ICRC and other international organisations, such as the UN Office for the Coordination of Humanitarian Affairs (OCHA) or initiatives such as the organisation Geneva Call,[32] are developing new tools and techniques to convince all parties to a conflict to adhere to certain rules protecting civilians and enabling humanitarian assistance.

Debates in the context of access to populations suffering from massive human rights violations are often associated with the responsibility to protect. The question is to what extent the responsibility for the protection of a population falls to the international community if a State is unwilling or unable to protect its citizens. Under the key term 'humanitarian intervention', a significant amount of scholarly work has focused on whether, in exceptional cases, it may be morally appropriate and legally justifiable that a coalition of States use military force to intervene for humanitarian purposes.

International military forces have always been involved in humanitarian action, although civil/military relations have been and remain tense, because the military always operates on a clear mandate in the interest of its commanding State or the international mission it is affiliated with. As such, military forces are never neutral. In the context of occupation, the occupying power has clear humanitarian duties. However, external military forces are today more often employed as part of foreign policy missions to assist other States in crisis with the provision of logistical support, such as during humanitarian operations. Moreover, international military forces often are providers of security for the local population and/or humanitarian operations as part of peacekeeping, peace enforcement missions or military escorts. In fact, civilian humanitarian action workers often share one operational space with armed forces.

The role of foreign military forces is often the subject of international negotiations and can be perceived ambivalently by the local population. The degree to which humanitarian organisations cooperate with military forces differs according to the organisations' own principles (see following section) and the context. In general, cooperation is easier in the context of natural disasters than in the context of armed conflict, in which host as well as third States might engage in hostilities. The host State plays an important role in the security and protection of humanitarian personnel.[33]

---

[32]Geneva Call is an NGO that engages armed non-State actors towards respect of international humanitarian norms, in particular those related to the protection of civilians in armed conflict (see: http://www.genevacall.org/).

[33]According to the Aid Worker Security Report 2012, attacks on aid workers are most prevalent in fragile and unstable States as well as in armed conflicts (cf. Stoddard et al. 2012).

4.3 Finances: Receivers and Donors of Humanitarian Action

States in crisis receiving international aid have generally been under-researched in humanitarian studies.[34] Harvey criticises the assumption of humanitarian organisations, that State structures are generally overwhelmed in times of conflict or disasters and that external assistance is therefore necessary and justified. He recalls that, in the 1970s and 1980s, donor States often provided direct bilateral support to governments. Due to the increased importance of civil society actors in the 1990s (and an increase in international military interventions), States affected by humanitarian crisis were mostly left out of the international coordination of humanitarian action. However, he notices a backshift to a more state-centric delivery of humanitarian action recently.

The majority of aid currently goes to a small number of countries with ongoing complex humanitarian crises. In 2013, Syria and neighbouring Lebanon and Jordan, affected by the Syrian refugee crisis, received 43% of international humanitarian assistance.[35] In 2014, acute emergencies in the Central African Republic, South Sudan, Iraq and States affected by the Ebola outbreak in West Africa accounted for 57% of humanitarian funding. Moreover, a number of countries experiencing protracted crises have received large amounts of assistance, such as the Occupied Palestinian Territories, Sudan, Ethiopia and Afghanistan. In contrast, a number of countries experiencing forgotten crises, such as Algeria/Western Sahara, Colombia and Myanmar, received less funding.[36]

The Development Assistance Committee (DAC) as one of the most important sub-structures of the Organization of Economic Cooperation and Development (OECD), has become the main platform for discussion and negotiation on donor strategies in the western hemisphere. DAC donors provide the majority of governments' international humanitarian assistance (over 90% since 2007).[37] However, the balance of humanitarian State-based financial structures is slowly shifting: while non-DAC donor contributions still fluctuate over time, they are generally on the rise and have cushioned the overall reduction in humanitarian financing from governments, for example, in 2012. Turkey, in particular, contributed US$1.6 billion in 2014, elevating it to the rank of fourth largest government donor that year after the United States (US$6 billion), the European Union (US$2.3 billion) and the United Kingdom (US$2.3 billion).[38]

---

[34]Harvey.

[35]Swithern et al. (2015), in: GHA 2015, p. 49, www.globalhumanitarianassistance.org/reports/.

[36]All numbers taken from the Global Humanitarian Assistance Report 2015, pages 49ff. When the most acute phase of emergencies is over, development funding may step in to provide for long-term support in reconstruction and rebuilding of society. For an overview on funding determinants, see for instance: Fink and Redaelli (2011); Fink and Redaelli (2011), pp. 741–757.

[37]*'94% of reported international humanitarian assistance from governments over the last decade and 90% (US$16.8 billion) in 2014'* (GHA-Report, 2015, p. 30).

[38]GHA 2015, pp. 2, 30, www.globalhumanitarianassistance.org/reports/.

International humanitarian institutions have placed much hope on new donors, such as the gulf countries and the BRICS since the early 2000, as they provided large amounts of funding to alleviate particular humanitarian crises (for example, in Haiti and Pakistan). However, the authoritarian character of certain regimes, and non-transparent decision-making in the distribution of donor funds, has also led to scepticism towards such donors on the part of traditional actors. Developing States and emerging powers increasingly engage in humanitarian action to gain international recognition or to wield soft power. However, their aims and principles in providing humanitarian action may differ from those of traditional donors. The latter tend to prefer channelling funds through multilateral organisations, whereas newly emerging donors are in favour of handing out bilateral support.[39]

Apart from government funding, an important percentage of international humanitarian action funds is provided by private donors, such as philanthropists, religious organisations, multinational companies or diaspora communities (for example, 24% in 2014).[40] The majority of aid in 2013 has been channelled through multilateral organisations (63%), NGOs (19%) and the Red Cross and Red Crescent Movement (8%).[41]

4.4 Coordination of Humanitarian Action

The UN takes the lead in the international coordination of humanitarian action, which is navigated through a complex system. A number of UN sub-organisations carry out different functions in the humanitarian system. They include the Emergency Relief Coordinator (ERC) at the Undersecretary level, the Office for the Coordination of Humanitarian Affairs (OCHA), United Nations High Commissioner for Refugees (UNHCR), United Nations (International)[42] Children's Emergency Fund (UNICEF), World Food Programme (WFP), Food and Agricultural Organization (FAO), United Nations Development Programme (UNDP) and World Health Organization (WHO).[43]

In 2005, a major reform of humanitarian coordination, known as the Humanitarian Reform Agenda, introduced a number of new elements to enhance predictability, accountability and partnerships.[44] The cluster approach was one of these new elements. Clusters are groups of humanitarian organisations, both UN and

[39]Binder and Meier (2011).

[40]GHA 2015, p. 42, www.globalhumanitarianassistance.org/reports/.

[41]*Id.*, p. 3.

[42]The name was shortened in 1953 but the acronym was retained.

[43]When dealing with humanitarian affairs, UN organisations also cooperate with the International Organization for Migration.

[44]For an overview on the development of international humanitarian coordination, see for instance Aderhold (2015), pp. 207–219.

non-UN affiliated, in each of the main sectors of humanitarian action, for example, water, health and logistics. They are designated by the Inter-Agency Standing Committee (IASC), chaired by the head of OCHA in its capacity as Emergency Relief Coordinator (ERC) and have clear responsibilities for coordination. Moreover, the IASC is a unique inter-agency forum involving key UN and non-UN humanitarian partners responsible for coordination and policy development, including in the development of the aforementioned self-binding rules and norms in humanitarian responses.

OCHA plays a key role in coordinating the various operational components of the humanitarian system. It works closely with global cluster lead agencies, the International Organization for Migration (IOM) and NGOs to develop policies, coordinate inter-cluster issues, disseminate operational guidance and organise field support. At the field level, OCHA helps ensure that the humanitarian system functions efficiently and in support of the Humanitarian Coordinator (HC). It provides guidance and support to the HC and Humanitarian Country Team and facilitates inter-cluster coordination. OCHA also helps to ensure coordination between clusters at all phases of the response efforts, including needs assessments, joint planning, monitoring and evaluation.

Since the early 1990s, regional organisations have also established humanitarian response units. For instance, the European Union Commission's Humanitarian Aid and Civil Protection Department (ECHO) is responsible for humanitarian action based on the 2007 European Consensus for Humanitarian Action. In a similar approach, many regional organisations have founded bodies designed to take rapid action when disaster strikes.[45] In some situations, regional organisations may be better suited to provide aid, for example where governments restrict access of humanitarian actors based on political constraints.[46]

At the same time, States have created bodies and mechanisms to respond to national disasters, as well as to coordinate national relief operations abroad. The way aid is coordinated at national levels depends predominantly on the respective State's political history and culture, its developmental level, as well as the degree to which States are either affected by humanitarian crises or act as donors of humanitarian action. States that have been heavily affected by natural disasters have sometimes learned from past experiences and thus developed very sophisticated national disaster response mechanisms (for example, Bangladesh). In a similar vein, cooperation between State and non-State humanitarian actors depends on the historical development of the political and administrative culture. For instance, in Germany, where civil society has become a strong political actor, coordination of humanitarian action, a responsibility of the Foreign Affairs Department, is performed in close cooperation with the major humanitarian NGOs based in the country.

---

[45] Zyck and Krebs (2013).

[46] For instance, in the case of Myanmar in 2008, international humanitarian interventions were partly rejected by the government, while regional offers of assistance were mostly accepted.

4.5 Humanitarian Non-governmental Organisations

The term 'transnational governance' reflects the fact that a growing number of non-State actors, such as NGOs, expert networks and multinational companies take part in international political affairs. This is especially true for post-conflict settings, where traditional State actors often lack the power and resources to assure humanitarian assistance, peace governance and post-conflict reconstruction. Consequently, humanitarian action is often coordinated by international (humanitarian) organisations.[47]

According to Labbé,[48] the majority of NGOs emerged in the twentieth century as a result of the experience of providing aid in times of war, for example, Save the Children (World War I), Oxfam & CARE (World War II), MSF (Biafra/Nigeria), Action Against Hunger (Cold War). In the 1980s, the evolution and development of NGOs increased rapidly. Different players have different concepts of the core humanitarian principles.[49] Hence, we can categorise organisations according to whether and how they adhere to the humanitarian principles.[50] Some of the oldest humanitarian organisations have religious roots, such as Caritas, Diakonie and Islamic relief. Larger religious organisations have professionalised rapidly and increasingly uphold the humanitarian principles.

Apart from religiously motivated NGOs, we differentiate *Dunantist* and *Wilsonian* actors in the humanitarian system.[51] While *Dunantists* strictly adhere to the humanitarian principles, *Wilsonians* work more in accordance with the foreign policies of their home States. Characteristically, Dunantists receive the majority of their funding from private sources (for example, MSF) to ensure independence from State policies. In contrast, some US-based *Wilsonian* organisations are mostly funded by the State. Despite the fact that the ICRC may also receive State funding, it is still considered the traditional custodian of international humanitarian law and strictly adheres to the humanitarian principles.

---

[47] Moran (2010).

[48] There are many approaches to categorising humanitarian actors, for instance according to the type of actor, differentiating between traditional and non-traditional actors according to Labbé (2012), http://www.google.de/url?sa=t&rct=j&q=&esrc=s&source=web&cd=9&ved=0CEwQFjAI&url=http%3A%2F%2Fwww.operationspaix.net%2FDATA%2FDOCUMENT%2F7549~v~Rethinking_Humanitarianism__Adapting_to_21st_Century_Challenges.pdf&ei=Qj9mVKG3IcSsPa3pgMgP&usg=AFQjCNGggkqEYW_giQ2UiR9K1MssqjSfuA&bvm=bv.79142246,d.ZWU.

[49] Slim (1997).

[50] Dijkzeul and Reinhardt (2013), pp. 77–105.

[51] The term '*Dunantist*' relates to Henry Dunant, the Swiss noble man, who gave birth to the idea of modern humanitarianism with his eye-opening account of the suffering of soldiers in the battle of Solferino in 1859 (Henry Dunant, 'A Memory of Solferino'). The term '*Wilsonian*' refers to the foreign aid policy of President Woodrow Wilsons.

A similar difference is reflected in multi-mandated versus strictly humanitarian NGOs, for example, Oxfam in contrast to MSF.[52] Multi-mandated NGOs carry out more development, conflict mitigation and human rights work in addition to their humanitarian operations. UN sub-organisations, as well as organisations cooperating closely with the UN, are bound by decisions of the UN Security Council and thus have difficulties in adhering to the humanitarian principles. The food organisations have to deal with the fact that food is a bulk good that needs to be paid for, and provided by, donor governments. They are therefore more government dependent than highly specialised medical organisations.

Moreover, an obvious divide can be observed between NGOs based in the global north, which receive the greatest share of humanitarian funding by their host States and the population of their home countries as opposed to local organisations based in the global south, which often depend on cooperation with international organisations or international NGOs to generate funds. At the same time, international partners need the knowledge of local partner organisations to implement their projects. The field of humanitarian NGOs has expanded rapidly since the 1990s in terms of numbers in NGOs and diversity. The increasing demand, the changing international political environment and a number of hurtful experiences in which humanitarian action got caught up have driven the sector to increasingly question its effectiveness and legitimacy.[53] Humanitarian organisations have thus begun to '[...] rationalise, bureaucratise, and professionalise'.[54]

5 Conclusion

As has been shown, global governance and humanitarian governance share certain features.[55]

First, norms and institutions are created to ease cooperation and coordination in humanitarian affairs to work towards the common goal of helping suffering populations. Moreover, loaded with the imperative to help, this is a highly normative and morally necessary and justified project as it is perceived as ultimately serving the greater good.

Second, as in other areas of international politics, we observe an increase in numbers and relevance of non-State actors, as well as governance processes shaped by a multitude of actors with at least partly competing interests.[56]

---

[52]Walker and Maxwell (2009).

[53]Harrell-Bond (1986).

[54]Barnett (2005) (723–740), p. 22.

[55]*Id.*, pp. 380ff. While underlining the similarities of global governance and humanitarian governance, Barnett advocates for widening the scope of research on humanitarian affairs to further understand how humanitarianism works.

[56]*Ibid.*

Third, international relations theories, as well as studying the development of organisations and institutions in the international system, can help to understand what motivates States to cooperate and how multilateral governance solutions in the shape of international organisations may work in humanitarian affairs. At the same time, many challenges, problems prevail, such as paternalism, politicisation and securitisation.

With the so-called *new wars,*[57] the context in which humanitarian action is taking place is changing. In contrast to interstate conflicts, nowadays, internal conflicts with various State and non-State parties are the dominant setting in armed conflicts. This leads to various complications and dilemmas.

First, aid organisations may, over time, replace State functions—which are not their aim. Although many evaluations and empirical studies highlight the importance of local knowledge (about social structures and hierarchies, discrimination, vulnerabilities, cultural norms and practices), humanitarians still do not use them to a sufficient extent. In theory, key words like 'capacity building', 'strengthening of local coping mechanisms' and 'resilience' are reproduced in countless policy documents, but the lack of cooperation and collaboration with local partners and representatives of the beneficiaries persists. Nevertheless, international NGOs usually depend on local partners for the implementation of projects. Humanitarian action should be delivered based on the principle of subsidiarity, that is, only after local resources and coping mechanisms have been exhausted. Instead, international humanitarian action frequently creates dependence on external interventions.[58] In some cases, the dependence on international humanitarian action and the powerful position of aid workers may lead to abuse of authority, increasing the vulnerability of victims. In reality, the degree of cooperation with local partners differs between organisations—today, many of them increasingly employ local personnel, reducing international personnel to a minimum. However, that does not fully solve the problem as local NGOs are dominated by—and personnel for international NGOs is frequently recruited from—the dominant educated elite, which may not always be familiar with local circumstances in crisis contexts. Moreover, corrupt elites and other parties to the conflict may also exploit aid. In sum, these conditions point to the consistently existing north versus south power assymetry in combination with prolonged dependencies of suffering populations in humanitarian action, which creates and reinforces paternalistic structures, or as Barnett puts it: 'Humanitarian governance operates with an emancipatory ethic that can justify and even legitimate acts of domination'.[59]

Second, humanitarian organisations have always been, and are increasingly perceived to be, political actors taking sides in conflicts, which threatens the principle of neutrality.[60] The perception of western international organisations by the local population differs: sometimes, western organisations are accorded an exaggerated degree of trust—whereas in other cases, their presence may increase

[57]Kaldor (2006).

[58]Müller (2013), pp. 147–157.

[59]Barnett (2012), p. 487.

[60]Cf. Weiss (1999).

tension and mistrust concerning western engagement. Moreover, humanitarian organisations are frequently viewed with scepticism, especially since the events surrounding 9/11. As a result of the global war on terror, national foreign policies have reinforced the claim to put national security interests first, by all means. This has thus led to a re-politicisation of humanitarian affairs.[61] The blurring of lines between civil and military actors, as well as multi-mandated organisations, which do not strictly adhere to the humanitarian principles and foreign policies making use of humanitarian action to pursue their national interests, threatens access to vulnerable populations and further increases the risk of politicising aid.[62]

At the same time, the international political discourse is increasingly dominated by security concerns. The increase in international military interventions poses a constant challenge for humanitarian civilian interventions with high risks for the security of humanitarian personnel. To further understand the politics of humanitarian action in world politics, we need to widen the scope of research both by breaking down disciplinary bound thinking and including more academics from the global south, where most humanitarian crises occur.

References

Aderhold E (2015) International coordination of humanitarian assistance. In: Heintze H-J, Thielbörger P (eds) From Cold War to cyber war: the evolution of the international law of peace and armed conflict over the last 25 years, pp 207–219

Audet F. Humanitarian space. In: Mac Ginty R, Peterson JH (eds) Routledge companion to humanitarian action. Routledge companions, pp 141–152

Barnett M (2005) Humanitarianism transformed. Perspect Polit 3(4):723–740

Barnett MN (2012) International paternalism and humanitarian governance. Global Constitutionalism 1(3):485–521

Barnett MN (2013) Humanitarian governance. Annu Rev Polit Sci 16(1):379–398

Baylis J, Smith S (eds) (2006) The globalization of world politics: an introduction to international relations, 6th edn. Oxford University Press, Oxford, United Kingdom

Binder A, Meier C (2011) Opportunity knocks: why non-Western donors enter humanitarianism and how to make the best of it. Int Rev Red Cross 93(884):1135–1149

Dallaire Ferland R. Istanbul dispatch: a first look back at the World Humanitarian Summit - Humanitarian Law & Policy. http://blogs.icrc.org/law-and-policy/2016/05/26/istanbul-dispatch/

DeMars WE, Dijkzeul D. The NGO challenge for international relations theory. Global Institution 92

Dijkzeul D, Lieser J (eds) (2013) Handbuch Humanitäre Hilfe. Springer, Heidelberg

Dijkzeul D, Reinhardt D (2013) Das internationale humanitäre System und seine Akteure. In: Dijkzeul D, Lieser J (eds) Handbuch Humanitäre Hilfe. Springer, Heidelberg, pp 77–105

Donini A (2010) The far side: the meta functions of humanitarianism in a globalised world. Disasters 34(Suppl 2):S220–S237. http://villierspark.org.uk/wp-content/uploads/2014/09/0061-Donini-2010-Meta-level-humanitarianism.pdf

[61]Cf. Audet, pp. 141–52 (147).

[62]Donini (2012).

Donini A (2012) The golden fleece: manipulation and independence in humanitarian action, 1st edn. Kumarian Press, Sterling
Dunant H. A Memory of Solferino
Fink G, Redaelli S (2011) Determinants of international emergency aid – humanitarian need only? World Dev 39(5):741–757
Harrell-Bond BE (1986) Imposing aid: emergency assistance to refugees. Oxford medical publications. Oxford University Press, Oxford [Oxfordshire], New York
Harvey P. Towards good humanitarian government: the role of the affected state in disaster response - HPG Policy Briefs 37
Heintze H-J (2015) Access to victims and humanitarian assistance. In: Heintze H-J, Thielbörger P (eds) From Cold War to cyber war: the evolution of the international law of peace and armed conflict over the last 25 years, pp 149–167
Kaldor M (2006) New & old wars, 2nd edn. Stanford University Press, Stanford
Karns MP, Mingst KA (2004) International organizations: the politics and processes of global governance. Lynne Rienner Publishers, Boulder
Keck ME, Sikkink K (1998) Activists beyond borders: advocacy networks in international politics. Cornell University Press, Ithaca
Labbé J (2012) Rethinking humanitarianism: adapting to 21st century challenges. http://www.operationspaix.net/DATA/DOCUMENT/7549~v~Rethinking_Humanitarianism__Adapting_to_21st_Century_Challenges.pdf
Moran MH (2010) Gender, militarism, and peace-building: projects of the postconflict moment. Annu Rev Anthropol 39(1):261–274
Müller O (2013) Almosenempfänger oder selbstbewusste Akteure? Die Rolle der lokalen Partner. In: Dijkzeul D, Lieser J (eds) Handbuch Humanitäre Hilfe. Springer, Heidelberg, pp 147–157
Oestreich JE (2011) Intergovernmental organisations in international relations theory and as actors in world politics. In: Reinalda B (ed) The Ashgate research companion to non-state actors. Ashgate research companion. Ashgate, Farnham, Surrey, England, Burlington, VT
Owen D, Strong TB (eds) (2004) The vocation lectures. Hackett, Indianapolis
Pfanner T. Editorial - IRRC March 2007 No 865. http://www.icrc.org/eng/resources/documents/article/review/review-865-p5.htm
Pries L (2008) Die Transnationalisierung der sozialen Welt: Sozialräume jenseits von Nationalgesellschaften. 1. Aufl. Edition Suhrkamp 2521. Suhrkamp, Frankfurt am Main
Robinson P (2015) News media and communication technology. In: Mac Ginty R, Peterson JH (eds) Routledge companion to humanitarian action. Routledge companions, pp 254–266
Rosenau JN, Czempiel EO (1992) Governance without government: order and change in world politics. Cambridge Studies in International Relations 20. Cambridge University Press, Cambridge [England], New York
Slim H (1997) Doing the right thing: relief agencies, moral dilemmas and moral responsibility in political emergemcies and war. Disasters 21(3):244–257
Stoddard A, Harmer A, Hughes M (2012) Aid Worker Security Report 2012: host states and their impact on security for humanitarian operations, Humanitarian Outcomes, December
Swithern S et al (2015) Global Humanitarian Assistance Report 2015: Executive-summary. Global Humanitarian Assistance Report
Swithern S et al Global Humanitarian Assistance Report 2015. www.globalhumanitarianassistance.org
Thakur R, Weiss TG (2009) R2P: from idea to norm—and action? Global Responsibility to Protect 1(1):22–53
Walker P, Maxwell DG (2009) Shaping the humanitarian world. Routledge global institutions. Routledge, Milton Park, Abingdon, Oxon, New York
Weiss T (1999) Principles, politics and humanitarian action. Ethics Int Aff 13
Zürn M, Zangl B (2004) Verrechtlichung: Baustein für Global Governance? Eine Welt Bd. 18. Dietz; Stiftung Entwicklung und Frieden, Bonn

Zyck SA (2013) Regional organisations and humanitarian action: November 2013. HPG Working Paper, Overseas Development Institute, Humanitarian Policy Group
Zyck SA, Krebs HB (2013) Localising humanitarianism: improving effectiveness through inclusive action - HPG Commissioned Reports - Briefing papers, November

Further Reading

Baylis J, Smith S (eds) (2006) The globalization of world politics: an introduction to international relations, 6th edn. Oxford University Press, Oxford, United Kingdom
DeMars WE, Dijkzeul D. The NGO challenge for international relations theory. Global institutions 92
Donini A (2012) The golden fleece: manipulation and independence in humanitarian action, 1st edn. Kumarian Press, Sterling
Dunant H. A Memory of Solferino
Fink G, Redaelli S (2011) Determinants of international emergency aid humanitarian need only? World Dev 39(5):741–757
Harrell-Bond BE (1986) Imposing aid: emergency assistance to refugees. Oxford medical publications. Oxford University Press, Oxford [Oxfordshire], New York
Heintze H-J, Thielbörger P (eds) From Cold War to cyber war: the evolution of the international law of peace and armed conflict over the last 25 years
Kaldor M (2006) New & old wars, 2nd edn. Stanford University Press, Stanford
Karns MP (2004) International organizations: the politics and processes of global governance. Lynne Rienner Publishers, Boulder. http://www.worldcat.org/oclc/53848373
Karns MP, Mingst KA (2004) International organizations: the politics and processes of global governance. Lynne Rienner Publishers, Boulder
Keck ME, Sikkink K (1998) Activists beyond borders: advocacy networks in international politics. Cornell University Press, Ithaca
Mac Ginty R, Peterson JH (eds) (2016) Routledge companion to humanitarian action. Routledge companions
Reinalda B (ed) (2011) The Ashgate research companion to non-state actors. Ashgate research companion. Ashgate, Farnham, Surrey, England, Burlington, VT
Rosenau JN, Czempiel EO (1992) Governance without government: order and change in world politics. Cambridge studies in International Relations 20. Cambridge University Press, Cambridge [England], New York
Slim H (1997) Doing the right thing: relief agencies, moral dilemmas and moral responsibility in political emergencies and war. Disasters 21(3):244–257
Weiss T. Principles, politics and humanitarian action
Walker P, Maxwell DG (2009) Shaping the humanitarian world. Routledge global institutions. Routledge, Milton Park, Abingdon, Oxon, New York

Uwe Andersen is Prof. Emeritus at Ruhr University Bochum (RUB), Germany, and Vice Executive Director of RUB's Institute for International Law of Peace and Armed Conflict (IFHV).

Katharina Behmer is Junior Researcher at RUB and the IFHV's General Manager.

Principles and Professionalism: Towards Humanitarian Intelligence

Andrej Zwitter

1 Introduction

Geopolitical challenges not only cause humanitarian crises; they can also be the source of failures in humanitarian action. Recent years have brought unique changes to the humanitarian landscape, from criminal and political threats, proliferation of actors in the international humanitarian sector, to professionalisation and accountability agendas imposed by international organisations and the humanitarian community itself.

This chapter outlines the most important political changes and challenges on the global stage, such as terrorism, the disappearance of humanitarian space, new actors besides traditional humanitarians and international coordination mechanisms.

Due to these changes and challenges, international humanitarian action is today more than ever in need of an advancement in analysis skills and strategic planning techniques in order to improve humanitarian projects and interventions.

At the same time, hesitation to learn from the experience and skills, which traditional intelligence analysis offers, stems in large part from a belief embedded in the culture of humanitarian action that denotes intelligence agencies negatively. However, the fact that intelligence analysis can provide exactly the skills and tools needed in the humanitarian field to improve project development and programming makes a strong case to use this experience for the professionalisation of humanitarian action. At the same time, it remains important that humanitarian actors keep a

---

This chapter is an adapted excerpt from the following book: Andrej Zwitter, *Humanitarian Intelligence: A Practitioner's Guide to Crisis Analysis and Project Design*, Rowman & Littlefield Publishers, New York, London 2016, Chapter 1, pp. 11–28. More information can be found on www.humanitarianintelligence.net. Reprinted with the permission of the publisher.

A. Zwitter (✉)
University of Groningen, Groningen, The Netherlands
e-mail: a.zwitter@rug.nl

© Springer International Publishing AG 2018

H.-J. Heintze, P. Thielbörger (eds.), *International Humanitarian Action*,
DOI 10.1007/978-3-319-14454-2_6

distance from intelligence actors. The concept of humanitarian intelligence is a way to strike the necessary balance in order to create a humanitarian intelligence tradecraft needed for analysis and intervention design that can save lives and improve safety and security of aid workers.

The foremost aim of this chapter is to show that humanitarian analysis needs are in many respects similar to traditional intelligence needs. Comparing both frameworks, this chapter covers the most important elements that constitute operational geopolitical parameters of humanitarian organisations.

Defining humanitarian intelligence means to first explain how the needs of humanitarian aid workers have changed over the last decades in political terms (2). Furthermore, it requires operationalising the humanitarian principles and the concept of 'humanitarian space' (3). The onset of the *global war on terrorism* (GWOT), specifically the effects of terrorism and counterterrorism on humanitarian action (4), and elements of professionalisation that have evolved in response to failures and lessons learned, (5) also need to be explained. Finally, once we understand the processes set in motion by experiences regarding success and failures, we can better grasp how international coordination mechanisms in humanitarian action evolved (6). Only then are we able to properly define humanitarian intelligence (7).

In other words, this chapter provides an intelligence perspective on the key geopolitical parameters that any humanitarian analyst, whether working for a small NGO or for a large international organisation, needs to understand and to a large degree also implement when planning operations.

2 The Changing Nature of Humanitarian Analysis Needs

Humanitarian action is not a new phenomenon. In fact, humanitarian aid in a structural and normatively embedded fashion has been provided to combatants since the onset of international law on the customs of armed conflict and the treatment of prisoners of war and those no longer capable to engage in acts of warfare (persons *hors de combat*).

The year 1864 marked a historical turning point, with Henri Dunant's founding of the International Committee of the Red Cross (ICRC), an organisation dedicated to alleviating suffering of persons *hors de combat*, prisoners of war and the civilian population. Subsequently, a number of international treaties were established to humanise warfare and protect the most vulnerable.

Another major turning point for the field of humanitarian action was the end of the Cold War, which led to a proliferation of humanitarian aid with the inclusion of many new non-governmental organisations (NGOs) and private groups dedicated to delivering aid to vulnerable populations affected by conflict or natural disasters.

The 1990s were marked by major humanitarian crises, in Somalia, Rwanda and Yugoslavia, to name but a few, many of which put humanitarian action to the test. For example, while the humanitarian intervention in Somalia helped in saving an estimated 100,000 lives, it also cost the lives of many soldiers and United Nations (UN) peacekeepers. Militia leaders used stolen food aid to generate cash and purchase weapons to ensure the loyalty of their followers, which perpetuated the conflict and created an imbalance of power that is shaping the Somali political landscape until today.[1]

While the goal of humanitarian aid workers and UN missions certainly was to alleviate suffering in all of these cases, the planning of many programmes and projects had serious omissions, which led to disastrous consequences for aid beneficiaries, the wider population and, eventually, entire nations. Consequently, researchers and analysts have justifiably criticised the conduct of the international community and humanitarian organisations for unintentionally prolonging conflicts and causing negative consequences for aid beneficiaries.[2] This prompted Hugo Slim to argue that

> [h]umanitarian aid obviously does have a dark side. Misapplied or not, the provision of help may well have negative repercussions beyond its original intention. The challenge for relief agencies is to determine the proper limits of their moral responsibility for this dark side, and then make all efforts to mitigate against it in their programmes.[3]

The international community and humanitarian organisations did take this critique very seriously and agonised over how to ensure that aid delivered would not yield unintended consequences. They set up standards, codes of conducts, as well as monitoring and reporting procedures, part and parcel of what is now known as the professionalisation of aid.

Another change in the field that affected the humanitarian community directly were the increasing attacks on humanitarian aid workers by terrorist organisations, especially in the wake of the post-9/11 conflicts in Afghanistan and Iraq, which were part of the larger GWOT, initiated by the United States of America (US) and its coalition of the willing. The effects of this change in the humanitarian operational space will be discussed in detail in the next section.[4]

In summary, the field of humanitarian action is under constant influence from a variety of factors that in part also determine analysis needs of rapid needs assessment teams, security experts, project design teams and project managers. The times in which humanitarian actors considered delivering food and makeshift shelters as sufficient means to fulfil their obligations are past. Today, humanitarian action is a major global industry, and States, as well as international organisations, are willing to spend massive amounts of money and in kind aid to help disaster and conflict stricken populations, which in turn attracts "for-and not-for-profit", faith-based and secular organisations alike. Foreign aid spending is also an important part of foreign policy strategies. They can put further pressure on aid organisations, for example in the form of donor interests, particularly when trying to utilise aid to achieve

---

[1]Clarke and Herbst (1996), pp. 70ff.

[2]Anderson (1999).

[3]Slim (1997), p. 256.

[4]Zwitter (2008), http://sites.tufts.edu/jha/archives/223; Macrae and Harmer (2003).

political goals. At the same time, humanitarians increasingly face safety and security risks, are required to provide better aid standards and have to comply with counterterrorism legislation.[5] Among the most important factors affecting humanitarian space and analysis needs are as follows:

- humanitarian principles and humanitarian space;
- effects of local-organised crime, terrorism and counterterrorism;
- professionalisation of humanitarian aid (standards of accountability); and
- coordination challenges among humanitarian stakeholders.

3 Humanitarian Space and Humanitarian Principles

Humanitarian space can be defined and understood in several ways. It may refer to the following:

- the operational space of humanitarian agencies necessary to meet humanitarian needs in accordance with the humanitarian principles;
- the space within which beneficiaries are able to uphold their rights to relief and protection;
- a sphere in which international humanitarian law is respected, allowing for unhampered aid relief; or
- humanitarian space as *a product of the dynamic and complex interplay of political, military and legal actors, interests, institutions and processes*.[6]

Most commonly, it simply denotes the 'humanitarian operating environment'.

There are several ways to achieve this operational space, generally either relying on military protection of aid workers or on the concept of humanitarian legitimacy (also called 'acceptance'). The latter depends, according to the ICRC, on the upholding of the humanitarian principles. Accordingly, Thürer explains that

> [t]he first issue is the subjective impartiality of the people who represent the organizations, the second being that of the structural characteristics of the organizations themselves – they must have room for manoeuvre with respect to the government and/or the parties to the conflict; independence and impartiality must be integral characteristics of the organization, and these characteristics must be guaranteed. Furthermore, their impartiality and independence must not only exist objectively, but must also be experienced and perceived by the outside world.[7]

Since their establishment in international humanitarian law, the humanitarian principles have become somewhat of a sacred vow to humanitarian aid agencies,

[5]For a detailed legal review of EU and US counterterrorism legislation concerning humanitarian and development aid see: Zwitter (2014), pp. 315–332.

[6]Collinson and Elhawary (2012), p. 1, http://www.odi.org/sites/odi.org.uk/files/odi-assets/publications-opinion-files/7643.pdf.

[7]Thürer (2007), p. 60.

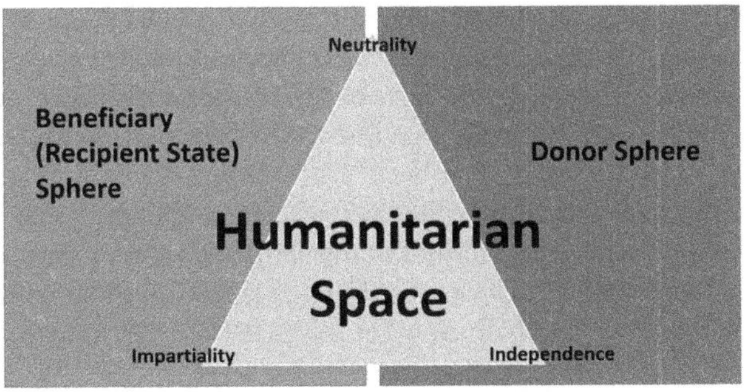

Fig. 1 Humanitarian space as consisting of humanitarian principles. Developed by the author, Andrej Zwitter. Reproduced by kind permission of the publisher from Andrej Zwitter, Humanitarian Intelligence: A Practitioner's Guide to Crisis Analysis and Project Design, Chapter 1, pp. 11–28 (Rowman and Littlefield, New York, London, 2016)

the UN humanitarian system and other stakeholders. To these actors, these principles are the all-encompassing norms that are or should be present in all humanitarian operations, although it has to be mentioned that not all actors always adhere to the principles or interpret them equally. Out of seven principles established at the XXth International Conference of the Vienna Red Cross in 1965, four are universally applicable[8]:

- *humanity*: to prevent and alleviate human suffering wherever it may be found;
- *impartiality*: to not discriminate on the basis of nationality, race, religious beliefs, class or political opinions; to relieve suffering, giving priority to the most urgent cases of distress;
- *neutrality*: to not take sides in hostilities or engage at any time in controversies of a political, racial, religious or ideological nature;
- *independence*: to act autonomously from States, international organisations and other authorities.

All four principles together form the *humanitarian space* (see Fig. 1).

Humanity is the overall objective, the reason underpinning all humanitarian work. It also guides actors to what should always be the prime directive where they face situations that require difficult decisions (so-called hard cases). The principles of impartiality, neutrality and independence guide the modus operandi of humanitarian operations. They determine the way humanity is to be achieved in external relations towards beneficiaries, donors and warring factions. This means that it requires humanitarian actors to set deliberate actions towards beneficiaries, donors and other stakeholders in order to be perceived as legitimate actors, which in turn is thought to achieve what is referred to as 'humanitarian space'.

[8]Pictet (1979), http://www.icrc.org/eng/resources/documents/misc/fundamental-principles-commentary-010179.htm.

Neutrality is the operational instrument in the field ensuring that nobody is being discriminated against. It is a principle that bridges the donor and the beneficiary sphere and prohibits an organisation's ideology from interfering with the principle of humanity, which posits the need of people as the sole determinant measure of aid distribution.

Impartiality refers to not taking sides between the opposing goals of parties in a conflict (this includes the international community and donor perspectives). As a principle located in the beneficiary or local sphere, it ensures that conflict parties do not oppose the delivery of aid to each other because both can benefit from the same advantage.

Independence serves to create an image of detachment from political goals, which are often present in the donor sphere. In order to ensure that aid agencies are perceived as truly impartial, they must be independent from donor and State interests (including democratisation and regime change agendas of States).

A violation of either of the principles can lead to stakeholders perceiving the humanitarian organisations as less neutral and may provide the former with cause to attacks, denial of access and other hindrances prone to limiting humanitarians' operational space. It is (sometimes wrongly) assumed that the principles and the *humanitarian space* they create to protect humanitarian aid workers also keep criminal entities in check.

However, coping with the threat of criminal actors, who simply aim to profit from aid and relief organisations, for example through kidnapping, carjacking, theft or sexual assault, often requires more than acceptance creating measures. Kidnapping in particular, the average global rate of which has risen by 28% in the 3 years before 2014,[9] increases the call for military protection or security details. *The challenge with a more protection-based approach, however, is that such measures must be carefully designed so as not to limit contact, and alienate the host community.*[10]

With regard to these criminal security issues, humanitarian organisations might have to resort to means of protection beyond acceptance-based security, which require a much more in-depth analysis of the local context and its stakeholders. The challenge is to continue to operate on the basis of the humanitarian principles while ensuring staff security and continuing to work closely together with the local population.

4 The Effects of Terrorism and Counterterrorism

The attacks on the World Trade Center and the Pentagon on 11 September 2001 had a profound effect on world politics, eventually leading to the interventions in Afghanistan and Iraq. The consequences of the politics of the GWOT did also not

---

[9]Aid Worker Security Report 2013 (2013), p. 4, http://aidworkersecurity.org/sites/default/files/AidWorkerSecurityReport_2013_web.pdf.

[10]*Id.*, p. 7.

halt before the humanitarian principles and the misuse of 'hearts and minds' practices by the invading forces. Intelligence agencies on the ground further blurred the lines between humanitarian organisations and enemy combatants.

Initially, after the first terrorist attacks struck the UN Office for the Coordination of Humanitarian Affairs (OCHA) in Baghdad in August 2003 and killed 22 people, including UN envoy Sergio Vieira de Mello, the humanitarian community hardly responded. Only a year later, when NGOs themselves became targets, starting with the kidnapping of two Italian aid workers (the 'two Simonas incident' as it was referred to in the NGO community), that the humanitarian community became aware of its own vulnerability and decided to respond by either keeping a low-profile or leaving the country altogether.[11] To illustrate the seriousness of the situation in numbers, during the year 2008, then UN Secretary General Ban Ki-Moon reported (UN staff, numbers in brackets: NGO staff) 25 (63) deaths from attacks, 490 (236) attacks, 160 (70) cases of detention by State authorities, 39 (103) incidents of unlawful detention by non-State actors, 263 (41) cases of assault, 546 (132) incidents of harassment, 578 (113) armed robberies, 119 (50) incidents of vehicle hijackings, etc.[12]

Consequently, the effects of terrorism and counterterrorism on humanitarian action cannot be underestimated. The US as one of the biggest humanitarian donors is particularly concerned that funds dedicated for aid could reach and unwillingly bankroll terrorist groups. International and regional organisations have their own concerns when it comes to the dual role they play with regard to the political nature of development aid, which conflicts with the neutral and impartial nature of humanitarian aid. These concerns and strategies to resolve them often do not match the NGOs' perception of the situation and their concerns for safety and security in the field. Local beneficiaries, in the meantime, are addressees of terrorist and counterterrorist operations and hearts-and-minds tactics and are recipients of humanitarian aid. In the years after 9/11, the impact of donor policies on humanitarian actors, encouraging the militarisation of aid, increasingly affected the image of humanitarian actors, questioning their impartiality and neutrality. There are, however, also important arguments in favour of the use of military support in humanitarian action, for example concerning the provision of humanitarians with the necessary transport and logistics or protecting civilians and aid workers from violence by State and non-State actors. In this regard, the military can often also be seen as a humanitarian actor itself, present in civil and military cooperation (CIMIC), together with other stakeholders such as UN agencies.

The two most common arguments for and against military protection of humanitarian aid workers are either diametrically opposed or constitute a vicious cycle: (1) humanitarian assistance requires military protection/involvement because of likely attacks, whereas (2) military involvement is a cause of the attacks against humanitarian aid workers. Advocates of the second argument usually demand a strict separation of military and humanitarian organisations. As an alternative

[11] Zwitter (2008).

[12] Ki-Moon (2008).

strategy to hardening targets by military protection, they commonly propose the creation of humanitarian space through acceptance.

The GWOT, even though the term has largely disappeared from public discourse, continues to affect the operation of humanitarian organisations in various ways. As regards funding of humanitarian actors, NGOs increasingly try to keep the origins of their funds secret and try to steer clear of implicit or explicit political agendas of donor States. This relates strongly to how NGOs position themselves vis-à-vis beneficiaries and the wider public. The GWOT also had an impact on programmes and projects: it led to the reduction of proximity of international NGOs to the field by the increasing use of implementing partners and steering of projects from secure locations (*remote controlling*); furthermore, NGOs tend to reduce their visibility in areas with hostile stakeholders.

The US has introduced the Partner Vetting System (PVS) for all organisations that apply for funding from USAID, which screens data on staff and implementing partners through CIA, FBI and NSA channels. This system has raised concern as being at best a big administrative burden to NGOs and at worst an infringement of privacy or even a potential security risk.[13] The PVS, together with terror lists of intergovernmental organisations and States, might help to monitor suspect entities, but in the perception of many humanitarian organisations it has also reduced humanitarian operational space and put humanitarians at risk of legal prosecution if they happen to be viewed as cooperating in any way with terrorist organisations, be it through direct assistance of people in need or in cases of negotiation for access to certain regions.

5 The Professionalisation of Humanitarian Aid

The trend towards professionalisation of aid can be attributed to the increasing awareness of the humanitarian community and other stakeholders that aid is not intrinsically beneficial because of the well-intentioned motivation underlying it, that when conducted unprofessionally it may result in negative (albeit unintended) consequences. Humanitarian organisations are increasingly under pressure to perform better, uphold standards and be accountable towards different stakeholders for local projects, funding, mandates and their overall mission.

For one, governmental and private donors expect their implementing partners to provide results for investment (*Has the organisation done what it promised to do to obtain funding*?)—this is in most cases a question of accounting. Beyond this point, the academic community has an important role in assessing and evaluating the successes and failures of aid organisations in disaster situations. Such assessment most often goes beyond mere accounting and asks questions of add-on *collateral damage* (unintended consequences of humanitarian action such as destruction of local markets), long-time impacts (such as aid dependency) or questions about

[13]Zwitter (2014).

cultural appropriateness, gender equality, beneficiary participation and ethics. The peer group of established humanitarian agencies, such as newcomers, and commercial relief contractors, such as DHL or Development Alternatives Inc., as well as the military, further increases the pressure on humanitarian organisations to professionalise their actions. Most importantly, however, a push originating from academics and donors for greater accountability towards the inclusion of beneficiaries at all stages of a relief project (planning, implementation, evaluation) raised the bar even higher. All these stakeholders put pressure on aid organisations to improve their performance, to be transparent in and to almost volunteer accountability to all interested parties.[14]

In the early 1990s, almost no common standards for humanitarian action besides international humanitarian law existed. The failure of many humanitarian projects during that time was in part attributed to the lack of standards of performance and accountability. Today, prompted by initiatives of the International Federation of the Red Cross and Red Crescent and OCHA, several important standards and codes exist. These are important as they set the parameters of operations. Some of the important codes and standards to be mentioned are as follows:

- *The Code of Conduct for The International Red Cross and Red Crescent Movement and NGOs in Disaster Relief*: this voluntary code of conduct was set up in 1994 and is a yardstick for self-governance of humanitarian organisations. It is assumed to be a minimum standard of professional conduct containing, among other elements, the humanitarian principles.[15]
- *The Sphere Standards (Humanitarian Charter and Minimum Standards in Disaster Response)* comprise widely recognised sets of common principles and universal minimum standards for disaster relief. The minimum standards are performance benchmarks in the following areas: water, sanitation and hygiene promotion (WaSH), food security, nutrition and food aid; shelter, settlements and non-food items; health services.[16]
- *The Core Humanitarian Standards (CHS)*, launched in December 2014 to replace the HAP 2010 Standards, the People in Aid Code of Good Practice and the Core Standards section of the Sphere Handbook,[17] covers the commitments shown in Table 1.
- The *Quality COMPAS reference framework* is a method of quality assurance developed on the basis of a six-year research project. It uses its own set of tools, offers training modules and consultancy services.[18] The COMPAS criteria and key processes (Table 2) are worth mentioning as they can be considered minimum quality criteria similar to the Core Standards[19]:

---

[14]Lancaster (1998); Stoddard (2009), pp. 246–266.

[15]http://www.ifrc.org/en/publications-and-reports/code-of-conduct/#sthash.M46QiRp2.dpuf.

[16]http://www.sphereproject.org.

[17]http://www.corehumanitarianstandard.org.

[18]http://www.compasqualite.org.

[19]Groupe URD (2009), p. 8, http://www.compasqualite.org/Setup/en/V9.06-EN_Quality_COMPAS_companion_book.pdf.

Table 1 Core Humanitarian Standards

1. 'Communities and people affected by crisis receive assistance appropriate and relevant to their needs.
2. Communities and people affected by crisis have access to the humanitarian assistance they need at the right time.
3. Communities and people affected by crisis are not negatively affected and are more prepared, resilient and less at-risk as a result of humanitarian action.
4. Communities and people affected by crisis know their rights and entitlements, have access to information and participate in decisions that affect them.
5. Communities and people affected by crisis have access to safe and responsive mechanisms to handle complaints.
6. Communities and people affected by crisis receive coordinated, complementary assistance.
7. Communities and people affected by crisis can expect delivery of improved assistance as organisations learn from experience and reflection.
8. Communities and people affected by crisis receive the assistance they require from competent and well-managed staff and volunteers.
9. Communities and people affected by crisis can expect that the organisations assisting them are managing resources effectively, efficiently and ethically.'

Developed by the author, Andrej Zwitter, citing CHS Alliance, Groupe URD and the Sphere Project: Core Humanitarian Standard on Quality and Accountability, p. 9 (2014), http://corehumanitarianstandard.org/files/files/Core%20Humanitarian%20Standard%20-%20English.pdf (accessed on 14 April 2017)

Table 2 COMPAS criteria and key processes

A. 'The project responds to a demonstrated need	B. The project achieves its objectives
C. The project removes or reduces the risk of negative impacts	D. The project aims for positive impacts beyond implementation
E. The project is consistent with the agency's mandate and principles	F. The project respects the population
G. The project is flexible	H. The project is integrated into its institutional context in an optimal manner
I. The agency has the necessary resources and expertise	J. The agency has the appropriate management capacity
K. The agency makes optimal use of resources	L. The agency uses lessons drawn from experience.'

Developed by the author, Andrej Zwitter, citing the COMPAS Criteria and Key Processes, http://www.compasqualite.org/en/compas-method/presentation-compas-method.php (accessed on 14 April 2017)

6 Coordination Challenges Among Humanitarian Stakeholders

Humanitarian action on the UN level dates back to the inception of the UN itself. In November 1943, a UN predecessor, the UN Relief and Rehabilitation Administration (UNRRA), was established. It was set up to provide aid to freed areas and to refugees. After the end of World War II, out of this organisation grew the two first UN aid agencies, today's UN High Commissioner for Refugees (UNHCR) and the UN International Children's Emergency Fund (UNICEF). During the Cold War, several others followed, including the World Food Programme (WFP, 1961) or the UN Development Programme (UNDP, 1965) to cater to humanitarian needs.[20] The proliferation of UN agencies with mandates relating to relief aid led to the need to coordinate and restructure the UN's humanitarian system in organisational and operational terms.

In 1991, the UN General Assembly (UNGA) responded to this need with its landmark Resolution 46/182,[21] which aimed at a consolidation of the UN system of humanitarian aid.

First, it established the operational principles, which from now on would be binding on all UN agencies delivering humanitarian aid: humanity, neutrality and impartiality.

Second, it established in accordance with general principles of international law (specifically the sovereignty of States) that primary responsibility for the initiation, organisation, coordination and implementation of humanitarian assistance lies with the States concerned. In terms of operational principles, the UNGA further added that linking relief, rehabilitation and development (LRRD) should be implemented as a fundamental principle within the UN humanitarian system as a whole. In structural terms, the resolution established coordination mechanisms for the organisation of actors, the consolidation of appeal processes for funding and overall strategy development:

- Inter-Agency Standing Committee (IASC),
- Emergency Relief Coordinator (ERC) as Under-Secretary General,
- Central Emergency Response Fund (CERF),
- Consolidated Appeals Process (CAP),
- Department of Humanitarian Affairs (DHA).

In 1998, the DHA was restructured by the Secretary General into OCHA, with an expanded mandate to include the coordination of all humanitarian responses on the UN level, policy development and humanitarian advocacy.[22]

[20] Zwitter (2011), pp. 53–55.

[21] UN General Assembly, Strengthening of the coordination of humanitarian emergency assistance of the United Nations, 19 December 1991, UN Doc. A/RES/46/182.

[22] OCHA, History of OCHA, http://www.unocha.org/about-us/who-we-are/history.

The failure to respond to the 2004 Darfur Crisis prompted the ERC to launch the Inter-Agency Real-Time Evaluation of the Humanitarian Response to the Darfur Crisis to develop lessons learned. It concluded that the humanitarian response to the Darfur Crisis was 'delayed and inadequate, primarily due to the inability of agencies to mobilize capacity and resources'.[23]

Frustration mounted with the response to the 2004/5 Indian Ocean tsunami, which eventually led the ERC to commission the Humanitarian Response Review (HRR). This report concluded that the overall system of humanitarian action (including the UN, Red Cross Movements, ICRC and NGOs) was in need of stronger humanitarian leadership to develop an overall strategy and a clustering of agencies into a sectoral coordination system in order to improve strategies on this level as well.[24]

This reform process led the IASC to develop a cluster approach with the following aims:

> At the global level, the aim of the cluster approach is to strengthen system-wide preparedness and technical capacity to respond to humanitarian emergencies by ensuring that there is predictable leadership and accountability in all the main sectors or areas of humanitarian response. Similarly, at the country level the aim is to strengthen humanitarian response by demanding high standards of predictability, accountability and partnership in all sectors or areas of activity.[25]

The cluster approach assigns leadership in different sectors of humanitarian aid to different organisations, which are particularly well versed in the specific area. These cluster leads coordinate the overall cluster strategy, develop preparedness and eventually become providers of last resort aid in case implementing partners fail to perform (with the exception of the ICRC). On a local level, these responsibilities contain more specifically the following[26]:

- establishment and maintenance of appropriate humanitarian coordination mechanisms;
- coordination with national/local authorities, State institutions, local civil society and other relevant actors;
- participatory and community-based approaches;
- needs assessment and analysis;
- emergency preparedness;
- planning and strategy development;
- application of standards;
- monitoring and reporting, etc.

Figure 2 illustrates the cluster approach as it is presently implemented.

[23]Humphries (2013), http://sites.tufts.edu/jha/archives/1976.

[24]Adinolfi et al. (2005), pp. 9–12.

[25]Guidance Note on Using the Cluster Approach to Strengthen Humanitarian Response (2006), p. 2, http://interagencystandingcommittee.org/working-group/documents-public/guidance-note-using-cluster-approach-strengthen-humanitarian-respon-0.

[26]*Id.*, p. 7.

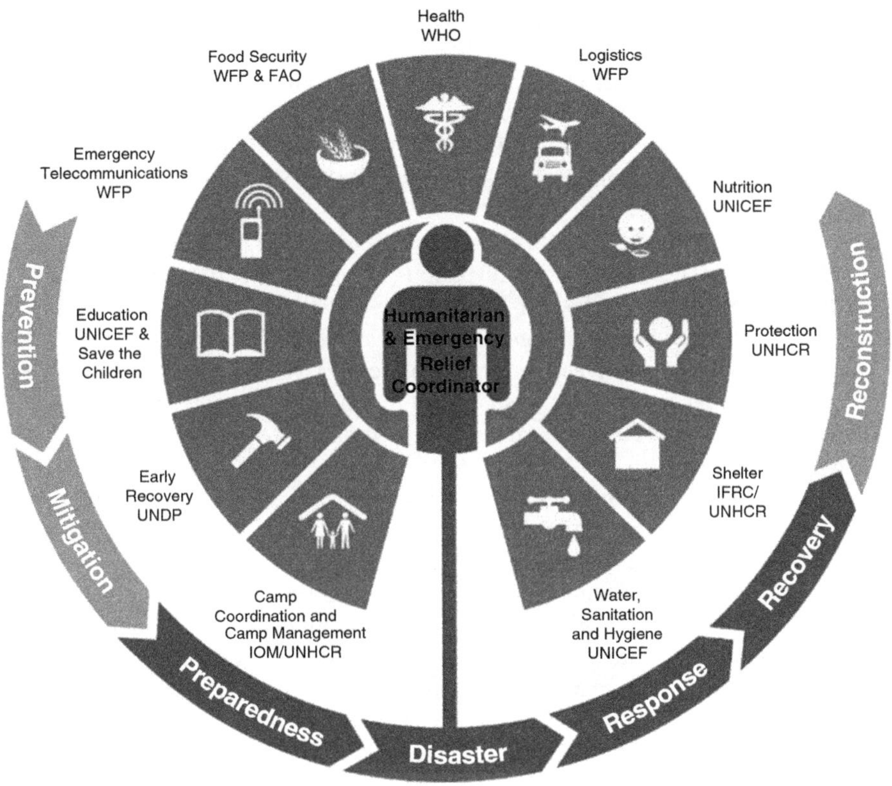

Fig. 2 Cluster approach. Reproduced by kind permission of the United Nations from UN Office for the Coordination of Humanitarian Affairs (OCHA)/Humanitarian Response, What Is the Cluster Approach, http://www.humanitarianresponse.info/coordination/clusters/what-cluster-approach (accessed on 14 April 2017)

As has been shown, the humanitarian community has invested much time to improve relief efforts and aid provision over the last decades. In this sense, standards and coordination mechanisms represent important elements that guide operation planning and need to be taken into account by humanitarian agencies.

7 Defining Humanitarian Intelligence

Helmuth von Moltke famously stated, ‘In war you will generally find that the enemy has at any time three courses of action open to him. Of those three, he will invariably choose the fourth’. As in other areas of intelligence analysis, humanitarian intelligence also aims to reduce uncertainty and risk by providing a basis for informed decision-making.

In general, intelligence analysis employs research methods similar to those used in market research or academic research. However, we can make three key distinctions between academic/market research and humanitarian and security intelligence.

First, in intelligence, accurate information is not readily available, and a wide range of methods and techniques must be deployed for data collection to compensate for that fact.

Second, concealment, deception and denial are routinely encountered during intelligence work. Actors are often suspicious of new third parties with potentially diametrically opposed agendas, which are met with secrecy or even hostility.

Third, intelligence bias with regard to anticipated deception and negative expectations regarding adversary actors tend to affect analytic interpretation. The fear that no information can be fully trusted (as it might be fed by counter-intelligence) can lead even to a point where analytical assessments have to yield to ad hoc intuitive decisions.

These three elements are common to humanitarian as well as traditional intelligence analysis. However, in many other respects, the tools and methods are quite different from traditional intelligence tradecraft. On the one hand, this has to do with limited capacities of humanitarian actors regarding signal intelligence; on the other hand, it is due to normative and operational standards specific to humanitarian action (for example, humanitarian principles). This is particularly true when it comes to accepted tools of recruiting informants and acquiring information. In terms of a general classification of intelligence, the following taxonomy of Hank Prunkun is very useful for humanitarian intelligence purposes[27]:

Tactical Intelligence

- is short-range or time limited;
- consists of patterns or operational mode activities.

Strategic Intelligence

- is considered to be a higher form of intelligence;
- provides a comprehensive view of a target or an activity;
- comments on future possibilities or identifies potential issues;
- provides advice on threats, risks and vulnerabilities;
- provides options for planning and policy development;
- assists in allocating resources; and
- requires extensive knowledge of the target or the area of activity.

Operational Intelligence

- provides immediate insight that supports an operation; and
- is oriented towards a specific target or an activity.

[27]Prunckun (2010), pp. 7–8.

To define 'humanitarian intelligence' is a matter of capturing the varieties of practices of humanitarian actors, trying to assess the status quo in a humanitarian crisis, the impact of humanitarian projects and programmes, as well as the underlying causes of persistent and complex emergencies. Humanitarian intelligence is then defined as 'the use of investigative and analytical techniques in service of rapid and continuous assessment, project and programme development, impact evaluation and learning'.

In terms of the above taxonomy, the intelligence needs regarding policy making and programme development are best comparable with strategic intelligence; project development requires skills in tactical intelligence, and the skills and information necessary for the daily work of the security officer in the context of the humanitarian operation would broadly fall into the area of operational intelligence.

In order to achieve consistency and inter-organisational compatibility of intelligence, coordinating bodies, such OCHA, have devised a variety of assessment tools and standards. This demand for mainstreaming of intelligence gathering and analysis is a consequence of the strong needs for coordination among different international, regional and local governmental and non-governmental organisations, and to some extent their common financing through centralised donor organisations such as the European Commission's European Civil Protection and Humanitarian Aid Operations (DG-ECHO) and USAID. Mainstreaming, however, remains difficult, in part due to the diversity of specialisations (food, health, shelter, WaSH, etc.), the different needs (project, programme, rapid-needs or impact assessment), the different standards applied (rights vs. needs-based approaches) and many other factors.

Distinct from other analytical techniques, humanitarian intelligence operates on specific key assumptions on security and safety:

- *increased risks*: routinely operating in volatile or hostile environments;
- *higher threat acceptance threshold*: negotiating access with potentially hostile parties;
- *operational security*: providing humanitarian space, including threats to physical and mental health of staff;
- establishing different tools and reporting formats for different clients (ECHO, diplomats, aid agencies, etc.);
- *target centric*: considering staff safety and security as of an equal concern as the livelihood of beneficiaries;
- *socio-cultural intelligence needs* for stakeholder interaction.

Humanitarian intelligence therefore focuses just as much on how to use humanitarian early warning indicators to assess risks, evaluate trends and provide early warning analyses as it does provide guidance on the operational design of humanitarian relief efforts. Another important aspect of humanitarian intelligence is that operational security depends on the intelligence analysis. This operational security is not simply an augmentation of an operation by adding a security feature but in fact means that operations needs to be designed in a way that ensures operational security intrinsically through every aspect of the project design. Humanitarian intelligence then goes beyond just giving advice on decision-making but requires the analyst to bridge analysis and project design through informing every single project design decision with the necessary piece of intelligence.

Since NGO's resources, unlike those of governments, are very limited, the same group of people is usually in charge of both humanitarian intelligence analysis and operations planning. This means that the intelligence analyst often also acts as project designer. Organisational capacities are in most cases a plus; however, they can also lead to bias concerning the evaluation of data and the needs for operations to succeed. Humanitarian intelligence analysis, therefore, is specifically under pressure to link all analytical steps as closely as possible to the project design process within the LogFrame. Humanitarian intelligence in the end has to tie neatly into the project cycle management as intertwining with the intelligence cycle.

Tactical humanitarian intelligence consists of rapid needs assessment (RNA) and field awareness intelligence for rapid relief aid (i.e., in military terms referred to as battlefield awareness, concerning, for example, accessibility of roads, mobility of beneficiaries or presence of criminal entities). Operational humanitarian intelligence, necessary in full-fledged projects, goes further. Most importantly, it includes, among other information, a stakeholder analysis that informs about the intentions of actors. Strategic humanitarian intelligence is mostly a policy tool and relevant for aid projects and programmes with a longer time frame than a two-week quick impact operation. The latter interacts with operational humanitarian intelligence due to the ongoing trend towards linking relief, rehabilitation and development (LRRD).

8 Conclusion

Humanitarian intelligence is closely related to traditional intelligence analysis. Like intelligence agencies, also humanitarian actors increasingly rely on Big Data, satellite imagery and automated analytics. However, while it shares common characteristics with military and security intelligence, it differs very much from both when it comes to humanitarian principles, operational parameters and the need to create a positive local perception, as well as the potential to engage with beneficiaries in a long-lasting collaboration. Humanitarian intelligence then must be particularly wary of the clandestine element that often accompanies the field of intelligence since trust by all stakeholders involved is one of the foremost elements that contribute to success and future collaboration. This element of trust is particularly expressed in the concept of accountability and the humanitarian principles that together form the backbone of professional humanitarian conduct.

References

Adinolfi C, Bassiouni DS, Lauritzsen HF, Williams HR (2005) Humanitarian Response Review. Independent report commissioned by the Under-Secretary-General for Humanitarian Affairs. Office for the Coordination of Humanitarian Affairs (OCHA), New York and Geneva, August

Aid Worker Security Report 2013 - The new normal: coping with the kidnapping threat. Aid Worker Security Database (AWSD). Humanitarian Outcomes, 2013. http://aidworkersecurity.org/sites/default/files/AidWorkerSecurityReport_2013_web.pdf

Anderson MB (1999) Do no harm: how aid can support peace or war. London

Clarke W, Herbst J (1996) Somalia and the future of humanitarian intervention. Foreign Aff 75 (2):70ff

Collinson S, Elhawary S (2012) Humanitarian space: a review of trends and issues. London, http://www.odi.org/sites/odi.org.uk/files/odi-assets/publications-opinion-files/7643.pdf

Groupe URD (2009) Quality COMPAS companion book. Version 9.06-EN. Groupe Urgence Réhabilitation Développement, Plaisians (France). http://www.compasqualite.org/Setup/en/V9.06-EN_Quality_COMPAS_companion_book.pdf

Guidance Note on Using the Cluster Approach to Strengthen Humanitarian Response. Interagency Standing Committee (IASC), New York, Geneva, November 24, 2006. http://www.humanitarianresponse.info/system/files/documents/files/IASC%20Guidance%20Note%20on%20using%20the%20Cluster%20Approach%20to%20Strengthen%20Humanitarian%20Response%20(November%202006).pdf

Humphries V (2013) Improving humanitarian coordination: common challenges and lessons learned from the cluster approach. J Humanit Assist, April 30, http://sites.tufts.edu/jha/archives/1976

Ki-Moon B, Safety and security of humanitarian personnel and protection of United Nations personnel. Report of the Secretary-General to the General Assembly, August 18, 2008

Lancaster W (1998) The code of conduct: whose code, whose conduct? J Humanit Assist, April 18, http://jha.ac/1998/04/18/the-code-of-conduct-whose-code-whose-conduct/

Macrae J, Harmer A (2003) Humanitarian action and the 'Global War on Terror': a review of trends and issues. HPG Report. Overseas Development Institute - Humanitarian Policy Group, July

OCHA, What is the cluster approach? | HumanitarianResponse. http://www.humanitarianresponse.info/coordination/clusters/what-cluster-approach

Pictet J (1979) The fundamental principles of the Red Cross: commentary. ICRC, January 1, http://www.icrc.org/eng/resources/documents/misc/fundamental-principles-commentary-010179.htm

Prunckun H (2010) Handbook of scientific methods of inquiry for intelligence analysis. Lanham

Slim H (1997) Doing the right thing: relief agencies, moral dilemmas and moral responsibility in political emergencies and war. Disasters 21(3):244–257

Stoddard A (2009) Humanitarian firms: commercial business engagement in emergency response. In: Steets J, Hamilton DS (eds) Humanitarian assistance: improving U.S.-European cooperation. Center for Transatlantic Relations, The Johns Hopkins University/Global Public Policy Institute, Washington, pp 246–266

Thürer D (2007) Dunant's pyramid: thoughts on the 'humanitarian space'. Int Rev Red Cross 89 (865):47–63

Zwitter A (2008) Humanitarian action on the battlefields of the global war on terror. J Humanit Assist (online Journal), October 25, http://sites.tufts.edu/jha/archives/223

Zwitter A (2011) The United Nations legal framework of humanitarian assistance. In: Heintze H-J, Zwitter A (eds) International law and humanitarian assistance: a crosscut through legal issues pertaining to humanitarianism. Springer Verlag, Berlin, Heidelberg, pp 51–69

Zwitter A (2014) Humanitarian action, development and terrorism. In: Saul B (ed) Research handbook on international law and terrorism. Edward Elgar, Cheltenham, pp 315–332

Zwitter A (2016) Humanitarian Intelligence: A Practitioner's Guide to Crisis Analysis and Project Design. New York, London

Further Reading

Collinson S, Elhawary S (2012) Humanitarian space: a review of trends and issues. Overseas Development Institute - Humanitarian Policy Group, London, April, http://www.odi.org/sites/odi.org.uk/files/odi-assets/publications-opinion-files/7643.pdf

Humphries V (2013) Improving humanitarian coordination: common challenges and lessons learned from the cluster approach. J Humanit Assist, April 30, http://sites.tufts.edu/jha/archives/1976

Slim H, Vaux T, Sandison P (2006) Key messages from ALNAP's review of humanitarian action, Report prepared for the Active Learning Network on Accountability and Performance in Humanitarian Assistance

Stoddard A (2003) Humanitarian NGOs: challenges and trends. In: Macrae J, Harmer A (eds) HPG Report 14, humanitarian action and the 'Global War on Terror': a review of trends and issues. Overseas Development Institute, Humanitarian Policy Group, London, July, pp 25–35

Rieff D (2002) Humanitarianism in crisis. Foreign Aff 81(6):111–121

Zwitter A (2015) Big Data and International Relations. Ethics and International Affairs 29(4): 377–389

Andrej Zwitter is Dean of University College Fryslân and Professor of International Relations and Ethics at the University of Groningen, the Netherlands, and Honorary Senior Research Fellow at Liverpool Hope University, UK, as well as Senior Fellow at the Centre for European Studies (CEFEUS), Politics and International Relation Department, Canterbury Christ Church University, UK. He is the co-founder of the International Network Observatory for Big Data and Global Strategy.

Part II
International Law

Public International Law

Elżbieta Mikos-Skuza

Public international law (PIL) today directly or indirectly impacts on every aspect of human life and is very much of a concern to professionals in a diverse range of specialisations, including in the field of humanitarian action. Regulations relating to human rights standards, the status of refugees, protection of victims of armed conflicts, international crimes, access to vulnerable populations in case of natural disasters, environmental matters, global communications, dispute resolution and management of interstate crises, among many others, all make up the realm of PIL.

This chapter focuses on those aspects of PIL that establish the international legal framework of humanitarian action. It identifies the particular characteristics of PIL that distinguish it from national law of States, as well as the main concepts and notions it shares with all specific disciplines relevant to humanitarian action.

It is also worthwhile mentioning at the very beginning that the role of PIL is not restricted to providing solutions in case of international problems but first and foremost to regulate international relations in such a way as to prevent crisis, avoid human suffering and thus reduce the need for humanitarian action in the first place.

1 What Is Public International Law?

In the past, PIL was defined as the body of law governing relationships between States—which for a long time remained its only subjects. Today, PIL is seen in a much broader light as there are bodies other than States that also have rights and obligations under PIL, particularly international intergovernmental organisations,

E. Mikos-Skuza (✉)
University of Warsaw, Warsaw, Poland
e-mail: e.mikos_skuza@wpia.uw.edu.pl

© Springer International Publishing AG 2018

H.-J. Heintze, P. Thielbörger (eds.), *International Humanitarian Action*,
DOI 10.1007/978-3-319-14454-2_7

such as the United Nations (UN) and humanitarian organisations within the UN system. There are also more and more regulations in PIL that concern the rights and obligations of individuals, particularly in the context of the protection of human rights and responsibility for war crimes, genocide, crimes against humanity and aggression. The unique international legal status of the International Committee of the Red Cross (ICRC), as well as the prior role of national liberation movements representing the interests of oppressed peoples exercising their right to self-determination, should also be emphasised.

The complex reality of today's international relations as expressed in the proliferation of drafters and addressees of international legal regulations challenges the traditional perception and definition of PIL. In his definition of PIL, Shearer takes account of these developments:

> International law may be defined as that body of law which is composed for its greater part of the principles and rules of conduct which States feel themselves bound to observe, and therefore, do commonly observe in their relations with each other, and which includes also:
>
> a. the rules of law relating to the functioning of international institutions or organizations, their relations with each other, and their relations with States and individuals; and
>
> b. certain rules of law relating to individuals and non-state entities so far as the rights or duties of such individuals and non-state entities are the concern of the international community.[1]

Another definition explicitly refers to the changing nature of PIL:

> Public international law can be described as composed of two layers: a traditional layer consisting of the law regulating coordination and cooperation between members of the international society – essentially the States and the organizations created by States – and a new layer consisting of the constitutional and administrative law of the international community of 6.5 billion human beings.[2]

However, despite the recognition of the role of non-State entities, PIL is still very much centred on State interests. Approximately 200 States in the world are the primary, sovereign subjects of PIL, and the status of all other subjects results from the will of States, most often expressed by way of agreements concluded between them.

The necessity for an international legal framework is a consequence of the fact that States and other subjects have varying, sometimes competing, interests and demands, whereas the international community requires regular and predictable conduct and behaviour to remain stable.[3]

PIL differs from private international law, which regulates *conflicts of laws*. While the former primarily concerns the relationship between States in so far as their official functions are concerned, the latter one relates to the activities of individuals and companies in their private dealings across national frontiers.

---

[1] Shearer (1994), p. 3.

[2] Sassòli et al. (2011).

[3] M. Koskenniemi, What is international law for? In: Evans (2014), pp. 89–114, also including numerous bibliographical references.

Examples of private international law dealings may include contracts concluded by humanitarian actors from one State carrying out international missions in another State, employing local staff or renting office space in that State. The legal issue in such a situation concerns the choice and/or determination of which State's domestic law applies to the private transnational contracts and potential disputes over their execution.

2 Public International Law and Municipal Law

In order to approach the nature of PIL, we must first understand the particular characteristics that distinguish PIL from municipal law.

Municipal law is usually identified with the existence of a central legislative body with the authority to establish laws for an entire community subordinated to this legislation, of a centralised system enforcing the law and of courts with compulsory jurisdiction to settle legal disputes and prosecute those who violate the law. These features, combined with the acceptance of a hierarchy of sources of law, are characteristic of any State's municipal law.

The concept of PIL differs substantially from an ideal national law in terms of the lawmaking process, the system of enforcement and the nature of the international judiciary.

2.1 The Absence of a Central Legislature

In municipal law, a supreme lawmaking body, such as a parliament, enacts legislation, which is hierarchically binding upon other subjects of domestic law.

PIL, on the other hand, has no central lawmaking authority. As its main subjects, States, are sovereign and equal, they themselves create the law that regulates their relationships with each other.

Hence, *State consent* is a crucial notion in PIL as no one international norm is binding upon States without their explicit or implicit consent. States express this consent mainly by concluding agreements accepted as binding on each other or by their established practices, which they recognise as legally binding custom. Even the most *self-evident* rules will not be binding if such consent is not given. For example, the prohibition of genocide is considered a rule of PIL not just because of its moral and political value but because of the wide acceptance by the international community of the Convention on the Prevention and Punishment of the Crime of

Genocide of 1948[4] and the customary nature of this obligation, confirmed by the International Court of Justice—the highest judicial authority in PIL.[5]

Lastly, even those bodies composed of all, or almost all, States in the world, such as the UN General Assembly (UNGA), have no legislative powers and cannot be considered *international parliaments.*

2.2 The Absence of Compulsory Law Enforcement

Municipal law is enforced by a police force and prosecutor's office. A breach of law can result in conviction and punishment in the form of a fine or imprisonment. In the case of a civil offence, such as a breach of contract, a party may be liable to pay compensation.

Contrarily, in PIL, there is no international police force to oversee obedience to the law. A State cannot be imprisoned or have a fine imposed on it for breaches of the law, however grave they may be. As is the case with lawmaking, there is no centralised law-enforcement agency. Consequently, enforcement of PIL is principally non-coercive and passes through diplomatic channels or via international pressure. The instances in which coercion is used are infrequent exceptions rather than the rule.

In case a State violates international norms, the customary rules on State responsibility for internationally wrongful acts, reflected in a non-binding document prepared by the UN International Law Commission,[6] provide that the State responsible for such act is under an obligation to cease that act, if it is continuing, and to offer appropriate assurances and guarantees of non-repetition.

The State is also obliged to make full reparation for the injury (both material and non-material) caused. Such reparation may take the form of restitution, compensation and satisfaction, either individually or in combination. Restitution means the re-establishment of the situation that existed before the wrongful act was committed. If damage cannot be made good by restitution, the State is under an obligation to offer financial compensation. Insofar as neither restitution nor compensation is possible, satisfaction should be given, which may consist in an expression of regret, a formal apology or another appropriate modality.

---

[4]Convention on the Prevention and Punishment of the Crime of Genocide, UNTS, Vol. 78, No. 277, http://treaties.un.org/doc/Publication/UNTS/Volume%2078/volume-78-I-1021-English.pdf. There are 147 States parties to this Convention.

[5]See: Advisory Opinion on Reservations to the Convention on Genocide, I.C.J. Rep. 1951, p. 15, at 23; Judgment in Barcelona Traction, Light and Power Co. (Belgium v. Spain), I.C.J. Rep. 1970, p. 3, at 32.

[6]Responsibility of States for Internationally Wrongful Acts, UN General Assembly Resolution 56/83 of 12 December 2001, annex, http://legal.un.org/ilc/texts/instruments/english/draft_articles/9_6_2001.pdf, Arts. 28–39.

Another way of enforcing PIL, particularly where a State is not willing to make reparation, is the imposition of sanctions adopted by States individually or collectively, with due consideration to the principle of the sovereign equality of States. Among such sanctions are suspensions or expulsions from international organisations. For example, the UN Charter provides that 'a member of the United Nations which has persistently violated the Principles contained in the present Charter, may be expelled from the Organization'.[7]

A wider spectrum of sanctions is foreseen in case of threats to the peace, breaches of the peace and acts of aggression.[8] They may take the form of 'complete or partial interruption of economic relations and of (. . .) communication, and the severance of diplomatic relations'. If the UN Security Council (UNSC) considers that such measures short of military force would be inadequate to ensure compliance with PIL, it may decide that military action shall be taken, including 'demonstrations, blockade, and other operations by air, sea, or land forces'.

In practice, the UNSC has imposed sanctions against States for violating PIL on several occasions. The examples include non-military sanctions against South Africa when it persisted in its policy of apartheid, trade restrictions against Iraq for its refusal to comply with the UN directives for disarmament following the Gulf War and also military action against Iraq in 1991, when it invaded and occupied Kuwait, against Bosnian Serbs in response to the siege of Sarajevo in 1995 or against the Gaddafi regime in Libya for committing crimes against humanity in 2011.

2.3 The Absence of a Compulsory Judicial System

Where municipal law is breached, the judiciary and a coercive penal system are available to react. Courts have mandatory jurisdiction that does not depend on good will and consent of parties to legal proceedings.

In PIL, courts and tribunals exist, but they are of a different nature than domestic judiciary. Some of them settle disputes arising between States; others hear cases brought by individuals against States violating human rights or try individuals who commit international crimes.

The competence of these tribunals always depends on State consent. No sovereign State can be compelled to appear before a court in any international proceedings. For example, the International Court of Justice (ICJ)—the principal UN

---

[7]Charter of the United Nations, adopted in San Francisco on 26th June 1945, http://treaties.un.org/doc/Publication/CTC/uncharter.pdf, Art. 6. The procedure of expulsion is construed in a manner that no State can be expelled against the will of one of the five permanent member States of the UN Security Council. Such an expulsion has never taken place.

[8]*Id.*, Arts. 41–42.

organ settling legal disputes and giving advisory opinions on legal questions, some of them relating to humanitarian problems[9]—is competent only if the case is referred to it by States or authorised organs satisfying all requirements provided for in Article 36 of the ICJ Statute[10] and in Article 96 of the UN Charter. More often than not, in the first stage of legal proceedings before the ICJ, States disagree as to whether the Court even has jurisdiction to hear the case.

The principle of State consent also applies to other tribunals. A person, claiming to be a victim of a violation of his or her human rights by a State, may apply to an international court against the State only if said State is a party to the treaty establishing this court and recognises its competence. For example, an individual is entitled to make claims before the European Court of Human Rights (ECtHR) on the basis of human rights set forth in the Convention for the Protection of Human Rights and Fundamental Freedoms, better known as the European Convention on Human Rights,[11] and may submit an application to the ECtHR in Strasbourg only if a violation was committed by a State that is party to the Convention—in other words, by a State that agreed to the establishment of the Court and submitted to its jurisdiction.

As regards tribunals established in order to prosecute individuals for the most serious crimes of international concern, such as the crime of genocide, crimes against humanity, war crimes and the crime of aggression, their competence is equally based on State consent, either directly or indirectly. For example, the 1998 Rome Statute of the International Criminal Court (ICC)[12] provides the Court jurisdiction insofar as States, on whose territory the crime was committed or of which the person accused of the crime is a national, have ratified the Statute. However, even if the State concerned is not a party to the Rome Statute, the UNSC may refer cases to the court. States indirectly consented to this procedure when they—becoming UN members—accepted the paramount role of the UNSC in international relations, Article 24 UN Charter conferring on it 'primary responsibility for the maintenance of international peace and security' and stipulating that 'the Security Council acts on their behalf'.

---

[9]See: Advisory opinions on the Legality of the Threat or Use of Nuclear Weapons, I.C.J. Rep. 1996, p. 226; Legal Consequences of the Construction of a Wall in the Occupied Palestinian Territory, I.C.J. Rep. 2004, p. 136; and judgments in: Case Concerning Military and Paramilitary Activities in and against Nicaragua (Nicaragua v. USA), I.C.J. Rep. 1986, p. 14; Cases Concerning Application of the Convention on the Prevention and Punishment of the Crime of Genocide (Bosnia and Herzegovina v. Serbia and Montenegro as well as Croatia v. Serbia), I.C.J. Rep. 2007, p. 43 and I.C.J. Rep. 2015, p. 118.

[10]The Statute of the ICJ is annexed to the UN Charter, of which it forms an integral part.

[11]European Convention on Human Rights, European Treaty Series No. 005, http://www.echr.coe.int/Documents/Convention_ENG.pdf.

[12]Rome Statute of the International Criminal Court, United Nations, Treaty Series, Vol. 2187, No. 38544, http://treaties.un.org/Pages/ShowMTDSGDetails.aspx?src=UNTSONLINE&tabid=2&mtdsg_no=XVIII-10&chapter=18&lang=en.

2.4 *Public International Law Is Real Law*

Its peculiar character is sometimes used to argue that PIL is not real law. Without going into the details of this academic debate,[13] it should be emphasised that the reality is that States conduct their affairs on the basis of the existence of PIL. Even in instances of breaches, the States concerned would not deny that there are existing legally binding obligations on them. They would rather argue their conduct to be consistent with the existing law as they interpret it. One may therefore conclude that States, even the most powerful ones, cannot do as they please. Instead, they obey PIL because it is in their interest to do so—either in their individual interest or in the interest of the wider international community and universal human values.

3 Subjects of Public International Law

The notion of legal personality is central to every legal system. It means that entities in a given system possess and exercise rights, discharge duties and have the capacity to maintain their rights by bringing claims.[14]

In municipal law, individual persons, as well as corporate and other entities established under domestic regulations, enjoy legal personality.

Contrarily, the principal subjects of PIL are States. It is through the permission of States that other actors in the international legal sphere have derived their own, independent legal international personality. These developments were acknowledged by the ICJ as early as 1949:

> The subjects of law in any legal system are not necessarily identical in their nature or in the extent of their rights, and their nature depends upon the needs of the community. Throughout its history, the development of international law has been influenced by the requirements of international life, and the progressive increase in the collective activities of States has already given rise to instances of action on the international plane by certain entities which are not States.[15]

The principal contexts in which the question of international personality has arisen are as follows:

- capacity to conclude valid agreements in the international sphere;
- capacity to make claims in respect of breaches of PIL; and
- capacity to bear international responsibility in case such breaches are committed by a given subject.

[13] See for details: S. Blay, The nature of international law, in: Blay and Piotrowicz (2005), pp. 6–21, including numerous bibliographical references.

[14] See for details: Crawford (2012), pp. 58–70, including numerous bibliographical references.

[15] Advisory Opinion on Reparation for Injuries Suffered in the Service of the United Nations, I.C.J. Rep. 1949, p. 174, at 178.

These concepts and notions are highly relevant to humanitarian action because the majority of PIL subjects are humanitarian donours, whose legal position therefore matters.

3.1 States

Despite the central importance of statehood to international legal system, there is no universally accepted definition of a State in PIL. The following criteria are considered necessary in order to establish a State's existence[16]:

- permanent population;
- defined territory—a State as an effectively established political community must be in control of a certain area, even if its frontiers are sometimes not fully defined;
- effective government, with centralised organs; and
- independence, represented by the capacity to enter into relations with other States. The question as to whether recognition by other States is an additional determinant of statehood cannot be discussed in detail here.

States are the most important donours of humanitarian assistance. It is estimated that they provide 60–75% (considering yearly fluctuations) of the total volume of global humanitarian aid.[17]

3.2 International Governmental Organisations

International governmental organisations are permanent associations of States with powers they may exercise independently of the member States themselves. These powers are exercised internationally—not just within one or more member States. There is no universally adopted definition of an international organisation, but certain elements are always present[18]:

- international treaty as a legal basis;
- States as members;
- permanent organs; and
- capacity to exercise the organisation's powers on the international plane.

[16]These criteria were defined in the Montevideo Convention on Rights and Duties of States of 1933, 165 League of Nations Treaty Series, p. 19. Although ratified by only 16 States, the Convention has acquired a meaningful influence on the interpretation of the notion of statehood.

[17]See annual reports, http://www.globalhumanitarianassistance.org.

[18]Crawford (2012), pp. 681–682.

Not every entity that operates in more than one State is a subject of PIL. There are increasing numbers of international non-governmental organisations (NGOs)—composed not of States but of individuals or associations whose cooperation is based on agreements registered in a State chosen by the members. NGOs are very active in different areas of international cooperation, including in humanitarian action.[19] Today's humanitarian sector is unthinkable without organisations such as CARE, Oxfam, Save the Children, World Vision, Doctors Without Borders and many others. However, these NGOS are not subjects of PIL. Their legal personality is limited to the domestic sphere. The same holds true for the legal status of multinational enterprises.

International intergovernmental organisations (IGOs) active in the field of humanitarian action include major world bodies such as the UN and its specialised agencies, regional bodies such as the European Union (EU) or the African Union, as well as institutions created for limited purposes in specific areas, such as the Committee on the Rights of the Child established under the 1989 Convention on the Rights of the Child.[20]

The UN, established in 1945, is accorded the most prominent role in the international system and conducts its tasks on the basis of the UN Charter.[21] The Charter contains a number of specific references to 'problems of humanitarian character', 'human rights', 'dignity and worth of the human person' or 'higher standards of living'.[22] As today all independent States are parties to the UN Charter and thus UN member States,[23] they have committed to combine their efforts to accomplish the aims stated in the Charter, including its humanitarian purposes.

The Charter establishes six principal UN organs: a General Assembly (UNGA), a Security Council (UNSC), an Economic and Social Council (ECOSOC), a Trusteeship Council,[24] an International Court of Justice (ICJ) and a Secretariat. Each of these organs is able to draw on the humanitarian provisions of the Charter[25]; however, the UNGA, ECOSOC and the Secretariat are of primary significance. The UNGA is composed of all UN members, making up the one forum where a matter may be brought before the entire international community. In

---

[19] Out of approximately 58,000 international NGOs active in different fields of international relations, there are about 260 registered with the UN Office for the Coordination of Humanitarian Affairs (OCHA)—http://www.uia.org.

[20] Convention on the Rights of the Child, United Nations, Treaty Series, Vol. 1577, No. 27531, http://treaties.un.org/doc/Publication/UNTS/Volume%201577/v1577.pdf.

[21] For a link to the text of the UN Charter, see http://treaties.un.org/doc/Publication/CTC/uncharter.pdf.

[22] See: Preamble and Arts. 1, 55, 56, 62, 76 UN Charter.

[23] There are 193 UN member States (as of 20th June 2016).

[24] This organ does not function anymore as the international trusteeship system ended in 1994.

[25] The UNSC may deal with humanitarian crises caused by an armed conflict while the ICJ may analyse legal issues of relevance for humanitarian action.

addition, one of the UNGA's main committees, the Third Committee, is competent to deal with humanitarian issues. With regard to ECOSOC, the ambit of its functions is very wide. It may initiate studies and reports and issue recommendations on various matters, including *for the purpose of promoting respect for, and observance of, human rights and fundamental freedoms for all.*[26] ECOSOC coordinates many of the activities of various specialised UN agencies, such as the World Health Organization (WHO), the Food and Agriculture Organization (FAO) or the International Organization for Migration (IOM). It should be emphasised that such specialised agencies are independent international organisations with their own legal personality. They do not share the UN's legal personality.

Within the complicated structure of the UN Secretariat, there is one office that merits special consideration from the perspective of humanitarian action: the UN Office for the Coordination of Humanitarian Affairs (OCHA). It plays a key role in the operational coordination of humanitarian assistance in partnership with national and international actors.

Lastly, the important role of different UN subsidiary organs, funds, programmes and semi-autonomous agencies within the UN system must not be neglected. They include the World Food Programme, the UN Children's Fund (better known as UNICEF), the UN High Commissioner for Refugees (UNHCR), the UN High Commissioner for Human Rights (OHCHR) or the UN Relief and Works Agency for Palestine Refugees in the Near East (UNRWA).

There are many IGOs that do not belong to the UN system but are recognised as subjects of PIL and play an important role in the field of humanitarian assistance, on a universal or regional level. With regard to the latter category, the role of the EU cannot be overstated. The tradition of relief assistance delivered by the European institutions is as long as the history of the European Communities themselves. In 1992, an effort was made to better coordinate such activities and the European Community Humanitarian Office (known as ECHO) was established. Since 2010, ECHO has been functioning as the European Commission's Directorate General for European Civil Protection and Humanitarian Aid Operations, ensuring rapid and effective delivery of EU relief assistance. As part of the EU, ECHO is not a separate subject of PIL.

3.3 The International Committee of the Red Cross

The International Committee of the Red Cross (ICRC) is a Swiss institution founded in 1863 in order to ensure protection and assistance for victims of armed conflict. Its mandate also encompasses humanitarian action during internal strife.

[26] Art. 62(2) UN Charter.

As an association governed by Swiss civil law, the ICRC falls outside the categories of subjects of PIL we have encountered so far. However, it is considered an international legal person whose *sui generis* status (status of its own kind) is recognised in international treaties, including the four Geneva Conventions of 1949 and their Protocols Additional of 1977,[27] which together make up the main body of international humanitarian law. They mandate the ICRC with several tasks, particularly as regards the protection of civilians and prisoners of war. In official documents adopted by international organisations, addressing specific armed conflicts or categories of victims, the ICRC is referred to separately, usually following the category of IGOs.[28]

The ICRC should not be mistaken for the International Red Cross and Red Crescent Movement of which it is but one, albeit highly important, component. Other parts of the Movement include National Red Cross and Red Crescent Societies, which may enjoy legal personality under the municipal laws of their respective countries, and the International Federation of Red Cross and Red Crescent Societies—an NGO coordinating the national societies' international activities. Hence, no Red Cross or Red Crescent institution, except for the ICRC, enjoys international legal personality.

The Holy See and the Maltese Order are also traditionally considered subjects of PIL because of their various activities, including humanitarian ones.

3.4 Individuals

Today, individuals enjoy substantial personality in the international sphere as a new category of subjects of PIL, although they still have a lesser procedural capacity than other international subjects. The development of active individual personality has to a great extent received its impetus through the human rights movement, principally in the context of the ability of individuals to assert their human rights and to bring claims for breaches of human rights treaties by States before international courts. Another evidence of individual international personality is that individuals may, under certain circumstances, be held accountable for international crimes by international tribunals.

Both of these situations are today regulated by two separate branches of PIL that developed mainly after World War Two: international human rights law and international criminal law.

---

[27]Geneva Conventions, UNTS, Vol. 75, Nos. 970–973, http://treaties.un.org/doc/Publication/UNTS/Volume%2075/volume-75-I-970-English.pdf, et sqq.; Protocols Additional to the Geneva Conventions, UNTS, Vol. 1125, Nos. 17512–17513, http://treaties.un.org/doc/Publication/UNTS/Volume%201125/volume-1125-I-17512-English.pdf, et sq.

[28]For details on the legal status of the ICRC, including numerous bibliographical references, see Sassòli et al. (2011), pp. 465–495.

4 Sources of Public International Law

The question of sources is fundamental in understanding PIL. It explains legal procedures and methods for the creation of binding rules on States and other subjects of PIL.[29] When tasked with outlining the sources of PIL, textbook authors usually refer to the enumeration contained in Article 38(1) ICJ Statute:

> The Court, whose function is to decide in accordance with international law such disputes as are submitted to it, shall apply:
>
> a) international conventions, whether general or particular, establishing rules expressly recognized by the contesting States;
> b) international custom, as evidence of a general practice accepted as law;
> c) the general principles of law recognized by civilized nations;
> d) (...) judicial decisions and the teachings of the most highly qualified publicists of the various nations, as subsidiary means for the determination of rules of law (...).

The wording of Article 38(1) suggests that it names the sources of ICJ decisions taken 'in accordance with international law' and not necessarily the sources of PIL itself. This is confirmed by the text of litera d).

Indeed, international tribunals do not have a lawmaking function. As the content of a judicial norm is often disputed, particularly where it involves a rule of custom, the ICJ is simply entitled to refer to earlier judicial decisions and judicial writings 'as subsidiary means for the determination of rules of law'. Similarly, the clause on 'general principles of law recognised by civilized nations' was included not as a separate source of law but in order to avoid the possibility of a lacuna, which may force the Court to declare there to be no treaty or established customary rule on the issue at hand, thus impeding it from reaching a decision.

On the other hand, the list contained in Article 38 ICJ Statute does not mention the role of international organisations in the creation of PIL as their special legal status was not yet recognised at the time the Statute was adopted.

The wording of Article 38(1) in phrases like 'conventions expressly recognised by the contesting States' and 'custom, as evidence of a general practice accepted as law' reflects the consensual character of PIL. These two main sources are created through the common consent of the main subjects of PIL, States.

4.1 International Treaties, Conventions and Other Agreements

International treaties, conventions and other agreements belong to the most important sources of PIL. A treaty is defined in Article 2(1)(a) of the Vienna Convention

---

[29]Legal scholars distinguish these formal sources of PIL from material sources, but the relevant debate is of a rather theoretical character—see Crawford (2012), pp. 1–3; H. Thirlway, The Sources of International Law, in: Evans (2014), pp. 117–120 and the extensive lists of bibliographical references provided by these authors.

on the Law of Treaties of 1969 (VCLT), the so-called *treaty on treaties*, as 'an international instrument concluded between States in written form and governed by international law, whether embodied in a single instrument or in two or more related instruments and whatever its particular designation'.[30]

The VCLT does not deal with unwritten international agreements (oral agreements are governed only by customary international law), nor does it cover international agreements involving international organisations. Such rules are the subject of the Vienna Convention on the Law of Treaties Between States and International Organisations or Between International Organisations of 1986,[31] which largely draws on norms of the VCLT.

Recent decades have seen a proliferation of treaties on almost every conceivable subject, including on those relevant for humanitarian action. Some of them have already been referred to in this chapter, for example the four Geneva Conventions of 1949 and their Protocols Additional of 1977, the Convention on the Prevention and Punishment of the Crime of Genocide of 1948, the European Convention on Human Rights and Fundamental Freedoms of 1950 or the Convention on the Rights of the Child of 1989. The list is much longer and includes such fundamental regulations as the Convention Relating to the Status of Refugees of 1951[32]; the International Covenant on Civil and Political Rights of 1966[33]; the International Covenant on Economic, Social and Cultural Rights of 1966[34]; and the Convention Against Torture and Other Cruel Inhuman or Degrading Treatment or Punishment of 1984.[35]

Some treaties not only impose humanitarian obligations on States and other actors but also allow individuals to bring complaints about their treatment under PIL.

4.2 *Customary International Law*

The definition of customary international law (CIL) provided in Article 38(1)(b) ICJ Statute emphasises the two requirements necessary to establish the

[30]Vienna Convention on the Law of Treaties, UNTS, Vol. 1155, No. 18232, http://treaties.un.org/doc/Publication/UNTS/Volume%201155/volume-1155-I-18232-English.pdf, Art. 2 (1)(a).

[31]This convention has not yet entered into force, pending further State ratifications. Its text is available at: http://legal.un.org/ilc/texts/instruments/english/conventions/1_2_1986.pdf.

[32]UNTS, vol. 189, No. 2545, http://treaties.un.org/doc/Publication/UNTS/Volume%20189/volume-189-I-2545-English.pdf.

[33]UNTS, vol. 999, No. 14668, http://treaties.un.org/doc/Publication/UNTS/Volume%20999/volume-999-I-14668-English.pdf.

[34]UNTS, vol. 993, No. 14531, http://treaties.un.org/doc/Publication/UNTS/Volume%20993/volume-993-I-14531-English.pdf.

[35]UNTS, vol. 1465, No. 24841, http://treaties.un.org/doc/Publication/UNTS/Volume%201465/volume-1465-I-24841-English.pdf.

existence of a customary norm—first, State practice, and second, acceptance of the practice as obligatory by the State concerned, often denoted with the Latin term *opinio iuris sive necessitates*.[36]

CIL may be created by all subjects of PIL; however, its traditional concepts were developed with regard to State practice and *opinio iuris*.

State practice is every activity of the organs and officials of States in a given area, namely what organs say and do in their official capacity. Such practice must be common, consistent and concordant, followed regularly under similar circumstances. It comprises not only active conduct but also abstention from acting. Taking into account the size of the international community, the practice does not have to encompass all States, nor does it have to be entirely uniform. However, there must be a sufficient degree of participation, especially by States whose interests are likely to be most affected by the rule in question. A State arguing that a given rule does not apply to it should be able to demonstrate its consistent opposition to the practice of other States and hence objection to that rule (*persistent objector*).

The idea of custom seems to suggest that customary norms are created over a rather lengthy period of time. However, the pace of change in all areas of human life has created a demand for a responsive legal framework. Therefore, what matters most is the intensity of State practice rather than the length of its duration. As the ICJ noted in its judgment in the North Sea Continental Shelf Case, 'the passage of only a short period of time is not necessarily (. . .) a bar to the formation of a new rule of customary international law' provided that 'within the period in question, short though it might be, State practice, including that of States whose interests are specially affected, should have been both extensive and virtually uniform'.[37]

The most difficult task in establishing the existence of a customary norm of PIL is the identification of its second element, namely common acceptance of the practice as an obligatory one by States. Indeed, a presumption of *opinio iuris* may be based on a wealth of State practice but not necessarily on a lack of practice. For example, the ICJ held that the fact that no nuclear weapons had been used since 1945 did not by itself render their use illegal on the basis of CIL, and referred directly to a perceived lack of *opinio iuris*.[38]

Another evidence of *opinio iuris* would be the codification of customary rules in the form of treaties that are subsequently universally accepted. The clearest

---

[36]There is a sizeable number of publications on customary international law—for relevant references, see Thirlway (1972) and Wolfke (1964).

[37]North Sea Continental Shelf Cases, Judgment, I.C.J. Reports 1969, p. 3, at 43.

[38]Advisory Opinion on Legality of the Threat or Use of Nuclear Weapons, I.C.J. Rep. 1996, p. 226, at 31–32.

example is the 1949 Geneva Conventions, which have now been ratified by virtually all States.[39]

Several customary rules, connected to the domain of humanitarian action, are universally accepted, such as the prohibitions on torture, genocide and racial discrimination.

4.3 International Organisations and the Development of International Law

IGOs play a significant role in the development of PIL rules. On the one hand, activities of governmental representatives at meetings of intergovernmental organisations can be qualified as State practice, or as evidence of *opinio iuris*, thus contributing to the formation of CIL. On the other hand, IGOs have the power to influence States' conduct in international relations either through non-binding recommendations (such as resolutions of the UNGA)[40] or even binding decisions (such as decisions of the UNSC).[41] In very exceptional cases, some (supranational) organisations have a lawmaking competence imposing new obligations on States parties,[42] although so far, this type of instrument has not been used in the domain of humanitarian action.

The practical significance of non-binding resolutions that formally cannot be regarded as sources of PIL has triggered the debate about so-called *soft law* or *soft rules*.[43] It is a convenient category comprising resolutions, which *prima facie* do not establish binding legal obligations, but are nevertheless designed to impact on the development of PIL. One of the best-known examples is the Universal Declaration of Human Rights of 1948—a formally non-binding UNGA resolution that became an international legal milestone, which set out for the first time the most fundamental human rights.[44] The history of this document proves that such resolutions

[39]There are 196 States parties to the Geneva Conventions (as of 20 June 2016).

[40]See for example UN General Assembly, Resolution 46/182 of 1991 on Strengthening of the coordination of humanitarian emergency assistance, UN Doc. A/RES/46/182.

[41]See for example UN Security Council, Resolution 827 of 1993, establishing the International Criminal Tribunal for the Former Yugoslavia, UN Doc. S/RES/827.

[42]Consider the regulations adopted by the Council of the European Union—see Art. 288 of the Treaty on the Functioning of the European Union, Official Journal of the European Union, C 81/1 of 2010.

[43]D.W. Greig, Sources of International Law, in: Blay and Piotrowicz (2005), pp. 85–90, including numerous bibliographical references.

[44]UN General Assembly, Resolution 217 (III), UN Doc. A/RES/217(III).

may over time develop from non-binding soft law into legally binding customary rules.

In the field of humanitarian action, many other soft rules exist in the form of declarations, guidelines or principles that are both regulatory and voluntary. *They are regulatory in that they create the hope or expectation that they will influence conduct and they are voluntary in that they create no legal commitments for the States concerned.*[45] Such documents are adopted by both IGOs and NGOs. Despite their provenance as legally non-binding, many of these documents are seriously taken into consideration in State practice.[46]

4.4 The Relationship Between Sources and Norms of International Law

The sources of PIL are equal in importance, which means that there is no supremacy of treaties over custom or of custom over treaties. Where treaty rules and customary norms collide, or have slight differences, one may have recourse to general principles of law—the special rule overrides the general rule and the later rule overrides the earlier rule. The lack of a hierarchy among sources, however, does not mean that there is no hierarchy among PIL norms. Two categories of norms enjoy supremacy over others.

First, the concept of peremptory norms of PIL (*ius cogens*) is universally recognised. *Ius cogens* is defined in Article 53 VCLT: it is a norm 'accepted and recognized by the international community of States as a whole as a norm from which no derogation is permitted and which can be modified only by a subsequent norm of general international law having the same character'.[47] A treaty that purports to derogate from such a norm is void. There is no authoritative catalogue of *ius cogens*, and its scope continues to raise controversy. The rules that attract the clearest support as *ius* cogens norms are the prohibition on the use of force and the prohibitions of genocide, racial discrimination and slavery.

The second category of norms superior to other rules are obligations of the UN member States contained in the UN Charter. Article 103 UN Charter provides that in the event of any conflict between such obligations and obligations under other international agreements, the Charter shall prevail.

[45] D.W. Greig, Sources of International Law, in: Blay and Piotrowicz (2005), p. 88.

[46] See for example Guidelines for the domestic facilitation and regulation of international disaster relief and initial recovery assistance, issued by the International Federation of the Red Cross and Red Crescent Societies, http://www.ifrc.org/en/what-we-do/idrl/idrl-guidelines.

[47] For a link to the text of the VCLT, see http://treaties.un.org/doc/Publication/UNTS/Volume%201155/volume-1155-I-18232-English.pdf.

5 Conclusion

A thorough understanding of particular characteristics of PIL that distinguish it from municipal law, of main concepts relating to subjects and sources of international law, is necessary to get acquainted with the legal framework of humanitarian action. The following chapters will address the issues mentioned above in greater detail, focusing on concrete branches of PIL that are particularly relevant in the context of humanitarian action.

References

Books and Reports

Blay S, Piotrowicz R (eds) (2005) Public international law. An Australian perspective. Oxford University Press, Melbourne

Crawford J (2012) Brownlie's principles of public international law. Oxford University Press, New York

Evans MD (ed) (2014) International law. Oxford University Press, New York

Sassòli M, Bouvier A, Quintin A (2011) How does law protect in war? ICRC, Geneva, open access at: http://www.icrc.org/casebook/doc/book-chapter/fundamentals-ihl-book-chapter.htm

Shearer IA (1994) Starke's international law. Butterworths, London

Thirlway H (1972) International customary law and its codification. Stijthof, Leiden

Wolfke K (1964) Custom in present international law. Ossolieneum, Wroclaw

Treaties and Statutes

Charter of the United Nations and Statute of the International Court of Justice of 1945;

Convention Against Torture and Other Cruel Inhuman or Degrading Treatment or Punishment of 1984, United Nations Treaty Series, vol. 1465, No. 24841;

Convention on the Prevention and Punishment of the Crime of Genocide of 1948, United Nations Treaty Series, Vol. 78, No. 277;

Convention on the Rights of the Child of 1989, United Nations Treaty Series, Vol. 1577, No. 27531;

Convention Relating to the Status of Refugees of 1951, United Nations Treaty Series, vol. 189, No. 2545;

European Convention on Human Rights and Fundamental Freedoms of 1950, European Treaty Series No. 005;

Geneva Conventions for the Protection of War Victims of 1949, United Nations Treaty Series, Vol. 75, Nos. 970-973;

International Covenant on Civil and Political Rights of 1966, United Nations Treaty Series, vol. 999, No. 14668;

International Covenant on Economic, Social and Cultural Rights of 1966, United Nations Treaty Series, vol. 993, No. 14531;

Montevideo Convention on Rights and Duties of States of 1933, 165 League of Nations Treaty Series, p. 19;
Protocols Additional of 1977 to the Geneva Conventions for the Protection of War Victims of 1949, United Nations Treaty Series, Vol. 1125, Nos. 17512-17513;
Statute of the International Criminal Court of 1998, United Nations Treaty Series, Vol. 2187, No. 38544.
Vienna Convention on the Law of Treaties of 1969, United Nations Treaty Series, Vol. 1155, No. 18232.

Cases

Barcelona Traction, Light and Power Co. (Belgium v. Spain), I.C.J. Rep. 1970, p. 3;
Case Concerning Military and Paramilitary Activities in and against Nicaragua (Nicaragua v. USA), I.C.J. Rep. 1986, p. 14;
Case Concerning Application of the Convention on the Prevention and Punishment of the Crime of Genocide (Bosnia and Herzegovina v. Serbia and Montenegro) I.C.J. Rep. 2007, p. 43;
Case Concerning Application of the Convention on the Prevention and Punishment of the Crime of Genocide (Croatia v. Serbia), I.C.J. Rep. 2015, p. 118.
Legal Consequences of the Construction of a Wall in the Occupied Palestinian Territory, I.C.J. Rep. 2004, p. 136.
Legality of the Threat or Use of Nuclear Weapons, I.C.J. Rep. 1996, p. 226;
North Sea Continental Shelf Cases, I.C.J. Reports 1969, p. 3;
Reparation for Injuries Suffered in the Service of the United Nations, I.C.J. Rep. 1949, p. 174;
Reservations to the Convention on Genocide, I.C.J. Rep. 1951, p. 15.

Further Reading

Aust A (2010) Handbook of international law. Cambridge University Press, Cambridge
Heintze H-J, Zwitter A (eds) (2011) International law and humanitarian assistance. A crosscut through legal issues pertaining to humanitarianism. Springer, Berlin
Klabbers J (2015) International law. Cambridge University Press, Cambridge
Shaw MN (2014) International law. Cambridge University Press, Cambridge
Spieker H (2015) The legal framework of humanitarian action. In: Gibbons P, Heintze H-J (eds) The humanitarian challenge. 20 years European Network on Humanitarian Action (NOHA). Springer – NOHA, Heidelberg

Elżbieta Mikos-Skuza is Senior Lecturer and Associate Professor at the Faculty of Law and Administration of the University of Warsaw, Poland. She also acts as Director of the NOHA Joint Master's Programme in International Humanitarian Action in Warsaw.

International Human Rights Law

Joana Abrisketa

1 The Process of Internationalisation of Human Rights

The experience of the League of Nations (1919–1945) is most similar to the United Nations (UN). Indeed, the UN in its current form was shaped by two major weaknesses of the League of Nations.

First, the League was not universal in nature since its members were never sufficient in number as to be truly globally representative (among others, the United States of America were never a member, and the Soviet Union was expelled from the League in reaction to its invasion of Finland in 1939).

Second, the League's fragility during World War II and its impotence in the face of the Nazi genocide prompted its dissolution and paved the way for the establishment of a new organisation by the conquering powers. Thus, the two guiding ideas underpinning the San Francisco Conference (held between April and June 1945) were, on the one hand, the determination to ensure the universal nature of the future structure and, on the other, the desire for the new organisation to last over time. The final result of the Conference was the Charter of San Francisco of 1945, the UN Charter.

Year 1945 was a key year in the development of international human rights law (HRL): with the establishment of the UN, symbolic of the evolution from traditional to contemporary public international law (PIL), the world witnessed the internationalisation of human rights. Traditional PIL, prior to 1945, was conceived as an instrument that exclusively regulated the relations between States: only States

The research on which this chapter is based received financial support from the Seventh Framework Programme of the European Commission (FP7/2007–2013), according to the terms of the Grant Agreement FRAME (n° 320000).

J. Abrisketa (✉)
University of Deusto, Bilbao, Spain
e-mail: joana.abrisketa@deusto.es

© Springer International Publishing AG 2018

H.-J. Heintze, P. Thielbörger (eds.), *International Humanitarian Action*,
DOI 10.1007/978-3-319-14454-2_8

were PIL subjects, and therefore only they were entitled to rights and owed obligations.[1] The scope of the *subjects* of PIL began to expand following the establishment of the first international organisation of a general nature (the League of Nations) and the subsequent recognition of different forms of legal personality. However, it was only with the inclusion of individuals in the UN Charter that natural persons first became subject to this manner of protection.

2 The Basis of the Regulatory System: The United Nations Charter

The internationalisation of human rights after World War II was effected primarily in response to the crimes commmitted by Nazi Germany and to the conviction that these crimes could have been avoided had there been an international system guaranteeing the protection of human rights. The UN Charter's preamble determines as its goals '[. . .] to reaffirm faith in fundamental human rights, in the dignity and worth of the human person, in the equal rights of men and women and of nations large and small'. Hence, the respect of fundamental rights, together with maintaining international peace and security, is the guiding idea that emerges from the preamble.[2]

Additionally, Article 1(3) UN Charter states that one of the main purposes of the organisation is '[t]o achieve international co-operation in [. . .] promoting and encouraging respect for human rights and for fundamental freedoms for all without distinction as to race, sex, language, or religion'. This is a programmatic standard in that it sets forth the UN's purpose and thereby determines the legitimacy of all actions it takes.[3] It should also be noted that the UN aims not merely to ensure the respect of human rights but also to achieve international cooperation in the development and stimulus of this interest common to all States.[4]

Finally, Article 55(c) UN Charter determines that '. . . the United Nations shall promote [. . .] universal respect for, and observance of, human rights and fundamental freedoms for all without distinction as to race, sex, language, or religion'.

This wording highlights that the inclusion of the principle of promotion of human rights in the UN Charter was a major landmark. However, despite its scale and scope, the mandate entrusted to the UN was limited by some major concerns: the Charter neither includes a definition of human rights, nor does it incorporate a basic inventory of those rights and set forth any basic mechanism to guarantee them. As a result, shortly after the creation of the UN, steps were taken to institute

[1]Buergenthal et al. (2009); Clapham (2007); Gómez Isa (1999), pp. 17–92; Wachsmann (2008).

[2]Alston and Goodman (2013), pp. 58–154.

[3]Pinto (1997), p. 16.

[4]*Ibid.*

de iure the principle of protection of the rights that was so vaguely set down in the Charter.

3 Major Instruments of International Human Rights Law

This subsection addresses three of the main international legal instruments targeting human rights: the Universal Declaration of Human Rights of 1948 and the International Covenants of 1966. These instruments together comprise the International Bill of Human Rights.

3.1 The Universal Declaration of Human Rights of 1948

Without exhaustively examining the process whereby the Universal Declaration was drafted, a very relevant aspect of its creation must be succinctly mentioned.[5] The Declaration was conceived, thanks to the endorsement of then US President Roosevelt, who, in his 1941 State of the Union Address known as the 'Four Freedoms Speech', planted the seed of the so-called universal *Magna Carta*. However, during the drafting of what would become the Universal Declaration, the Western bloc ignored the interest that President Roosevelt evinced in 'freedom from want' and 'freedom from fear', to such a degree that the countries comprising this bloc suggested including only civil and political rights on the basis of the essentially individualistic connotation of these concepts in the eighteenth and nineteenth centuries. It was only in the face of manifest opposition by the Socialist bloc and the pressure exerted by Latin American States that their Western counterparts agreed to include a series of economic, social and cultural rights in the Universal Declaration. The Socialist bloc countries were distrustful and sceptical throughout the entire drafting period and only consented to cooperate after the West agreed to include the protection of social and economic rights. Nevertheless, in view of the fact that its proposals were for the most part turned down, the Socialist bloc abstained from voting for the sum total of the text that was adopted by the UNGA on 10 December 1948.

Focusing on the contents of the Declaration, the Frenchman René Cassin, one of its founding fathers, observed that it rested upon four fundamental pillars. The first includes the rights of the person (the right to equality and the right to life, to freedom and to safety). The second pillar comprises the rights of the individual within the scope of his relations with the social groups of which he is a member (the right to a private and family life, the right to marry, freedom of movement within

[5]For a Commentary on the Universal Declaration of Human Rights, see Afredsson and Eide (1999).

the State or abroad, the right to a nationality, the right to own property and freedom of religion). The third pillar includes political rights, exercised in order to contribute to the establishment of State bodies or to participate in political activities (freedom of thought and of assembly, the right to active and passive suffrage, the right to access the government). Finally, the fourth pillar encompasses rights exercised in the economic and social arena, i.e., within the scope of labour relations (the right to work, the right to fair compensation and the right to rest and leisure) and the right to education.[6]

Nevertheless, the Universal Declaration was not proclaimed as an international treaty and therefore not a legally binding document. As it was a resolution (in the guise of a Declaration) adopted by the UNGA, it obtained the legal nature of a *recommendation* without the force of law inherent to an international treaty.[7] Thus, shortly after the Declaration's adoption, the international community began work to include the rights contained in the Universal Declaration in a new binding and enforceable treaty.

3.2 The International Covenants of 1966

The discrepancies between the two global power blocs became evident during the drafting of what was to become the great treaty on human rights. Indeed, the initial idea was to draft one single covenant that would comprise the totality of the rights contained in the Universal Declaration. However, after lengthy debates, the UNGA requested the Commission on Human Rights to draw up two separate documents—one was to include civil and political rights and the other economic, social and cultural rights—both of which were to contain as many similar provisions as possible so as to energetically reflect the single nature of the desired end.

In 1966, the International Covenant on Civil and Political Rights (ICCPR) and the International Covenant on Economic, Social and Cultural Rights (ICESCR) were adopted. The two documents have an analogous structure, and some of their respective articles are either identical or very similar.

The ICCPR includes the rights that are commonly identified as so-called *first-generation* human rights: the right to life, the right to freedom from torture, the right to freedom and safety, the right to movement and residence, the right to legal and judicial guarantees, the right to a legal personality, the right to private and family life, the right to freedom of thought and of speech, the right to freedom of assembly, as well as political and family-related rights.[8] Furthermore, two Optional Protocols

---

[6]Cassin (1951), pp. 237–367.

[7]Oraá and Gómez (1997), p. 77.

[8]On this issue, see Cassese (2012), pp. 136–143 and Lillich (1984), pp. 115–169.

complement the ICCPR: the First Optional Protocol of 1966[9] deals with the right of individuals to file complaints before the Human Rights Committee; the Second Optional Protocol of 1989[10] aims at the abolition of the death penalty.

The ICESCR includes rights that are often referred to as 'second generation' human rights. These include, among others, the right of all men and women to work, to form and join a trade union, to social security and protection, to physical and mental health, and to enjoy education, science and culture.[11] Its Optional Protocol, which sets forth the individual complaint mechanism, was adopted in 2008 and entered into force in 2013.[12]

The major difference between the two Covenants of 1966 lies in the fact that their States parties enter into different obligations. The wording used to set out obligations differs from one Covenant to the other: the ICCPR targets obligations of result, whereas the ICESCR pursues a specific obligation of conduct. However, despite the fact that initially references were made to the different degrees of compliance, the Committee on Economic, Social and Cultural Rights (CESCR) stated in 1990 that the ICESCR implies both the steady accomplishment of the obligations, as well as their immediate effect.[13]

However, the *official* position as regards these two sets of rules is that both types of rights are *universal, indivisible and interdependent and interrelated. The international community must treat human rights globally in a fair and equal manner, on the same footing, and with the same emphasis.*[14]

In practice, while most governments support the equal status and relevance of economic, social and cultural rights, they fail to take steps to strengthen those rights in their domestic legal orders.

---

[9]Optional Protocol to the International Covenant on Civil and Political Rights, adopted and opened for signature, ratification and accession by UN General Assembly Resolution 2200A (XXI) of 16 December 1966, entry into force on 23rd March 1976.

[10]Second Optional Protocol to the International Covenant on Civil and Political Rights, aiming at the abolition of the death penalty, adopted and proclaimed by UN General Assembly Resolution 44/128 of 15 December 1989.

[11]Eide (2001), pp. 9–28.

[12]Optional Protocol to the International Covenant on Economic, Social and Cultural Rights, adopted on 10 December 2008 during the sixty-third session of the General Assembly by resolution A/RES/63/117 of 10 December 2008, entered into force on 13 May 2013.

[13]Committee on Economic, Social and Cultural Rights, General Comment No. 3, The nature of States parties' obligations (Fifth session, 1990), U.N. Doc. E/1991/23, annex III, 4rd December 1990.

[14]Vienna Declaration, Adopted by the World Conference on Human Rights in Vienna on 25 June 1993 para 5, http://www.ohchr.org/EN/ProfessionalInterest/Pages/Vienna.aspx.

4 Defining Features of the Treaties on Human Rights

The treaties on human rights are agreements entered into by States, while individual human beings are the ones protected by these rights.[15] More specifically, one of the rights that individuals are entitled to is access to international authorities—judicial and non-judicial alike—to uphold those rights against the State.

Further, the nature of obligations contained in the human rights treaties is essentially objective. The treaties referred to are not synallagmatic, which denotes reciprocal compliance between States and individuals with the obligations in question. Hence, the general principle of international law that exempts one subject of PIL from complying with obligations it owes to another party, which is in violation of said rules, is not applicable. Non-compliance with the contents of a treaty on human rights, therefore, warrants neither the suspension of the treaty nor the termination thereof by other States parties. Human rights treaties create *erga omnes* obligations, which continue to exist at all times.

To conclude this summary of the most characteristic features of HRL, it should be stressed that there are two fundamental levels on which this legal framework has evolved: the regulatory or substantive level and the institutional level whereby the rules have to be applied.[16]

The first level marks certain rights as human rights and focuses on the construction of rules and standards. In the articulation of this regulatory dimension, there is a clear interaction between domestic law and PIL. It was indeed during the initial stages of codification that international treaties adapted the concepts of itemising the rights and freedoms in question from national constitutions (the Constitution of the French Fourth Republic, the Constitution of Italy 1947 and the Basic Law for the Federal Republic of Germany 1949—the most influential constitution of all). The 1948 Declaration of Human Rights and the European Convention for the Protection of Human Rights and Fundamental Freedoms of 1950 are telling examples. These international instruments in turn inspired Eastern and Central European States to include fundamental rights in their national constitutions throughout the 1990s. The Cold War over, these countries adapted their State models to the ones in place in the democracies of Western Europe.

The second level, the institutional dimension, referring to the specific implementation of rules designed to protect human rights, is of a clearly international nature. The institutional mechanisms in place strive to monitor the substantiation of violations of HRL carried out in the jurisdictions of States parties to human rights treaties. They provide guarantees of non-repetition, to assure reparations and to persuade against the perpetration of new violations at an international level.

---

[15] Pinto (1997), p. 57.

[16] Álvarez, N., La evolución de los derechos humanos a partir de 1948: hitos más relevantes, in: Gómez Isa (1999), pp. 93–178.

5 International Systems to Protect Human Rights

5.1 *Treaty Mechanisms*

There are currently 10 international treaties on human rights, adopted under UN auspices, each of which provides for the establishment of a separate Committee (or human rights treaty body) to safeguard States' compliance with their rules. All treaty bodies are made up of independent experts of recognised competence in human rights, whose names are put forward by the States parties and are then voted on. The composition of treaty bodies reflects different regional groups, and the number of members ranges between 10 and 25:

- The International Covenant on Civil and Political Rights establishes the Human Rights Committee (CCPR).
- The International Covenant on Economic, Social and Cultural Rights establishes the Committee on Economic, Social and Cultural Rights (CESCR).
- The International Convention on the Elimination of All Forms of Racial Discrimination establishes the Committee on the Elimination of All Forms of Racial Discrimination (CERD).
- The Convention on the Elimination of All Forms of Discrimination Against Women establishes the Committee on the Elimination of All Forms of Discrimination Against Women (CEDAW).
- The Convention Against Torture and Other Cruel, Inhuman or Degrading Treatment or Punishment establishes the Committee Against Torture (CAT).
- The Optional Protocol of the Convention Against Torture establishes the Subcommittee on the Prevention of Torture and Other Cruel, Inhuman or Degrading Treatment or Punishment (SPT).
- The Convention on the Rights of the Child establishes the Committee on the Rights of the Child (CRC).
- The International Convention on the Protection of the Rights of All Migrant Workers and Members of Their Families establishes the Committee of Migrant Workers (CMW).
- The International Convention on the Rights of Persons with Disabilities establishes the Committee on the Rights of Persons with Disabilities (CRPD).
- The Convention for the Protection of All Persons from Enforced Disappearance establishes the Committee on Enforced Disappearances (CED).

The mandate common to all of these committees is to monitor whether member States implement the conventions, through the examination of the reports sent periodically by the parties themselves (State reporting). All member States are obliged to submit an initial comprehensive report during the first year after the treaty becomes effective and afterwards every four or five years, depending on the treaty. In their reports, States parties must describe the juridical, administrative and legal measures they have adopted to ensure compliance with the respective treaty. The aim is to verify the progress achieved, to detect problems, to assess needs and to plan necessary policies. In accordance with this procedure, the pertinent committee (known as the treaty body) may decide to examine the status of implementation of a given treaty irrespective of whether it has already received the report or not. In this case, the treaty body will present to the member State a list of concerns, inviting it to send a delegation to the Human Rights Council. Oftentimes, it is sufficient for the treaty body to notify a State that it will examine its current status of compliance to persuade it to present its report.

In specific cases, the committees created by virtue of the treaties may receive and examine complaints from individuals who believe their rights have been violated, subject to certain conditions (individual communications). Additionally, some of the treaty bodies may initiate investigations if they receive reliable information containing well-grounded details about relevant violations, if member States have acknowledged separately and individually the treaty body's competency in this regard.

Finally, each treaty body publishes its interpretation of the respective treaty provisions in the form of *general comments* or *general recommendations*. This hermeneutical undertaking to clarify the content of HRL treaties has been essential in the implementation of specific human rights that were proclaimed in very broad terms.

Four of the treaty bodies were established or had their competencies expanded after 2000.[17] This means that, over the last decades, the expansion of the system has been significant regarding several aspects: the number of treaty bodies, the number of their sessions, the number of their experts and the number of their decisions.[18] In addition, States are obliged to fulfil their reporting obligations under the different treaty regimes, which has become an overlapping reporting burden.[19]

5.2 United Nations Human Rights Special Procedures

Under the UN Human Rights Special Procedures, experts (*Special Rapporteurs* or *Working Groups*) analyse, monitor and advise on issues pertaining to human rights, either with regard to specific allegations (thematic mandates) or with the aim of examining the situation in a specific State (country mandates). The scope of each Special Procedure is determined by the specific decision creating it, but the tasks of the Rapporteurs and Working Groups are usually similar in that they carry out country visits, take action with regard to specific cases by communicating directly

[17]The Optional Protocol of the Convention against Torture, which established the Subcommittee on the Prevention of Torture and other Cruel, Inhuman or Degrading Treatment or Punishment was adopted in 2002; the Conventions on the Rights of Persons with Disabilities and the Convention on Enforced Disappearances were adopted in 2006 and the Committee on the Rights of the Child adopted its third Protocol on a communications procedure in 2011.

[18]Pillay (2012).

[19]Egan (2013), pp. 209–243.

with the governments concerned, and even contribute to the development of the legal framework within the capacity of their mandate. Unlike the UN treaty mechanisms, which were established by virtue of the respective conventions, Special Procedures undertake their activities whether a State has ratified the pertinent treaty or not. Also, it is not necessary to have exhausted domestic remedies to access these procedures.[20]

When the mandate holders of Special Procedures interact directly with governments, they take action in cases of violations that have occurred, that are currently occurring or that will foreseeably occur. The process involves communicating with the government in question through the Office of the United Nations High Commissioner for Human Rights (OHCHR). Mandate holders request information and data regarding allegations of human rights violations, the adoption of preventive measures or call for the beginning of an investigation. Communications in general are known as 'urgent appeals' if the information provided relates to an ongoing violation or a violation that will foreseeably take place and as a Complaints Procedure Form when the information provided deals with already-committed violations.

Most of the mandates in existence until June 2006 were created upon the initiative of the then Commission of Human Rights and approved by the United Nations Economic and Social Council (ECOSOC). After 19 June 2006, when the United Nations Human Rights Council was created in substitution of the Commission on Human Rights, the Council was called upon to assume, review, improve and rationalise all mandates, mechanisms, functions and responsibilities of the Commission in order to maintain an effective system of Special Procedures.[21]

6 The United Nations Human Rights Council

The intergovernmental nature of the former UN Commission on Human Rights—made up of 53 members chosen according to geographical representation, including the permanent members of the UN Security Council (UNSC)—led the Commission to politicise the handling of the cases, resulting in a series of discriminatory selective decisions that ultimately resulted in the Commission's loss of credit.[22] Consequently, the UN undertook a reform of the system in 2006. Two catalysts lay behind this change of course.

First, Western countries agreed that the function of the Commission on Human Rights, the nature of which was notoriously political, had to be modified.

[20]Office of the High Commissioner for Human Rights, Working with the United Nations Human Rights Programme. A Handbook for Civil Society, New York and Geneva 2008, p. 107.

[21]Office of the High Commissioner for Human Rights, Manual of Operations of the Special Procedures of the Human Rights Council, Geneva, 2008, p. 4.

[22]Alston (2006), pp. 185–224.

Second, there was a perception that the UN had to be reformed in its entirety, underlined by then Secretary General Kofi Annan, who sought to finalise his mandate in 2006 through a significant reform. Since other reforms, especially regarding the make-up of the UNSC, were not possible, it was clear that the reform would have to be carried out via a lesser body. Although the reform was indeed required, the reason why it was actually undertaken was not essentially the desire to improve the protection and safeguarding of human rights but rather the desire to camouflage the fact that other attempts at renewal within the UN framework had not been accomplished.

Hence, the UN Human Rights Council was established, created by the UNGA as an intergovernmental body made up of 47 member States and in charge of strengthening the promotion and protection of human rights on a global level.[23] The Council has the ability to make recommendations to the UNGA, insofar as it is a subsidiary body of the UN, which the Commission on Human Rights was not.

The UNGA decided that the Council would avail itself of a new mechanism to assess the human rights situations in all UN member States: a universal periodic review (UPR), the major innovation of the newly created body. UNGA Resolution 60/251 provided that the Council should

> [u]ndertake a universal periodic review, based on objective and reliable information, of the fulfilment by each State of its human rights obligation and commitments in a manner which ensures universality of coverage and equal treatment with respect to all States; the review shall be a cooperative mechanism, based on an interactive dialogue, with the full involvement of the country concerned and with consideration given to its capacity-building needs; such a mechanism shall complement and not duplicate the work of treaty bodies.[24]

In contrast to the assessments of the United Nations Commission on Human Rights, which were selective in nature, the new mechanism ensures that every UN member State is periodically evaluated.[25] UPR serves to assess the human rights situations in the 192 United Nations' member States every four years.[26] As a starting point, the UPR uses information derived from different sources:

- information prepared by the State under review (the National Report);
- a compilation prepared by the OHCHR containing information from treaty bodies, Special Procedures and other relevant bodies; and
- a summary, also prepared by the OHCHR, containing information from civil society (NGOs, different national human rights associations, women's groups, trade unions and religious groups).

The actual review consists of a dialogue (the so-called added value) of three hours' duration that the State under review engages in with the UPR Working Group, made up of the 47 members of the Council on Human Rights. After this

[23] UN General Assembly Resolution 60/251, UN Doc A/RES/60/251, 15 March 2006.

[24] *Ibid.*

[25] Alston (2006), pp. 185–224; Freedman (2011), pp. 289–309.

[26] Every year 42 States are reviewed.

dialogue, a troika of rapporteurs (made up of three members of the council) and the UPR Secretariat prepare a report containing the questions posed during the dialogue and the recommendations made, noting those which the State has accepted. Finally, the working group accepts the report and sends it to the Council for approval.

Very succinctly, criticism of UPR centres on two aspects: first, the review is presented by member States, and second, there is no guarantee that representatives of civil society can participate fully.

Concerning the assessment carried out by the States, it is of note that human rights treaties generally foresee the existence of bodies that are specifically tasked to monitor compliance with obligations. As we have seen, these bodies are made up of independent experts who do not respond to the interests of any specific State. Thus, the scope of compliance with human rights rules is assessed with a guarantee of objectivity. However, within the framework of UPR, it is State delegations that study human rights in the State under review. Since all States are subject to this same review process, it is not improbable that they will avoid adopting harsh positions in order to not receive strong criticism themselves.[27]

As regards the limited participation of civil society, in contrast to the procedures in place for reviews carried out by human rights treaty bodies, UPR procedure stipulates that NGOs must submit relevant information prior to the presentation of the State report. Hence, the organisations do not have the possibility of questioning the information provided by the State or of contributing further analyses to counter the State's positions. In turn, NGOs may be present during the review, but they may not make any declarations or ask the State under review questions. This makes it impossible for civil society to directly pose fundamental questions regarding the status of human rights in the State under review.

References

Books and Reports

Afredsson G, Eide A (eds) (1999) The Universal Declaration of Human Rights. A common standard of achievement. Martinus Nijhoff, London

Buergenthal T, Shelton D, Stewart D (2009) International human rights in a nutshell, 4th edn. Thomson Reuters

Clapham A (2007) Human rights. A very short introduction. Oxford University Press

Oraá J, Gómez F (1997) La Declaración Universal de los Derechos Humanos. Instituto de Derechos Humanos, Universidad de Deusto

Pillay N (2012) Strengthening the United Nations human rights treaty body system. A Report by the United Nations High Commissioner for Human Rights, Office of the High Commissioner for Human Rights, Geneva

[27]Cowan and Billaud (2015), pp. 1175–1190; Smith (2013), pp. 1–31; Vengoechea-Barrios (2008), pp. 101–116.

Pinto M (1997) Temas de derechos humanos. Editores del Puerto, Buenos Aires
Wachsmann P (2008) Les Droits de L'Homme, 5th edn. Dalloz

Articles and Book Chapters

Alston P, Goodman R (2013) The human rights regime: background and birth. Comment on international dimension of human rights regime. In: International human rights. Oxford University Press
Alston P (2006) Reconceiving the United Nations human rights regime: challenges confronting the new UN Human Rights Council. Melb J Int Law 7:185–224
Cassese A (2012) A plea for a global community grounded in a core of human rights. In: Cassese A (ed) Realizing Utopia: the future of international law. Oxford University Press
Cassin R (1951) La Déclaration universelle et la mise en oeuvre des droits de l'homme. Recueil des cours de l'Académie de Droit International de La Haye 79(II):237–367
Cowan J, Billaud J (2015) Between learning and schooling: the politics of human rights monitoring at the Universal Periodic Review. Third World Quarterly 36:1175–1190
Egan S (2013) Strengthening the United Nations human rights treaty body system. Hum Rights Law Rev 13:209–243
Eide A (2001) Economic, social and cultural rights as human rights. In: Eide A, Krause C, Rosas A (eds) Economic, social and cultural rights, 2nd rev. edn. Nijhoff, Dordrecht
Freedman R (2011) New mechanisms of the UN Human Rights Council. Neth Q Hum Rights 29:289–309
Gómez Isa F (1999) La Declaración Universal de Derechos Humanos: algunas reflexiones en torno a su génesis y a su contenido. In: Gómez Isa F et al (eds) La Declaración Universal de Derechos Humanos en su cincuenta aniversario. Un estudio interdisciplinar, Universidad de Deusto, Bilbao
Lillich R (1984) Civil rights. In: Meron T (ed) Human rights, international law: legal and policy issues. Oxford University Press
Smith R (2013) To see themselves as others see them: the five permanent members of the Security Council and the Human Rights Council's universal periodic review. Hum Rights Q 35:1–31
Vengoechea-Barrios J (2008) The universal periodic review: a new hope for international human rights law or a reformulation of errors of the past? Revista Colombiana de Derecho Internacional 12:101–116

UN Documents

Committee on Economic, Social and Cultural Rights, General Comment 3, The nature of States parties' obligations (Fifth session, 1990), U.N. Doc. E/1991/23, annex III, 4rd December 1990.
Office of the High Commissioner for Human Rights, Manual of Operations of the Special Procedures of the Human Rights Council, Geneva 2008.
Office of the High Commissioner for Human Rights, Working with the United Nations Human Rights Programme. A Handbook for Civil Society, New York and Geneva 2008.
Optional Protocol to the International Covenant on Civil and Political Rights, adopted and opened for signature, ratification and accession by General Assembly resolution 2200A (XXI) of 16 December 1966 and entered into force on 23rd March 1976.
Optional Protocol to the International Covenant on Economic, Social and Cultural Rights, adopted on 10 December 2008 during the sixty-third session of the General Assembly by resolution A/RES/63/117 of 10 December 2008 and entered into force on 13rd May 2013.

Second Optional Protocol to the International Covenant on Civil and Political Rights, aiming at the abolition of the death penalty, adopted and proclaimed by General Assembly resolution 44/128 of 15 December 1989 and entered into force on 11th July 1991.
UN General Assembly Resolution 60/251, UN Doc A/RES/60/251, 15 March 2006.
Vienna Declaration, Adopted by the World Conference on Human Rights in Vienna on 25 June 1993 para 5., http://www.ohchr.org/EN/ProfessionalInterest/Pages/Vienna.aspx.

Further Reading

Alston P, Goodman R (eds) (2012) International human rights
De Schutter O (2014) International human rights law – cases, materials, commentary, 2nd edn. August

Joana Abrisketa is Associate Professor of Public International Law at Deusto University, Spain, where she previously acted as Director of the NOHA Joint Master's Programme in International Humanitarian Action.

International Humanitarian Law

Renata Vaišvilienė

1 Concept and Sources of International Humanitarian Law

Public international law (PIL) regulates the relations among international subjects: States, international organisations and, to a lesser degree, individuals (whose status as a subject is limited to a particular area of application), as well as other entities, such as the Holy See, by granting rights and imposing obligations. Despite the existence of the obligation to settle disputes peacefully,[1] and the obligation to refrain from the threat or use of force against the territorial integrity or political independence of any State,[2] armed conflicts are still a reality and in need of international regulation.

International humanitarian law (IHL) is a branch of PIL with the purpose of limiting the use of violence in armed conflict in order to protect those who do not or no longer directly participate in hostilities and to restrict the means and methods of warfare. The main goal of armed conflict is to weaken the military potential of the enemy, which is why IHL seeks to restrict the amount of violence necessary to reach this goal. Hence, IHL is the branch of PIL that indicates not only when armed violence may be used but also how.

However, IHL does not generally prohibit the use of violence, focusing instead on its consequences and the need to protect vulnerable persons. Further, IHL applies irrespective of the rationale behind a conflict. It presumes that the aims of the parties engaging in conflict are rational and do not contradict IHL, so that each party to the conflict must adhere to and is protected by IHL. IHL also does not prohibit belligerents from overcoming the other party to the conflict. Furthermore,

[1]Art. 33 UN Charter.

[2]*Id.*, Art. 2(4).

R. Vaišvilienė (✉)
Vilnius University, Vilnius, Lithuania
e-mail: renata.vaisviliene@tf.vu.lt

© Springer International Publishing AG 2018

H.-J. Heintze, P. Thielbörger (eds.), *International Humanitarian Action*,
DOI 10.1007/978-3-319-14454-2_9

the limited possibilities to control the correct implementation of IHL lead to the unfortunate result that the protection of IHL in practice does not benefit all those affected by armed conflict.

IHL accords protection based on the all-important principle of humanity.[3] In its Advisory Opinion on the Legality of the Threat or Use of Nuclear Weapons, the International Court of Justice (ICJ) indicated these main principles of IHL:

- protection of the civilian population and objects, implying the distinction of combatants and non-combatants;
- prohibition to cause unnecessary suffering to combatants, providing that the use of weapons is not unlimited.[4]

The full range of basic rules governing armed conflict and protection of its victims comprises the following IHL principles:

- distinction between civilians and combatants;
- prohibition to attack people *hors de combat* (Fr. 'out of the combat'), incapable of continuing to fight;
- prohibition to inflict unnecessary suffering;
- principle of necessity; and
- principle of proportionality.

The principles and regulations of IHL are embodied in the wide range of sources of IHL, the development of which began several millennia ago, with works such as Sun Tzu's *The Art of* War,[5] the Code of Manu,[6] works of ancient Greece[7] and Rome,[8] the Old Testament[9] or Islamic law[10] and further evolved during the Middle Ages.[11] Many others were to follow. During the American Civil War, Professor Francis Lieber, at the behest of Union President Abraham Lincoln, prepared the Lieber Code of 1863, which regulated the conduct of Union forces in battle and paved the way for similar code, culminating in IHL.

The codification of the customs and rules of IHL can be traced back to the nineteenth century, which is rather early in comparison with other areas of PIL. The development of the modern sources of IHL began with the adoption of the First Geneva Convention (GC) for the Amelioration of the Condition of the Wounded in

[3]'*The principle of humanity stands out on its own in the doctrine of the Red Cross, and all other principles hang from it.*' Pictet (1956), pp. 14–31.

[4]Report of the International Court of Justice 1 August 1996–31 July 1997, General Assembly Official Records, Fifty-Second Session Supplement No. 4 (A/52/4), para. 78.

[5]Tzu (2005), The Art of War, fourth century BC.

[6]The Laws of Manu (1991), fourth–second century BC.

[7]See, The Odyssey, Bk I, lines 260-3 ed. Lattimore (1965), p. 34.

[8]See, Phillipson (1911), pp. 21–23.

[9]See, The Book of Deuteronomy, XX, pp. 19–20.

[10]See, Siyar (1966).

[11]See for example *Corpus juris canonici*, 1500. See, Keen (1965).

Armies in the Field of 1864, many provisions of which derived from existing customary rules and practices.

The idea to adopt a unified approach towards the protection of victims of armed conflict was induced by an initiative of Swiss businessman Henry Dunant, which he laid out in his book *A Memory of Solferino* published in 1862.[12] Dunant narrates the horrors he witnessed during the battle of Solferino of 1859, which opposed French, Italian and Austrian forces in northern Italy. He was most shocked by how wounded soldiers had simply been abandoned on the battlefield. On the spot, he gathered local inhabitants to provide shelter and medical aid for victims of the battle. Dunant subsequently called on States to create a convention and enshrine principles that would ensure legal protection for the wounded.

This initiative eventually culminated in the foundation of the International Committee of the Red Cross (ICRC) in Geneva (1863), which began to promote IHL and organised a conference in view of drafting the First GC in 1864.

This treaty was the beginning of what came to be known as Geneva Law, a body of law designed to protect the victims of armed conflict. In 1868, the Declaration relating to Explosive Projectiles was adopted in Saint Petersburg, fostering the development of Hague Law, built on the principle of reciprocity between belligerent parties. Contrary to Geneva Law, Hague Law combined all provisions related to limitations or prohibitions of specific means and methods of warfare. Later, the international community recognised that the developing body of IHL needed to adapt to the reality of contemporary armed conflicts, and more conventions were adopted. Whereas the Hague Conventions of 1899 and 1907 codified laws and customs of war,[13] others, such as the Geneva Conventions of 1906 and 1929,[14] were devoted to the amelioration of the conditions of victims of armed conflict.

The sources of modern IHL are the four Geneva Conventions (GCs) of 1949[15] and their three Additional Protocols (APs).[16] The GCs are an extrapolation of the previous provisions of Geneva Law, whereas the first two APs of 1977 cover provisions of Geneva and Hague Law, leading to a convergence of both frameworks. The APs further develop rules of the GCs and adapt IHL to new and unconventional situations of warfare, which, albeit, have become the norm today. The four GCs and Additional Protocol I (AP I) apply to international armed conflict (IAC), which pins States against each other. Additional Protocol II (AP II) regulates the rules of warfare in non-international armed conflict (NIAC), opposing State forces and organised non-State actors or two or more groups of non-State actors.

---

[12]Dunant (1989).

[13]Hague Conventions II of 1899 and IV of 1907.

[14]1906 Geneva Convention on the Wounded and Sick in Armies in the Field, 1929 Geneva Convention on the Treatment of Prisoners of War.

[15]1949 Geneva Conventions (GCs): (I) on the Wounded and Sick in the Field, (II) on the Wounded, Sick and Shipwrecked at Sea, (III) on the Treatment of Prisoners of War and (IV) on the Protection of Civilian Persons.

[16]1977 Additional Protocols (APs) I, II to the GCs. 2005 AP III to the GCs.

Additional Protocol III of 2005 (AP III) introduces an additional distinctive humanitarian emblem alongside the Red Cross and Red Crescent: the red crystal.

Despite the widespread ratification of these main treaties, customary norms of IHL remain important as they fill the gaps left by treaty law and apply to States that may not have ratified particular conventions. Moreover, customary IHL strengthens the protection of victims in NIAC as the codified rules regulating NIAC are substantially less numerous than those applying to IAC. One of the most general examples of customary IHL is the famous *Martens Clause*, which acts as a sort of umbrella rule and provides that '[. . .] in cases not covered by the law in force, the human person remains under the protection of the principles of humanity and the dictates of the public conscience'.[17]

2 Application of International Humanitarian Law

IHL applies from the beginning of any armed conflict, whether of international or non-international character. The rules of IHL, however, do not apply to internal disturbances that are marked by serious disruptions of domestic order resulting from isolated or sporadic acts of violence, such as riots, but that do not reach the level of armed conflict. Moreover, provisions of IHL referring to implementation, such as the obligation of disseminating information on the laws of armed conflict, also apply in times of peace.

As regards terminology, the notion of 'war' must be distinguished from that of armed conflict, which is used today in IHL. The term war is an expression of the classic understanding that a state of war only begins with a corresponding declaration. Pictet's Commentary to GC I indicates:

> It remains to ascertain what is meant by "armed conflict". The substitution of this much more general expression for the word "war" was deliberate. One may argue almost endlessly about the legal definition of "war". A State can always pretend, when it commits a hostile act against another State, that it is not making war, but merely engaging in a police action, or acting in legitimate self-defence. The expression "armed conflict" makes such arguments less easy. Any difference arising between two States and leading to the intervention of armed forces is an armed conflict [. . .], even if one of the Parties denies the existence of a state of war. It makes no difference how long the conflict lasts, or how much slaughter takes place. [. . .] If there is only a single wounded person as a result of the conflict, the Convention will have been applied as soon as he has been collected and tended, [. . .].[18]

The International Criminal Tribunal for the former Yugoslavia (ICTY) confirmed this reading in the 1995 Tadic case, stating that 'an armed conflict exists

[17] Art. 1(2) AP I and the preamble to AP II, at para. 4; This clause was first introduced in 1899 at The Hague Conference and can be found in the preambles to Hague Conventions II, IV and, although only implicitly, in GCs I-IV, Arts. 63/62/142/158 respectively.

[18] See Pictet (1952), p. 32.

whenever there is a resort to armed force between States [. . .]'.[19] However, it is important to remember that this *first shot* rule only applies to situations of IAC, with the exception of certain cases that do not fulfil the criteria of IAC but to which the law regulating IACs nevertheless applies. In this vein, Common Article 2 GCs stipulates that IHL applies 'to all cases of partial or total occupation of the territory of the High Contracting Party even if the said occupation meets with no resistance'. Article 1(4) AP I stipulates that the Protocol also covers

> conflicts in which peoples are fighting against colonial domination and alien occupation and against racist regimes in the exercise of their right of self-determination, as enshrined in the Charter of the United Nations and the Declaration on Principles of International Law concerning Friendly Relations and Co-operation among States in accordance with the Charter of the United Nations.

To trigger an NIAC, the level of intensity of internal violence is required to be higher than in the case of IAC with its *first shot* rule. The ICTY has required 'protracted armed violence between governmental authorities and organized armed groups or between such groups within a State'[20] in order for a situation to reach the level of NIAC. This is because States are very cautious about qualifying a violent confrontation as NIAC due to the range of obligations therefore imposed on them, which would not apply in cases of internal unrest below the threshold of NIAC. Unfortunately, Common Article 3 GCs does not provide indications as to the lowest possible level of armed confrontation required in order for IHL to apply.

Terrorist acts are also covered by the provisions of IHL where they form part of an armed conflict. However, terrorist acts committed outside this context fall outside the scope of IHL. In many instances, classifying the action of terrorists poses difficulties and is highly contested.

The application of IHL ends with the *general close of military operation*.[21] In the case of NIAC, AP II refers to the 'end of the armed conflict'[22] as the moment when IHL ceases to apply. In practice, contemporary armed conflicts are often protracted crises that may continue to rage for a long time, albeit at lower intensity. Ceasefires are also frequently unstable. Hence, armed conflicts rarely end with *debellatio*, a clear defeat of one side. To stay abreast of these circumstances, IHL continues to apply to direct post-conflict consequences of armed conflict.[23]

---

[19] ICTY, Prosecutor v. Tadic, IT-94-1-AR72, Appeals Chamber, Decision 2 October 1995 Part A, para. 70.

[20] *Ibid.*

[21] GC IV, Art. 6(1) and (2); AP I, Art. 3(b).

[22] Art. 2(2) AP II.

[23] See Art. 5 GC I, Art. 5 GC III, Art. 6(3) GC IV, Art. 3(b) AP I, Art. 2(2) AP II.

3 International and Non-international Armed Conflict

Historically, PIL developed within the framework of interstate relations. Similarly, IHL was at the beginning not concerned with internal armed conflicts that were assumed to fall under the sovereign domestic jurisdiction of States. After the adoption of AP II in 1977, however, certain NIACs became part of the theatre of conflict regulated by IHL.

IAC is defined in Common Article 2 GCs, as well as Article 1 AP I, and denotes a situation of armed clashes between two or more States, also including occupations,[24] as well as wars of national liberation.[25]

Article 1 AP II defines an NIAC as comprising all types of conflict outside the scope of AP I. The same article further states that such conflict

> takes place in the territory of a High Contracting Party between its armed forces and dissident armed forces or other organized armed groups which, under responsible command, exercise such control over a part of its territory as to enable them to carry out sustained and concerted military operations and implement this Protocol.

It is important to note that this definition does not apply to the wider range of situations covered by Common Article 3 GCs. Hence, certain types of internal conflict are only covered by Common Article 3 GCs, not by the narrower scope of AP II. The ICTY has replaced the requirement of a conflict's protracted character by the requirement of intensity. It emphasised that NIACs must reach a sufficiently high degree of organisation and level of violence in order to be identified as such.[26]

Legal regulation of both types of armed conflict differs in terms of broadness, specialisation and institutional supervision. The law of IAC is codified with specialised rules and well-established international supervision mechanisms, whereas NIAC is much less regulated as existing provisions are of a more general character and the framework lacks institutional supervision.

Despite the formal differences that characterise both regimes, there is a tendency to reduce the gap in the regulation of IAC and NIAC. The 2005 ICRC study on customary IHL,[27] the result of ten years of research, found that 136 (arguably even 141) out of 161 codified rules of IHL also formed part of customary IHL. Although

---

[24]Art. 2(1) GC I-IV: '[. . .] *the present Convention shall apply to all cases of declared war or of any other armed conflict which may arise between two or more of the High Contracting Parties, even if the state of war is not recognized by one of them. The Convention shall also apply to all cases of partial or total occupation of the territory of a High Contracting Party, even if the said occupation meets with no armed resistance*'.

[25]Art. 1(4) AP I: '*The situations referred to in the preceding paragraph include armed conflicts in which peoples are fighting against colonial domination and alien occupation and against racist ré gimes in the exercise of their right of self-determination* [. . .].'

[26]ICTY, Prosecutor v. Tadic, IT-94-1-AR72, Appeals Chamber, Decision 2 October 1995, Part E, paras. 49 and 60; ICTY, Prosecutor v. Ljube Boškoski and Johan Torčulovski, IT-04-82-T, Judgement 2 July 2008, paras. 177–206.

[27]International Humanitarian Law (1996), pp. 194–222.

most of them are based on AP I norms that only directly apply to IAC, as norms of custom, they equally apply to NIAC.

From a humanitarian point of view, the protection of the victims of NIAC must equal the one accorded to victims of IAC, especially given that most conflicts in today's world are NIACs. Moreover, according to Common Article 3(4) GCs, the application of these norms to NIAC does not make an NIAC international in character. Even where the parties agree to submit themselves to all of the laws regulating IAC during their struggle, as Common Article 3 (3) GCs encourages them to do, this does not turn an NIAC into an international conflict.

4 Principle of Distinction

The most fundamental principle of IHL, the principle of distinction, mandates that armed conflict must only take place between members of the armed forces of the belligerents and should not affect civilians. This requirement stems from the need to identify who those participating in hostilities can attack as the principle of distinction mandates that only the enemy's military potential may be targeted. Accordingly, persons lawfully participating in the hostilities, referred to as combatants, must be distinguished from persons *hors de combat* (for example, the wounded) and people not involved in the hostilities (civilians[28]).

The protection of civilians encompasses the obligation to treat them humanely at all times and to protect them especially against all acts of violence or threats thereof, as well as against insults and public curiosity.[29] Any State must safeguard civilians under its jurisdiction and refrain from ill-treating them, for example by confiscating their property or hindering their access to food, water, shelter or medical assistance.[30]

Special groups of civilians requiring particular care are children, women, families, the elderly,[31] refugees and the displaced.[32] Children must be protected from assault, receive care and be prevented from taking part in hostilities (while they are under 15 years of age). They must also not be left on their own and be separated from adults in case of arrest. Further, the death penalty may not be administered to children below the age of 18.[33] Women must be treated equally to men, but due to their objective vulnerability preferential treatment should be afforded. In this vein,

[28]The definition of civilians is enshrined in Art. 50 AP I, which states '*A civilian is any person who is not a member of armed forces*'.

[29]Art. 27 GC IV.

[30]See Arts. 13–26 GC IV, Arts. 72–79 AP I, in particular Art. 75.

[31]See Arts. 44, 45 and 49 GC III; Arts. 27(3), 85(2) and 119(2) GC IV.

[32]See Arts. 23, 44 GC IV; Art. 70 AP I.

[33]See Art. 76 GC IV; Art. 77 AP I.

women are accorded special respect of their sexual integrity[34] and due attention in case of pregnancy or nursing.[35] Each party to a conflict must facilitate family reunifications wherever possible[36] and alleviate other needs by establishing hospitals and safety,[37] neutral[38] or demilitarised zones.[39]

The principle of distinction must be observed at all times. However, the 'civilianization'[40] of modern armed conflicts is increasingly causing difficulties for the implementation of the principle of distinction. Asymmetric warfare[41] and the emergence of new actors, such as the engagement of private military and security companies,[42] lead to greater implication of civilians participating in hostilities and result in the loss of their protection from being directly attacked. However, generally, where a person's status is in doubt, that person shall be considered a civilian.[43]

A combatant is a person who takes a direct part in the hostilities of an armed conflict[44] as a member of the armed forces *stricto sensu* (Lat. 'in the restricted sense') recognised and identified by the State that controls the armed forces in question according to national law. The definition of combatants *lato sensu* (Lat. 'in the broad sense') covers members of a group who fulfil the following requirements[45]:

- being commanded by a person responsible for his subordinates;
- having a fixed distinctive sign recognisable at a distance;
- carrying arms openly;
- conducting operations in accordance with the laws and customs of war.

AP I adapts these requirements to the increased need for regulation of national liberation movements and guerrilla warfare. Article 43 AP I states that armed forces of a party to a conflict comprise organised groups and units under the command of that party, even if the latter is represented by a government or an authority not recognised by the opposing party. In order to qualify as armed forces, troops must be subject to an internal disciplinary system, which can ensure compliance with the rules of IHL.

---

[34]Art. 27 GC IV.

[35]See for example Arts. 89 and 132 GC IV, Art. 76(3), AP I Art. 6(4) AP II.

[36]See Art. 74 AP I.

[37]See Art. 14 GC IV.

[38]See Art. 15 GC IV.

[39]See Art. 60 API.

[40]See Wenger and Mason (2008).

[41]For details, see Pfanner (2005).

[42]For details, see Percy (2012).

[43]This has been stated by, among others, the ICTY and the International Crimina Court, see: http://ihl-databases.icrc.org/customary-ihl/eng/docs/v2_rul_rule5.

[44]GC III Art. 4.

[45]Art. 1 Hague Convention IV, Art. 4(A)(2) GC III.

The requirements relating to organisation, responsibility and compliance with the law of armed conflict equally apply to national liberation movements and their forces. Recognising, however, that there are situations in armed conflicts in which combatants cannot be distinguished from other participants to the conflict, due to the nature of the hostilities, they nevertheless retain their combatant status if they carry arms openly (a) during each military engagement and (b) during such time as they are visible to the adversary while engaged in military deployment preceding the launching of an attack in which they are to participate.

Combatant status is also conferred upon inhabitants of non-occupied territory who on approach of an enemy spontaneously take up arms to resist the invading forces. This is also the case where defensive forces have not had time to constitute themselves as regular armed units, provided they carry arms openly and respect the laws and customs of war (*levée en masse*). All other persons do not have the right to kill combatants and can therefore not lawfully participate in hostilities the way combatants do.

Combatants do not lose their status under IHL even if they violate the law of armed conflict, unless they fail to distinguish themselves from the civilian population.

Combatants captured by enemy forces are accorded prisoner of war (POW) status. The belligerent party detaining POWs has full jurisdiction over them. The captured is a prisoner of a capturing State. It is under an obligation to respect the rights accorded to POWs in GC III. POWs must at all times be treated humanely[46] and may not be prosecuted for mere participation in hostilities. Becoming a POW is not a punishment but entails preventing combatants from further participation in the armed conflict. If in doubt about whether someone is to be granted POW status, this is presumed to be the case until the person's real status has been determined. POW status is also granted to persons accompanying armed forces, including those belonging to non-combat groups such as aircraft/ship crews or war correspondents. However, spies and mercenaries do not receive POW status when captured.

The two major categories of defenceless persons in IHL are persons *hors de combat* and civilians. The amount of protection applicable to them varies but does not depend on whether they had earlier taken part in hostilities or not. Civilians who take a direct part in hostilities may be targeted by combatants. The ICRC's *Interpretive Guidance on the Notion of Direct Participation in Hostilities under International Humanitarian Law*[47] provides details on when civilians may be qualified as directly participating. Belligerent parties have the right to make sure that POWs do not rejoin the battle. As they are not considered military targets, their protection stems from the basic principle of distinction.

[46]Art. 13 GC III.

[47]See Melzer (2009); http://www.icrc.org/eng/assets/files/other/icrc-002-0990.pdf.

5 Means and Methods of Warfare

The definition of *means* of warfare within the scope of IHL encompasses weapons and weapons systems or platforms employed for the purposes of attack, as well as, more generally, all equipment used during the conduct of hostilities. *Methods* of warfare denote the conduct of hostilities and concern the way in which the means are used. Such methods include tactical or strategic ways of conducting hostilities, not related to any specific weapons and which are intended to overwhelm or surprise and ultimately weaken the enemy. The laws of IHL governing means and methods of warfare contain two types of norms: general principles banning certain effects and specific rules addressing particular weapons or methods.

The main principle of IHL in this regard limits the rights of the parties to the conflict to choose such means or methods.[48] This restriction is based on the main principles of IHL, the distinction of civilian and military objectives, prohibition to cause unnecessary suffering and the principle of proportionality. Some methods of warfare are always prohibited, whereas others are forbidden only if the result of their use would violate these principles. Likewise, the use of certain means, namely weapons, is prohibited under any circumstances due to their inherent characteristics, whereas others may be used, subject to limitations. Such restrictions are listed in the GCs and their Aps, as well as other international instruments. Certain methods of warfare directly contradicting the principles of IHL are considered grave breaches of the law of armed conflict and war crimes. Article 85 AP I provides a non-exhaustive list of such methods.

6 Legal Status and Protection of Humanitarian Workers

IHL ensures protection of humanitarian workers, which derives from the purpose of their activity during armed conflict and the key elements of their work—independence and neutrality. The GCs and their APs distinguish between two main groups of humanitarian workers—those affiliated with the International Red Cross and Red Crescent Movement and those working within independent humanitarian organisations.

Legal protection of Red Cross and Red Crescent Movement affiliates is due to the medical aid they provide to the sick and wounded, combatants as well as civilians. To this end, IHL mandates the use of the Red Cross, Red Crescent and Red Crystal emblems and prescribes special attention by States parties towards them. The emblems may only be used as protective signs by medical services of regular armed forces,[49] National Red Cross and Red Crescent Societies,[50] civilian

---

[48] Art. 35 AP I.

[49] Art. 38 GC I.

[50] Art. 26, 42, 44 CG I.

hospitals and other medical facilities recognised as such by the government and authorised to display the emblems as protective symbol.[51] The emblems may also serve to mark persons as well as vehicles or other machinery of impartial international humanitarian organisations,[52] so long as they remain under the control of the parties to the conflict. The GCs and their APs demand that States legislate on the authorisation of these emblems.

IHL also provides protection to medical personnel, administrative support staff and religious attendants who work to protect the wounded, sick and shipwrecked[53]:

- Personnel is not to be attacked on the battlefield and must be allowed to perform its medical or religious duties.[54]
- Fallen into the hands of the adverse party, medical and religious personnel are not to be considered POWs and may only be detained if they are to take care of POWs held by the respective State party.[55]

GCs I and IV provide protection to civilians caring for sick and wounded combatants and/or civilians.[56] AP I further expands the category of persons (permanent or temporary personnel, military or civilian) protected by virtue of their medical or religious functions.[57] Aid societies are granted the same protection if they meet the requirements laid out in the Conventions.[58]

Humanitarian workers affiliated with independent humanitarian organisations that deploy humanitarian assistance may act in armed conflict under the protection of IHL.[59] The ICJ defined humanitarian assistance in the Nicaragua case as

> [a]n essential feature of truly humanitarian aid is that it is given "without discrimination" of any kind. In the view of the Court, if the provision of "humanitarian assistance" is to escape condemnations as an intervention in the internal affairs of Nicaragua, not only must it be limited to the purposes hallowed in the practice of the Red Cross, namely "to prevent suffering", and "to protect life and health and ensure respect for the human being"; it must also, and above all, be given without discrimination to all in need in Nicaragua....[60]

The legal protection that humanitarian workers are accorded under IHL includes protection from attack and mistreatment while in the hands of the opposing party. The scope of protection depends upon the applicable IHL provisions pertaining to the nature of the conflict. As civilians, humanitarian workers benefit from the

---

[51] Art. 18 GC IV.

[52] Art. 9 AP I.

[53] Arts 24 and 25 GC I; Arts. 36 and 37 GC III.

[54] See Arts. 24–27 GC I; Arts. 36 and 37 GC II; Arts. 15–20 AP I; Art. 9 AP II.

[55] See Arts. 28 and 30 GC I; Art. 37 GC II; Art. 33 GC III.

[56] See Art. 18 GC I, Art. 20(1) GC IV.

[57] See Art. 8(c) and (d) AP I.

[58] See Arts. 26 and 27 GC I; Art. 25 and 36 GC II; Art. 9(2) AP I.

[59] See Common Art. 3 GCs; GC I-III Art. 9, GC IV Art. 10; GC IV Art. 59, 61.

[60] ICJ, Military and Paramilitary Activities in and against Nicaragua (Nicaragua v. United States of America), Judgement, ICJ Rep. 1986, para. 243.

principle of distinction, applicable both in IAC and NIAC. Violation of this principle constitutes a war crime.[61] Unfortunately, in practice, humanitarian workers travelling with armed escorts risk being identified with armed groups and become more vulnerable to possible attacks.

7 Access to Humanitarian Relief During Armed Conflict

The notion of access to humanitarian relief is not defined in IHL. It is generally understood as the right to receive international protection and relief from an impartial humanitarian relief operation. Such action is subject to the consent of the State or parties concerned and does not prescribe coercive measures in the event of refusal, however unwarranted.[62]

The main legal basis for a right to access to humanitarian relief is a customary rule of IHL, which states that '[t]he parties to the conflict must allow and facilitate rapid and unimpeded passage of humanitarian relief for civilians in need, which is impartial in character and conducted without any adverse distinction, subject to their right of control'.[63] The application of other legal grounds depends on the nature of the armed conflict in question. During IAC, the provisions of the GCs and AP I apply. Article 23 GC IV stipulates that States must 'allow the free passage of all consignments of medical and hospital stores intended only for civilians and the free passage of all consignments of essential foodstuffs, clothing and tonics intended for children under fifteen, expectant mothers and maternity cases'. The belligerents must also ensure rapid and unimpeded passage of all relief consignments, equipment and personnel.[64] While the provisions of GC IV are somewhat limited regarding vulnerable groups or types of goods and supplies, AP I applies to the entire civilian population. It is forbidden to delay forwarding consignments and diverting them from the purpose for which they are intended under AP I. However, certain exceptions for the benefit of the population or urgent necessity are allowed.[65] Parties to the conflict are also obliged to take positive action to protect relief consignments and to facilitate their rapid distribution, as well as to encourage and facilitate effective international coordination of relief action.[66]

In times of occupation, the occupying power must either ensure that the civilian population receives essential supplies or accept relief from external actors.[67]

---

[61]Rome Statute of the International Criminal Court, A/CONF.183/9, 17 July 1998 and also reprinted in ILM, Vol. 37, 1998, Art. 8(2)(b)(iii).

[62]A definition formulated by OCHA: http://www.who.int/hac/about/reliefweb-aug2008.pdf.

[63]Rule No. 55 in Henkaerts (2005).

[64]See Art. 70(2) AP I.

[65]Art. 70 (3)(c) AP I.

[66]Art. 70 (4) and (5) AP I.

[67]Art. 59 (1) GC IV.

AP II does not pronounce on access to humanitarian assistance for NIAC.[68] However, the ensuing legal gap between IAC and NIAC regarding this issue is closed by customary rules, including the requirement to respect and protect humanitarian assistance personnel and objects and to ensure free movement of authorised humanitarian assistance personnel.[69]

Both AP I and II require consent of the parties concerned to humanitarian relief.[70] Such consent, however, may not be withheld arbitrarily,[71] and a refusal must be based on valid reasons. Where a lack of relief would amount to hunger and starvation, a party's refusal to accept relief is invalid and may amount to a war crime.[72] In NIAC, the consent of non-State armed groups is not officially required. However, in practice, consent of these actors becomes relevant for implementation of relief efforts where non-State armed groups control or operate in the territory concerned.

8 Responsibility for Breaches of International Humanitarian Law

IHL not only regulates the conduct of belligerent parties in conflict. It also sets obligations and provides mechanisms to implement and enforce its provisions. Common Article 1 GCs stipulates that States must respect the Convention at all times. States also have an obligation to supress violations of IHL. The GCs and AP I list the most serious violations, which should be punished as grave breaches of IHL.[73] Serious infringements listed amount to war crimes. War crimes were first defined in the London Charter,[74] which established the post-World War II Nuremberg Tribunal in its annex, which stated that

> violations shall include, but not be limited to murder, ill-treatment or deportation to slave labour or for any other purpose of civilian population of or in occupied territory, murder or ill treatment of prisoners of war or persons on the seas, killing of hostages, plunder of public or private property, wanton destruction of cities, towns or villages, or devastation not justified by military necessity.[75]

[68] Art. 18 (2) AP II.

[69] Rules No. 31, 32; Rule No. 55, See Art. 70(2) AP I.

[70] Art. 70 (1) AP I, Art. 18 (2) AP II.

[71] Art. 23 GC IV, Art. 70 (3) AP I.

[72] Art. 54 AP I, Art. 14 AP II.

[73] See Art. 49 and 50 GC I, Art. 50 and 51 GC II, Art. 129 and 130 GC III, Art. 146 and 147 GC IV, Art. 85 AP I.

[74] See also Rome Statute of International Criminal Court, See Art. 70(2) AP I, Art. 8 where the definition is wider—in addition listing all the possible offences listed in the GCs and AP I.

[75] The London Charter, Art. 6(b).

This list is not exhaustive and leaves room for other infringements, such as executing a spy without trial or disregarding an offer to surrender. War crimes do not require widespread or systematic commission, so that any single act may constitute a war crime, given that it is directly linked with a situation of armed conflict.

As IHL itself neither proscribes penalties nor establishes criminal procedure mechanisms, States have to address war crimes at the national level. The principle of *aut dedere aut judicare* (Lat. 'extradite or prosecute') requires the initiative to prosecute possible offenders to be given to the other related State.[76]

States parties to the Geneva Conventions should also start criminal or disciplinary proceedings for infringements below the level of war crimes. Since national proceedings can only go ahead when national laws criminalise such acts, States should already enact corresponding legislation in times of peace.[77]

According to the GCs, every State has the obligation to join the search for persons alleged to have committed, or to have ordered, grave breaches of IHL and shall bring such persons to justice before its own courts, regardless of their nationality.[78] This is an obligation under the principle of universal jurisdiction, which has evolved as a mean to avoid immunity of offenders. However, a risk of possible negative consequences should be kept in mind when exercising universal jurisdiction. Unbridled universal jurisdiction could challenge the global legal order and deprive individuals of their rights when used in a politically motivated manner or for vexatious purposes.[79]

At the international level, States are responsible for actions committed by their armed forces.[80] Therefore, States must require their military commanders to prevent or suppress breaches of IHL and keep control of their subordinates.[81] The fact that a breach of the GCs or of AP I or II is committed by a subordinate does not exempt his superiors from penal or disciplinary responsibility if they had reason to know that he was going to commit such a breach and did not take preventive measures.[82] Subordinates bear the responsibility for related consequences but may claim extenuating circumstances.

The concept of grave breaches of IHL does not apply to NIACs. However, international instruments,[83] judicial decisions[84] and the literature imply that serious

---

[76]In general, criminal law of a State applies only to acts committed within its territory or by its own nationals.

[77]Art. 49 GC I, Art. 50 GC II, Art. 129 GC III, Art. 146 GC IV, Art. 80 AP I.

[78]Art. 49 (2), Art. 50 (2) GC II, Art. 129 (2), GC III, Art. 146 (2) GC IV.

[79]Bassiouni (2008), p. 153.

[80]Art. 91 AP I.

[81]Art. 87 AP I.

[82]Art. 86 (2) AP I.

[83]ICTY Statute, UN Doc. S/RES/827 (May 25, 1993), Interpretation of Art. 3 in ICTY, Prosecutor v. Tadic, IT-94-1-AR72, Appeals Chamber, Decision 2 October 1995 Part A, para. 70; UN Statute of ICTR, UN Doc. S/RES/955 (November 8, 1994) Art. 4; Rome Statute of the International Criminal Court, Art. 70 (3)(c) AP I, Art. 8(2)(c), 8(2)(e).

[84]ICTY, Prosecutor v. Tadic, IT-94-1-AR72, Appeals Chamber, Decision 2 October 1995 Part A, para. 70 and more cases listed in Sassòli et al. (2011), p. 60.

violations of the law on NIAC is covered by customary norms of IHL, which are equal in scope to the rules of the GCs and AP I.

Most importantly, the international community has taken steps to establish international judicial bodies with the mandate to prosecute individuals for war crimes and other international crimes. This topic is discussed in the next chapter.

References

Books and Reports

Dunant H (1989) A Memory of Solferino. International Committee of the Red Cross, Geneva

International Humanitarian Law (1996) From law to action: report on the follow-up to the international conference for protection of war victims. Int Rev Red Cross, No. 311, March–April

Keen M (1965) The laws of war in the late middle ages. London

Melzer N (2009) Interpretive guidance on the notion of direct participation in hostilities under International Humanitarian Law. ICRC; http://www.icrc.org/eng/assets/files/other/icrc-002-0990.pdf

Phillipson C (1911) The international law and custom of ancient Greece and Rome, vol 2. London

Pictet J (1952) Commentary of the first Geneva Convention for the amelioration of the condition of the wounded and sick in armed forces in the field. International Committee of the Red Cross, Geneva

Pictet J (1956) Red Cross principles. ICRC, Geneva

Report of the International Court of Justice 1 August 1996–31 July 1997, General Assembly Official Records, Fifty-Second Session Supplement No. 4 (A/52/4)

Sassòli M, Bouvier A, Quintine A (2011) How does law protect in war? vol I. ICRC, Geneva

Siyar S (1966) The Islamic law of nations, early 9th century, translated by Majid Khadduri. Baltimore

Tzu S (2005) The art of war, translated by Thomas Cleary. Boston and London

The Laws of Manu (1991) Translated by Wendy Doninger and Brina Smith. London

Articles and Book Chapters

Bassiouni MC (2008) Universal jurisdiction for international crimes: historical perspectives and contemporary practice. In: Bassiouni MC (ed) International criminal law, vol II. Martinus Nijhoff Publishers, Leiden

Henkaerts J-M (2005) Study on customary International Humanitarian Law: a contribution to the understanding and respect for the rule of law in armed conflict. Int Rev Red Cross, No. 857, 31 March

Homer (1965) The Odyssey, Bk I, lines 260–263, translated by Richmond Lattimore. New York

Percy S (2012) Regulating the private security industry: a story of regulating the last war. Int Rev Red Cross, No. 887

Pfanner T (2005) Asymmetrical warfare from the perspective of humanitarian law and humanitarian action. Int Rev Red Cross, No. 857

Wenger A, Mason S (2008) The civilianization of armed conflict: trends and implications. Int Rev Red Cross, No. 872

Treaties and Statutes

Charter of the United Nations, 24 October 1945, 1 United Nations Treaty Series XVI.
Convention (II) with Respect to the Laws and Customs of War on Land and its annex: Regulations concerning the Laws and Customs of War on Land. The Hague, 29 July 1899.
Convention (IV) respecting the Laws and Customs of War on Land and its annex: Regulations concerning the Laws and Customs of War on Land. The Hague, 18 October 1907.
Convention for the Amelioration of the Condition of the Wounded and Sick in Armies in the Field. Geneva, 6 July 1906.
Convention for the Amelioration of the Condition of the Wounded and Sick in Armies in the Field. Geneva, 27 July 1929.
Convention relative to the Treatment of Prisoners of War. Geneva, 27 July 1929.
Geneva Convention for the Amelioration of the Condition of the Wounded and Sick in Armed Forces in the Field (First Geneva Convention), 12 August 1949, 75 United Nations Treaty Series 31.
Geneva Convention for the Amelioration of the Condition of Wounded, Sick, and Shipwrecked Members of Armed Forces at Sea (Second Geneva Convention), 12 August 1949, 75 United Nations Treaty Series 85.
Geneva Convention Relative to the Treatment of Prisoners of War (Third Geneva Convention), 12 August 1949, 75 United Nations Treaty Series 135.
Geneva Convention Relative to the Protection of Civilian Persons in Time of War (Fourth Geneva Convention), 12 August 1949, 75 United Nations Treaty Series 287.
Protocol (I) Additional to the Geneva Conventions of 12 August 1949, and relating to the protection of victims of international armed conflicts, 1125 United Nations Treaty Series 3.
Protocol (II) Additional to the Geneva Conventions of 12 August 1949, and relating to the Protection of Victims of Non-International Armed Conflicts, 1125 United Nations Treaty Series 609.
Protocol (III) Additional to the Geneva Conventions of 12 August 1949, and relating to the Adoption of an Additional Distinctive Emblem, 2404 United Nations Treaty Series 261.
Rome Statute of the International Criminal Court, 17 July 1998, 2187 United Nations Treaty Series 3.
The London Charter for the Computer-Based Visualisation of Cultural Heritage.

UN Documents

Statute of the International Criminal Tribunal for the former Yugoslavia, UN Doc. S/RES/827, 32 ILM 1192.
Statute of the International Criminal Tribunal for Rwanda, UN Doc. S/RES/955, 33 ILM 1598.

Cases

ICJ, Military and Paramilitary Activities in and against Nicaragua (Nicaragua v. United States of America), Judgment, ICJ Rep. 1986.
ICTY, Prosecutor v. Ljube Boškoski and Johan Tarčulovski, IT-04-82-T, Judgement 2 July 2008.
ICTY, Prosecutor v. Tadic, IT-94-1-AR72, Appeals Chamber, Decision 2 October 1995.

Further Reading

Gasser H-P (1993) International humanitarian law: an introduction. Henry Dunant Institute. Paul Haupt Publishers, Geneva

Green LC (2008) The contemporary law of armed conflict, 3rd edn. Manchester University Press

Kalshoven F, Zegveld L (2001) Constraints on the waging of war: an introduction to International Humanitarian Law. International Committee of the Red Cross

Sassòli M, Bouvier AA (2011) How does law protect in war? vol I. ICRC, Geneva

Renata Vaišvilienė is Lecturer at the Public Law Department, Faculty of Law of Vilnius University, Lithuania, and Director of Lithuania's NOHA branch.

International Criminal Law

Pierre Thielbörger

1 International Criminal Law and Human Rights Law

The term international criminal law (ICL) already indicates that this body of law is made up of two distinct elements. It is a mixture of both public international law (PIL) and domestic criminal law. The fusion of these two fields of law makes ICL truly unique.

On the one hand, ICL is part of PIL because it rests on the same sources: treaties, customary international law (CIL) and—to some extent—general principles of law (Article 38 of the International Court of Justice's Statute (ICJ Statute)). ICL is at the same time at odds with PIL because the subjects function differently in both legal orders: ICL deals with individuals, while PIL is mainly concerned with States and international organisations.

On the other hand, ICL carries significant characteristics of domestic criminal law, dealing with punishing individuals for having committed crimes. At the same time, ICL is fundamentally different from domestic criminal law as the application of criminal law is usually based on a State's national territory and jurisdiction. Criminal law is usually detached from the international legal plane because a State only has the sovereignty to punish its own citizens (active personality principle)[1] for committing crimes, or any person if they commit crimes on that State's territory (territorial principle).[2]

ICL thus combines elements of PIL and domestic criminal law while at the same time being at odds with both of these fields. In this way, ICL is best understood as a

[1]Ipsen (2014), pp. 582, 585; v. Arnauld (2014), p. 532 at para. 1273.

[2]Cassese et al. (2013), p. 274; Ipsen (2014), p. 584; v. Arnauld (2014), p. 532 at para. 1272.

P. Thielbörger (✉)
Ruhr University Bochum, Bochum, Germany
e-mail: pierre.thielboerger@rub.de

© Springer International Publishing AG 2018

H.-J. Heintze, P. Thielbörger (eds.), *International Humanitarian Action*,
DOI 10.1007/978-3-319-14454-2_10

body of PIL that imposes criminal responsibility directly onto individuals instead of leaving it to domestic criminal prosecution.

ICL is sometimes also said to be the logical mirror of international human rights law (HRL).[3] This is only partly true. It is true insofar as both fields of law put the individual into the focus, not (as is usually the case in PIL) the State: while HRL accords the individual powerful basic rights towards the State, ICL imposes specific duties on the individual, namely the duty not to commit certain fundamental crimes. Only in this case is the prosecution lifted from the national level to the international level. In this way, the Rome Statute of the International Criminal Court[4] emphasises in its preamble and Articles 1 and 5 (1) that ICL only deals with 'the most serious crimes of concern to the international community as a whole'. Just as rights and duties can be considered two sides of the same coin, HRL and ICL can be too: HRL accords (international) rights to the individual, whereas ICL imposes an international duty on it.

However, there are also aspects in which ICL and HRL do not simply mirror one another. Most importantly, ICL only applies to exceptional cases—the threshold at which a case is lifted from the level of national jurisdiction to international tribunals is enormously high. While any commitment of an international crime will always violate HRL in one way or another, the opposite is often not true. Certainly, not every human rights violation amounts to an international crime.[5]

2 The Origins of International Criminal Law

The Westphalian system, developed by the treaty of Westphalia in 1648, which ended the Thirty-Year War, which had ravaged Europe, acts to secure the peaceful coexistence of sovereign and equal States, a goal also enshrined in Article 2 (1) UN Charter. Nevertheless, this system has often been criticised as being blind towards the individual. Within this classical concept, the individual is solely mediated through the State, for instance in the form of *diplomatic protection*: a State claims rights violations of its nationals abroad not as violations of that individual but rather as a violation of the State itself.[6] Indeed, PIL—in its traditional conception—accords rights and duties to States, not to individuals.

---

[3]Pires (1995), pp. 133–136; Tulkens (2011), pp. 577–578.

[4]Rome Statute of the International Criminal Court, 17 July 1998, in: UNTS 2187 (2004), p. 3.

[5]Cryer et al. (2014), p. 14.

[6]Permanent Court of International Justice, Case of the Mavrommatis Palestine Concessions, Judgement of 30 August 1924, Series A No. 2, p. 12. A different course is taken by the ICJ in its Diallo judgement (ICJ, Case Concerning Ahmadou Sadio Diallo (Republic of Guinea v. Democratic Republic of the Congo), Judgement of 19 June 2012, I.C.J. Reports 2012, pp. 324, 344 at para. 57, in which the court states that reparation is paid to compensate Mr. Diallo (not Guinea) for the injury caused. This is in some ways at odds with the classical understanding of diplomatic protection which assumes a right of the State, not the individual.

2.1 *The Nuremberg and Tokyo Tribunals*

With the end of World War II in 1945, this thinking changed. During and after the war, the conviction ripened that political redress (as represented by the Treaty of Versailles after World War I) was not sufficient to bring closure to conflict. A legal response was also considered necessary, in particular the prosecution of surviving high-ranking Nazi Imperial Japanese officials by an international criminal legal procedure.

A few months after the end of the war, the Allies (USA, Soviet Union, United Kingdom and France) signed the London Agreement,[7] which regulated the prosecution and punishment of the major war criminals of the European Axis. This agreement was included as an annex to the Charter of the International Military Tribunal at Nuremberg (hereinafter 'Nuremberg Charter').[8] The tribunal started its proceedings against high-ranking political and military Nazi leaders on 20 November 1945 in Nuremberg (hereinafter 'Nuremberg trials'). The tribunal consisted of one judge per allied State (Article 2 Nuremberg Charter). The Nuremberg trials were to deal with the very limited number of crimes listed in Article 6 Nuremberg Charter: crimes against the peace, war crimes and crimes against humanity. In a very similar manner, the Allies also conducted an International Military Tribunal for the Far East in Tokyo (Japan). The judges' bench of the Tokyo tribunal—like the Nuremberg one—was exclusively made up of judges from the four allied States. The Tokyo tribunal started its work on 3 May 1946 and prosecuted Japanese individuals for crimes committed on the Asian continent.[9]

Both tribunals—as politically desirable as they might have been—have faced severe criticism from a legal perspective.

First, the composition of judges failed to include judges from neutral States. In this way, they were not international but essentially western tribunals.

Second, both tribunals dealt exclusively with German and Japanese war criminals; crimes committed by the allied forces were excluded from jurisdiction. In this way, it may be argued that both tribunals exercised one-sided justice imposed by the victors (*Siegerjustiz*).

Third, some of the crimes tried in Nuremberg and Tokyo had not been previously explicitly defined as such. It is hard to argue that sentencing defendants under penal norms specifically designed for the trials does not violate one of criminal law's golden rules, the principle of *nullum crimen sine lege* (lat. 'no crime without pre-existing penal law').[10] The Nuremberg judges recognised this obvious problem with their jurisdiction. They nevertheless justified it with reference to the

---

[7]Agreement for the prosecution and punishment of the major war criminals of the European Axis, 8 August 1945, in: UNTS 82 (1951), p. 280.

[8]Annex to *id.*, p. 284.

[9]Werle and Jessberger (2014), pp. 10–11.

[10]This principle is discussed in detail in Sect. 3.1 of this chapter.

exceptional cruelty of the Nazi crimes: actions so heinous as to clearly amount to severe crimes that required punishment—even without their previous codification.[11]

2.2 The International Tribunals for the Former Yugoslavia and Rwanda

Because of this serious criticism and, even more importantly, as a result of PIL's paralysis during the Cold War, it took a long time for ICL to take its next crucial steps. The 1990s saw some of the worst atrocities since World War II. The international community's ensuing outrage led to the creation of two international bodies to prosecute crimes committed: the International Tribunal for the Former Yugoslavia (ICTY) in 1993 and the International Tribunal for Rwanda (ICTR) in 1994. Given their very similar composition, these two tribunals are often described as 'sister-tribunals',[12] indeed two sisters that were brought up very far apart from each other with the ICTY based in The Hague (the Netherlands) and the ICTR located in Arusha (Tanzania). After their official *expiration date* in 2015, pending cases are now dealt with by an international transitional tribunal, the International Residual Mechanism for Criminal Tribunals,[13] also located in The Hague. The inception of the two tribunals for the former Yugoslavia and Rwanda and the reasons for their establishment are remarkable.

First, both the genocide and ethnic cleansing of Muslim men and boys in the former Republic of Yugoslavia, as well as the genocide committed by the Hutu majority in Rwanda against the Tutsi minority and the butchering of moderate Hutus, are hardly comparable with any other crimes committed since World War II. These crimes certainly screamed for international criminal prosecution.

Second, both tribunals were not created by an international treaty involving the successor States of Yugoslavia or Rwanda, which would certainly have been the most common way. Instead, they were established by two UN Security Council (UNSC) resolutions.[14] Article 41 UN Charter enables the UNSC to 'decide what measures not involving the use of armed force are to be employed to give effect to its decisions'. While the majority of legal scholars have by now endorsed this approach of the UNSC, some authors severely doubt that the creation of an international tribunal truly fell within the council's mandate under Article 41 UN Charter.[15]

[11] International Military Tribunal, Nazi Conspiracy and Aggression: Opinion and Judgment, Washington 1947, p. 49.

[12] Møse (2005), pp. 920–927; Zacklin (2004), pp. 541–542.

[13] UN Security Council, Resolution 1966, UN Doc. S/RES/1966, 22 December 2010.

[14] UN Security Council, Resolution 827, UN Doc. S/RES/827, 25 May 1993 (establishing the ICTY) and Resolution 955, UN Doc. S/RES/955, 8 November 1994 (establishing the ICTR).

[15] See, for instance, Arangio-Ruiz (2000), pp. 609, 722; Lamb (1999), pp. 361, 376.

On the one hand, the UNSC can only make use of the means of Articles 39–42 UN Charter if it has previously found an 'act of aggression, a breach of the peace or a threat to the peace' (Article 39 UN Charter) to have occurred. Thus, the council would have needed to find that international criminal tribunals for Yugoslavia and Rwanda were necessary to restore international peace and security or to prevent them from being threatened in the future. To assume this was the case might indeed appear far-fetched: criminal justice is mainly a punitive rather than a preventive measure. What is more, the UNSC regularly addresses *de iure* States in its resolution, while the establishment of a criminal tribunal *de facto* targets individuals.

On the other hand, the list of coercive non-military means in Article 41 UN Charter, although quite extensive, is not exhaustive,[16] as emphasised by the word 'including'. Thus, the UNSC may choose one of the means listed in Article 41 UN Charter—or any other non-military means that it might deem appropriate. There is no cogent reason apparent *per se* why this should not also include the establishment of a criminal tribunal. The UNSC is generally accepted to have a very wide margin of discretion in choosing the means necessary to maintain international peace and security.[17]

2.3 Other International and Hybrid Criminal Tribunals

Further international or *hybrid*—partly international, partly domestic—criminal courts followed shortly after this initiative of the UNSC.

In the Special Court for Sierra Leone (2002),[18] the government of that State set up a court in cooperation with the UN in order to prosecute individuals for serious violations of international humanitarian law (IHL) and domestic law during Sierra Leone's civil war (1991–2002). The court operated offices in Freetown (Sierra Leone), The Hague (the Netherlands) and New York City (USA). Its most famous case is certainly the one against Charles Taylor, who in 2012 became the first convicted African Head of State and was sentenced to 50 years in prison.[19]

The Extraordinary Chambers in the Courts of Cambodia (Khmer Rouge Tribunal)[20] were established by an agreement of the Cambodian government and the UN in 2003

[16]Krisch (2012), p. 1305, para. 14; Wilson (2014), p. 84; v. Arnauld (2014), p. 443 at para. 1036 and p. 445 at para 1042.

[17]Krisch (2012), para. 14; Wilson (2014), p. 84.

[18]Agreement between the United Nations and the Government of Sierra Leone on the Establishment of a Special Court for Sierra Leone, 16 January 2002, in: UNTS 2178 (2004), p. 138.

[19]Special Court for Sierra Leone, Prosecutor v. Charles Ghankay Taylor, Case No. SCSL-03-01-T, Trial Chamber II, Judgment of 18 May 2012, http://www.rscsl.org/Documents/Decisions/Taylor/1285/SCSL-03-01-T-1285.pdf; and Case No. SCSL-03-01-A, Appeals Chamber, Judgment of 26 September 2013 (essentially conforming the Trial Chamber's judgment), http://www.rscsl.org/Documents/Decisions/Taylor/Appeal/1389/SCSL-03-01-A-1389.pdf.

[20]Agreement between the United Nations and the Royal Government of Cambodia concerning the Prosecution under Cambodian Law of Crimes Committed during the Period of Democratic Kampuchea, 6 June 2003, in: UNTS 2329 (2005), p. 1.

to try senior leaders of the Khmer Rouge regime that had devastated Cambodia between 1975 and 1979. It is a so-called hybrid court as it is set up within the framework of the Cambodian legal system but has many international legal characteristics. For instance, judges are both Cambodian and nationals from other States, and the applicable law is also a mixture of Cambodian law and PIL.[21]

The Special Tribunal for Lebanon (2007)[22] was established for the international prosecution of the assassination of Rafiq Hariri on 14 February 2005, who served as Prime Minister of Lebanon from 1992–1998 and 2000–2004. Mr. Hariri was killed in a terrorist attack by a car bomb, the perpetrators of which have never been found. The tribunal has its seat in Leidschendam-Voorburg, near The Hague (the Netherlands), as well as an office in Beirut (Lebanon). It was established by an agreement between the Lebanese government and the UN in 2006, following a UNSC resolution.[23] Like the Khmer Rouge Tribunal in Cambodia, it is a hybrid court as it applies both national and international laws. Since it began to operate in 2009, the tribunal has issued four arrest warrants to the authorities of Lebanon against Hezbollah members.[24] All suspects, however, remain at large. The procedures are thus led *in absentia*, meaning without the accused being present: an approach that is certainly unusual in criminal proceedings. Another important facet of this tribunal is that the suspects are *de facto* charged with *terrorism*.[25] The tribunal is the first international court to include such a charge in its investigative work, despite the

[21]See, *id.*, Art. 3 and Art. 9 in conjunction with Art. 3 of the Law on the Establishment of Extraordinary Chambers in the Courts of Cambodia for the Prosecution of Crimes committed during the Period of Democratic Kampuchea, 10 August 2001, NS/RKM/0801/12, http://www.skpcambodia.com/Laws%20&%20Regulations%20of%20the%20Kingdom%20of%20Cambodia/Tribunals/KR%20trial%20law-final-after-amend-Eng.pdf.

[22]Agreement between the United Nations and the Lebanese Republic on the Establishment of a Special Tribunal for Lebanon, 22 January 2007 and 6 February 2007, in: UNTS 2461 (2007), p. 257.

[23]UN Security Council, Resolution 1664, UN Doc. S/RES/1664, 29 March 2006; see also UN Security Council, Resolution 1757, UN Doc. S/RES/1757, 30 May 2007 (endorsing the agreement).

[24]The warrants to arrest Mr Salim Jamil Ayyash, Mr Mustafa Amine Badreddine, Mr Hussein Hassan Oneissi, and Mr Assad Hassan Sabra, respectively, each including transfer and detention order, of 28 June 2011, are available at the Tribunal's website: http://www.stl-tsl.org. On 11 February 2014, the Trial Chamber issued an oral ruling to join the case against Hassan Habib Merhi with the case against the four accused mentioned above.

[25]See Art. 2 (a) of the Statute of the Special Tribunal for Lebanon, declaring the provisions of the Lebanese Criminal Code relating to the prosecution and punishment of acts of terrorism and others to be applicable. The text is attached to the Agreement between the United Nations and the Lebanese Republic on the Establishment of a Special Tribunal for Lebanon, 22 January 2007 and 6 February 2007, in: UNTS 2461 (2007), pp. 293, 294.

difficulties that PIL has experienced over the last years in elaborating a legal definition of the term 'terrorism'.[26]

The International Crimes Tribunal of Bangladesh (2009) investigates the genocide committed in 1971 by the Pakistani Army and local groups during the Bangladesh Liberation War. It is based on the International Crimes (Tribunals) Act of 1973,[27] which is largely compatible with the standards required under PIL. As with the Special Tribunal for Lebanon, trials held *in absentia* are possible.

Lastly, the Extraordinary African Chambers in the Senegalese Courts constitutes special chambers for the prosecution of former Chadian President Hissène Habré and affiliates for international crimes within the legal framework of the Senegalese judicial system.[28]

2.4 The International Criminal Court

Finally, since 2002, the International Criminal Court (ICC) has taken up its operations. It must by now be considered the most important of all international criminal courts and tribunals. It aims to cover not a specific time frame or region but strives to become the universal court in charge of all international criminal prosecutions.

The ICC is the first independent, treaty-based and truly international criminal court. The treaty establishing this court—the Rome Statute (RS)[29]—was drafted in 1998 and entered into force on 1 July 2002. The court started its operations with an inaugural session on 11 March 2003; its seat is The Hague in the Netherlands (Article 3 (1) RS).

While the RS currently has 139 signatory States and 124 States parties (including all South American States, most European States and many African States),[30] some important States have explicitly not supported it so far. The United States has signed but not ratified the treaty (which would be necessary for its legal effects to unfold), Russia most recently repealed its signature and China never signed the RS. Some of these States have even displayed somewhat hostile behaviour towards the jurisdiction of the ICC. Famously, in 2002, the US Congress adopted the

[26]See Art. 2 of the proposed Comprehensive Convention on International Terrorism. For the text of the draft convention see Appendix II to UN General Assembly, UN Doc. A/59/894, 12 August 2005. This definition remains, however, largely contested, see for instance the Kuala Lumpur Declaration on International Terrorism of 3 April 2002, Annex II to UN General Assembly, UN Doc. A/56/911, 8 April 2002, which emphasises that also the motivation should be part of the definition, while the proposed Convention put an emphasis exclusively onto the means employed.

[27]Act No. XIX of 20 July 1973, http://bdlaws.minlaw.gov.bd/pdf_part.php?id=435.

[28]Chambres Africaines extraordinaires, http://www.chambresafricaines.org/.

[29]See Rome Statute of the International Criminal Court, 17 July 1998, in: UNTS 2187 (2004), p. 3.

[30]Status of the Rome Statute, including signatures, ratifications and withdrawals, http://treaties.un.org/Pages/ViewDetails.aspx?src=TREATY&mtdsg_no=XVIII-10&chapter=18&clang=_en.

'American Service-Members' Protection Act'.[31] This piece of legislation states that should a US citizen or a 'covered allied person' ever be tried by the ICC, the US President would have the authority 'to use all means necessary and appropriate' to free that person. This is understood as also giving authority to invade the premises of the ICC and return that US citizen or covered allied person back to the USA, which is why the act has also been termed 'The Hague Invasion Act'.

The court has 18 judges (Article 36 (1) RS) and consists of three different legal divisions: the pre-trial division, the trial division and the appeals division (Article 34 lit. b) RS). It also has an office of the prosecutor (Article 34 lit. c) RS) and a registry (Article 34 lit. d), 43 RS). The presidency rotates and is currently held by Argentinian Judge Silvia Fernández de Gurmendi; Gambian lawyer and former Minister of Justice Fatou Bensouda heads the office of the prosecutor. The election of Fatou Bensouda was hoped to be a significant breakthrough for the ICC's general acceptance. Not only is Bensouda the first woman to hold the position but also the first individual from the African continent.

Previously, the court had been criticised as a court for the prosecution of African nationals instead of a truly global criminal court.[32] While this criticism has to be taken seriously, as the acceptance by African States is certainly crucial for the court's future success, it overlooks two important factors.

First, the ICC has by now commenced several preliminary investigations outside of Africa, for instance in Afghanistan, Colombia, Georgia, Honduras, Iraq, Palestine, South Korea, Ukraine and Venezuela.

Second, and even more importantly, the investigations and trials conducted so far often relied on the explicit request of the respective African States. Out of 10 situations the prosecutor is currently investigating, five were referred to the court by the respective States.[33]

Thus, there is not much ground to claim that the ICC has imposed its investigations one-sidedly on African States; it is rather the case that many African States have actively sought the court's help. Nevertheless, over the course of 2016, several African States, including South Africa, Burundi and Gambia, have announced their withdrawal from the RS.

[31]American Service-members' Protection Act of 2002, 2 August 2002, http://web.archive.org/web/20031015053419/http://www.state.gov/t/pm/rls/othr/misc/23425.htm.

[32]Mbaku (2014), p. 9, http://www.brookings.edu/~/media/Research/Files/Reports/2014/foresight-africa-2014/03-foresight-international-criminal-court-africa-mbaku.pdf?la=en; du Plessis et al. (2013), http://www.chathamhouse.org/sites/files/chathamhouse/public/Research/International%20Law/0713pp_iccafrica.pdf; Akande (2009), http://www.ejiltalk.org/africa-and-the-international-criminal-court./.

[33]For an overview of situation and cases, see the ICC's webpage at: http://www.icc-cpi.int/en_menus/icc/situations%20and%20cases/Pages/situations%20and%20cases.aspx.

3 Some General Principles of Criminal Law

Before dealing *in extensio* with the jurisdiction of the ICC, it is worth recapitulating some basic features that distinguish criminal law from public or civil law.

3.1 *Nullum Crimen, Nulla Poena sine Lege*

It is well accepted in criminal law that any behaviour that is up for prosecution must have been a criminal offence at the time it occurred. Often the two principles of *nullum crimen sine lege* (lat. 'no crime without law') and *nulla poena sine lege* (lat. 'no punishment without law') are mixed up. In truth, however, they are two distinct principles.

On the one hand, the *nullum crimen* principle—the more important of the two—demands that a person must not be convicted if the accused could not have reasonably been aware at the time of his/her action that this behaviour was criminal in nature.[34] This principle is not a new development in ICL. Article 15 of the International Covenant on Civil and Political Rights (ICCPR) of 1966 states that '[n]o one shall be held guilty on account of any act or omission which did not constitute a criminal offence, (...) at the time when it was committed'. Both the Nuremberg Charter and the Tokyo Charter were heavily criticised for violations of exactly this principle.[35] The judges in Nuremberg defended their jurisdiction by claiming that the crimes in question were so horrific that nobody could have reasonably assumed them to be in accordance with the law.[36]

Some authors have claimed an even stronger variant of the *nullum crimen* principle, demanding that criminal conviction requires a written law.[37] Certainly, this principle would indeed hold true in many national criminal legal orders. Thus, CIL would be generally excluded as a source of ICL as per the principle of *nullum crimen sine lege scripta* (lat. 'no crime without written law'). The ICTY has, however, explicitly rejected this stricter form of the *nullum crimen* principle;[38] some authors have further emphasised that international (criminal) law, in contrast

---

[34]ICTY, Prosecutor v. Mitar Vasiljević, Case No. IT-98-32-T, Trial Chamber II, Judgment of 29 November 2002, para. 193, http://www.icty.org/x/cases/vasiljevic/tjug/en/vas021129.pdf; ICTY, Prosecutor v. Milan Milutinović *et al.*, Case No. IT-99-37-AR72, Appeals Chamber, Decision on Dragoljub Ojdanić's Motion Challenging Jurisdiction—Joint Criminal Enterprise of 21 May 2003, paras. 37–42, http://www.eccc.gov.kh/sites/default/files/documents/courtdoc/00207160-00207178.pdf.

[35]See Sect. 2.1 of this chapter.

[36]Nuremberg International Military Tribunal (1947), pp. 172, 217.

[37]Degan (2005), pp. 45, 67; Olásolo (2007), p. 301.

[38]Most prominently ICTY, Prosecutor v. Dusko Tadic aka 'Dule', Case No. IT-94-1, Appeals Chamber, Decision on the Defence Motion for Interlocutory Appeal on Jurisdiction of 2 October 1995, paras. 139–144, http://www.icty.org/x/cases/tadic/acdec/en/51002.htm.

to many domestic legal orders, does not always require a written source,[39] as also evidenced by Article 38 (b) ICJ Statute.

In order to nevertheless do justice to the *nullum crimen* principle, the RS of the ICC incorporates the so-called *elements of crime*, which include detailed definitions of the enumerated crimes. Article 22 RS also explicitly emphasises two specific elements of the *nullum crimen* principle: non-retroactivity (Article 22 (1) RS) and clarity of the law (Article 22 (2) RS).

On the other hand, the *nulla poena* principle requires defined penalties to be attached to the different criminal norms. For the RS, this principle was addressed in Article 23, which states that a person must be punished in accordance with the statute. Thus, possible punishments are clearly elaborated in the RS. The situation was less clear with regard to the ICTY and the ICTR. Both tribunals were required to have recourse to the practice of prison sentences of the respective states in which the crimes had occurred.[40] However, this would have enabled the tribunals in extreme cases to impose the death penalty, which existed in Yugoslavia and Rwanda at the time the crimes were committed. To exclude this possibility, the statutes of the ICTY and ICTR emphasised that recourse to national law related only to terms of imprisonment (thus implicitly excluding other forms of punishment such as the death penalty).[41]

3.2 *In Dubio Pro Reo*

Human rights are often interpreted broadly by courts and scholars in a way that maximises the protection of the individual.[42] This can be understood as a legitimate interpretation in light of Article 31 lit. c) Vienna Convention on the Law of Treaties (VCLT): an interpretation of each individual human right in light of the object and purpose of the human rights treaty as a whole. In that way, human rights treaties are often very liberally interpreted, going beyond what the drafters originally had in mind.

However, this does not hold true for ICL, whose treaties also serve the rights of suspects and the accused. An expansive interpretation of the rights of one side tends to result in a restrictive interpretation of the other side's rights. Hence, in ICL, a

[39]Cassese et al. (2013), pp. 73–74.

[40]Art. 24 (1) S. 2 of the Statute of the ICTY, annexed to UN Security Council, Report of the Secretary-General Pursuant to Paragraph 2 of Security Council Resolution 808 (1993), UN Doc. S/25704, 3 May 1993, p. 36; and Art. 23 S. 2 of the Statute of the ICTR, annexed to UN Security Council, Resolution 955, UN Doc. S/RES/955, 8 November 1994 (establishing the ICTR).

[41]Art. 24 (1) S. 1 of the ICTY's Statute, and Art. 23 S. 1 of the ICTR's Statute, both UN Security Council, Resolution 827, UN Doc. S/RES/827, 25 May 1993 (establishing the ICTY) and Resolution 955, UN Doc. S/RES/955, 8 November 1994 (establishing the ICTR).

[42]Cryer et al. (2014), p. 13.

broad interpretation of the listed crimes is much more problematic than in the case of HRL.

What is more, where there is indeed ambiguity in the law or in the evidence gathered, this must be taken into account in a favourable light for the accused rather than to his/her disadvantage: *in dubio pro reo* (lat. 'when in doubt, for the accused'). Thus, the interpretation of crimes under PIL has to be restrictive (rather than expansive) as the rights of the accused might otherwise be infringed; extreme cases might result in a scenario in which the *nullum crimen* principle is violated. In a similar manner, Article 22 (II) (2) RS emphasises that in case of ambiguity, a norm shall be interpreted in favour of the person under investigation or prosecution.

3.3 Ne bis in Idem

The principle *ne bis in idem* (lat. '*not twice for the same*') requires that nobody be punished twice for the same crime. This principle is not yet generally accepted as custom applying between all States, but rather restricted to municipal State jurisdiction. This is confirmed by Article 14 (7) ICCPR, which states that no one shall be liable to be tried or punished again for an offence for which he has already been finally convicted or acquitted in accordance with the law and penal procedure of each State. The European Union (EU) has gone one step further and established a transnational *ne bis in idem* principle for its member States under Article 50 EU Charter of Fundamental Rights.[43]

The ICC's RS goes even further than the EU, establishing three variants of the *ne bis in idem* principle, which stipulate as follows: the ICC cannot convict twice for the same crime (horizontal prohibition, Article 20 (1) RS), a national court cannot sentence where the ICC has already made a decision (downward prohibition, Article 20 (2) RS) and the ICC cannot convict where a national court has already done so (upward prohibition, Article 20 (3) RS).[44]

4 The International Criminal Court's Jurisdiction Under the Rome Statute

Turning from general principles of criminal law to the particular jurisdiction of the ICC, a number of problems, both procedural and substantive, arise.

[43]See Art. 50 of the Charter of Fundamental Rights of the European Union, 18 December 2000, in: Official Journal of the European Union (2010), C 83/02.

[44]For the specific problem of upward prohibition of *ne bis in idem*, see also the principle of complementarity, see Sect. 4.1.2 of this chapter. See, also, Surlan (2005), http://www.esil-sedi.eu/sites/default/files/Surlan_0.PDF.

4.1 Criminal Procedure

Some procedural requirements can be summarised very briefly. These include questions of who can be tried before the ICC (jurisdiction *ratione personae*; generally speaking: individuals), what the eligible time period for crimes to be prosecuted is (jurisdiction *ratione temporis*, only after the entry into force and after ratification of the RS) and which crimes the court may investigate (jurisdiction *ratione materiae*, only crimes defined in the RS).

Other procedural requirements are more complex. These include the modes in which jurisdiction is established, the relationship between the ICC's jurisdiction and national jurisdiction and issues surrounding the principle of immunity.

4.1.1 Ways to Establish Jurisdiction

The ICC does not have jurisdiction over just any international crime. Quite to the contrary, the principle of non-intervention as derived from the sovereign equality of States (Article 2 (1) UN Charter) accords States' jurisdiction over their territory and their citizens. Only if a State consents to international criminal prosecution is a case lifted from the national to the international sphere. The first two modes to establish the court's jurisdiction reflect this requirement of State consent.

First, jurisdiction can arise if the accused is a citizen of a State that has either previously ratified the RS or that has recognised the jurisdiction of the ICC *ad hoc* (for the case at hand only, Article 12 (2) lit. b), (3), and Article 13 RS). The accused's nationality is thus one possible link to establish the ICC's jurisdiction.

Second, the court also has jurisdiction if an alleged crime was committed on the territory of a State that has either previously ratified the RS or that accepts the jurisdiction of the ICC *ad hoc* (Article 12 (2) lit. a), (3); Article 13 RS). Thus, the territory of the State on which the alleged crime took place may also be a link for the establishment of the ICC's jurisdiction.

Both links are very much in line with the idea of the active personality principle and the territorial principle. States are accepted to hold jurisdiction over their citizens and over their territory; this includes the right to conduct criminal prosecution. The significant resistance that many governments have levelled against the jurisdiction of the ICC is in part explained by the fact that these two principles do not always function in accordance with each other.

We can easily imagine cases in which the territorial sovereignty of one State collides with the personal jurisdiction of another State, for example where a citizen of a non-signatory State commits a crime on the territory of a signatory State. Assuming all formal conditions are met, the latter finding would suffice to justify the ICC's jurisdiction over such a citizen committing crimes in the territory of a signatory State. In that case, the outspoken and repeated protests of the non-signatory home State of the perpetrator could not hinder the establishment of such jurisdiction of the ICC. In essence, a State would have to tolerate the prosecution of one of its citizens in The Hague against its explicit will—an idea that appears almost unimaginable to sovereign nations, especially superpowers like the USA. There are also other issues at play: Israel, for example, is concerned about future cases against its citizens since Palestine has acceded to the RS,[45] and the prosecutor has opened a preliminary investigation for cases on Palestinian soil.[46]

The third alternative to establish the court's jurisdiction is by way of referral of a situation to the ICC by the UNSC (Article 13 lit. b) RS). The status of the UNSC and its mandate to maintain international peace and security justify this exceptional possibility of establishing jurisdiction for the ICC without State consent. This constellation has so far occurred twice: once in the case of Darfur in 2005[47] and once in the case of Libya in 2011.[48] Establishing jurisdiction without State consent can lead to difficult questions, for example, the parallel validity of provisions of the RS (such as immunity[49]) as CIL, where the statute itself cannot be directly applied without State ratification.

4.1.2 The Principle of Complementarity

While the ICTY and the ICTR both enjoy general primacy over national law and national courts,[50] the ICC does not. Instead, it fulfils a complementary function to national criminal jurisdiction. The ICC would simply be overburdened if it were to deal with all international crimes on a global scale. Thus, according to Article 17 (1) RS, the court shall only determine a case admissible if a State that would otherwise hold jurisdiction over the case is either unwilling or unable to genuinely carry out the investigation or prosecution.

Unwillingness can mean that either a State has undertaken proceedings only for the purpose of shielding a person from international criminal responsibility (Article 17 (2) lit. a) RS), there is an unjustified delay in the proceedings undertaken (Article 17 (2) lit. b) RS) or the proceedings are not conducted independently or impartially (Article 17 (2) lit. c) RS).

Inability is given in a case of total or substantial collapse or unavailability of any national judicial system. This can be, *inter alia*, the case if a State is unable to obtain the accused or the necessary evidence and testimony (Article 17 (3) RS).

---

[45]M. Abbas, Declaration Accepting the Jurisdiction of the International Criminal Court, 1 January 2015, http://www.icc-cpi.int/iccdocs/PIDS/press/Palestine_A_12-3.pdf; UN Secretary-General, Depositary Notification of Accession to the Rome Statute by the State of Palestine, UN Doc. C. N.13.2015.TREATIES-XVIII.10, 15 January 2015.

[46]ICC Press Release, The Prosecutor of the International Criminal Court, Fatou Bensouda, opens a preliminary examination of the situation in Palestine, 16 January 2015, http://www.icc-cpi.int/en_menus/icc/press%20and%20media/press%20releases/Pages/pr1083.aspx.

[47]UN Security Council, Resolution 1593, UN Doc. S/RES/1593, 31 March 2005.

[48]UN Security Council, Resolution 1970, UN Doc. S/RES/1970, 26 February 2011.

[49]Immunity is discussed in detail in Sect. 4.1.3 of this chapter.

[50]Art. 9 (2) of the ICTY's Statute and Art. 8 (2) of the ICTR's Statute, both UN Security Council, Resolution 827, UN Doc. S/RES/827, 25 May 1993 (establishing the ICTY) and Resolution 955, UN Doc. S/RES/955, 8 November 1994 (establishing the ICTR).

4.1.3 The Principle of Immunity

Rules of immunity have traditionally hindered the exercise of ICL before national courts. In the Yerodia case,[51] for instance, Belgium had issued an international arrest warrant with Interpol against the then foreign minister of the Democratic Republic of Congo, who was accused of genocide. When Congo accused Belgium of having illegally issued the arrest warrant before the ICJ, the court sided with Congo, emphasising that the immunity of Yerodia blocked the issuance of an arrest warrant.[52] Similarly, in the cases on the former Chadian President Habré[53] and former Chilean President Pinochet,[54] it was confirmed that persons holding public office could only be held responsible after the end of their mandate.

International criminal jurisdiction is regularly designed to overcome this problem of immunity. Article 7(2) ICTY Statute, Article 6(2) ICTR Statute and most importantly Article 27(2) RS (*no immunity principle*) state that immunities shall not bar international criminal courts from exercising their jurisdiction over persons otherwise enjoying immunity. Indeed, criminal procedures were started against heads of State on several occasions while they were still holding public office. Such was the case of Slobodan Milošević (Yugoslavia) before the ICTY,[55] Charles Taylor (Liberia) before the Special Court for Sierra Leone,[56] as well as Laurent Gbagbo (Ivory Coast), Uhuru Kenyatta, William Ruto and Joshua Sang (all three Kenya) before the ICC.[57] Similarly, arrest warrants were issued against Omar al Baschir (Sudan) and Muammar Gaddafi (Libya) by the ICC.[58]

---

[51] ICJ, Arrest Warrant of 11 April 2000 (Democratic Republic of the Congo v. Belgium), Judgement of 14 February 2002, I.C.J. Reports 2002. p. 3.

[52] *Id.*, p. 29 at para. 70.

[53] ICJ, Questions relating to the Obligation to Prosecute or Extradite (Belgium v. Senegal), Judgment of 20 July 2012, I.C.J. Reports 2012. p. 422.

[54] United Kingdom House of Lords, Regina v. Bartle and the Commissioner of Police for the Metropolis and Others Ex Parte Pinochet and Regina v. Evans and Another and the Commissioner of Police for the Metropolis and Others Ex Parte Pinochet, Judgment of 24 March 1999, in: I.L.M. 38 (1999), p. 430.

[55] ICTY, Prosecutor v. Slobodan Milošević., Case No. IT-02-54: http://www.icty.org/case/slobodan_milosevic/4.

[56] Special Court for Sierra Leone, Prosecutor v. Charles Ghankay Taylor, Case No. SCSL-03-1: http://www.rscsl.org/Taylor.html.

[57] ICC, Prosecutor v. Laurent Koudou Gbagbo, Case No. ICC-02/11-01/12; Prosecutor v. Uhuru Muigai Kenyatta, Case No. ICC-01/09-02/11; Prosecutor v. William Samoei Ruto and Joshua Arap Sang, Case No. ICC-01/09-01/11; for all cases at the trial stage, see http://www.icc-cpi.int/en_menus/icc/situations%20and%20cases/cases/Pages/cases%20index.aspx.

[58] ICC, Prosecutor v. Omar Hassan Ahmad Al Bashir, No. ICC-02/05-01/09, Pre-Trial Chamber I, First Warrant of Arrest of 4 March 2009 and Second Warrant of Arrest of 12 July 2010, http://www.icc-cpi.int/en_menus/icc/situations%20and%20cases/situations/situation%20icc%200205/related%20cases/icc02050109/Pages/icc02050109.aspx; Prosecutor v. Muammar Mohammed Abu Minyar Gaddafi, Pre-Trial Chamber I, Warrant of Arrest of 27 June 2011, http://www.icc-cpi.int/iccdocs/doc/doc1099321.pdf.

With regard to the ICC, the cases in which a situation is transferred to the court by the UNSC remain particularly difficult. The RS—and with it the no-immunity principle of Article 27 (2) RS—is not directly applicable if a State has not ratified it. Nevertheless, the prosecutor may start investigations on the explicit request of the UNSC. The question then is whether and in how far Article 27 (2) RS has become part of CIL.[59]

4.2 *Substantive Law*

The ICC's jurisdiction covers four international crimes: genocide, crimes against humanity, war crimes and aggression.

4.2.1 Genocide (Article 6 Rome Statute)

Genocide has been referred to as the 'crime of crimes'.[60] The term genocide is a combination of Greek and Latin: *genos* being Greek for 'race', while *caedere* means 'to kill' in Latin.[61] Coined by Raphael Lemkin as a reaction to the mass killings of Jews by the Nazis in World War II,[62] the term featured first in UN General Assembly (UNGA) Resolution 96(I) of 1946[63] and shortly after in the Genocide Convention of 1948.[64] The ICJ has made clear that the prohibition of genocide is one of the rare norms in PIL from which no derogation is permitted (Article 53 S. 2 VCLT, *ius cogens*).[65]

Article 6 RS, in direct replication of Article II Genocide Convention, defines genocide as

> . . . any of the following acts committed with intent to destroy, in whole or in part, a national, ethnical, racial or religious group, as such:
> (a) Killing members of the group;
> (b) Causing serious bodily or mental harm to members of the group;
> (c) Deliberately inflicting on the group conditions of life calculated to bring about its physical destruction in whole or in part;

[59] Thielboerger (2011) and Frau (2011).

[60] Schabas (2009).

[61] See the definition of '*genocide*' at: http://www.oxforddictionaries.com/definition/english.

[62] Lemkin (1944), pp. 79–82.

[63] UN General Assembly, Resolution 96 (I), UN Doc. A/RES/96(I), 11 December 1946.

[64] Art. 2 of the Convention on the Prevention and Punishment of the Crime of Genocide, 9 December 1948, in: U.N.T.S. 78 (1951), p. 277. The Convention entered into force on 12 January 1951 and currently (April 2017) has 147 parties, see http://treaties.un.org/Pages/ViewDetails.aspx?src=TREATY&mtdsg_no=IV-1&chapter=4&lang=e for the Convention's status.

[65] ICJ, Armed Activities on the Territory of the Congo (Democratic Republic of the Congo v. Uganda), Judgement of 19 December 2005, I.C.J. Reports 2005, pp. 168, 202 at para. 64.

(d) Imposing measures intended to prevent births within the group;
(e) Forcibly transferring children of the group to another group.

Article 6 RS enumerates certain objective elements, such as killing or causing physical or mental harm. It also prescribes, however, that any of these acts must be carried out 'with intent to destroy, in whole or in part, a national, ethnical, racial or religious group' (*subjective element*) in order to qualify as genocide. Two elements in the definition of genocide are noteworthy.

First, ethnic cleansing will most often, maybe surprisingly, not qualify as genocide. Usually, ethnic cleansing focuses not on the partial or complete destruction of a group but on its relocation.[66] Ethnic cleansing might often fall within the scope of crimes against humanity, but it generally does not constitute genocide, although it targets a specific ethnic group.

Second, the crime of genocide must be carried out with the *intent*, a highly condensed form of will, to destroy a group. This high threshold has made it very difficult for international criminal tribunals to prove genocidal intent, most recently in the Croatia-Serbia Genocide case before the ICJ.[67] One of the rare instances where such intent was confirmed by an international tribunal is the attack on the city of Srebrenica by Bosnian Serbs, which the ICJ examined in a 2007 case pinning Bosnia and Herzegovina against Serbia and Montenegro.[68]

4.2.2 Crimes Against Humanity (Article 7 Rome Statute)

Most statutes of international criminal tribunals include definitions of crimes against humanity.[69] However, these definitions are inconsistent and have generated substantial confusion about the term for a long time.[70]

Article 7 RS now clarifies that

[66] v. Arnauld (2014), p. 544 at para. 1304.

[67] ICJ, Application of the Convention on the Prevention and Punishment of the Crime of Genocide (Croatia v. Serbia), Judgement of 3 February 2015, para. 441 (dismissing Croatia's claim) and para. 515 (dismissing Serbia's counter-claim), http://www.icj-cij.org/docket/files/118/18422.pdf.

[68] ICJ, Application of the Convention on the Prevention and Punishment of the Crime of Genocide (Bosnia and Herzegovina v. Serbia and Montenegro), Judgment of 26 February 2007, I.C.J. Reports 2007, pp. 43, 155–166 at paras. 278–297.

[69] Art. 6 (c) of the Charter of the International Military Tribunal at Nuremberg, Agreement for the prosecution and punishment of the major war criminals of the European Axis, 8 August 1945, in: UNTS 82 (1951), p. 280; Art. 5 (c) of the International Military Tribunal for the Far East, 19 January 1946, in: T.I.A.S. 1589; Art. 5 of the ICTY's Statute, UN Security Council, Resolution 827, UN Doc. S/RES/827, 25 May 1993 (establishing the ICTY) and Resolution 955, UN Doc. S/RES/955, 8 November 1994 (establishing the ICTR); and Art. 23 S. 1 of the ICTR's Statute, UN Security Council, Resolution 827, UN Doc. S/RES/827, 25 May 1993 (establishing the ICTY) and Resolution 955, UN Doc. S/RES/955, 8 November 1994 (establishing the ICTR).

[70] Bassiouni (1994), pp. 457, 471.

> 1. (...) 'crime against humanity' means any of the following acts when committed as part of a widespread or systematic attack directed against any civilian population, with knowledge of the attack:
>
> (a) Murder; (...)
> (c) Enslavement;
> (d) Deportation or forcible transfer of population; (...)
> (f) Torture;
> (g) Rape, sexual slavery, enforced prostitution, forced pregnancy, enforced sterilization, or any other form of sexual violence of comparable gravity; (...)
> (i) Enforced disappearance of persons; (...)
> (k) Other inhumane acts of a similar character intentionally causing great suffering or serious injury to body or to mental or physical health.

Given the logic of Articles 6–8 *bis* RS, Article 7 RS should have been listed as the last of the four crimes. It acts in many ways as a residual crime covering aspects of the other three crimes while at the same time being much broader in scope.

Crimes against humanity differ from the crime of genocide in a number of ways. First, the threshold of the subjective element is certainly lower: no *intent* is needed to fulfil the subjective element of crimes against humanity; *knowledge* of the facts that constitute the crime is sufficient. Second, with regard to the objective elements, the target group is different. Crimes against humanity are offences against the civil population in general, not necessarily against one specific group. Third, the required level of organisation behind the crimes committed is set higher than in the case of genocide: a *systematic or widespread attack* against a civilian population is necessary. In this way, crimes against humanity are best understood as an *umbrella crime*. Rather than targeting one specific act—the concept seeks to criminalise an organised policy that lies behind a set of different crimes.

4.2.3 War Crimes (Article 8 Rome Statute)

War crimes connect ICL with IHL, the topic of the previous chapter.[71] Not all violations of IHL, however, constitute war crimes. Only grave violations of IHL create international individual liability. While Article 2 ICTY Statute and Article 4 ICTR Statute contain rather general and extendible regulations on war crimes, the drafters of the ICC's RS decided to include an exhaustive list of cases that constitute war crimes.

It includes an enumeration of more than 500 individual elements of crime. Although commendable from the perspective of the *nullum crimen sine lege principle*,[72] the article's drafting has created a convoluted paragraph that is hard to handle in practice. What is more, given that the list was clearly meant to be

[71] See chapter 3 on international humanitarian law.

[72] This principle is discussed in detail in Sect. 3.1 of this chapter.

exhaustive, there is little room for adjusting Article 8 RS to new developments in IHL or to new modes of warfare.

As is common in IHL, Article 8 RS strictly divides armed conflicts into two categories: international armed conflicts (Article 8(2) lits. a) and b) RS) and non-international armed conflicts (Article 8 (2) lits. c) and e) RS). Many of the listed elements of crime, however, apply to both forms of armed conflict.

The wording that the ICC 'shall have jurisdiction in respect of war crimes in particular when committed as part of a plan or policy or as part of a large-scale commission of such crimes' is very unfortunate. Far from aiming to exclude the punishability of individuals in cases where such plan or policy is absent, it was instead meant as an appeal to the court to focus particularly on the prosecution of crimes committed as a result of such plan or policy but did not intend to leave other war crimes unpunished.

4.2.4 Aggression (Article 8 *bis* Rome Statute)

While the statutes of Nuremberg and Tokyo included *crimes against peace*[73] in order to prosecute political leaders for having led their countries into fully fledged wars, the statutes of the ICTY and ICTR did not include such crimes as both conflicts started within one State. Given that *crimes against peace* or *crimes of aggression* specifically target political leaders, the inclusion of this crime was particularly controversial. Article 5 (2) RS (initial version) emphasised that the ICC could only exercise jurisdiction over such crimes once States parties had agreed on a definition of aggression.

For a long time, it seemed as though States would not be able to agree on the elements of aggression, and many observers believed that this crime would actually never find its way into the jurisdiction of the ICC. However, in the first review session on the RS in Kampala (Uganda) in 2010, States parties agreed on the new Article 8 *bis* RS.[74] It adopts the definition of UNGA Resolution 3314 of 1974[75] nearly fully for its definition of the crime of aggression.

Nevertheless, many caveats remain even after the inclusion of Article 8 *bis* RS. Most of them are listed in Article 15 RS itself: before the ICC can exercise

[73]Art. 6 (a) of the Charter of the International Military Tribunal at Nuremberg, Agreement for the prosecution and punishment of the major war criminals of the European Axis, 8 August 1945, in: UNTS 82 (1951), p. 280; Art. 5 (a) of the Charter of the International Military Tribunal for the Far East, 19 January 1946, in: T.I.A.S. 1589.

[74]Review Conference of the Rome Statute of the International Criminal Court, Kampala, 31 May–11 June 2010, Resolution RC/Res.6, 11 June 2010 (adopted by consensus), in: Official Records, p. 17: http://asp.icc-cpi.int/iccdocs/asp_docs/ASP9/OR/RC-11-Part.I-ENG.pdf.

[75]UN General Assembly, Resolution 3314 (XXIX), UN Doc. A/RES/3314 (XXIX), 14 December 1974.

jurisdiction over the crime of aggression, a two-thirds majority of signatory States is needed (Article 15 *bis* (3) and 15 *ter* (3)), retroactive application is specifically excluded (Article 15 *bis* (2) and 15 *ter* (2)) and States can even generally exclude the applicability of that crime against their citizens or subject to their State territory and jurisdiction (Article 15 *bis* (4) RS). Thus, although the crime of aggression has finally been included in the RS, there is not much hope that it will become a well-functioning part of the Statute.

5 Conclusion

ICL is one of the most fascinating and vibrant parts of PIL. While it is not a new field of law (the Nuremberg and Tokyo trials as a reaction to World War II took place in the late 1940s), it has recently experienced a steep ascent. With the international criminal tribunals for Rwanda and particularly the former Yugoslavia perceived as rather successful, an even more ambitious project became feasible: the establishment of a general international criminal court. What seemed an audacious dream two decades ago has become reality: the ICC took up its work in 2002.

When discussing the future of ICL, one refers, in fact, to the future of this very court. As much as it is fervently praised as a breakthrough for international criminal justice by some, it is at the same time bitterly condemned as an instrument of intervention in States' internal affairs by others. It will be crucial for the court to convince the sceptics of its value in order to become a truly universal court.

That is why it is important to very seriously consider the concerns and withdrawals of some African States over the last years. The support of African nations is crucial for the court's future development. It must never become an instrument of western democracies to bring African leaders to international justice: such a perception of the court would, indeed, be the end of the ICC. The appointment of Fatou Bensouda was in this way a first step in trying to reduce the simmering distrust of African States against the court.

Similarly, the court must also take the concerns expressed by the USA and Israel seriously—even if these concerns are at times expressed in provocative rather than constructive ways. The court must be particularly careful towards if and how it addresses potential cases in the Palestinian territories against Israeli citizens. Whether the court likes it or not, it is not only a legal but also a highly political and politicised institution, certainly more so than any national criminal court. In this way, the court must at all times remain keenly aware of its double responsibility as a legal and as a political institution. To balance and reconcile these two responsibilities will be the main challenge for the ICC in the years to come.

References

Books and Reports

v. Arnauld A (2014) Völkerrecht, 2nd edn. Heidelberg
Cassese A et al (2013) International criminal law, 3rd edn. Oxford
Cryer R et al (2014) An introduction to international criminal law and procedure, 3rd edn. Cambridge
Ipsen K (2014) Völkerstrafrecht. In: Ipsen K (ed) Völkerrecht, 6th edn. Munich
Schabas W (2009) Genocide in international law: the crime of crimes, 2nd edn. Cambridge
Werle G, Jessberger F (2014) Principles of international criminal law, 3rd edn. Oxford
Wilson G (2014) The United Nations and collective security. London

Articles and Book Chapters

Akande D (2009) Africa and the International Criminal Court. In: EJIL: Talk!, http://www.ejiltalk.org/africa-and-the-international-criminal-court./
Arangio-Ruiz G (2000) On the Security Council's "Law-Making". Rivista di Diritto Internazionale 83:609
Bassiouni MC (1994) "Crimes Against Humanity": the need for a specialized convention. Columbia J Transnat Law 31:457, 471
Degan V-D (2005) On the sources of international criminal law. Chin J Int Law 4:45, 67
Frau R (2011) Gaddafi vor Gericht? – Der Internationale Strafgerichtshof erlässt die ersten drei Haftbefehle in der Libyen-Situation. In: Bofaxe, No. 388D, 29 June 2011
Krisch N (2012) Article 41. In: Simma B et al (eds) The Charter of the United Nations, vol II, 3rd edn. Oxford
Lamb S (1999) Legal limits to the United Nations Security Council powers. In: Goodwin-Gill GS, Talmon S (eds) The reality of international law: essays in honour of Ian Brownlie. Oxford, pp 361, 376
Lemkin R (1944) Axis rule, axis rule in occupied Europe: laws of occupation, analysis of government, proposals for redress. Washington, pp 79–82
Mbaku J (2014) International justice: the International Criminal Court and Africa
Møse E (2005) Main achievements of the ICTR. J Int Crim Justice 3:920–927
Nuremberg International Military Tribunal (1947) Judgment and sentences of 1 October 1946. Am J Int Law 41:172
Olásolo H (2007) A note on the evolution of the principle of legality in international criminal law. Crim Law Forum 18:301
Pires A (1995) Quelques obstacles à une mutation du droit pénal. Revue Générale du Droit 26:133–136
du Plessis M, Maluwa T, O'Reilly A (2013) Africa and the International Criminal Court
Surlan T (2005) *Ne bis in idem* in conjunction with the principle of complementarity in the Rome Statute
Thielboerger P (2011) Haftbefehl gegen Muammar al-Gaddafi – Keine Immunität vor dem IStGH? In: Short Essays on International Humanitarian Law (Bofaxe), No. 387D, 29 June 2011
Tulkens F (2011) The paradoxical relationship between criminal law and human rights. J Int Crim Justice 9:577–578
Zacklin R (2004) The failings of ad hoc international tribunals. J Int Crim Justice 2:541–542

Treaties and Statutes

Agreement between the United Nations and the Government of Sierra Leone on the Establishment of a Special Court for Sierra Leone, 16 January 2002, in: United Nations Treaty Series 2178 (2004), p. 138.

Agreement between the United Nations and the Lebanese Republic on the Establishment of a Special Tribunal for Lebanon, 22 January 2007 and 6 February 2007, in: United Nations Treaty Series 2461 (2007), p. 257.

Agreement between the United Nations and the Royal Government of Cambodia concerning the Prosecution under Cambodian Law of Crimes Committed during the Period of Democratic Kampuchea, 6 June 2003, in: United Nations Treaty Series 2329 (2005), p. 1.

Agreement for the prosecution and punishment of the major war criminals of the European Axis, 8 August 1945, in: United Nations Treaty Series 82 (1951) p. 280.

Annex to the Agreement for the prosecution and punishment of the major war criminals of the European Axis, 8 August 1945.

American Service-Members' Protection Act, 116 Stat. 820, 2 August 2002.

Charter of Fundamental Rights of the European Union, 18 December 2000, in: Official Journal of the European Union (2010), C 83/02.

Convention on the Prevention and Punishment of the Crime of Genocide, 9 December 1948, in: U.N.T.S. 78 (1951), p. 277.

International Crimes (Tribunals) Act of 1973, Act No. XIX of 20 July 1973.

Law on the Establishment of Extraordinary Chambers in the Courts of Cambodia for the Prosecution of Crimes committed during the Period of Democratic Kampuchea, 10 August 2001, NS/RKM/0801/12.

Rome Statute of the International Criminal Court, 17 July 1998, in: United Nations Treaty Series 2187 (2004) p. 3.

Cases

ICC, Prosecutor v. Laurent Koudou Gbagbo, Case No. ICC-02/11-01/12; Prosecutor v. Uhuru Muigai Kenyatta, Case No. ICC-01/09-02/11.

ICC, Prosecutor v. Muammar Mohammed Abu Minyar Gaddafi, Pre-Trial Chamber I, Warrant of Arrest of 27 June 2011.

ICC, Prosecutor v. Omar Hassan Ahmad Al Baschir, No. ICC-02/05-01/09, Pre-Trial Chamber I, First Warrant of Arrest of 4 March 2009 and Second Warrant of Arrest of 12 July 2010.

ICC, Prosecutor v. William Samoei Ruto and Joshua Arap Sang, Case No. ICC-01/09-01/11.

ICJ, Application of the Convention on the Prevention and Punishment of the Crime of Genocide (Bosnia and Herzegovina v. Serbia and Montenegro), Judgment of 26 February 2007, I.C.J. Reports 2007, pp. 43, 155-166.

ICJ, Application of the Convention on the Prevention and Punishment of the Crime of Genocide (Croatia v. Serbia), Judgment of 3 February 2015.

ICJ, Armed Activities on the Territory of the Congo (Democratic Republic of the Congo v. Uganda), Judgment of 19 December 2005, I.C.J. Reports 2005, pp. 168.

ICJ, Arrest Warrant of 11 April 2000 (Democratic Republic of the Congo v. Belgium), Judgment of 14 February 2002, I.C.J. Reports 2002. p. 3.

ICJ, Case Concerning Ahmadou Sadio Diallo (Republic of Guinea v. Democratic Republic of the Congo), Judgment of 19 June 2012, I.C.J. Reports 2012.

ICJ, Questions relating to the Obligation to Prosecute or Extradite (Belgium v. Senegal), Judgment of 20 July 2012, I.C.J. Reports 2012. p. 422.

ICTY, Prosecutor v. Dusko Tadic aka "Dule", Case No. IT-94-1, Appeals Chamber, Decision on the Defence Motion for Interlocutory Appeal on Jurisdiction of 2 October 1995.

ICTY, Prosecutor v. Milan Milutinović *et al.*, Case No. IT-99-37-AR72, Appeals Chamber, Decision on Dragoljub Ojdanić's Motion Challenging Jurisdiction – Joint Criminal Enterprise of 21 May 2003.
ICTY, Prosecutor v. Mitar Vasiljević, Case No. IT-98-32-T, Trial Chamber II, Judgment of 29 November 2002.
ICTY, Prosecutor v. Slobodan Milošević., Case No. IT-02-54, see: http://www.icty.org/case/slobodan_milosevic/4.
Permanent Court of International Justice, Case of the Mavrommatis Palestine Concessions, Judgment of 30 August 1924, Series A No. 2.
Special Court for Sierra Leone, Prosecutor v. Charles Ghankay Taylor, Case No. SCSL-03-01-T, Trial Chamber II, Judgment of 18 May 2012.
Special Court for Sierra Leone, Case No. SCSL-03-01-A, Appeals Chamber, Judgment of 26 September 2013.
United Kingdom House of Lords, Regina v. Bartle and the Commissioner of Police for the Metropolis and Others Ex Parte Pinochet and Regina v. Evans and Another and the Commissioner of Police for the Metropolis and Others Ex Parte Pinochet, Judgment of 24 March 1999, in: I.L.M. 38 (1999), p. 430.

UN Documents

Kuala Lumpur Declaration on International Terrorism of 3 April 2002, Annex II to UN General Assembly, UN Doc. A/56/911, 8 April 2002.
Proposed Comprehensive Convention on International Terrorism, Appendix II to UN General Assembly, UN Doc. A/59/894, 12 August 2005.
Statute of the ICTR, annexed to UN Security Council, Resolution 955 UN Doc. S/RES/955, 8 November 1994.
Statute of the ICTY, annexed to UN Security Council, Report of the Secretary-General Pursuant to Paragraph 2 of Security Council Resolution 808 (1993), UN Doc. S/25704, 3 May 1993.
UN General Assembly, Resolution 96 (I), UN Doc. A/RES/96(I), 11 December 1946.
UN General Assembly, Resolution 3314 (XXIX), UN Doc. A/RES/3314 (XXIX), 14 December 1974.
UN Secretary-General, Depositary Notification of Accession to the Rome Statute by the State of Palestine, UN Doc. C.N.13.2015.TREATIES-XVIII.10, 15 January 2015.
UN Security Council, Resolution 827, UN Doc. S/RES/827, 25 May 1993.
UN Security Council, Resolution 955, UN Doc. S/RES/955, 8 November 1994.
UN Security Council, Resolution 1593, UN Doc. S/RES/1593, 31 March 2005.
UN Security Council, Resolution 1664, UN Doc. S/RES/1664, 29 March 2006.
UN Security Council, Resolution 1757, UN Doc. S/RES/1757, 30 May 2007.
UN Security Council, Resolution 1966, UN Doc. S/RES/1966, 22 December 2010.
UN Security Council, Resolution 1970, UN Doc. S/RES/1970, 26 February 2011.

Other

International Military Tribunal, Nazi Conspiracy and Aggression: Opinion and Judgement, Washington 1947, http://www.stl-tsl.org.
Status of the Rome Statute of the International Criminal Court, http://treaties.un.org/pages/ViewDetails.aspx?src=TREATY&mtdsg_no=XVIII-10&chapter=18&lang=en.

M. Abbas, Declaration Accepting the Jurisdiction of the International Criminal Court, 1 January 2015, available at: http://www.icc-cpi.int/iccdocs/PIDS/press/Palestine_A_12-3.pdf.
ICC Press Release, The Prosecutor of the International Criminal Court, Fatou Bensouda, opens a preliminary examination of the situation in Palestine, 16 January 2015, available at: https://www.icc-cpi.int/Pages/item.aspx?name=pr1083.
International Military Tribunal for the Far East, 19 January 1946, in: T.I.A.S. 1589.
Review Conference of the Rome Statute of the International Criminal Court, Kampala, 31 May – 11 June 2010, Resolution RC/Res.6, 11 June 2010, in: Official Records, p. 17.

Further Reading

Cassese A (2013) Cassese's international criminal law, 3rd edn
Crawford J (2012) International criminal justice. In: Brownlie's principles of public international law

Pierre Thielbörger is Professor for German Public Law and Public International Law and Managing Director of the Institute for International Law of Peace and Armed Conflict (IFHV) at Ruhr University Bochum, Germany. He currently serves as President of the NOHA General Assembly.

Disaster Law

Ronan McDermott

1 The Fragmented Nature of Disaster Law

A wide range of legal and regulatory issues arise in crises that are precipitated by natural and technological disasters. These include the determination of the role and responsibility of States in offering and/or accepting assistance, the free movement of relief workers, goods and equipment, as well as ensuring that the range of actors involved in humanitarian assistance is accountable to beneficiary governments and communities.

Despite the central importance of law to the management of natural and technological disasters, the existing body of law is relatively fragmented when compared with the regime for armed conflict provided by international humanitarian law (IHL). This fragmentation is characterised by the varied geographic scope of the legal instruments that govern disasters (bilateral, regional and universal); these legal instruments often either leave gaps or create overlaps. It is also quite fragmented in terms of the mode of instrument in which this area is primarily regulated; while IHL is highly codified, disaster law relies heavily on a range of soft law instruments in addition to the existing hard law instruments.

2 Definition and Scope of Application of Disaster Law

Disaster law refers to the legal provisions that govern the range of challenges that arise from natural and technological disasters occurring in peacetime. Until relatively recently, the scope of the field was generally considered to be limited to legal

R. McDermott (✉)
University College Dublin, Dublin, Ireland
e-mail: ronan.mcdermott@ucd.ie

© Springer International Publishing AG 2018

H.-J. Heintze, P. Thielbörger (eds.), *International Humanitarian Action*,
DOI 10.1007/978-3-319-14454-2_11

provisions concerning the disaster response phase of the disaster management cycle.[1] However, this chapter conceives of disaster law more broadly to include legal provisions concerning not only disaster response but also other disaster management phases, including disaster risk reduction and preparedness. The rehabilitation and reconstruction phases are governed by the general rules of international law and therefore are not addressed in this chapter.

There are a wide range of definitions of disaster in disaster law instruments.[2] Most of the existing *hard law* norms in the field deriving from treaties and other sources of international law relate to disasters with transboundary impacts, i.e. disasters that require international assistance. However, recently a range of norms, soft law in nature, have been created by the international community that also address recurrent, smaller-scale disasters that do not necessarily require international assistance as part of the response but that nonetheless cumulatively impose considerable costs in terms of human lives and property.[3] This chapter will thus also address those norms that have been developed by the international community that, although not legally binding, do nonetheless inform domestic disaster management regimes.

3 Emergence and Early Development of Disaster Law

A possible explanation for the relative fragmentation and underdevelopment of disaster law svis-à-vis IHL is that historically natural and technological disasters, unlike armed conflicts, have not generally been considered a core concern of the international community.[4]

The League of Nations produced a Convention establishing the International Relief Union in 1927. The Convention aimed, according to its preamble, 'to render aid to each other in disasters, to encourage international relief by a methodical co-ordination of available resources, and to further the progress of international law in the field'.[5] However, the International Relief Union had a limited impact, and its work ended with the onset of World War II.

The immediate post-war development of disaster law was chiefly characterised by the adoption of bilateral treaties on disaster assistance.[6] Another attempt to create a comprehensive and universal disaster law instrument came with the submission in 1984 by the UN Secretary General of the text of a Draft Convention

---

[1]See, for example Hoffman (2003), pp. 13–20.

[2]Fisher (2007), p. 23.

[3]Concerning soft law, see van Hoof (1983).

[4]It should be noted, however, that as early as 1758 the Swiss diplomat and legal scholar Emer de Vattel noted the duty of States to come to the assistance of others experiencing famine, as '*assisting in such a dire situation is so central to humanity that no civilized nation would fail entirely to do so*'. Cited in Fisher (2007), p. 25.

[5]Fidler (2005), pp. 458–473 at 464.

[6]Fischer (2003), pp. 24–44 at 24–25.

on Expediting the Delivery of Emergency Assistance to the Economic and Social Council.[7] Ultimately, however, the text failed to receive sufficient support and remained in draft form.

4 Bilateral, Regional and Global Disaster Law Mechanisms

Contemporary disaster law remains highly fragmented in the absence of a universal and comprehensive instrument and thus relies on a range of mechanisms concluded at different levels of governance (bilateral, regional and global) that address a wide range of issues relating to disaster management.

4.1 Bilateral Disaster Law Treaties

Bilateral treaties that regulate disaster management form the bulk of the existing international instruments relating to disasters.[8] For the most part conceived in terms of the provision of mutual assistance, such treaties, with a few exceptions,[9] are generally concluded between neighbouring States.

De Guttry provides a typology of disasters regulated by bilateral treaties.[10] The first category of treaties regulates all types of major natural and technological disasters. The second category of treaties relates to specific kinds of disaster, for example forest fire control. A further category of treaties has an even narrower scope of application and regulates disasters occurring in a predefined geographic area, for example disasters occurring in a mountainous border region or maritime disasters occurring in waters adjacent to an international border.

Bilateral treaties can address a range of disaster management issues, including the management of requests and offers of assistance, risk assessment and reduction, damage and loss assessment, monitoring systems, education and training, emergency management and planning, engineering and social problems, and technological information exchanges.[11] It has been asserted that the general trend in terms of the content of the various bilateral disaster law treaties is from agreements concerning particular hazards and/or narrow aspects of disaster management towards the pursuit of more general frameworks for mutual assistance.[12]

---

[7]Office of the UN Disaster Relief Coordinator, Convention on Expediting the Delivery of Emergency Assistance (Draft), UN Doc. A/39/267/Add.2 E/1984/96/Add.2, of June 18, 1984.

[8]Fisher (2007), p. 80.

[9]See, for example Italy and Russia.

[10]de Guttry (2012), pp. 11–12.

[11]*Id.*, p. 12.

[12]Fischer (2003), p. 24.

4.2 Regional Disaster Law Mechanisms

Arrangements for disaster management at the regional level have proliferated in recent years. An advantage that regional organisations in disaster management possess is the trust and familiarity that these fora provide for the member States concerned. Such an advantage can facilitate the agreement of effective common policies that are tailored to the particular needs of the regions concerned.[13] The form of cooperation varies greatly across regions and ranges from political dialogue through information exchange to harmonisation, training and joint operations. Ferris and Petz have investigated the forms of cooperation engaged in by 13 regional organisations.[14] All thirteen of the organisations investigated have held regional intergovernmental meetings concerning disaster risk management and a regional DRR framework or convention. Twelve of the 13 organisations have ratified a regional disaster management framework convention. A lesser but not insignificant number of organisations have developed regional disaster relief insurance and other financial mechanisms, operational response capacities and agreed military protocols. Despite considerable cooperation across a range of disaster-management-related issues, only two regional organisations (the European Union and the Organisation of American States) have developed either a treaty mechanism or a set of guidelines for facilitating and regulating disaster response.

4.3 Global Multilateral Disaster Law Instruments

There are few instruments at the global level that regulate disaster management in peacetime; those that do exist tend to be sectorial in the sense that they merely form part of broader international regimes (for example, customs or civil aviation regimes), address only particular disaster threats or address only a particular type of actor or aspect of a relief operation.

[13]Haver and Foley, https://www.humanitarianoutcomes.org/sites/default/files/Backgroundpaper2RegionalandInternationalInitiatives.pdf.

[14]Ferris and Petz, http://www.brookings.edu/~/media/Research/Files/Reports/2013/02/regional%20organizations%20disasters%20ferris/REGIONAL_DISASTER_MECHANISMS_2013.pdf. The thirteen regional organisations are: the African Union; Economic Community of West African States; Southern African Development Community; Organisation of American States; Central American Integration System; Caribbean Community and Common Market; the Andean Community; the League of Arab States; South Asian Association for Regional Cooperation; Association of Southeast Asian Nations; European Union; Council of Europe; and the Secretariat of the Pacific Community.

4.3.1 Broad International Regimes Addressing Disaster Issues

There are a number of established international regimes that address disaster relief in an incidental manner. Although these regimes often have counterparts at the bilateral and regional levels, only the global regimes are outlined here.

Obstacles to the free movement of relief items, goods and equipment, either through delays caused by customs procedures or the costs incurred by customs taxes and duties, can hamper an international relief effort. Such obstacles often arise in the context of the inundation of the customs offices of disaster-affected States by such relief items, goods and equipment. The broad international regime governing customs has striven to address this.

The 1970 World Custom Organisation (WCO) Recommendation to Expedite the Forwarding of Relief Consignments in the Event of Disasters recommended States to allow the 'admission free of import duties and taxes'[15] of relief consignments intended as gifts to victims of a disaster. A temporary admission regime is also recommended for equipment used in a relief effort, provided that such goods are subsequently re-exported.[16] Paragraph 6 of Annex J.5 to the Kyoto Convention contains similar provisions to those provided by the WCO Recommendation. However, few States have participated in the Annex, which, even within the framework of an international treaty, is formulated in terms of a recommendation.[17] The same lack of State participation characterises annexes B.3 and J.5 to the revised 1999 International Convention on the Simplification and Harmonisation of Customs Procedures, which simplify customs procedures and waive fees. Despite the range of initiatives undertaken at bilateral and regional levels, as well as at the universal level, to facilitate cross-border movement of relief material, it has been asserted that States retain considerable discretion in practice in introducing legislation and regulation to facilitate foreign relief consignments.[18]

The broad international regimes governing civil aviation and maritime transport also contain disaster-related norms. In terms of civil aviation, the Convention on International Civil Aviation provides that States parties shall facilitate relief flights undertaken by civil aircraft.[19] Regarding civil maritime transport, the Annex to the

[15]WCO doc. T2-423, 8th June, 1970, para. 5.

[16]*Id.*, para. 6.

[17]Adinolfi (2012), p. 539.

[18]*Id.*, p. 546.

[19]Chapter 8.8 of Annex 9 to the Convention on International Civil Aviation (Chicago, 7th December 1944) additionally provides that: '*Contracting States shall facilitate the entry into, departure from and transit through their territories of aircraft engaged in relief flights performed by or on behalf of international organisations recognised by the UN or by or on behalf of States themselves and shall take all possible measures to ensure their safe operation. Such relief flights are those undertaken in response to natural and man-made disasters which seriously endanger human health or the environment, as well as similar emergency situations where UN assistance is required. Such flights shall be commenced as quickly as possible after obtaining agreement with the recipient State.*'

1965 Convention on the Facilitation of Maritime Traffic has been amended to provide in Sections 7.8–7.10 for the facilitation of the arrival and departure of ships engaged in disaster relief work, including the facilitation of the entry and clearance of persons, cargo, material and equipment required to deal with disaster situations.

4.3.2 Mechanisms Addressing Specific Hazards

Although a comprehensive and universal legal regime does not currently exist at the global level, a number of regimes have developed that are directed towards addressing particular natural and technological hazards. Such hazards include infectious diseases, nuclear accidents, industrial pollution, civil transport and maritime/aviation accidents. It can be asserted that these hazards have the potential to create negative externalities for neighbouring States, thereby generating incentives for States to regulate.[20] The regime governing nuclear accidents and infectious diseases are outlined in more detail below.

The threat posed by nuclear accidents has obvious cross-border implications. However, apart from the instruments that establish the International Atomic Energy Agency, some bilateral treaties and some agreements entered into by international organisations and member States, there was no universal instrument that strove to regulate this threat until 1986.[21] The Chernobyl nuclear accident precipitated the adoption by the international community of two treaties relating to nuclear safety and to emergency preparedness and response, respectively.[22] A range of other treaties provide further regulation concerning preparedness and response, safety and security, and liability for nuclear damage.[23]

The transboundary nature of infectious diseases and other threats to public health has resulted in the development of a body of legal norms given effect by treaties, the regulations of a number of international organisations, as well as soft law instruments.[24] Under its constitution, the World Health Organization (WHO) is given considerable powers to 'take emergency measures within the functions and financial resources of the organisation to deal with events requiring immediate action'.[25]

---

[20] Fidler (2005), p. 460.

[21] Gioia (2012), pp. 85–102, at p. 86.

[22] Convention on Assistance in the Case of a Nuclear Accident or Radiological Emergency (Vienna, 26 Sept. 1986); Convention on Early Notification of a Nuclear Accident (Vienna, 26 Sept. 1986).

[23] Gioia (2012), pp. 85–102.

[24] Venturini (2012), pp. 45–64, at p. 57.

[25] Art. 28(i) WHO Constitution, http://www.who.int/governance/eb/who_constitution_en.pdf.

In 2005, the World Health Assembly adopted a new version of the International Health Regulations (the Regulations), which entered into force on 15 June 2007.[26] The Regulations provide that States parties must notify WHO of any event that may constitute a public health emergency. The WHO Director General is given the power to determine the existence of an international emergency and to issue recommendations.

4.3.3 Mechanisms Addressing Particular Aspects of Disaster Relief

A final category of universal disaster law instruments contains those instruments that address particular aspects of disaster relief or govern the activities of particular relief actors. One of the few examples within this category and one of the only dedicated global disaster law treaties to have been adopted in the latter half of the twentieth century is the Convention on the Provision of Telecommunication Resources for Disaster Mitigation and Relief Operations.[27] The convention details the procedures for offering and requesting telecommunications assistance.[28] It also details the privileges and immunities that telecommunication providers enjoy, including immunity from arrest, detention and legal process and exemption from taxation and other charges.[29]

4.3.4 The International Law Commission's Draft Articles on the Protection of Persons in the Event of Disaster

Looking to the future, the UN International Law Commission (ILC), which is mandated to promote the progressive development of PIL and its codification, has issued a set of draft articles concerning the protection of persons in the event of disaster.[30] Although the concrete consequence of the Draft Articles remains unclear, they can contribute to confirming the content of the rules and principles of international law in this regard.[31] Human dignity in disaster settings is given prominence in Draft Article 5, and although international human rights law has

---

[26]The 2005 International Health Regulations are the successor to the preceding 1969 International Health Regulations.

[27]Fidler (2005), p. 465.

[28]Art. 4, Convention on the Provision of Telecommunication Resources for Disaster Mitigation and Relief Operations (Tampere, 18th June 1998).

[29]*Id.*, Art. 5.

[30]Report of the International Law Commission on the work of its sixty-eighth session, 2 May–10 June and 4 July–12 August 2016, UN Doc. A/71/10 chap. IV, paras 38–49.

[31]Boyle and Chinkin (2007), pp. 160–162.

always been applicable in disaster settings,[32] Draft Article 6 makes this explicit.[33] The draft articles also address the rights and duties of States to seek and provide assistance.

5 Soft Law Instruments

As mentioned above, disaster law is not only fragmented in terms of its geographic scope. It is also fragmented in terms of the various types of instruments contained within this body of law. Therefore, there are a significant number of soft law instruments that provide guidance of non-legally binding nature. These instruments strive to regulate the humanitarian sector as a whole or particular actors engaged in disaster management.

5.1 Soft Law Instruments Addressed to States

A range of soft law instruments have been adopted that are addressed to States.

Recognising the fragmented nature of disaster law as outlined above, the International Disaster Response Law Guidelines of the International Federation of the Red Cross (IFRC) has drawn on the wide range of existing standards and has supplemented these with novel elements to create a comprehensive but non-legally binding guidance document known as the Guidelines for the Domestic Facilitation and Regulation of International Disaster Relief and Initial Recovery Assistance (the IDRL Guidelines).[34] Guidance is provided to governments concerning how to ensure legal preparedness for an international relief effort. The IDRL Guidelines seek to address both obstacles to the provision of humanitarian relief (in sectors including customs, immigration, transport), as well as potential quality and accountability shortfalls.

Another important initiative has been the Hyogo Framework for Action[35] and its successor instrument, the Sendai Framework for Disaster Risk Reduction

[32]Kent (2011), pp. 137–138.

[33]See Report of the International Law Commission on the work of its sixty-eighth session, 2 May–10 June and 4 July–12 August 2016, UN Doc. A/71/10 chap. IV, para 48.

[34]The IDRL Guidelines were unanimously adopted in 2007 by States parties to the Geneva Conventions and Red Cross and Red Crescent actors at the 30th International Conference of the Red Cross and Red Crescent. See Resolution 4, 30th International Conference of the Red Cross and Red Crescent 30IC/07/R4. The IDRL Guidelines have also been endorsed several times in UN General Assembly resolutions.

[35]UNISDR, Hyogo Framework for Action 2005–2015: Building the Resilience of Nations and Communities to Disasters. Extract from the final report of the World Conference on Disaster Reduction (A/CONF.206/6), Geneva 2007.

2015–2030.[36] The latter's overarching priorities are to galvanise UN member States in better understanding disaster risk, strengthening disaster risk governance to manage disaster risk, investing in disaster risk reduction for resilience, enhancing disaster preparedness for effective response and to *Build Back Better* in recovery, rehabilitation and reconstruction.

The conditions under which military and civil defence assets may be deployed are detailed in the Guidelines on the Use of Foreign Military and Civil Defence Assets in Disaster Relief (the Oslo Guidelines). The deployment of military assistance is governed by the principle of complementarity; only if civilian and/or humanitarian resources are insufficient should military assistance be provided.[37] Military assistance ought to be provided at no cost to the receiving State or party.[38] In principle, military and civil defence personnel deployed on disaster relief missions will do so unarmed and in national uniforms,[39] and such personnel ought to have a clearly defined legal status.[40]

5.2 *Soft Law Instruments Addressed to Other Humanitarian Actors*

A wide range of technical standards exist that serve to guide the relief activities of humanitarian actors, including UN agencies, the Red Cross Movement and non-governmental organisations (for example, the Sphere Project[41]). Codes of conduct for relief personnel have also been created (for example, Code of Conduct for the International Red Cross and Red Crescent Movement and Non-Governmental Organisations in Disaster Relief). The Core Humanitarian Standard, which was published in December 2014, strives to consolidate a number of key guidelines in the humanitarian sector through the detailing of a set of nine commitments to communities and people affected by crisis.[42]

---

[36]UNISDR, Sendai Framework for Disaster Risk Reduction 2015–2030 (A/CONF.224/CRP.1), Geneva 2015.

[37]Guidelines on the Use of Foreign Military and Civil Defence Assets, in: Disaster Relief, p. 24.

[38]*Id.*, p. 27.

[39]*Id.*, p. 29.

[40]*Id.*, pp. 30–31. A wide range of bilateral status of forces agreements (SOFAs) and visiting forces agreements (VFAs) exist, which sometimes have specific provisions with regard to disaster relief assistance. See Fisher (2007), p. 80.

[41]Walker and Purdin (2004), pp. 100–111; Tong (2004), pp. 176–189; Darcy (2004), pp. 112–123; Gostelow (1999), pp. 316–325.

[42]The Foreword to the Core Humanitarian Standard states that '*[i]t is the intention of the boards of HAP International, People In Aid and the Sphere Project that the CHS will replace the 2010 HAP Standard in Accountability and Quality Management, the People In Aid Code of Good Practice in the Management and Support of Aid Personnel and the Core Standards section of the Sphere Handbook*'.

6 Conclusion

Similar to many other bodies of international law, disaster law is characterised by considerable fragmentation. Although it may well be unlikely, and possibly undesirable, that a universal and comprehensive disaster law treaty is concluded, the prospects for building consensus among the international community concerning key disaster law issues have been increased by recent initiatives such as the ILC Draft Articles and the development of the Common Humanitarian Standard. The increasing engagement of regional organisations with disaster issues is to be welcomed, as are efforts to ensure coherence between regional and global humanitarian and disaster management regimes. Disaster law may still be regarded as in its infancy, and challenges undoubtedly remain in ensuring the necessary legal preparedness to support efficient and effective disaster management. Nonetheless, the international community is increasingly resorting to a range of legal and policy instruments in various multilateral fora to address the growing challenges posed by natural and technological disasters.

References

Books and Reports

Adinolfi G (2012) Customs obstacles to relief consignments under international disaster response law. In: de Guttry A, Gestri M, Venturini G (eds) International disaster response law. The Hague, Netherlands

Boyle A, Chinkin C (2007) The making of international law. OUP

Ferris E, Petz D In the neighborhood: the growing role of regional organizations in disaster risk management, http://www.brookings.edu/wp-content/uploads/2016/06/REGIONAL_DISASTER_MECHANISMS_2013.pdf

Fisher D (2007) Law and legal issues in international disaster response. Geneva

Haver K, Foley C Regional and international initiatives, Background paper 2 prepared for the International Dialogue on Strengthening Partnership in Disaster Response, http://www.alnap.org/resource/10841

Venturini G (2012) International disaster response law in relation to other branches of international law. In: de Guttry A, Gestri M, Venturini G (eds) International disaster response law. The Hague, pp 45–64

Articles and Book Chapters

Darcy J (2004) Locating responsibility: the Sphere Humanitarian Charter and its rationale. Disasters 28(2):112–123

Gioia A (2012) Nuclear accidents and international law. In: de Guttry A, Gestri M, Venturini G (eds) International disaster response law. The Hague, pp 85–102

Gostelow L (1999) The Sphere Project: the implications of making humanitarian principles and codes work. Disasters 23(4):316–325

de Guttry A (2012) Surveying the law. In: de Guttry A, Gestri M, Venturini G (eds) International disaster response law. The Hague, Netherlands
Fidler D (2005) Disaster relief and governance after the Indian Ocean tsunami: what role for international law? Melb J Int Law 6:458–473
Fischer H (2003) International disaster response law treaties: trends, patterns and lacunae. In: International disaster response laws, principles and practice: reflections, prospects and challenges. Geneva, pp 24–44
Hoffman M (2003) What is the scope of international disaster response law? In: International disaster response laws, principles and practice: reflections, prospects and challenges. Geneva, pp 13–20
Kent G (2011) The human right to disaster mitigation and relief. Environ Hazard 3:137–138
Tong J (2004) Questionable accountability: MSF and Sphere in 2003. Disasters 28(2):176–189
Walker P, Purdin S (2004) Birthing sphere. Disasters 28(2):100–111

Treaties and Statutes

Convention on Assistance in the Case of a Nuclear Accident or Radiological Emergency (Vienna, 26 Sept. 1986).
Convention on Early Notification of a Nuclear Accident (Vienna, 26 Sept. 1986).
Convention on the Provision of Telecommunication Resources for Disaster Mitigation and Relief Operations (Tampere, 18 June 1998).
Guidelines on the Use of Foreign Military and Civil Defence Assets in Disaster Relief.
WHO Constitution, http://www.who.int/governance/eb/who_constitution_en.pdf.

UN Documents

Office of the UN Disaster Relief Coordinator, Convention on Expediting the Delivery of Emergency Assistance (Draft), UN Doc. A/39/267/Add.2 E/1984/96/Add.2, 18 June 1984.
UN General Assembly, Resolution 60/195, UN Doc. A/RES/60/195, 2 March 2006.
UN International Law Commission, Report of the International Law Commission on the work of its sixty-sixth session (5 May – 6 June and 7 July to 8 August 2014) UN Doc A/CN.4/L.831.
UNISDR, Hyogo Framework for Action 2005–2015: Building the Resilience of Nations and Communities to Disasters. Extract from the final report of the World Conference on Disaster Reduction (A/CONF.206/6). Geneva 2007.
van Hoof, G., Rethinking the sources of international law, Deventer 1983

Further Reading

Caron D, Kelly M, Telesetsky A (eds) (2014) The international law of disaster relief. Cambridge
de Guttry A, Gestri M, Venturini G (eds) (2012) International disaster response law. The Hague
Fisher D (2007) Law and legal issues in international disaster response. Geneva

Hoffman M (2003) What is the scope of international disaster response law? In: International disaster response laws, principles and practice: reflections, prospects and challenges. Geneva, pp 13–20

Zwitter A, Lamont CK, Heintze H-J, Herman J (eds) (2014) Humanitarian action: global, regional and domestic legal responses. Cambridge

Ronan McDermott is a Research Fellow at the Centre for Humanitarian Action, University College Dublin, Ireland.

Protection of Refugees and Minorities

Hans-Joachim Heintze and Charlotte Lülf

1 Introduction

The right to humane treatment entails the entitlement of the civilian population to receive humanitarian assistance. If a conflict party does not provide civilians under its control with relief supplies, humanitarian and impartial relief actions shall be undertaken, without any adverse distinction between civilians. This applies more or less to all armed conflicts and also in peacetime in the event of natural disasters. The International Disaster Response Law Guidelines of the International Federation of the Red Cross (IFRC) similarly state that in disaster situations, when the affected State determines that a disaster situation exceeds national coping capacities, that State's government should seek international and/or regional assistance to address the needs of affected persons.[1]

Any humanitarian assistance must address the special needs of vulnerable groups. This entails, on the one hand, a prohibition on discrimination and, on the other hand, positive measures to meet the special requirements of such groups. Refugee and Minority law are two distinct fields of Public International Law that govern the protection of certain defined vulnerable individuals and groups. Their protection, in law and in the field, has been a challenge for humanitarian action and beyond, not solely due to practical obstacles but also due to the disputed scope of their legal entitlements. The evolvement of the two fields has started decades ago, both on the international and regional levels, the protection of their beneficiaries is widely codified, and the pertinent legal instruments are being monitored by

[1] International Federation of the Red Cross and Red Crescent Societies, Guidelines for the Domestic Facilitation and Regulation of International Disaster Relief and Initial Recovery Assistance, 2007.

H.-J. Heintze • C. Lülf (✉)
Ruhr University Bochum, Bochum, Germany
e-mail: Hans-Joachim.Heintze@rub.de; charlotte.luelf@ruhr-uni-bochum.de

© Springer International Publishing AG 2018

H.-J. Heintze, P. Thielbörger (eds.), *International Humanitarian Action*,
DOI 10.1007/978-3-319-14454-2_12

national, regional and international actors and build the normative foundation for protection measures in the field. Yet, contemporary developments again reflect the difficulties to implement existing legal obligations and the disputes about their scope of application. Against this background, the chapter provides an introduction into the development of the two fields of law and their most prominent instruments and offers an overview on substantive rights as well as regional developments.

2 International Refugee Law

With the changing nature of armed conflicts, large-scale natural disasters and the economic struggle of countries, new displacement patterns have emerged that challenge the traditional architecture of the international legal system and the responsibility of States towards citizens and aliens.

The legal debate has always been strongly influenced by the classical separation of people with refugee status under the Convention on the Status of Refugees of 28 July 1951 (hereafter Refugee Convention) and the wide range of displaced persons leaving their State of origin due to generalised situations of violence, environmental change or economic downfall, all of which are not commonly covered by the Refugee Convention. Due to the absence of a comprehensive migration law branch, the situation of these migrants is considered under HRL or international labour law but not under refugee law. This seperation between the two branches was mirrored in the work and mandate of the United Nations High Commissioner for Refugees (UNHCR) and its counterpart, the International Organization for Migration (IOM). However, the last decades have proven that no easy distinction between voluntary and involuntary displacements can be made, and the distinction between those that fulfil the definition of international refugee law and those that do not is blurred in practice.

Apart from the international protection established, States have made use of regional international law and national domestic mechanisms to temporarily adopt protection measures in cases of serious natural disasters or armed conflict situations that expand the scope of protection for persons in flight, albeit geographically limited.[2]

2.1 *The Historical Development of International Refugee Law*

Refugee protection became a matter of international politics and international law for the first time in the early twentieth century.[3] While people fleeing their home

[2]See McAdam (2005), McAdam (2012) and Plender and Mole (2000).

[3]Hathaway (2012), p. 177.

countries had previously been protected by various national laws concerning aliens, a systematic international framework was envisaged only in the aftermath of World War I. The League of Nations addressed the issue of migration and refugees during the 1920s and established an Office of the High Commissioner for Russian Refugees and a High Commissioner for Refugees Coming from Germany.[4]

Following the dismantling of the League of Nations due to its inability to ensure peace and security, the Allied Forces took the initiative of establishing a United Nations Relief and Rehabilitation Administration in 1944 and an International Refugee Organization in 1947.[5]

The events of World War II, as well as the emerging Cold War, strengthened the idea that the international community would need to assume responsibility for the protection of fundamental rights if States failed in their responsibility towards their citizens. With the Universal Declaration of Human Rights of 1948 codifying that *everyone has the right to seek and to enjoy in other countries asylum from persecution* (Article 14 (1)), the commitment and objective to institutionalise assistance was further strengthened.

The roots of the contemporary refugee protection framework lie in the establishment of the Office of the UNHCR. With its statute annexed to United Nations General Assembly (UNGA) Resolution 428 (V) of December 1949, this body was founded to address the massive numbers of displaced persons following World War II on a temporary basis. With the adoption of the 1951 Refugee Convention, the main legal instrument and cornerstone of the refugee law framework was drafted and entered into force. These post-war developments still form the basis of today's international refugee framework.

2.2 Legal Instruments and Sources of Refugee Protection

The 1951 Refugee Convention is the universally applicable cornerstone of international refugee law that establishes primary standards for people deprived of the benefits of nationality and citizenship. It is considered to *represent a milestone in the emergence of a global will to address problems of forced displacement.*[6] Apart from classical refugee law, the framework interacts considerably with cognate fields of international law (PIL), in particular HRL, IHL and ICL,[7] all of which are discussed in the various chapters of this textbook.

[4]First international instruments were drafted such as the 1928 Arrangement relating to the Legal Status of Russian and Armenian Refugees, followed by the 1933 Convention relating to the International Status of Refugees.

[5]UNHCR, An Introduction to International Protection, 1 August 2005, www.unhcr.org/3ae6bd5a0.pdf.

[6]*Id.*, p. 9.

[7]Relevant treaties include *inter alia* the Convention against Torture and Other Cruel, Inhuman or Degrading Treatment or Punishment (1984), the International Bill of Rights or the 1949 Geneva Conventions.

The 1967 Protocol to the Refugee Convention marked a critical shift in the evolution of refugee law insofar as it lifted the temporal and geographical limitations initially contained in the Refugee Convention. Until 1967, its application was limited to refugees fleeing before 1951 and events occurring in Europe. At the time of writing, the Convention and the Protocol have been ratified by 145 and 146 States, respectively.[8]

Apart from the Refugee Convention, regional initiatives to address specific geo-political issues of displacement have resulted in the drafting and entry into force of further treaties and declarations.[9] These include the 1969 Organisation of African Unity Convention Governing the Specific Aspects of Refugee Problems following Decolonialisation in Africa in the late 1950s, the 1984 Cartagena Declaration for Latin American Countries or the Bangkok Principles of 1966, revised in 2001. Although both latter documents are legally non-binding, most countries in the respective regions do apply them and have incorporated their provisions into national legislation.[10] In Europe, the Council of Europe in particular has acted as a pioneer in the development of refugee and asylum law through its recommendations and resolutions.[11] Furthermore, the European Union (EU) has established a unique supranational framework of harmonised asylum laws. Article 78 of the Treaty on the Functioning of the European Union codifies the goal to establish a common policy on asylum, subsidiary protection and temporary protection in accordance with the Refugee Convention, including a common status, procedures and standards. These are further elaborated by the various instruments of secondary law such as the directives on qualification, reception conditions, procedures, return and the Dublin regulations.[12]

These conventions are complemented by fundamental principles of refugee law of customary nature, such as the principle of non-refoulement as well as by other

[8]See for a list of ratifications and signatures, UN Treaty Collections Database, http://treaties.un.org/Pages/ViewDetailsII.aspx?src=TREATY&mtdsg_no=V-2&chapter=5&Temp=mtdsg2&clang=_en.

[9]Still supported development, see *The Executive Committee encourages States and UNHCR to continue to promote, where relevant, regional initiatives for refugee protection and durable solutions, and to ensure that regional standards which are developed conform fully with universally recognized protection standards and respond to particular regional circumstances and protection needs.* UNHCR, Executive Committee Conclusions, General Conclusion on International Protection, 17 October 1997, N° 81 (k).

[10]UNHCR, Protecting Refugees: A Field Guide for NGOs, p. 17.

[11]See the 1947 Resolution on Asylum to Persons in Danger of Persecution, the 1980 European Agreement on Transfer of Responsibility for Refugees, the 1981 Recommendation to Member States on the Protection of Persons Satisfying the Criteria in the Geneva Convention who are not Formally Recognised as Refugees or the European Convention on Human Rights.

[12]For more information on the EU asylum instruments, see http://ec.europa.eu/dgs/home-affairs/what-we-do/policies/asylum/index_en.htm. For more on the interaction of international refugee law and European asylum law, see Battjes (2006).

soft law instruments,[13] such as UNGA resolutions, for example the Declaration on Territorial Asylum 2312 (XXII) of 14 December 1967,[14] and the conclusions of UNHCR's governing Executive Committee. Although some principles and regulations are specifically designed to address refugee matters, most of the protection awarded finds its counterpart in HRL, for instance the Universal Declaration of Human Rights, the International Covenant on Civil and Political Rights (ICCPR) or the European Convention on Human Rights.[15]

2.3 *Refugees in International Law*

As the international framework centres on the Refugee Convention, its legal definition of the term refugee must be examined. To be eligible for protection as a refugee under the Convention and its Protocol, a person must fulfil the criteria set forth in Article 1 A(2) Refugee Convention, which stipulates that a refugee is any person who

> [. . .] owing to well-founded fear of being persecuted for reasons of race, religion, nationality, membership in a particular social group or political opinion, is outside the country of his nationality and is unable or, owing to such fear, is unwilling to avail himself of the protection of that country; or who, not having a nationality and being outside the country of his former habitual residence as a result of such event, is unable or, owing to such fear, is unwilling to return to it.

The definition encompasses six elements.[16]

Alienage, *being outside of the country of nationality* or *being outside of the country of his former habitual residence*, distinguishes *de jure* refugees from internally displaced people (IDPs) and marks the shift of factual responsibility from the State of origin to the receiving host State. This element is interpreted to include, both, persons fleeing owing to fear of being persecuted as well as *sur place refugees*, people whose fear of persecution in case of return developed while already beeing outside of their country of origin.[17]

---

[13]Soft law mechanisms in the field of refugee protection include the London Declaration of International Law Principles on Internally Displaced Persons (2000) and the Guiding Principles on Internal Displacement (1998).

[14]A prominent example is the 1967 UN General Assembly Resolution on Territorial Asylum, reiterating people's right to seek asylum and the granting of such as a humanitarian and non-political act.

[15]Right to life, liberty and security of person, freedom from torture, or cruel, inhuman and degrading treatment or punishment, freedom from arbitrary arrest and detention, to name just a few.

[16]For a detailed assessment and clarification of the elements, see UNHCR, Handbook on Procedures and Criteria for Determining Refugee Status under the 1951 Convention and the 1967 Protocol relating to the Status of Refugees, HCR/IP/4/Eng/REV.1 Geneva, 1992, http://www.unhcr.org/publications/legal/3d58e13b4/handbook-procedures-criteria-determining-refugee-status-under-1951-convention.html.

[17]Hathaway (2012), p. 184.

The refugee's fear of persecution entails both a subjective and objective element.[18] The Refugee Convention does not define persecutory acts, which may include a wide range of conduct and deprivation of basic civil and political rights such as torture, assault, detention or other restriction of political or social expression.[19] Persecution is a potential or actual violation of life, freedom or other substantive rights of a person.[20] The actors carrying out persecution in the Refugee Convention's scope include both State and non-State agents.[21] Situations in which States prove unable or unwilling to prevent persecution by others are also comprised. The five grounds for persecution limit the application of the Refugee Convention to persecution *on account of* a specific discriminatory nature. Although the grounds can overlap, they establish an exhaustive list, and no other discriminatory grounds than those explicitly stated trigger the definition and the protection regime.

Persecution based on race covers all identifiable ethnic groupings, while persecution for religion reasons targets persons because of their belief system or its manifestation in the public and private sphere. The criterion of nationality concerns grounds based on memberships to ethnic, religious, cultural or linguistic communities. In particular, with regard to social groups and holders of a certain political opinion, advances have been made over recent years to expand the scope of these categories through jurisprudence and adjustment to modern needs.[22] Social groups are identified by sharing a common characteristic or by being perceived as sharing one. The substance of the ground of political opinion can be deduced from, *inter alia*, Article 19 of the Universal Declaration and Article 19 of the ICCPR and should be interpreted broadly.[23] Typically it relates to holding views that oppose the State, the government or public policies.[24]

Other additional grounds for fleeing one's home country motivated by economic reasons or environmental disasters are not covered by the Refugee Convention and will only trigger refugee protection if occurring in conjunction with one of its five grounds.

---

[18]For more details, see: The Michigan Guidelines on Well-Founded Fear, University of Michigan Law School, March 2004, http://www.refugee.org.nz/fear.html.

[19]Goodwin-Gill (1998), pp. 66 f.

[20]D. Kugelmann, Refugees, 2010, p. 2, http://opil.ouplaw.com/view/10.1093/law:epil/9780199231690/law-9780199231690-e866?rskey=06ax1f&result=1&prd=EPIL.

[21]*Id.*, pp. 70 f.

[22]See Hathaway (2012), p. 178 and more detailed studies on jurisprudential developments in Coll and Bhabha (eds) (1992), Lambert (1995) and Symes and Jorro (2003).

[23]*Everyone has the right to freedom of opinion and expression; this right includes freedom to hold opinions without interference and to seek, receive and impart information and ideas through any media and regardless of frontiers* (Art. 19 Universal Declaration of Human Rights).

[24]Goodwin-Gill (1998), p. 49.

Refugees must be distinguished from IDPs,[25] or other types of migrants, including people fleeing natural disasters or generalised violence in their countries of origin. Although not covered by the Refugee Convention, certain other groups are, nonetheless, considered by the UNHCR as persons of concern. Over the last decades, UNHCR's mandate has been extended by the UNGA to cover not only refugees but also IDPs, stateless persons, people fleeing conflict or serious disturbances of public order, as well as returnees and include them in the operational protection scheme of the Office.[26]

2.4 Exceptions to Refugee Protection

While the inclusion clause of Article 1A Refugee Convention establishes criteria to identify persons coming within its scope, Articles 1D and 1E contain exclusion clauses limiting refugee eligibility.[27] This clause refers to persons that would normally qualify as refugees but are denied protection, either because they are protected through a specialised organisation such as the United Nations Relief and Works Agency for Palestine Refugees in the Near East (UNRWA) or because of full protection by their country of residence. Article 1F provides for the exclusion of refugee status for persons who have committed an international crime, such as war crimes, or crimes against humanity; who have committed a serious non-political crime outside the country of refuge prior to being admitted to the country as a refugee; or who are guilty of acts contrary to the principles and purposes of the UN.[28]

These grounds are exhaustive and to be applied restrictively.[29] International refugee law was designed to temporarily shift the responsibility of protection from

---

[25]IDPs are defined in the 1998 guiding principles on internal displacement as *person or groups of persons who have been forced or obliged to flee or to leave their homes or places of habitual residence, in particular as a result of or in order to avoid the effects of armed conflict, situations of generalized violence, violations of human rights or natural or human-made disasters and who have not crossed an internationally recognized State border.*

[26]UNHCR, Note on the Mandate of the High Commissioner for Refugees and His Office, http://www.unhcr.org/526a22cb6.html.

[27]G. Gilbert, Current Issues in the Application of the Exclusion Clauses, in: Feller et al. (eds) (2003).

[28]These crimes include crimes against the peace, war crimes, crimes against humanity; serious non-political crimes or acts contrary to the purposes and principles of the UN. For more information see Hathaway (2012), p. 189.

[29]On Terrorism: US Department of Justice, Office of the Attorney General, Matter of S-K-, 23 I&N 936 (BIA 2006); War Crime and Crimes against Humanity: United States Supreme Court, Negusie v. Holder, 555 U.S. 511, 2009; Grand Chamber of the Court of Justice of the European Union, Joined Cases C-57/09 and C-101/09 Bundesrepublik Deutschland v. B und D, 9 November 2010, ECR I-000; Particularly serious crime: UK High Court, R (on the application of) ABC (a minor) (Afghanistan) v. Secretary of State for the Home Department, 6 December 2011, EWHC 2937.

the home State to the host State for as long as the former State or the State of habitual residence is unable or unwilling to ensure protection. Therefore, the 1951 Convention in Article 1C contains a cessation clause, terminating refugee status and therewith protection, if persons voluntarily accept the protection of their country of origin, reacquire the nationality of their home State after having been stripped of it, acquire a new nationality and therewith protection of that State, voluntarily re-establish themselves in the country from which they fled or the circumstances leading to recognition as refugees have otherwise ceased to exist.[30]

Large-scale displacement in Asia and Africa has led to consensus on the drafting of regional refugee instruments designed to address the specific situation of refugees and other forced migrants.[31] Consequently, both the OAU Convention as well as the Cartagena Declaration expand the definition of refugee to include persons who

> owing to external aggression, occupation, foreign domination or events seriously disturbing public order in either part or the whole of [their] country of origin or nationality, [are] compelled to leave [their] place of habitual residence in order to seek refuge in another place outside [their] country of origin or nationality[32]

and

> persons who have fled their country because their lives, safety or freedom have been threatened by generalized violence, foreign aggression, internal conflicts, massive violation of human rights or other circumstances which have seriously disturbed public order.[33]

While these regional treaties and declarations are limited in their geographical scope, they extend the personal scope of application and thereby encompass a much broader group of protectees.

2.5 The Rights of Refugees

According refugee rights protection rights is attributed to the inherent nature of being a refugee and not dependent on a formal determination of the refugee status: *Recognition of his refugee status does not (...) make him a refugee but declared*

---

[30]UNHCR, Handbook on Procedures and Criteria for Determining Refugee Status under the 1951 Convention and the 1967 Protocol relating to the Status of Refugees, HCR/IP/4/Eng/REV.1 Geneva, 1992, http://www.unhcr.org/publications/legal/3d58e13b4/handbook-procedures-criteria-determining-refugee-status-under-1951-convention.html, p. 18.

[31]Arboleda (1991), pp. 185–207.

[32]Art 1 (2) OAU Convention Governing the Specific Aspects of Refugee Problems in Africa, http://www.achpr.org/files/instruments/refugee-convention/achpr_instr_conv_refug_eng.pdf.

[33]Conclusion 3 Cartagena Declaration on Refugees, https://www.oas.org/dil/1984_cartagena_declaration_on_refugees.pdf.

him to be one. He does not become a refugee because of recognition, but he is recognized because he is a refugee.[34]

The rights codified in Articles 2, 3 and 4 Refugee Convention, however, distinguish between different levels of entitlement, i.e., for refugees under a State's jurisdiction, refugees physically present in the State's territory, refugees lawfully present, refuges lawfully staying and refugees durably resident in the receiving State.[35]

The basic obligation flowing from the Refugee Convention is the principle of non-refoulement contained in Article 33, which forbids States from returning refugees to *frontiers of territories where his life or freedom would be threatened on account of his race, religion, nationality, membership of a particular social group or political opinion.*

Beyond the principle of non-refoulement, the fundamental rights established for refugees are heavily intertwined with and mirrored in HRL.[36] Refugees, generally, enjoy comparable rights to regular citizens of the receiving State concerning social security, labour or assistance as laid down in Articles 23 and 25 Refugee Convention. Further rights include the right to freedom of movement and the receiving State's obligation to issue travel documents; the right to liberty and security of the person, discussed in particular with regard to the detention of asylum seekers; and the right to family life, access to courts, regulations on employment and welfare, such as housing and public education.

3 Implementation and Enforcement of Refugee Law

International refugee law primarily establishes binding obligations for the signatory States of the relevant legal conventions based on international treaty law and the general principle of *pacta sunt servanda*—treaties are binding and must be performed in good faith.[37]

Obligations of States include cooperation with the UNHCR, in accordance with Article 35 Refugee Convention and Article 2 of its 1967 Protocol. Parties to the Convention and Protocol are obliged to cooperate with the UNHCR in the exercise of its functions and the implementation of the treaty. Furthermore, States parties need to inform the UNHCR about the national legislation that they have adopted to

[34]UNHCR, Handbook on Procedures and Criteria for Determining Refugee Status under the 1951 Convention and the 1967 Protocol relating to the Status of Refugees, HCR/IP/4/Eng/REV.1 Geneva, 1992, http://www.unhcr.org/publications/legal/3d58e13b4/handbook-procedures-criteria-determining-refugee-status-under-1951-convention.html, p. 28.

[35]Hathaway (2005), pp. 154 ff.

[36]See in detail, E. Lauterbach/D. Bethlehem, The Scope and Content of the Principle of Non-Refoulement: Opinion, in: Feller et al. (eds) (2003); UNHCR, UNHCR Note on the Principle of Non-Refoulement, November 1997, http://www.refworld.org/docid/438c6d972.html.

[37]Art. 26, Vienna Convention on the Law of Treaties.

ensure the implementation of the Convention.[38] While the UNHCR monitors the implementation of the Refugee Convention, the Office also works on durable solutions to end the displacement cycle. These durable solutions for refugees include voluntary repatriation, the return in safety and dignity to countries of origin, local integration to the host community or resettlement to a third State that is willing to admit them on a permanent basis.

Typically, the determination of refugee status is conducted by the national authorities of the receiving State, which leads to a diversity of different procedures and regulations. There are, furthermore, countries that are either not signatories of the Refugee Convention and its Protocol or unable to address and process asylum claims.[39] In these cases, the UNHCR carries out these determinations through its field offices.

Under normal conditions, asylum claims are processed on an individual basis. However, in certain cases of mass influx, single nation States and also the UNCHR will afford *prima facie* refugee status to members of the group as it was the case with people from southern and central Iraq or people fleeing the Syrian conflict.[40]

Some States and regions, most importantly the EU, have drafted common standards to unify and harmonise their legislation as regards immigration. However, even in the highly communitarized EU, the implementation of EU asylum law within the member States is not uniform. The principles regulating the European mechanisms have been heavily criticised as enabling the European States to circumvent their obligations towards refugees by outsourcing and offshoring their border and migration control mechanisms, and the legal instruments of the Common European Asylum System are under the constant scrutiny of national and regional courts, the UNHCR and NGOs working in the field of migration and refugee protection.

4 Minority Rights

Ethnic conflicts constitute serious threats to the peace and stability of international relations. The violent conflicts during the separation of Yugoslavia and the successor States of the Soviet Union are an indicator of the danger inherent in ethnic conflicts and the suppression of minorities. Due to political abuse of ethnic tensions, thousands of lives have been lost and millions of people have been forced to flee their homes. To address these recurring situations and crises, the international

[38]For a detailed analysis of the supervisory responsibilities of the UNHCR, see W. Kälin, Supervising the 1951 Convention Relating to the Status of Refugees: Article 35 and Beyond, in: Feller et al. (eds) (2003).

[39]Non-signatories include Afghanistan, Eritrea, India, Iraq, Lebanon, Libya, Pakistan, Syria and Ukraine among others.

[40]UNHCR, Resettlement Handbook, Geneva 2011, p. 77.

community and regional initiatives have codified specific legal protections for minorities.

4.1 Historical Development

Historical examples justify the consideration of minorities as vulnerable groups and therefore give them special importance in humanitarian crises and special attention by humanitarian action. Further, from a legal perspective, minority conflicts are not just internal affairs of States because they often disrupt regional peace and stability. Hence, a whole body of international law addresses minority rights.

After World War I, minority protection was internationalised by a system of peace treaties and the League of Nations because not all European peoples were able to exercise their right to self-determination and to establish their own independent States. Instead, the victorious powers formed multi-ethnic States like Czechoslovakia and Yugoslavia. To mitigate the consequences of the non-implementation of American President Wilson's Fourteen Points, which aimed to guarantee political independence and territorial integrity of all States, they decided to establish a minority protection system through several post-World War I treaties. It is often seen as an effort to satisfy minorities whose claims to self-determination had not been realised.

These territorial adjustments created new minorities in the newly established States. The concept of minority protection was seen as the second-best solution and resulted in the victorious powers concluding five minority treaties and four peace treaties that were tailored towards the specific situation within these States.

However, the precondition for the success of these minority norms was a readiness by States to cooperate. Following World War I, European States were not ready for the intensive international cooperation that was required to make the treaties work, insisting on sovereignty and a path of intolerant nationalism. Under these conditions, the envisaged minority protection system was untenable and consequently collapsed.[41]

Concerning the legal method applied in the minority and peace treaties after World War I, the treatment of minorities was addressed in terms of collective rights. Many provisions had group dimensions by conferring rights upon minority organisations. This approach was later misused by the Nazis to justify their territorial expansion into Czechoslovakia.

Against this historical background, States rejected any protection system for minorities in the post-World War II period. According to the new UN approach, minority rights became part of the system of human rights protection. In the 1950s, the UN considered the effective protection against discrimination in combination with general human rights a sufficient framework to ensure minority rights. The

[41]Eide (2005), p. 36.

dominant motivation for this was the fear of nationalist and secessionist movements. Some States also argued that according rights to certain groups would have negative consequences for the society, as well as minorities themselves. Special minority status, it was thought, would hinder nation building by putting entire groups in a separate category. However, in 1953, while the ICCPR was drafted, the UN Human Rights Commission began work on an article for the protection of minorities. The idea was to amend the provisions concerning human rights and non-discrimination by including an article on minority specific rights. The result of these discussions now constitutes Article 27 ICCPR, which reads:

> In those States in which ethnic, religious or linguistic minorities exist, persons belonging to such minorities shall not be denied the right, in community with the other members of their group, to enjoy their own culture, to profess and practice their own religion, or to use their own language.

4.2 *Holders of Minority Rights*

The wording of Article 27 ICCPR has given rise to many problems of interpretation, especially because the rights that the norm mentions are not available to the minorities as group rights.

Instead, the holders of these rights are individuals belonging to minorities. This constitutes a renunciation of the traditional approach of according groups collective rights. The switch was justified with the claim that minorities were subjects not of international but of domestic law.[42] The formulation is in line with the human rights approach of the ICCPR because human rights are individual rights.

However, Article 27 contains a collective element, reflected in the passage *in community with the other members of their group*. Thus, many scholars argue that the article may still be regarded as protecting a collective right.[43] At least, certain rights may be thought of in part as collective rights exercisable individually.[44] It is quite obvious that cultural rights require the recognition of collective rights since traditions and institutions can be kept only by a group as such.[45] The Human Rights Committee explains the supplementary quality of Article 27, which protects persons belonging to minority groups in addition to the rights the ICCPR grants to all individuals in general. The Committee argues in its General Comment 23 that this protection

> is directed towards ensuring the survival and continued development of the cultural, religious and social identity of the minorities concerned, thus enriching the fabric of society

[42]Nowak (1993), p. 495.

[43]Sieghart (1983), p. 377.

[44]Thornberry (1992), pp. 173–176.

[45]Hailbronner (1992), p. 133.

> as a whole. Accordingly [...] these rights must be protected as such and should not be confused with other personal rights conferred on one and all under the Covenant.[46]

Another issue of interpretation concerns the role of the State. According to the wording of Article 27 ICCPR, it is the State that must not deny the right of persons to enjoy their own culture. In this way, the State protects the existence of cultural communities. Ultimately, however, it is up to the State to determine which groups constitute minorities because there is still no generally accepted definition of a minority in PIL. The term is defined neither by Article 27 ICCPR nor by the 1992 Declaration on the Rights of Persons Belonging to National or Ethnic, Religious and Linguistic Minorities. Therefore, States maintain a high level of discretion and a considerable margin of appreciation in according minority status to groups and employ the concept in different ways.

Minority rights instruments do not clarify who can identify the relevant groups or determine which individuals belong to them. This power of the State contradicts the human right to self-identification, both at a group and personal level.

In PIL, it is sometimes controversial whether a group qualifies as a minority, evidencing a need for clear criteria. Some definitions discussed by academia containing the essential characteristics of minorities may help. These definitions have gained wide acceptance as the report of UN Special Rapporteur on the Prevention of Discrimination and Protection of Minorities, Francesco Capotorti, confirms.

Capotorti refers to objective and subjective characteristics.[47] An objective criterion for a minority is the existence of a population group with ethnic, religious or linguistic features that differ from the rest of the population. This group must be less numerous than the rest of the population in a multinational society. Being a non-dominant group in society is another objective criterion to constitute a minority. Dominant minorities are not vulnerable and therefore not entitled to special protection. The third criterion is that the members of the minority hold the citizenship of their country of residence, as well as long-standing ties with that State. Some experts criticise this last criterion and also consider immigrant groups as minorities because the enjoyment of minority rights, as with human rights generally, should not be narrowed by a nationality requirement. The Human Rights Committee, for its part, has denounced the nationality requirement in its General Comment 23. Just as members of minority groups need not be citizens, they need not be permanent residents: *Thus, migrant workers or even visitors constituting such minorities are entitled not to be denied the exercise of those rights* (Paragraph 5.2). While the inclusion of migrant workers was welcomed in the literature, such an inclusion was seen as unrealistic and difficult to defend.[48]

---

[46]Human Rights Committee, General Comment No. 23, Art. 27, 6 April 1994, UN-Doc. CCPR/C/21/Rev.1/Add.5.

[47]F. Capotorti, Study on the Rights of the Persons Belonging to Ethnic, Religious and Linguistic Minorities, 1979, UN-Doc. E/CN.4/Sub.2/384/Rev.1.

[48]Henrard, http://opil.ouplaw.com/view/10.1093/law:epil/9780199231690/law-9780199231690-e847?rskey=W2t5z2&result=1&prd=EPIL, para. 11.

The objective criteria are supplemented by a subjective one, which requires that the person concerned wishes to preserve his or her minority identity. This approach is consistent with the human rights dimension of minority protection and leads to the consequence that a person can choose to assimilate. However, the precondition is the decision of the person to choose freely to be treated as a member of the minority group or not. To avoid State abuse, it should not too easily be accepted that a group or person does not want to hold on to the minority identity.

4.3 Content of Minority Rights

The Human Rights Committee's General Comment 23 gives an impressive interpretation of the obligations of States:

> Although article 27 is expressed in negative terms, that article, nevertheless, does recognize the existence of a "right" and requires that it shall not be denied. Consequently, a State party is under an obligation to ensure that the existence and the exercise of this right are protected against their denial or violation. Positive measures of protection are, therefore, required not only against the acts of the State party itself, whether through its legislative, judicial or administrative authorities, but also against the acts of other persons within the State party.

Article 27 ICCPR outlaws discrimination against persons belonging to minorities and provides them protection and special rights. The goal is to secure the cultural survival of the minorities and to undertake specific protective measures according to the specific situation. States are obliged to provide assistance, including financial support, to ensure the survival of minorities. The following minority rights are of special importance:

- use of a minority language by members of the minority group and among themselves;
- publication of newspapers and books;
- use of a minority language to publicly express views;
- establishment of institutions such as schools and cultural organisations;
- effective opportunities for children to acquaint themselves fully with the language and culture of their group; and
- effective exercise of all fundamental human rights without discrimination.

Minorities must be ensured substantive equality and safeguarding of their minority identity. This means not only formal equality by treating everybody exactly the same but also considering all relevant circumstances. This may at times also justify differential treatment. The 1992 UN Declaration emphasises more explicitly the rights to identity and to substantive equality. The document moves away from the negative formulation of Article 27 ICCPR and avoids clauses like 'where possible' and 'where appropriate', which were used by States as excuses for inactivity in the promotion of minority rights. While the Declaration is not legally binding, it is of political importance and underlines the political interest of the international community to realise all human rights for everybody.

5 The European Dimension of Minority Protection

The dissolution of both the Soviet Union and Yugoslavia were accompanied by bloody confrontations. Violations of minority rights were one of the grounds for the hostilities. It became obvious that Europe was in need of new instruments in the field of minority protection. The Organization for Security and Co-Operation in Europe (OSCE) was a pioneer in this regard at the end of the Cold War.

A breakthrough was the Concluding Document of the Copenhagen Meeting of the then Conference on the Human Dimension of the then Commission on Security and Cooperation in Europe (CSCE) of 29 June 1990, which combined principles of democracy and positive obligations on States to protect and promote minority identities. During the CSCE meeting in 1990, it was recognised that the treatment of minorities was directly relevant to stability in Europe. In 1992, the Netherlands made a revolutionary proposal for the establishment of the post of the CSCE High Commissioner on National Minorities (HCNM). The respect for minority rights is in principle no longer exclusively an internal affair of the OSCE States. While the HCNM is not intended to side with minorities, the institution can act as an instrument of early warning and conflict resolution.

This legal situation is underscored by general PIL, which also recognises the rights of the suppressed to resist massive violations of minority rights, such as serious discrimination. Under these circumstances, the affected national minority can be entitled to make use of its right to self-determination.[49] This would undoubtedly be a very extreme conclusion to draw, and it poses the question of how serious a violation of minority rights has to be to provide proportional justification for a claimed right to secession. This question remains contested.

The underlying problem of proportionality highlights the difficulty of distinguishing between the legitimate right of resistance and terrorism. It is understandable that the right of decision was not given to the HCNM. The first HCNM, Max van der Stoel, rightly argued that the mandate *doesn't deserve the beauty prize for clarity*.[50] But this also implies flexibility and gives the Commissioner a great deal of freedom. Despite the formal restrictions of the mandate and the political sensitivity of the issues, there was room for a pragmatic interpretation.[51] One of the ways to exploit this freedom was the appointment to work out recommendations concerning different minority rights issues. These recommendations are collections of best practices in the fields of education rights,[52] linguistic rights,[53] effective

[49]Doehring (2002), p. 57, para. 36.

[50]van der Stoel (1999), p. 13.

[51]Ghebali (2009), p. 114.

[52]OSCE, The Hague Recommendations regarding the Education Rights of National Minorities, October 1996.

[53]OSCE, The Oslo Recommendations regarding the Linguistic Rights of National Minorities, February 1998.

participation in public life[54] and the use of minority languages in the broadcast media.[55] One can consider these documents as starting points for future standard setting.

In the COE framework, two legally binding treaties on minority issues entered into force. The first one is the 1992 European Charter for Regional or Minority Languages and the 1995 Framework Convention on National Minorities. The latter treaty is the first legally binding instrument on this topic and contains a catalogue of special minority rights.

6 Conclusion

The legal protection of both refugees and minorities has been on the international agenda for decades and has led to various binding and non-binding legal instruments to enshrine their rights on the international and regional level, as well as at the domestic level. This chapter has provided an overview of these two fields of PIL. Although heavily codified and implemented in numerous States under the supervision of international and regional State and non-State organisations, their application is still challenged during and after contemporary crises triggered by armed conflicts and natural disasters around the world. The protection of vulnerable groups, in particular, depends on the continuous reappraisal of existing laws in the light of contemporary challenges, its evolution and adaption to new situations, and the awareness of opportunities and limits by all actors involved.

References

Books and Reports

Coll G, Bhabha J (eds) (1992) Asylum law and practice in Europe and North America: a comparative analysis. Washington

Feller E, Türk V, Nicholson F (eds) (2003) Refugee protection in international law. UNHCR's Global Consultations on International Protection, CUP, Cambridge

Goodwin-Gill GS (1998) The refugee in international law, 2nd edn. OUP, Oxford

Hathaway JC (2005) The rights of refugees under international law. CUP, Cambridge

Lambert H (1995) Seeking asylum: comparative law and practice in selected European countries. Dordrecht

McAdam J (2005) Complementary protection in international refugee law. Oxford University Press, Oxford

[54]OSCE, The Lund Recommendations on the Effective Participation of National Minorities in Public Life, September 1999.

[55]OSCE, Guidelines on the Use of Minority Languages in the Broadcast Media, October 2003.

McAdam J (2012) Climate change, forced migration, and international law. Oxford
Sieghart P (1983) The international law of human rights. Oxford
Symes M, Jorro P (2003) Asylum law and practice. Haywards Heath
Thornberry P (1992) International law and the rights of minorities. Oxford University Press, Oxford

Articles and Book Chapters

Arboleda E (1991) Refugee definition in Africa and Latin America: the lessons of pragmatism. Int J Refug Law 3(2):185–207
Battjes H (2006) European asylum law and international law. In: Immigration and asylum law and policy in Europe series. Martinus Nijhoff Publishers, Leiden
Doehring K (2002) Self-determination. In: Simma B (ed) The Charter of the United Nations, a commentary. Oxford
Eide A (2005) Historical and global perspective. In: Weller M (ed) The rights of minorities. Cambridge
Ghebali V-Y (2009) The high commissioner on national minorities after 15 years: achievements, challenges and promises. Secur Hum Right 20
Hailbronner K (1992) The legal status of population groups in a multinational state under public international law. In: Dinstein Y, Tabory M (eds) The protection of minorities and human rights. Dordrecht
Hathaway JC (2012) Refugees and asylum. In: Opeskin B, Perruchoud R, Redpath-Cross J (eds) Foundations of international migration law. Cambridge
Henrard K, Minorities, international protection. In: Max Planck Encyclopedia of Public International Law [MPEPIL], online version, access: http://opil.ouplaw.com/view/10.1093/law:epil/9780199231690/law-9780199231690-e847?rskey=W2t5z2&result=1&prd=EPIL
Nowak M (1993) CCPR Commentary, Article 27. Kehl
Plender R, Mole N (2000) Beyond the Geneva Convention: constructing a *de facto* right of asylum from international human rights instruments. In: Nicholson F, Twomey P (eds) Refugee rights and realities. Evolving international concepts and regimes. Cambridge
van der Stoel M (1999) Peace and stability through human and minority rights. Baden-Baden, p 13

Other

Cartagena Declaration on Refugees, https://www.oas.org/dil/1984_cartagena_declaration_on_refugees.pdf.
International Federation of the Red Cross and Red Crescent Societies, Guidelines for the Domestic Facilitation and Regulation of International Disaster Relief and Initial Recovery Assistance, 2007.
OAU Convention Governing the Specific Aspects of Refugee Problems in Africa, http://www.achpr.org/files/instruments/refugee-convention/achpr_instr_conv_refug_eng.pdf.
UNHCR, Handbook on Procedures and Criteria, http://www.unhcr.org/publications/legal/3d58e13b4/handbook-procedures-criteria-determining-refugee-status-under-1951-convention.html

Further Reading

Goodwin-Gill GS, McAdam J (2007) The refugee in international law, 3rd edn. Oxford University Press

Henrard K (2013) Minorities, international protection. Max Planck Encyclopedia of Public International Law

Vedsted-Hansen J (ed) (2015) The refugee law reader. Cases, documents, and materials, 7th edn. Hungarian Helsinki Committee

Weller M (2005) The rights of minorities. A commentary on the European Framework Convention for the protection of national minorities. Oxford University Press

Hans-Joachim Heintze is Professor for Public International Law at the Institute for International Law of Peace and Armed Conflict (IFHV) and Director of the NOHA Joint Master's Programme in International Humanitarian Action at Ruhr University Bochum, Germany.

Charlotte Lülf is Lecturer and Research Associate at the Institute for International Law of Peace and Armed Conflict (IFHV) and teaches in the among others legal modules of the NOHA Joint Master's Programme in International Humanitarian Action.

Part III
Public Health

Learning Objectives

This part of our textbook aims for students to:

- Understand basic terminology and concepts related to public health;
- Understand the basic patterns of excess mortality and morbidity, which can be expected in various emergency and refugee situations, as well as their determinants; and
- Know standard technical/managerial approaches to provide public health, especially as provided by consensus documents.

We add a section on challenges, dilemmas, do's and don'ts at the end of each subchapter to help place this consensus in perspective.

Basic Concepts and Current Challenges of Public Health in Humanitarian Action

Siri Tellier, Andreas Kiaby, Lars Peter Nissen, Jonas Torp Ohlsen, Wilma Doedens, Kevin Davies, Dan Brun Petersen, Vibeke Brix Christensen, and Niall Roche

Research assistance: Nick Skenderian, MSc Global Health student, University of Copenhagen.

Reviewer: Rudi Coninx, Humanitarian Policy and Guidance, WHO.

Editors: Siri Tellier and Niall Roche.

S. Tellier (✉)
University of Copenhagen, Copenhagen, Denmark
e-mail: stellier@sund.ku.dk

A. Kiaby
DanChurchAid, Yangon, Myanmar
e-mail: anki@dca.dk

L.P. Nissen
ACAPS/University of Copenhagen, Geneva, Switzerland
e-mail: lpn@acaps.org

J.T. Ohlsen
Haukeland University Hospital, Bergen, Norway
e-mail: jonastorp@gmail.com

W. Doedens
United Nations Population Fund, Pers Jussy, France
e-mail: doedens@unfpa.org

K. Davies
Danish Red Cross, Copenhagen, Denmark
e-mail: kd4uhere@yahoo.co.uk

D.B. Petersen
Zealand University Hospital, Koege, Denmark
e-mail: danbrun@gmail.com

V. Brix Christensen
Copenhagen University Hospital, Copenhagen, Denmark
e-mail: brixchr@dadlnet.dk

N. Roche
Trinity College Dublin, Dublin, Ireland
e-mail: roche.niall@gmail.com

© Springer International Publishing AG 2018

H.-J. Heintze, P. Thielbörger (eds.), *International Humanitarian Action*,
DOI 10.1007/978-3-319-14454-2_13

1 Introduction

Siri Tellier

1.1 General Concepts and Approaches

A disaster is commonly defined as 'a serious disruption of the functioning of a society, causing widespread human, material, or environmental losses, which exceed the ability of the affected society to cope using its own resources'.[1]

This definition, by the United Nations Office for Disaster Risk Reduction (UNISDR) disaggregates the concept of disaster into three aspects: the event (disruption), the impact (losses) and the response (cope) and thereby lays the foundation for analysing what can be done to address each aspect, reducing risk. It is also the definition currently used by the World Health Organization (WHO). More recently, UNISDR has defined disaster as

> a serious disruption of the functioning of a community or a society at any scale due to hazardous events interacting with conditions of exposure, vulnerability and capacity, leading to one or more of the following: human, material, economic and environmental losses and impacts.[2]

The annotation to this definition provides:

> The effect may test or exceed the capacity of a community or society to cope using its own resources, and therefore may require assistance from external sources, which could include neighbouring jurisdictions, or those at the national or international levels.[3]

This definition opens up for further analysis, for example moving away from a blanket assumption that the community or society cannot cope.

The literature often refers to 'natural' vs 'man-made' disasters. This categorisation is not consistently applied, but the term 'natural' disaster is often used to refer to earthquakes or hurricanes and sometimes droughts, epidemics and technological disasters, whereas 'man-made' disasters often refer to armed conflict. This approach is increasingly criticised as many 'natural' disasters are influenced by human action (for example, deforestation leading to mud slides or, conversely, strict building codes limiting the damage caused by earthquakes). Disaster management focuses more and more on societal factors that influence risk and vulnerability in order to identify measures for disaster risk reduction.

---

[1]WHO, Health Action in Crisis – definitions, http://www.who.int/hac/about/definitions/en/ (accessed 2017.03.08).

[2]United Nations Office for Disaster Risk Reduction (UNISDR), Terminology on Disaster Risk Reduction, http://www.unisdr.org/we/inform/terminology (accessed 10.03.2017).

[3]*Ibid.*

Rather than categorising a disaster as either man-made or natural, it is perhaps more relevant to identify whether or not it involves armed conflict as this is more significant for its root causes, impact, as well as what response would be appropriate. Thus, a complex (political) emergency is commonly defined as 'a situation with complex social, political and economic origins which involves the breakdown of state structures, the disputed legitimacy of host authorities, the abuse of human rights and possibly armed conflict, that creates humanitarian needs'.[4] The term 'is generally used to differentiate humanitarian needs arising from conflict and instability from those that are the result of natural disaster'.[5]

The terms 'disaster', 'complex emergency', 'humanitarian crisis' and many others are at times applied rather inconsistently. Here, we will use the initial definition of 'disaster' as an umbrella working definition for the type of scenario in which public health measures come into play.

Another term that has come into use over the last decade is that of 'fragile states', sometimes referred to as 'failed states', 'fragile situations' or 'chronic disasters'. There is no agreed definition of the term (or indeed that the term refers to a whole nation State), but there is some agreement on its fundamental characteristics. Thus, the World Bank notes:

> State policies and institutions are weak in these countries, making them vulnerable in their capacity to deliver services to their citizens, to control corruption, or to provide for sufficient voice and accountability. They face risks of conflict and political instability [... and] (t)wo billion people live in countries where development outcomes are affected by fragility, conflict and violence.[6]

In such situations, health systems are challenged, making it more difficult to prevent or respond to disasters, including 'natural' disasters such as epidemics. In parallel, the term 'resilience' has appeared. The UNISDR defines it as

> [t]he ability of a system, community or society exposed to hazards to resist, absorb, accommodate to and recover from the effects of a hazard in a timely and efficient manner, including through the preservation and restoration of its essential basic structures and functions [...].[7]

To build resilience, it is important to understand the societal conditions that may turn a hazard into a disaster. 'Humanitarian Action' is based on the concept of 'disaster' as defined above, namely that the society concerned cannot cope with the impact of a hazardous event and therefore needs external assistance. The vulnerability or coping capacity of the affected society—whether it is more or less fragile,

[4]WHO, Health Action in Crisis – Definitions, referring to a definition by ALNAP, http://www.who.int/hac/about/definitions/en/ (accessed 10.03.2017).

[5]*Ibid.*

[6]World Bank (2005), p. v, http://documents.worldbank.org/curated/en/907971468327613700/pdf/34790.pdf.

[7]UNISDR, Terminology on Disaster Risk Reduction, http://www.unisdr.org/we/inform/terminology (accessed 10.03.2017).

more or less resilient—is central to deciding whether humanitarian action is indeed necessary and what form it should take.

It also leads to one of the key challenges of humanitarian action: how a large number of external humanitarian actors should coordinate their actions. A new epoch in international humanitarian action began with the adoption by the United Nations General Assembly of Resolution 46/182 to strengthen coordination of humanitarian emergency assistance. The resolution provides that 'humanitarian assistance should be provided with the consent of the affected country and in principle on the basis of an appeal by the affected country'[8] and that '[i]nter-governmental and non-governmental organizations working impartially and with strictly humanitarian motives should continue to make a significant contribution in supplementing national efforts'.[9]

In practice, local authorities may be temporarily unable to coordinate the flow of external assistance, and it remains a contentious issue. Over the last two to three decades, a great amount of effort has been put into the harmonisation of approaches. This section therefore frequently refers to widely used standards of the so-called Sphere Project and the guidelines of the Inter Agency Standing Committee (IASC).

The WHO defines 'health' as 'a state of complete physical, mental and social well-being and not merely the absence of disease or infirmity'[10] and public health as '[t]he science and art of promoting health, preventing disease, and prolonging life through the organized efforts of society'.[11]

Public health in humanitarian action (PHHA) builds on these definitions, addressing both preventive and curative measures and both determinants of health, such as nutrition, water, sanitation and hygiene promotion (WaSH) or environmental health, as well as essential health services, such as treatment of injury, control of communicable and non-communicable diseases, and also mental health. Measures such as these, which seek to meet basic needs, are often referred to as 'relief'. In emergencies, human rights abuses that jeopardise life in dignity (for example, gender-based violence) also become public health concerns. Measures to address these issues are usually grouped under the term 'protection'.

There is broad agreement that the overall objective of PHHA, at least in the acute phases of emergency response, is to prevent excess mortality and morbidity and assist those affected by disaster to lead lives in dignity. Mortality is seen as a key measure to analyse how an emergency is evolving.[12] This overall focus on mortality is informed by the dramatic increase in mortality levels that have been observed in

[8]UN General Assembly, 78th Plenary meeting (1991), Strengthening of the coordination of humanitarian emergency assistance of the United Nations, A/RES/46/182, para. 3.

[9]*Id*, para. 5.

[10]WHO (1948): http://www.who.int/governance/eb/who_constitution_en.pdf.

[11]WHO (1998), p. 3 (adapted from the Acheson Report, London, 1988), http://www.who.int/healthpromotion/about/HPR%20Glossary%201998.pdf.

[12]The Sphere Project (2011).

the past, rising to 40–50 times the normal level among refugees, for example those fleeing the Rwandan genocide.[13]

To quantify *excess mortality and morbidity*, the usual approach is to estimate pre-disaster mortality/morbidity levels (for protracted emergencies, sometimes the mortality rate in neighbouring countries is used as a proxy) to arrive at a *baseline mortality*. This is then compared with levels observed during the emergency, to determine *excess mortality*.

The metrics most commonly used to assess mortality are mortality in the overall population and mortality in children under five since, in emergencies, children under five have seen some of the greatest levels of excess mortality.

The threshold level for classifying a situation as an Acute Public Health Emergency (APHE) is often set at levels exceeding one death/10,000 people/day or two deaths of children under five/10,000 children under five/day. These levels were suggested in 1990, when they represented a doubling of baseline levels of mortality in developing countries. Since then, mortality levels have declined. Therefore, some standards such as those of the Sphere Project suggest that the threshold level should also be reduced and be calculated for each emergency as a doubling of the relevant baseline level of mortality.[14]

The standard levels are probably best applied as a way to focus surveillance attention on excess mortality rather than as a fixed level, and they may not be equally relevant for all emergencies.

Even in calmer times, resources are rarely sufficient to meet public health needs, and usually, the response must be prioritised, according to which factors cause the greatest amount of harm, and where a response can do the most to prevent such harm. In disasters, prioritisation becomes especially relevant as health problems may grow rapidly at the same time as local resources to deal with them may be decimated.

Prioritisation is in principle based on risk analysis. Risk analysis is utilised in many fields, but here we will refer to one form of *risk equation* adapted to public health[15]:

$$R = H \times E \times V/C$$

where R signifies risk (for example, the risk of excess deaths due to measles), H signifies hazard (for example, the likelihood and extent of a measles epidemic), E signifies exposure (for example, crowded conditions in refugee camps, leading to higher exposure), V signifies vulnerability (for example, malnutrition, which greatly increases case fatality) and C signifies coping capacity (for example, due

[13]Checchi and Roberts (2005); Toole and Waldman (1990), pp. 3296–3302; Salama et al. (2004), pp. 1801–1813.

[14]Checchi and Roberts (2005); Toole and Waldman (1990), pp. 3296–3302; The Sphere Project (2011).

[15]Boudreau (2009), p. 30; Johns Hopkins and IFRC (2008).

The former source refers to $R = H \times V/C$ whereas the latter source adds E to the equation.

to vaccination). It should be noted that the intention is not to give a mathematically precise formula, but rather an interrelationship.

Prioritisation has developed over time based on experience. Médecins Sans Frontières (MSF) proposed an early listing in 1997, which included 10 actions, such as assessment and measles vaccination. The listing of what to include as priority public health measures has evolved over time. For example, reproductive health issues, or mental health and psychosocial support, have now been included, and most recently, non-communicable diseases are beginning to receive attention.[16] Here, we will follow the listings as given in the Sphere Handbook.

Within many essential health services, detailed guidelines have been developed, with a view to harmonising approaches, notably by the IASC and the Sphere Project.

The time factor is significant in disasters, influencing both the human impact and the appropriate response. Disasters range from 'sudden-onset' (sometimes referred to as 'rapid-onset') events such as earthquakes, which may last seconds, to slow-onset or chronic situations such as droughts, or protracted armed conflict, which may last years or decades.

Over time, frequent reference has been made to the 'disaster cycle' (Fig. 1), reflecting a basic concept of societies shifting between times of what is often termed 'normalcy' and sudden or slow-onset disaster. This cycle is reflected in disaster management: urgent response to the onset of a sudden or slow-onset disaster (for example, surgery), transits into recovery assistance activities (for example, rehabilitation from surgery), mitigation and prevention during non-disaster phases (for

Fig. 1 The disaster cycle. Reproduced by kind permission of the publisher from D.E. Alexander, How to write an Emergency Plan (Dunedin Academic Press, Edinburgh, 2016)

[16]Toole and Waldman (1990), pp. 3296–3302; The Sphere Project (2011); MSF (1997), pp. 43–54; Demaio et al. (2013).

example, improving building codes and practices) and, lastly, preparedness and surveillance (for example, mapping the location of disabled persons who may need assistance in case of an earthquake) in view of coming or impending disasters.

The concept of the disaster cycle has been widely used over the last 30–40 years, with scholars debating its origin. The concept has been challenged since it may provide a somewhat simplistic and sequential impression of the stages of a disaster. However, it remains an important analytical framework.

Disaster preparedness is essential, if quick and effective action is to be taken. Yet disasters are very diverse and often develop in unpredictable ways. Therefore, preparedness is often based on an *all-hazards approach*, with certain standard elements in place, which can then be adjusted as the emergency unfolds.

Decisions must be taken very quickly, often based on incomplete information. Therefore, situation assessment and information management are essential, both at the stage of initial rapid assessment (IRA) and throughout the later process. This includes establishing key demographic and epidemiological indicators.

To strengthen preparedness, a practical PHHA approach is to develop standard preparedness elements based on past experience. One example is the Interagency Emergency Health Kit (IEHK), an agreed list of medicines, pre-packaged and sometimes pre-positioned. The kit is intended to serve 10,000 people for 3 months, at either community, regional or referral clinic/hospital level, based on a standard demographic composition. As information about the specific situation is collected and analysed, such elements can be flexibly deployed and adjusted over time.

1.2 Challenges, Dilemmas, Dos and Don'ts

A central challenge of humanitarian action is to establish its overall goal and level of ambition. During acute phases of an emergency, the stated objective is a return to *normalcy*. During times of recovery, and especially in mitigation or development phases, the objective may be to 'build back better', reducing vulnerability and increasing coping capacity of populations and their health systems in a sustainable manner. The objective of disaster response is to return to normalcy, whereas the objective of mitigation/development may be to change that *normalcy*.

This simple point can be contentious. For example, should a targeted emergency feeding programme aim to give beneficiaries' perfect nutritional levels if the surrounding population has high levels of malnutrition and yet receives no aid? Should an emergency health programme provide services free of cost or subsidise construction of latrines if the surrounding population has to pay for services or receives no subsidies, in accordance with governmental policy? Should humanitarian action address only injury due to an earthquake or also life-threatening injury from traffic accidents, or should they also advocate for a change in building codes to prevent future injury?

This is an eternal and real dilemma. Global frameworks have arguably paid too little attention to the interaction between humanitarian and development assistance, as well as how to facilitate early recovery. The new UN Sustainable Development Goals adopted by the UN General Assembly in September 2015[17] repeatedly refer to the importance of resilience to natural disasters, which may increase attention. The Sendai Framework for Disaster Risk Reduction, adopted in March 2015, also stresses the need for resilience and 'building back better', notably mentioning improved health not only as a goal in humanitarian response but also as a factor that increases resilience.[18]

Another challenge has been referred to above: how to balance between preparing for generic disasters and ensuring that the response is context specific and culturally suitable. Continual follow-up assessment of responses is essential to help navigate this dilemma.

Finally, one may question the overall focus of humanitarian action on saving lives. What about saving livelihoods?

2 Basic Demographic and Epidemiological Concepts

Siri Tellier

Demography is the quantitative study of the structure (age, sex, location) of populations, changes therein (mortality, fertility, migration) and the determinants and consequences of these characteristics.

> Epidemiology is the study of the distribution and determinants of health-related states or events (including disease), and the application of this study to the control of diseases and other health problems.[19]

Given the overriding objective to prevent excess mortality, it is important to establish baseline levels. The two most important ones are as follows:

- *crude death rate (CDR)*: number of deaths per 1000 population (as of mid-year) per year (sometimes expressed as per cent, for example 1% of the population dying in any given year);
- *under-five mortality (U5M)*: proportion of children dying before the age of five, expressed per 1000 live births (sometimes as per cent, for example 10% of children under five dying before they reach their 5th birthday).

In emergencies, mortality levels can change dramatically within days. In such cases, recourse to yearly rates is insufficient, and emergency metrics have been established that are more time sensitive and simple to calculate:

- *crude mortality rate (CMR)*: deaths per 10,000 population per day;
- *under-five mortality rate (U5MR)*: deaths of children <5 per 10,000 children <5 per day.

---

[17]UN General Assembly Resolution, Transforming our world: the 2030 Agenda for Sustainable Development A/RES/70/1, http://www.un.org/ga/search/view_doc.asp?symbol=A/RES/70/1.

[18]UN, Sendai Framework for Disaster Risk Reduction 2015–2030, A/CONF.224/L.22015.

[19]WHO, Health Topics, Edpidemiology, http://www.who.int/topics/epidemiology/en/.

Comparing emergency and baseline metrics is simple for crude mortality. A CMR of 1/10,000 population per day translates into a CDR of 36.5/1000/year or 3.65%. Present global levels of mortality are around 10/1000 or 1% per year in most countries. Thus, the emergency level represents 3–4 times the baseline level in most countries.

As regards U5M, the comparison is more complicated and confusing. The emergency metric, U5MR, is a simple rate: a level of 2/10,000/day translates into a rate of 73/1000/year. If maintained over 5 years, this results in 36.5% of children dying before the age of five. For the baseline metric, U5M is a cumulative proportion. The global average stands at less than 5% of children dying before the age of five. As it is complicated to calculate U5M life expectancy, and unrealistic to do so in an emergency, the U5MR metric is useful, as long as it is not simply compared to U5M.

Other important concepts related to mortality and morbidity include the following.

Case Fatality, Sometimes Referred to as Case Fatality Rate (CFR) Proportion of people diagnosed with an illness who die from it. It is usually applied to acute, short-term illnesses such as cholera, which can be observed over a limited period. CFR varies greatly depending on the vulnerability of the population and the quality of response and is therefore a useful monitoring indicator. For example, case fatality to measles may be as high as 10–30% in malnourished children living in high-exposure refugee settings, whereas it may be 1% in well-nourished children with lower exposure.

Attack Rate Proportion of people who fall ill after a specified exposure. It is often expressed as a percentage (for example, 10% of the refugees in the camp were diagnosed with cholera during the most recent epidemic).

Case Definition Set of diagnostic criteria that must be fulfilled to identify a case of a particular disease. Case definitions can be based on clinical, laboratory, epidemiological or combined clinical and laboratory criteria. When a set of criteria is standardised for purposes of identifying a particular disease, it is referred to as a 'standard case definition'.

Proportional Mortality It refers to the proportion of all deaths due to a specific cause.

Incidence It is the number of new cases of a disease during a specified period of time, divided by the population number at risk during that period.

Prevalence Number of existing cases of disease at a given point in time divided by the population at risk. The time period is chosen to fit the situation.

Ratio It is a comparison of two numbers, where the denominator and numerator do not necessarily refer to the same population (for example, *sex ratio* refers to the number of males per 100 females).

Rate Measure of the speed or frequency with which an event occurs within a defined population that is at risk in a defined time frame. The numerator refers to the same population as the denominator (for example, U5MR refers to the number of deaths of children under five, divided by the number of children under five).[20]

Disability-Adjusted Life Years (DALYs) Sum of years of life lost (YLL) to premature mortality within a population and years lived with disability (YLD).[21] This metric was developed for the first 'global burden of disease' study, capturing not only fatalities but also years lived with disability.

Mortality and morbidity may be the most obvious metrics, but others are equally important. They include the following:

Crude Birth Rate (CBR) It refers to the number of live births per population of 1000 (mid-year) per year.

Children Different sources use different age groupings or do not indicate a precise age—for example, 'women and children' is a meaningless metric unless it is clear whether the age grouping refers to children aged 0–4 (under five), 0–17 (under 18) or something else. The Convention on the Rights of the Child is generally taken to refer to children as anyone aged under 18 (that is, minors).

Refugee is defined as a

> [P]erson who [. . .] owing to a well-founded fear of being persecuted for reasons of race, religion, nationality, membership of a particular social group or political opinion, is outside the country of his nationality, and is unable to or, owing to such fear, is unwilling to avail himself of the protection of that country or return there because there is a fear of persecution. . .. .[22]

Internally Displaced Persons (IDPs): these are

> [P]ersons or groups of persons who have been forced or obliged to flee or to leave their homes or places of habitual residence, in particular as a result of or in order to avoid the effects of armed conflict, situations of generalized violence, violations of human rights or natural or human-made disasters, and who have not crossed an internationally recognized State border.[23]

Household It refers to one or more persons living together who make common provision for food or other essentials.[24]

Health Facility Utilisation Rate It is the number of outpatient visits per year (may also be calculated for a shorter period).

Number of Consultations/Clinician/Day This pertains to the number of first-time or repeated visits per full-time equivalent clinician per day.

---

[20]Checchi et al. (2007).

[21]WHO, Metrics: Disability-Adjusted Life Year (DALY), http://www.who.int/healthinfo/global_burden_disease/metrics_daly/en/.

[22]Art. 1 (A)(1)(2).Convention of 1951 relating to the Status of Refugees and its 1967 Protocol.

[23]Guiding Principles on Internal Displacement (E/CN.4/1998/53/Add.2), 1998, Principles and Scope.

[24]*Cf.* UN Statistics Division, http://unstats.un.org/unsd/demographic/sconcerns/fam/fammethods.htm#A1 (accessed 17 January 2017).

3 The Overall Human Impact of Emergencies

Siri Tellier

3.1 Concepts and Baseline Situation

In 2015, the global population stood at about 7.4 billion. The annual number of deaths was approximately 55 million, resulting in a global crude death rate (CDR) of around 8/1000 or, in approximate terms, about 1%.[25] This rate is fairly constant across populations since higher-mortality populations also tend to be younger.

Out of those deaths, in 2015, around 20% were due to what is commonly referred to as 'group 1' diseases (communicable diseases, maternal/perinatal and nutritional disorders), 70% resulted from 'group 2' diseases (non-communicable diseases (NCDs), esp. cardiovascular disease, cancer, diabetes and chronic obstructive pulmonary disease (COPD)) and around 10% were due to a group 3 disease (injury).[26]

Several types of transition influence the evolution of these overall levels and the environment in which PHHA is delivered. The most important of these are as follows.

Demographic Transitions Populations in most countries are ageing and increasingly live in urban areas. Almost all future population growth will take place in urban areas of developing countries, and population will be of older ages.[27] This shift is a main contributor to the increase in NCDs.

Epidemiologic Transitions Most countries, including high-, middle- and low-income countries (HMLICs), have undergone a shift from group 1 to group 2 diseases as the main cause of death. This is due not only to the success of controlling group 1 diseases but also to increasing risk factors associated with ageing and urbanisation. A few decades ago, close to 20% of children died before the age of five, mostly from communicable diseases and malnutrition. Vaccination, antibiotics and improved nutrition and WaSH, as well as general development, have contributed to cutting the U5MR to less than 5%.

Disaster Transitions Many sources point to an observed, and/or expected, increase in the numbers of people affected by extreme weather, especially floods and storms.

---

[25]UN World Population Prospects, the 2015 Revision; http://esa.un.org/unpd/wpp/DataQuery//dataquery/ (accessed on 10 March 2017).

[26]Global Burden of Disease 2015 Mortality and Causes of Death Collaborators (2016), pp. 1459–1544.

[27]UN World Population Prospects 2015; http://esa.un.org/unpd/wpp/DataQuery//dataquery/ (accessed on 10 March 2017).

There is some variance in what pathways are identified as the cause of such increases—because the number of events has grown or because populations are increasingly concentrated in urban areas vulnerable to such events.[28] Seismic events (earthquakes, tsunamis) are still responsible for the largest number of deaths, but their prevalence seems to remain at a constant level.[29]

Observers also note a shift from international conflicts of defined duration to longer-term, low-intensity situations of violence, often in urban settlements, in *fragile* contexts, and with many involving non-State actors.[30] In recent years, several MICs, rather than LICs, have experienced large-scale emergencies and situations of conflict, with Iraq and Syria being prime examples.

Response Transitions Since 1991, the number of international actors in humanitarian assistance and funding has increased rapidly. Thus, in the aftermath of the 2010 earthquake in Haiti, several hundred international NGOs engaged in relief efforts. Funding has increased from less than 1% of official global development assistance (ODA) to around 10%, although shortfalls remain.[31] A combination of increasing concerns about security, as well as technological innovation, is leading to a rapidly changing role of web-based tools, in collecting information as well as in developing responses—what some observers have termed 'cyber-humanitarianism'.[32] There is also a move toward providing cash or vouchers rather than goods such as food because it is less demanding in terms of logistics and may prove less disruptive for local markets. Emerging donors, including the private sector, increase both the complexity and opportunities of humanitarian action. Transitions provide an increasingly complex image of how the emergency landscape is forecast to change and what the humanitarian consequences might be. The growing number of emergency and fragile situations, leading to population movements, poses major challenges. Lessons from situations such as the Ebola pandemic have added to the evidence base, including by providing one more example that the expressed goal of *involving* local communities has not succeeded,[33] yet is crucial for building resilience. This fact may heighten awareness that anthropological approaches may be useful—where not necessarily bringing in foreign anthropologists but building on local knowledge.[34]

---

[28]Véron and Golay (2015).

[29]IDMC (2014).

[30]Spiegel et al. (2010), pp. 341–345; IDMC/NRC/UNHCR (2015).

[31]Pan American Health Organization (PAHO) (2010) and Telford and Cosgrave (2006).

[32]OCHA (2012).

[33]ALNAP et al. (2015).

[34]WHO (2015a) and DuBois et al. (2015).

3.2 Levels and Possible Pathways to Excess Mortality and Morbidity

Emergencies can cause dramatic increases in mortality.[35] Historically, the big killers were starvation and epidemics, both of which claimed millions of lives. For example, the Spanish flu of 1918 is estimated to have killed 25–50 million people (more than World War I). Famine caused an estimated 20–40 million deaths in China between 1958 and 1961. Conflicts in the twentieth century (especially the two World Wars), are estimated to have claimed a total of 50–100 million lives.[36]

In recent decades, death tolls as a result of disasters are estimated to be lower than these historical levels. Some of the highest fatality numbers occurred during the Rwandan genocide (estimated to have caused 500,000–1,000,000 deaths) or starvation in the Democratic People's Republic of Korea in the mid-1990s (estimated to have resulted in similar numbers). Since 2000, the 2004 Indian Ocean tsunami and the earthquake in Haiti in 2010 are estimated to have caused 200–300,000 deaths each. The conflict in Syria was estimated to have caused around 200,000 deaths in 2014,[37] with newer numbers even higher, but also highly contested.

As horrendous as these numbers are, the one thing that may be encouraging is that recent death tolls are not as high as those seen in more distant history.

As is always the case in epidemiology, it is important to disaggregate these overall death tolls to help identify the pathways leading to excess mortality and morbidity, and ways in which to disrupt those pathways. The level and cause of any death toll are influenced by many variables. Below are some.

Type of Disaster Droughts may cause starvation, whereas injury is the main cause of death in earthquakes.[38] Historically, communicable diseases have caused especially high levels of death. There is growing recognition that this may change, at least where such diseases occur in the wake of natural disasters, as long as health systems remain in place and displacement is limited.[39]

Phase of Disaster Most deaths in the early phases of conflict are related to violence, whereas in later phases, for example after massive displacement, deaths due to communicable diseases may increase, as protective structures break down (for example, WaSH).[40]

Age/Sex After the 2005 tsunami hit Sri Lanka, one study indicated that children under five had the highest mortality, and females aged 20–40 had much higher

---

[35]Checchi and Roberts (2005); Toole and Waldman (1990), pp. 3296–3302.

[36]Alexander (2006), pp. 1–23.

[37]Price et al. (2014).

[38]Doocy et al. (2013), p. 36.

[39]The Sphere Project (2011); Guha-Sapir et al. (2007), pp. 1338–1341.

[40]Guha-Sapir et al. (2005).

mortality rates than males of the same age.[41] In LMICs, average female mortality has been found to be higher than male mortality in natural disasters. Average female mortality rates are often more elevated in natural disasters, while male mortality rates may be higher in armed conflict.[42] During the 2011 cholera epidemic in Haiti, men were dying at higher rates than women. This was interpreted to be due to men attending cholera treatment centres less frequently than women as men were ill informed about the symptoms of cholera, mistaking them for those of HIV.[43]

Battle/Non-battle Deaths One major challenge in calculating death tolls in armed conflict is to determine how many deaths are directly due to battle injury as opposed to deaths indirectly caused by conflict, especially group 1 causes such as malnutrition or disease. An oft-heard statement is that out of the total number of deaths that World War I caused, 90% concerned combatants and only 10% civilians, whereas the opposite is true for World War II. Although the origin and evidence base of this quote are difficult to trace, several recent studies do estimate levels of indirect deaths in conflict to be many times higher than direct battle deaths.[44]

Physical/Economic Environment Generally, LICs have higher death tolls than MHICs in otherwise similar disasters. Beyond the human impact, it should be noted that economic losses are higher for HICs in absolute terms but lower as a proportion of GDP.[45] Thus, the 2011 Japan and 2010 Haiti earthquakes caused approximately 16,000 and 200,000 deaths respectively, but Japan incurred $200 billion in damages compared to Haiti's $2 billion.

Resilience of Populations/Health Systems Sri Lanka experienced little post-tsunami mortality in 2005, despite warnings that epidemics should be expected. This has been attributed to a resilient health care system, a strong civil society and an educated population.[46] Health systems that are overwhelmed by one type of disaster (for example, Ebola), and where trust in the health system is low, may result in deterioration in health services for other areas, such as maternal health, as the population avoids seeking clinical care.[47]

Forced displacement is a major risk factor. In recent decades, refugee numbers gradually declined and stood at around 15 million, whereas the number of IDPs gradually increased to around 25 million.[48] However, the recent crisis in Syria has

[41]Tellier (2014), p. 22, http://www.acaps.org/search?search_query=demographic+profile&=%E2%9A%B2.

[42]*Ibid.*

[43]DG ECHO Thematic Policy Document no. 6: Gender – Different Needs, Adapted Assistance, July 2013, p. 6, http://ec.europa.eu/echo/files/policies/sectoral/gender_thematic_policy_document_en.pdf.

[44]Geneva Declaration Secretariat (2008), p. 174; Lacina and Gleditsch (2005), pp. 145–166.

[45]Wisner et al. (2004).

[46]Munasinghe (2007), pp. 9–11.

[47]Lyengar et al. (2015).

[48]UNHCR (2014), pp. 2–3.

led to about four million refugees and nine million IDPs (out of a total pre-conflict population of around 20 million). For 2015, this brings the global total of people forcibly displaced as a result of persecution, conflict, generalised violence or human rights violations to around 65 million. This is often misrepresented as being the greatest refugee crisis since World War II. The United Nations High Commissioner for Refugees (UNHCR) and the World Bank have published a correction to that misunderstanding: it is the largest number of refugees since the early 1990s, but with respect to IDPs, whose numbers are only estimated since 1989, the comparison cannot be made.[49] UNHCR identifies situations involving more than 25,000 refugees for more than 5 years as major protracted refugee situations.[50] Using this definition, nearly two-thirds of refugees in the world today—over six million people—are caught in protracted refugee situations. With displacement, life-sustaining coping capacities that populations have built up over centuries (food production, quality WaSH, shelter and family support) may disappear. Recent studies indicate that, within displaced populations, refugees generally have the best health indicators; IDPs have the worst, with those who have not fled conflict areas occupying an intermediate position. The interpretation is that refugees fall under the protection of organisations such as the UNHCR. Those remaining in their homes may still have access to some of the life-support mechanisms that they had before the conflict. However, IDPs often reside in areas where they have little means to support themselves but may indeed have fled because they are at odds with parties to the conflict, so that they cannot expect help.[51]

A group thus far receiving little attention is that of persons displaced by sudden or slow- onset *natural* disaster, including climate change. The terminology and definition are not clear. People concerned are sometimes referred to as '*climate* migrants', 'climigrants' or 'environmental refugees'. Given the difficulties in defining these groups, it is perhaps not surprising that there are as yet few estimates of their numbers. Recent studies estimate the number of people displaced by slow-onset natural disasters to have doubled over the last decades. Such populations are, to some extent, in a governance limbo—no convention or declaration or international organisation is devoted to their protection.[52]

Lastly, the issue of morbidity receives less attention than mortality. However, there is some development, for example, with the increased attention to mental health and psychosocial support, which may not cause death and yet cause major problems, not least in situations of protracted displacement. The 2015 Sendai Framework refers to the importance of chronic disease, maybe indicating increased

[49]World Bank/UNHCR (2016). Forcibly Displaced: Toward a development approach supporting refugees, the internally displaced, and their hosts ADVANCE EDITION. © 2016 International Bank for Reconstruction and Development/The World Bank 1818 H Street NW, Washington, DC 20433.

[50]UNHCR, EC/54/SC/CRP.14, paras. 3–5.

[51]CRED (2013), see p. 6 for a summary of the situation described above.

[52]DMC, Norwegian Refugee Council (2011).

attention by the international humanitarian community.[53] Attention to other chronic non-communicable diseases such as diabetes or heart disease has increased greatly since the beginning of the Syrian crisis, given that the affected population is higher income, as well as older and more urbanised than was the case in earlier crises, and therefore had higher levels of NDCs and also had received better treatment pre-crisis. The inclusion in the Sustainable Development Goals may also help focus attention.

3.3 Challenges, Dilemmas, Dos and Don'ts

Levels of mortality, morbidity and other health-related metrics are extremely difficult to estimate yet are often quoted with misleading precision. For example, excess deaths in the Democratic Republic of Congo are estimated at between 200,000 and over four million, depending on the method of determination used.[54]

Furthermore, the emphasis in recent decades has been on mortality. This chapter discusses public health in humanitarian action, so we can hardly suggest that the study of mortality is unimportant. However, other health metrics, including for morbidity (for example, DALYs), arguably deserve higher prominence than they receive today. Tackling root causes remains a challenge for preparedness.

4 Governance in Humanitarian Action

Andreas Kiaby and Siri Tellier

4.1 The Role of Governance in Humanitarian Action

What makes governance in humanitarian action different from governance in more stable times? To answer this question, let us return to the working definition of disaster, established in Sect. 1, which requires calling a situation a disaster when it is a hazardous event, when it has great impact and when it may be beyond the coping capacity of the society concerned. One major question follows from this definition: if a society is unable to cope with the disaster, what happens to the rules that have governed that society so far?

---

[53] UN, Sendai Framework for Disaster Risk Reduction 2015–2030, A/CONF.224/L.22015.

[54] Coghlan et al. (2006), pp. 44–51; Coghlan et al. (2009), pp. 88–96; Lambert and Lohle-Tart (2009), http://adrass.net/WordPress/wp-content/uploads/2010/09/Excess-Death-Toll-in-DRC-1998-2004-diffusion.pdf.

During crises, especially in times of conflict, questions abound: is there a legal obligation to provide aid to victims in need? If so, who must fulfil this obligation and according to which standard? To what extent is the State affected by disaster allowed to restrict or deny such help? What rules and principles govern external aid and interventions where the State is unwilling or unable to care for people within its territory? Can States intervene in another State to provide humanitarian support without that State's consent? How can the government cope not only with the disaster but with the international actors?

In peacetime, the obligations of a State during natural disasters towards the population on its territory are primarily regulated by national laws. This means that national laws also define the humanitarian response (sometimes referred to as disaster response law), including issues related to health care. These laws and policies may concern entitlement to free government health care, what is considered to be the right to abortion, qualifications required to practise medicine or rules governing the import of medication.

However, national laws may be at odds with States' international obligations, so that humanitarian operators must find a way to strike the right balance and ensure that every response contributes to the respect, protection and fulfilment of international obligations while considering national specificities.

A key human rights document concerning health care is the International Covenant on Economic, Social and Cultural Rights (ICESCR) of 1966. It establishes the right to health (Article 12) and binds signatory States to 'take steps, individually and through international assistance and cooperation' to achieve the full realisation of this right. This is a direct obligation on States parties to seek and provide international assistance in order to achieve human rights obligations related to health, food, education and shelter. Refusing to request and facilitate such assistance on an arbitrary basis and in times of crisis may, in fact, amount to a violation of human rights law.

There are several reasons why States choose to restrict international assistance during conflict. Security-related concerns, real or not, are among the main grounds. In some cases, denial of consent for humanitarian relief, or constraints imposed on the delivery of such, may even be part of a military strategy of starving the enemy or the civilian population. Another important constraint on humanitarian access is the growing perception over the past years that humanitarian aid has become more and more politicised.

The Geneva Conventions (GCs), the core of international humanitarian law (IHL), have been universally ratified, indicating consensus on the obligations of States to assist and protect their civilian populations against the effects of armed conflict and to grant impartial humanitarian actors access to conflict areas to deliver aid and relief (what is often referred to as 'humanitarian space').The obligation to ensure respect for the GCs means that all States must do everything in their power to end violations of IHL, for example by exercising their influence over their armed forces and by facilitating the delivery of impartial, neutral and independent humanitarian aid, such as health care services and medicine.

Other relevant IHL provisions relate to the respect and protection of humanitarian and medical relief personnel and objects and to the prohibition to use starvation of the civilian population as a method of warfare.

States have expressly recognised that impartial humanitarian organisations have an important role to play in addressing humanitarian needs. Public international law, including IHL, has over time recognised that humanitarian services cannot be regarded as either unlawful interference in domestic affairs of a State or as an unfriendly act. However, impartial efforts must be distinguished from so-called *humanitarian interventions* or actions related to the *responsibility to protect*, which are controversial and highly politicised concepts. Although IHL is relatively clear about the issue of access for humanitarian actors to conflict areas,[55] the reality is that access has to be negotiated on a daily, if not hourly, basis in many current conflicts, for example in Syria.

The humanitarian principles of neutrality, impartiality and independence are reflected in many different cultures and documents and codified particularly in the GCs and a number of UN Security Council and UN General Assembly Resolutions. They are widely cited as the basis for humanitarian action. Impartial action means that the greatest amount of aid is given to those with the greatest need without unlawful discrimination (such as on the basis of political affiliation or ethnicity).

In order to fulfil their mandate impartially, humanitarian organisations must be able to act independently of other interests, such as the priorities of their donors. To receive access to populations in need, organisation and their staff must be perceived as neutral, exemplified by the trust of all parties to the conflict and must refrain from becoming embroiled in controversies.

International refugee law and principles related to IDPs are also relevant where such populations are present. The Refugee Convention came into force in 1951 in the aftermath of World War II, with large populations of refugees.[56] The 1998 Guiding Principles on Internal Displacement were developed in response to the observations that conflicts were increasingly internal and of longer duration, resulting in large numbers of IDPs. However, the Guiding Principles are not yet legally binding.[57] In recent decades, a number of initiatives to protect specific populations are being created.[58]

[55]Arts. 23 GC IV and Art. 70(2) AP I.

[56]UNHCR (2011).

[57]Guiding Principles on Internal Displacement (E/CN.4/1998/53/Add.2), 1998, Principles and Scope.

[58]ICRC (2015), pp. 1–4.

4.2 Challenges, Dilemmas, Dos and Don'ts

Regardless of whether humanitarian relief is sanctioned by law and whether consent has been given or not, the ability to operate depends on the situation on the ground. You as a humanitarian actor are often confronted with practical questions. Do the militia members manning checkpoints trust and respect you? Do the local village chiefs consent to male medical staff providing medical treatment for women of the village? Do you feel your professional ethics dictate you to act in a manner that is not in accordance with national laws? The way actors in conflict perceive you and your actions will often be more crucial than the applicable laws.

Compliance with relevant international obligations is particularly challenging. What do you do when a State's national law is on your side but its rule of law is weak and no one seems to comply? Often, negotiation skills and persuasion, using a mix of arguments drawing on law, religion and local culture may be more appropriate than reciting the GCs. Another dilemma lies in conflicts between humanitarian organisations' moral values and national laws, even where those laws do not violate international norms. For example, how would you react if you were a medical doctor faced with a victim of gang rape who wishes to have an abortion in a country where abortion is illegal under all circumstances, even to save the mother's life? How would you balance when to report and go public with your knowledge of massive human rights abuses with the risk of the government throwing you out of the country for publicly displaying its crimes? The targeting of medical staff shows that such questions are delicate to navigate in often hostile environments and that the humanitarian space is in jeopardy.[59]

5 International Coordination of Humanitarian Aid

Lars Peter Nissen and Siri Tellier

5.1 The Evolution of the International Humanitarian System

The idea that one should help people in need is central to many religions and cultures, but internationally organised humanitarian aid is a relatively recent development. It poses new dilemmas, with one of the most common being that it may be seen as interfering with the concept of national sovereignty.

The first major efforts to provide material assistance to victims of armed conflict were undertaken by the International Committee of the Red Cross (ICRC), founded

[59] ICRC (2011).

in 1863. It provided health care to injured soldiers on the battlefield who were considered *hors de combat*. As noted above, this was only possible because the States concerned had acceded to the GCs, providing the humanitarian space necessary for such action. Over the next decades, many humanitarian organisations emerged. Much later, in 1991, another game-changing milestone came, triggered by images of humanitarian workers handing loaves of bread to Kurdish refugees fleeing the First Gulf War. With the end of the Cold War in 1991 and new challenges looming, new possibilities for joint action seemed possible. UN General Assembly Resolution 46/182[60] called on the UN to take a more active role in coordinating international humanitarian assistance and established structures for the following:

- leadership (including what is now called the Emergency Relief Coordinator, heading the UN Office for Coordination of Humanitarian Action (OCHA));
- operational and technical coordination (including the already mentioned Inter-Agency Standing Committee (IASC)); and
- funding mechanisms (including what is now called the Central Emergency Response Fund (CERF) and the Consolidated Appeals Process (CAP)).

The IASC, as a coordinating body, includes UN organisations as well as well other major actors, including the Red Cross/Red Crescent Movement and several non-governmental organisations (NGOs), either as full members or standing invitees.

In response to the experiences gained over the last decades, the system has undergone major changes. Major inter-agency evaluations of the response to large-scale humanitarian crises such as the Rwandan genocide in 1994, the Indian Ocean tsunami of 2004, the 2010 earthquake in Haiti, and floods in Pakistan have all had an effect.

The 1994 Rwandan experience focused attention on the need to develop common operational standards and guidelines (for example, IASC guidelines, as well as the Sphere Project, which by now includes hundreds of NGOs, as well as Red Cross/Red Crescent members). In addition to harmonising approaches, such standards also provide a basis to hold humanitarian actors accountable. The Humanitarian Accountability Partnership is another effort at standardising Humanitarian Accountability and Quality Management.

In the wake of the response to the 2004 tsunami, which revealed major operational gaps, and taught humanitarians some severe lessons, a major humanitarian reform was initiated by the then UN Emergency Relief Coordinator, Jan Egeland. To meet the challenges, a *cluster* system was developed (see Part I, Chapter 6, Figure 2 of this textbook), which grouped organisations and assigned leadership duties. For example, WHO is the global lead of the *health cluster*, UNICEF leads WaSH and nutrition, UNHCR heads the protection cluster and UNHCR and IFRC co-lead the shelter cluster. Within clusters, certain organisations may be assigned to

[60] UN General Assembly, 78th Plenary meeting (1991), Strengthening of the coordination of humanitarian emergency assistance of the United Nations, A/RES/46/182, para. 3.

take on special roles: for example, the United Nations Population Fund (UNFPA) is the unofficial lead on reproductive health within the health cluster and on sexual and gender-based violence (SGBV) within the protection cluster. At the local level, operational leadership may also be transferred to another organisation if the global lead has limited capacity.

An increasing focus on local capacity, risk reduction and 'building back better' also fed into the 2005 Hyogo Framework of Action: Building the Resilience of Nations and Communities to Disasters and its follow-up—the 2015 Sendai Framework of Action on Disaster Risk Reduction. It focuses on the issue of health issues, not only as an effect of disasters but also to improve the disaster resilience of communities.

The 2010 earthquakes in Haiti and floods in Pakistan focused attention on the need for extraordinary effort in extraordinary situations, termed 'level 3 emergencies'. The 'transformative agenda' was adopted to try to meet this challenge, as well as to follow up on the humanitarian reform process in general. More recently, then UN Secretary General Ban Ki-moon convened a World Humanitarian Summit (WHS) to follow up on these developments. The WHS was held in Istanbul on 23–24 May 2016, with a focus on four themes:

- humanitarian effectiveness;
- reducing vulnerability and managing risk;
- transformation through innovation; and
- serving the needs of people in conflict.

If one were to point to the most concrete result of the conference, it might be the emphasis on *localisation*, which means that funding streams should increasingly be channelled through local organisations, to build capacity.

5.2 *Challenges, Dilemmas, Dos and Don'ts*

Coordination remains an area of enormous progress despite the equally enormous challenges that remain. Some of these will be explored in the coming sub-chapters, when we turn to operational issues. These include essential health services (for example, communicable disease control), protection (for example, with respect to sexual and gender-based violence), as well as determinants of health (for example, WaSH).

As mentioned above, in any disaster, prioritisation of actions is crucial. An early attempt at listing such priorities is MSF's *Refugee Health*[61] of 1997. The 2011 Sphere Handbook builds on this work, adding mental health, reproductive health, as well as the beginnings of issues related to non-communicable diseases, and emphasising health systems.

[61]MSF (1997), p. 174.

6 Assessing Humanitarian Needs

Jonas Torp Ohlsen and Siri Tellier

The importance of assessing humanitarian needs is underlined in several instruments. For example, Sphere Handbook core standard number 3 states that '[t]he priority needs of the disaster-affected population are identified through a systematic assessment of the context, risks to life with dignity and the capacity of the affected people and relevant authorities to respond'.[62] This point is reiterated in the Core Humanitarian Standard.[63] There are also a large number of guidelines, which detail the conduct of such assessments, both by content and organisation,[64] including the Multicluster/Sector Initial Rapid Assessment (MIRA).[65] This chapter reflects on the key recommendations of some of these instruments.

6.1 Why Assessments?

Disasters are by their nature chaotic and dynamic, the result of a change from a *normal* situation to an evolving crisis. Demographic and epidemiological data are central in order to assess both the baseline situation as well as the extent of the change caused by the disaster concerned. Information management is one of the most basic skills of humanitarian action.

Specifically, data from such assessments serve, among others, to

- guide operational responses; estimate the overall scale with regard to three dimensions: geography, sector and affected population group; assess needs; monitor progress, including performance, outcomes and impact;
- report to the outside world, advocate for appropriate intervention, raise funds, account for their utilisation; and
- inform security assessments.

Data are essential to give the basis for targeting and prioritisation. One of the most common challenges is that the parties concerned may question why aid is given to one group rather than another. Data can sometimes help to show that such choices are indeed *needs based* and thereby *impartial*.

[62]The Sphere Project (2011), Core Standard No. 3.

[63]Groupe URD HI (2014).

[64]Global Health Cluster Rapid Health Assessment Guidelines, 2007.

[65]IASC (2012).

6.2 When Should Assessments Take Place?

Assessment should be a continuous process, not a one-off event. Data are assembled

- *prior to a crisis*, globally (for example *rules of thumb* or *standard populations*, which can be used as a basis for global preparedness such as health kits) or locally (for example, early warning systems, surveillance);
- *in the first hours after conflict begins or disaster strikes*, before field data can be collected (for example, based on web-based secondary data to adjust global *standard populations* to the local situation and establish baselines);
- *in the first days after the event*: primary data collected in the field can be used as input for an initial rapid assessment; such assessments are often qualitative and not statistically significant;
- *over the next few weeks/months*: sector-specific surveys, including elaboration of statistically sophisticated quantitative data; Fig. 2 is a representation of this timeline.

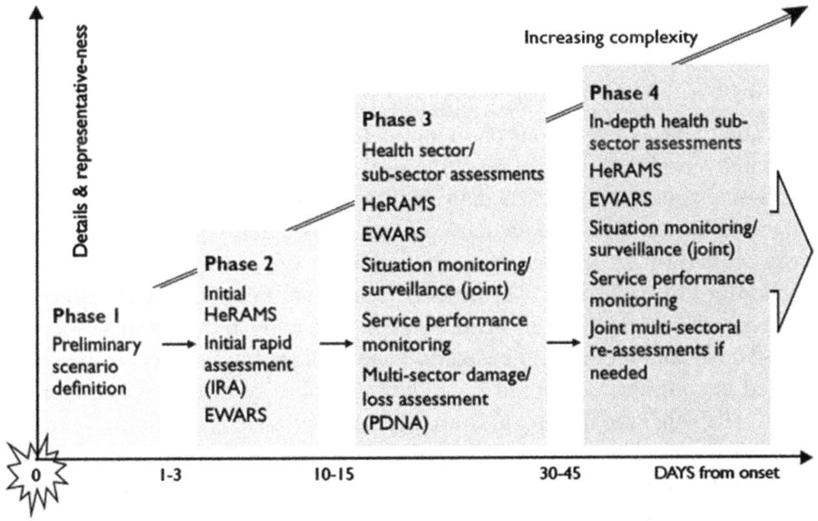

Fig. 2 Phases of data collection, analysis and planning following a major, sudden-onset crisis. Reprinted by kind permission of the WHO from WHO Health Cluster, Provisional Version, Chapter 3, Assessment and Health Situation Monitoring, p. 72, Copyright (2009), http://www.who.int/hac/network/global_health_cluster/chapter3.pdf?ua=1 (accessed on 14 April 2017)

6.3 Basic Principles of Data Assessment

Basic principles include the following, which are well known but inconsistently applied:

- *Do no harm* (do not collect data that hurt the respondent or enumerator).
- *Prioritise* (collect only the data that you need).
- *Adjust to a time frame*.
- *Triangulate* (collect data from different sources: compare them, distinguishing differences due to diverse methods from differences due to trends over time and place).
- *Be aware* of how data are presented to the population (empower people, do not cause panic).
- *Plan carefully* (think about what data and logistics are needed).
- *Coordinate* (do not duplicate what others have collected).

Additionally, as the Assessment Capacities Project (ACAPS) suggests, there are three important principles[66]:

- Know what you need to know. Collect only data which are needed.
- Make sense, not data. Don't collect new data if you can analyse existing data to get the answer you need.
- Don't be precisely right, be approximately right.

As Gilbert Burnham personally suggested to me once, in January 2010: 'public health is about making decisions on incomplete information'. Keeping this in mind, shortcuts and simplified ways of reaching useful data may need to be applied. Here, we emphasise collecting baseline data, including those available from the Internet, and this is for a reason. Local data are often of poor quality and difficult to access, and even more difficult and dangerous to collect *de novo*. For example, on average, about one-third of births and two-thirds of deaths are not adequately registered.

However, there has been an upsurge in high-quality big data available on the Internet. Those data are usually based on local sources but have been analysed and interpreted according to standard procedures, are easily available and sometimes less politically sensitive than local sources. We emphasise *high quality* sources—as is always the case for data, it is important to carefully choose the source, for example the UN and the CIA World Factbook may not be equally acceptable as a source, even if the data they present are the same.

[66]ACAPS Director, Lars Peter Nissen, MIT center for civic media, October 2012 http://civic.mit.edu/blog/mstem/talking-fast-at-crisismappers-the-ignite-talks, accessed 2017.03.11.

Table 1 Demographic profiles of five countries, 2010–2015

	Japan	Brazil	Niger	Afghanistan	Iran
Population, million	126	200	20	32	79
Total fertility rate	1.4	1.8	7.5	5	1.9
Crude birth rate, %	0.8	1.5	5	3.4	1.9
Crude death rate, %	1	0.7	1.3	0.8	0.5
Under 5 mort./1000	3	24	127	92	22
Mat. mort. ratio/100,000 live births	5	56	590	400	23
Children <5, % (aged 0–4)	4	7.5	22	15	9
Women of rep. age, % (15–49)	21	27	20	23	28
'Older' people, % (60+)	33	12	4	4	9

Developed by the authors, Siri Tellier and Jonas Torp Ohlsen, based on data from the United Nations. From World Populations Prospect: The 2012 Revision, Volume II: Demographic Profiles, by United Nations, Department of Economic and Social Affairs © 2013. Reprinted with the permission of the United Nations. http://esa.un.org/unpd/wpp/Publications/Files/WPP2012_Volume-II-Demographic-Profiles.pdf (accessed on 14 April 2017)

6.4 *What/How: Demography*

Priority humanitarian operational action as outlined above includes such relief measures as providing tents for households, measles vaccinations for children under 5/under 15, age-appropriate food distribution or providing birthing kits and emergency obstetric care for pregnant women. For each of these cases, it is important to determine the demographic composition of the population. Such data are also needed as a denominator for other rates, for example mortality. To determine the demographics at pre-crisis times, *standard populations*, such as those provided in the Sphere Handbook,[67] are widely used.

However, country demographic profiles may vary greatly. For an indication of possible ranges, see Table 1 for five country profiles for the period of 2010–2015.[68]

As a pre-crisis rule of thumb, CBRs are usually in the range of 1% for HICs, 2% for MICs and 4–5% for LICs. CDRs are more uniform around 1% (±0.5%). The percentage of children under five is generally approximately five times the CBR (for example, $5 \times 1.5\% = 7.5\%$ for Brazil). Mortality rates are almost uniformly higher for males than for females, especially in the age group 0–4, and the proportion of women of reproductive age is 25% (±5%). Generally, there is little reason to use regional averages as even the demographic profiles of neighbouring countries can differ significantly (for example, Afghanistan and Iran in Table 1). When a crisis occurs, these rules of thumb may have to be refined within minutes, by producing a country-specific demographic profile from web-based data, as given above. Where humanitarian action moves into primary data collection, it may be

[67] The Sphere Project (2011).

[68] United Nations Department of Economic and Social Affairs' World Populations Prospect 2012, Volume II: Demographic Profiles, http://esa.un.org/unpd/wpp/Publications/Files/WPP2012_Volume-II-Demographic-Profiles.pdf.

sufficient to use an approximation of 20% of children aged 0–4 rather than conducting large-scale surveys, which may (or may not) arrive at slightly more precise numbers, but which may also leave out many respondents, and may not account for the fact that many people do not know their precise age.

Shortcuts and triangulation methods may be used to compensate for poor data quality, such as categorising any person shorter than 105–110 cm as under 5 years of age or estimating the number of deaths from the number of graves at the site. Some key methods and data references for a more detailed understanding of this matter can be found in the suggested reading section at the end of the public health part.

6.5 What/How: Epidemiology

As per the above-mentioned principles, before beginning the collection of primary data, available secondary data should be assembled. In the first weeks after a crisis, primary qualitative data may be useful if collected in a systematic manner, down to the anecdotal level. Primary quantitative data should preferably be statistically significant. Given the effort involved in collecting primary quantitative data, one should only set out to gather this type of data if all other data seem insufficient. When compiling data, preparation is crucial:

- Think through what data are needed—prepare dummy tables (draft final report).
- Pilot questionnaires and interview technique to ensure questions are understood and acceptable within the respective setting. Translate and back translate to ensure wording is accurate.
- Enumerators must be well trained—language skills are essential.
- Logistics as well as security considerations are key.

Qualitative methods include the following.

Health Walk Observe marketplaces, clinics, fields, pharmacies and note who visits them, what the prices are, whether markets are selling relief goods and get a feel for the current general atmosphere. You could use a systematic questionnaire (or simply take notes).

Focus Group Discussions Ensure that key populations with specific needs, who might otherwise not be heard, are included (for example, women).

In-depth Interviews with Key Informants These may include religious/community leaders, health staff, clients, private pharmacy owners, etc.

Rumour Management Collecting and assessing rumours is a recognised component of epidemiological intelligence. You may (carefully) establish it as part of your health information system, for example by asking health personnel and others to report *cases of acute, watery diarrhoea* (suspect cholera).

Quantitative methods, based on sampling (ideally statistically significant), are usually based on a statistical analysis of what the necessary sample size should be, and the households (individuals) are chosen thereafter depending on the situation according to the following methods.[69]

Convenience Sampling Pick out any sample you find conveniently accessible. Such samples are unlikely to be representative.

Purposive Sampling Pick respondents from each of the groups you find most significant. They will often be outliers, for example the poorest group, orphans, etc. Again, these samples will not be representative but can provide you with important information.

Snowball Sampling Interview one person who can help you identify the next person of importance to your analysis. Again, this method will not lead to representative results.

Simple Random Sampling You can use this method if you know the population size and specific locations (for example, address, registry) so that you can select households randomly. However, this is rarely the case in crisis.

Systematic Sampling You know what you need, for example a 10% sample, and households are arranged in an orderly manner, for example tents or street numbers. You may pick the first household randomly (for example, choose a number between 1 and 10) and then interview every 10th household.

Multistage Cluster Sampling You know the overall population size, but households are not systematically numbered. Here, you would first subdivide into divisions and then into clusters and, lastly, randomly identify the needed number of households within each cluster.

Assessments should be ongoing, and you can feed data obtained by using the methods described above into a health information system to complement service data from health service points.

6.6 Challenges, Dilemmas, Dos and Don'ts

Despite the many existing guidelines on the importance of sharing and harmonising data, humanitarian organisations have generally not followed this advice. Instead, they produce a profusion of uncoordinated reports. There is also criticism that the data collected do often not focus sufficiently on the most pressing issues, for example injury after earthquakes.[70] One of the reasons often mentioned for the lack of coordination is that organisations try to keep data to themselves as prime data enhance their visibility, which in turn makes it easier to obtain funding. Several studies have examined the usefulness of assessment results and data gathering for the planning of operations. They found that agencies, to a certain extent, do not use their data very

---

[69] IFRC (2013) and MSF (2006).

[70] PAHO (2010).

well; that initial assessments (which are supposed to be prepared in the first 72 h) are often prepared very late; and that there is significant overlap between assessments.[71]

7 Cooperation with Local Health Systems

Jonas Torp Ohlsen and Siri Tellier

Despite the fact that local health systems may temporarily be unable to cope with the effects of humanitarian crises, it is a guiding principle of humanitarian action that international actors should closely cooperate with local health systems (and populations) wherever possible.

7.1 Concepts and Baseline Situation

The WHO has proposed to approach health systems based on the so-called six building blocks (see Fig. 3).

This approach suggests analysing health systems according to the following components.

Health Service Delivery Health services can be provided in various ways, for example via accessible and acceptable service delivery points, often arranged in a three-tier system. For example, there may be one primary service delivery point per

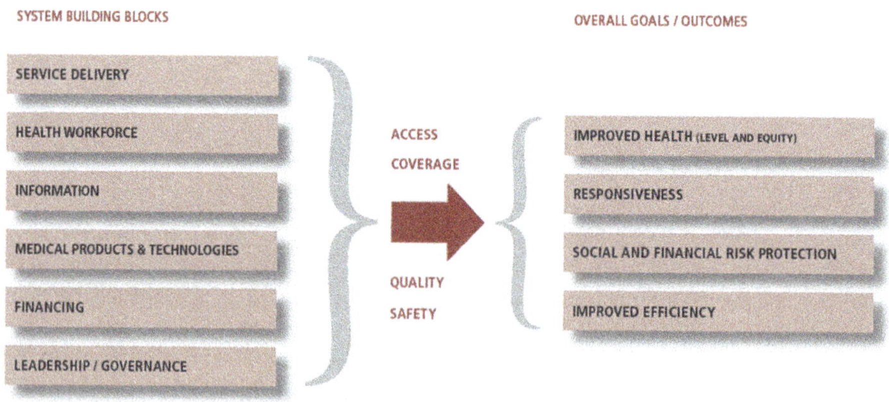

Fig. 3 The six building blocks of a health system: aims and desirable attributes. Reprinted by kind permission of the WHO from WHO, Everybody's Business: Strengthening Health Systems to Improve Health Outcomes. WHO's Framework for Action, Introduction, p. 3, Copyright (2007), http://www.who.int/healthsystems/strategy/everybodys_business.pdf (accessed on 14 April 2017)

[71]Olin and von Schreeb (2014) and Garfield et al. (2011).

population of 10,000; one secondary point per 50,000; and one tertiary/referral point for every population of 250,000.

Human Resources The health field is often regulated in terms of qualifications required to practise. In addition, in many countries, traditional health personnel (for example, traditional birth attendants—TBAs) are major providers, and need to be taken into account, even if they may not be part of the official health system.

Drugs and Medical Supplies These items are in principle regulated by essential drug lists, protocols for prescription or regulations for disposal of outdated drugs. In many States, private pharmacies are *de facto* not only the main source of drugs but also the most used health facility.

Health Financing In LICs, total health expenditure (THE) may be as low as 20 USD per capita per year, compared to 6000 USD in High HICs such as the US. Populations in LICs pay a higher-than-average proportion of THE out of their own pockets, and in some fragile contexts there is often almost no public, taxpayer-financed access to health services.

Health Information Management This may include health information systems (for example, service statistics), surveillance systems and research.

Leadership and Coordination Public health may be planned and regulated by governments or professional organisations.

7.2 Fragility and Resilience of Health Systems in Emergency Situations

In emergencies, the above components of any existing health system may no longer function because the physical infrastructure has been destroyed, because the health providers have been killed or displaced or because the supply of drugs is interrupted. Therefore, humanitarians should map the status of the components and seek ways to build on them wherever possible.

The temptation is often to build parallel systems, and that may indeed be necessary, but such systems make it more difficult to transit to post-emergency recovery. As mentioned above, many local regulations and legal frameworks will remain in force during an emergency and should be followed. The role of traditional healers as well as private pharmacies in the society concerned should be considered. The performance of a health system may be jeopardised when its capacity is swamped. The 2014 Ebola epidemic in West Africa negatively affected the utilisation of all other, non-Ebola-related health services, so that, for example, attendance at maternity clinics declined. To bridge the gap, mobile clinics were established to reach women unwilling to go to health clinics.[72] Some health systems

[72]Bolkan et al. (2014).

seem more resilient than others to the effects of disasters. For example, against all odds, the health system in Sri Lanka apparently continued to function after the 2004 tsunami.[73]

Finally, the sensitive topic of disposal of dead bodies can be a challenge for the health system. It is an important issue to tackle in a dignified manner, and, not least in the light of experience from the Ebola crisis, new guidelines refer exactly to safe and dignified burial. Although it may seem insensitive at first glance, we will refer to this question in sub-chapter 16 on 'waste management'.[74]

7.3 Challenges, Dilemmas, Dos and Don'ts

How should one engage with the local health system? Will engagement delay or jeopardise the quality of service delivery? In case of no engagement, what are the costs of building up a parallel system, possibly jeopardising local trust in the national health system?

How should one engage with local populations? One of the most frequently cited recommendations is to encourage community participation. Yet it is also one of the least followed,[75] with identified reasons being both that it will delay/hamper response and, at times, that it may jeopardise neutrality.

The recommendation to work with local health systems often poses a dilemma if one wants to maintain high standards and be perceived to be neutral. At times, local standards are of unacceptable technical or ethical level (for example, discriminatory). On the other hand, parallel systems may cause a drain of human resources from the existing system and have potential issues of sustainability, lack of competence building and problems of exit strategy. Jealousy may arise if the surrounding population is receiving less relief than the affected population.

Standards are not only an issue for national health systems. Foreign medical assistance staff does not always conform to optimal standards with respect to technical skills, knowledge of medical context or experience working in resource-limited situations. Sometimes too many and sometimes too few staff is deployed. There have been many attempts to rectify this with core humanitarian standards, and most recently the WHO has developed guidelines for foreign medical teams.[76] The same is true for medical products—at times, drugs have been dispatched that were inappropriate for the local situation, that were past their expiration date or with insufficient instructions (for example, not in the local language). The WHO inter-agency health kits are one attempt to overcome this challenge.

---

[73]Munasinghe (2007).

[74]WHO, PAHO, ICRC, IFRC (2006).

[75]ALNAP et al. (2015).

[76]WHO (2013).

Case in Point: Nepal—Please Send No More Dogs
Two weeks after the April 2015 earthquake, Nepal issued a plea to international organisations to stop sending search and rescue teams. So far, 76 teams, comprising some 2242 staff members and 135 trained dogs, had arrived and found 16 bodies.[77] The Nepalese Health Ministry also asked that no more international health staff be deployed since enough medical personnel were available. Any additional staff would have to undergo screening by the WHO.

8 Communicable Diseases and Outbreak Control

Jonas Torp Ohlsen and Siri Tellier

8.1 Concepts and Baseline Situation

Infectious diseases are caused by a pathogen (prion, virus, bacteria, fungus, parasite). The route of infection varies—for instance, directly from one individual to another (for example, measles), indirectly through a vector (for example, malaria) or through the soil (for example, tetanus). The terms 'contagious', 'communicable' and 'infectious' are at times used interchangeably. However, in the humanitarian action framework (such as the Sphere Project), it is more common to use the term 'communicable' disease (CD), which we shall also apply throughout this chapter.

Globally, deaths due to communicable disease have declined over the last two decades and now constitute less than 20% of total deaths.[78] Progress has been particularly rapid for children under five, who were historically the group with the highest death rates. The total number of deaths of children under five has dropped from 12.4 million in 1990 (U5M close to 20%) to less than 6 million in 2015 (U5M less than 5%).[79] The main killers of children used to be diarrhoeal diseases, measles and pneumonia, with under-nutrition being a contributing factor.

Improved nutrition, water and sanitation, increased levels of vaccination, as well as general improvements in living standards and health services, have reduced both the number of cases of these diseases and also their case fatality rates. The neonate age group of children has made the least progress, with pre-term birth and low birthweight remaining problematic, as they are linked to the more complex issues involved in antenatal and obstetric care.

---

[77]Thomsen (2015).

[78]Global Burden of Disease (GBD) 2015, Mortality and Causes of Death Collaborators (2016), pp. 1459–1544.

[79]UNICEF, Levels and Trends in Child Mortality – Report 2015, Report of the Inter-Agency Working Group on Child Mortality, http://www.childmortality.org/files_v20/download/igme%20report%202015_9_3%20lr%20web.pdf, p. 1.

8.2 Pathways to Excess Mortality and Morbidity in Emergencies

Not all emergencies result in outbreaks of CDs, but especially those involving conflict and/or displaced populations, risk poor WaSH, insufficient food, uncontrolled vectors, poor housing, crowding and poor access to health care. Thus, diseases may become more prevalent or reappear, including diarrhoeal diseases, measles, acute respiratory infections, as well as malaria,[80] with children under five at special risk. This chapter provides an overview of the most common CDs relevant to emergencies.

8.2.1 Measles

Baseline Global measles control has seen great progress in the last decades. The estimated number of deaths attributed to measles was at 134,000 in 2015, representing a 79% reduction from the 2000 levels. Globally, measles vaccination has increased from 73% to 85% in the same period.[81] There is wide variation in levels by country, but some are now close to levels often recommended (for example, the Sphere Handbook recommends 90–95%[82]). Particularly important is the improvement in nutritional levels as malnourished children have much higher case fatality than well-nourished children.[83] This, along with general improvements in health care and economic growth in low-income countries, helps explain the progress in measles mortality reduction.

Excess Risk Prevention and treatment of measles is often prioritised as it is one of the most infectious diseases known (spreading by air-borne droplets) and because displaced persons are at a higher risk of exposure (as a result of crowding), vulnerability (due to malnutrition) and lack of coping (restricted access to health care and vaccinations).[84]

Case Definition[85]*:*

- *clinical*: any person in whom a clinician suspects measles infection *or* any person with fever *and* a maculopapular rash (i.e., non-vesicular) *and* cough, coryza (i.e., runny nose or conjunctivitis, for example red eyes);
- *laboratory criteria for diagnosis*: presence of measles-specific IgM antibodies.

---

[80]Hershey et al. (2011).

[81]WHO Media Centre, Measles, http://www.who.int/mediacentre/factsheets/fs286/en/ (accessed on 10.03.2017).

[82]The Sphere Project (2011).

[83]*Ibid.*

[84]MSF (1997).

[85]WHO (2009).

Management and Outbreak Control Treatment of individual cases comprises general supportive care (fluid, nutrition), vitamin A (reduces mortality) and potentially antibiotics for secondary bacterial infections. Both pre-emptively and as outbreak control, vaccination coverage should be kept above 90%, with the target age group generally being 6 months to 5 years, potentially extending to 15 years based on outbreak analysis. This should include the distribution of vitamin A.[86]

8.2.2 Malaria

Baseline The global level of malaria deaths was estimated at around 429,000 in 2015,[87] a 29% decrease of mortality since 2000,[88] attributed to massive scaling up of measures such as insecticide-treated nets (ITNs) and treatment with artemisinin combination therapies (ACTs), also supported by the much wider availability of rapid diagnostic kits over the last decade. Malaria is concentrated in sub-Saharan Africa, where 92% of deaths occur. The majority of malaria deaths occur in children under 5 years of age.[89]

Excess Risk This includes displaced population,[90] poor environmental sanitation, children and pregnant women.[91]

Case Definition[92]*:*

- *uncomplicated malaria (species: P. falciparum, malaria, ovale, vivax)*: persons with fever or history of it within the last 48 h, with or without nausea, vomiting, diarrhoea, headache, back pain, chills, myalgia, where other obvious causes of fever have been excluded;
- *complicated malaria (species: P. falciparum)*: persons with fever and symptoms as for uncomplicated malaria but with associated signs of disorientation, loss of consciousness, convulsions, severe anaemia, jaundice, haemoglobinuria, spontaneous bleeding, pulmonary oedema, shock;
- *laboratory confirmation*: rapid test (often widely available) or microscopy.

Management and Outbreak Control This involves adequate antimalarial treatment, by mouth or injection according to severity. Transmission reduction includes

---

[86]MSF (2013).

[87]GBD 2015, Mortality and Causes of Death Collaborators (2016).

[88]*Ibid.*

[89]WHO (2016).

[90]Williams et al. (2013), p. 121.

[91]WHO Media Centre, Malaria, http://www.who.int/mediacentre/factsheets/fs094/en/ (accessed on 10 March 2017).

[92]WHO (2005).

insecticide-treated nets, vector control (environmental sanitation, indoor residual spraying, larviciding), active case finding in the community.

8.2.3 Cholera and Other Diarrhoeal Diseases

Baseline The total number of global deaths from diarrhoeal diseases has decreased from 1.7 million in 2005 to around 1.3 million in 2015,[93] generally attributed to improved WaSH and better treatment. With oral rehydration salts (ORS), CFR has been massively reduced.[94] Although many pathogens may cause diarrhoea, cholera (vibrio cholera) is of special concern in crises due to its potential for large outbreaks.

Case Definition[95]*:*

- *clinical*: in a cholera non-endemic area—a patient over five who develops severe dehydration or dies from acute watery diarrhoea; in a cholera endemic area—a patient aged 5 years or more who develops acute watery diarrhoea, with or without vomiting;
- *laboratory confirmation*: vibrio cholera 01 or 0139 isolated from patient with diarrhoea.

Protocol for Treatment Oral rehydration (ORS) or intravenous fluids according to severity. Antibiotics are of limited value for cholera but relevant for bloody diarrhoea (dysentery). Recent evidence may indicate a role for oral cholera vaccination in the prevention and management of outbreaks.[96]

8.2.4 Acute Respiratory Infections

Baseline Acute respiratory infections (ARIs) cover a vast spectrum from mild to life-threatening diseases. Many different pathogens may cause infection. Severe forms of the disease are often bacterial. Several ARI pathogens are preventable by vaccination.[97]

---

[93]GBD 2015, Mortality and Causes of Death Collaborators (2016).

[94]Munos et al. (2010), pp. i75–i87.

[95]WHO, Prevention and control of cholera outbreaks: WHO policy and recommendations, http://www.who.int/cholera/technical/prevention/control/en/index1.html. Accessed on 3 May 2017.

[96]Grandesso et al.(2014), pp. 1625–1635; Luquero et al. (2014), pp. 2111–2120.

[97]WHO/UNICEF (2015).

Excess Risk One comparative study shows high percentages of excess morbidity and mortality (20–35% proportional mortality), as well as case fatality (up to 30–35%), due to ARI in humanitarian settings.[98] However, drawing a valid comparison with baseline rates is difficult due to differences in definitions.[99]

Case Definition (for Childhood Pneumonia) Cough and/or difficulty breathing, with fast breathing and/or chest indrawings. If *danger signs* are present, this indicates severe disease.[100] It also includes any case of fever with cough and rapid breathing.

Protocol for Treatment Oral or injectable antibiotics according to severity; oxygen provision (scarce resource due to logistical challenges); rehydration, nutrition.[101] Active case finding and early referral are important.

8.2.5 Outbreak Preparedness and Control

Arguably, any emergency should be analysed to determine whether outbreaks are likely and to evaluate the response capacity of the health system.[102] An outbreak preparedness plan (general or disease specific) should be developed, available (for example, hard copy) and understood by involved parties. Training should be conducted, and it should contain the following:

- coordination/leadership (who, what role, when convened);
- case definitions and management protocols;
- list of contacts for reporting, testing—authorities/the WHO/reference labs;
- stocks of drugs, protective equipment—not necessarily vaccines if cold chain dependent; kits, for example diarrhoeal disease or haemorrhagic fever kits, are commonly stocked;
- plans for procurement of additional commodities;
- plans for isolation facilities; and
- materials for sampling and shipping of samples (in compliance with IATA rules).

Potential outbreaks can be identified by epidemiological surveillance, single-case alerts from health structures within the community or *rumour-checking*. Diseases with epidemic potential (measles, cholera, shigellosis, haemorrhagic fevers) require immediate reporting.[103]

Epidemiological investigations should include clarification of signs and symptoms (verbal autopsy for deceased persons), relevant sample taking and shipping to reference labs, investigations of potential exposure and mapping of cases in time

[98] Bellos et al. (2010).

[99] *Ibid.*

[100] WHO (2014), p. 19.

[101] MSF (2016), p. 71.

[102] The Sphere Project (2011) and WHO (2005).

[103] See *id.* at p. 319 for 10 key steps to investigate potential outbreaks of disease.

and space. Populations that may be at risk should be identified, and the potential scale of outbreak should be analysed.[104]

Outbreak control measures generally comprise the following:

- isolation and treatment of cases;
- proper management of dead bodies and medical waste;
- transmission/source reduction; often cross-sectional with a focus on WASH, environmental sanitation and vector control;
- vaccination campaigns where relevant (measles, consider for cholera);
- health promotion (HP) and community involvement, for example on general hygiene, disease-specific measures, active/early case finding;
- close epidemiological surveillance (using HIS) to characterise the outbreak and evaluate quality of care (CFR $< 1\%$ goal in cholera).

9 Reproductive Health, HIV/AIDS and Sexual and Gender-Based Violence

Wilma Doedens and Siri Tellier

9.1 Concepts

In 1994, the International Conference on Population and Development agreed on a concept of reproductive health referring to a state of complete physical, mental and social well-being related to the reproductive system throughout the life cycle. It includes the ability to go through pregnancy and deliver a healthy infant; the right to freely decide on the timing, number and spacing of children (including issues related to infertility); eliminating unsafe abortion; prevention and cure of sexually transmitted infections, including HIV/AIDS, as well as health in relation to sexuality. It is sometimes referred to as sexual and reproductive health and rights (SRHR). Given the sometimes contentious nature of SRHR, this consensus is important.

Concepts

Maternal mortality ratio (MMR): this refers to maternal deaths per 100,000 live births.

Neonatal (newborn) deaths: these are deaths during the first 28 days of life.

Skilled birth attendant (SBA): accredited health professionals trained in midwifery skills. SBAs are distinguished from traditional birth attendants (TBAs), often

[104]WHO (2012).

community members who traditionally support women in giving birth, irrespective of skills.

Emergency obstetric care (EmOC): this involves life-saving health care to prevent maternal and newborn mortality.[105]

Contraceptive prevalence: this pertains to the percentage of women aged 15–49, married or in union, who use, or whose partners use, any method of contraception.

Unmet need for family planning: this involves that proportion of women aged 15–49 years, married or in union, who report not wanting any more children or wanting to delay the birth of their next child for at least 2 years but who do not use any method of contraception.

Total demand for contraception: it is the sum of contraceptive prevalence and unmet need.

Infertility: it is a disease of the reproductive system defined by the failure to achieve a clinical pregnancy after 12 months or more of regular unprotected sexual intercourse (*infecundity*).

Traditional/modern means of contraception: traditional means of contraception include withdrawal or lactational amenorrhoea, whereas modern means refer to methods available at clinics or pharmacies, such as sterilisation, hormonal methods or intrauterine devices. All methods have failure rates, but given that modern methods have lower failure rates than traditional ones, the term 'effective methods' is often used as a synonym for 'modern'.

HIV/AIDS: it is short for human immunodeficiency virus/acquired immune deficiency syndrome. The majority of infections are sexually transmitted.

ART/HAART: it means anti-retroviral therapy and highly active ART.

Sexually transmitted infection (STI): previously referred to as sexually transmitted disease (STD), the use of terminology has changed in recognition of the fact that many cases of STIs are asymptomatic, especially in women. Reproductive tract infections (RTIs) overlap with STIs but refer to the location rather than the manner of transmission.

Sexual and gender-based violence (SGBV): both the acronym and the definition of SGBV are not universally agreed on, including among UN organisations. Alternative acronyms currently in use include GBV (gender-based violence) or VaW (violence against women). Some actors object to the term 'gender' as it refers to socially ascribed roles, which they consider relativistic. IASC uses the term GBV. We refer to SGBV as we deem it the most inclusive term. It is taken to involve acts against another person that are based on socially ascribed gender roles, harmful, against that person's will, of a sexual, physical, traditional, socio-economic emotional or psychological nature.[106]

---

[105]UNFPA, Standards in emergency obstetric and newborn care, http://www.unfpa.org/resources/setting-standards-emergency-obstetric-and-newborn-care.

[106]Tellier (2016).

9.2 Baseline Situation

9.2.1 Maternal/Neonatal Health

One estimate puts the global number of maternal deaths in 2015 at 275,000, which represents a reduction of 44% compared to 1990.[107] The levels of maternal mortality demonstrate higher disparities within and among countries than almost any other health indicator, with 99% of deaths occurring in LMICs.[108] It is estimated that roughly up to 40% of women may develop complications during child birth, 15% of which may be life threatening.

Most studies show that around 70–80% of maternal deaths stem from direct obstetric conditions, such as post-partum haemorrhage (making up about a third of these deaths), hypertension/eclampsia, sepsis, abortion and miscarriage.[109] The remainder, indirect causes such as malaria, AIDS and heart disease, can aggravate pregnancy conditions. In addition to fatalities caused by complications, a far greater number of women experience morbidities, including fistula and uterine prolapse. Reproductive health includes the health of the newborn, and estimates assume that 2.6 million stillbirths and 2.7 million neonatal deaths occur every year.[110]

Up until the mid-1990s, the understanding was that risk factors for complications of childbirth were to a great extent predictable and that TBAs could be trained to provide pregnant women with the necessary care.

However, it is now assumed that the direct conditions mentioned above can develop unpredictably and suddenly and that any response requires a higher level of skills and clinical surroundings than TBAs are able to provide. Basic skilled EmOC is provided by skilled birth attendants who are trained to deal with complications through so-called signal functions.

These include administering drugs such as oxytocin (to contract the uterus to stop haemorrhage), antibiotics (to counter sepsis), magnesium sulphate (to counter convulsions caused by eclampsia), conducting interventions such as manual removal of the placenta, removal of retained products of conception, assisted vaginal delivery preferably with vacuum extractor (to assist in prolonged labour), as well as basic neonatal resuscitation care to assist newborn babies. Comprehensive EmOC is typically delivered in hospitals and includes these basic signal functions plus caesarean sections, safe blood transfusion and higher-level care for sick or low birthweight newborns. Complications can develop quickly (for example, haemorrhage can result in death in 1–2 h), and reliable transport and cost are key challenges, causing delays in seeking and obtaining health care.

---

[107]GBD 2015, Mortality and Causes of Death Collaborators (2016).

[108]Tellier (2016) and Say et al. (2014).

[109]Tellier (2016) and Say et al. (2014).

[110]Tellier (2016) and Say et al. (2014).

9.2.2 Contraception

The global contraceptive prevalence rate (CPR) among married or in-union women stood at 64% in 2015.[111] However, there is much disparity in CPR among and within countries, with a rate of 40% in least-developed countries and the lowest, in sub-Saharan Africa, at 24%.[112]

The methods used also vary significantly. Consider that, in Albania, most couples use traditional methods, whereas injectable hormonal methods are common in Uganda. In India, sterilisation is the most common form of contraception. Nevertheless, there is international consensus that approaches should focus on *unmet need*, that is, providing effective contraception to women who do not wish to become pregnant yet but are not using effective methods of contraception.

The issue of infertility has received relatively little attention at the global level. There are few comparable estimates, but levels for lifetime experience of clinical infertility as defined above generally hover around 16–26%.[113] This is true in both LICs and HICs, although the proportion of secondary infertility resulting from poor health care (for example, infections) is higher in LICs.[114]

9.2.3 STIs, HIV/AIDS and SGBV

Globally, the WHO estimates an annual incidence of 499 million new cases of treatable bacterial and protozoal STIs (syphilis, gonorrhoea, chlamydial genital infections and trichomoniasis).[115] In addition, millions are affected by mostly incurable viral infections. New HIV infections peaked at 3.1 million in 199 and decreased to 2.3 million in 2012.[116] AIDS-related deaths have dropped from 2.1 million in 2004 to 1.6 million in 2012.[117] Sub-Saharan Africa still has the highest levels for most indicators but has also seen the greatest levels of improvement, whereas other regions, such as Eastern Europe, still experience rising levels.[118]

The human papillomavirus (HPV) contributes to a large number of cases of cervical cancer every year, which result in 270,000 deaths.[119]

---

[111]UN Population Division (2015), p. 1, http://www.un.org/en/development/desa/population/publications/pdf/family/trendsContraceptiveUse2015Report.pdf (accessed 10 March 2017).

[112]*Ibid.*

[113]Tellier and Obel (2015), http://www.globalhealthminders.dk/wp-content/uploads/2015/05/GHM-Infertility-Brief.pdf.

[114]Tellier (2016).

[115]*Ibid.*

[116]*Ibid.*

[117]*Ibid.*

[118]*Ibid.*

[119]*Ibid.*

An infection with one STI increases the risk of becoming infected with another due to higher exposure to risks, for example skin lesions providing easier transmission, and secretions with high levels of white blood cells. Risk factors for increased incidences of STIs/HIV include unprotected sex with multiple concurrent partners, drug use by injection, lack of infection prevention in health settings, as well as mother to child transmission.

Treatment of AIDs has changed radically over time as drugs and treatment strategies have become more effective and prices, including for antiretroviral treatment (AVR), decreased. ARV drugs have contributed to a reduction in transmission[120] since persons who are HIV positive but receive drugs transmit HIV at very low levels. Treatment is now also used to prevent HIV transmission after an act of unprotected intercourse or after occupational exposure.

Levels of SGBV are notoriously difficult to estimate. Recent global prevalence figures indicate that 35% of women worldwide have experienced either intimate partner violence or non-partner sexual violence in their lifetime widely among countries.[121] Risk factors for both becoming a perpetrator and/or a victim include lower levels of education, exposure to child maltreatment or experiences of family violence, harmful consumption of alcohol and drugs, attitudes accepting towards violence and gender inequality.

9.2.4 Excess Mortality/Morbidity

For maternal/neonatal mortality, one basic point concerns not what is different but what remains the same. At least during the first 9 months after an acute onset emergency, women continue to have babies more or less at the same rate as before, with similar need for EmOC. For example, in the case of Niger, one could expect a CBR of about 5%. Within an affected population of one million, there would be an average of 140 births per day, of which 15% would need EmOC, including a percentage of at least 5% requiring caesarian section. In addition, there may be increases in communicable disease outbreaks, for example cholera or hepatitis E, leading to miscarriages and foetal loss or malaria and malnutrition, causing anaemia, which increases the risk of death from post-partum haemorrhage.

Concerning STIs and HIV/AIDS, there is limited conclusive evidence to indicate an inevitable increase in emergencies. However, there are many risk factors, for example reduced access to health services, family disruption or displacement to a region with higher prevalence of HIV/AIDS.

As regards SGBV, reliable estimates are hard to obtain, partially because survivors/victims find it difficult or dangerous to report. For example, estimates for the 1994 Rwanda crisis state that between 100,000 and 250,000 women were

[120]*Ibid.*

[121]UN Women, Facts and Figures, http://www.unwomen.org/en/what-we-do/ending-violence-against-women/facts-and-figures (accessed on 20 February 2017).

raped. In Liberia, estimates are at 40,000 (1989–2003). Estimates of up to 60,000 rapes have been produced for the wars in Yugoslavia (1992–1995).[122]

Many risk factors leading to increases in SGBV in disasters, especially complex emergencies, have been identified. These situations can weaken protective societal institutions, such as police and health care, and issues including displacement and violence may disrupt the dynamics of communities or families that usually act as protective circles. All of these factors increase levels of domestic violence. Once people fall victim to SGBV, their impetus to seek help may be jeopardised due to fear of the offender and fear of stigma. Where livelihoods are destroyed, the likelihood of vulnerable persons entering the market for transactional sex also rises.[123]

9.3 Existing Approaches and Guidelines

Reproductive health is contentious, in particular where it touches on issues such as abortion and sexuality, including sexual orientation. More than most areas of health, it is closely related to both personal dignity and choice, as well as to physical health. Therefore, in humanitarian settings with multiple actors, the approach towards reproductive health has been influenced by human rights, with a strong component of both protection and relief. At the 1994 UN Conference on Population and Development in Cairo, all 179 attending States agreed by consensus on a definition of reproductive health. It is universally applicable as it is based on wording derived from the human rights framework, including the Convention on the Elimination of all Forms of Discrimination Against Women. Hence, it applies equally to refugees, internally displaced persons and others living in humanitarian settings.

The international community has increasingly focused on addressing the gravity of sexual violence in armed conflict. UN Security Council Resolutions 1325, 1820, 1888 and 1889 on Women, Peace and Security affirm the unique needs, perspectives and contributions of women and girls in conflict settings. For the first time in history, reproductive health was recognised at the Security Council level, with Resolution 1889 explicitly referencing the need to ensure women and girls access to reproductive health services and reproductive rights to achieve better socio-economic conditions in post-conflict situations.

---

[122]Vu et al. (2014), http://currents.plos.org/disasters/article/the-prevalence-of-sexual-violence-among-female-refugees-in-complex-humanitarian-emergencies-a-systematic-review-and-meta-analysis/; UN, UN outreach programme on genocide in Rwanda, http://www.un.org/en/preventgenocide/rwanda/about/bgsexualviolence.shtml.

[123]IASC (2005), p. 100, http://www.unhcr.org/453492294.pdf.

SRHR, and in particular SGBV, require a multi-sectoral integrated approach. Personnel from sectors such as protection, health, nutrition, WaSH, camp planning, education and community service all have an important role to play in the process.

Strategic and Operational Policy Given their contentious nature, SRHR are relative newcomers to the health services considered essential in emergencies. The issue was not included in the 1997 MSF listing of health priorities. In 1995, an Inter-agency Working Group (IAWG) with more than 100 members from UN and NGO circles was established, producing a field manual on RH in emergencies for testing in 1996 and a full-fledged version in 1999. An update was produced in 2010.[124] It is not a fully fledged IASC manual but remains a version for field review, reflecting its contentious nature, for example related to abortion. IASC for its part has also developed instruments, including successive versions of the HIV/AIDS guidelines[125] and SGBV guidelines.[126]

One of the RH Field Manual's central operational concepts is the Minimum Initial Service Package (MISP). The MISP is intended to be put in place as soon as possible during the first phases of an emergency, before any in-depth analysis of the local situation can take place. It prioritises the actions required to prevent excess mortality and morbidity in the first months of a crisis by setting out five objectives:

- *Ensure* that the health sector/cluster identifies an organisation and an RH officer to lead the implementation of the MISP.
- *Prevent and manage* the consequences of sexual violence (for example, improve security related to WaSH, take care of victims).
- *Reduce* HIV transmission: ensure safe blood transfusion practice, facilitate and enforce respect for standard (universal) precautions, make free condoms available.
- *Prevent* excess maternal and newborn morbidity and mortality: ensure availability of basic and comprehensive EmOC, including newborn care services; establish a referral system to higher-level care where needed; provide clean delivery kits to visibly pregnant women when access to a health facility is not possible.
- *Plan* for comprehensive RH services, integrated into primary health care (PHC), as the situation permits.

There has been a gradual shift in approaches over time. For example, in the 1990s, actors were reluctant to provide treatment for AIDS, given cost and complexity in providing continuity of care. As the costs of treatment decreased while simplicity of administering treatment increased, a 2007 UNHCR guideline proposed a decision tree that recommended initiating ART treatment in cases where funding was available for 12 months to train providers with adequate supervision and protocols, assure confidentiality and ensure access by host populations.[127]

---

[124]IASC (2010b).

[125]IASC (2010a).

[126]IASC (2005).

[127]UNHCR (2007), http://www.unhcr.org/uk/488495642.pdf.

Within the health cluster (headed by the WHO at the global level), UNFPA is often responsible for SRHR. Given that RH care is commodity dependent, 13 reproductive health kits have been developed by the IAWG and are managed by UNFPA to support the implementation of the MISP. These kits provide supplies for 3 months and target the community and primary health care level (with a population coverage of 10,000), health centre and hospital level (with a population coverage of 30,000) or referral hospitals (covering a population of 150,000). They are composed on the basis of a demographic/epidemiologic standard population (see sub-chapter 4 for average numbers):

- adult males: 20%;
- women of reproductive age (WRA): 25%;
- CBR: 4%;
- complicated abortions/pregnancy: 20%;
- vaginal tears/delivery: 15%;
- caesarean section: 20%;
- WRA using contraception: 15% (oral: 30%, injectables: 65%).

The kits can be ordered from UNFPA.[128] Dignity kits are provided by UNFPA under the protection cluster. They include menstrual hygiene materials, compiled for each setting, based on preliminary discussions with affected women and girls on menstrual protection practice.

Within the protection cluster, headed by UNHCR, UNFPA is responsible for SGBV. The multi-sectoral, survivor-centred programming approach to prevent and respond to SGBV includes camp design (for example, placement of latrines), protection systems for women and girls, making available medical services (emergency contraception, STI and HIV prevention), psychosocial support for survivors and informing the community of available services.

9.4 Challenges, Dilemmas, Dos and Don'ts

SRHR remains a sensitive issue. Experience tells that local authorities may not always be aware of existing international agreements on the topic. Therefore, humanitarian workers should familiarise themselves with global and national policies and instruments. Other lessons from implementation of the MISP include the following:

- Appointment of a strong, respected coordinator is essential. Roles and responsibilities must be clearly divided between humanitarian actors.
- Contraception is important—people use all available methods during an emergency.

[128]UNFPA (2011).

- Where abortion is legal, safe abortion care should be made available (abortion is only completely illegal in six States, but service providers may not know the law).[129]
- Syndromic diagnosis and treatment of STIs should be applied and provided without laboratory testing. Patients should receive a protocol presenting them with clinical symptoms and signs for an STI.
- Ensure that culturally appropriate menstrual protection materials (usually packed with other toiletries in *hygiene or dignity kits*) are distributed to women and girls.

Recent reviews of MISP implementation note increased awareness but also continuing logistical issues and delays in moving toward comprehensive RH programming.[130] Global policies, such as those laid down in UN Security Council Resolution 1325, are an important step but have been criticised for securitising and/or victimising women rather than empowering them.

10 Non-communicable Diseases

Siri Tellier

10.1 Concepts and Baseline Situation

Non-communicable diseases (NCDs) represent a wide range of illnesses, but this chapter refers to four particular NCDs. These are the focus of global consensus documents such as the WHO's Global Action Plan for the Prevention and Control of NCDs 2013–2020 and include cardiovascular diseases, diabetes (Type 2), cancers and chronic respiratory diseases. Besides their non-communicable nature (one cannot catch an NCD from another person, although there are exceptions), these four diseases also share four common, modifiable risk factors—tobacco use, physical inactivity, unhealthy diets and the harmful use of alcohol.

Baseline Mortality As mentioned in the introduction, major transitions in demography (ageing and urbanising populations) and in epidemiology (improved control of communicable diseases, maternal, perinatal and nutritional disorders), as well as the globalisation of food systems, have resulted in a worldwide shift in the burden of disease. Today, NCDs are responsible for 40 million deaths per year globally (or seven in every 10), ending far more lives than communicable diseases and other

[129] Tellier (2016).

[130] *Ibid*; Onyango et al. (2013), pp. 342–356; Chynoweth (2015).

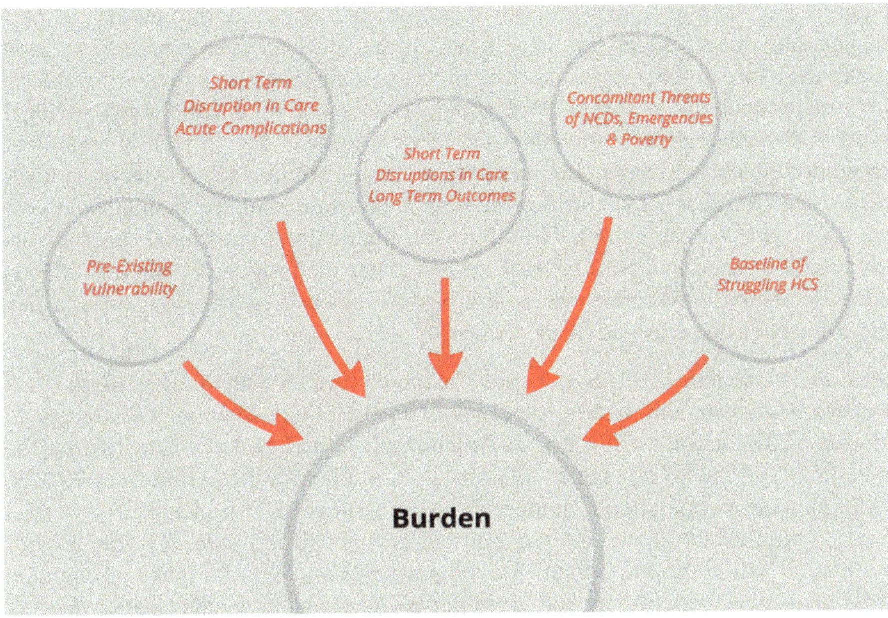

Fig. 4 Pathways to excess mortality and morbidity in emergencies. Developed by the author

factors.[131] The increase in NCDs began in HICs, associated with economic development, but is now also accelerating in LMICs where 87% of 'premature' deaths from NCDs already occur.[132] Therefore, the baseline epidemiology concerning any population in crisis will be different today from what it would have been just a few decades ago. As many recent disasters and population movements have occurred in MICs (such as Iraq or Syria) rather than in LICs, the rise and relevance of NCDs are becoming more prominent. In most situations, NCDs will require long-term care, in particular, at the primary care level. This care is not usually expensive and may cost just a few dollars a month per person but is critical to ensuring secondary prevention of further disease and associated complications.

Excess Mortality Several pathways to excess mortality in emergencies have been identified (see Fig. 4). Due to their chronic or long-term nature, NCDs often represent a unique demand on health systems, requiring consistent care over many years. Unlike more acute conditions, even short interruptions in decade-long treatments can lead to heightened levels of morbidity, sometimes with permanent impacts. Persons with an NCD may be more exposed to crises (for example, if they have mobility problems or, through associations with poverty, may be living in temporary or more vulnerable housing or suburbs), more susceptible to its effects (for example, persons with diabetes are at greater risk of injury developing into

[131]GBD 2015, Mortality and Causes of Death Collaborators (2016).
[132]*Ibid.*

gangrene) or less able to cope (for example, because of interruptions in their medications due to the crisis). Conditions in post-disaster situations may include higher exposure to risk factors (such as tobacco or alcohol use or marketing among displaced populations due to psychological stressors or a breakdown in legal frameworks, respectively) or longer-term consequences due to lack of treatment for communicable diseases (for, example untreated streptococcus infections leading to heart disease), malnutrition or nutritional treatment for malnutrition (for example, rapid nutritional rehabilitation with high-calorie nutritional supplements has been identified as a possible risk for longer-term obesity and diabetes). Maternal malnutrition may contribute to low birthweight babies, which again is a risk factor for later diabetes and heart disease.[133]

General Approaches NCDs generally received limited attention until the last decades. However, this is now changing. The WHO has developed a strategy to combat NCDs, and the UN General Assembly held a High-Level Meeting on the issue in 2011. The WHO created a Global Action Plan for the period from 2013 to 2020, as well as operational guidelines, such as the WHO package for essential non-communicable disease interventions in primary health care in resource-poor settings.[134] While the Millennium Development Goals (MDGs) make no mention of NCDs or their risk factors, the Sustainable Development Goals (SDGs) do.

Emergency Approach The response to NCDs in emergency situations is less advanced but is developing and changing rapidly. NCDs may not cause the quick increase in mortality, which could be expected from diseases such as cholera or measles. Further, since NCDs often are chronic, treatment in emergency situations is jeopardised for logistical and financial reasons, not least in mobile populations.

The 2011 version of the inter-agency emergency health kit did not include drugs related to NCDs, such as insulin,[135] and no IASC guideline on NCDs exists. However, both are under revision as this book went to print. Guidelines such as the 2011 Sphere Handbook include only a few references, which suggest ensuring continuation of drug treatment.

However, there is increasing attention to the fact that a more concerted approach needs to be found.[136] There is also attention towards the very real dilemmas related, for example, to prioritisation of cost.[137] There is further special focus on interaction with other priority areas, for example disability and ageing populations. Typhoon Haiyan, which struck the Philippines in 2013, and the long-term conflict in Syria have increased attention towards NCDS. The populations of both States received comparatively good health care and had a relatively high median age prior to their

[133]Demaio et al. (2013); Roberts et al. (2012), http://www.who.int/bulletin/volumes/90/1/11-098863/en/ (accessed on 31 January 2017).

[134]WHO (2010).

[135]WHO (2011b).

[136]Chan and Kim (2011), pp. 111–114.

[137]Spiegel et al. (2014), pp. 290–297.

respective natural disasters. The baseline situation and population thus had particular health vulnerabilities, where a large proportion of people were already receiving required treatment for NCDs.

According to a Health Access and Utilisation Survey published by UNHCR in October 2014, approximately 15% of Syrian refugees, aged 18 years or older, suffered from at least one chronic condition, and medical care was a major reason cited by refugees for returning to Syria, a trend that MSF studies have since confirmed.[138] Such an epidemiological context presents unique challenges for an emergency health response.

10.2 Challenges, Dilemmas, Dos and Don'ts

Increased attention towards people living with NCDs in emergencies is recent, and most challenges still lie ahead. There is limited high-quality evidence on epidemiology, beyond a few small-scale examples. There is also little consensus on strategic or operational guidelines, except a recommendation to avoid interruption of medication. Operational responses also require a substantial number of commodities and/or funding that are currently not made available for such undertakings. Lastly, logistical and cost-related challenges abound.

Some authors suggest using an approach that aims to integrate the treatment of NCDs into programmes to tackle other chronic, infectious diseases. That way, one could use some of the established decision trees, for example those for HIV/AIDS.

The important issue of treating host populations alongside those particularly affected by disaster poses ethical dilemmas, on which no consensus has yet been reached.

Nevertheless, there are positive signs. For example, the WHO has established and soon will update a framework of evidence-based *best buy* interventions for NCDs. These are cost-effective and easily implemented individual and population-based interventions designed to reduce risk factors and the overall burden of NCDs, and may be adaptable to emergencies. Several humanitarian organisations are seeing it as a priority to identify a realistic way forward.[139] The Sendai Framework in para 30(k) notably refers to chronic diseases, helping to open up discussion.[140]

---

[138] MSF (2014), http://www.doctorswithoutborders.org/news-stories/field-news/treating-chronic-diseases-among-syrian-refugees.

[139] WHO (2011a).

[140] UN, Sendai Framework, para. 30(k).

11 Mental Health and Psychosocial Support

Kevin Davies and Siri Tellier

11.1 Concepts and Baseline Situation

As mentioned above, the metric of disability-adjusted life years (DALYs), introduced in the 1990s,[141] captures not only fatalities but also years lived with disease. One of the most important effects of introducing the metric was that it drew attention to mental health problems, which do not necessarily kill but may cause major disability.

In 2010, mental and substance use disorders accounted for 7.4% of all DALYs worldwide and were the leading cause of YLDs worldwide. This percentage is made up of the following disorders: depressive disorders accounted for 40.5%, anxiety disorders for 14.6%, illicit drug use disorders for 10.9%, alcohol use disorders for 9.6%, schizophrenia for 7.4%, bipolar disorder for 7.0%, pervasive developmental disorders for 4.2%, childhood behavioural disorders for 3.4% and eating disorders for 1.2%.[142] Dementia, a similar disorder, was not included in the statistics. The burden of disorders increased by 37.6% between 1990 and 2010,[143] mostly driven by population growth and ageing. Although few deaths are attributed directly to such disorders (with the exception of self-harm), they do pose a significant challenge.[144] These figures have been been disputed on methodological grounds by some authors who argue that they "underestimate the burden of mental illness by more than a third" citation (Vigo et al. 2016).

11.2 Excess Mortality and Morbidity

The complete disruption of *normalcy* by a disaster can be expected to cause excess mortality and morbidity.[145] For example, consider that among Manhattan residents directly affected by the 9/11 attacks, high rates of probable post-traumatic stress disorder (PTSD) (7.5%) and major depression (9.7%) were diagnosed 1 month after the events.[146] Given that mental illness in emergencies may, to a large extent, constitute normal and reversible reactions to external events, various measures have

[141]WHO, Health Topics, Edpidemiology, http://www.who.int/topics/epidemiology/en/.

[142]WHO, Health Statistics, Estimates for 2000–2015, http://www.who.int/healthinfo/global_burden_disease/estimates/en/index2.html.

[143]Murray et al. (2012), pp. 2197–2223.

[144]Whiteford et al. (2013), pp. 1575–1586.

[145]Mollica et al. (2004), pp. 2058–2067.

[146]Galea et al. (2003), pp. 514–524.

been developed to assess the mental situation of victims. The simplified distress scale may serve as an example. It focuses on stress rather than disorder and incorporates a number of additive components[147]:

- events;
- disruption of daily functioning;
- reactions (for example, confusion, worry, fear); and
- symptoms.

The Global Burden of Disease Study brought increased attention to mental health. Yet, in LMICs, health systems devote a very low percentage of their already limited financial resources to MHPSS. In this regard, the 1990s saw a growing focus on psychological first aid.

The tsunami disaster of 2004 and subsequent events increased the international community's attention towards the issue.

The IASC guidelines of 2007 were an important achievement in bringing a coherent approach. They refer to 'mental health and psycho-social support' (MHPSS), explicitly including both specialised medical approaches as well as more basic support. The guidelines' *intervention pyramid* (see Fig. 5) provides several rules of thumb to assess the severity of problems, as well as the type of assistance needed, which has since been further developed.[148]

The intervention pyramid complements a model developed by Agger & Strang, emphasising factors that promote individual well-being and resilience (*Psycho-social wellbeing model*), going beyond the traditional focus of mortality and morbidity in disasters and highlighting the relationship between human capacity, social ecology/support system, as well as culture and values of the population at hand.[149]

It also builds on five evidence-based principles in MHPSS interventions identified by Hobfall et al., further supporting the well-being model, and areas for intervention in the immediate and mid-term phases of a post traumatic event: (1) promote safety, (2) promote calming, (3) promote self- and collective efficacy, (4) promote connectedness and (5) promote hope.[150]

Various rules of thumb estimate (very approximately) that around 10% of populations suffer from preexisting conditions that require clinical care, 20–40% have been exposed to aggravated situations (lack of protection/violence) and require paraprofessional care and 50–70% may be temporarily affected and in need of community/family support but return to normalcy once their basic needs are met.[151] In 2010, a follow-up assessment guideline was produced. MHPSS is

[147]IASC (2007), http://www.who.int/mental_health/emergencies/guidelines_iasc_mental_health_psychosocial_june_2007.pdf.

[148]*Id.*, pp. 12–13.

[149]Strang and Ager (2003), pp. 2–12.

[150]Hobfoll (2009), pp. 229–243.

[151]IASC (2007), http://www.who.int/mental_health/emergencies/guidelines_iasc_mental_health_psychosocial_june_2007.pdf.

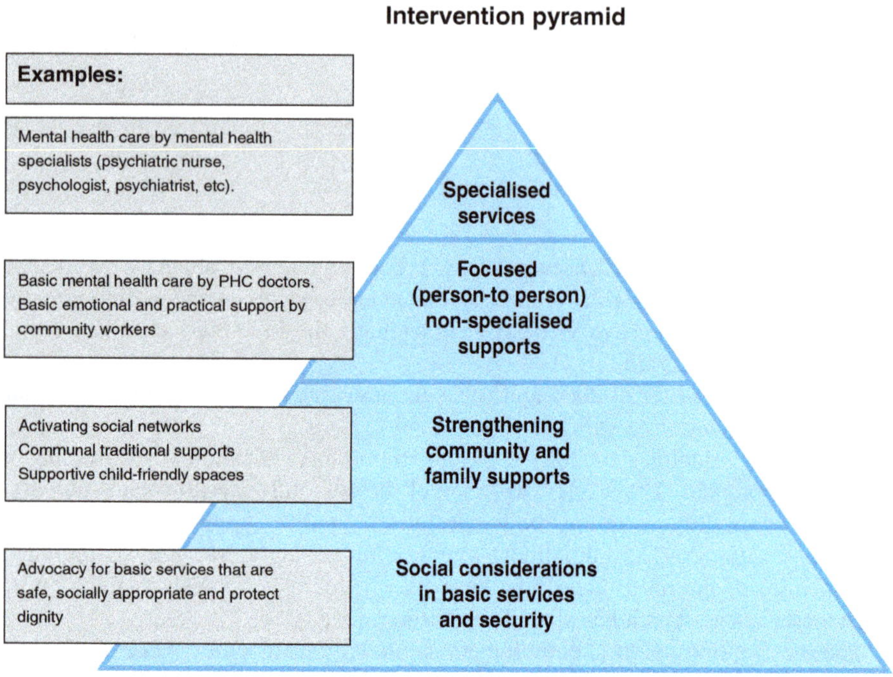

Fig. 5 Intervention pyramid. Reprinted by kind permission of the WHO from IASC Guidelines on Mental Health and Psychosocial Support in Humanitarian Emergencies. What Should Humanitarian Health Actors Know?, Introduction, p. 3, Copyright (2010), http://www.who.int/mental_health/emergencies/what_humanitarian_health_actors_should_know.pdf (accessed on 14 April 2017)

increasingly seen as a standard part of emergency response. The *emergency response units* of the IFRC in Haiti in 2010 may serve as an example.

11.3 Challenges, Dilemmas, Dos and Don'ts

Wessels et al. have analysed many MHPSS approaches to date and identified widespread violations of the 'do no harm' imperative in emergency contexts. Prominent issues include contextual insensitivity to issues such as security, humanitarian coordination and the inappropriate use of various methods; the use of an individualistic (Western) orientation that does not necessarily fit the context and culture of the populations affected; an excessive focus on deficits and victimhood that can undermine empowerment and resilience; the use of unsustainable, short-term approaches that breed dependency, create poorly trained psychosocial workers and lack appropriate emphasis on prevention; and the general imposition of outsider approaches.[152]

A 2014 review of the guidelines credited them with assisting in creating an overall improvement in the quality of MHPSS response. However, many challenges remain, including inter-agency competition, lack of coordination and an imbalance in funding between the more clinical approaches positioned at the top level of the IASC pyramid, generally supported by the WHO and medical organisations, and more community and socially based interventions, often supported by organisations such as UNICEF/UNHCR. Lastly, it is problematic that external funding at times establishes systems that are not sustainable.[153]

12 Forms of Injury and Treatment

Dan Brun Petersen and Siri Tellier

12.1 Concepts and Baseline Situation

Concepts

Multiple casualty event: an incident in which the number of casualties overextend but do not overwhelm the health system. Priority is accorded to the most life-threatening cases.

Mass casualty event: an incident in which the number of casualties overwhelms the health system. Priority is accorded to treating people with the greatest chance of survival.

Triage: it is the process of categorising patients according to the severity of their injuries/illness, prioritising treatment by availability of resources and the patient's chances of survival.

Penetrating trauma or blunt trauma: it involves trauma (not) involving skin penetration.

First aid medical care for injury: it refers to the treatment of injury by way of non-operative functions, prior to transfer to a referral centre for more advanced functions, such as advanced surgery.

[152]Wessells (2009), pp. 842–854.

[153]IASC Reference Group on Mental Health and Psychosocial Support in Emergency Settings, Review of the Implementation of the IASC Guidelines on Mental Health and Psychosocial Support in Emergency Settings, 2014.

Baseline The variety of forms and methods of treatment highlight the challenge for PHHA actors to make decisions as to who should receive priority of medical attention where needs overstretch given capacities and how to augment these capacities in order to treat as many patients as possible.

The global burden of disease due to injury (group 3 diseases) makes up less than 10% of all deaths. This includes unintentional (3–4 million a year) as well as intentional deaths, the latter of which includes self-inflicted harm (about one million) interpersonal (about half a million) and collective violence (on average about 200,000 a year).[154] Injury due to exposure to the forces of nature accounted for another average of around 100,000 deaths over the last decade.[155]

Group 1 deaths (communicable disease, nutritional conditions, perinatal and maternal deaths) disproportionately affect children under the age of five. Group 2 (NCDs) mostly affect persons over 45. However, Group 3, intentional or unintentional injury, mostly affects young adults, especially males. For that group, they are the leading cause of death. Young males are the demographic group that has experienced the least improvement in mortality over the last decades,[156] and increasing urbanisation and motorisation could make it difficult to address this issue. The main immediate causes of death due to injury are damage to the central nervous system and substantial blood loss.

12.2 Excess Mortality and Morbidity: Levels and Pathways

The level and type of injury incurred vary according to the specific type of emergency and phase in which injury was suffered.

In rapid-onset natural disasters, such as earthquakes, fractures and crush syndrome are frequent. Crush syndrome occurs when muscle tissue is crushed, and the body subsequently attempts to rid itself of the waste products, flooding the kidney and causing renal failure. During droughts and heat waves, heat exhaustion and heat stroke contribute to excess mortality. Fatal hypothermia can be caused both by low temperatures and exposure to water. Volcanoes cause both burns and problems related to inhalation of fumes.

In conflict and post-conflict situations, mines and unexploded ordnance can result in both penetrating and blunt injury. This distinction is important with respect to the risk of infection. The time factor is particularly crucial in alleviating the consequences of injury: what is sometimes referred to as the 'golden hour' captures the fact that breakdowns of the central nervous system or respiratory failure may happen within minutes and massive bleedings within hours.

[154] GBD 2015, Mortality and Causes of Death Collaborators (2016).

[155] *Ibid.*

[156] Gillespie et al. (2014), pp. 1003–1017.

12.3 Approaches for Response

There is no single approach that encapsulates how to best respond to injury in emergency situations, although several organisations, such as the WHO,[157] have developed guidelines. As for other essential health services, in a rapidly changing and overwhelming emergency situation, continuing assessment of the seriousness of the situation and the capability to respond are crucial. Assessment involves making tough decisions: is the victim's condition life or limb threatening? Is it salvageable? Are resources and time available to conduct treatment? Should and could the case be referred?

Some assessment and triage tools are included in Advanced Trauma Life Support (ATLS), which builds on the main risk factors mentioned above. It is used to prioritise action for individual patients or patient populations, by following the ABCDE steps:

A:. Airway—if airways are blocked, remove the obstruction (for example, suction, tube).
B:. Breathing—if breathing is irregular, use ventilation, a tube, oxygen.
C:. Circulation—if there is massive bleeding, compress to control bleeding, use a tourniquet, provide IV fluids to restore circulating volume.
D:. Disability—immobilise to prevent injury (splint).
E:. Exposure—ensure that the patient is protected from hot/cold (blankets).

Throughout the procedure, treat wounds, provide tetanus vaccination if it has not already been done and provide pain killers.

In situations involving mass casualties, a system of prioritisation will often include categorising patients according to the following criteria:

T1 Red	(serious, treatable);
T2 Yellow	(less serious, can wait);
T3 Green	(not serious, must wait);
T4 Black	(life threatening but not salvageable).

12.4 Challenges, Dilemmas, Dos and Don'ts

Surgical teams can be geared towards treating combat injuries. However, the proportion of injury due to violence is relatively limited with many cases the result of emergencies such as natural disasters. Non-intentionally caused injury (for example, traffic accidents, obstetric) suffered outside conflict settings may increase and soon account for the majority of cases. Thus, surgical teams must adapt their

157 WHO_HAC (2007).

priorities accordingly.[158] However, prioritisation efforts are hampered by extremely poor data, for example because assessments do not classify death or deteriorating health due to injury.[159]

13 Nutrition

Vibeke Brix Christensen and Siri Tellier

13.1 Concepts and Baseline Situation

Concepts

Malnutrition: malnutrition refers to either over-nutrition or under-nutrition. Under-nutrition may be due to a lack of micronutrients (vitamins and minerals, especially vitamin A and zinc) or a lack of macronutrients (protein, carbohydrates, fats). Extreme malnutrition may result in marasmus (extreme thinness, with children under 18 months especially affected) and kwashiorkor (two-sided oedema, swelling due to fluid retention, particularly prevalent in children of the same age group).

Stunting/wasting: stunting refers to low height relative to age (usually the result of chronic malnutrition), whereas wasting refers to low weight as related to height.

Z-score: the *Z*-score represents a standard deviation—for example, if a person's nutritional *Z*-score stands at 0, he or she is at the median level. If it stands at −1, his or her score is one standard deviation below the mean. For example, a person's weight to height ratio may, for example, lie within the lowest 5%. A *Z*-score of −2 indicates that the respective person is within the lowest 1%, and a *Z*-score of −3 signifies that he or she belongs to the lowest 1/1000 of the population.

SAM: severe acute malnutrition—*Z*-score for weight to height is below −3.

MAM: moderate acute malnutrition—*Z*-score for weight to height is below −2.

MUAC: mid-upper-arm circumference—the MUAC measure[160] is a long strip with a series of colour bands. It is used to screen children with various nutritional levels, to help detect the seriousness of their condition and thereby help to indicate the most apt form of treatment. It is based on the finding that the MUAC is rather stable across the age levels of 6–59 months (and therefore

[158] Chu et al. (2010), pp. 262–263.

[159] PAHO (2010).

[160] For an illustration, see: https://www.unicef.org/supply/files/Mid_Upper_Arm_Circumference_Measuring_Tapes.pdf.

can be applied without knowing the patient's exact age). A green band (>125 mm) indicates a normal state of nutrition, yellow (115–125 mm) signifies a moderate level of malnutrition, whereas red (<115 mm) represents severe malnutrition and risk of death. The 115 mm cut-off point is an indicator of marasmus and highlights a need for special feeding.

Body mass index (BMI): weight (in kg)/height (in metres) × 2—a value below 18.5 signals underweight, whereas a value over 25 indicates overweight, and over 30 obesity.

Baseline Malnutrition is increasingly recognised as a contributor to disease rather than an outright main cause of death. Historically, starvation killed a large number of people, whereas today, death from starvation has become rare. The proportion of children under five who are stunted was estimated at a quarter in 2012, down from 40% in 1990, with the highest rates in South Asia. Despite this improvement, undernutrition is still estimated to be a contributing factor in close to 50% of all child deaths.[161] It reduces the resilience and immune defences of the child, increases case fatality rates for CDs such as measles and contributes to impaired mental development. Malnutrition particularly affects young children since the strongest growth happens within the first 3 years of life.

Over-nutrition and obesity, risk factor for many NCDs, are also increasing, often due to the transitions mentioned in sub-chapter 3, especially urbanisation. Obesity affects both children and adults and is globally estimated to be responsible for more deaths than underweight.[162] However, there is great disparity among different populations. Thus, in Syria in 2012, close to 40% of females aged 20 and above were estimated to be obese (and close to 30% of children under five were estimated to be stunted), whereas the corresponding numbers for Japan were around 3% for each.[163]

13.2 *Pathways to Excess Mortality and Morbidity in Emergencies*

Disasters and conflicts may destroy food production and other livelihoods. Such situations put a strain on health systems and lead to increased levels of stress for caregivers, who may be unable to care for children, all of which increases the risk of malnutrition. Displaced populations in particular may run the risk of incurring negative nutritional effects as a result of particular nutritional factors, including increasing use of unhealthy food and reduced levels of exercise, which may further obesity.

[161] WHO, Media Centre, Children: reducing mortality, http://www.who.int/mediacentre/factsheets/fs178/en/ (accessed on 10 March 2017).

[162] *Ibid.*

[163] WHO Country health profiles, http://www.who.int/countries/en/ (accessed on 10 March 2017).

One important correlation is between maternal starvation and child health. There is robust evidence that highly undernourished pregnant women may also give birth to low birthweight babies, who may be at risk of developing NCDs (diabetes, heart disease) later in life. There is also some evidence, although less robust,[164] that suggests that these persons' own children are low birthweight, in other words a transgenerational epigenetic effect.

13.3 Existing Approaches and Guidelines for Response

Nutrition is an area of humanitarian action that has seen great advances over the last decades. Both the means to monitor levels and screen patients, as well as feeding programmes and products, have undergone major changes.[165]

In order to prevent malnutrition, breastfeeding of infants is recommended during their first 6 months. If women continue to partially breastfeed children until they reach the age of 2 years, this alone would prevent around 20% of child deaths, mostly those occurring as a result of pneumonia or diarrhoeal disease. Feeding programmes usually aim at providing 2100 kcal per adult, (10% protein and 17% fat), with the precise composition determined by age and living situation. Aggravating circumstances include cold weather (under 10°C), poor health conditions (a situation where CMR is above 1/10,000), as well as individual factors such as pregnancy.

Concerning treatment, the focus lies on SAM and MAM rather than micronutrient deficiencies or stunting since they are most likely to develop following an emergency, are most easily identified and cause the highest levels of excess mortality, whereas they can be relatively easily treated.

Rapid assessment is extremely important, even if often conducted under difficult conditions, where simplified methods of screening are necessary. For both SAM and MAM, patients are identified by MUAC screening, weight/height measurements are conducted to determine their respective *Z*-score and observations are made to detect possible oedema. The same is true for adults (using the BMI measurement). Children with SAM (*Z*-scores above three) require treatment in a health care facility. Hence, special feeding products have been developed, such as plumpy'nut (see Fig. 6) or BP100 (see Fig. 7). In cases of MAM, feeding can usually take place at the home or community level and includes training of caregivers.

Supplemental feeding programmes have had great positive effect, but there is also some evidence that rapid recovery from malnutrition may lead to adverse health effects during later stages in life, for example NCDs.

---

[164] Stein and Lumey (2000), pp. 641–654; Painter et al. (2008), pp. 1243–1249.

[165] Young et al. (2004), pp. 1899–1909.

© Nutriset 2013

Fig. 6 Plumpy'nut package. Reproduced by kind permission of copyright owner, Nutriset

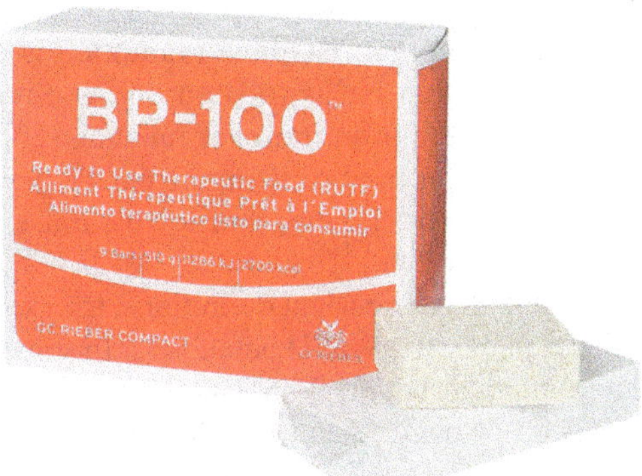

Fig. 7 BP-100 package. Reproduced by kind permission of GC Rieber from http://www.gcrieber-compact.com/product-range/malnutrition/treatment-severe/bp-100/

14 Environmental Health, Including Water, Sanitation and Hygiene

Niall Roche and Siri Tellier

Environmental health/WaSH is one of the key public health priorities in any humanitarian context and is a sector that is often populated by engineering professionals but demands a range of *softer* skills to complement those delivering the *hardware*. Environmental health/WaSH staff comes from a variety of disciplines.

Environmental Health In 2006, the WHO defined environmental health, sometimes referred to as environment and health, as 'A conceptual domain covering the interrelationship between human health and the environment, linking improvement of human health, now and in future generations, to the protection, restoration and improvement of environmental quality'.[166] This definition goes beyond the normal interpretation of WaSH in that it has the scope to address many other environmental determinants of health. It is mainly focused on the interaction between human health and the built environment and addresses not only the communicable disease

[166] WHO Europe (2006), p. 10, http://www.euro.who.int/__data/assets/pdf_file/0019/130177/E88308.pdf.

burden, which WaSH normally works to address, but also the ever-increasing non-communicable disease burden.

WaSH WaSH has been defined in different ways but is generally regarded as including all aspects of water supply, sanitation (excreta management, waste management and drainage), plus hygiene promotion. Sub-sectors of WaSH as outlined in the Sphere Project Handbook (2011) are hygiene promotion, water supply, excreta disposal, vector control, solid waste management and drainage.

Sanitation Sanitation was officially defined during the International Year of Sanitation in 2008 and is 'the collection, treatment and disposal or reuse of human excreta, domestic wastewater and solid waste and associated hygiene promotion'.[167]

Hygiene Promotion Hygiene promotion is essentially a sub-component of wider health promotion but is focused on the environmental or WaSH determinants of health. One definition from Ferron et al. (2000), defines hygiene promotion as 'the planned and systematic attempt to enable people to take action to prevent water and sanitation related illness, and to maximise the benefits of improved, water and sanitation facilities'.[168]

Despite these clear-cut definitions, the existing literature does not provide a clear indication of what WaSH actually is. In some organisations, the sub-components of environmental health/WaSH will include vector control, medical waste disposal, provision of bathing and laundry facilities, food safety, shelters, responder safety and even radiation. Regardless of the sub-components listed in various places, the key to sound environmental health, like any other public health intervention in humanitarian action, is to properly assess the health risks and to address them in a prioritised fashion.

For the purposes of this section, the key components of environmental health and WaSH deemed most relevant in humanitarian action are as follows:

- water supply;
- excreta management;
- liquid and solid waste management, including dead body management;
- health and hygiene promotion;
- vector control;
- housing/shelter and settlement/site planning; and
- control of pollution with a focus on household air quality.

Housing/shelter and settlement/site planning fall under the responsibility of the shelter cluster,[169] but due to the role of overcrowding in the transmission of many communicable diseases in particular, we also include it here.

[167]See definition developed for the International Year of Sanitation 2008 by the Water Supply and Sanitation Collaborative Council, cf. http://www.unece.org/fileadmin/DAM/env/water/meetings/wgwh/Firstmeeting_2008/IYS.pdf.

[168]Ferron et al. (2000)—cabdirect.org.

[169]Davis and Lambert (2002); The Global WASH Cluster, http://washcluster.net/.

Baseline There has been a great deal of progress in WaSH, yet globally around 660 million people are not using an improved source of water.[170] One billion are practising open defecation, and only 19% use soap after using the toilet.[171]

Evidence Base The evidence base for the effect of WaSH and wider environmental health on the communicable disease burden dates back more than 150 years to the 1850s, when John Snow (the father of epidemiology) advised authorities in London to take the handle off the Broad Street handpump, the effect of which was a marked decline in the incidence of cholera. Readers of the BMJ (British Medical Journal) in a vote declared *sanitation* the most important medical advance since 1840, when the journal was founded. In many respects, WaSH has become the 'forgotten foundation of health'.

Relative Effect of Different Components While the broad evidence of the effect of WaSH on health has been known for a long time, the relative impact of its different components is currently best encapsulated by Fewtrell et al.'s Systematic Review of 2005. It determined with respect to diarrhoea (the second biggest killer of children under five and one of the four key communicable diseases in emergencies) that handwashing with soap as an intervention delivers the biggest reduction in incidence (as much as 47%), followed by water quality at the household and sanitation, which, in turn, is followed by water quantity. Providing good quality water at the source (like a handpump), while important, delivers the least amount of impact in terms of reduced incidences of diarrhoea. It is important to remember this when determining what aspects of WaSH and wider environmental health to emphasise.

The 'F' Diagram (Fig. 8) Much of the work in WaSH centres around the 'F' diagram, which helps to illustrate the areas of focus within WaSH in order to prevent the transmission of pathogens through the faecal-oral route.

15 Water Supply: The Water Safety Chain

Niall Roche and Siri Tellier

The key concept to capture with regard to water supply is the 'Water Safety Chain', which focuses attention on the need to protect and possibly treat water from the source all the way to the point of consumption or point of use. The following outlines the different stages in water supply provision to ensure that beneficiaries are enabled to have access to safe water in sufficient quantities.

---

[170]Progress on Sanitation and Drinking Water – 2015 update and MDG Assessment, UNICEF and WHO, 2015.

[171]Freeman et al. (2014).

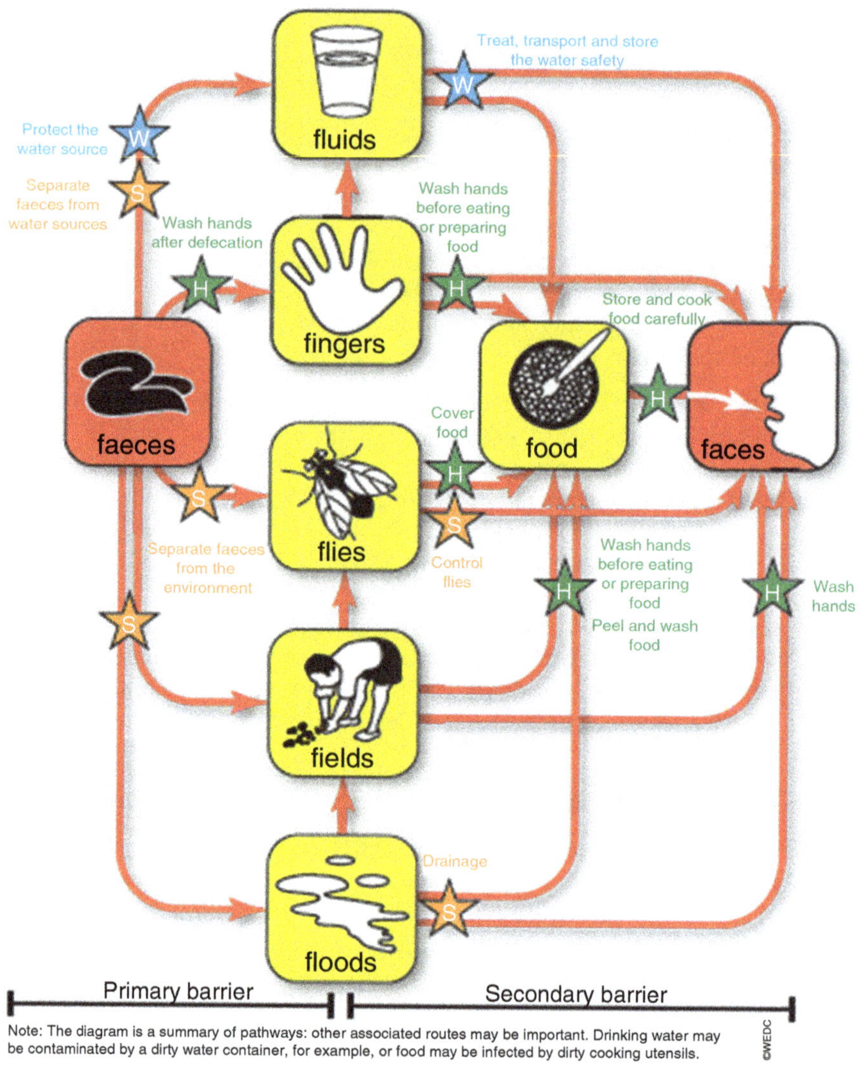

Fig. 8 The 'F' diagram. Reproduced by kind permission of The Water, Engineering and Development Centre (WEDC) from WEDC, The 'F' Diagram, Poster 04, http://wedc.lboro.ac.uk/resources/posters/P004_The_F_Diagram.pdf (accessed on 14 April 2017)

15.1 Water Sources and Demand

Water essentially comes from four different sources:

- surface water (rivers, lakes and ponds);
- ground water (wells, boreholes, tube wells, springs);
- rainwater; and
- sea water (which can be desalinated).

Daily demand for water varies among the regions of the world, populations and cultures, but need is determined by the variety of uses people have for water, some of which take place outside the home. Domestic water need generally refers to water for the purposes of (1) drinking, (2) washing (of cooking utensils, clothes and personal) and (3) cooking. The Sphere Project Handbook assigns an absolute minimum standard of 15 l of water per person per day for these purposes.[172] Consider that daily demand in Ireland for domestic water is 150 l per person per day, illustrating how varied demand can be.

Beyond domestic needs, water has a multitude of uses, including but not limited to water for construction (mud blocks, for example); drinking water for animals (a cow may consume up to 40 l of water in a day); water for irrigation of crops, including vegetables; water for religious purposes (needed before praying); water for excreta management (water is needed to flush many types of toilets), plus the added demand for water at institutions such as schools, hospitals, cholera treatment centres, administrative centres, etc.

In humanitarian contexts, where affected populations engage in crop production, the demand for water can be up to 70 times the water needed for domestic purposes, and therefore those responsible for allocating water supply need to take account of the varying demand for water for different purposes, which may also fluctuate over the seasons. Management of water calls for what is termed integrated water resources management (IWRM), where household water demand is just one part of the entire equation.

15.2 Source Selection, Advantages and Disadvantages

Choosing water sources to utilise in a humanitarian situation will depend on a number of key criteria that include but are not limited to the following:

- the number of people in need of water and their culture;
- the uses of water needed and the quality of water needed for each use (for example, water for consumption will need to be of the highest quality, whereas water for bathing could be of a lower quality);
- the standards to be applied, which must be suited to the context, which may differ between nations;
- the phase of the emergency that humanitarians find themselves in as development of groundwater sources may take time;
- construction issues surrounding finance, human resources and material resources needed to develop a source;
- operation and maintenance issues to sustain a particular source; and
- environmental sustainability of the source.

[172]The Sphere Project (2011).

Each source has certain advantages and disadvantages. Surface water sources tend to be easy to access, and it is often easier to quantify the amount of water available. However, surface water sources are easily contaminated, and the water will need treatment. Groundwater sources tend to provide water of a high quality (microbiological quality at least) but are often more difficult to access. Rainwater provides water of a good quality if collected in a clean manner but may not be available all year round.

15.3 Construction and Protection of Sources and Sustainable Supply

Most surface water sources are naturally occurring rivers or lakes, but in some cases such sources are also constructed. For example, constructed ponds are a common feature in Cambodia, and in parts of Eritrea micro dams have been built to capture and retain rainwater as an adaptation measure in response to climate change. As with any source, protecting it from contamination is paramount, and surface water sources can be protected by keeping concentrations of people away from the source, fencing to prevent human and animal access and the provision of platforms to enable people to have access to water without entering and potentially transmitting schistosomiasis and guinea worm.

Ground water sources such as wells are either dug or drilled. *Shallow wells* of less than 10 m can easily be dug but beyond that depth tend to be drilled and may extend to depths of 45–60 m and sometimes beyond 100 m. Springs can be developed by the construction of a spring protection box. Shallow wells often have open access where people use a rope and bucket to collect their water. However, such wells can be protected through a series of progressive steps ultimately leading to the fitting of a handpump.

Part of the sustainability question is dealt with under environmental sustainability, but one of the biggest challenges with respect to water supply in later phases of an emergency and in recovery is the sustainability of operation and maintenance through community participation. Some of the issues that need to be addressed under this question include the level of community contribution expected, including financial contributions, the choice of technology, the availability of spare parts, skilled pump mechanics to repair non-functioning handpumps and the role of the government in monitoring and technical support.

15.4 Water Transport, Storage and Distribution

The stages in a water supply system include the following[173]:

- abstraction and transmission;
- storage;

[173]Davis and Lambert (2002).

- treatment; and
- distribution.

The chain of supply may not follow the stages in this order, with treatment, for example, sometimes preceding storage (at the household level, for example). However, whatever chain is followed, the ultimate aim is to ensure that the available water is fit for human consumption.

Water is transported to an affected population in one of two ways, either by trucking or through a pipeline, if not directly accessed from a source by those affected. Pipes come in various types and sizes and may extend for several kilometres depending on the distance from the source to the people being served.

If people are accessing water from a source directly, they may collect and transport it in a variety of containers made from different materials and of various sizes. Standard *jerrycans* used for collection tend to be made of plastic with a capacity of 15–20 l.

Storage of water for supply to a community can be in reservoirs or large storage tanks. Storage tanks vary in size and construction from bladder tanks to the Oxfam tanks, which can reach capacities of 95,000 l.

From storage facilities, water is directed to a distribution point or series of distribution points. For treated water, this is often achieved through tap stands (often containing 4–6 taps) with each tap expected to serve 250 people. If water is accessed directly from a well or borehole (fitted with or without a handpump), the ratio can be higher, often one well per 500 people served. Distribution points should, of course, be accessible not only in terms of distance (the sphere standard is 500 m) but also in terms of time so that people do not spend significant quantities of time queuing for water.

15.5 Water Treatment at the Community and Household Level and Testing

In order to render water safe for human consumption, it may be necessary to treat it. In general, surface water sources need the most amount of treatment to ensure that faecal coliforms are not present. There are four stages to the treatment process, and depending on the quality of the raw water accessed, up to all stages may need to be followed. They are as follows:

- coagulation (using ALUM (aluminium sulphate)) and flocculation;
- sedimentation;
- filtration; and
- disinfection.

The three stages prior to disinfection aim to remove as much organic matter and pathogens from the water as possible in order to maximise the disinfectant (normally chlorine) applied. In humanitarian contexts, the chlorine product procured for disinfection normally comes in granular form and would be known as

HTH (high-test hypochlorite) delivered in concentrations of 55–70%. Chlorine can be applied to batches of water as in trucks or can be delivered continuously in water treatment plants. To be effective, the chlorine normally needs a contact time of 30 min. Water that is supplied to communities either through trucks or pipelines should contain a residual chlorine level of 0.2–0.5 mg/l at the point of use. This excess is provided to deal with any post-treatment contamination that may occur during transmission to the point of use. Normally, a swimming pool comparator is used to determine if there is chlorine residual in the water at the point of use and the level of residual present. It should be noted that the treatment of water in this way only deals with microbiological quality and does not remove chemical impurities in the water.

At the household level, there are a number of treatment options, including boiling, household filters, solar disinfection and chlorine-based products that often come in liquid or tablet form. Some products for use at the household level combine flocculation and chlorination actions.

Water must be tested to ensure that it is safe for human consumption in accordance with the WHO Guidelines on Drinking Water Quality or National Equivalents. Often, water is tested at the point the source is identified and before the source is developed. There are three broad sets of parameters tested: physical parameters such as colour, taste and smell; microbiological parameters as an indicator of faecal contamination; and chemical parameters such as iron and arsenic, to name just two. Special kits are available to test key parameters in the field, which is particularly important for microbiological testing, as samples need to be analysed soon after collection.

A key temptation in water supply is to aim strictly for the sphere standard of 15 l per person per day and not to contextualise the situation and adapt the standard aimed for in accordance with cultural practices and demand for water beyond the needs for domestic purpose. A second key challenge is to ensure that the issue of gender is adequately mainstreamed into planning for water supply as the majority of the burden for collecting, transporting and storage lies with women and children.

16 Excreta and Waste Management

Niall Roche and Siri Tellier

16.1 Excreta Management

16.1.1 Concepts

Some people view excreta as public enemy number one. This is perhaps not surprising considering that 1 g of faeces contains a reported 10 million viruses, one million bacteria, one thousand parasite cysts and one hundred parasite eggs.[174] As with water, the concept of the 'sanitation safety chain' ensures that excreta once produced are kept from coming in contact with the human population either directly or indirectly. The following section will mainly deal with the options available to do so, explain key principles to consider, as well as touch upon ways to improve *sanitation coverage* in later phases.

In the majority of cases, excreta management is referred to as sanitation, and in the context of development goals reference is often made to 'basic sanitation', 'improved sanitation' and the 'sanitation ladder'. Over time, people move up the sanitation ladder from open defecation to the complete separation of excreta from human contact through a system of sewers.

Diarrhoea and intestinal parasites are the key illnesses that excreta management aims to prevent, but one needs to be mindful of the link with environmental enteropathy (a condition that shows no clear clinical signs but contributes to reduced nutritional outcomes). In terms of terminology, some now suggest that we refer to faecally transmitted infections to help capture environmental enteropathy, diarrhoeal diseases and intestinal parasites. The importance of excreta management is exemplified by the events that took place in Goma, Zaire (today's Democratic Republic of the Congo), in 1994, where there was only one latrine for every 1029 inhabitants, and over a 3-week period a total of over 45,000 people died from cholera.

16.1.2 What Latrines Do: Components and Options

Latrines, the term most often used to describe toilets in resource-poor settings, serve a number of functions. They not only protect health but should also provide comfort, privacy and safety for users. A latrine has three principle components:

- a pit, often 2–3 m deep, which may be unlined or lined (to prevent the soil from collapsing);
- a floor slab or platform that is often set up for sitting, although more often than not for squatting;
- a superstructure or housing facility the user enters.

In the early phases of many emergencies, toilets simply do not exist (such as in the case of refugees fleeing to a greenfield site), or where they do, they may be damaged and in need of repair or have to be adapted to suit the situation faced. The following outlines the options for managing excreta and essentially follows steps along the sanitation ladder. Successful provision of toilets/latrines may depend on knowing what step on the sanitation ladder those affected are on in times of normalcy:

[174] UNICEF and LSHTM (1999).

- open defecation—in some situations this may be a normal practice for the affected;
- defecation fields—an immediate and short-term solution;
- communal latrines—a medium-term solution but difficult to maintain and which poses protection issues;
- family latrines—a medium- to long-term solution, often provided at the ratio of one latrine for 20 people, equivalent to four families and considered the target to reach in order to enhance cleaning of latrines and extend their lifespan.

In public health terms, the ventilated improved pit (VIP) latrine is a preferred technical option to control flies in pit latrines, but resources may not suffice to provide this type of latrine. Once fully used, many pit latrines can simply be covered with soil, and a new pit may be dug, with the option of reusing the floor slab and possibly the superstructure.

The lifespan of a latrine depends on several factors, including the number of users, the volume of the pit, the sludge accumulation rate for each user and the infiltration capacity of the soil. As a rough estimate, consider that each person produces approximately 175 g of excreta per day, and a standard pit latrine may last for up to a maximum of 6 months.

Not all excreta are disposed of, and in some cultures the reuse of excreta may be a cultural norm. Certain latrines may include options that allow for the recovery of excreta and urine for reuse, often as a fertiliser. These types of latrines are known as composting latrines, Ecosan latrines or urine diversion latrines.

In some contexts, such as urban environments or areas with high water tables, excreta management options can be limited. Buckets or bag options (one is known as the pee poo bag) or the use of portable toilets may be feasible solutions to this problem.

Portable toilets and some pit latrines need to be emptied from time to time. When this happens, the excreta have turned into what has become known as faecal sludge. The proper management of faecal sludge is critical to ensure that human contact with the sludge is kept to a minimum, both for the workers removing the sludge from latrines, septic tanks or portable toilets as well as for the general public.

Toilets may also need to be provided and/or managed at institutional and public areas, especially schools, health centres, hospitals, market areas and administrative offices, which may need additional support to mount this challenge.

16.1.3 Cross-Cutting Issues

There are a number of key cross-cutting issues relevant to excreta management in addition to the issues of protection, environment and responder safety already mentioned.

Gender issues are of equal importance: normally, latrines are demarcated along gender lines with a larger number of latrines allocated to women, whereas men are often provided with urinals. Depending on the methods used, special waste or washing facilities may be provided in toilets to support menstrual hygiene.

Toilets must be accessible to all sections of the community, including the elderly, the disabled and the young children. The excreta of very young children may have to be additionally managed through the provision of nappies and/or potties, possibly included under a hygiene kit.

As with any development in humanitarian action, effective planning is key to successful excreta management. Participation of the affected in all stages of the project cycle will contribute to success. Understanding existing cultural norms and practices is particularly important, one example being the need to establish beforehand whether the population to be served consists of 'washers' or 'wipers', terms denoting the preferred method of anal cleansing.

The background situation with respect to *sanitation* coverage may be very low when one considers how many people do not use *basic* or *improved* sanitation as we now move towards targets set under the Sustainable Development Goals. In the context of Linking Relief and Rehabilitation to Development (LRRD), one may have to implement excreta management activities along the lines of higher development. Many countries have now adopted the CLTS (Community-Led Total Sanitation) approach to sanitation, in which communities are *triggered* to build their own sanitation facilities without any subsidies or inputs from external agents. Social marketing of sanitation is another common approach that utilises the 4 Ps of marketing where the toilet (product) is sold (at the right price) in a market (in the right place) through marketing (promotion).

16.1.4 Challenges, Dilemmas, Dos and Don'ts

Excreta management should not be seen as an isolated public health priority. Poorly designed or maintained latrines are a breeding ground for flies, a key vector of disease. Toilets are also important to ensure protection and dignity and have a role to play in menstrual hygiene management.

Do not assume that once faecal sludge has been removed from a latrine or portable toilet it will be disposed of in a proper manner. One must ensure that faecal sludge is managed properly all the way to the end of the sanitation safety chain.

Reaching a defined ratio of latrines to users (for example, 1:20) does not equal success. Excreta management is about more than outputs in the form of latrines constructed; it is also about use, proper operation and maintenance of these facilities, the elimination of open defecation and proper decommissioning of facilities once the emergency is over.

16.2 Waste Management

16.2.1 Concepts

Waste is not only unsightly and often smelly but has the potential to pose serious public health risks to populations affected by disaster, whereas other waste, such as the rubble generated following an earthquake, may simply inhibit access to affected areas and limit the effectiveness of the overall humanitarian response. The following health risks are associated with waste:

- Waste provides a source of harbourage and food for flies, rats, dogs, snakes and other scavengers, many of whom are vectors of communicable diseases, flies being perhaps the most important.
- Waste may also provide a breeding site for mosquitos, such as *aedes aegypti* or the tiger mosquito, responsible for the transmission of dengue fever. They are often found breeding in pools of water inside waste tyres.
- Waste may pose a fire risk and source of pollution if burned.
- Waste may pose a risk of physical injury.
- Waste may also contribute to the pollution of water sources.
- Waste may block drains and contribute to flooding events.

16.2.2 Types of Waste and Strategies for Dealing with Them

For the purposes of this chapter, we outline the following categorisations of waste:

- storm water (a significant issue in monsoon-affected countries);
- solid waste, which can be sub-categorised into (1) domestic/household waste, (2) hazardous waste, (3) vegetation/soil/sediment, (4) relief waste (plastic bottles, fish tins, etc.) and (5) demolition waste;
- wastewater (sometimes known as sullage or grey water) from kitchens, bathhouses and laundry;
- health care waste.

Storm water drainage problems can be prevented or solved in a number of ways. Linking again to site selection, it is important to try and identify sites that are not prone to flooding and have sufficient slope to allow for drainage. Drainage must be planned in accordance with the expected rainfall and either removed or harvested as a potential source of water. Once constructed, drains need to be kept clear and not allowed to block up with silt or other solid waste.

Solid waste can come in a variety of forms, and most implementing agencies engaged with waste management will deal with solid waste from the domestic environment, which may be broadly classified into organic (compostable) and inorganic material (glass, plastic, etc.). Hazardous waste can cover a multitude of types, including waste oil, batteries, pesticides, asbestos, etc.

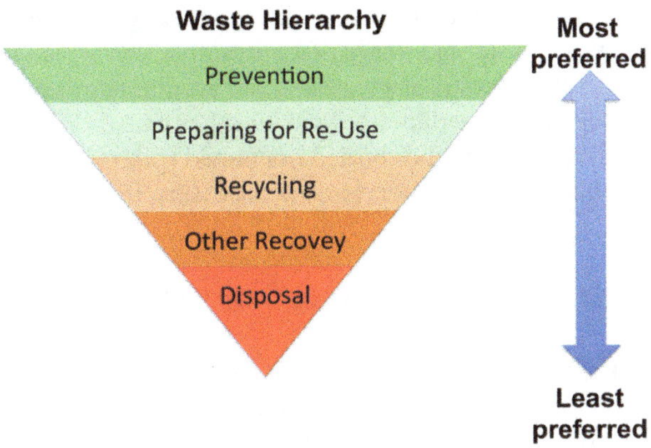

Fig. 9 Good waste management hierarchy. Reproduced by kind permission of Carbon Footprint Ltd from www.carbonfootprint.com, http://www.wastefootprint.com/ (accessed on 14 April 2017)

The principal strategy to good waste management is to try and follow the waste hierarchy (see Fig. 9), which aims to prevent the generation of waste in the first place, passes through minimisation, reuse, recycling and, lastly, disposal, the least favoured option.

Humanitarian agencies in keeping with mainstreaming the environment into their actions have a responsibility to reduce or minimise the amount of waste they generate. Reuse of materials may be common in some emergency contexts where, for example, bricks could be reused in construction. Recycling is another option, a good example being the crushing of rubble following an earthquake for use as an aggregate in the making of concrete or a road surface. Organic waste at the household level can be made into compost for the cultivation of crops.

Disposal of waste is the least favoured but often a necessary and expensive action to undertake. The stages of solid waste disposal cover collection (household bins, for example), transport and disposal. Disposal normally passes by one of two ways: burning or burying. In the majority of cases, it is buried either on-site or off-site in a landfill.

Deciding how to dispose of solid waste depends on a number of factors, including the types of waste generated and locally available options to deal with such waste. In many cases, there may be opportunity to segregate the waste and follow a decision pathway for each type of waste, to reuse it, recycle it or dispose of it.

Wastewater can be generated from a number of sources, including overflows from tap stands, household and communal washing areas (i.e., public showering rooms) and possibly centralised kitchens. Such waste, if not directed into a public drainage system or water course, can be utilised as a resource for irrigation or disposed of as is the norm in a soak pit. Kitchen waste in particular may contain oils and fats, which need to be removed before discharge into the drainage system.

Dealing with health care waste requires specialist expertise as parts of it are medical or clinical waste. This concerns about 10–25% of the waste generated at health care facilities. The remaining general waste can be dealt with like other categories of solid waste, for example burned or buried. Medical waste can be subdivided into a number of different categories, including infectious waste, pathological waste and sharps (for example, syringes, scalpels, etc.). Segregation of waste at the point of generation or accumulation is key, with sharps needed to be segregated immediately. As with other categories of waste, medical waste can be burned/incinerated or buried/contained (placentas in a placenta pit). Incineration to achieve certain temperatures is necessary for some categories of medical waste.

16.2.3 'Managing the Dead': Or 'Safe and Dignified Burial'?

Classically, the issue of burying the deceased was discussed within the category of waste management. This chapter is an opportunity to interject a comment on how insensitive this placement may seem to the communities affected and how, beyond the emotional aspects, this vantage point may affect operational issues. The Ebola pandemic is one recent event that has drawn attention to the critical role of burial practices in response to the epidemic.

To some people, the management of the dead is a waste management issue while understanding the emotional sensitivity surrounding the issue. Sudden-onset events like genocide, an earthquake or epidemics like Ebola or cholera may lead to very high numbers of deaths. In general, the dead do not pose an immediate risk to physical health unless the cause of death is a highly infectious disease like Ebola or cholera. Hence, the priority for humanitarians should be on the survivors.

Following a disaster, WaSH personnel are often designated to deal with the dead. The first priority then is to ensure the safety of those undertaking this task. The staff has to be aware of the risks in handling dead bodies and accessing those bodies in often dangerous circumstances. They should be provided with PPE, be enabled to wash and change clothes after work, have first aid available and be vaccinated to ensure that they are covered against diseases like tetanus. Where bodies are recovered, facilities should be available to store them, identify them and deal with them in a culturally sensitive way. Information has to be managed and communicated carefully. Families and relatives of the deceased must receive support. In the majority of cases, the issue of burial should be approached in accordance with the customs and norms of the respective societies.

The exception may be in relation to *infectious dead*, who may have died from infections such as Ebola, Marburg or cholera. Special precautions must be taken when handling infectious dead. Such precautions may include extra PPE for handlers, the use of body bags (bodies in West Africa during the Ebola crisis of 2014/2015 were double bagged), the use of a disinfectant (a 2% chlorine solution), limited or no contact with the body and immediate burial. Facilitating dialogue with communities, informing the family about the process will help alleviate fear and facilitate acceptance.[175]

[175]WHO (2015b).

16.2.4 Challenges, Dilemmas, Dos and Don'ts

In resource-poor settings, waste is often seen more as a commodity to be exploited than disposed of, and the recovery of waste from landfill sites often becomes a means of livelihood. This fact should be considered in waste management planning. Special reference also needs to be made to the fact that certain categories of waste should not be reused or recycled. One-time-use syringes, for example, must be disposed of.

Humanitarians should not be in a rush to dispose of the dead in mass graves for fear of an epidemic. Such a frenzied approach may lead to resistance from communities, which have been known to hide bodies in order to avoid mass burial. Such burials may also cause other problems for relatives of the deceased who may not be able to properly grieve or prove a relative's death to insurance companies.

17 Health and Hygiene Promotion

Niall Roche and Siri Tellier

17.1 Concepts

Hygiene promotion is an essential component of WaSH but is often seen as something that is tacked on to the more prominent and tangible components of providing water, excreta and waste management facilities. An early global WaSH cluster meeting once indicated that many people did not understand the purpose of hygiene promotion, its expected outcomes and the common ways in which it is implemented. As a concept, hygiene promotion is essentially a sub-component of wider health promotion. The Ottawa Charter of 1986 defined health promotion as 'the process of enabling people to increase control over their lives so that they may maintain and improve their health…'.[176]

Promoting health in its widest sense addresses many of the social determinants of health, including peace, access to education, food, income and equity and not just some of the more direct determinants such as access to safe water. There are several different approaches to health promotion, which is not limited to formal education. For example, the Irish Road Safety Strategy promotes health through a reduction in road deaths and injuries through what is referred to as the 4 E's. Education is one of them, but road safety is also promoted through engineering (making roads safer), enforcement (for example, of laws that punish people for drinking and driving) and evaluation

[176] WHO Europe (1986), http://www.euro.who.int/__data/assets/pdf_file/0004/129532/Ottawa_Charter.pdf?ua=1.

(to measure performance). Similar approaches can be taken to promote health in humanitarian contexts. Many of them refer to the combination of *hardware* (engineering work) and *software* (education work) to deliver on health objectives.

Hygiene promotion as defined by Ferron et al. is 'the planned and systematic attempt to enable people to take action to prevent water and sanitation related illness, and to maximise the benefits of improved water and sanitation facilities'.[177] Hygiene education can therefore be viewed as part of wider hygiene promotion with the purpose of providing knowledge and information and developing the necessary skills (for example, making ORS to treat diarrhoea) so that people can make an informed choice about their health behaviour.

The terminology used with respect to health and hygiene promotion includes behaviour change communication (BCC), information, education, communication (IEC), and dialogue and action. The term 'Dialogue and Action' in particular helps to stress that health/hygiene promotion starts by engaging with affected populations to understand existing beliefs and behaviours in a spirit of true participation in the programme development process.

A common framework used to help understand the interrelationship between different components is the Hygiene Improvement Framework (see Fig. 10) as it refers to not only access to hardware and hygiene promotion but also the enabling environment. In humanitarian contexts, the enabling environment may be regarded as the commitment and capacity of implementers to conduct hygiene improvement effectively.

17.2 Communication Channels

Much of what we call health or hygiene promotion tends to actually be health/hygiene education with the provision of hardware captured under the water and sanitation parts of WaSH. The provision of non-food items to further enable people to utilise the knowledge they have been given may form a part of the hygiene promotion response or be delivered under other clusters.

17.2.1 Steps in Health/Hygiene Promotion

The key steps to planning and implementing effective hygiene promotion activities require you, as humanitarians, to do the following:

- Make contact with communities in a spirit of participation ensuring you do not bypass leadership. Make special efforts to consider marginalised/vulnerable groups.
- Deepen understanding of the community, including gathering baseline data, identifying risks, understanding motivational factors towards certain behaviours and family dynamics in the household.

[177]Ferron et al. (2000), p. 12.

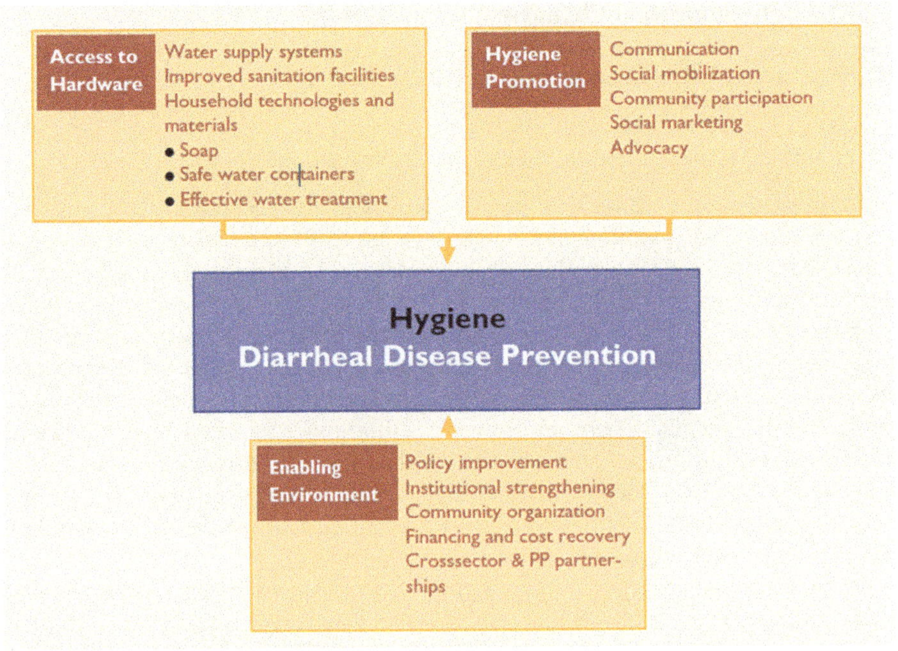

Fig. 10 The hygiene improvement framework. Reprinted by kind permission of the WHO from WHO, Sanitation and Hygiene Promotion.Programing Guidance, Figure 1, page 2, Copyright (2005), http://www.who.int/water_sanitation_health/hygiene/sanhygpromo.pdf (accessed on 14 April 2017), and by kind permission of USAID from USAID et al., The Hygiene Improvement Framework: A Comprehensive Approach for Preventing Childhood Diarrhea, page 10, (2004), http://www.ehproject.org/PDF/Joint_Publications/JP008-HIF.pdf (accessed on 14 April 2017)

- Identify target groups, be it mothers, children, men, etc. Some may be regarded as your primary audience (i.e., children), while others will be secondary (i.e., parents).
- Define your objectives and indicators for measuring progress and impact.
- Decide on outreach structure and human resource requirements. Many personnel may already exist within the health system and be known as community health workers or similar.
- Decide on the methods to use (usually a combination of mass media and interpersonal methods) and settings to target (community health clubs, for example) and prepare (IEC) materials. These materials must be pre-tested to ensure understanding of the message.
- Initiate training of staff and the community.
- Monitor progress utilising the community as much as possible.

17.2.2 Communication Channels

Hygiene promotion tends to be delivered in two ways:

- through mass media; and
- through a people-centred or interpersonal approach.

Mass media are a convenient way to deliver health messages, and numerous avenues can be utilised, including radio, posters, leaflets, campaigns (such as the annual campaign for Global Handwashing Day on 15 October each year), street theatre, social marketing or social media and other technology-related methods, such as texting health messages to community members. In this way, it is possible to convey simple messages, to support behavioural change if other enabling factors (handwashing stations, for example) are present and thus to put specific health issue on the public agenda. There are, however, limitations to mass media impacts. Maximum levels of effectiveness can be reached if media strategies are integrated into wider campaigns, such as advisory campaigns (taking place, for example, in a doctor–patient setting) or group sessions (for example, teachers and school children or imam/priest and religious followers).

In interpersonal settings of hygiene promotion, the status of the messenger is of great importance. That person must be someone who the recipient of the information respects and will believe, such as is usually the case with doctors, who are generally regarded as trustworthy.

17.2.3 Measuring Health/Hygiene Promotion

Part of the challenge with respect to health/hygiene promotion lies in measuring the level of change achieved through promotion. Tap stands and toilets are somewhat easy to count as an output, but successful health/hygiene promotion is not measured simply by the number of leaflets distributed or the number of hygiene sessions conducted by community health workers. Measuring success is more complicated and requires significant qualitative and quantitative research skills.

The key hygiene behaviours promoted in humanitarian contexts tend to focus around handwashing with soap at critical times and after going to the toilet, safe disposal of excreta and safe storage of water at the household level. All of this behavioural advice addresses key risks for communicable disease, associated with emergencies. Other behaviour that should be promoted may include sleeping under a bednet to prevent malaria and keeping children out of the reach of cooking fires to limit exposure to household air pollution. Some of these are specific to WaSH, while others are not. Hence, they are mentioned here under the joint heading of health and hygiene promotion.

Implementers of hygiene promotion measure performance through Knowledge Attitude and Practice (KAP) surveys in which baseline knowledge, attitude and practice levels are measured at the beginning of any response. This baseline is later used to compare changes in knowledge, attitudes and behaviours at or near the end of the intervention from an end-line KAP survey. Unfortunately, KAP surveys are prone to social desirability bias (meaning respondents provide answers that they think the enumerator would like to hear), which can lead to giving misleading results in terms of the behaviour examined, for example handwashing. To overcome this bias, it is recommended to measure performance through formative research that includes tools such as structured observation, household surveys, behaviour trials, in-depth interviews and focus group discussions to help triangulate findings.

17.2.4 Hygiene Related Non-food Items

A large number of health/hygiene non-food items (NFIs) may be distributed as part of an emergency response. More recently, the mechanisms are changing to include cash or vouchers so that beneficiaries can procure the items they need for themselves. Standard items often considered important to distribute that *enable* or support behaviour change include water containers (jerrycans) for transport and storage of water (some with a built-in tap to aid handwashing), household water treatment products such as disinfection tablets, mosquito nets and hygiene kits. The latter may contain soap, toothbrushes, toothpaste, nail cutters, sanitary pads and razors, etc. Determining what the exact content of hygiene-related distributions should include is tricky. Whereever possible, distribution should be based on prior consultation with the affected populations.

17.3 Challenges, Dilemmas, Dos and Don'ts

Every culture has its specific approaches towards hygiene. Hence, one must not assume that once people have received certain information they will change their behaviour. Behavioural change is a complicated process, and many forces determine motivation towards a certain behaviour, deviating from that behaviour or adopting a different type of behaviour. Soap manufacturers, for example, sell soap not by promoting its health benefits but, more often than not, by indicating how fresh and beautiful you may feel after using it. The importance of understanding one's *market* cannot be overemphasised. Inconsistent or unadjusted messaging risks not achieving the hygiene promotion objectives. It is therefore important to understand beliefs and customs around hygiene and to harmonise messaging among actors and over time.

18 Vector Control, Settlement Planning and Household Air Pollution

Niall Roche and Siri Tellier

18.1 Vector Control

18.1.1 Concepts

Vector control refers to the prevention and control of diseases spread through vectors such as mosquitoes and flies. Two of the four big killers in emergencies, diarrhoeal diseases and malaria, are spread in this way. Flies (which physically transport pathogens from excreta to food, for example) transmit diarrhoeal diseases, whereas anopheles mosquitoes pick up parasites from the blood of infected individuals, spreading malaria by enabling the parasite to undergo life cycle changes in the mosquito. Other common disease vectors include rats, fleas, cockroaches, mites, lice and ticks.

The key to vector control is integrated vector management, which demands a wide public health approach. Vector control is not just about spraying chemicals but also includes drainage (to limit breeding sites), good engineering (of latrines to control flies) waste management (to limit access to food for rats), working towards behavioural changes (sleeping under a bednet, covering water jars) and even animal husbandry (to limit the potential spread of zoonotic diseases that are spread from animals to humans (for example, Crimean-Congo haemorrhagic fever spread from donkeys to humans in Afghanistan via ticks).

18.1.2 Strategies for the Control of Vectors

The stepped strategy outlined below can help determine what interventions to engage in and at what moments. At the height of an epidemic, you, as a humanitarian, may skip some of the steps and tackle the immediate problem if large numbers of the adult vector are present:

- *Know your enemy*, which entails understanding as much as possible about the vector to be targeted—where does it lay its eggs, what types of environments does it breed in and where does it like to rest? Some mosquitos prefer to rest indoors, making indoor residual spraying a feasible option.
- *Prevent the vector from breeding in the first place*: drainage work and the removal of waste can limit a vector's breeding opportunities.

- *Control the vector as early as possible in its life cycle*: mosquito larvae are easier to target than mosquitoes flying around. Larvicides may be added to water storage jars to control the mosquito responsible for dengue fever.
- *Control of the adult vector*: thermal fogging and indoor residual spraying may be implemented to control mosquitos, whereas rats may be caught in traps or poisoned, and fleas may be controlled by dusting.
- *Personal protection* includes the use of bed nets, repellents and coils. Vaccination is feasible for some vector-borne diseases, and even treatment is a form of prevention as it removes the source of infection.

18.1.3 Bednets and Indoor Residual Spraying with Respect to Malaria

Bednets, also known as insecticide-treated nets (ITNs) or long-lasting insecticidal nets (LLINs), and indoor residual spraying (IRS) alongside intermittent preventive treatment for pregnant women (IPTp) are primary tools for the control of malaria. Bednet coverage in sub-Saharan Africa, where the majority of deaths occur, has increased substantially in recent years due to the impact of the Global Fund. IRS may be implemented using a variety of different insecticides, including DDT. Ideally, IRS (where the chemical is sprayed on wall surfaces of domestic dwellings) should take place in advance of the malaria transmission season and continue its effect over many months.

18.1.4 Challenges, Dilemmas, Dos and Don'ts

End-user compliance with respect to using bednets effectively is a challenge and again linked to behavioural communication and enabling targeted groups to use the nets. Factors that can contribute to uptake include previous experience in using nets, the time of year in which distribution takes place, colour, mesh size, type of housing people, as well as shape of the nets.

18.2 Household Air Pollution

Household air pollution (HAP), sometimes referred to as indoor air pollution, is not listed as a public health priority with respect to humanitarian situations. However, in a context where air pollution in general, and HAP more specifically, is one of the biggest risk factors to health and the single biggest risk factor in Asia, one could argue that there is some justification to address it. People affected by disasters tend to be the poorest in already vulnerable situations, often relegated to using the dirtiest fuels such as crop waste and dung to cook and, in some cases, heat their homes.

The WHO estimated that, in 2012, air pollution accounted for seven million deaths globally (one in every eight), and HAP alone accounted for 4.3 million with over 580,000 of those deaths occurring in sub-Saharan Africa.[178] Put in perspective, this is nearly three times the number of deaths attributed to HIV and AIDS.

Inefficient cooking fires, using dirty fuels in unventilated environments often occupied by the most vulnerable (women and children) and other like-minded behaviour produce a cocktail of pollutants, including particulates and carbon monoxide. The health impacts are also numerous, including cancer, chronic obstructive pulmonary diseases and acute lower respiratory infections. People living in poverty and those affected by disaster are often exposed to pollution levels that far exceed those that would be considered safe in an industrial environment.

Solutions to household air pollution can be found at three levels:

- tackling the source of pollution by switching to cleaner fuels such as LPG (liquid petroleum gas) or kerosene—in many contexts, this is simply not a feasible option in the short term;
- adjusting the living environment by supporting the use of more fuel-efficient stoves (may be distributed as part of NFI distribution), improving ventilation in shelters and supporting the cooking of food outdoors;
- improving behaviours around cooking/heating through health education and promotion—information provided may include advice on keeping children away during cooking, drying fuel properly before use and simply using a lid on the cooking pots, which can reduce cooking time substantially.

One should not assume that just because others are not addressing household air pollution and it is not considered WaSH that it is not an issue deserving of attention in the context of public health interventions. Impacts extend beyond health, to include protection of the environment through reducing levels of fuel needed and protection of vulnerable people, as women would not have to spend time at risk in the bush collecting fuelwood, where HAP is properly addressed.

18.3 Shelter/Housing and Site/Settlement Planning

In the majority of cases, people displaced by crisis or disaster decide themselves where they are going to stay during the crisis. However, in many cases, sites can be identified and prepared in advance. For example, as part of its contingency plan for dealing with floods, the Government of Malawi has preselected *evacuation sites* suitable to house displaced people affected by floods. Site selection is critical as many of the public health problems associated with camps are attributable to unfavourable selection of sites (located in a flood-prone zone or in an area where

[178]WHO Media Centre, 7 million premature deaths annually linked to air pollution, http://www.who.int/mediacentre/news/releases/2014/air-pollution/en/ (accessed on 10 March 2017).

malaria is endemic) and/or poor site planning that fosters overcrowding, producing conditions suitable to the spread of communicable diseases. Poor planning may also constitute a great source of stress and psychological harm to beneficiaries.

While it may be practically impossible to find sites that meet all the criteria suitable for the protection of public health, one must identify criteria that need to be considered and select sites fulfilling the most critical. For example, following the 11 September attacks, large sites on Pakistani soil were identified and prepared in advance of an anticipated influx of refugees from Afghanistan. The criteria of security, water supply and access (all year round) were considered the most critical determinants in approving suitable sites. Other criteria may include sufficiency of space (typically 45 square metres per person) for each person to be housed, including space for potential new arrivals, elevation to ensure optimal drainage, soil conducive to the digging of pit latrines, location of the water table to access water but also opportunities of limiting contamination of ground water supplies and vegetative cover to help keep dust levels down around health centres and provide shade.

Site planning is an additional part of the equation and must be conducted with great care. From a WaSH perspective, good site planning alone can enable affected populations to access the services they need and protect them from harm. For example, site planning that fails to account for latrines from the beginning creates a number of potential problems that could be avoided, such as forcing implementing agencies to place latrines on the edge of camps. This may discourage some people from using them as they may deem them to be too far away from their dwellings, as well as generating a protection risk.

An often-overlooked challenge with respect to camps concerns issues arising once they are vacated. In these cases, much of the camp infrastructure needs to be decommissioned. Particular care must be applied where pit latrines are concerned. Staff engaged in closing down latrines needs to be adequately protected from the risk of infection, and latrines need to be backfilled with additional soil to allow for settlement and thereafter be marked and possibly mapped.

References

Alexander D (2006) Globalization of disaster: trends, problems and dilemmas. J Int Aff 59(2): 1–23

ALNAP, Brown D, Donini A (2015) Rhetoric or reality? Putting affected people at the centre of humanitarian action

Bellos A, Mulholland K, O'Brien KL, Qazi SA, Gayer M, Checchi F (2010) The burden of acute respiratory infections in crisis-affected populations: a systematic review. Conflict Health 4:3

Bolkan HA, Bash-Taqi DA, Samai M, Gerdin M, von Schreeb J (2014) Ebola and indirect effects on health service function in Sierra Leone. PLoS Curr Outbreaks 6:1

Boudreau T (2009) Solving the risk equation people-centred disaster risk assessment in Ethiopia. In: Humanitarian Practice Network Network Paper No. 66, p 30

Chan E, Kim J (2011) Chronic health needs immediately after natural disasters in middle-income countries: the case of the 2008 Sichuan, China earthquake. Eur J Emerg Med 18(2):111–114

Checchi F, Roberts L (2005) Interpreting and using mortality data in humanitarian emergencies: a primer for non-epidemiologists. In: Humanitarian Practice Network Paper No. 52
Checchi F, Gayer M, Grais RF, Mills E (2007) Public health in crisis - affected populations: a practical guide for decision makers. London
Chu K, Trelles M, Ford N (2010) Rethinking surgical care in conflict. Lancet 375(9711):262–263
Chynoweth SK (2015) Advancing reproductive health on the humanitarian agenda: the 2012–2014 global review. Conflict Health 9(Suppl 1)
Coghlan B, Brennan RJ, Ngoy P, Dofara D, Otto B, Clements M et al (2006) Mortality in the Democratic Republic of Congo: a nationwide survey. Lancet 367(9504):44–51
Coghlan B, Ngoy P, Mulumba F, Hardy C, Bemo VN, Stewart T et al (2009) Update on mortality in the Democratic Republic of Congo: results from a third nationwide survey. Disaster Med Public Health Prep 3(2):88–96
Convention Relating to the Status of Refugees of 1951, United Nations Treaty Series, vol 189, no 2545
CRED (2013) People affected by conflict 2013 – humanitarian needs in numbers
Davis J, Lambert R (2002) Engineering in emergencies: a practical guide for relief workers, 2nd edn. London
Demaio A, Jamieson J, Horn R, de Courten M, Tellier S (2013) Non-communicable diseases in emergencies: a call to action. PLoS Curr 5
DMC, Norwegian Refugee Council (2011) Displacement due to natural hazard-induced disasters: global estimates for 2009 and 2010
Doocy S, Daniels A, Packer C, Dick A, Kirsch T (2013) The human impact of earthquakes: a historical review of events 1980–2009 and systematic literature review. PLoS Curr Disasters 36
DuBois M, Wake C, Bennett C (2015) The Ebola response in West Africa - exposing the politics and culture of international aid. Humanitarian Polloy Group Working Paper, October 2015
Ferron S, Morgan J, Marion OR (2000) Hygiene promotion, a practical manual for relief and development, recently revised
Freeman MC, Stocks ME, Cumming O, Jeandron A, Higgins JP, Wold J, Pruss-Ustun A, Bonjour S, Hunter PR, Fewtrell L, Curtis V (2014) Hygiene and health: systematic review of handwashing practices worldwide and update of health effects
Galea S, Vlahov D, Resnick H, Ahern J, Susser E, Gold J et al (2003) Trends of probable post-traumatic stress disorder in New York City after the September 11 terrorist attacks. Am J Epidemiol 158(6):514–524
Garfield R, Courtney B, Chataigner P, Walton-Ellery S (2011) Common needs assessments and humanitarian action. Humanitarian Practice Network, London
Geneva Declaration Secretariat (2008) The global burden of armed violence, p 174
Gillespie DOS, Trotter MV et al (2014) Divergence in age patterns of mortality change drives international divergence in lifespan inequality. Demography 51(3):1003–1017
Global Burden of Disease 2015 Mortality and Causes of Death Collaborators (2016) Global, regional, and national life expectancy, all-cause mortality, and cause-specific mortality for 249 causes of death, 1980–2015: a systematic analysis for the Global Burden of Disease Study 2015. Lancet 388(10053):1459–1544
Global Health Cluster Rapid Health Assessment Guidelines (2007)
Grandesso F, Allan M, Jean-Simon PS, Boncy J, Blake A, Pierre R et al (2014) Risk factors for cholera transmission in Haiti during inter-peak periods: insights to improve current control strategies from two case-control studies. Epidemiol Infect 142(8):1625–1635
Groupe URD HI (2014) People in aid and the sphere project. Core humanitarian standard on quality and accountability
Guha-Sapir D, Degomme O, Phelan M (2005) Darfur: counting the deaths, mortality estimates from multiple survey data. CRED working paper
Guha-Sapir D, van Panhuis WG, Lagoutte J (2007) Short communication: patterns of chronic and acute diseases after natural disasters - a study from the International Committee of the Red

Cross field hospital in Banda Aceh after the 2004 Indian Ocean tsunami. Trop Med Int Health 12(11):1338–1341

Guiding Principles on Internal Displacement (E/CN.4/1998/53/Add.2) (1998)

Hershey CL, Doocy S, Anderson J, Haskew C, Spiegel P, Moss WJ (2011) Incidence and risk factors for malaria, pneumonia and diarrhea in children under 5 in UNHCR refugee camps: a retrospective study. Conflict Health 5(24)

Hobfoll S (2009) Five essential elements of immediate and mid-term mass trauma intervention: empirical evidence. Focus Psychiatry Online 7(2):229–243

IASC (2014) Reference group on mental health and psychosocial support in emergency settings. Review of the implementation of the IASC guidelines on mental health and psychosocial support in emergency settings

ICRC (2011) Health care in danger - making the case. ICRC, Geneva

ICRC (2015) Prevention and criminal repression of rape and other forms of sexual violence during armed conflicts. Advisory Service on International Humanitarian Law, pp 1–4

IDMC (2014) Disaster-related displacement risk: measuring the risk and assessing its drivers

IDMC/NRC/UNHCR (2015) Disaster-related displacement risk: measuring the risk and addressing its drivers

IFRC (2013) Baseline basics

Inter-Agency Standing Committee (2005) Guidelines for gender-based violence interventions in humanitarian settings: focusing on prevention of and response to sexual violence in emergencies. Geneva

Inter-Agency Standing Committee (2007) IASC guidelines on mental health and psychosocial support in emergency settings

Inter-Agency Standing Committee (2010a) Guidelines for addressing HIV in humanitarian settings. Geneva

Inter-Agency Standing Committee (2010b) Inter-agency field manual on reproductive health in humanitarian settings - 2010 revision for field review. Geneva

Inter-Agency Standing Committee (2012) Multi-Cluster/Sector Initial Rapid Assessment (MIRA)

Johns Hopkins, IFRC (2008) Public health guide for emergencies

Lacina B, Gleditsch NP (2005) Monitoring trends in global combat: a new dataset of battle deaths. The demography of conflict and violence/La démographie du conflit et de la violence. Eur J Popul/Revue Européenne de Démographie. 21(2/3):145–166

Lambert A, Lohle-Tart L (2009) Overmortality in Congo (DRC) during the 1998–2004 conflicts: an estimate of excess deaths scientifically based on demographic methods

Luquero FJ, Grout L, Ciglenecki I, Sakoba K, Traore B, Heile M et al (2014) Use of Vibrio cholerae vaccine in an outbreak in Guinea. N Engl J Med 370(22):2111–2120

Lyengar P, Kerber K, Howe C, Dahn B (2015) Services for mothers and newborns during the Ebola outbreak in Liberia: the need for improvement in emergencies. PLoS Curr Outbreaks

Mollica RF, Cardozo BL, Osofsky HJ, Raphael B, Ager A, Salama P (2004) Mental health in complex emergencies. Lancet 364(9450):2058–2067

MSF (1997) Refugee health an approach to emergency situations. 43–54, 309

MSF (2006) Rapid health assessment of refugee or displaced populations

MSF (2013) Management of a measles epidemic. 2013 edition

MSF (2014) Treating chronic diseases among Syrian refugees, 16 April 2014, http://www.doctorswithoutborders.org/news-stories/field-news/treating-chronic-diseases-among-syrian-refugees

MSF (2016) Clinical guidelines – diagnosis and treatment manual. 2016 edition, p 71

Munasinghe M (2007) The importance of social capital: comparing the impacts of the 2004 Asian Tsunami on Sri Lanka, and Hurricane Katrina 2005 on New Orleans. Elsevier. Ecol Econ 64:9–11

Munos MK et al (2010) The effect of oral rehydration solution and recommended home fluids on diarrhoea mortality. Int J Epidemiol 39:i75–i87

Murray CJL, Vos T, Lozano R, Naghavi M, Flaxman AD, Michaud C (2012) Disability-adjusted life years (DALYs) for 216 diseases and injuries in 21 regions, 1990–2010: a systemic analysis for Global Burden of Diseases Study 2010. Lancet 380:2197–2223

OCHA (2012) WEB: humanitarianism in the network age

Olin E, von Schreeb J (2014) Funding based on needs? A study on the use of needs assessment data by a major humanitarian health assistance donor in its decisions to allocate funds. PLOS Curr Disasters

Onyango MA, Hixson BL, McNally S (2013) Minimum Initial Service Package (MISP) for reproductive health during emergencies: time for a new paradigm? Global Public Health 8(3): 342–356

PAHO (2010) Health response to the earthquake in Haiti, January 2010 - lessons to be learned for the next massive sudden-onset disaster. Pan American Health Organization, Washington

Painter R, Osmond C, Gluckman P, Hanson M, Phillips D, Roseboom T (2008) Transgenerational effects of prenatal exposure to the Dutch famine on neonatal adiposity and health in later life. Br J Obstet Gynaecol 115(10):1243–1249

Price M, Gohdes A, Ball P (2014) Updated statistical analysis of documentation of killings in the Syrian Arab Republic

Roberts B, Patel P, McKee M (2012) Noncommunicable diseases and post-conflict countries. Bull World Health Organ 90(1)

Salama P, Spiegel P, Talley L, Waldman R (2004) Lessons learned from complex emergencies over past decade. Lancet 364:1801–1813

Say L et al (2014) Global causes of maternal death: a WHO systematic analysis. Lancet Global Health 2(6):e323–e333

Spiegel PB, Checchi F, Colombo S, Paik E (2010) Health-care needs of people affected by conflict: future trends and changing frameworks. Lancet 375(9711):341–345

Spiegel P, Khalifa A, Mateen FJ (2014) Cancer in refugees in Jordan and Syria between 2009 and 2012: challenges and the way forward in humanitarian emergencies. Lancet Oncol 15(7): e290–e297

Stein A, Lumey L (2000) The relationship between maternal and offspring birth weights after maternal prenatal famine exposure: the Dutch Famine Birth Cohort Study. Hum Biol 72(4): 641–654

Strang A, Ager A (2003) Psychosocial interventions: some key issues facing practitioners. Intervention 1(3):2–12

Telford J, Cosgrave J (2006) Joint evaluation of the international response to the Indian Ocena Tsunami. Synthesis report. Tsunami Evaluation Coalition, London

Tellier S (2014) Demographic profile, using secondary data. ACAPS 22, http://www.acaps.org/search?search_query=demographic+profile&=%E2%9A%B2

Tellier S (ed) (2016) Sexual and reproductive health and rights: agreements and disagreements. A background document of the evidence (July 2016 edition). Working Group on Sexual and Reproductive Health, July 2016, Copenhagen, 6th edn

Tellier S, Obel J, Infertility. Global Health Minders (May 2015), http://www.globalhealthminders.dk/wp-content/uploads/2015/05/GHM-Infertility-Brief.pdf

The Global WASH Cluster, http://washcluster.net/

The Sphere Project (2011) Sphere handbook – humanitarian charter and minimum standards for disaster response. The Sphere Project, Geneva

Thomsen CB (2015) Lande sender overflødige redningshold til Nepal. Politiken. 6 May 2015

Toole M, Waldman RJ (1990) Prevention of excess mortality in refugee and displaced populations in developing countries. JAMA 263(24):3296–3302

UN High Commissioner for Refugees (2014) UNHCR global trends 2013. UNHCR, Geneva

UN High Commissioner for Refugees, Protracted Refugee Situations, 10 June 2004, EC/54/SC/CRP.14, http://www.refworld.org/docid/4a54bc00d.html, last accessed 28 February 2017

UN Population Division (2015) Trends in contraceptive use worldwide, p 1, http://www.un.org/en/development/desa/population/publications/pdf/family/trendsContraceptiveUse2015Report.pdf

UN, Sendai Framework for disaster risk reduction 2015–2030. A/CONF.224/L.22015
UN Statistics Division, http://unstats.un.org/unsd/demographic/sconcerns/fam/fammethods.htm#A1
UN, UN outreach programme on genocide in Rwanda accessed 2015 041 9. Available from: http://www.un.org/en/preventgenocide/rwanda/about/bgsexualviolence.shtml
UN Women, Facts and Figures, http://www.unwomen.org/en/what-we-do/ending-violence-against-women/facts-and-figures
UN World Population Prospects, the 2015 Revision; http://esa.un.org/unpd/wpp/dataquery/
UNFPA (2011) Manual: inter-agency reproductive health kits for crisis situations, 5th edn
UNFPA. Standards in emergency obstetric and newborn care. Available from: http://www.unfpa.org/resources/setting-standards-emergency-obstetric-and-newborn-care
UNHCR (2007) UNHCR's strategic plan for HIV and AIDS 2008–2012, http://www.unhcr.org/uk/488495642.pdf
UNHCR (2011) The convention of 1951 relating to the status of refugees and its 1967 protocol, 189 U.N.T.S. 150
UNICEF and LSHTM (1999) Towards better programming, a manual on hygiene promotion
UNICEF, Levels and trends in child mortality – Report 2015, Report of the Inter-Agency Working Group on Child Mortality, http://www.childmortality.org/files_v20/download/igme%20report%202015_9_3%20lr%20web.pdf
UNISDR, Terminology on disaster risk reduction: http://www.unisdr.org/we/inform/terminology (accessed on 2017.03.10)
Véron J, Golay V (2015) Can environmental migration be measured? Popul Soc 552
Vigo D, Thornicroft G, Atun R (2016) Estimating the true global burden of mental illness. Lancet Psychiatry 3(2):171–178
Vu A, Adam A, Wirtz A, Pham K, Rubenstein L, Glass N, et al (2014) The prevalence of sexual violence among female refugees in complex humanitarian emergencies: a systematic review and meta-analysis. PLoS Curr 6
Water Supply and Sanitation Collaborative Council, cf. http://www.unece.org/fileadmin/DAM/env/water/meetings/wgwh/Firstmeeting_2008/IYS.pdf, accessed on January 31, 2017
Wessells MG (2009) Do no harm: toward contextually appropriate psychosocial support in international emergencies. Am Psychol 842–854
Whiteford HA, Degenhardt L, Rehm J, Baxter AJ, Ferrari AJ, Erskine HE et al (2013) Global burden of disease attributable to mental and substance use disorders: findings from the Global Burden of Disease Study 2010. Lancet 382(9904):1575–1586
WHO (1998) Health promotion glossary, WHO/HPR/HEP/98.1, p 3, http://www.who.int/healthpromotion/about/HPR%20Glossary%201998.pdf
WHO (2005) Communicable disease control in emergencies - a field manual
WHO (2007) Everybody's Business: strengthening health systems to improve health outcomes. WHO's framework for action. WHO, Geneva
WHO (2009), Response to measles outbreaks in measles mortality reduction settings: immunization, vaccines and biological
WHO (2010) Package of essential non-communicable disease interventions of primary health care in low-resource settings
WHO (2011a) Prevention and control of NCDs: priorities for investment
WHO (2011b) The Interagency Emergency Kit 2011. WHO, France
WHO (2012) Outbreak surveillance and response in humanitarian emergencies. Geneva
WHO (2013) Classification and minimum standards for foreign medical teams in sudden onset disasters
WHO (2014) Revised WHO classification and treatment of pneumonia in children at health facilities: evidence summaries, p 19
WHO (2015a) Report of the Ebola Interim Assessment Panel
WHO (2015b) Safe and dignified burial protocol
WHO (2016) World Malaria Report

WHO Europe (1986) Ottawa Charter for Health Promotion, http://www.euro.who.int/__data/assets/pdf_file/0004/129532/Ottawa_Charter.pdf?ua=1, accessed on 31 January, 2017
WHO Europe (2006) Environment and health – an international concordance on selected concepts, p 10, http://www.euro.who.int/__data/assets/pdf_file/0019/130177/E88308.pdf, accessed on 31 January, 2017
WHO, Health topics, edpidemiology, http://www.who.int/topics/epidemiology/en/
WHO Media Centre, 7 million premature deaths annually linked to air pollution, http://www.who.int/mediacentre/news/releases/2014/air-pollution/en/ (accessed on 10 March 2017)
WHO, Media Centre, Children: reducing mortality, http://www.who.int/mediacentre/factsheets/fs178/en/. (accessed on 10 March 2017)
WHO Media Centre, Malaria, http://www.who.int/mediacentre/factsheets/fs094/en/ (accessed on 10 March 2017)
WHO Media Centre, Measles, http://www.who.int/mediacentre/factsheets/fs286/en/ (accessed on 10 March 2017)
WHO, Metrics: Disability-Adjusted Life Year (DALY), http://www.who.int/healthinfo/global_burden_disease/metrics_daly/en/ (accessed on 10 March 2017)
WHO, PAHO, ICRC, IFRC (2006) Management of dead bodies after disasters: a field manual for first responders
WHO, Prevention and control of cholera outbreaks: WHO policy and recommendations, http://www.who.int/cholera/technical/prevention/control/en/index1.html (accessed on 3 May 2017)
WHO. Health action in crisis - definitions, http://www.who.int/hac/about/definitions/en/
WHO. Preamble to the Constitution of the World Health Organization as adopted by the International Health Conference, New York, 19–22 June 1946, and entered into force on 7 April 1948, http://www.who.int/governance/eb/who_constitution_en.pdf
WHO/UNICEF (2015) Ending preventable child deaths from pneumonia and diarrhoea by 2025 the integrated Global Action Plan for Pneumonia and Diarrhoea (GAPPD)
WHO_HAC (2007). Mass casualty management systems: strategies and guidelines for building health sector capacity
Williams HA et al (2013) Discourse on malaria elimination: where do forcibly displaced persons fit in these discussions? Malar J 12:121
Wisner B, Blaikie P, Cannon T, Davis I (2004) At risk: natural hazards, people's vulnerability and disasters. Routledge, London
World Bank (2005) Fragile states – good practice in country assistance strategies, p v, http://documents.worldbank.org/curated/en/907971468327613700/pdf/34790.pdf
Young H, Borrel A, Holland D, Salama P (2004) Public nutrition in complex emergencies. Lancet 364(9448):1899–1890

Further Reading

Section 1

Sphere Project (2011) Sphere handbook – humanitarian charter and minimum standards for disaster response. Geneva
Inter-Agency Standing Committee (2009) Health cluster guide: a practical guide for country-level implementation of the health cluster. Geneva
Boudreau T (2009) Solving the risk equation people-centred disaster risk assessment in Ethiopia. Humanitarian Practice Network 66. London
UN, Sendai Framework for Disaster Risk Reduction 2015–2030, A/CONF.224/L.22015, 18 March 2015

PAHO (2010) Health response to the earthquake in Haiti: lessons to be learned for the next massive sudden-onset disaster. Washington
Brown D, Donini A (2015) Rhetoric or reality? Putting affected people at the centre of humanitarian action. ALNAP Study, London
Alexander D (2006) Globalization of disaster: trends, problems and dilemmas. J Int Aff 59(2): 1–23
Spiegel P, Checchi F, Colombo S, Paik E (2010) Health-care needs of people affected by conflict: future trends and changing frameworks. Lancet 375:341–345
Salama P, Spiegel P, Talley L, Waldman R (2004) Lessons learned from complex emergencies over past decade. Lancet 364:1801–1813

Section 2

Checchi F, Roberts L (2005) Interpreting and using mortality data in humanitarian emergencies: a primer for non-epidemiologists. Humanitarian Practice Network 52. London
Tellier S (2014) Demographic profile, using secondary data, ACAPS

Section 3

Demaio A, Jamieson J, Horn R, de Courten M, Tellier S (2013) Non-communicable diseases in emergencies: a call to action. PLoS Curr 5
Checchi F, Gayer M, Grais RF, Mills E (2007) Public health in crisis—affected populations: a practical guide for decision makers. Humanitarian Practice Network 61. London
Véron J, Golay V (2015) Can environmental migration be measured? Popul Soc 552, Paris
Internal Displacement Monitoring Centre (2014) Disaster-related displacement risk: measuring the risk and assessing its drivers. Geneva
Price M, Gohdes A, Ball P (2014) Updated statistical analysis of documentation of killings in the Syrian Arab Republic
Doocy S, Daniels A, Packer C, Dick A, Kirsch T (2013) The human impact of earthquakes: a historical review of events 1980–2009 and systematic literature review. PLOS Curr Disasters
Guha-Sapir D, Degomme O, Phelan M (2005) Darfur: counting the deaths, mortality estimates from multiple survey data. CRED Network
Geneva Declaration Secretariat (2008) Global burden of armed violence. Geneva
UNHCR (2014) Global trends 2013. UNHCR, Geneva
CRED (2013) People affected by conflict: humanitarian needs in numbers. Brussels

Section 4

ICRC (2015) Prevention and criminal repression of rape and other forms of sexual violence during armed conflicts, pp 1–4
ICRC (2011) Health care in danger: making the case. Geneva
Danish Red Cross (2004) Handbook on the practical use of international humanitarian law. Copenhagen
ICRC (2014) ICRC Q&A and Lexicon on humanitarian access

Section 5

Michael M (2007) Global health cluster rapid health assessment guidelines

Inter-Agency Standing Committee (2012) Multi-Cluster/Sector Initial Rapid Assessment (MIRA). Geneva

Olin E, von Schreeb J (2014) Funding based on needs? A study on the use of needs assessment data by a major humanitarian health assistance donor in its decisions to allocate funds. PLoS Curr Disasters

Garfield R, Courtney B, Chataigner P, Walton-Ellery S (2011) Common needs assessments and humanitarian action. Humanitarian Practice Network 69. London

Section 6

World Health Organization (2007) Strengthening health systems to improve health outcomes: WHO's framework for action. Geneva

Bolkan H, Bash-Taqi D, Samai M, Gerdin M, von Schreeb J (2014) Ebola and indirect effects on health service function in Sierra Leone. PLoS Curr Outbreaks

Munasinghe M (2007) The importance of social capital: comparing the impacts of the 2004 Asian Tsunami on Sri Lanka, and Hurricane Katrina 2005 on New Orleans, Elsevier. Ecol Econ 64:9–11

World Health Organization (2011) The Interagency Emergency Kit 2011. Geneva

Lyengar P, Kerber K, Howe C, Dahn B (2015) Services for mothers and newborns during the Ebola outbreak in Liberia: the need for improvement in emergencies. PLOS Curr Outbreaks

Section 7

UN (2014) The Millennium Development Goal Report 2014. United Nations, New York

World Health Organization (2005) Communicable disease control in emergencies: a field manual. Geneva

Section 8

Hershey C, Doocy S, Anderson J, Haskew C, Spiegel P, Moss W (2011) Incidence and risk factors for malaria, pneumonia and diarrhea in children under 5 in UNHCR refugee camps: a retrospective study. Conflict Health 5

Luquero F, Grout L, Ciglenecki I, Sakoba K, Traore B, Heile M, Diallo AA, Itama C, Page AL, Quilici ML, Mengel M, Eiros J, Serafini M, Legros D, Grais R (2014) Use of Vibrio cholerae vaccine in an outbreak in Guinea. N Engl J Med 370:2111–2120

Bellos A, Mulholland K, O'Brien K, Qazi S, Gayer M, Checchi F (2010) The burden of acute respiratory infections in crisis-affected populations: a systematic review. Conflict Health 4

Section 9

UNFPA (2014) Standards in emergency obstetric and newborn care, http://www.unfpa.org/resources/setting-standards-emergency-obstetric-and-newborn-care
Tellier S, Lund S (2014) Sexual and reproductive health and rights: agreements and disagreements - a policy brief. Working Group on Sexual and Reproductive Health. Copenhagen
Tellier S, Obel J (2015) Infertility, global health minders
Vu A, Adam A, Wirtz A, Pham K, Rubenstein L, Glass N, Beyrer C, Singh S (2014) The prevalence of sexual violence among female refugees in complex humanitarian emergencies: a systematic review and meta-analysis. PLoS Curr 6
Inter-Agency Standing Committee (2005) Guidelines for gender-based violence interventions in humanitarian settings: focusing on prevention of and response to sexual violence in emergencies. Geneva, http://www.unhcr.org/453492294.pdf
Inter-Agency Standing Committee (2010) Inter-agency field manual on reproductive health in humanitarian settings. Geneva
Inter-Agency Standing Committee (2010) Guidelines for addressing HIV in humanitarian settings. Geneva
UNFPA (2011) Manual: inter-agency reproductive health kits for crisis situations. New York
Onyango M, Hixson B, McNally S (2013) Minimum Initial Service Package (MISP) for reproductive health during emergencies: time for a new paradigm? Global Public Health 8:342–356
Chynoweth S (2015) Advancing reproductive health on the humanitarian agenda: the 2012–2014 global review. Conflict Health 9

Section 10

Roberts B, Patel P, McKee M (2012) Non-communicable diseases and post-conflict countries. Bull World Health Organ 90
World Health Organization (2010) Package of essential non-communicable disease interventions of primary health care in low-resource settings. Geneva
Chan E, Kim J (2011) Chronic health needs immediately after natural disasters in middle-income countries: the case of the 2008 Sichuan, China earthquake. Eur J Emerg Med 18:111–114
Spiegel P, Khalifa A, Mateen F (2014) Cancer in refugees in Jordan and Syria between 2009 and 2012: challenges and the way forward in humanitarian emergencies. Lancet Oncol 15:290–297
MSF (2014) Lebanon: treating chronic diseases among Syrian refugees

Section 11

Mollica R, Cardozo B, Osofsky H, Raphael B, Ager A, Salama P (2004) Mental health in complex emergencies. Lancet 364:2058–2067
Inter-Agency Standing Committee (2007) IASC guidelines on mental health and psychosocial support in emergency settings. Geneva
Strang A, Ager A (2003) Psychosocial interventions: some key issues facing practitioners. Intervention 1:2–12
Hobfall S, Watson P, Bell C, Bryant R, Brymer M, Friedman MJ, Friedman M, Gersons B, de Jong J, Layne C, Maguen S, Neria Y, Norwood A, Pynoos R, Reissman D, Ruzek J, Shalev A, Soloman Z, Steinberg A, Ursano R (2009) Five essential elements of immediate and mid-term mass trauma intervention: empirical evidence. Focus Psychiatry Online 7(2):229–243

World Health Organization (2007) Mass casualty management systems: strategies and guidelines for building health sector capacity. Geneva
Chu K, Trelles M, Ford N (2010) Rethinking surgical care in conflict. Lancet 375:262–263
Wessells M (2009) Do no harm: toward contextually appropriate psychosocial support in international emergencies. Am Psychol 842–854
Inter-Agency Standing Committee (2014) Review of the implementation of the IASC guidelines on mental health and psychosocial support in emergency settings: how are we doing?

Section 12

Black R, Victora C, Walker S, Bhutta Z, Christian P, de Onis M, Ezzati M, Grantham-McGregor S, Katz J, Martorell R, Uauy R (2013) Maternal and child undernutrition and overweight in low-income and middle-income countries. Lancet 382:427–451
Painter R, Osmond C, Gluckman P, Hanson M, Phillips D, Roseboom T (2008) Transgenerational effects of prenatal exposure to the Dutch famine on neonatal adiposity and health in later life. Br J Obstet Gynaecol 115:1243–1249
Young H, Borrel A, Holland D, Salama P (2004) Public nutrition in complex emergencies. Lancet 364:1899–1909
Jones K, Berkley J (2013) Severe acute malnutrition and infection. CMAM Forum
Briend A, Maire B, Fontaine O, Garenne M (2012) Mid-upper arm circumference and weight-for-height to identify high-risk malnourished under-five children. Matern Child Nutr 8:130–133

Section 13

Sanitation and Hygiene Applied Research for Equity (SHARE), London School of Hygiene and Tropical Medicine, http://www.shareresearch.org/
WASH Plus–Supportive Environments For Healthy Communities, USAID, http://www.washplus.org/
Bartram J, Cairncross S (2010) Hygiene, sanitation and water: the forgotten foundations of health. PLoS Med 7
International Rescue Committee, International Water and Sanitation Centre, http://www.ircwash.org/
The Global WASH Cluster: Water, Sanitation, Hygiene, http://washcluster.net/

Section 14

WHO, UNICEF, Joint Monitoring Programme, http://www.wssinfo.org (06-May-2015)
Water Engineering and Development Centre, http://wedc.lboro.ac.uk/, Loughborough University, http://wedc.lboro.ac.uk/
WaterAid, Sustainability Framework, 2011

Sections 15 and 16

Harvey P (2007) Excreta disposal in emergencies: a field manual, WEDC

WHO, PAHO, ICRC, IFRC (2006) Management of dead bodies after disasters: a field manual for first responders

Section 17

Kar K, Chambers R (2008) Handbook on community-led total sanitation

Ferron S, Morgan J, O'Reilly M (2000) Hygiene promotion: a practical manual for relief and development

Section 18

World Health Organization (2006) Fuel for life: household energy and health. Geneva

Davis J, Lambert R (2002) Engineering in emergencies: a practical guide for relief workers. London

Siri Tellier is an External Lecturer at the Department of Public Health at the University of Copenhagen, Denmark.

Andreas Kiaby is Country Director of DanChurchAid Myanmar.

Lars Peter Nissen is Director of ACAPS and a Visiting Professor at the University of Copenhagen, Denmark.

Jonas Torp Ohlsen is a Medical Doctor at Haukeland University Hospital in Bergen, Norway.

Wilma Doedens is a Technical Advisor with the United Nations Population Fund in Geneva, Switzerland.

Kevin Davies is a Cognitive Behavioural Psychotherapist and currently works for the Danish Red Cross.

Dan Brun Petersen is Head of Department at Emergency Department at Zealand University Hospital in Koegen, Denmark.

Vibeke Brix Christensen is a Medical Doctor at the Department of Pediatrics and Adolescent Medicine, Global Health Unit, University Hospital Copenhagen, Denmark.

Niall Roche is a WaSH/Environmental Health Consultant and Adjunct Assistant Professor at the Centre of Global Health at Trinity College, Dublin, Ireland.

Part IV
Anthropology

Anthropology and Humanitarianism?

Ulrika Persson-Fischier

How is anthropology relevant to humanitarianism? This short introduction is intended to give students some tools to provide their own answers to this question.

We can distinguish two different ways in which anthropology can be of importance to humanitarianism: anthropology *in* humanitarianism and anthropology *of* humanitarianism.

Anthropology in humanitarianism refers to the ways that anthropology and its concepts, perspectives, theories, methodologies and experiences of studying culture and societies all over the world can be applied in humanitarian action, i.e., how anthropology can make humanitarian action better, more effective, more receptive to local needs and so forth.[1]

Anthropology of humanitarianism refers to what anthropology has learnt by turning its investigating eye towards humanitarianism itself, its work, organisations, ethics, to help humanitarians understand what it is they are actually doing, to make eventual contradictions, problems and inconsistencies apparent.[2] In the first instance, this anthropology of humanitarianism may simply seem to be a critique, but there is more to it than that; if administered properly, this critique holds potential to understand and improve.

Anthropology in humanitarianism and the anthropology of humanitarianism represent two different ways in which anthropology may be useful to humanitarianism, and both have their value. It may even be argued that either one would be insufficient without the other; the former may be used for encounters with humanitarian victims, the latter for understanding the humanitarian aid worker. Humanitarian action contains both dimensions. Keep them in mind throughout your

[1]For more on this aspect of anthropology see: Eriksen (2010).

[2]For more on this aspect of anthropology see: Bornstein and Redfield (2011).

U. Persson-Fischier (✉)
Uppsala University, Uppsala, Sweden
e-mail: Ulrika.Persson-Fischier@angstrom.uu.se

© Springer International Publishing AG 2018

H.-J. Heintze, P. Thielbörger (eds.), *International Humanitarian Action*,
DOI 10.1007/978-3-319-14454-2_14

studies—and beyond. Many times, students have told me that they continued to discuss dimensions of humanitarianism in anthropological terms long after their anthropology course and that their understanding of anthropology deepened over time. On occasion, their anthropological training would lead them to turn to one another in other contexts saying: 'Now that is an anthropological perspective!' One group of students even suggested using anthropological concepts to improve evaluations of humanitarian projects. Anthropology is not something you are done with once your studies are over; it may continue to influence the way you understand, think about and act within the humanitarian field for the rest of your career.

1 What Is Anthropology?

Anthropology is the study of *man* (Gr. *anthropos*). Anthropologists study humans, culture and societies all over the world. This means that anthropology does not have a specific subject matter as its object of study, like most other academic disciplines, for example law or medicine. As long as it involves humans, anything and everything can be the object of study for anthropologists. In this vein, both the humanitarian victim (anthropology in humanitarianism) and the humanitarian worker (the anthropology of humanitarianism) can be part of the subject matter that anthropologists study. Anthropology is not the only discipline that studies humans. Others such as psychology and biology do as well. How does anthropology differ from such disciplines? Psychology focuses on individuals, whereas biology examines what is common to all humans, exploring man as a species. Anthropology instead focuses on groups of people and what interactions take place between people in such groups. Unlike psychology, anthropology is less interested in the processes within the mind of individuals than in the interactions between people in groups. Unlike biology, anthropology is less interested in what is common to all humans than in what differs between groups.[3]

But how does anthropology differ from sociology, a field that is also interested in groups? Sociology, with its founder Emile Durkheim, started as an attempt to understand modern society; the industrial, urbanised, secular society that developed after the industrial revolution at the end of the nineteenth century in Western Europe and North America. Anthropology, on the other hand, emerged in the wake of the experiences of travellers and explorers, and with colonisation, as the study of the non-modern societies of the world; these have been referred to in different ways—primitive, traditional, exotic savage, indigenous—most of which are no longer socially acceptable. Whatever label we decide to put on the above-mentioned academic fields, anthropology started as the study of societies outside urban, industrial, secular centres of the world, and this makes it unique. No other discipline has systematically studied these social formations and the cultural ideas

[3]For an elaboration on this point, see for example Hannerz (1996).

that guide them. This is equivalent to what anthropology can contribute to humanitarianism: an understanding of the non-western, non-industrialised, non-urban, non-secular victim of humanitarian disasters.[4]

The origins of anthropology in the study of non-modern societies also shape the ways that anthropologists study modern societies. Through the study of the non-modern, anthropology has gained insights, developed theories, concepts and methods that enable anthropologists to see things that sociology, with its focus on modern society, cannot see. Hence, the experiences from the study of the non-modern help anthropology study the modern, being one way in which anthropology differs from sociology.

However, if anthropology does not have a specific object of study, how do we know that we are using an anthropological perspective? If medicine is defined by its study of specific medical fields and law by its study of legal norms and codes, how can we say that something is distinctively anthropological? Since anthropology studies anything that relates to humans, it is not specific objects of study that define it but rather particular perspectives, concepts, methods and modes of representation that are the core of anthropology. These methods are what enable us to distinguish an *anthropological perspective* from the one found in other fields. This chapter will discuss some of the most important anthropological ones.

2 Holism: How the Social, the Material and the Symbolic Are Related

A holistic perspective is one of the conceptual points of departure for the field of anthropology. Anthropology starts from the idea that a part cannot be understood separately from the whole and that different parts of society and culture are interrelated; they interact and depend upon one another. Without an understanding of the whole, the understanding of any part will be insufficient.

As anthropology sees it, there are three dimensions of human action: the material, social and symbolic dimensions. The material dimension refers to how humans organise their physical surroundings, how we procure food and deal with waste, infrastructure, architecture and all the other material substance that surrounds us. The social dimension refers to the ways that humans act in relation to one another, the formal and informal, conscious and unconscious ways that we behave. The symbolic dimension, lastly, refers to how social modes of conduct and the material world around us get infused with meaning, how some objects become beautiful and other things ugly, why some modes of behaviour are wrong and others correct. This is basically what anthropologists understand as culture, and will be discussed further on.

[4]For more on the history and background of anthropology, see Kuper (1996) and Moberg (2012).

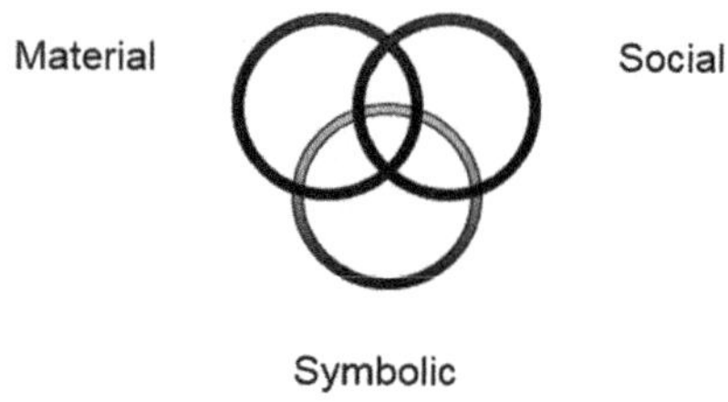

Fig. 1 The holistic perspective. Developed by the author, Ulrika Persson-Fischier

From a holistic perspective, the material, social and symbolic dimensions make up a whole (see Fig. 1), in which all parts are interrelated. To understand even one part, we have to understand the whole. It also means that all dimensions affect one another. If something changes in one dimension, the others will change, too.

Let us exemplify holism. Imagine a development project. To promote empowerment and independence of women in an African village, we build a water pump in the middle of the village. At present, women have to walk 5 km every day to get water from a well, and we hope that a water pump in the village will save these women time so that they will be able to engage in economic activities like vegetable farming or sewing and sell the products for a profit, giving them some economic independence. Eventually, the water pump is built.

One year later, we return to evaluate our project. To our dismay, we learn that, during this time, there has been an alarming increase in witchcraft accusations and even several killings of women accused of being witches. We are horrified by these occurrences but at the same time believe that this could not have had anything to do with the water pump. Without analysing the facts from a holistic perspective, it may seem as if the arrival of the water pump and the killings were completely unrelated issues. Employing a holistic perspective, however, we can start to unfold how all these events are related.

The material dimension of having to walk 5 km to get water involved a social dimension in this society. As women walked to the well, they chatted and gossiped with one another, discussing what happened in the village, talking about accidents, illnesses, injuries and deaths. In this way, social conflicts within the village were managed and contained. *Gossiping* thus prevented conflicts from escalating into violence.

Once the women did not have to walk for hours every day any more, gossiping disappeared and with it a social outlet and conflict management system. The absence of this social interaction activated a symbolic system that had always been present in this village, as in many other communities around the world, lingering beneath the surface: the belief in witchcraft. Witchcraft is a belief system that seeks to explain the ultimate cause of things, including misfortune, accidents, illnesses and deaths. For example, in our case, all villagers agree that the reason why the tree fell upon and crushed my cattle was because termites had eaten up the tree. But why did the tree fall exactly at the moment my cattle were standing under it? To find an explanation for inexplicable occurrences—which science cannot provide—people tend to turn to belief systems, such as fate, religion, chance and randomness, or witchcraft.[5]

Witchcraft beliefs are widespread all over the world. They centre around the idea that evil spirits are capable of entering human bodies and make them practise witchcraft, actions that may cause neighbours to fall ill, an enemy's cattle to succumb to disease, children to become sick, crops to fail and so on. The persons affected may be unaware of the spirit within, hence not *know* that they are performing witchcraft. According to such belief systems, to determine whether witchcraft has taken place, and who the responsible witch is, an oracle must be consulted that will use divination to determine what has happened. Following such a *trial,* the witch may be punished. Punishment can, for example, be a fine in kind, like cattle, functioning as a sort of *tax* and wealth redistribution system or, on rare occasions, where social conflicts escalate, extreme measures, such as killing the witch.

This is what has happened in our village. Our small change of the material setting, the water pump, changed the social dimension and the function of *gossip*. The function of this institution, as a social outlet that manages conflicts, disappeared. This in turn activated a symbolic system of understanding misfortune, which negatively affected the women that we sought to help. It would be very difficult to understand the interrelations between these events without assuming a holistic perspective. This must not lead us to conclude that we should not try to change things or improve people's living conditions but that when doing so, we require deeper insight into how material, social and symbolic dimensions of societies go together.

3 Methodological Relativism

Another core perspective in anthropology is relativism. From an anthropologist's point of view, we do not understand the term in the sense most commonly referred to, as normative relativism, which claims we should refrain from judgement as everything is equally good (or bad) or we should not judge others by our own standards. That is a different argument, with which some anthropologists agree whereas others do not.

Methodological relativism is a relativism that requires that we, when trying to understand another individual or community, temporarily leave our own norms behind and refrain from judging according to our standards. This approach provides an effective means to understand other peoples or cultures. It is gaining understanding by putting ourselves in other persons' shoes, trying to see the world from their perspective. Anthropologists believe that this form of relativism is a necessary step to gain a deep understanding of others. Only after acquiring this form of

[5]See for example Tambiah (1990).

understanding can we possibly—if that is what we intend to do—judge the value of something.

The fieldwork I have conducted in Siberia may provide an example. Siberia is one of the most poverty-stricken areas in Russia, marginalised, poor and socio-economically vulnerable. There is a lack of industry, infrastructure and jobs, and an elevated rate of unemployment and alcoholism, with other social problems abounding. One of my informants and friends there, a young woman in her twenties, was still unmarried and, like most other singles, lived with her parents to get by, even though she had a good job. She worked as a university teacher; her mother was a cardiologist at the hospital and her father a local government administrator. They each earned 2000 roubles a month, which is a very low salary for highly qualified professions. Pooling their resources together, they just about managed to make ends meet. One day I went shopping with this family. They bought a new jacket for my friend. It was not a warm coat to cope with the extreme temperatures (up to minus 40 °C) that occur in Siberia but a pink leather jacket with tuffs, suitable for autumn and fashionable for a couple of seasons, which cost 10,000 roubles: my friend had bought a jacket worth five months her salary.

Without employing a relativist perspective to grasp the situation, anyone's imminent reaction may be to conclude that the family must be mad. How could they spend such a large amount, considering my friend cannot even afford to live on her own, in a region marked by extreme poverty and unemployment? Surely, they ought to have spent this money on more useful things than on luxury goods? Would it not evidently have been better to either save the money in the bank, buy a good old-age insurance, get additional education to improve job prospects or renovate the house? At least, this is how we would approach the scenario from a non-relativist perspective. If we, however temporarily, leave our own ideas about rationality and reason behind and try to see the world with the eyes of the family in question, we may perceive different considerations, which might indeed make their priority seem perfectly reasonable and rational.

All the things we believe this family ought to have rather spent their money on—education, renovation, health care and so on—are not things that can be achieved with financial means alone, not in this society. The family would surely be best advised to follow our conventional wisdom in a place like Sweden, but not in post-Soviet Siberia and many other places around the world. In those cases, to receive access to education or health care, you need contacts: friends, relatives and acquaintances rather than money alone. How do you then meet and maintain contacts and social networks? By constantly reconfirming that you belong to their social group, that you are part of them. How do you do this? In this particular place, clothes and looks are an important key. This may be related to the Soviet experience of being unable to make many of the important decisions about your life yourself: where to live or which career to pursue. Clothing and appearance may have been one of the few things of which the individual was in control in Soviet times, and today appearance is still very important in Russia. It is one way to mark who you are and to what group you belong.

A relativist perspective may therefore help us realise that putting a lot of money into luxury clothing is in fact a way to find access to all the things we consider poverty-stricken people should prioritise—jobs, income, housing, health care and investing in a secure future. Putting five months of salary into a coat may, from a relativist's point of view, then suddenly appear as a fully rational and reasonable kind of investment into social security. However, it is only by temporarily ridding ourselves of our normative judgement that this will become apparent. After we have gained understanding through this process, we are still perfectly free to criticise, to deem this system ineffective, as it forces people to put their resources into luxury consumption to achieve basic security. But the cure for this problem will be very different based on a relativist understanding. It is the system that makes people act the way they do, and in a different system, people would be free to use their resources differently. Without our relativist methodology, we would try explaining to this family how irrational their actions are. Through our relativist understanding, we see how futile such an attempt would be since for this family, it is quite rational to pay five months of salary for a jacket to advance in the system they actually live in.[6]

4 Comparing for Understanding

Anthropology has a comparative ambition. Since anthropology studies various societies and cultures all over the world, the discipline collects a broad range of comparative material. On the one hand, anthropology studies diversity, the many different forms of culture and society that exist on our planet. One of its strengths is that by analysing this diverse material, anthropology can relativise many tenets we view as *natural* or necessary parts of human life. Whatever social institutions, practices or belief systems you claim must be universal, the anthropologist will find a counterexample, some society or culture, which thinks or does things differently, and which still functions. Hence, the anthropologist will accept very few things as *natural*.

One the other hand, among all this diversity and beneath the bewildering difference of practices and belief systems, the anthropologist studies commonalities, deeper structures that reappear in different shapes within human institutions. So beneath the surface of practices that appear to have nothing in common, the anthropologist may detect a common structure and by describing that structure also provide a new understanding of phenomena that we thought we knew.

One example of this is how anthropology can argue that Christmas presents, American Indian potlatch and humanitarian aid are really about the same thing. In 1925, the anthropologist Marcel Mauss wrote his famous book *The Gift* on the diversity of practices of gift giving from around the world, which at the surface

[6]For an elaboration on rationality, see Wilk and Cliggett (1996).

seemed to have nothing in common.[7] By comparing practices, Mauss managed to discover their underlying functions and provided us with an understanding of what is at stake in these apparently different and unrelated gift rituals.

Using Mauss's observation, we can detect a variety of practices as forms of gift giving. Christmas presents are an obvious example. American Indian Potlatch is another. The latter designates native big feasts that were initially banned by United States authorities. One village would work very hard over a long time to compile a large number of gifts of all kinds, such as food, hunting gear, clothes and jewellery. They would then invite their neighbouring village over for a big party—finally setting fire to all the gifts. The authorities deemed this practice to be completely meaningless and destructive, prohibiting it. Humanitarian aid is another example of gift giving. The humanitarian worker offers the victims of conflict and disaster the gift of help.

What Mauss did was to compare different forms of gift giving to detect what function it fulfilled in each case. His conclusion was that gift giving, the redistribution of material goods, is not about change of ownership over things at all but about creating and maintaining social relationships and, hence, also about power. From this perspective, offering gifts activates a reciprocal system and maintains social bonds and relationships. Anthropologically speaking, there can never be a *free* gift. Gifts always require a counter-gift, and as long as that debt is present, the social relationship becomes one of social debt and power. The one who receives the gift becomes indebted to the giver, and immediately a social relationship of power forms. The receiver is indebted until the gift is reciprocated. Presenting gifts is thus an important social institution because it creates social bonds between people and not because it involves material goods. Gift giving takes on different shapes in different contexts because societies differ, but the social function remains the same.

Exchanging Christmas presents is an example of gift giving that can create a social bond between equals: as long as the gifts are of equal (perceived) value, no one becomes indebted to the other, but the function of the gifts is to confirm the continuity of the relationship. On the other hand, where Christmas gifts are of very unequal (perceived) value, the result is different. If gift giving were merely about changing ownership of material objects, we would hold the recipient of the more expensive gift to be the winner. However, anyone who has ever been in the situation of receiving a much more expensive gift than he or she has given knows that the opposite is in fact the case. The person who has offered the more expensive gift is perceived as the *winner*, socially speaking, because the receiver becomes indebted, until a gift of equal or higher value is reciprocated.

This was the function of potlatch. The greater the feast and the more beautiful the gifts given, the more prestige the giver attained, whereas the receiver became indebted. By offering material goods to others, one can thus gain prestige, honour and other immaterial goods. In that sense, gift giving is about power. And this makes humanitarian aid a bit more complicated than we may think. We might want

[7] Mauss (2001 [1925]).

to view the humanitarian gift as free, given without ulterior motives. But from an anthropological perspective, even humanitarian aid will by necessity involve social indebtedness, whatever the humanitarian aid givers want to actually achieve, no matter how altruistic they act. This process lies within the social institution of giving, no matter how individuals involved would like their action to be understood. The problem with the humanitarian gift is that it is a gift that can never be repaid. It necessarily creates indebtedness to the humanitarian aid giver that will last forever. Hence, one aspect of the gratitude that the aid receiver will express to the aid giver is the imbalanced power relationship that the gift has created between the giver and the receiver.

This is not to say that the humanitarian gift is a bad thing. It is a necessary thing, only somewhat more complicated that we may think at first glance. One way to improve aid giving may be to take this aspect of gift giving into consideration. Further, there may be ways for us humanitarians to let conflict and disaster victims repay their perceived debt, to equalise our relationship. They might like to give the aid worker something very valuable, like the story of their life or token gifts. In those situations, it may be a good idea to accept such gifts, rather than to refuse them, even if we do not wish to intrude on their private lives or believe that they should keep material belongings for themselves, as they actually need them. After all, there are more important things at stake than token gifts: equality and dignity.

Marcel Mauss showed us that what on the surface seems to be about handing over things instead is about social indebtedness and power. And it is only thanks to the globally comparative project of anthropology that he managed to do so. It is only with the help of the bewildering diversity that we can make out common structures between things that may not seem to be related at first glance. Since anthropology contains all this material from all over the world, it can, by comparison, help us understand issues, we believe to see through, in a new way. This method of comparison can lead to the discovery of the real function of many more social practices, gift giving being but one example.[8]

5 Culture in Everyday Life

We now turn to one of anthropology's preferred analytical concepts: culture. The concept of culture is used in many other disciplines, and it also appears in contexts outside of academia. Because the concept of culture has been used in many different ways, anthropologists have sometimes thought it better to abandon it altogether.[9] However, it keeps reappearing, thus indicating that it is essential to anthropology. This will be illustrated in the following chapters of this section.

[8]For another intriguing example that has become extremely influential within anthropology, see Douglas (2002). It will surely change the way you understand the term '*dirt*'.

[9]See Hannerz (1996), p. 234 for an elaboration on this point, and on the concept of culture.

There are numerous definitions of culture, maybe as many as there are anthropologists. Whereas *culture* previously was used as a noun—we talked about a culture, as bounded, fixed and whole—anthropologists now rather treat it as an adverb, the cultural, symbolic, meaning-making aspect of any given context. Anthropologists realised that the (globalised) world does not consist of bounded *cultures* as everywhere symbolic worlds mix and collective meaning-making systems overlap.

Today, culture is thus treated as an important aspect of any situation, and there is a reason why anthropologists keep insisting on studying culture and pointing out its importance. The reason is that people in general are quite unaware of their own culture and how it effects their actions and their thinking. That is why the study of culture is still one of anthropology's most important contributions.

What then is culture anthropologically speaking? Rather than proposing yet another definition of the term, we will start with an example. Imagine you are a parent and want to spend a nice day out with your child. You think that going to the zoo would be a good idea, to let your child see lions, tigers and elephants. You invest a lot of time, energy and money in this project. However, once you reach the zoo, you are in for a disappointment. Instead of marvelling at the animals, your small child immediately runs to the zoo kiosk, nagging about ice cream. You believe your trip has been a failure as your child has not realised that it is lions, tigers and elephants that make the zoo special rather than ice cream, which you could buy anywhere. Hence, you return home thinking that this was a waste of time, energy and money. A few years later, the two of you visit the zoo again. And this time, as if by magic, your child immediately runs to see the lions, tigers and elephants. You are satisfied; a success at last, your child has 'got it'.

Such a mundane example is maybe not what we immediately associate with culture. More often, we may think about culture in terms of world views, religions, ethics and morals rather than everyday life situations. But it is in such situations that culture is most at play, manifesting itself not as explicit, consciously stated *world views* but simply as assumptions about how things are. It is self-evident to us that the focus at a zoo should be animals, not ice cream.

Each and every one of us lives in one and the same world. Still, our ideas about what is good and bad, what is beautiful and ugly and what is important in different situations vary. The reason is that culture makes us focus on certain aspects of life, while other issues simultaneously remain out of sight so we do not even notice them. Culture directs our attention and tells us what should be at the centre of our attention, what should be in the foreground and what should remain in the background.

Culture abounds everywhere equally; there is not more culture in some contexts than in others. Neither is it the case that *immigrants* have more culture than receiving countries nor that culture is more abundant in *traditional* societies than industrialised ones. It is only that we notice culture more easily among others than among ourselves since we take our own culture for granted.

Culture is neither individual or chosen nor explicit or conscious. The reason our child directed his or her attention to the animals during the second visit to the zoo is not because we have told him or her that animals are the main attraction of a zoo. The child has simply learnt that this is the case by growing up in our society, among us. Our social settings infuse us with culture, without us even noticing it. Culture is thus not something that we individually choose to follow, nor do we actually know our own culture very well. We are simply not aware of this culture surrounding us because it is simply the way we perceive how things *are*. Therefore, we rarely need to make culture explicit or conscious; it is implicit and unspoken.

Anthropologists understand culture not so much as something developed by *thought*, or controlled by the mind, but more as emotional reactions, situated in our guts, under our skin. Consider you were to enter a bus in Uppsala, Sweden. There is only one person on the bus as you embark. Which is the one seat you will most likely not take? It will usually be the seat next to the other passenger. Choosing that particular seat would be considered antisocial behaviour in this social context. Similarly, if you were the one to sit alone on a bus and one more person entered and sat down beside you, how would you react? Probably with a feeling of discomfort, maybe even fear, a gut reaction, not a conscious thought. You probably would not realise your reaction to be based on culture but simply feel that the person sitting beside you is strange, perhaps even dangerous. However, if you were to take the bus in a different part of the world, say on the way to our African village mentioned above, to examine the water pump we built, the opposite may be true. If you do not sit down next to the only person on the bus besides you, and engage in conversation, you may be considered weird and antisocial.

Even if culture is symbolic, and as such affects us on a mental level, it produces very tangible effects in the material and social world since culture makes us act and, hence, shapes the world. Even though we cannot access the minds of other people, we can study their culture and examine how it shapes the way they act; that is culture's social and material effects.

Since culture relates more to gut feelings than rational thought, it is very difficult to change it by rational argument. Culture is deeply embedded in us, situated under our skin, unspoken, implicit. And since we simply are not aware of most of our culture—since we are inclined to believe that a certain set of social rules is simply how things are—it is difficult to deal with culture through rational argument.

It is easier to take note of the culture of others than one's own culture. Therefore, it is easy to jump to the conclusion that to take the culture of other, culturally different, persons into consideration or *dealing with culture conflict* is about getting to know *their* culture and being sensitive to *their* culture. It is easy to forget that, in all such situations, a meeting of cultures is at play, *theirs* and *ours*, and that without getting to know and dealing with *our* culture in the first place, we will not achieve much. This means that when we deal with *local culture* as part of humanitarian work, this should involve immersing ourselves in both the culture of the humanitarian victims and our culture as humanitarian workers. This is one reason why the anthropology of humanitarianism is as important as anthropology in humanitarianism.

But if culture is about how we perceive things to be, is it not equally important to find out how things actually are? Consider the example of two well-known symbols: first, the crucifix, to all appearances a cultural symbol, a symbol of a world view that explains life to us, why things happen, what they mean, why things go wrong and what we should do to prevent misfortune in the future (things went bad as a punishment from God; if we follow his commandments in the future, things will be better). It is a cultural symbol that has social and material effects as it shapes our actions; it instructs believers what they should do, when and with whom and coordinates peoples' actions (go to Sunday mass, pay your tenth to the church).

Now, consider a second symbol, the watch, which also functions as a cultural symbol; it tells us why things go bad and how to prevent misfortune in the future (I was late; I must be on time next time), and it shapes our actions, what we do, when and with whom (be at work from 8 a.m. to 5 p.m., take the bus home at 5:08 p. m., spend the weekend with my family).

Both, the crucifix and the watch, function as cultural symbols, and equally so. However, what if we counter by saying that religion is something you believe in whereas the clock just shows what is? If I were to wear a crucifix around my neck, it is imaginable that, although rude, someone might come up to ask me, 'So, do you believe in God? Do you really know that God exists? Can you prove that God exists?'—to which I would have to answer, 'No, I cannot prove that God exists'. On the other hand, if I were wearing a watch on my wrist, it is difficult to imagine anyone asking the following questions: 'So, do you believe in time? Do you really know what time is? Can you prove that it exists?' Nevertheless, my answer would most likely be similar to the one given in response to the questions about God: 'No, I do not know what time is, and I cannot prove its existence'. We would hardly find it reasonable to even ask these questions, simply because *time* is cultural and something we take for granted.

Hence, even if some people may be able to prove that time exists and understand its nature, this is not the reason time has the power over us that it does. It has this power over us because we allow it, because we believe in it, the same way many of us believe in religion. It is through its cultural rather than factual power that time rules our lives. The real nature of reality is beside the point here. Symbols may function as cultural, whether or not they represent facts, and it is not its true value that determines whether a symbol will be successful as a cultural symbol or not.

This means that when dealing with culture—which happens very often as any human context involves culture—truth, rational argument, knowledge, information and even education will have little effect. One aspect of Western culture is that it tends to believe in the power of knowledge and information, putting faith in education. However, information alone is often not powerful enough to alter behaviour. The reason why people smoke is hardly because they are unaware that it is dangerous for their health. The reason why people do things is more often than not that culturally desired outcomes are at stake or because the system they live in rationalises seemingly irrational actions. This was the case of my friend who put five months of salary into a jacket. Telling her this was a bad idea would hardly have prevented her from doing it.

6 Anthropological Methods: Fieldwork, Participant Observation and Ethnography

Anthropological experience shows that there is often a marked discrepancy between how people say they act and how they actually act. This is not because people tend to lie when it comes to their own actions but because people are often unaware of what they actually do. Part of the reason is that culture shapes our self-perception to such a large degree. We aim to be particular persons; we aspire to certain traits and positions. When we talk about what we do, culturally defined ideals influence how we choose to carry and present ourselves. What we really do can be something quite different. Consider, for example, the idealistic notions of humanitarianism found in treaties and resolutions and how different the reality of providing humanitarian aid in the field can be. Both the real and the ideal are important, but different, parts of the humanitarian experience.

In a sense, this is a gloomy picture; if people say one thing and actually do another, acting on the basis of unconscious affiliation to a particular culture, wouldn't they then, so to speak, not even know why they act as they do? How can we then ever study and understand anyone? Simply interviewing people and conducting surveys is apparently not sufficient. These methods are important but will not take you all the way.

This chapter began with explanations of several theoretical concepts. However, this does not mean that anthropology started with developing a set of abstract theories and then set out to collect empirical material. The opposite was the case. Anthropology began with the collection of empirical material and only derived its concepts on the basis of results from the field. It thus, to a large extent, refers to fieldwork and ethnography. Anthropology has grown out of methodological practices that investigate both what people say they do and what they actually do. Anthropologists use fieldwork, participant observation and writing ethnography to conduct their research.

By both listening to what people say, and observing what they actually do, both professed ideals and real actions can be discerned. Anthropologists go about this by living together with the people they study, following their daily routine, for an extended period of time, often years. Such actions are part of fieldwork and participant observation as described by anthropologist Clifford Geertz.[10] Anthropologists transcribe these observations in a process called ethnography.

I conducted both fieldwork and participant observations for almost a year in Siberia, where I lived with my friend Tanya. We shared a bunk bed, with me on the top bunk and her and her daughter on the bottom bunk. I participated in Tanya's and her friends' and family's life, doing what they did. To a large extent, this meant drinking tea, going to the sauna and digging potatoes as these were their main activities. This is not to say my study was dedicated entirely to tea drinking,

[10]For more elaborations on fieldwork and participant observation, see Amit (1999) and Robben and Sluka (2011).

frequenting saunas or potato growing. The theme was 'Post-Soviet transformation among the indigenous peoples of northern Russia'. My research thus concerned a much more abstract and political issue than the practical and mundane activities I often engaged in during my stay. If I had simply asked people about *post-Soviet transformations*, I would have received one—idealised—answer, whereas through sharing their daily activities conversing and chats, I got another—real—answer. Hence, fieldwork and participant observation are a way to experience how the persons studied practice and act out things in everyday life, and participating in seemingly mundane activities can be a window to learning about many aspects of the local society, which go far beyond the activities themselves.

After I returned from my stay in Siberia, I wrote an ethnography about my experiences. The term ethnography refers to both the method of collecting material and the mode of presenting it. It attempts to give the reader a sense of the lives of the informants, as if one stood in their shoes. Descriptions engaging all five senses, quotes and examples are especially important. Writing an ethnography is in a way similar to the approach I have chosen in trying to write this text, using as little specialised vocabulary as possible and supporting my arguments with examples so that anyone is able to understand it.[11]

Fieldwork, participant observation and ethnography characterise and, to a large extent, define anthropology. Although anthropology *invented* these methods, they are today used in many other disciplines. The invention of these methods came about by mere chance. Bronislaw Malinowski, the father of long-term fieldwork, conducted his first field research quite involuntarily. As a Polish national living in Australia, which fought on the side of the British, the enemy, during World War I, he was considered an *enemy national* and not allowed to leave Australia. As a result, he decided to dedicate his time to conducting research on the Pacific Trobriand Islands for several years, becoming the first person to engage in modern fieldwork. This resulted in the classic ethnography *Argonauts of the Western Pacific*, published in 1922.[12] Since that time, there has been an extensive development of fieldwork, participant observation and ethnography within anthropology, but the basic idea has remained the same: going somewhere; living with locals; talking to them, preferably in their own language; sharing their daily activities; doing what they do; and later describing the experiences in text.

This particular methodology means that as an academic discipline, anthropology differs in significant ways from natural science and quantitative social science.[13] For one thing, anthropology is inductive, not deductive. Rather than developing a hypothesis that is then to be proved or disproved empirically, anthropologists let fieldwork experiences guide the course of their investigation. So depending on what they learn from informants, they may end up somewhere completely different from where they started.

[11] A few examples of interesting ethnographies include: Abu-Lughod (1999), Farella (1990) and Shostak (2009).

[12] Malinowski (1922).

[13] For a more thorough discussion, see Michrina and Richards (1996).

In my own case, fieldwork led me to question one of the fundamental categories that my research proposal was based upon: that of *indigenous peoples*. On the basis of what I learnt from digging potatoes and drinking tea, I came to the conclusion that rather than something that simply *exists* out there, *indigenous peoples* can be better understood as mental categories by anthropologists, who project them on the world. This had not in any way been my initial hypothesis. I had never thought along these lines before beginning my fieldwork. The realisation came about as a result of my field experience.

In a natural scientific tradition, it would be a problem to diverge from an initial hypothesis, but in anthropology it is expected. This is because anthropology aims to create understanding rather than proving hypotheses. Anthropologists can rarely claim that their findings are *statistically significant*, the way other social sciences may argue. This is not what anthropologists try to achieve.

Instead, anthropology has the potential to discover truly new insights, the unexpected and unknown, things we never even thought about asking. But this requires a very open mind, curiosity, humility in relation to informants and the realisation that everything needs to be investigated—especially that which is familiar and which you think you already know.

In this way, fieldwork has the potential to alter your own world view. This is often a painful process, during which you have to question yourself and the ideas you take for granted. Living with people for a long time in a foreign setting gets under your skin; it may be difficult but also immensely rewarding. You will certainly never be the same again. Despite the process often being painful, the change affected is often for the better. The same is probably true for humanitarian fieldwork. It is not only a job; it will ruffle and upset you. Hence, humanitarian work may be both painful and rewarding.

It is clear that, in anthropology, the social person of the anthropologist is crucial for the success of any study. Anthropology differs from the natural sciences in the way that subjective bias is necessary and good, not something to avoid. In anthropological fieldwork, you will be your own methodological tool. It takes a human to understand another human. This means that your own subjectivity and empathy as an anthropologist, i.e. bias, is what enables you to understand other people. But that same bias will also make you misinterpret and misunderstand others. Therefore, subjectivity is considered bad and something to avoid in natural and quantitative sciences. Anthropology deals with these problems of bias in a different way, through constant reflexivity.

The process is as follows: as your experiences in fieldwork lead your understanding into a certain direction, you will encounter difficulties, issues that contradict this understanding. Having to face such challenges is usually a sign that your bias is tricking you. You then need to reflect on your own bias; what is it about my subjective person that makes me misunderstand this situation? Is it the fact that I am a woman, single mother of two teenage sons, middle aged, educated, urban, secular, etc. that instils certain prejudices in me? Am I interpreting this situation on the basis of my own perspective rather than on the basis of what the world looks like from the perspective of those whose culture I am here to study? Am I not practising methodological relativism? Such reflexions on your own bias may enable you to overcome challenges in fieldwork, and the process will deepen your understanding. Anthropological fieldwork and participant observation are qualitative, interpretative methods in the hermeneutic process of continuously deepened, but never absolute, understanding.

Yet if anthropological methods are steeped in subjective bias, and you never reach a clear answer, only continuous, deepened understanding, how can the quality of anthropological knowledge be assessed? How does one determine that one anthropological study is better than the other? Validation in disciplines using qualitative methods is very different from validation in disciplines using quantitative methods. The latter determines quality through replication of a particular study. If I do the same as you did and reach the same result, this means your study is of sound quality.

This form of validation requires a study to be made within a controlled environment, not in real time and in real-life situations, so that it can be replicated at all. This is not the case with anthropology. Since we do fieldwork in real time, engaging in the lives of real people, it is principally impossible to replicate studies. Even if you were to travel to the same place where I did fieldwork and talk to the same people I talked to, your current situation will be different from the one I experienced, and you will be a different social person than me. Hence, the result must also deviate from mine. Replication is therefore not an option to validate anthropological studies.

Anthropology is validated differently, through consistency of description. If the ethnography I write makes sense, is internally consistent, helps to explain more things than other ethnographies do, is able to incorporate additional empirical and theoretical material and still remains consistent, then it is an ethnography of high quality.

It was through this same mode of validation that I realised that the idea of indigenous peoples simply *existing* cannot be maintained but is better understood as a mental construction of the anthropologists, who project it onto the world. This adapted way of viewing indigenous peoples helped me make more sense of my experience in the field, and more sense of the particular culture of people I met in Siberia.

These aspects of inductivity, bias, subjectivity, challenge, hermeneutic circle, validation through consistency and understanding all fit well into the spectrum of studies on humanitarianism. They can be practised both in humanitarianism and in the scrutiny of humanitarianism. Any humanitarian can use them in their everyday work. This method may indeed be the greatest contribution of anthropology to humanitarianism.

But there is one point at which anthropology and humanitarianism diverge: time. Anthropologic work progresses slowly. Fieldwork, participant observation and writing ethnography require a lot of time. Humanitarianism, on the other hand, is a race against time. Humanitarians must rapidly assess situations and make quick decisions. They cannot go through a year of fieldwork, investigation and writing ethnography before deciding on a course of action.

This divergence between anthropology and humanitarianism is not easily overcome and leads to a host of questions. Can anthropologists and humanitarians cooperate? Can anthropologists work for humanitarian organisations? Can humanitarians use anthropological methods and material? There are no straightforward answers to these questions. It is certain that humanitarians cannot afford to sit and wait for a year before deciding what to do. That would increase, rather than decrease, human suffering. Despite the differences, maybe even contradictions just outlined, there are still ways in which anthropologists and humanitarians could cooperate. As anthropologists have already studied many cultural contexts around the world, humanitarians may use existing ethnographies when entering new fields or cooperate with anthropologists who have worked or currently work in these fields. Anthropologists might also conduct studies for humanitarian organisations in geographical areas that often encounter humanitarian disasters. It is even imaginable to have a pool of anthropologists, who could switch between organisations, as their regional competencies are needed.

Nevertheless, as I have tried to convey in this introduction, the most important contribution of anthropology is not specific regional field experience but providing core concepts and perspectives, both in theory and method. These can be learnt and used by anyone. My hope is therefore that you, the students, will develop a bit of an anthropologist mindset and in your future careers use anthropological methods and concepts, where the situation requires and enables you to do so. In some situations, anthropology will provide valuable and useful tools and, in other situations, offer completely different perspectives and practices.

7 Conclusion

In this chapter, we have discussed some core notions and concepts, which together make up and shape the distinct character of anthropology. By keeping these concepts in mind during your studies of anthropology, and beyond in your work as a humanitarian, you will be able to come up with your own answers to the question of how anthropology may be of interest to humanitarian aid, and, more importantly, how you will choose to make it relevant.

References

Abu-Lughod L (1999) Veiled sentiments. Honour and poetry in a Bedouin society. University of California Press, Berkley

Amit V (1999) Constructing the field. Ethnographic fieldwork in contemporary world. Routledge, London

Bornstein E, Redfield P (eds) (2011) Forces of compassion: humanitarianism between ethics and politics. School for Advanced Research Press, Santa Fe

Douglas M (2002) Purity and danger: an analysis of concept of pollution and taboo. Routledge, London

Eriksen TH (2010) Small places, large issues: an introduction to social and cultural anthropology. Pluto Press, London

Farella J (1990) The main stalk: a synthesis of Navajo philosophy. The University of Arizona Press, Tucson

Hannerz U (1996) Transnational connections: culture, people, places. Routledge, London

Kuper A (1996) Anthropology and anthropologists: the modern British school. Routledge, London and New York

Malinowski B (1922) Argonauts of the Western Pacific: an account of native enterprises and adventures in the Archipelagoes of Melanesian New Guinea. Routledge and Kegan, London

Mauss M (2001 [1925]) The gift. Routledge, New York

Michrina BP, Richards C (1996) Person to person. Fieldwork, dialogue, and the hermeneutic method. State University of New York Press, Albany

Moberg M (2012) Engaging anthropological theory: a social and political history. Routledge, London and New York

Robben ACG, Sluka JA (2011) Ethnographic fieldwork: an anthropological reader. Wiley, Oxford

Shostak M (2009) Nisa - the life and words of a !Kung woman. Harvard University Press, Cambridge

Tambiah SJ (1990) Magic, science, religion, and the scope of rationality. Cambridge University Press, Cambridge

Wilk RR, Cliggett LC (1996) Economies and cultures: foundations of economic anthropology. Westview, Oxford

Further Reading

Chernoff J (2003) Hustling is not stealing. Stories of an African bar girl. University of Chicago Press, Chicago

Finnström S (2008) Living with bad surroundings: war, history, and everyday moments in northern Uganda. Duke University Press, Durham

Harris M (1979) Cultural materialism: the struggle for a science of culture. Random House, New York

Höjdestrand T (2009) Needed by nobody: homelessness and humanness in post-socialist Russia. Cornell University Press, Ithaca

Maček I (2009) Sarajevo under siege. Anthropology in wartime. University of Pennsylvania Press, Philadelphia

Ong A (1999) Flexible citizenship: the cultural logics of transnationality. Duke University Press, Durham

Robben C (ed) (2010) Iraq at a distance: what anthropologists can teach us about the war. University of Pennsylvania Press, Philadelphia

Ulrika Persson-Fischier holds a PhD of social anthropology and is a Lecturer at the Division of Industrial Engineering and Management of Uppsala University, Sweden.

Anthropological Perspectives

Odina Benoist

Anthropology in a broad sense can be defined as the study of diversity through time and across space. It comprises two main fields: biological anthropology, which deals with biological diversity, and sociocultural anthropology, which deals with sociocultural diversity. Table 1 compares the characteristics of both anthropological approaches. This chapter explores the second field.

What perspective should anthropologists adopt in their work in order to achieve an accurate comprehension of sociocultural diversity? How should they proceed when entering a social universe so far unknown to them? What means should they implement to succeed in seeing the world through the eyes of the members of the society studied, to understand facts using their way of thinking, to feel as they feel? How do anthropologists manage to seize the meaning that another society gives to matters like birth, death, war or natural disaster? Assuming an anthropological perspective implies, on the one hand, a particular way of conducting fieldwork on the basis of in-depth surveys and participant observation, as Bronislaw Malinowski proposed to do from his own experience in the Trobriand Islands in the 1910s. Later on, fieldwork underwent a rapid and general diffusion in anthropology, and anthropologists have steadily improved and enriched fieldwork techniques throughout the twentieth century. These fieldwork techniques are discussed in the previous chapter.

Following an anthropological perspective implies, on the other hand, becoming familiar with some conceptual tools that should guide the anthropologist in fieldwork, both during the data collection phase and during the subsequent analysis of the data that he or she will present in a report, article or book. Conceptual tools in anthropology are diverse. This chapter will present some tools judged essential in order to deal with otherness, i.e., notions that may be useful in any situation where

O. Benoist (✉)
Aix-Marseille University, Aix-en-Provence, France
e-mail: odina.benoist@univ-amu.fr

© Springer International Publishing AG 2018

H.-J. Heintze, P. Thielbörger (eds.), *International Humanitarian Action*,
DOI 10.1007/978-3-319-14454-2_15

Table 1 Biological and sociocultural anthropologists

Biological anthropologists seek to understand how humans adapt to diverse environments; how biological and cultural processes work together to shape growth, development and behaviour; and what causes disease and early death. In addition, they are interested in human biological origins, evolution and variation. They give primary attention to investigating questions having to do with evolutionary theory, our place in nature, adaptation and human biological variation. To understand these processes, biological anthropologists study other primates (primatology), the fossil record (palaeoanthropology), prehistoric people (bioarchaeology) and the biology (e.g., health, cognition, hormones, growth and development) and genetics of living populations.	**Sociocultural anthropologists** examine social patterns and practices across cultures, with a special interest in how people live in particular places and how they organise, govern and create meaning. A hallmark of sociocultural anthropology is its concern with similarities and differences, both within and among societies, and its attention to race, sexuality, class, gender and nationality. Research in sociocultural anthropology is distinguished by its emphasis on participant observation, which involves placing oneself in the research context for extended periods of time to gain a first-hand sense of how local knowledge is put to work in grappling with practical problems of everyday life and with basic philosophical problems of knowledge, truth, power and justice. Topics of concern to sociocultural anthropologists include such areas as health, work, ecology and environment, education, agriculture and development, and social change.

Reproduced by kind permission of the American Anthropological Association from What is Anthropology?, http://www.americananthro.org/AdvanceYourCareer/Content.aspx?ItemNumber=2150 (accessed on 14 April 2017)

one could be faced with cultural diversity, which is often much more difficult to seize and to deal with than it may seem. We thus first examine the concept of *culture* before dealing with the distinction between an emic approach and an etic approach to culture. We lastly explore the concepts of ethnocentrism and cultural relativism.

1 Understanding Culture

1.1 Defining Culture

The term culture has different meanings. It was introduced in the field of anthropology in the last decades of the nineteenth century and became more prevalent over the course of the twentieth century. The first anthropological definition of culture was proposed in 1871 by the British anthropologist Edward B. Tylor (1832–1917): 'Culture or Civilization, taken in its wide ethnographic sense, is that complex whole which includes knowledge, belief, art, morals, law, custom, and any other capabilities and habits acquired by man as a member of society.'[1]

[1]Tylor (1871), p. 1.

A representative of cultural evolutionism, which had the objective of conceiving a history of mankind in which every society should have its place, Tylor provided a definition where culture appears as 'a neutral term that may be applied to the whole mankind and that allows to finish with a certain approach to 'primitives' that considered them as beings apart'.[2] Many other definitions followed Tylor's, two of which we explore next.

On the basis of the opposition between nature and culture, Melville Herskovits (1895–1963) wrote: 'Culture is the man-made part of the environment.'[3] The image of the garden may illustrate this point: many people like gardens because they love nature. However, does a garden solely reflect nature? Flowers, trees and earth do. On the other hand, arranging flowers and pruning hedges in a certain way, growing foreign species, pulling out certain plants because we consider them to be weeds are cultural actions that shape the nature contained in a garden.

Clifford Geertz's (1926–2006) definition of culture focuses on the meaning of cultural facts, on the symbolic dimension, that is an inherent characteristic of culture. Geertz defines culture as 'an historically transmitted pattern of meanings embodied in symbols, a system of inherited conceptions expressed in symbolic forms by means of which men communicate, perpetuate, and develop their knowledge about and their attitudes toward life'.[4] Culture is thus the web of significance that man has spun and to which he is suspended[5]; culture is a context that allows people to explain their actions, their thoughts, their feelings.[6] Geertz makes a clear distinction between social structure and culture. He does not disregard the study of social structure, which he defines as the 'economic, political, and social relations among individuals and groups',[7] but he considers culture, that is only the pattern of meanings embedded in symbols, to be the object of the study of anthropology.

In sum, culture provides society with a common framework of references that explains the meaning of beliefs and practices. Culture thus guides the actions of people in social life. It would be wrong, however, to assume that culture acts as a programme operating on passive human beings. Culture guides human action but does not determine it. As a matter of fact, the reasons for certain types of actions and decisions that one takes depend on culture, but other decisions and actions may be due to economic constraints, social class or political affiliation. This should never be forgotten. It is true that acquaintance with the culture of a community allows for a better understanding of community members' real lives. However, social life cannot be reduced to an explanation that only takes into account cultural references. Even though individuals, under certain circumstances, are likely to act according to their cultural references, they will, on other occasions, act as members

[2]Cuche (1996), p. 16. Translation by author.

[3]Herskovits (1948), p. 17.

[4]Geertz (1973), p. 89.

[5]*Id.*, p. 5.

[6]*Id.*, p. 14.

[7]*Id.*, p. 362.

of a social class or according to ethnic belonging, religious beliefs, political factors or economic constraints.

1.2 Universality and Specificity of Culture

According to the definitions discussed, culture is an essential attribute of the human condition, and in this sense, it is universal. Every human being, in contrast to other living beings, has a culture.[8] Culture is thus something that unifies mankind. In this sense, we refer to *culture* in singular form.

However, culture, this distinctive feature of human condition, appears in human history as a diversity of cultures. This means that whereas culture unifies humans and differentiates them from all other living beings, it also differentiates human communities from each other: although all societies explain how the world was created, why the sun rises every day, what the sense of life and of death is and so on, these explanations vary from one society to another. We thus speak of 'cultures', in the plural form.

What do differences between cultures consist of? More specifically, when do differences between two communities lead us to speak of the existence of two distinct cultures? French anthropologist Claude Levi-Strauss replies to this question in the following way:

> What is called a 'culture' is a fragment of humanity which, from the point of view of the research at hand and of the scale on which the latter is carried out, presents significant discontinuities in relation to the rest of humanity. If our aim is to ascertain significant discontinuities between, let us say, North America and Europe, then we are dealing with two different cultures; but should we become concerned with significant discontinuities between New York and Chicago, we would be allowed to speak of these two groups as different cultural units.[9]

This implies that the term 'culture' is a concept, which must be applied according to the investigation that the researcher wishes to carry out, and that 'cultures' are not 'things' that have been predefined once and for all. Culture is thus an intellectual construct developed by the researcher on the basis of behaviour that he or she observes and of meanings that individuals express in a given community. Culture is thus a construct corresponding to an observed reality.

[8]However, this idea should be reviewed on account of recent research concerning cultural behaviour of animal communities.

[9]Lévi-Strauss (1963), p. 295.

1.3 *Permanence and Dynamics of Culture*

Transmissibility is a key feature of culture, meaning it is passed on from one generation to the next. Parents instil in their children what their own group considers to be *good* behaviour, *correct* practices and those values the children *should* make their own. Individuals are thus shaped by the culture of their own group from the very first years of their life, and without being aware of it, they learn to perceive these behaviours, practices and values as evidence of their very humanity—i.e., as natural facts—instead of perceiving them as what they really are, a way of thinking and acting that has been conditioned by their community—i.e., as cultural facts. This is why we can say that transmission of culture is a social process that is intimately associated to a process of naturalisation of culture.

Transmissibility implies reproduction of culture: general practices, thoughts and feelings of a community are those of the elders of the group and come from the distant past. However, such reproduction does not suppose that the cultural features of a society remain forever the same as the transmission of tradition is always accompanied by a certain degree of change. This is because culture is dynamic, although the pace of change varies from one community to another. Alongside norms and practices that are maintained, others are modified more or less significantly or even disappear, while some innovations find their place within this whole we refer to as culture.

It is thus essential to take into account the two dimensions that characterise culture: permanence and change. In fact, culture clearly shows the aspect of permanence over the passage of time, while change is reflected by its reproduction. For example, despite considerable differences, seventeenth century and present French culture demonstrate a continuity, which makes French culture recognizable; however, these observable differences between the cultural framework of two periods, separated by a long and eventful history, also explain the fact that a Frenchman of the twenty-first century cannot identify anymore with many attitudes and values that characterised seventeenth century French culture.

2 The 'Emic' and 'Etic' Approaches to Culture

References to the 'etic' and 'emic' approaches to culture are numerous in anthropological literature. These terms were coined by the American linguist Kenneth Pike (1912–2000) in an attempt to transpose conceptual tools of linguistics into the study of culture.

On the basis of the distinction between the respective aims of phonetics and phonemics, Pike created the notions of 'etic' and 'emic', by keeping just the last part of the names of these two branches of linguistics. Phonetics is the study of language as a system of material sounds, focusing on the acoustic dimension of language regardless of its speakers' perception, and it is based on data gathered from objective observations and measurements. Phonemics is the study of language as a system of significant sounds, or a system of phonemes; it centres on phonemic contrasts that are relevant for speakers (for example, an English speaker distinguishes 'tip' and 'dip' as different words with different meaning because 't' and 'd' are two different phonemes in English) and thus necessarily takes into account the specific features of individual languages. Each of these branches of linguistics implies a specific perspective as regards the study of sounds in language. Both approaches are complementary as well as equally necessary to this study.

It is this double perspective of linguistics that Pike, in the 1950s, proposed to extend to the study of culture.[10] Despite criticism, essentially by American anthropologists, the distinction emic/etic is still widely used in Anglophone social sciences: when considering the beliefs and practices of members of a society, researchers may adopt two different but complementary perspectives.

The emic perspective, which Pike refers to as 'internal' or 'domestic',[11] is the one that corresponds to the inner workings of society: researchers try to penetrate society by studying concepts that are meaningful for social actors and explanations that they themselves offer about their own behaviour and practices; the aim is to understand the viewpoint of members of the society under study, to see the world through their eyes.

The etic perspective, which Pike refers to as 'external' or 'alien',[12] is external to society: the researcher analyses a cultural fact by using concepts that are meaningful for him or her but not for the people directly concerned by that cultural fact; the aim is to highlight a number of factors that appear to be 'invisible' to the social

---

[10]In: Language in Relation to a unified Theory of the Structure of Human Behavior (Summer Institute of Linguistics, Glendale, California 1954, p. 8), Kenneth Pike defined the etic and the emic approaches as follows:

> There are two basic standpoints from which a human observer can describe human behavior, each of them valuable for certain specific purposes. In the one, the etic approach to the data, an author is primarily concerned with generalized statements about the data, such that he (a) classifies systematically all comparable data, of all cultures in the world, into a single system; (b) provides a set of criteria to classify any bit of such data; (c) organizes into types the elements so classified; (d) studies, identifies and describes any newly found data in reference to this system which has been created by the analyst before studying the particular culture within which the new data have been found.
>
> In contrast to the etic approach an emic one is in essence valid for only one language (or one culture) at a time – or, more specifically, for only one minimum dialect at a time or for the relatively homogeneous and integrated behavior of people of one culture area or culturally defined class of people; it is an attempt to discover and to describe the pattern of that particular language or culture in reference to the way in which the various elements of that culture are related to each other in the functioning of that particular pattern, rather than an attempt to describe them in reference to a generalized classification derived in advance of the study of that particular culture.

[11]*Id.*, p. 10.

[12]*Ibid.*

actors' eyes, allowing for general comparisons or to formulate a theory. Let us look at an example.

In many Latin American societies, which have been influenced by Spanish folk culture since colonial times (by cultural legacy or by acculturation), people recognise a folk illness called *susto* (Span. 'fright'). Beyond some general features, the specific perception of this illness varies from one society to another. Taking an emic perspective, let us first examine some elements that characterise *susto* in a mestizo society in the Chaco region of northern Argentina.[13] This illness, which in this area affects almost exclusively young children, can be caused by any strong and sudden experience of fear. According to the belief, such a shock has two consequences: first, a worm supposed to reside inside the human spine climbs to the neck of the victim, which is painful enough to cause convulsions; second, a vital quality abandons the body of the victim (our interlocutors expressed this fact in terms of loss of spirit, strength and even the name of the victim). However, the root cause of this illness lies in the fragility of the spirit (the vital quality) of children affected. Hence, the treatment administered to victims aims to fortify them against fragility: when the healer sprays holy water from his own mouth in the form of a cross on the child's face, and makes it breathe in the smoke emanating from burned rosemary, incense and myrrh, he transfuses to the child the *force of God* (contained in holy water, the cross and the elements burned), as well as part of the force of his own body (which he emits from his mouth). An herbal tea, made from plants classified as 'hot', then transmits supplementary force to the child as people in this society perceive a close link between force and *hot* elements (*hot* food and *hot* remedies that transmit heat to the body, independently of their temperature in degrees). Christian baptism is regarded as a prevention of *susto* because of the *force of God* that this practice communicates to the child.

The contrast between force and fragility is a key explanatory axis of illness and treatment in this society, but it also concerns several other spheres, including the life cycle, annual cycle, lunar cycle and gender differences. An individual's body and spirit are naturally fragile at birth and become stronger with age, over the course of the cycle of life; this explains the fact that, in this society, *susto* affects almost exclusively children. As for gender differences, women's body and spirit are naturally more fragile than men's; this explains the fact that when *susto* exceptionally affects an adult, it will be a woman.

Our example illustrates how, on the basis of an emic perspective, a society explains a cultural fact and establishes links between different domains.

In other Latin American societies, mainly adults are affected by *susto*. Such is the case in Mexico, where Arthur Rubel, Carl O'Nell and Rolando Collado have studied *susto* not to deepen its cultural meaning but to investigate its significance as regards morbidity; this required an etic approach. The researchers centred on three culturally and linguistically different groups in order to be able to draw general conclusions. The three groups were settled in the state of Oaxaca, Mexico:

[13] Sturzenegger (1999).

Zapotecs, Chinantecs and Ladinos. All groups explained *susto* as the consequence of a frightful experience that results in the loss of vital force: the *alma* (soul) among Ladinos, the *bi* (strength, voice, respiration) among Chinantecs and the *espírit* (a vital force that is distinct from the soul that departs from the body with death) among Zapotecs. As part of the treatment of *susto*, all three groups accomplish the soul-calling ritual, a widespread practice in which the healer calls the soul by the patient's name and persuades it to return.

The researchers' goal was then to see what *susto* as sickness reflected in terms of pathology. Given that symptoms recurrently invoked were loss of appetite, weight and physical strength, restlessness during sleep, apathy during waking hours, depression and introversion, as well as lack of motivation for daily work,[14] Rubel assumed, in 1964, that there was a link between *susto* and stress: in Spanish American societies, *susto* would thus be a way to respond to a stressful situation.[15] The interdisciplinary study that Rubel carried out 20 years later with O'Nell and Collado broadened the initial view by taking into consideration interactions between clinical facts and social phenomena. Surveys then focused not on the cultural explanations for *susto* but on the victims' psychological state and quality of social relationships, as well as on their physical and psychiatric health. The study showed that any link between *susto* and psychiatric disorders was invalid, but it not only confirmed the soundness of the first hypothesis but also provided evidence that individuals identifying themselves as victims of *susto* also suffered from a greater number of diseases and had a higher mortality rate than the rest of the population.[16]

In this case, the researchers adopted an etic approach: variables taken into account did not make sense within the cultural framework of studied societies but were external to it. Meaningful in a foreign medical culture, these variables proved to also be fully relevant to reach a medical *diagnosis* from the observation of individuals affected by a disorder that modern medicine does not recognise.

A similar double standpoint analysis could be applied to the study of needs among a population in the wake of a natural disaster. An NGO could make such a study based on a list of shortcomings that international organisations generally view as 'needs' and that can allow comparisons to be made between different regions and time periods. This would correspond to an etic perspective because the needs have been defined from the outside and serve, according to an internationally accepted kind of analysis, to measure the extent of a crisis, to establish the diagnosis of a situation, to make comparisons between situations. From an emic perspective, we would leave out such lists and would take the time for an in-depth investigation by making sure that people can freely express themselves on whether they feel needs and what they are. Both inquiries have necessarily different objectives—which may eventually be complementary—and they will surely result in strikingly different results. Table 2 lists the main aspects of emics and etics.

[14]Rubel (1964), p. 270.

[15]*Id.*, p. 280.

[16]Rubel et al. (1991) [1984], pp. 112–120.

Table 2 Emics and etics

Emics and Etics represent two perspectives for viewing cultural phenomena	
Emics	Etics
Emics is derived from 'phonemics'—sounds that native speakers recognise as being distinct and significant in distinguishing meaning.	Etics is derived from 'phonetics'—sounds that are distinguished by linguists but may or may not be meaningful to native speakers.
Emic knowledge represents views of thoughts and behaviour from the perspective of the participants.	Etic knowledge represents views of thoughts and behaviour from the perspective of the observer/researcher.
Emic descriptions are regarded as meaningful and appropriate by members of the culture being studied.	Etic accounts and descriptions are expressed in terms of categories that are regarded as meaningful and appropriate by the community of scientific observers.
Emic knowledge may not be applicable for generating scientific theories.	Etic knowledge must be applicable for generating theories of cross-cultural differences and similarities.
Emic knowledge achieves the status of 'emic' by passing the test of native consensus.	Etic knowledge is obtained through direct observation or elicitation or through participants trained by the observers.
Emic descriptions describe what is culturally meaningful rather than what is theoretically significant.	Etic descriptions do not have to be meaningful or appropriate to native informants to be deemed valid.

Reproduced by kind permission of the publisher from Harris, Marvin; Johnson, Orna, Cultural Anthropology, 5th Ed., Copyright 2000. Pearson Education, Inc., New York, New York

3 Ethnocentrism: The Belief in the Superiority of One's Own Culture

3.1 Defining Ethnocentrism

Concisely, ethnocentrism is a feeling of self-centredness that makes people regard the rest of the world through their own conceptual patterns. This term was coined by the American sociologist William Graham Sumner (1840–1910), who defined ethnocentrism as

> the technical name for this view of things in which one's own group is the center of everything, and all others are scaled and rated with reference to it. [...] Each group nourishes its own pride and vanity, boasts itself superior, exalts its own divinities, and looks with contempt on outsiders. Each group thinks its own folkways the only right ones, and if it observes that other groups have other folkways, these excite its scorn.[17]

Ethnocentrism is therefore a universal attitude. Every society views itself as a centre surrounded by a boundary beyond which mankind is less accomplished than inside. Members of traditional societies often refer to themselves as 'the men', 'the

[17]Sumner (1906), p. 13.

excellent', 'the beautiful people', 'the real people', whereas they talk about neighbouring groups by using names that depreciate their human quality, denigrating, for example, their appearance or their behaviour, such as 'ground-monkeys' or 'lousy eggs'.[18] Thus, the groups we often hear of referred to as Eskimos do not use this term to refer to themselves. *Eskimo* is the name that was given to them by Algonquians, their neighbours, in whose language it means 'those who eat raw meat'. This corresponded indeed to Eskimos' eating habits, but as these habits were for Algonquians a manifestation of *barbaric* behaviour, the term is manifestly pejorative. The Eskimo, on the other hand, call themselves 'Inuit' (sing. 'Inuk'), which means 'people' or 'persons'. We can also mention the fact that the languages of traditional societies often lack a general equivalent to the term 'human being': they only have ethnic appellations for their own group and for the different groups with whom they regularly or occasionally enter into contact.

The same difficulty in conceiving the idea of the oneness of mankind through cultural diversity concerned the so-called *historic* societies. The concepts of 'barbarian' and 'savage', formerly widespread, reflect a denial of cultural diversity. The term 'barbarian' in ancient Greece and Rome referred to those who were not part of Greek or Roman culture. 'Savage', in Western tradition, has been used to declassify from 'culture' and reclassify as parts of 'nature' those societies considered to not have attained advanced levels of civilisation. A savage animal or a savage plant is an *undomesticated* one. Qualifying a society as savage is a way of asserting that it is has remained in a natural state, devoid of any culture of its own.

Anthropology was marked in its early days, in the second half of the nineteenth century, by the ethnocentric attitude that pervaded an evolutionary model. Ethnocentrism consisted in ranking societies on the basis of cultural diversity.

The theory of cultural evolution coupled cultural diversity with different stages of a social development similar to the ages of life. This theory proposed a model of graded civilisational stages defined by the degree of technological development achieved by societies. The perceived link between technological progress and achievements in other social fields, accounting for the place of Western civilisation at the top of the pyramid, betrays Western society's feeling of superiority. However, it is important to remark that, from this perspective, cultural differences simply represent the state of the art at a particular moment in time. It may change since, following the theory of cultural evolution, every people has the intellectual capabilities to reach the highest civilisational stage.

This view lies at the opposite side of a racist position, according to which the innate biological faculties of a people determine the level of its civilisational possibilities. Racism is a historically dated ideology founded on pseudo-scientific assumptions, which ranks peoples on the basis of supposed biological capacities and for which differences between populations are impossible to overcome. Ethnocentrism, in contrast, is a universal attitude derived from the feeling that one's culture is preferable to those of others.

[18]Lévi-Strauss (1952), p. 12.

3.2 Consequences of Ethnocentrism

Ethnocentrism is not neutral as regards social relationships; it has both positive and negative implications. Its positive consequences concern the integrity of the group: firstly, ethnocentrism serves to maintain a sense of group solidarity by promoting people's pride; secondly, solidarity among individuals effectively builds up force for defending the group against external aggression or danger; finally, people's pride is a mechanism to preserve culture.

Ethnocentrism appears to be a normal sociological fact that has an essential social function as it assures cultures' continued existence, as explained by Jean-Pierre Simon:

> Ethnocentrism should be considered a fully normal fact, which makes possible, in fact, the existence of every ethnic group as such, ensures the preservation of its existence, constitutes a defence mechanism for the in-group against the outside world. In this sense, a certain degree of ethnocentrism is necessary for the survival of any ethnic group, since it appears that such a group cannot but disintegrate and vanish without the feeling widely shared by its members of the excellence and the superiority, at least in some aspect, of its language, its ways of living, feeling and thinking, its values and religion. The total loss of ethnocentrism leads to assimilation by adoption of the language, the culture, the values of a community regarded as superior.[19]

This view is fully shared by Melville J. Herskovits (1895–1963), even if it did not prevent him from becoming one of the major mentors of cultural relativism, which he theorised:

> The primary mechanism that makes for the evaluation of culture is ethnocentrism. Ethnocentrism is the point of view that one's own way of life is to be preferred to all others. Flowing logically from the process of early enculturation, most individuals have this feeling about their own culture, whether they verbalize it or not. Outside the stream of Euroamerican culture, particularly among nonliterate peoples, this is taken for granted rather than phrased in any precise terms. In this form, ethnocentrism is to be viewed as a factor making for individual adjustment and social integration. For the strengthening of the ego, identification with one's own group, whose ways are implicitly accepted as best, is all-important.[20]

Ethnocentrism's negative consequences concern the relationships between different groups. Problems essentially derive from the promotion of one group over others and are likely to be a source of social conflict. These negative consequences often affect the unity of complex societies; in this sense, ethnocentrism fits together with self-belongingness. In a multicultural society, it can become a cause of fragmentation if one group strongly manifests a sense of superiority over others.

We should never forget that the intercultural encounter is an encounter between two or more ethnocentrisms, which implies a double reason for misunderstanding and disagreement. Such difficulties are all the more important when there is a strong cultural divide between the groups that come into contact. This may, in extreme

[19] Simon (1993), pp. 57–63. Translation by author.

[20] Herskovits (1948), p. 68.

cases, lead to a point where the feeling of otherness implies doubts about the human condition of the members of another group. Claude Lévi-Strauss reports an anecdote that highlights the misfortune of two blind ethnocentrisms:

> [. . .] curious situations arise in which two parties at issue present a tragic reflection of one another's attitude. In the Greater Antilles, a few years after the discovery of America, while the Spaniards were sending out Commissions of investigation to discover whether or not the natives had a soul, the latter spent their time drowning white prisoners in order to ascertain, by long observation, whether or not their bodies would decompose.[21]

Ethnocentrism can have negative consequences even when accompanied by positive feelings. This is the case for those who work in development without asking themselves questions that could lead them to reconsider some of their practices. As the previous chapter describes in detail, we are accustomed to the gift of charity, to the generous gift, without the expectation of anything in return. This kind of gift is non-existent in the vast majority of traditional societies, where the motivation behind offering gifts is not generosity but the desire to initiate or seal a link with another individual. Such a gift implies reciprocity; it requires that the recipient of a gift provide a counter-gift to the donor so that a lasting link is established. Some development projects that include transfers of goods, which could be seen as gifts, fail to take this specificity into account. Such unintended ethnocentrism can lead to misunderstandings between development workers and local populations.

4 Cultural Relativism or the Equivalence of Cultures

4.1 Defining Cultural Relativism

The glory years of the theory of evolution and its theoretical model on the history of human societies were followed by a strong reaction on the part of anthropologists who, having adopted fieldwork and having therefore been in close contact with traditional societies, found that the evolutionary model was not helpful when trying to understand everyday life in these societies.

The perspective that emerged in this context, mainly based upon the experience of the American anthropologist Franz Boas (1858–1942), was to study a society in itself, avoiding to draw comparisons or to establish hierarchies. Since each culture is unique, any culture's wealth lies in its specificity, and cultural facts should be explained not in relation to any one model but within the context of the culture itself. Boas thus promoted an attitude of respect towards cultural difference and was the first to conjure the way of thinking we refer to today as cultural relativism, even if he never used this expression. Cultural relativism was subsequently explored by his disciple Melville Herskovits, who stated:

---

[21] Lévi-Strauss (1952), Simon (1993), p. 12.

> Cultural relativism is in essence an approach to the question of the nature and role of values in culture. It represents a scientific, inductive attack on an age-old philosophical problem, using fresh, cross-cultural data, hitherto not available to scholars, gained from the study of the underlying value-systems of societies having the most diverse customs. The principle of cultural relativism, briefly stated, is as follows: Judgments are based on experience, and experience is interpreted by each individual in terms of his own enculturation. Those who hold for the existence of fixed values will find materials in other societies that necessitate a reinvestigation of their assumptions. Are there absolute moral standards, or are moral standards effective only as far as they agree with the orientations of a given people at a given period of their history? We even approach the problem of the ultimate nature of reality itself.[22]

The theory of cultural relativism thus postulates the equivalence of all cultures. In other words, every culture, every world view, is as valid as any other. This does not imply denying the reality of technological progress of certain societies or even refusing the possibility of ranking cultures on the basis of certain individually considered quantifiable criteria (for example, number of working hours per day or week). For an anthropologist, adhering to cultural relativism means to recognise that it is not possible to make any intellectual or moral judgement concerning the values disclosed by a particular belief system or a particular form of social organisation as values depend on the particular society where they have been established. This produces an ethical relativism, for which

> there are no 'true' moral standards for everybody, or universal principles of duty or moral commitment. Any truth is contingent; it is part of a social, cultural and historical context. As it is unfeasible to determine absolute principles, moral judgments on the good and the evil are only possible within a given culture.[23]

4.2 *Criticism of Cultural Relativism*

Cultural relativism has been considered for several decades as a dogma that almost no anthropologist dared to challenge. However, this dogma has been gradually undermined for reasons paradoxically relating to ethics.

Anthropologists, in their desire to be respectful towards the peoples they studied, abstained from judging the relative merits of these peoples' culture as opposed to Western culture. Following decolonisation and the end of European rule, the populations of newly independent states themselves did not appear to doubt the *superiority* of some aspects of Western culture, mainly technology and accessibility to education and to health care, which led to development.

Former colonies that had just gained independence eagerly pursued development. In certain cases, such nations actually accused anthropologists of perpetuating colonial domination by putting too much emphasis on the significance of

[22] Herskovits (1955), Chapter 19, p. 353.

[23] Massé (2000), p. 15. Translation by author.

tradition, by excessively promoting outdated practices that in their view appeared as an obstacle to development. Thus, cultural relativism was challenged by the very people who were supposed to benefit from it.

Criticism from anthropologists themselves only appeared somewhat later. It is worth noting the contribution of American medical anthropologist Ruth Macklin in her book *Against Relativism*,[24] in which she posed significant objections to ethical relativism while distinguishing herself from an attitude of moral absolutism, stating that

> [t]o acknowledge the existence of universal ethical principles is not a commitment to moral absolutism. Ethical principles always require interpretation when they are applied to particular social institutions, such as a health care system or the practice of medicine. In the particulars, there is ample room to tolerate cultural diversity.[25]

She thus distinguishes cultural relativism from a flexible tolerance that we should take into account when we are confronted with cultural diversity. At the same time, she adopts, from the outset of her book, a position that objects to the unthinking acceptance of diversity, the respect of traditional practices or values just because they form part of tradition:

> What I intend to show is that some things are relative, others are not. A convincing argument against ethical relativism need not conclude that nothing is relative, only that certain types of actions and practices – chiefly, those that violate human rights – are not. Because I reject the extremist version of ethical relativism, the task before me is to construct a plausible argument by way of rebuttal. One strategy toward that end will be to distinguish between explanation and justification. It is one thing to provide an explanation of why an individual or an entire culture holds certain beliefs and acts in certain ways. It is quite another thing to provide a justification for those beliefs and actions. Another strategy is to ask whether the consequences of traditional practices provide an objective basis for making ethical judgments. If a cultural practice produces manifest suffering or produces lifelong physical disability, there are good grounds for judging that practice to be ethically wrong. A well-known example is the historical practice in China of foot-binding women.[26]

This extract from Ruth Macklin's book warrants several comments.

The ancient custom of bandaging Chinese women's feet illustrates a practice that a part of society, not subjected to it, may have esteemed to be valuable (in this case, men, for whom women with tiny feet matched a certain canon of beauty), while it caused suffering to another part (said women). Arguing today, on behalf of cultural relativism, that this custom, considered as positive in traditional Chinese culture, should have been kept would support the viewpoint of groups that dominate society at the expense of those who wish to change oppressive practices. Similar examples of traditional practices that victimise the most vulnerable segments of a society, which are, moreover, those for whom it is most difficult to make oneself heard, still

---

[24]Macklin (1999).

[25]*Id.*, pp. 273–274.

[26]*Id.*, p. 24.

abound in a large number of societies. They include, among many others, stoning, female genital mutilation or infanticide.

Cultural relativism argues that each culture may determine itself whether a practice or standard is right or wrong. However, the anthropologist does not observe a culture as if it were a *disembodied* abstract entity, but as it is practised and experienced in a living society. Any anthropologist quickly observes that societies are composed of groups and social categories whose viewpoints, interests and wishes are not homogeneous. A correctly realised anthropological study does not consist in highlighting the dominant norm of society, or the one that most faithfully represents tradition. Instead, it aims to listen and to transcribe the voice of every social group and category, to make apparent the complexity of divisions and of solidarity links, of consensus and dissension when analysing any culture.

On the one hand, not to take into account this complexity denotes a conservative position, insofar as there are neglected individuals who are likely to bring a social change, to implement the dynamics of society. Incidentally, since Western anthropologists, within their own societies, are more often than not part of sectors that support change against tradition, promoting the opposite attitude in a society different from their own is surprising, to say the least.

On the other hand, unhinged cultural relativism reveals an attitude of contempt towards those who are caught in disadvantaged positions on account of traditional norms and practices. For instance, the promotion of traditional medicines is today fairly frequent in many indigenous societies. Encouraging such promotion on account of respect for these societies' traditional knowledge, advocating traditional care, may appear in this context a mere front for an attitude of disdain towards indigenous life, especially considering that health indicators clearly highlight the epidemiological gap between societies with and without access to modern medicine.

The strategy of distinguishing between explanation and justification enables us to avoid the problematic consequences of cultural relativism. A situation is explained on the basis of an observation; it is justified on the basis of standards that differentiate the acceptable from the unacceptable. Ruth Macklin stresses and clarifies this distinction precisely because cultural relativism, for which cultural norms and practices find their justification in culture, left it aside, giving rise to ambiguity on what it really means to say that a standard or a value is relative.

Observing different societies, we realise that value systems and concepts related to what is right and wrong, good and bad, are as diverse as the societies they are a part of. One of the first lessons of anthropology is that universal values do not exist. All societies have a sense of what is right. However, whereas some may associate a rightful societal order with equality, others might prefer a hierarchical order, characterised by (legalised) inequality. Herskovits mirrored this observation when he wrote: 'The very definition of what is normal or abnormal is relative to the cultural frame of reference.'[27]

[27] Herskovits (1948), p. 354.

It is, however, one thing to state that cultural diversity is evident in all areas: in how to build houses, organise kinship systems and worship gods, as well as in the relativity of values. It is another thing—and this corresponds to the framework of cultural relativism—to affirm the equivalence of value systems, which could lead to the justification of extreme behaviour, for example, of a father killing his daughter, seemingly in line with the standards of his culture, if he considers her to have sullied the family honour. In other words, the mere fact of noticing, and of stating, that values are relative does not mean that someone is an adherent to cultural relativism. That someone would become an adherent only if he or she considers that any action is justified, which can be explained according to the traditions of the person performing it.

4.3 The Anthropologist's Attitude

Relativism was born from a concern for equality and from a purpose of respect and neutrality but is not indeed ideologically neutral. An attitude of relativism may even account for the tolerance of situations that neglect the observance of human rights.

In this respect, Ruth Macklin wonders what the limits of tolerance should be. Why should we, in relation to other societies, tolerate and advocate tolerance of situations that we would find intolerable in our own? Tolerance often comes at a cost: the protection of traditional culture may imply the acceptance of degrading practices and conditions, and those who pay this price are, in general, individuals who belong to the most vulnerable sectors of those societies whose cultures supposedly need to be safeguarded. Therefore, only a flexible and limited conception of tolerance seems tenable.

The position accorded to cultural relativism and the limits of tolerance should be evaluated in each context as the situations concerning traditional practices and values are extremely complex and diverse. Such an evaluation should take into account several points.

First, it is important to keep in mind that assuming the equivalence of values and morality systems may lead us to mask the relationship of forces between those who suffer on account of tradition and those who benefit from it.

Second, the appeal of cultural relativism often lies in the idea that it expresses and supports attitudes of open-mindedness, whereas rejection of cultural relativism is thought to reveal dogmatism and narrow-mindedness. However, a position of cultural relativism may, in fact, lead us to justify those who are authoritarian and dogmatic in their own society.

Third, it seems necessary to distinguish between the respect of cultural differences and the mechanical consent of practices for which the sole justification is to exist and to be part of tradition. A naive and unthinking relativism is just an easy way out, but it is not the kind of response that complex situations require.

5 Conclusion

Anthropology as a discipline was born in the second half of the nineteenth century, when early scientific works dealing with cultures, then regarded as 'exotic', reflected an idea that dates from the distant past. It stated that people belonging to different cultures are in fact different. Anthropology was then led by the evolutionary stream for which mankind was a whole, but which at the same time explained the history of mankind through the filter of ethnocentrism and regarded Western civilisation as being superior to all others. Throughout the twentieth century, anthropology has followed on its path, hand in hand with a movement of thought that gradually led it to see in a member of another culture not someone different but someone equal: anthropology, born of an interest in difference, has thus become a discipline concerned with diversity. Ethnocentrism has been criticised, although its positive aspects have been outlined at the same time. Cultural relativism has for a long time also been strongly advocated for as an unquestionable truth by anthropologists because it supports equality. More recently, this *unquestionable* truth has been challenged as cultural traditions often oppress individuals subjected to them, undermining their human rights.

References

Cuche D (1996) La Notion de Culture dans les Sciences Sociales. La Découverte, Paris

Geertz C (1973) The interpretation of cultures. Basic Books, New York

Herskovits M (1948) Man and his works. The science of cultural anthropology. A.A. Knopf, New York

Herskovits M (1955) Cultural relativism and cultural values. In: Herskovits M (ed) Cultural anthropology. A.A. Knopf, New York

Lévi-Strauss C (1952) Race and history. UNESCO, Paris

Lévi-Strauss C (1963) Structural anthropology. Basic Books, New York

Macklin R (1999) Against relativism. Cultural diversity and the search for Ethical Universals in Medicine. Oxford University Press, New York

Massé R (2000) Les limites d'une approche essentialiste des ethnoéthiques: pour un relativisme éthique critique. Anthropologie et Sociétés 24(2):13–33

Pike K (1954) Language in relation to a unified theory of the structure of human behavior. Summer Institute of Linguistics, Glendale

Rubel A (1964) The epidemiology of a folk illness: Susto in Hispanic America. Ethnology 3:270

Rubel A, O'Nell CW, Collado-Ardón R (1991 [1984]) Susto: a folk illness. University of California Press, Berkeley pp 112–120

Simon J-P (1993) Ethnocentrisme. Pluriel-Recherches 1:57–63

Sturzenegger O (1999) Le mauvais œil de la lune. Ethnomédecine créole en Amérique du Sud, Karthala, Paris

Sumner W (1906) Folkways: A study of the sociological importance of usages, manners, customs, mores, and morals. Ginn and Co., Boston, p 13

Tylor E (1871) Primitive culture. John Murray, London, p 1

Further Reading

Cowan J, Dembour M-B, Wilson R (eds) (2001) Culture and rights: anthropological perspectives. Cambridge University Press, Cambridge
Geertz C (1983) Local Knowledge. Further essays in interpretive anthropology. Basic Books, New York
Harris M, Johnson O (2000) Cultural anthropology, 5th edn. Allyn & Bacon
Kuper A (1999) Culture. The anthropologist's account. Harvard University Press, Cambridge
Malinowski B (1944) A scientific theory of culture and others essays. The University of North Carolina Press, Chapel Hill
Maquet J (1964) Objectivity in anthropology. Curr Anthropol 5:47–55
Massé R (2003) Valeurs universelles et relativisme culturel en recherche internationale: les contributions d'un principisme sensible aux contextes socioculturels. Autrepart 28:21–35
Shweder RA, Levine RA (eds) (1984) Culture theory: essays on mind, self and emotion. Cambridge University Press, Cambridge
Sperber D (1985) On anthropological knowledge: three essays. Cambridge University Press, Cambridge

Odina Benoist is Senior Lecturer in anthropology and Researcher at the Laboratoire Interdisciplinaire de Droit des Médias et des Mutations Sociales (LID2MS), part of the Faculty of Law and Political Science of Aix-Marseille University, France.

Armed Conflicts and Humanitarian Crises: Insights from the Anthropology of War

Kristina Roepstorff

1 Introduction

Interstate and intrastate armed conflicts have declined in number since the 1990s. According to the Uppsala Conflict Data Program (UCDP), the year 2013 saw 33 ongoing armed conflicts in 25 locations worldwide—a decrease of almost 37% in comparison to the peak in the immediate post-Cold War period. Of these armed conflicts, seven were categorised as wars, namely conflicts with at least 1000 battle-related deaths in a year.[1] This is the good news. The bad news is that despite a general decrease in armed conflicts, people around the world continue to suffer from their effects. News of ongoing and new armed conflicts accompanied by shocking pictures of people in plight make it into our living rooms on a daily basis. As of 2016, 65.6 million people where forcibly displaced worldwide as a result of persecution, conflict, violence, or human rights violations, and in February 2015, 12.2 million people—nearly half of the population—were in need of humanitarian assistance in war-torn Syria alone.

[1]Organisations and research projects use different thresholds to define armed conflict and war and therefore produce divergent assessments of global trends. The Uppsala Conflict Data Program (UCDP), which is linked to the Department of Peace and Conflict Research at Uppsala University, provides one of the most used data sources on armed conflicts. It defines armed conflicts as 'contested incompatibility, which concerns government and/or territory where the use of armed force between two parties, of which at least one is the government of a state, results in at least 25 battle-related deaths'. Wars, accordingly, are high-intensity armed conflicts with more than 1000 battle-related deaths.

K. Roepstorff (✉)
Otto-von-Guericke University Magdeburg, Magdeburg, Germany

University College Dublin, Dublin, Ireland

Ruhr-University Bochum, Bochum, Germany
e-mail: kristina.roepstorff@ovgu.de

© Springer International Publishing AG 2018

H.-J. Heintze, P. Thielbörger (eds.), *International Humanitarian Action*,
DOI 10.1007/978-3-319-14454-2_16

Yet numbers tell us little about the experience of people who live in the midst of armed conflicts and the impacts of humanitarian crises on virtually all aspects of society. In such contexts, the political and violent nature of these complex humanitarian emergencies poses significant challenges for humanitarian action. Experiences from humanitarian crises such as in Bosnia, Rwanda, Afghanistan and Syria have sparked debates among scholars and practitioners about the extent to which humanitarian principles can be upheld in situations of armed conflict. These debates were accompanied by the realisation that humanitarian action, despite good intentions, might have negative impacts on the conflict context itself. With humanitarian aid workers increasingly becoming targets of violence, the provision of humanitarian assistance in armed conflicts requires a deep understanding of the very context in which this intervention takes place in order to avoid causing harm and to ensure the protection of both humanitarian workers and the affected population.

The anthropology of war covers a broad range of topics of high relevance to understand contemporary armed conflicts and humanitarian crises. Looking beyond the immediate facts of the situation and highlighting the social dimension of armed conflicts, it allows grasping the broader context in which humanitarian crises occur. With the discipline's comparative and holistic outlook, anthropology thus offers important insights into causes, dynamics and effects of armed conflicts. Over the last 150 years, anthropologists have produced a growing ethnographic database on how material, institutional and cultural factors explain war and its effects, resulting in a rich body of empirically substantiated theories. Thereby, anthropological scholarship on war is far from systematic and homogenous. Covering the many aspects of the interrelationships between war, violence and society, anthropological scholarship in this field is vast, diverse and ever evolving.

This chapter only provides a glimpse of some of the many debates and themes in the anthropology of war. It presents several important anthropological approaches to explaining the causes and effects of war, introduces themes that emerged in anthropological scholarship on contemporary armed conflicts and links the anthropology of war to an anthropology of peace. In a final section, the chapter addresses the controversy regarding the role of anthropologists in armed conflicts and the challenges of conducting field research in war zones.

2 Anthropological Perspectives on Armed Conflict

The anthropological study of armed conflict differs from the perspectives of other disciplines, such as political science or law, in that it examines war as a social practice that is deeply embedded within the broader cultural context in which it occurs. In studying war, anthropologists are mainly concerned with its social dimensions. They ask questions, such as: how do cultural beliefs relate to the practice and experience of armed conflict? What are the norms and rules that govern warfare in different societies? How does armed conflict relate to other factors, including ecology, economy, kinship, gender, values and politics?

Although early anthropologists of the nineteenth century did not study war as such, their ethnographic accounts of small-scale societies include informative descriptions of feuding, raiding and warfare practices, offering important findings of cross-cultural variations in conflict resolution, the use of violence and the waging of war. With later anthropologists studying the phenomenon of war more explicitly, a lively debate has produced new valuable insights into the social dimensions of conflicts, violence and war. Dominant themes that emerged are questions concerning the universality and inevitability of war, evolutionary accounts of primitive/tribal versus modern warfare, the causes and practices of warfare and the effects of armed conflict on sociocultural systems.[2] More recently, new conflicts in the aftermath of the Cold War, the attacks on 11 September 2001, the so-called 'global war on terror' and the wars in Afghanistan, Iraq and Syria have provoked new debates and research in anthropology and related disciplines.

2.1 *Violence and War as Social Institution*

Conflicts, which form an inevitable part of daily life, may be settled peacefully or violently. The anthropology of law deals with comparative research on the different norms and institutions that exist in societies for settling conflicts among its members to maintain or restore order. Research in this field shows how norms, institutions and taboos by which the use of violence is controlled differ from society to society. What is regarded as legitimate and appropriate use of violence by one society may well be regarded as excessive and brutal by another. This insight of anthropology is also important for humanitarian workers who may have to get to terms with practices they find appalling. This does not mean that one has to accept violent behaviour, but that one needs to understand how norms governing violence are embedded within broader sociocultural contexts.

Ethnographic studies of different societies have analysed the practices of homicide, capital punishment, raiding, feuding and warfare and how they are embedded within and shaped by particular societies' belief systems, norms and institutions. The anthropology of war specifically deals with highly escalated conflicts that elude the normal mechanisms of control and order and where armed violence becomes a means of conflict resolution within a society or between societies. Bronislaw Malinowski, one of the most influential anthropologists of the twentieth century, has provided a prominent definition of war as 'the use of organized force between two politically independent units, in pursuit of [each unit's] policy'.[3] War can thus be understood as a long-term struggle for political ends within particular social contexts in which groups use, or threaten to use, lethal force against each other in pursuit of their aims. This implicates that warfare—in contrast to other forms of violent behaviour—is a form of collective (armed) violence used for collective

---

[2]For an overview of the development of the anthropology of war, see: Otterbein (1999), pp. 794–805; Gusterson (2007), pp. 155–175.

[3]Malinowski (1941), pp. 521–550.

rather than merely individual ends. Thereby war is generally associated with the breakdown of order, viewed as an abnormality occurring outside of the social realm and lacking rules of its own.

One of the most important contributions of anthropologists has been to challenge this common understanding of violence and warfare as something exceptional that does not form part of ordinary social reality. They have argued that perceiving violence war as something inherently bad or abnormal detaches it from its social context—the very context we need to place it in, if we want to understand its causes, practices, experiences and effects. Rather, violence and war needs to be understood in relation to existing patterns of violence within a given society.[4]

Indeed, violence and war are intimately linked concepts, whereby violence is a broader phenomenon of which warfare presents a particularly severe form. Just like culture in general, patterns and practices of violence and warfare are not static but may change over time and may adapt to changing conditions at the local, regional, national or international level. Anthropologists have thus been particularly interested in finding explanations for the varying frequency, intensity, forms and meanings of violence and war across time and space.

2.2 *Primitive Versus Modern Warfare*

Due to the discipline's long-standing primary focus on indigenous and exotic peoples outside of Europe, early anthropological studies of war have frequently focused on primitive, stateless or acephalous (headless) societies. Assuming that primitive man was man in his natural state, anthropologists deliberated the causes of war in primitive societies and debated the evolution of war from simple to state societies.

Contrasting primitive or tribal warfare with modern warfare practised by large-scale societies, many early—but also later—anthropological studies analysed and explained the phenomenon of war within an evolutionary theoretical framework. For instance, in 1915, Hobhouse et al. published a study that placed its cross-cultural comparison of war and the treatment of captured soldiers within an evolutionary theoretical framework, arguing that the killing of prisoners taken in war decreased with higher levels of subsistence technology.[5] Malinowski, on the other hand, held that warfare evolved as a means to pursue national policies and differentiated six 'cultural phases in the development of organized fighting'.[6] In the same vein, linking warfare to a high level of sociopolitical complexity, numerous anthropologists have argued that war as collective violent action only emerged with increasing social stratification and organisation. Warfare was associated with chiefdoms and states, whereas more egalitarian band and tribal societies were believed to settle their

[4]To gain a deeper understanding of this, see Richards (2005).

[5]Hobhouse et al. (1915).

[6]See Malinowski (1941), pp. 521–550.

(smaller) disputes by way of self-redress, homicide and feuds. If warfare played any role, it was considered to be more sportive and ritualistic in nature. Consequently, non-lethal tribal warfare was commonly contrasted with lethal warfare waged by modern nation states.[7] Thus, a dominant theme in the anthropology of war is the differentiation between primitive and modern warfare and the ways in which the modern state system and the emergence of military specialists and technological innovation have changed not only the motives and rules but also the magnitude of wars. In fact, witnessing the destructive forces of World War I and World War II, many anthropologists regarded large-scale wars and genocides as modern phenomena and claimed that traditional primitive societies were more peaceful.

2.3 *The 'Myth of the Peaceful Savage'*

Although from the 1920s on anthropological research on war was increasingly influenced by the anti-evolutionism of Franz Boas—often referred to as the father of modern anthropology who introduced culture as its primary analytical concept—and cultural relativist approaches, evolutionary accounts dominated well into the 1950s. Out of these evolutionary explanations of the origins of war emerged the myth of the peaceful savage and a romanticisation of hunter-gatherer societies.

Hence, another dominant theme in the anthropology of war is the debate revolving around the claimed 'warlike' or 'peaceful' nature of humans and societies. In what can be seen as a clear extension of the Hobbes-Rousseau controversy of the Enlightenment period, beliefs about human nature and war are implicitly reflected in the interpretation of ethnographic data. A tendency among ethnographers to ignore evidence of violence and warfare, presenting the people they studied as essentially peaceful—or essentially inclined to engage in warfare—resulted in contradictory research findings.

While some scholars produced ethnographies to prove the human predisposition to violence and war, others saw human nature as essentially peaceful and wars as a social construction. These two opposing positions defined the discipline's discourse on war and violence for a long time, resulting in a number of ethnographies on warlike and peaceful societies and still fuel controversy to this date.[8] Understanding war as a social construction and cultural institution, as famously described by Margaret Mead—a student of Boas—has, however, become the dominant view in the anthropology of war.

Despite the long-standing debate on the subject, no single explanation for the variance in violence and warfare has been found. In fact, there is no consensus among scholars on what exactly constitutes violence and war. Some have even argued that the constitutive and dynamic nature of violence and war renders any attempt to define the phenomenon futile and that studying violence requires a

[7] For more information on this debate, see: Reyna and Downs (1994).

[8] Instructive to gain an understanding of this controversy: Kelly (2000) and Keeley (1996).

dynamic approach to grasp its procedural nature, the way it shapes people and their perceptions, the way it finds its expression in everyday life, as well as its underlying functions and dynamics.[9] More recently, scholars have shifted their attention to studying the conditions under which wars occur and the impact they have on society.

Anthropologists have shown how wars are not only products of social reality but also producers of the same by altering notions of solidarity, identity and social hierarchy.[10] This insight from the anthropology of war is significant for humanitarian action as it draws attention to the dynamic nature of violence and warfare, the way it is embedded in a specific sociocultural system and how the sociocultural system itself may change as a consequence. Pre-assumptions and perceptions of the context in which humanitarian actors intervene may thus have to be altered and adapted on an ongoing basis in order to understand the complex interrelation of culture, society and armed conflict. It also helps humanitarian aid workers to reflect on what they see and experience when deployed in the field.

2.4 Causes and Effects of Armed Conflict

Anthropology, like other disciplines, seeks to explain why societies wage wars. Particularly prominent are materialist explanations that see competition over scarce resources such as land or food as the fundamental causes of war.[11] One of the shortcomings of these accounts is that they explain the variations in the incidence of wars on the basis of the rational-choice paradigm. This, however, fails to explain the importance of other factors such as identity, culture and socio-psychological motivations. The 'greed versus grievance' debate in the explanation of ethnic conflicts is linked to this: 'greed' refers to the argument that people engage in armed conflicts because of economic rewards based on rational cost-benefit calculations; 'grievance' stands for the view that people fight over issues of identity (ethnicity, religion, social class, etc.). Today, most scholars agree that both factors contribute to armed conflicts and wars.

Approaches within the social-structural tradition understand warfare mainly as an ordering principle of social relations and social structures. As anthropologist Max Gluckman concluded from his research on political systems among African tribes, social relations that are formed through marriage alliances, trade networks, gift exchange and so forth play an important role in limiting the frequency and intensity of warfare.[12] Moreover, anthropologists have argued that war may

[9]Robben and Nordstrom (1995).

[10]Rao et al. (2011) offers a collection of interesting case studies that examine the ways in which wars are not only products of specific sociocultural contexts, but produce cultural practices.

[11]See for instance Ferguson (1984).

[12]Gluckman (1956).

enhance social stability by maintaining intra-group solidarity vis-à-vis a common enemy. Correspondingly, societies with relatively fragile social ties between groups have been found to be especially prone to higher levels of violence and warfare.

Another, phenomenological, line of research in the anthropology of war is primarily concerned with the interpretation and translation of systems of meaning. Research that falls within this category attributes the variations in the nature and frequency of war to cultural differences in values and beliefs and studies the meanings and memories attached to war in particular societies. Ethnographic studies in this line of research have shown how memories about past injuries preserved by refugee communities or in institutionalised form as museums or war memorials are often selective and function as a mobilising force for collective violent action.[13] Anthropologists have further examined how living in a chronic state of fear affects the social fabric of societies and daily lives of people: neighbours and friends turn into enemies, families are separated by flight or forced conscription, with a general sense of hopelessness and trauma as effects of war on society.[14] Other topics in this line of research include the gendered dimensions of the practice and representation of violence and war, the body and symbolic performances of war and violence, as well as the adequacy of applying Western notions—such as childhood or trauma—to non-Western contexts. As such, anthropology poses critical questions regarding conventional approaches in international humanitarian action.

Moreover, the 1990s saw an increasing recognition that primitive wars could not be understood separately from the colonial encounter. In what has been termed the 'tribal zone', anthropologists have argued that the contact between state and non-state societies has exacerbated warfare within and between them.[15] Similarly, studies on contemporary ethnic and religious conflicts in Europe, Asia and Africa examined the legacies of colonial domination and the role of nationalism in these conflicts.

2.5 *Anthropology and Contemporary Armed Conflicts*

The end of the Cold War saw an increase in intrastate conflicts that were no longer dominated by the geopolitical and ideological battles between the East and the West. A controversy emerged as to whether they presented a qualitatively new sort of war. According to the new war thesis, post-Cold War intrastate conflicts are seen as being characterised by a change of actors, a massive increase of civilian casualties and development of new war economies. Where weak or failed states have lost their monopoly to conduct legitimate violence, various non-state actors that

[13]See for example Malkki (1995).

[14]See Green (1994), pp. 227–256; Robben and Suarez-Orozco (2000).

[15]Ferguson and Whitehead (2000).

mobilise around ethnic, racial or religious identities challenge its authority and claim state power. Though regular armies still participate in these contemporary conflicts, a multitude of other actors, such as insurgents, paramilitary groups, local warlords, criminal gangs and mercenary groups, are also involved, making such conflicts more complex and uncertain to predict. War economies are mostly based on illegal trade in arms, drugs, natural resources and human trafficking.[16] Whereas the distinction between old and new wars remains disputed, conflicts in the Balkans, Sierra Leone, Rwanda, Darfur or Afghanistan and a growing concern about international terrorism have informed research that addresses the complexities of the contexts in which contemporary armed conflicts and humanitarian crises unfold and in which humanitarian actors operate.

Moving away from the distinction between the primitive and the modern, anthropologists too turned towards studying contemporary armed conflicts. The debate revolving around new wars during the 1990s generated research on ethno-political conflicts, genocide and terrorism, among other things. Anthropological studies of ethno-political conflicts and genocide critiqued essentialist notions of identity, challenging common perceptions of these conflicts as originating in ancient tribal hatreds and linking them to the experience of colonialism, the emergence of nationalism and the dynamics of globalisation.[17] In their research on terrorism, anthropologists have focused not only on the victims of terrorist attacks but also on the experience of perpetrators and the transnational linkages of cultures of violence and terror.

Thus, over the last decades, a rich body of in-depth ethnographic studies on contemporary armed conflicts has emerged, addressing questions of the organisation of war, ritual aspects of warfare, its socio-economic consequences and the causes and experiences of organised and collective violence. Generally, anthropologists agree that mono-causal explanations fail to provide an accurate account of a phenomenon as complex as armed conflicts and humanitarian crises. While, at first sight, practices and experiences of violence may appear similar across the world, the everyday experience of war, its causes, expressions and effects are always situated within a particular sociocultural context. Hence, there is broad consensus within the discipline that war has to be understood as a historically and locally situated practice that is not only a destructive but also a productive part of social reality.

How are these findings relevant for humanitarian action? This field of inquiry is only emerging, and further debate and research is needed. However, we can maintain that only by understanding the everyday practice of war can we also develop meaningful efforts for peacebuilding and conflict transformation, breaking spirals of violence and addressing root causes of armed conflicts and humanitarian crises.

[16]Kaldor (1999).

[17]Recommended readings on these topics include: Eller (1999) and Hinton (2002).

2.6 Anthropology of Peace

As noted above, anthropologists argue that conflicts form an inevitable part of daily life and may be settled peacefully or violently. So far, we have dealt with the sociocultural reality of violence and war. However, getting along, reconciling and peacemaking are very common and important aspects of social behaviour. If only a few anthropologists have studied the phenomena of war and violence, even less attention has been paid to the phenomenon of peace. Yet anthropology has a track record of investigating conflict resolution practices in different societies. Ethnographic studies of societies in various parts of the world show a wealth of peaceful means by which conflicts are settled, including self-redress, avoidance, toleration, negotiation and third-party intervention.[18] Anthropology's insights into the relationship between culture and conflict resolution has thereby informed theoretical models of mediation and reconciliation and has been put into practice by people working on conflict transformation and peacebuilding.[19]

One of the dominant approaches in the anthropology of war (and peace) that has been already addressed is the classification of societies according to their perceived peaceful and violent natures. Thus, anthropologists have asked why some societies oppose aggressiveness, violence and warfare while others tolerate it. Focusing on peaceful societies, they have examined how their particular belief systems and world views foster non-violent attitudes and behaviour. Moreover, they have studied the various structures and societal organisation that promote peacefulness and harmony among their members, for example by discouraging competition and self-focus.[20]

More recently, ethnographic studies focusing on everyday experiences of violence have exposed the simultaneous existence of suffering and laughter, fear and hope. By doing so, they have challenged a narrow conceptualisation of war as being apart from the ordinary and have placed it in the daily lived experience of people. War and peace are then not exclusive but coexisting social realities. Thinking of war and peace as a continuum instead of as a sharp dichotomy allows a shift from explaining the causes of war to analysing processual aspects of the practices of war and peace.[21] Anthropology may thus not only provide unique insights into the causes, dynamics and effects of war but also shine light on the potential for peace. For this reason, anthropologists are often sceptical of internationally driven peacebuilding interventions. Emphasising the local potential for peace, anthropologists have focused on peacebuilding activities at the grass-roots level, including studies on the role of ritual for peacebuilding and reconciliation.[22] As anthropologists have shown, if war is a social construct, so is peace.

---

[18]See Fry (2006).

[19]Important works in this field include: Avruch (1998) and Lederach (1997).

[20]See Sponsel (1996), pp. 95–125.

[21]Richards (2005). Instead of advancing a sharp dichotomy between war and peace, this edited volume advances the argument that we should think of war and peace as a continuum.

[22]See Schirch (2005) and Ross (2002).

3 Anthropologists in Armed Conflicts and Humanitarian Crises

This chapter has so far focused on anthropological research on violence and war. Another related topic of high relevance is how anthropologists work in contexts of armed conflict and humanitarian crises and the ethical implications this has on their actions. Anthropologists may work in these contexts in several ways, all of which give rise to particular questions and concerns. They may act as staff of humanitarian organisations or be embedded in counter-insurgency operations, conduct research in conflict zones and provide recommendations for policymakers.

Two themes that have provoked debate within the discipline will be addressed in this part of the chapter: the role of anthropologists within the military—or military anthropology—and the role of anthropologists as researchers in and on war.

3.1 Anthropologists and Counter-Insurgency

In the aftermath of 9/11, and with the US military recruitment of anthropologists for their operations in Afghanistan and Iraq, a renewed debate on the role of anthropologists in counter-insurgency operations emerged. Believing that the war on terror would benefit from anthropologists' language skills and familiarity with the sociocultural context of certain areas of operation, the CIA and military institutions sought to contract a number of them. The rise of what has been termed 'military anthropology'—referring to the increasing recruitment and use of services of anthropologists for military goals—has prompted a heated debate on the academic and professional ethics of anthropologists. While some anthropologists responded enthusiastically, other anthropologists cautioned against the harm that such initiatives would do to the credibility and neutrality of the discipline.[23] Especially the practice of the United States military of embedding anthropologists within the controversial Human Terrain System (HTS) in Iraq and Afghanistan has come under critique. The HTS is designed to provide military commanders and personnel with an understanding of the local population in the regions in which they are deployed.

Anthropologists' collaboration with the military and intelligence is, however, nothing new. As early as 1919, Franz Boas criticised anthropologists who acted as spies during World War I. The role of anthropologists in counter-insurgency in Latin America and Southeast Asia in the 1960s also provoked a debate on the discipline's ethics and professionalism.[24] In 1971, the American Anthropological Association took a clear stand against these kinds of covert services from

[23]For details on this controversy, see: Lucas (2009).

[24]Wakin (1992).

anthropologists by adopting the Principles of Professional Responsibility, which have been further developed in 2009 and 2012.

But if anthropologists with their contextual knowledge may help counter terrorism, war and suffering, why shouldn't they lend their services to the national security apparatus? Or are there alternative strategies to use anthropological knowledge to mitigate the suffering imposed on civilian populations without jeopardising the integrity of the individual anthropologists and the discipline in general? The relationship between anthropology and the military is complex and multifaceted, as personal accounts of anthropologists working in this field reveal.[25] The issue remains highly controversial and raises a whole set of ethical questions, not least about the responsibility and credibility of anthropology as an academic discipline that produces important insights of practical relevance. Could similar ethical questions arise in the context of humanitarian action?

3.2 *Fieldwork in Conflict Zones*

Conducting field research in conflict zones and during humanitarian crises raises a whole set of ethical and security issues. Participant observation and collecting information in volatile contexts do not only endanger anthropologists but also increase the vulnerability of their informants and the local population.

Prolonged field research in local communities affected by war is difficult and dangerous. In 1995, Robben and Nordstrom published an edited volume entitled Fieldwork under Fire: Contemporary Studies of Violence and Survival. The collection of essays covers various aspects of conducting fieldwork in zones of violence and war. Focusing on everyday experiences, the authors give voice to those affected by violence and war, including perpetrators, victims, profiteers and the researchers themselves. Apart from the obvious questions of security—of the researcher, the informants and the local people—it raises a number of theoretical, ethical and methodological questions. One of the most fundamental questions in this regard is how anthropologists in such contexts cope with witnessing violence and suffering first-hand. They may even become targets of aggression and violence themselves. With an increasing number of anthropologists conducting research on armed conflicts and humanitarian crises, questions of protection and dealing with trauma need to be addressed within the discipline.

Methodologically, the issue arises how fear and silencing—both common features of conflict environments—may affect the research process and research outcomes. Field researchers in situations of armed conflict need to constantly separate facts from rumours. While questions concerning data reliability and the subjectivity of perceptions and interpretations are not unique to this field of research, in contexts of armed violence that are characterised by a heightened degree of uncertainty and

---

[25]Rubinstein et al. (2012).

fear, rumours spread easily, and it is often difficult to differentiate between truth and falsehood. Anthropologists should be sensitive to this and reflect this in their evaluation of data.

Another central issue in conducting research in contexts of armed conflict concerns the presentation of research findings: how does an ethnographer write about armed conflict without producing a pornography of violence?[26] Should anthropologists bear witness to the terror and violence they encounter during field research, even if it compromises their safety? Anthropologists have done so in the past and continue to do so, but the question is not easily answered. Apart from security concerns, anthropologists from the Global North speaking or writing on behalf of people affected by armed conflicts and humanitarian crises in the Global South may unwittingly reinforce existing power relations and postcolonial discourse. On the other hand, it may be argued that, precisely because of their privileged status, anthropologists who witness injustices have the responsibility to bear witness.[27] Ultimately, each person has to decide for himself.

4 Conclusion

War, international terrorism, ethno-political conflict and insurgency not just happen out of the blue but are highly organised events and have to be understood in the social contexts in which they occur. Mono-causal explanations fail to provide an accurate account of a phenomenon as complex as armed conflicts and humanitarian crises. A contextual approach to understanding the occurrence and dynamics of armed conflicts and wars in specific situations is needed to allow for conflict-sensitive humanitarian action. Understanding war as part of the social reality of human beings and lived experiences, anthropology can offer humanitarian actors important insights into the social dimensions of war. Anthropological research on war shows how it is not only a social construct but also constitutive of social reality. If war is a social construct, so is peace. War and peace are not exclusive but coexist in the shared experience of people. The best analytical approach to understanding armed conflicts and humanitarian crises is through an examination of actual practices of war and peace in particular localities. Only by understanding the everyday practice of war can meaningful efforts for peacebuilding and conflict transformation be developed. For anthropologists working in contexts of armed conflicts and humanitarian crises, a number of ethical and methodological questions arise that need to be addressed both on an individual level as well as within the discipline at large.

[26]For a though-provoking reflection on this and related issues, see Daniel (1996) and Waterston (2008).

[27]See for instance Scheper-Hughes (1992).

References

Avruch K (1998) Culture and conflict resolution. US Institute of Peace Press, Washington

Daniel E (1996) Charred Lullabies: chapters in an anthropology of violence. Princeton University Press, Princeton

Eller J (1999) From culture to ethnicity to conflict: an anthropological perspective on international ethnic conflict. University of Michigan Press, Ann Arbor

Ferguson R (1984) Warfare, culture, and environment. Academic Press, Orlando

Ferguson R, Whitehead N (2000) War in the tribal zone: expanding states and indigenous warfare. American Research Press, Santa Fe

Fry D (2006) The human potential for peace. An anthropological challenge to assumptions about war and violence. Oxford University Press, New York

Gluckman M (1956) Custom and conflict in Africa. Blackwell, Oxford

Green L (1994) Fear as a way of life. Cultur Anthropol 9:227–256

Gusterson H (2007) Anthropology and militarism. Annu Rev Anthropol 36:155–175

Hinton A (2002) Annihilating difference: the anthropology of genocide. University of California Press, Berkeley

Hobhouse L, Wheeler G, Ginsberg M (1915) The material culture and social institutions of the simpler peoples: an essay in correlation. Chapman & Hall, Ltd., London

Kaldor M (1999) New & old wars. Organized violence in a global era. Polity Press, Cambridge

Keeley L (1996) War before civilization: the myth of the peaceful savage. Oxford University Press, Oxford

Kelly R (2000) Warless societies and the origin of war. University of Michigan Press, Michigan

Lederach JP (1997) Building peace: sustainable reconciliation in divided societies. United States Institute of Peace Press, Washington

Lucas G (2009) Anthropologists in arms: the ethics of military anthropology. AltaMira Press, Plymouth

Malinowski B (1941) An anthropological analysis of war. Am J Sociol 46:521–550

Malkki L (1995) Purity and exile: violence, memory and national cosmology among hutu refugees in Tanzania. University of Chicago Press, Chicago

Otterbein K (1999) A history of research on warfare in anthropology. Am Anthropol 101: 794–805

Rao A, Bollig M, Böck M (2011) The practice of war: production, reproduction and communication of armed violence. Berghahn Books, New York

Reyna S, Downs S (1994) Studying war: anthropological perspectives. Gordon and Breach, Philadelphia

Richards P (2005) No peace, no war: an anthropology of contemporary armed conflicts. Ohio University Press, Athens

Robben A, Nordstrom C (1995) Fieldwork under fire: contemporary studies of violence and survival. University of California Press, Berkeley

Robben A, Suarez-Orozco M (2000) Cultures under siege: collective violence and trauma. Cambridge University Press, Cambridge

Ross F (2002) Bearing witness: women and the South African Truth and Reconciliation Commission. Pluto Press, London

Rubinstein R, Fosher K, Fujimura C (2012) Practicing military anthropology: beyond expectations and traditional boundaries. Kumarian Press, Sterling

Scheper-Hughes N (1992) Death without weeping: the violence of everyday life in Northeast Brazil. University of California Press, Berkeley

Schirch L (2005) Ritual and symbol in peacebuilding. Kumarian Press, Bloomfield

Sponsel L (1996) The natural history of peace: a positive view of human nature and its potential. In: Gregor T (ed) A natural history of peace. Nashville

Wakin E (1992) Anthropology goes to war: professional ethics and counterinsurgency in Thailand. University of Wisconsin Press, Madison

Waterston A (2008) An anthropology of war: views from the frontline. Berghahn Books, New York

Further Reading

Otterbein K (1999) A history of research on warfare in anthropology. Am Anthropol 101:794–805

Reyna S, Downs S (1994) Studying war: anthropological perspectives. Gordon and Breach, Australia

Richards P (2005) No peace, no war: an anthropology of contemporary armed conflicts. Ohio University Press, Athens

Robben A, Nordstrom C (1995) Fieldwork under fire: contemporary studies of violence and survival. University of California Press, Berkeley

Waterston A (2008) An anthropology of war: views from the frontline. Berghahn Books, New York

Kristina Roepstorff is a Research Associate at Otto-von-Guericke University Magdeburg and NOHA Sessional Instructor at the Centre for Humanitarian Action at University College Dublin and the Institute for International Law of Peace and Armed Conflict (IFHV) at Ruhr-University Bochum.

Forced Migration and Refugee Settings from an Anthropological Perspective

Relinde Reiffers

1 Introduction

In 2015, more than 65.3 million people were forcibly displaced worldwide due to conflict, disaster and insecurity, with 40.8 million people internally displaced within their own countries.[1]

This chapter explores what forced migration means from an anthropological perspective, both within the framework of humanitarian action, specifically legal and political aspects, as well as from the perspective of affected communities. To analyse the consequences of displacement and its relation to notions of home and identity, I use the situation of Bhutanese refugees in Nepal as a case study.

2 The Meaning of Forced Migration

Migrants, in many cases, lack citizenship of their host country, usually form part of a minority of migrants and refugees there and often live in circumstances of destitution, whereas their situation may originally have been very different, in their country of origin. According to Eriksen, a lot of anthropological research on migration has focused on aspects of discrimination and disqualification, strategies for the maintenance of group identity and the relationship between immigrant and majority cultures. George and Olwig add that attention has been increasingly geared towards the transnational relationship between migrants' communities of origin and

[1]United Nations High Commissioner for Refugees (2016), Global Trends, Forced Displacement in 2015, http://www.unhcr.org/576408cd7.pdf, p. 2.

R. Reiffers (✉)
University of Groningen, Groningen, The Netherlands
e-mail: R.A.Reiffers@rug.nl

© Springer International Publishing AG 2018

H.-J. Heintze, P. Thielbörger (eds.), *International Humanitarian Action*,
DOI 10.1007/978-3-319-14454-2_17

the sociocultural environment in host countries.[2] This way, diaspora communities that always originate from communities of origin give a sense of belonging to people in many different places of the world. Cultural identity is of major importance among migrants.

Authenticity and tradition can play a role within and outside minorities of migrant communities. In his study of a multi-ethnic English neighbourhood, Bauman found that options related to emphasising or using, for instance, ethnicity, nationality, gender, age, community and neighbourhood in different contexts are highly different and subject to debate. Thus, multiple identities, roles and views can be used for different reasons and for various aims both within and outside a group.

The International Association for the Study of Forced Migration (IASFM) defines forced migration as 'a general term that refers to the movements of refugees and internally displaced people (those displaced by conflicts) as well as people displaced by natural or environmental disasters, chemical or nuclear disasters, famine, or development projects'.[3]

The study of forced migration is multidisciplinary and incorporates a wide variety of perspectives ranging from the academic, governmental and aid sector to local perspectives. Forced Migration Online (FMO) suggests a framework that can be used to address different types of forced migration and types of migrants. According to FMO, three types of forced migration can be identified[4]:

- *Conflict-induced displacement* concerns people who are forced to flee their homes due to conflict, civil war, violence and persecution on the ground of nationality, race, political opinion or social group.
- *Development-induced displacement* relates to people who are compelled to move as a result of policies or projects aiming to enhance development, such as dams, roads, mining and conservation reserves.
- *Disaster-induced displacement* refers to people displaced as a result of natural disasters (floods, earthquakes), environmental change (deforestation, global warming) and man-made disasters (industrial accidents).

Those researching or working with displaced groups often use different main terms to describe these groups. This distinction can be essential in determining which rights these displaced groups have and to what kind of protection they are entitled. Moreover, the background of these different groups can determine causes and needs when designing humanitarian interventions related to prevention and protection. IASFM distinguishes between the following types of people forced to flee their homes:

- *Refugees*: the legal definition of a refugee is enshrined in the 1951 United Nations Convention Relating to the Status of Refugees. Article 1 of the

[2]Eriksen (2010), pp. 299 and 319.

[3]IASFM, http://www.efms.uni-bamberg.de/iasfm/mission.htm.

[4]FMO, http://www.forcedmigration.org/about/whatisfm.

Convention defines a refugee as a person residing outside his or her country of nationality, who is unable or unwilling to return because of a 'well-founded fear of persecution on account of race, religion, nationality, membership in a political social group, or political opinion'. A large number of states have signed the 1951 Refugee Convention and/or its 1967 Protocol, pledging to protect refugees and not return them to a country where they may be persecuted. Article 33 (1) of the 1951 Convention codifies the international law principle of non-refoulement:

> No Contracting State shall expel or return ('refouler') a refugee in any manner whatsoever to the frontiers of territories where his life or freedom would be threatened on account of his race, religion, nationality, membership of a particular social group or political opinion.

Those recognised as refugees have a clear legal status and are entitled to the protection of the UNHCR.

- *Asylum seekers* are people who have moved across an international border in search of protection under the 1951 Refugee Convention but whose claim for refugee status has not yet been determined.
- *Internally displaced persons* (IDPs) are 'persons or groups of persons who have been forced or obliged to flee or to leave their homes or places of habitual residence, in particular as a result of or in order to avoid the effects of armed conflict, situations of generalized violence, violations of human rights or natural or human-made disasters, and who have not crossed an internationally recognized State border'.[5]
- *Development displacees* are people who have been compelled to move as a result of policies and projects aiming to enhance development, such as dams, roads, mining, deforestation and conservation reserves.
- *Environmental and disaster displacees* are people displaced as a result of natural disasters (floods, earthquakes), environmental change (deforestation, global warming) and man-made disasters (industrial accidents).
- *Smuggled people* are migrants moved illegally for profit. They are part of an unequal commercial transaction. As it has become more and more difficult to cross borders as an asylum seeker, migrants have increasingly drawn upon services of smugglers.
- *Trafficked people* are moved by deception or coercion for the purposes of exploitation. The profit in trafficking people comes from the sale of their sexual services or labour in the country of destination. Trafficked persons may be prevented from leaving or be bound by debt or threat of violence.[6]

---

[5]Guiding Principles on Internal Displacement (E/CN.4/1998/53/Add.2), 1998, Principles and Scope.

[6]FMO, http://www.forcedmigration.org/about/whatisfm.

3 An Anthropological Conceptualisation of Forced Migration

Anthropology can contribute to exploring variations in the behaviour of different groups of displaced people, as well as to the functioning of the humanitarian sector in settings of displacement, by contributing to a deeper understanding of the design and implementation of humanitarian programmes. The Refugee Studies Centre at the University of Oxford suggests that an anthropological conceptualisation of forced migration consists of four characteristics.

First, the anthropological approach is based on in-depth empirical analysis, providing insight into a displaced community or several subgroups within a displaced community.

Second, it focuses on the micro level, examining what various (political, economic) processes mean to displaced people within certain contexts.

Third, the anthropological approach analyses the perspective of the displaced and aims to understand what meaning people give to social phenomena.[7]

Fourth, the anthropological approach explores the humanitarian system and response to forced migration. An anthropological approach can give a nuanced contribution to the analysis of forced migration, adding to the legal conceptualisation that is often used.

A very significant anthropological debate in forced migration relates to the relationship between place, space and identity formation. These are essential notions in anthropology and even more so as regards forced migration and displacement.

Therefore, ever greater attention is paid to the changing nature of forced migrants' identity and the way they react with agency to their new environment. Migrant's agency is essential for their strategies, future plans and ability to settle in a new environment.[8]

4 An Anthropological Perspective of Forced Migration and Displacement

The anthropologist Colson's overview of forced migration and the anthropological response show that the study of forced migration is now a major research area within the field. Since the 1970s, anthropologists have increasingly studied the effects that the arrival of large groups of displaced people has on host populations. Other anthropologists have studied the humanitarian community as it exerts a

[7] International Summer School in Forced Migration Participant's Handbook, Refugee Studies Centre, University of Oxford 2010, pp. 16–17.

[8] Molles (2013), p. 17.

strong influence on the experience of displaced people. Colson stated that, in addition to studying forced migration, anthropologists have attempted to ameliorate the situation of displaced people through the creation of agencies that give a voice to the displaced, such as the Refugee Studies Centre of Oxford.[9] E.V. Daniel notes that an anthological approach to refugee studies is relatively new, with the establishment of the Refugee Studies Centre being a major event linking the two research fields, and discusses the intersection between anthropology and the discourse surrounding refugees and displacement.[10]

The term refugee can have very different meanings in different settings, cultures and approaches. As Daniel argues, it is the anthropologists' task to navigate these different understandings.[11] Hence, anthropologists are charged with the responsibility to understand the life of a displaced person, to interpret what it means to have experienced traumatic events and betrayals of trust and to convey these experiences to the wider world.

4.1 Social Networks, Identities and Community Perspectives

An omnipresent component of forced migration and displacement is radical change and the loss of familiar circumstances, community structures and social networks. These processes affect former structures built on trust and reciprocity. The social fabric of a community, particularly displaced communities, is usually destroyed when it is affected by conflict. Pre-existing social structures may not function anymore, and time, coupled with active community level interventions, is necessary to rebuild the social fabric and a sense of trust and mutual understanding and agreement. The use of narrative theatre, for instance, may be beneficial in rebuilding a community. Such theatre can support the strength of people by stimulating a dialogue within the community. By discussing and addressing problems of the community in a theatre setting, creative and appropriate problem solving can take place, which may contribute to rebuilding trust and cooperation.

Narrative theatre focuses on conflict-affected communities, in which trust and dialogue may have diminished. Narrative theatre aims to create an environment where people can meet, discuss their problems and work towards realistic outcomes acceptable to all members of the community. This approach builds on the strengths and skills available in communities. In a *theatre setting*, facilitated by community workers, people dramatise and discuss problems leading to agreed solutions and actions. This way, dialogue is encouraged and trust can be rebuilt and strengthened.[12]

---

[9]Colson (2003), pp. 14–15.

[10]Daniel (2002).

[11]*Id*, p. 279.

[12]Sliep (2009), p. 7.

Such an approach was successfully employed in Burundi, where conflict had forced people to flee to neighbouring Tanzania. During their absence, other people sometimes claimed their homes and land. Once people returned to their villages after the conflict had ended, they faced problems related to their homes and lands. A Burundian NGO, in cooperation with an international NGO, introduced the narrative theatre approach in the communities. It turned out to be beneficial for communities and their returnees, to discuss the issues, search for solutions and rebuild trust again.[13]

In a setting of displacement, everything changes, including people's roles in life. This affects their identities. Since people define themselves in terms of the roles they play, *loss of role structures means that they cannot know who they are or who anyone else is until new roles are constructed and people assigned to them.*[14]

Identity also relates to membership of a group based on ethnicity and nationality. These types of identity are not fixed but are fluid and are part of a continuous process.

As Anderson has shown, nations must be seen as communities, which are 'imagined because the members of even the smallest nation will never know most of their fellow-members, meet them, or even hear of them, yet in the minds of each lives the image of their communion'.[15] He further states that, nevertheless, people identify themselves with the nation as a community to such an extent that they are willing to fight or even die for this community.

Thus, a setting of displacement provides both challenges and opportunities. The result is often a redefinition of roles that community members assume due to their new surroundings. Even deeply entrenched roles, such as those attached to gender, may change, sometimes enhancing underlying difficulties. For instance, where women in refugee camps take on roles that were previously the domain of men, it may leave the latter depressed, feeling devaluated, which may lead to family violence. Issues such as old age and loss of family members further affect identities. For example, in the wake of the death of parents and a disruption of social structures due to displacement, it may happen that the eldest child of a household may have to take care of his or her younger brothers and sisters. In such cases, the child assumes the roles of both father and mother and takes on a new identity.

However, the notion of home is very important in terms of identity and belonging. Where displaced people have dwelt in camps for decades and identities are ruptured, they may create a shared history and, possibly, a myth of returning to their home one day, grounding their identity in memories of the past. For example, in Palestine and Lebanon, many displaced Palestinians have embraced the key as their common symbol. Many of them have guarded the keys of their Palestinian homes, believing that one day they will be able to return.

[13]Healing communities programme of the NGOs War Trauma Foundation and Centre Ubuntu.

[14]Colson (2003), p. 8.

[15]Anderson (1983).

4.2 Refugees, Space and Place: The Micro Level

Refugee camps form social and cultural complexities in which new identities crystallise, as Agier describes in his anthropological analysis of refugee camps as urban ethnographic cases.[16] He suggests that the humanitarian system creates the social and political non-existence of aid recipients.

The recognition of refugees only as victims influences their identity. Refugee camps can thus be viewed as 'non-places', which are characterised by loss of memory, relationships and identity. At the same time, refugee camps also provide opportunities for reworking identities, influencing different classes, finding work and social positions.[17] Agier has conducted ethnographic research in the UNHCR-administered Dadaab refugee camp in Kenya, which hosts more than 300,000 refugees, predominantly of Somali origin, but is also home to Sudanese, Ethiopian, Eritrean and Ugandan nationals. Refugees are grouped into blocks according to citizenship, ethnicity and clan. Differences in activities and allocation of resources create social differentiations within the camps, which is exacerbated by the interventions of UNHCR and other NGOs. For instance, minorities can access loans for craft activities or as volunteers for NGOs. While some groups within the camps sometimes seek to remind these minorities of their inferior status, the opportunities present may also help minorities reach a new status. All of these dynamics are part of an ethnic chessboard within the refugee setting.

Anthropologist Malkki compared the situation of refugees in camps and in urban areas. She found that in refugee camp, community identity is reinforced, whereas 'the refugees who settle individually in towns produce more cosmopolitan forms of identity and their ethnic attachment loses its mythico-historical roots'.[18] By creating different forms of identity, both ethnic and non-ethnic, a camp does not manage to turn into a genuine space of urban sociability. Agier concludes that the camps, due to their character as emergency shelters, become spaces of waiting. Each refugee must redefine his or her place to retain a minimum of identity.[19] The unfinished character of life in camps entails uncertainty and leads to incompleteness of the process of integration.

Bauman underlines that through his ethnographic work, Agier returns human subjectivity to the refugees, helping them regain control of their lives.[20] This ethnographic approach demonstrates that both anthropologists and refugees can provide perspectives, which add value to the design and implementation of humanitarian interventions.

Refugees in camps must learn to live in the here and now. They find themselves in a transitory stage, which does not lead to a socially defined state.

---

[16] Agier (2002), pp. 317–341 and 318.

[17] *Id.* pp. 322–323.

[18] Malkki (2002), pp. 351–360.

[19] Agier (2002), p. 337.

[20] Bauman (2002), pp. 343–349.

Malkki describes displacement as a problem of organisation. Refugees are staying in camps where order is provided. Refugee camps, in this sense, are devices of care and control. According to the 1951 Refugee Convention, refugees are guaranteed freedom of movement and the right to asylum, but this is often considered as unrealistic in practice, given geopolitical realities. Malkki questions the construction of ideal-typical figures of the refugee camp and the refugee. Depending on the specific situation, a refugee may experience his or her refugee status as either providing protection or posing constraint.[21]

Many refugee communities have resided in camps for decades, up to 20 or 50 years, awaiting conflicts in their home regions to subside or the outcome of political negotiations to bear fruit, not able to stay or return, not knowing what will happen to them, unable to make plans for the future. In order to bring an end to this so-called *warehousing* of refugees (a situation where refugees are housed in one place for years on end due to lack of agreement or decisions on how to resolve the situation), the international community has established voluntary resettlement programmes to third countries. On the one hand, these programmes offer an opportunity for a new start in the United States, Australia or Europe for families and a future for their children. On the other hand, embarking on this road entails many new challenges, including leaving the region and social context in which people have lived for a long time. It is particularly challenging for elderly people to leave everything behind, move to a new country with whose culture or language they are often unfamiliar. Moreover, in many cases, family members who stay behind place high expectations on the resettled family members to find work or study, which these people often cannot meet, especially in a short time frame.

In many disaster-affected regions, family and community ties are very strong, which can pose extra challenges to families scattered over the world.

4.3 The Humanitarian Sector Related to Displacement

There have been increasing calls from anthropologists and also from the humanitarian sector (for example, during the World Humanitarian Summit 2016) for greater involvement of the beneficiaries of aid in determining their fate and the way humanitarian aid is provided. De Waal argues for a democratisation of the aid encounter, placing decisions on use of aid in the hands of recipients.[22] This means talking with beneficiaries instead of about them.

The situation of Ethiopian refugees in a camp in neighbouring Sudan during the Ethiopian famine in 1985 provides an illustrative case. These refugees went on a hunger strike, demanding permission to leave the camp and return home to the Ethiopian highlands. At the time, aid workers were puzzled as to why refugees

[21] Malkki (2002).

[22] de Waal (1997), pp. 623–639.

would wish to return to a difficult and dangerous situation. It has now been understood that the refugees wanted to return to their homelands, which would have enabled them to cultivate the land attached to their homes for the coming year and return to a degree of normalcy. This example emphasises the importance of fieldwork-based anthropology in relief and development contexts.[23]

Anthropologist Harrell-Bond has analysed interactions between helpers and refugees, addressing political forces. She stresses the need for a rights-based humanitarianism. This requires a shift from the approach of charity, which often portrays refugees as victims, to recognising them as survivors who demonstrate strength by pursuing their lives.[24] Harrell-Bond concludes that it is encouraging that NGOs begin to rely more on codes of conduct and minimal standards in the delivery of aid but stresses that it is essential to have systems of accountability towards refugees in place and to aim for capacity building driven from the grass-roots structures themselves.

5 The Case of Bhutanese Refugees in Nepal

The following summary of an exemplary case is based on the article ‘Psychological support for Bhutanese refugees in Nepal’.[25] For more than 20 years, thousands of Bhutanese refugees have lived in refugee camps in Eastern Nepal, in an uncertain and challenging situation. Now, the possibility of resettlement is bringing even more challenges into their lives. In recognition of this situation, a local NGO (TPO Nepal) provides psychosocial support to this group in collaboration with UNHCR and other humanitarian agencies.

The relationship between the northern Bhutanese (Drukpa) and southern Nepali-speaking Bhutanese (Lhotshampas) populations was relatively free of conflict until the early 1990s. At that time, more than 80,000 Lhotshampas were forced to flee to Nepal from Bhutan, following the introduction and enforcement of restrictive citizenship laws, and a ‘One Nation, One People’ government policy.[26] Bhutan claims that this group left willingly and denies that they were ever citizens. The refugees, however, claim that they were forced to leave Bhutan because of their ethnicity. As a consequence of this process, many people lost their nationality and are currently stateless. The government of Nepal, concerned about the implications of the refugee influx for national security, has been unwilling to allow refugees’ permanent residence. Yet, even though Nepal is not a signatory to the 1951 Refugee

[23]de Waal (2002).

[24]Harrell-Bond (2002), pp. 51–85.

[25]Based on Reiffers et al. (2013), pp. 169–179, http://www.interventionjournal.com/sites/default/files/Psychosocial_support_for_Bhutanese_refugees_in.5.pdf.

[26]Hutt (1996), pp. 397–420.

Convention, the government has allowed the refugees to *temporarily* stay in refugee camps.[27]

From 1993 until today, there have been 14 bilateral negotiations between Bhutan and Nepal to find a suitable solution, but none has produced results.[28] Due to increasing international discussions on the *warehousing* of refugees, as well as donor fatigue, some members of the international community have agreed to facilitate a process of resettlement to the United States, Canada, Australia, New Zealand, Norway, Denmark, the Netherlands and the United Kingdom.[29]

Under the resettlement programme, which was launched in 2007, more than 50,000 refugees from Bhutan have now left Nepal to start a new life elsewhere. The UNHCR and partner organisations continue to seek solutions for the remaining 60,000 refugees. According to UNHCR, more than 49,000 people among the remaining refugee population have expressed an interest in resettlement. Other refugees, however, prefer to either repatriate to Bhutan or stay in Nepal. The international community hopes that Bhutan and Nepal will allow these smaller groups to either remain or return as humanitarian interventions are to be phased out after the conclusion of the resettlement programme.

In the meantime, international and national humanitarian agencies continue to provide services related to health care, education and other needs within the Nepalese refugee camps. There were originally seven camps, but due to the resettlement process mentioned above and the ensuing decrease of the refugee population, the camps are now being consolidated. Conditions in the camps remain challenging; they are overpopulated and prone to security risks related to conflict and violence. Continuing uncertainty about the future and a protracted stay in the camps have also fuelled frustration and distress, which in turn impact psychosocial well-being. In order to offer the refugee community psychosocial support, TPO Nepal has designed a programme with the aim of improving psychosocial well-being and reducing psychosocial distress among Bhutanese refugees. This programme is implemented in close coordination with UNHCR and camp-based organisations (CBOs) from the refugee community to provide a range of psychosocial support to address psychosocial distress, with attention to cultural values.

A needs-based assessment among Bhutanese refugees in the camps showed that they experience various stressors related to basic needs and shelter, as well as resettlement opportunities and procedures.[30] According to this assessment, 'fear and insecurity, conflict in the family, confusion, substance abuse, stress and anxiety, worry about culture and religion, fear of separation and suicidal ideation are some of the key psychosocial problems prioritized by respondents'.[31] Another assessment identified suicide as a major problem and confirmed that the number

[27] Adelman (2008).

[28] Sharma (2009), www.ksl.edu.np.

[29] Loescher and Milner (2005).

[30] Luitel et al. (2009).

[31] Ibid.

of suicides among Bhutanese refugees in Nepal is disproportionately high.[32] Living in a refugee camp for 20 years, after having gone through difficult experiences and without any clarity in terms of the future, creates many challenges.

While there are educational and medical facilities in the camps, and refugees have been able to organise themselves within various forms and contribute to activities, rendering life meaningful has proved to be difficult. Additionally, refugees are not officially allowed to work and therefore unable to provide for their families. Even so, some of them do work as farmers, tradesmen, tailors or teachers in the informal sector, or within the camps.

Resettlement to third countries provides an opportunity to study and work, and brings hope. This new dimension, however, has created complex situations for families. Young people are eager to start a new life and create a better future for themselves and their children. However, many elderly people have no wish to migrate again and prefer to wait for an opportunity to either return to Bhutan or stay in Nepal. Within families, this has created tension and conflict resulting in some people either migrating or staying against their wishes. Families can be separated for years because part of a family may be eligible to resettle, whereas others may need to wait for the completion of a long process due to complicating factors, such as severe (mental) health problems, divorce or mixed marriages between refugees and local people from Nepal or India.

Ongoing uncertainty and family conflicts may also lead to various psychosocial problems, such as depression or suicide. There are very regular reports of attempted or committed suicides by refugees who see no other way out. Difficulty in giving meaning to one's life, or dealing with problems, can result in other negative impacts, such as substance abuse or increase in domestic violence.

The psychosocial care programme aims to enhance community resiliency at the grassroots level with wider participation of the refugee community in the design and implementation of activities. The programme includes awareness raising to increase mental health literacy in the community; psychosocial counselling; classroom-based interventions in which children from vulnerable families are involved in after-school activities related to music, dance and play in order to learn to communicate differently and gain more self-esteem; and group interventions, such as women's empowerment groups. For interventions on specialised mental health care, people are referred to other specialised aid agencies. A group of psychosocial counsellors participated in a training course on psychosocial issues and support. They now provide psychosocial counselling in counselling centres in the camps, or in people's huts. The counsellors are supported and supervised by clinical psychologists. In order to strengthen early identification of psychosocial problems, ensure timely referrals and provide suitable care, members of the refugee population have also been trained to work as community psychosocial workers (CPSWs) or classroom-based intervention (CBI) facilitators. They provide basic

[32]Schinina (2011).

psychosocial services. Their presence helps create a continuous flow of knowledge and support into the camps.

Counsellors are involved with psychosocial counselling, psycho-education and awareness-raising campaigns, assisted by the CPSWs. They support people in dealing with their problems and assist them in finding new ways to cope. The main components of psychosocial counselling include problem solving in the family or community, symptom management, psychological education, emotional support in relationships and development of personal skills. Family-oriented supportive counselling is provided through home visits, with a focus on parental capacities and psychological-education sessions, aiming to increase the well-being of families.

For the coming years, it is recommended to continue the psychosocial services at the camp level and to create or link these to existing psychosocial services in host communities. Refugees remaining in Nepal can then also benefit from the shared care facilities, which is essential as the ones who stay behind are often the most vulnerable, such as the elderly and people with severe illnesses or mental disorders. Involvement of the host community can contribute to the creation of a social care network for both communities. Developed interventions in support of the refugee community should ideally be integrated and embedded into existing care interventions and structures in the region, taking into account both culturally acceptable and international standards.[33]

It would be helpful to explore possible linkages with psychosocial organisations in states where refugees resettle in order to develop a system of handing over cases and sharing experiences, as well as support. This is of particular importance for suicide prevention and strengthening the (psycho)social situation of vulnerable refugees who might need support in the process of becoming citizens and fully engaging in their new home.[34]

6 Conclusion

Today, enormous amounts of people find themselves displaced, away from home, in a humanitarian disaster setting. Such situations affect them in many ways. Due to displacement, insecurity and uncertainty, people's identity and well-being are strongly affected while they try to give meaning to the world around them. This is where the anthropological perspective is important in terms of supporting people to identify their views and needs, conveying them within the humanitarian sector.

Displacement often incurs radical change; people lose their community structures, social networks and homes, which can have physical, psychological and

[33]Jordans and Sharma (2004), pp. 171–180.

[34]Reiffers et al. (2013).

spiritual effects. Further, people may experience loss of identities and roles, posing both challenges and opportunities to them.

Being displaced places many challenges on families, such as the Bhutanese families who have resided in camps in Nepal for more than 20 years. Resettlement programmes to third countries can provide solutions for some families. However, many families are also challenged by leaving their homes again, by processes that tear apart families and by relocating (elderly) people into new place contexts where everything is different and a sense of belonging needs to be found again.

An anthropological perspective of the humanitarian sector stresses that decisions on aid should more often be placed in the hands of aid recipients, in consultation with beneficiaries, instead of decisions about them. With that, it is essential to aim for capacity building to be driven from the grassroots structures themselves.

Ethnographic research and views can support people in getting back to managing their lives again. Anthropologists and affected people can provide a view of the situation and perspective of people in humanitarian settings, which is of paramount importance for the appropriate design and implementation of any humanitarian interventions.

References

Adelman H (2008) Protracted displacement in Asia: no place to call home. Ashgate, Hampshire

Agier M (2002) Between war and city. Towards an urban anthropology of refugee camps. Ethnography 3(3):317–341

Anderson B (1983) Imagined communities: reflections on the origins and spread of nationalism. Verso, London

Bauman Z (2002) In the lowly nowherevilles of liquid modernity. Ethnography 3(3):343–349

Colson E (2003) Forced migration and the anthropological response. J Refugee Stud 16(1):14–15

Daniel EV (2002) The refugee: a discourse on displacement. In: Exotic no more: anthropology on the frontlines. Chicago University Press

de Waal A (1997) Democratizing the aid encounter in Africa. Int Aff (Royal Institute of International Affairs) 73(4):623–639

de Waal A (2002) Anthropology and the aid encounter. In: Exotic no more: anthropology on the frontlines. Chicago University Press

Eriksen TH (2010) Small places, large issues, an introduction to social and cultural anthropology. Pluto Press, London

Forced Migration Online (FMO). www.forcedmigration.org. Accessed 20 Jan 2015

Harrell-Bond B (2002) Can humanitarian work with refugees be humane? Hum Rights Q 24:51–85

Hutt M (1996) Ethnic nationalism, refugees and Bhutan. J Refugee Stud 9:397–420

International Summer School in Forced Migration Participant's Handbook, Refugee Studies Centre, University of Oxford 2010, pp 16–17

Jordans MJD, Sharma B (2004) Integration of psychosocial counselling in care systems in Nepal. Intervention 2:171–180

Loescher G, Milner JH (2005) Protracted refugee situations: domestic and international security implications. Routledge, London

Luitel NP, Karkai K, Prasai B, Jordans M (2009) Psychosocial issues of Bhutanese refugees. Compilation of findings of qualitative study. TPO Nepal, Kathmandu

Malkki LH (2002) News from nowhere: mass displacement and globalized problems of organization. Ethnography 3(3):351–360

Molles ED (2013) Identity and immigrant integration in Western Europe's "New" migration cities, the cases of Dublin and Madrid. Josef Korbel J Adv Int Stud 5:17

Reiffers R et al (2013) Psychosocial support for Bhutanese refugees in Nepal. Intervention 11 (2):169–179. http://www.interventionjournal.com/sites/default/files/Psychosocial_support_for_Bhutanese_refugees_in.5.pdf

Schinina G, Sharma S, Gorbacheva O, Mishra AK (2011) 'Who am I?' Assessment of psychosocial needs and suicide risk factors among Bhutanese refugees in Nepal and after third country resettlement. International Organization for Migration, United Nations High Commissioner for Refugees, Bureau of Population, Refugees and Migration, Geneva

Sharma N (2009) Bhutanese refugee situation: an assessment of Nepal-Bhutan bilateralism. Kathmandu School of Law, Bhaktapur. www.ksl.edu.np

Sliep Y (2009) Healing communities by strengthening social capital: a narrative theatre approach. War Trauma Foundation, Diemen, p 7

The International Association for the Study of Forced Migration (IASFM). www.iasfm.org, http://www.efms.uni-bamberg.de/iasfm/mission.htm

United Nations High Commissioner for Refugees (2016) UNHCR Global Trends 2015. UNHCR, Geneva. http://www.unhcr.org/576408cd7.pdf.de

Further Reading

Agier M (2002) Between war and city. Towards an urban anthropology of refugee camps. Ethnography 3(3):317–341. http://faculty.washington.edu/plape/citiesaut11/readings/Agier%20BETWEEN.pdf

Bauman Z (2002) In the lowly nowherevilles of liquid modenity. Ethnography 3(3):343–349

Colson E (2003) Forced migration and the anthropological response. J Refugee Stud 16(1). http://web.mnstate.edu/robertsb/308/forced%20migration%20and%20the%20anthropological%20response.pdf

Malkki LH (2002) News from nowhere, mass displacement and globalized problems of organization. Ethnography 3(3):351–360. http://www.mcrg.ac.in/AddReading/2008/H_maalki_camps.pdf

Relinde Reiffers is a Lecturer of anthropology, who teaches in the NOHA Joint Master's Programme in International Humanitarian Action at the University of Groningen, the Netherlands.

An Anthropological Perspective on the Timeline of Humanitarian Interventions

Juan Carlos Gumucio-Castellon

This chapter deals with the main temporal stages of humanitarian programmes and the interlinked contexts within which these stages unfold, proceeding from early identification of humanitarian risks to the linking with development execution of humanitarian aid as a participative and empowering effort.

In the multidisciplinary field of humanitarian assistance, anthropology plays a role at all stages, from the initial concerted efforts to identify possible or probable upcoming critical or disastrous situations to the implementation of steps and measures designed to attain sustainable development for the areas and populations affected.

The temporal stages of humanitarian action are considered here from an anthropological perspective, i.e. early identification of risks, risk reduction and preparedness, rapid reaction in the face of emergency or disaster and, finally, linking humanitarian action to development when it comes to reconstruction efforts in disaster zones. The process is perhaps best characterised as a circle rather than a straight line.

1 Early Identification of Probable Future Hazards

Processes that may eventually lead to humanitarian crises, including degradation or loss of habitat, increased levels of social conflicts and climate change, among others, should be identified as early as possible. In many cases throughout different regions, ranging from the Kalahari over the Sahel and Central America to the Amazon and others, the anthropologic insights into specific conditions obtained

J.C. Gumucio-Castellon (✉)
Uppsala University, Uppsala, Sweden
e-mail: jc.gumucio@gmail.com

© Springer International Publishing AG 2018
H.-J. Heintze, P. Thielbörger (eds.), *International Humanitarian Action*,
DOI 10.1007/978-3-319-14454-2_18

through ethnographic research can be of great value to humanitarians. For instance, the inhabitants of the Central African rainforest, already facing various challenges such as deforestation and poaching, may today be facing a severe reduction of rainfall:

> The Congolese forest, with its drier conditions and higher percentage of semi-evergreen trees, may be more tolerant to short-term rainfall reduction than are wetter tropical forests, but for a long-term drought there may be critical thresholds of water availability below which higher-biomass, closed-canopy forests transition to more open, lower-biomass forests.[1]

Those directly affected by such impending changes would be the various low-density rainforest groups in the area, collectively known as Pygmies, but well differentiated by anthropologists as the Mbuti, Aka, Baka and Twa.

As in any other discipline, the context—academic, political and otherwise—in which this kind of ethnographic knowledge is obtained is highly contested, with various uncertainties and perils. The former may be illustrated by the work of Paul Farmer, professor of Anthropology at Harvard Medical School and Chair of Global Health and Social Medicine at Harvard in Haiti. Farmer's well-documented early warnings of a catastrophe waiting to happen in Haiti went unheeded until the earthquake struck in 2010. As to the perils, the dangers faced by Napoleon Chagnon, both in the field among the Amazonian Yanomamo and then in the academy, are poignantly described in his recent book *Noble Savages*, providing much food for thought.[2]

2 Implementation of Risk Reduction Programmes

Reducing risk and vulnerability through enhanced preparedness is essential to preserving life.[3] Moreover, as the Global Assessment Reports (GARs) published by the United Nations Office for Disaster Risk Reduction (UNISDR)[4] from 2009 onwards have established, disaster risk will continue to rise, making enhanced preparedness essential.

In the effort to minimise disaster impact and losses while confronting risky ecological, political and economic processes and pitfalls, concerned anthropologists have to combine research on general issues, such as poverty reduction and decreased vulnerability, with local/regional forms of knowledge and best practices. As a matter of fact, the possibilities and potentials of these alternative forms of knowledge are often not immediately apparent to outsiders. As James Boon puts it:

[1]Zhou et al. (2014), pp. 86–90; http://www.nature.com/nature/journal/v509/n7498/full/nature13265.html.

[2]Chagnon (2013).

[3]European Consensus on Humanitarian Aid, p. 24.

[4]UNISDR, Global Assessment Report 2015, http://www.unisdr.org/we/inform/gar.

> Those who bemoan anthropology's scientific shortcomings underestimate its characteristic accomplishments: discovering subtlety, pattern, dialectics and innuendo in human matters, that viewed by agencies of analysis outside of anthropology appear merely misguided and laughable.[5]

Adequate channels of information can be more complex than what initially meets the eye, linguistically or otherwise. Suppose, for instance, there was a need to distribute information regarding volcanic eruptions and evacuation to indigenous Mapuche populations in southern Chile and Argentina. Agents from disciplines unrelated to anthropology might not be aware that the local language *Mapudungun* has several distinct orthographic variants and at least an equal number of phonological ones.[6] This kind of knowledge directly impacts on the way information needs to be prepared.

Preparedness also suffers from the human tendency to forget. What has been called the last great subsistence crisis in the western world happened after the colossal volcanic eruption of Mount Tambora, in 1816, on the island of Sumbawa, Indonesia. A year without summer followed, and the consequences were severe, not only in Southeast Asia but also in eastern parts of North America and across Europe, with famine, bread riots and epidemics. According to B. McGuire, although our knowledge of the potential hazards of volcanism has increased over the last 200 years, much remains to be done.[7]

3 The Disaster or Emergency Situation

When rapid action and early recovery are of the essence, the anthropologically trained agent will often be able to contribute to humanitarian efforts in several ways.

First, anthropologists are trained to establish rapid and close relationships with host communities. This community closeness refers to a technical and well-informed understanding of the implications of social formations such as super class, section, subsection, clan, moiety, cognation, etc., as well as patterns of affiliation and disintegration of social harmony and conflict.[8] In other words, anthropology needs to look for social heterogeneity most often found beneath an apparent and superficial homogeneity: 'Anthropologists can be extremely effective in presenting valuable insights, demonstrating the ranges of variation within seemingly homogeneous groupings'.[9]

---

[5]Boon (1982), p. 47.

[6]Carbonell et al. (2005), pp. 111–137.

[7]McGuire (2015), pp. 26–27.

[8]Godelier (2011), p. 123f.

[9]Ervin (2002), p. 108.

Second, anthropologists learn to avoid the pitfalls of simplifying complex issues that can be tempting for agents working with emergency protocols, tight schedules and limited resources. As I witnessed in Lombok, Indonesia, a system of latrines or waste disposal that is erected without proper consultancy with local practices will most often remain unused.

Third, anthropological knowledge of specific surroundings facilitates communication; familiarity with the specific meaning and implications of local terms and concepts provided by an anthropologist helps to make local knowledge congruent and an active part of the aid effort as expressed in agreed protocols and codes of conduct. Inversely, such mediation allows for protocols and procedures to be optimally implemented within specific sociocultural settings. In other words, and in terms of the conventional distinction, it is a mediation between the logic of the *emic* and the logic of the *etic*.[10]

One may liken this to an informed mediation between the categories of *ethnos* and *demos*, as in the interplay between traditional-kinship-based and modern-social-contract-based political decision mechanisms, common and codified law and adjudication systems, with multiple possibilities for a combination of secular and religious, private and public dimensions. The same holds true for the highly complex interplay of various medicinal systems, traditional, alternative and/or allopathic, in many places.

4 Reconstruction and the Link with Development

If anthropology is a relatively new facet of humanitarianism, development has long been a key concept in applied anthropology and was already well established as a subfield by the early 1980s.[11] The 2002 edition of the Encyclopaedia of Social and Cultural Anthropology includes a detailed entry on development but not on humanitarianism.[12] As Pierre Minn explains:

> Humanitarianism has received relatively little scrutiny from anthropologists, but the same is not true for development, which has attracted significant attention in the form of ethnographic studies as well as theoretical analyses and reflection. Much of the literature in this area is directly relevant to the topic of humanitarianism, and can serve as an important resource for the emerging domain.[13]

The relation to development work is also a controversial aspect of humanitarian action:

[10] I.e., the difference between culture-specific and universal models of understanding.

[11] Hoben (1982), pp. 349–375.

[12] Barnard and Spencer (eds) ([1996] 2003).

[13] Minn (2007).

> The humanitarian instrument lacks follow-through: there are few examples of an international assistance programme moving forward smoothly from the emergency phase into rehabilitation and development. It saves lives but fails to restore livelihoods or rehabilitate economies. In other words, the system has not mastered transition.[14]

In some cases, reconstruction, not to mention development, has to be postponed because of prolonged crises or failures of assistance programmes. For example, the sustained effort to remedy the disastrous consequences of the ongoing Sidjoarto mudflow in eastern Java, where approximately 40,000 persons were displaced, was not met with success. There is much controversy as to how to mitigate the effects of this severe crisis.[15] Similarly, many reconstruction programmes have been in place in Haiti since the earthquake of 2010 with little success.[16] There is also considerable overlap between emergency aid, reconstruction and development:

> While development and humanitarian assistance are two distinct phenomena, they are not without significant overlap. Much of the activities described as 'development' (improving the lives of impoverished populations through education, health care, agriculture, etc.) can be (and often are) glossed as humanitarian activities, and vice-versa. In addition, both development and humanitarian projects, despite their differences, entail relationships between individuals and institutions in wealthy and impoverished countries, and have developed sizable infrastructures to facilitate these relationships and the processes that emerge from them.[17]

In the phase of post-conflict or post-disaster reconstruction leading to development, the anthropologist will rely heavily on a communicative and holistic concept of culture, understood here as the processual combination of the social, cognitive and material dimensions of life. In this way, taking due consideration of the caveats mentioned above, the anthropologically trained agent will consider the implications of social structures, various classifications, symbolic systems and other cognitive domains, as well as the constraints and possibilities of local material and economic conditions. All this will permit an informed focus on factors such as community participation, social dynamics, relativity and possible sources of misunderstanding (Instituto de Derechos Humanos 2000).

Community participation is one of the main factors enhancing the adequate congruence of reconstruction programmes with local needs and aspirations. This has broad implications, from general considerations, such as in whose interests a certain reconstruction programme is really being implemented, to more direct specifics, such as the choice or combination of appropriate qualitative and quantitative measurement tools. *Community members may prefer statements of a verbal or qualitative nature; decision makers may want facts bolstered by numbers.*[18]

---

[14]Hyder (2007).

[15]Wayman (2011), http://www.smithsonianmag.com/science-nature/the-worlds-muddiest-disaster-1603529/?no-ist; A.R. Fitrianto, Shrimp Farmers' Innovation In Coping With The Disaster (A Case Study In Sidoarjo Mud Volcano Disaster Toward Shrimp Farmers' Responses), http://www.sciencedirect.com/science/article/pii/S2212567112003322.

[16]Farmer (2011) and Schuller (2010).

[17]Minn (2007).

[18]Ervin (2002), p. 196.

Community demands are not infrequently disregarded. For example, in the wake of the great earthquake and tsunami of 2004, inhabitants of the Nicobar Islands were, in the first place, concerned with gathering tools to rebuild their homes. However, the roughly 60 NGOs that descended on those remote settlements had their own priorities and agendas, and consequently locals were swamped by items, including radios, junk food and gas stoves, in the absence of liquefied gas canisters. Nicobarese culture is based on joint families of 40–50 people, but the concept of providing aid or building houses for extended families was unknown to the agents of the Indian government, so 7000 *modern* tin houses for nuclear families were commissioned. No wonder social ecologist Simron Jit Singh, present at the time, says he witnessed how a flood of aid destroyed a culture.[19]

In the same way, social dynamics, when not taken into account, can wreck well-intentioned but ill-informed reconstruction programmes:

> ….. distinguishing with elaborate precision, the contexts – marriage, worship, and to an extent diet, law and education – within which men are separated by their dissimilitudes, and those – work, friendship, politics, trade – however warily and however conditionally, they are connected by them.[20]

Certainly, such knowledge cannot be rapidly acquired as it would appear, for instance, in the list of motivating factors recommended by Richard D. Lewis while negotiating a deal in India. He states:

> Make yourself familiar with Indian family arrangements, e.g. brothers and sons usually living under one roof, look at things from their point of view, develop a tolerance for ambiguity – it is common in Asia, make yourself familiar with the respective positions of men and women and the system of arranged marriage, etc.[21]

In reality, learning about this kind of deep structural patterns, not least the subtle semantics of ambiguity, takes up considerable time as innuendo, and implicit traits of communication are usually not immediately apparent but discernible only after protracted fieldwork that takes months and years. To engage ambiguity is, according to Redfield and Bornstein, one of the gifts of anthropology, the result of working

> …in a gray zone between analytic registers, one initiated by the ambiguous, ambitious and varied roles that ethnographers have with human practice: as participant observers, expert witnesses, moral spectators, consultants, activists, critics, historians, outsiders, engaged sympathizers, and active members.[22]

These kinds of insights can otherwise be obtained through documentary and archival studies, such as that of John Pemberton on the historical roots of authenticity in central Java, where the manifestation of a sense of traditional royal Javanese culture employs many elements borrowed from the Dutch colonial

[19]O'Neill (2015), pp. 34–35.

[20]Geertz (1983), p. 67.

[21]Lewis (2006), p. 440.

[22]Bornstein and Redfield (2010), p. 26.

presence and other European prestige-laden tokens: 'Regardless of how many Spanish figurines, French chandeliers, Italian sculptures or Dutch portraits might be crammed into the Kraton Surakarta,[23] it would all eventually, be viewed as "authentically Javanese".'[24] In the aftermath of the 2010 eruption of the Merapi volcano in that same region, such insights were relevant for a proper understanding of the sociocultural landscape of the region. They now need to be considered together with relevant modern concepts in order to form a coherent and meaningful whole in the context of reconstruction.

Further, the anthropologically trained agent needs to dispose of a sense of relativity. He or she will be aware that anthropology, as James Boon puts it, 'forestalls any culture's sense of its own inevitability',[25] acknowledging the importance and significance of the range of variation on the understanding of the nature of humanitarian aid, be it local, traditional, modern, secular or religious.

For instance, in areas with a prevalence of traditional Muslim concepts of charity, this means taking due consideration of *zakat* and *sadaqa*. As Hyder explains:

> Zakat is obligatory and payable only to Muslim beneficiaries who are specified in the Qur'an (Sura 9, verse 60); zakat therefore does not really qualify as being the equivalent of humanitarian aid in modern terms. Sadaqa, especially one particular kind designated as sadaqat al-tatawwu' (alms of spontanaiety) is voluntary and can be given to Muslim and non-Muslim alike without further specification of their status or need. This type of sadaqa is therefore more akin to humanitarian aid in modern terms.[26]

One must carefully evaluate whether these concepts are being considered, even where their logic might differ from the contemporary ideal of humanitarian assistance of inclusiveness and non-discrimination.[27] As it is, the interface between these Muslim humanitarian concepts and non-confessional humanitarian assistance remains to a large extent unexplored. At the same time, these divergent aspects should not be overplayed:

> Whatever the points of difference, they seem to have little impact on humanitarian operations in Muslim countries. OIC members welcome humanitarian agencies to their meetings as observers, have passed helpful resolutions (for example expressing appreciation of UNHCR's work), and in general have good relations with international humanitarian agencies, both as contributors and as recipients. Thus there seems to be broad agreement on the underlying purposes.[28]

There are many possible sources of misunderstanding between anthropology and humanitarian aid. A general principle would be that humanitarianism rests on the notion that the common human moral community to which we all belong consists of

[23]The royal palace in Surakarta/Solo.

[24]Pemberton (1994), p. 67.

[25]Boon (1982), p. 47.

[26]Hyder (2007).

[27]*Ibid.*

[28]*Ibid.*

individuals capable of free communication and, in principle, able to interact and collaborate according to rules of mutual respect.[29]

In practice, in intercultural settings with interdisciplinary teams of agents operating in the field, communication and collaboration often require solid professional support to facilitate intercultural understanding. In this context, the anthropologically trained agent contributes ethnographic inside expertise with reference to specific cases, situations, locations, groups, etc., thus facilitating for other members of the team a better understanding of local beneficiaries and affected individuals' demands and expectations.

5 Conclusion

Finally, anthropologists and specialists from other disciplines, lawyers, medical doctors and nurses and even economists, who also perceive and analyse the intricacies of sociocultural patterns, have much in common. Acknowledging the high frequency of assault on women in India, Amartya Sen points to the fact that this terrible form of violence is related to brute force, as well as to the level of permissiveness of a set of negative attitudinal factors. This shows that any programme of social reform to combat physical violence against women thus needs to take into account educational, cultural and political factors.[30]

As any other aid practitioner, the anthropologist confronts the fundamental question of the justification of the humanitarian approach and the meaning of an effort that is positioned within the boundaries of a field of action characterised by a unified and integral sense of a single human moral community. In other words, it is the sense of obligation to help people in need that follows from a shared moral space.[31]

As to its inner logic and reason, humanitarianism is positioned between the two polarities of morality and politics,[32] justice and heartfelt caring, constituting itself within that field around a core of integrity and empowerment. Rather than the mobilisation of compassion over justice,[33] humanitarianism is the interplay of compassion with justice, of rights with emotions, of violence and trauma with suffering. It is not a matter of translating or replacing one set of values or categories for another but a matter of interaction and dialectics in the context of a politics of compassion. It would thus appear that the essence of humanitarianism is to guard a sense of integrity, an experience, a sense of ownership and empowerment.

[29]Cortina (2010), p. 130.

[30]Sen (2005), p. 237.

[31]Cortina (2010), p. 58.

[32]NOHA, Anthropology in Humanitarian Assistance, 1998, 2nd edn., p. 4.

[33]Fassin (2012).

Therefore, one way to characterise humanitarianism is to see it as mandated by a feeling of obligation (the duty to help) born of a sense of solidarity, which impels the agent to a professionally informed experience of caring, helping and healing. At the same time, the heartfelt condition of this solidarity makes it, following Jean Watson, so unitary to its various manifestations that the members of the host community, the beneficiaries, feel these manifestations as if they were their own from the very beginning, a sense of ownership that empowers recipients and restores them to the same statutory level as the caring humanitarian agent.[34] This leads the humanitarian effort to its logical circular conclusion, which is also a preparedness for a new cycle, considering that rupture, trauma and suffering are not the exception but rather the rule.[35]

Finally, what started as an apparent timeline shows itself to, in reality, be a circular process that, following Adela Cortina,[36] is incomplete without the element of democratic and participative reciprocal education.

References

Barnard A, Spencer J (eds) ([1996] 2003) The encyclopedia of social and cultural anthropology. Routledge, London

Boon J (1982) Other tribes, other scribes. Symbolic anthropology in the comparative study of cultures, histories, religions and texts. Cambridge University Press, Cambridge

Bornstein E, Redfield P (2010) An introduction to the anthropology of humanitarianism. In: Redfield P, Bornstein E (eds) Forces of compassion. Humanitarianism between ethics and politics. SAR Press, Santa Fe

Carbonell J, Lavie A et al (2005) Language technologies for humanitarian aid. In: Cahill KM (ed) Technology for humanitarian action. Fordham University Press, New York

Chagnon N (2013) Noble savages. My life among two dangerous tribes – the Yanomamö and the anthropologists. Simon & Schuster, New York

Cortina A (2010) Justicia cordial. Minima Trotta, Madrid

Ervin A (2002) Applied anthropology. Tools and perspectives for contemporary practice. Allyn and Bacon, Boston

European Consensus on Humanitarian Aid, The humanitarian challenge. DG humanitarian aid (ECHO). European Commission, Brussels

Farmer P (2011) Haiti after the earthquake. Perseus Group, Philadelphia

Fassin D (2012) Humanitarian reason. A moral history of the present. University of California Press, Berkeley

Geertz C (1983) Local knowledge. Further essays in interpretative anthropology. Basic Books, New York

Godelier M (2011) The metamorphosis of kinship. Verso, London

Hoben A (1982) Anthropologists and development. Annu Rev Anthropol 11:349–375

Hyder M (2007) Humanitarianism and the Muslim world. J Humanit Assist, August

[34]Watson (2012), Burlington, 2nd edn., Ch. 8.

[35]NOHA, Anthropology in Humanitarian Assistance, 1998, 2nd edn., p. 10.

[36]Cortina (2010), p. 94.

Instituto de Derechos Humanos (2000) La antropologia en la ayuda humanitaria. Instituto de Derechos Humanos. Universidad de Deusto
Lewis R (2006) When cultures collide. Leading across cultures. Nicholas Brealey International, Boston
McGuire B (2015) Natural disaster amnesia. Threats we choose to forget. New Scientist 3014, 27/3
Minn P (2007) Toward an anthropology of humanitarianism. J Humanit Assist, August
O'Neill S (2015) I watched a flood of aid destroy a culture. New Scientist 3013, 23/3
Pemberton J (1994) On the subject of "Java". Cornell University Press, Ithaca
Schuller M (2010) Haiti's disaster after the disaster: the IDP camps and cholera. J Humanit Assist, December
Sen A (2005) The argumentative Indian. Picador, New York
Watson J (2012) Human caring science. A theory of nursing. Jones & Bartlett, London
Wayman E (2011) The World's Muddiest Disaster Earth's most violent mud volcano is wreaking havoc in Indonesia. Was drilling to blame? And when will it end? The Smithsonian, December
Zhou L et al (2014) Widespread decline of Congo rainforest greenness in the past decade. Nature 509

Further Reading

Abram D (1997) The spell of the sensous. Vintage Books, New York
Barnett M (2008) Humanitarianism in question. Politics, power, ethics. Cornell University Press, New York
Hoffman PJ, Weiss TG (2006) Sword & salve. Confronting new wars and humanitarian crises. Rowman & Littlefield Publ. Inc, Oxford
Kottak CP (2000) Anthropology. The exploration of human diversity, 8th edn. McGraw Hill, Boston
Macionis JJ (2009) Society, the basics. Pearson Education International, London
Minear L, Smith H (eds) (2007) Humanitarian diplomacy. Practitioners and their craft. United Nations University Press, New York

Juan Carlos Gumucio-Castellon is a former Lecturer of Anthropology at Uppsala University, Sweden.

Part V
Management

Managing Humanitarian Action: An Introduction

Pat Gibbons

Global Humanitarian Assistance reached record levels in 2014 at $24.4 billion; however, that same year, the highest level of global humanitarian need was also evidenced with an excess of 200 million people affected by disasters.[1] The trend of humanitarian need outstripping supply is a persistent and growing problem over recent years. The extent of the problem was manifest in 2015, when the shortfall in the UN's humanitarian appeal reached 40%.[2] Many and varied theories are being offered on how to address this deficit; however, the need for improved *management* (planning, organising, controlling and coordinating global humanitarian resources[3]) in pursuit of the global humanitarian goal (to save lives, alleviate suffering and support life with dignity for all disaster-affected peoples[4]) has consistently featured high on the humanitarian agenda.

Humanitarian management is a varied and complex process that is complicated by many factors, not least the global humanitarian context—the range of disasters in terms of typology and geographic spread, together with the dynamism that typifies the new generation of disasters; the diversity of humanitarian actors in terms of values, policies and ways of working; and the complexity of the working environments typified by breakdown in societal institutions and where humanitarian action is constantly evolving to its complex, dangerous and/or stressful milieu.

[1] Global Humanitarian Assistance (GHA) (2015).

[2] World Humanitarian Summit Secretariat (2015).

[3] These functions are well documented as the '*classical functions of management*', which were established by Fayol in 1949 and continue to shape management textbooks and management education.

[4] '*Saving lives, alleviating suffering and supporting/ maintaining life with dignity for disaster affected people*' is a well-established goal of humanitarian action.

P. Gibbons (✉)
University College Dublin, Dublin, Ireland
e-mail: pat.f.gibbons@ucd.ie

© Springer International Publishing AG 2018

H.-J. Heintze, P. Thielbörger (eds.), *International Humanitarian Action*,
DOI 10.1007/978-3-319-14454-2_19

This introductory chapter to the management section describes the contemporary humanitarian management context and posits some of the future challenges for the *humanitarian system*.

1 The Global Humanitarian Context

Despite tremendous advances in science to improve both quality and quantity of life, all evidence suggests that human suffering from the impacts of armed conflicts and other types of disasters has reached unprecedented levels. Over 60 million people are currently displaced from their homes due to conflict and violence, while in excess of 200 million people affected by disasters annually require humanitarian assistance. The economic costs of disasters and natural hazards have grown year on year and now exceed $300 billion per annum.[5] The humanitarian challenge to meet the needs of people affected by or vulnerable to crises is likely to grow in scale and complexity. The causal factors for current and predicted humanitarian need include poverty, hunger, disease, water shortages, climate change, population growth, unplanned rapid urbanisation, mass migration and food insecurity.[6]

There is little doubt that data suggesting large increases in the level of humanitarian need is partially explained by improved data collection methodologies. However, one should not be surprised by these worrying statistics given that almost a fifth of the world's population survive on less than a $1 a day, a similar percentage of the global population is living in fragile States that are prone to repeated violent conflicts[7] and approximately half of the world's population is living in urban settings, and this is projected to grow to two-thirds by 2050—an increasing percentage of this population are slum dwellers.[8] Furthermore, it is important to consider that more than 85% of UN humanitarian appeals over the past decade were in support of people affected by armed conflict. While the number of active conflicts in the world has stabilised, the impact and protracted nature of conflicts have worsened.[9]

The recognised failure of the international community to reach out to disaster-affected populations prompted the UN Secretary General to organise a World Humanitarian Summit (WHS) to address the magnitude of current and future global humanitarian challenges. The results of this 2016 Summit are calling for a new and coherent approach to address root causes of disasters, increasing political diplomacy for prevention and conflict resolution and bringing humanitarian,

[5]UNISDR, Global Assessment Report 2015.

[6]World Humanitarian Summit Secretariat (2015).

[7]OECD (2014).

[8]World Humanitarian Summit Secretariat (2015).

[9]OCHA (2013).

development and peacebuilding efforts together.[10] The core responsibilities and commitments made by various stakeholders at the WHS highlight the need for collective response towards a new 'Agenda for Humanity'.

2 Diversity of Humanitarian Actors and Management Challenges

The proliferation of humanitarian actors in terms of size and scope of operations over the past 25 years is well documented.[11] Significant efforts have been made to enhance global management among these diverse actors by initiatives such as the UN's Humanitarian Reform Programme in 2005 and the Transformative Agenda in 2011. These early initiatives have consistently sought to improve partnerships, coordination, coherence, financial accountability and leadership in a bid to enhance the effectiveness of humanitarian action.

In more recent years, greater efforts have been made to view core humanitarian actors as part of a *humanitarian system*.[12] The State of the Humanitarian System Report 2015 defines this humanitarian system as 'the network of interconnected institutional and operational entities through which humanitarian assistance is provided when local and national resources are insufficient to meet the needs of the affected population'.[13] It goes on to identify the institutional and operational entities as follows:

- local, national and international NGOs;
- UN humanitarian agencies;
- the International Red Cross and Red Crescent Movement;
- recipient government agencies with responsibility for crisis response;
- humanitarian arms of regional intergovernmental organisations;
- donor government agencies and offices that provide humanitarian funding and coordination.

In addition, this *humanitarian system* frequently works with non-core actors that also participate in humanitarian response, but unlike the above-listed core humanitarian actors, humanitarian action is not their core function. Such non-core actors include military forces, religious institutions, private sector entities and diaspora groups.[14]

[10]World Humanitarian Summit – Chair's Summary (2016).

[11]Gibbons (2010), pp. 11–27; Taylor et al. (2012), ALNAP (2015).

[12]"*System*" – *a group or combination of interrelated, interdependent or interacting elements forming a collective entity*' (Collins Dictionaries 2015).

[13]ALNAP (2015), p. 18.

[14]*Id.*, p. 19.

While all humanitarian core actors purport to be governed by a common set of fundamental humanitarian principles, namely humanity, impartiality, neutrality and independence,[15] the challenges to coordinate this diverse group should not be underestimated. One might argue that the key to understanding the complexities of managing this stakeholder mix is to appreciate the different governance and management characteristics that are particular to *groupings* within this mix.

At the risk of oversimplifying this issue, three groupings can be discerned in line with three broad sectors (public, private and voluntary sectors). These different sectors view core organisational values concerned with governance, management and accountability quite differently. Local, national and international NGOs are characteristically voluntary in character, while the UN, recipient governments, regional intergovernmental organisations and donor governments are bound by public sector values. The Red Cross and Red Crescent Movement, while not identified as an NGO, combines elements of public sector provision, given its role as custodian of international humanitarian law, and also employs typically voluntary sector characteristics in the delivery of humanitarian action through the Federation and the National Societies. The private sector is not governed by the humanitarian principles and has quite different governance and management values to both the public and voluntary sectors, yet it is an increasingly active stakeholder in the provision of humanitarian action. Figure 1 presents the relationship between governance, management and the customer for each of the three sectors.

The private sector is governed by paid officials whose primary responsibility is to their shareholders, to ensure that they get a return on their investment. In the case of the public sector, the government is ultimately responsible to their voters, who they seek to satisfy in order to get re-elected. In contrast, the voluntary sector, by definition, is governed by a voluntary board that gives their time and expertise in the interest of the common good.

The management function also varies considerably between sectors. The company, in the case of the private sector, is charged with the production of goods and services that meet customers' needs and wants. The success of the company largely hinges on its ability to provide the customer with the right product at the right price, and company management is frequently rewarded with bonuses and other incentives when they meet agreed targets. The company's health is largely dependent on satisfied customers who buy the product and/or services. In the event that the company does not meet the needs and/or wants of the customer, the products and/or services will not be bought, and the company will be forced to close in a relatively short time period. Management in the public sector is charged with providing a range of services to the public, who show their satisfaction by using the services. Customers are legally obliged to pay for public services through various taxation policies.

Public sector organisations are typically bureaucratic and highly hierarchical with staff enjoying secure jobs. Workers in the public sector, while not in a position

[15]OCHA (2013).

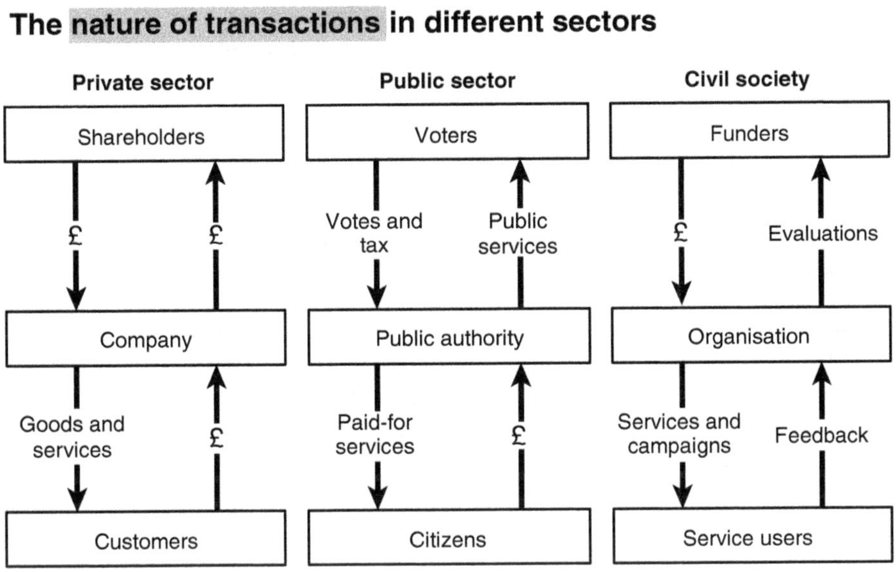

Fig. 1 The nature of transaction in different sectors. Reproduced from Managing Without Profit—Leadership, governance and management of civil society organisations (2017) by Mike Hudson and by kind permission of the publishers, The Directory of Social Change, 352 Holloway Road, London N7 6PA www.dsc.org.uk from whom copies may be purchased

to receive bonuses in the same way as the private sector, enjoy job security, and rewards for productivity come in the form of better working conditions and/or promotion. In theory, satisfied customers demonstrate their satisfaction by returning elected representatives to power. Dissatisfied public service customers may opt in the short term to use alternative services from the private sector if affordable and eventually register their dissatisfaction by voting in a new public representative over time.

The voluntary sector is largely associated with providing services to people *in need*, especially in those areas where the public sector is unable or unwilling to meet the needs of its constituents. Voluntary sector organisations are usually dependent on healthy public and private sectors for funding and donations to provide their services. Funding is typically provided on the basis of short-term contracts of between 1 and 5 years, which in turn complicates management and continuity of service provision. Given the dependence on donors for funding, the relationship between management and the customer is fundamentally different. The customers of voluntary sector services rarely have the financial or political powers afforded to customers of private companies and/or public sector customers. They seldom enjoy the same choices available to those in other sectors either because of the lack of alternative service providers or their poor spending power, to the extent that in some cases they are referred to as beneficiaries rather than customers. Instead, the power rests with the donors and funders of voluntary sector service suppliers. Frequently, voluntary sector organisations are accused of being more concerned with satisfying the donor rather than the customer, and therefore accountability tends to be to the donor and funders rather than the customer whom they purport to serve.

If one were to apply this broad organisational conceptual framework to analyse the humanitarian action enterprise, the private sector has a limited but growing influence on global humanitarian action. Private sector companies are generally recognised as non-core humanitarian actors given that, while they contribute significantly to humanitarian action, provision of products and services on the basis of humanitarian need can never be their primary function. In 2014, the private sector contributed approximately one-quarter of global humanitarian assistance,[16] provided by individuals, companies, corporations, trusts and foundations. Traditionally, the vast majority of private sector engagement in humanitarian action concerned funding voluntary sector organisations to provide much-needed goods and services by way of corporate social responsibility (CSR). However, humanitarian CSR engagement by private sector entities, which is typically evidenced as philanthropic and financial donations, is evolving to a *shared value* approach in which businesses aim to make economic as well as social gains. This shared value approach is regarded as necessary to capitalise on existing private sector expertise and also to advance private sector engagement in the humanitarian enterprise.

Many mainstream humanitarian agencies have developed operational partnerships with private sector entities; examples of private sector engagement in recent years include a private mobile telephone company erecting a cellular tower inside a refugee camp in Liberia, an outdoor sporting company designing a new solar-powered lamp and phone charger that is now distributed in natural disasters but also marketed commercially as sporting goods, a credit card company foundation collaborating with WFP to create an *e-food* system (cash and voucher transfer system).[17] It is envisaged that private sector engagement in humanitarian action will grow in terms of scale and scope of action. The report from the high-level panel on finance, convened as part of the WHS consultative process, concluded:

> Beyond governments, the humanitarian community must harness the power of business to deliver its key skills and capabilities. Business is still a modest factor in humanitarian activities, yet has the creativity and capacity at scale to provide new solutions to risk management, support aid delivery, create jobs, and modernise transparency and accountability. Involving staff in humanitarian action is also motivational, and companies need to be encouraged – from insurance and digital cash to logistics and telecommunications – to get involved in providing their relevant skills and capacity for delivering life-saving assistance.[18]

The public sector has dominated humanitarian funding over the past 25 years. In the post-Cold War period and following the UN's decision to take a more proactive

[16]Global Humanitarian Assistance (GHA) (2015), p. 4.

[17]Gibbons et al. (2014).

[18]UN's High Level Panel on Humanitarian Financing (2016), p. vi.

role to support disaster-affected people globally by establishing the Department of Humanitarian Affairs in 1991, humanitarian aid grew in significance among the political donor aid community from comprising approximately 5% of the total ODA budget in 1989 to 8% between 1994 and 1998 and 10.5% in 2000.[19] It then hit a *glass ceiling* throughout the 2000s when, while continuing to rise in absolute terms, it remained at approximately 11% of ODA. The global humanitarian budget has increased over this period, and in 2014 it reached approximately $24.5 billion, of which about three-quarters are provided by donor governments.[20]

The vast majority of humanitarian assistance, approximately 90%, comes from the OECD DAC countries. Approximately 70% of donor funding is directed through UN agencies and the Red Cross Red Crescent Movement, while most of the remainder is delivered through the NGO community.[21] Governments are continuously challenged to justify increases in overseas aid budgets to their customers/voters, especially when the economy is going through stressful periods and when there are increased welfare demands at home. Governments have increasingly justified the increases in ODA on the basis of its potential to enhance overseas trade; however, this juxtaposition contravenes the very notion of humanitarian aid, which by its very definition should be driven by the needs of disaster-affected people and not the political or security interests of donors/funders. Similarly, some might contend that the increased funds available to humanitarian action served to fuel a huge increase in aid providers, who themselves are constituents of these donor governments. This in turn places added pressures on governments that are frequently challenged to ensure that resources are used to the best possible effect in the interest of affected people and not the interests of their own national NGOs. It is estimated that less than 3% of humanitarian assistance is channelled directly to disaster-affected countries.[22]

At the WHS, donors and humanitarian partners announced agreement on a Grand Bargain that incorporates a cost-saving measure that will result in up to $1 billion saving to humanitarian action over the next 5 years. Included was a commitment to channel 25% of financing to national and local responders as directly as possible by 2020.[23] The jury is out on how this will be achieved in the future.

There were approximately 4840 aid providers in 2014,[24] the vast majority of which are NGOs. The majority of these are national and local NGOs that operate within their own national boarders, whereas the lion's share of humanitarian

[19]HPG Report 11 (2002).

[20]Global Humanitarian Assistance (GHA) (2015).

[21]ALNAP (2015).

[22]Global Humanitarian Assistance (GHA) (2015).

[23]WHS – Chair's Summary (2016), p. 7.

[24]ALNAP (2015).

funding goes to UN agencies, international NGOs (INGOs)[25] and the Red Cross Movement. The recent State of the Humanitarian System Report estimated that the top five INGOs receive over 30% of all funds channelled through the NGO sector. The make-up of the NGO sector varies considerably from INGOs with thousands of employees that operate across countries similar to a multinational (for example, Save the Children has an estimated 14,000 staff working in 120 countries) to small organisations with a handful of staff. They also vary considerably in their mandate and expertise. The vast majority of NGOs enjoy a dual mandate, delivering both development aid and humanitarian aid. This is especially true for national and local organisations in lesser-developed countries that rarely recognise the development–humanitarian divide. NGOs are constantly challenged to address the ever-increasing humanitarian demands globally. The rapid growth in the number and range of voluntary sector organisations has posed many well-documented challenges, the more common of which include the following:

- It is difficult to establish and maintain the motivation of a voluntary board, which is invariably comprised of busy people with limited opportunity to provide financial incentives.
- There is increased competition between NGOs that vie for funding from a limited number of sources.
- Given this limited funding, some would argue that NGO policy and strategy are too frequently driven by donor demands rather that customer needs.
- The voluntary sector is frequently criticised for its lack of professionalism, especially when one applies public and/or private sector indicators of good management practice.
- The big message coming from the extensive consultations in the run up to the WHS was that more needs to be done to place affected people at the centre of the humanitarian effort. This would suggest that the aid community is either unwilling or unable to engage meaningfully with affected people.

3 The Complexity of the Operating Environment

Humanitarian action, by definition, operates in chaotic and dangerous environments where organisations seek to save lives, alleviate suffering and support life with dignity for disaster-affected people. While international human rights law suggests that all disaster-affected populations have a right to humanitarian assistance, access

[25] INGO – International Non-Governmental Organisation – The United Nations Economic and Social Council (ECOSOC) defines an INGO as '*any organization which is not established by inter-governmental agreement*' (Resolution 288 (X) 27 February 1950), '*including organizations which accept members designated by government authorities, provided that such membership does not interfere with the free expression of views of the organizations*' (Resolution 1296 (XLV) of 25 June 1968).

for humanitarian actors is not given and needs to be negotiated with national authorities.[26]

Humanitarian actors frequently find themselves in a compromised position. On the one hand, they are largely dependent on donors whose priorities may rest with political interests rather than the interests of the neediest affected populations, while, on the other hand, they also have to negotiate access to affected populations with authorities and warring parties that may have little respect for international law. While these challenges are not new, all evidence suggests that the operating environment is becoming more insecure, and aid workers are increasingly being targeted in their efforts to deliver aid. A recent Aid Security Report found that in 2014, 329 aid workers were victims of serious attacks.[27]

Humanitarian organisations are continuously challenged to develop ever more sophisticated strategies to retain a presence alongside disaster-affected people in a bid to provide humanitarian protection and assistance. Unlike other stakeholders such as military or political officials who share this space, humanitarian actors have few means available to them other than humanitarian principles that serve to guide humanitarian action and provide and maintain humanitarian space. While much of the debate surrounding humanitarian space focuses on legal and geopolitical arguments, management too has its part to play. All core actors in the humanitarian system are defined by their core function, namely to save lives, alleviate suffering and support life with dignity for disaster-affected people. The fundamental principles of this system were established in UN General Assembly Resolutions 46/182 and 58/114.[28] These fundamental principles have been further interrogated and reaffirmed by the global humanitarian community as recently as 2014–2015, during the extensive consultation process in preparation for the WHS.[29]

While the humanitarian principles are not management tools per se, they give guidance to humanitarian operations that serve to provide humanitarian actors with a distinct identity recognised in international humanitarian law (through the substantive principles namely humanity and impartiality) and to maintain the confidence of all through their actions (through the derived principles namely neutrality and independence). Such is the importance of the humanitarian principles that the humanitarian community has, on several occasions, established structures, codes of conduct and standards to operationalise humanitarian action in line with the principles. Most notable among these are the following.

The Inter-Agency Standing Committee (IASC), 1991 It was established as a global humanitarian forum by UN General Assembly Resolution 46/ 182 as the primary mechanism for inter-agency humanitarian coordination.[30] In line with Article 38 of

[26]Gillard (2013), pp. 351–382; Wagner (2005), pp. 24–27.

[27]Humanitarian Outcomes (2015).

[28]OCHA (2013).

[29]World Humanitarian Summit Secretariat (2015).

[30]Inter-Agency Standing Committee, http://interagencystandingcommittee.org/.

Resolution 46/182, it comprises the main operational relief agencies from the United Nations with standing invitation to the international components of the Red Cross/Red Crescent (RCRC) Movement and the International Organization for Migration (IOM). It can also invite relevant international non-governmental organisations on an ad hoc basis. The IASC currently comprises nine members (FAO, OCHA, UNDP, UNFPA, UNHCR, UN-Habitat, UNICEF, WFP and WHO) and nine standing invitees (ICRC, ICVA, InterAction, IFRC, IOM, Office of the RSG on the rights of IDPs, OHCHR, SCHR and the World Bank).[31] The IASC has evolved considerably since its establishment in 1992 to become the main global humanitarian coordination mechanism, and this evolution was in no small way facilitated by the introduction of the Humanitarian Reform Programme 2005 and the Transformative Agenda 2010. The IASC engages with a plethora of working groups and subsidiary bodies. These working groups and their associated task teams convene to shape policy, proffer guidelines and strategies on contemporary humanitarian challenges. Current issues under consideration include humanitarian financing, accountability to affected people, the relief- development nexus and protection priority.[32]

The Code of Conduct for the Red Cross and Red Crescent Movement and NGOs in Disaster Relief, 1994 This Code of Conduct was prompted by the proliferation of organisations engaging in humanitarian assistance with limited experience or knowledge of the challenges to deliver humanitarian aid. The RCRC Movement, together with eight of the world's biggest humanitarian organisations, established the Code to safeguard humanitarian standards and behaviour in times of disasters—especially in conflicts. This Code comprises 10 points of principle, which all humanitarian actors should adhere to in their disaster-response work, and goes on to describe the relationships that agencies working in disasters should seek with donor governments, host governments and the UN system. The first four principles refer directly, in varying degrees, to the four humanitarian principles: humanity, impartiality, neutrality[33] and independence. The other six points of principle relate to knowledge and years of experience in the field. Most of the later six points of principles build on the idea of respect for affected populations, their culture and capacities, and they too identify with the need for accountability to those they assist,

[31] *Ibid.*

[32] *Ibid.*

[33] There is no direct reference to neutrality in point of principle 3—especially when compared with the other three principles. Those responsible for drafting it have been very clear on their reasons for this. Dorothea Hilhorst in her 2004 review of the Code—A Living Document?—which is cited in the text—was clear on this point: Reference to neutrality was left out to accommodate the principles of justice and human rights that are cherished by many organisations. The article does not explicitly call upon agencies to be neutral in the sense of 'refraining from taking sides in hostilities or engage in controversies of a political, racial, religious or ideological nature', but it is hard to see how taking sides in hostilities could be separated from using aid to further political standpoints. Principle 3 thus appears to be ambiguous, and gives little guidance to NGOs working in conflict situations.

as well as to those from whom they accept resources. However, these points of principle are not reflected in the fundamental humanitarian principles.[34] The value of the Code of Conduct was (re)assessed in 2004 and was found to be '... still of great potential value in articulating a set of shared principles for humanitarian organisations'.[35]

The Sphere Standards, 1997 The Sphere Standards are the result of an initiative of the humanitarian community (in particular, NGOs and the RCRC Movement) that, in the aftermath of the Rwandan Genocide, sought to promote and develop a set of universal standards for humanitarian relief. In essence, the Sphere Standards attempt to lay down a set of minimum standards for what victims of disasters need to survive with dignity across a range of basic needs, including water and sanitation, nutrition, food aid, shelter and site planning, and health services.[36] Driven by a resolve similar to the Code of Conduct, the Sphere Standards are prefaced by a Humanitarian Charter, which creates the all-important link between victims' needs and rights as laid down in international human rights law, refugee law and international humanitarian law. The Sphere Standards are also similar to the Code of Conduct in that it served to bring together a diverse group of humanitarian actors, which were growing exponentially at the time both in numbers and scale of operations, to agree to universal standards that were largely accepted and used by donors, UN agencies, host governments and NGOs alike.[37] The Sphere Standards are further credited with the beginnings of efforts to improve professionalism in the delivery of aid and a new focus on the need for humanitarian action to be accountable to their customers. The Sphere Standards continue to be used as a main reference point of minimum standards for all operational organisations and have been revised and updated in 2003 and 2009/10 to include sections on protection.[38]

People in Aid, 1997 This was also an initiative borne out of the Rwandan genocide on the part of the growing humanitarian NGO community aimed at promoting best practices in human resource management.[39] To achieve this, People in Aid established a code with seven principles, governed by the main principle that 'people are central to the achievement of our mission'.[40] It served to spark a debate on providing necessary infrastructure to enhance professionalism in the delivery of aid by putting in place a code of good practice in the management and support of personnel who work in dangerous environments, often with limited job security.

---

[34]International Federation of the Red Cross and Red Cresent Societies (IFRC) (2015), Code of Conduct, http://www.ifrc.org/en/publications-and-reports/code-of-conduct/.

[35]Hilhorst (2005), pp. 351–369.

[36]Walker and Maxwell (2009).

[37]*Ibid.*

[38]The Sphere Project (2011).

[39]Walker and Maxwell (2009).

[40]People in Aid (2003) http://www.dochas.ie/sites/default/files/People_In_Aid_Code.pdf.

This initiative was frequently seen as the beginning of humanitarian organisations establishing systems on internal accountability that facilitate adherence to standards, accountability and financial propriety.[41] In 2014, People in Aid merged with the Humanitarian Accountability Partnership International to form the Core Humanitarian Standards Alliance, discussed below.

Active Learning Network for Accountability and Performance in Humanitarian Action (ALNAP), 1997 ALNAP is generally regarded to be a product of the Joint Evaluation of Emergency Assistance to Rwanda (JEEAR)—an evaluation commissioned by Western governments and universally recognised for its professionalism and rigour that aimed to learn from the experiences of the Rwanda genocide in 1994. Based on the premise that evaluations of this nature could go on to significantly enhance competence in the delivery of aid and coherence in the *system*, a group of academics, consultants, UN agencies and NGOs went on to establish ALNAP in 1997. It continues to provide a space for academics, practitioners and policymakers to review and influence the state of the humanitarian system and has since broadened its governance base to include representatives from all major humanitarian actor groupings.[42]

Good Humanitarian Donorship, 2003 This initiative aims to enhance the coherence and effectiveness of donor actions, as well as their accountability to beneficiaries, implementing organisations and domestic constituencies, with regard to the funding, coordination, follow-up and evaluation of such actions. The number of donor governments that have subscribed to GHD has grown from 17 in 2003 to 40 in 2014. Among the 23 principles that comprise the GHD principles of good practice is an affirmation of donors' commitment to the four humanitarian principles, to strengthen humanitarian systems and to build on local capacities and to respect accountability to affected population, as well as their own constituencies.[43] While all efforts to engage in principled humanitarian action have to be welcomed, there is an ever-increasing call for improved standards to monitor commitment to these principles—something that has been repeated in all the aforementioned professional joint evaluations; there is no reason to believe that GHD should be any different. One might assume that the creation of *institutional space*—or providing a space for departments/units within their respective political institutions with the required level of independence to prioritise humanitarian principles over the goals of the institution—would be central to political engagement in humanitarian action. This has been one of the very positive outcomes of the Hyogo Framework for Action (2005) as many governments have demonstrated their

[41]Walker and Maxwell (2009).

[42]ALNAP (2016).

[43]Good Humanitarian Donorship (2013) Principles and Good Practice of Humanitarian Donorship, http://www.ghdinitiative.org/ghd/gns/principles-good-practice-of-ghd/principles-good-practice-ghd.html.

commitment to disaster risk reduction and institutional support for disaster risk management. This in turn has facilitated efficient and effective engagement with the authorities at all levels for internal as well as external actors.

Humanitarian Accountability Partnership International (HAP), 2003 HAP was established to strengthen accountability of humanitarian organisations towards those affected by crisis situations and to facilitate improved performance within the humanitarian sector. The ultimate goal of HAP was to uphold the rights and dignity of disaster-affected people by making humanitarian organisations more accountable. Central to HAP's strategy was the establishment of principles to guide humanitarian actors to be more accountable to their intended beneficiaries through self-regulation, compliance verification and quality assurance certification.[44] Later in 2014, HAP merged with People in Aid to the Core Humanitarian Standards Alliance, which is discussed below.

Humanitarian Reform, 2005 OCHA and the IASC took a very significant step towards consolidating a *humanitarian system* with the Humanitarian Reform Initiative.[45] The process took place at a time when there was growing frustration on the part of UN and non-UN humanitarian actors to deal in a timely, appropriate or effective way with the crises in Darfur and South Sudan. The humanitarian reform agenda aimed to strengthen humanitarian response by introducing new measures to enhance response capacity, accountability, predictability and partnership. It provided an ambitious effort by the international humanitarian community to reach more beneficiaries, with more comprehensive, needs-based relief and protection, in a more effective and timely manner. It specifically sought to enhance coordination through a cluster system. At the core of the cluster system is the drive to strengthen in-country coordination, to sharpen advocacy on key humanitarian issues and principles and to increase and strengthen partnerships for humanitarian action.

Transformative Agenda, 2010 Following 5 years of the Humanitarian Reform Initiative and with the accumulated knowledge and experience gleaned from the Haiti earthquake and the Pakistan floods, OCHA and the IASC adopted the Transformative Agenda (TA). It focuses on three key areas—leadership, coordination and accountability—while retaining a commitment to the four humanitarian principles. The areas of leadership and coordination build on and reinforce the commitment to the cluster approach. The TA advocates greater empowered leadership and the active participation of host authorities in local communities. This value of accountability to vulnerable locals, while not new, is poorly developed in comparison to agencies' well-established commitment of accountability to donors with frameworks such as results-based management. The existing principles of humanity and impartiality promote values such as respect and cooperation, but nowhere in the

[44]Centre on Conflict, Development and Peacebuilding (2016).

[45]International Council of Voluntary Agencies (2016).

foundational principles is there an explicit reminder that humanitarian actors be accountable to the population they purport to serve.

Core Humanitarian Standards, 2014 In 2014, the Humanitarian Accountability Partnership (HAP) International, People in Aid and the Sphere Project formed the Joint Forces Initiative and published the Core Humanitarian Standard on Quality and Accountability.[46] This document was the result of a yearlong consultative process that targeted more than 2000 humanitarian workers worldwide and involved a diverse range of humanitarian stakeholders, including NGOs, governments, the UN, donor agencies and academia. The Core Humanitarian Standard proposes a set of nine commitments[47] that can be voluntarily adopted by organisations and individuals to guide or even evaluate their work.[48] The CHS advocates for a principled approach to accountable high-quality humanitarian action that places respect for the fundamental rights of affected people at the centre. From a management perspective, the CHS offers the additional utility of analysing each of the nine commitments proffering action and envisaged organisational responsibilities to guide action. Humanitarian actors have constantly adapted to the changing demands of the global disaster context.

The common denominator among all the codes, standards and reforms has been a commitment to the fundamental humanitarian principles. This commitment has been reaffirmed and reinforced in the consultative process leading up to the WHS,[49] as well as the WHS itself.[50] Some would argue that humanitarian initiatives tend to be reactionary in nature in that they continuously adapt to changed contexts and argue for greater forward thinking towards a more transformative approach to deal with existing risks and threats to accommodate preventative action. The humanitarian principle will continue to shape humanitarian action into the future and will remain the foundation to guide policy and practice.

[46]Groupe URD, HAP International, People In Aid and the Sphere Project, Core Humanitarian Standard on Quality and Accountability, 2014.

[47]The Nine Commitments of the CHS are (1) Humanitarian response is appropriate and relevant, (2) Humanitarian response is effective and timely, (3) Humanitarian response strengthens local capacities and avoids negative effects, (4) humanitarian response is based on communication, participation and feedback (5)complaints are welcomed and addressed, (6) humanitarian response is coordinated and complimentary (7) humanitarian actors continuously learn and improve (8) staff are supported to do their job effectively, and are treated fairly and equitably (9) resources are managed and used responsibly for their intended purpose.

[48]Groupe URD, HAP International, People In Aid and the Sphere Project, Core Humanitarian Standard on Quality and Accountability, 2014.

[49]World Humanitarian Summit Secretariat (2015), p. xii.

[50]WHS – Chair's Summary (2016).

4 Managing Humanitarian Action in the Future

The UN Secretary General urged the humanitarian community to 'commit to taking forward this Agenda for Humanity and use it as a framework for action, change and mutual accountability'[51] to shape the WHS discussions. This document was informed by an extensive global consultative process that included 8 regional consultations; 151 national stakeholder consultations; 400 plus written submissions; 23,000 plus people consulted; 5500 comments received online; and 19 consultations with the private sector.[52] The results of this humanitarian consultative process, together with the results of other global aid summits, including the Sendai Framework for Disaster Risk Reduction (March 2015), the Sustainable Development Goals (New York, September 2015) and the UN Climate Change Conference COP21 (Paris, December 2015), all contributed to the Agenda for Humanity.

The consultative process for the WHS, which engaged the global humanitarian community in particular, is still one of the best barometers of future trends in humanitarian action management. It identified five major areas for action in the future. These five major action areas were established as the foundation on which stakeholders would build *commitments, partnerships and transformative actions*[53] to deliver change in the future. They comprise the following.

Dignity Dignity means to empower disaster-affected people to cope and recover by enabling them to be the primary agents of their own response and ensuring aid is appropriate and relevant to all. National and international actors will be encouraged to build on local coping mechanisms and protection strategies. Humanitarian actors should look for innovative ways to engage meaningfully with affected people, adopt aid mechanisms that support greater choice and increase accountability to the people they serve. While respecting cultural difference, humanitarian actors will support greater gender equality in their response, recognise and address the pervasive nature of gender-based violence and promote gender balance in leadership roles. All efforts will be made to limit the effects of disasters on the livelihoods of marginalised groups, especially children of school-going age, the disabled, elderly and all those with special needs.

Safety Protection and the rights of all individuals will be placed at the centre of humanitarian response. All efforts will be made to prevent and end conflicts by increasing political engagement, putting an end to violations of international law and encouraging the principled delivery of humanitarian aid. Protection strategies should adopt a coordinated approach that builds on local efforts that affected people have established to protect themselves and the agreed mandates of other

[51]UN (2016), Annex to the Report of the Secretary-General for the World Humanitarian Summit, http://consultations.worldhumanitariansummit.org/bitcache/5a7c81df22c7e91c35d456a1574aa6881bb044e4?vid=569102&disposition=inline&op=view.

[52]World Humanitarian Summit Secretariat (2015), p. 8.

[53]*Id.*, page 9.

stakeholders. Humanitarian action can never be employed as a substitute/alternative to political inertia to prevent, respond to or end conflict. Humanitarian action will be principled, and those with leadership responsibilities will be held accountable for their actions. All efforts are and will be made to ensure the safety and security of staff, with the required competences to apply security management systems, and maintain proximity to the customer/affected people.

Resilience There must be investments in preparedness, managing and mitigating risk, reducing vulnerability, finding durable solutions for protracted displacement and adapting to new threats. New and improved mechanisms are being sought to (re)position the principled delivery of humanitarian action alongside other aid sectors, including development, climate change and peacebuilding. The challenge is to develop a framework that allows humanitarian actors to address immediate life-saving needs alongside engaging in issues that impact the causes and consequences of disasters. Humanitarian actors are now being asked to engage more actively to address the root causes of disasters and also to enhance the connectedness and sustainability of their actions. There are many who challenge this notion of 'mission creep' on the premise that previous experiences such as integrated missions and comprehensive approaches, which sought to bring diverse stakeholders together to improve coherence in the delivery of aid, frequently resulted in the politicisation and instrumentalisation of humanitarian aid. The challenge will be for this new framework to facilitate humanitarian actors to retain humanitarian agency space that allows them to deliver principled humanitarian action. Governments are being asked to shift their thinking from managing crises to managing risk. It is envisaged that more attention will be committed to disaster risk reduction and preparedness mechanism, both by way of long-term agreements and financial resources. In the same vein, more attention will be given to preventing predictable disasters, not only those associated with climate change but also demographic challenges, displacement and urbanisation.

Partnerships The preferred means of engagement for humanitarian actors are diverse and inclusive of partnerships that place the needs of vulnerable people at the centre while respecting both the humanitarian principles and applicable international and national laws. These partnerships will promote the sharing of information and stronger relations with local actors to enhance the relevance and appropriateness of humanitarian action. It is envisaged that improved partnerships will also facilitate improved monitoring and develop a culture of continuous learning and adaptation, which in turn will promote the application of innovation to keep pace with the dynamic nature of the humanitarian context.

Finance Financial means are necessary to bridge the existing resource deficit and enhance the efficient utilisation of resources to preserve life, dignity and the resilience of disaster-affected people. This is planned to be achieved by not only increasing the aid budget but also improving efficiency, accountability and transparency of aid financing. New ways are being sought to enhance greater coherence and collective bargaining among aid donors in what is being muted as the 'Grand

Bargain'. It is hoped that this approach will also serve to put affected people at the centre of humanitarian action and address some of the existing bottlenecks that impede efficacy in humanitarian action, including expanding unearmarked and multi-annual funding, expanding direct funding to local organisations and increasing direct funding to affected governments for risk financing.

5 Conclusion

Management in humanitarian action has evolved considerably in response to many factors, not least the ever-challenging responsibility to reach out to the growing numbers of disaster-affected people globally. One might view the evolutionary path of the humanitarian system through a similar lens as Tuckman's model, which suggests that groups go through several stages in arriving at team-like characteristics with everyone working towards a common goal.

The first of these periods, also referred to as the forming phase, was prompted by the UN's engagement in humanitarian action in 1991 with the establishing of the IASC and adopting the system's foundational principles. It continued right up until 1998 with the establishment of OCHA.

The second period, or the storming phase, was complicated by many factors, including the changing disaster context, the proliferation of agencies and organisation with disparate mandates and values operating in a shared space, and the reactionary nature of the evolving system with limited regulations that tend to be adaptive rather than transformative.

It could be argued that we are now experiencing a third, voluntary period, the normative phase, which was very much prompted by the increasing deficit between humanitarian need and supply, and the realisation that change in the system is required. This phase began in 2013 with calls for a first-ever gathering of all humanitarian stakeholders to set an agenda for humanitarian action post 2016. The UN has now synthesised the commitments from this gathering, the WHS, held in Istanbul in May 2016, and developed a new Agenda for Humanity with five core responsibilities. They include global leadership to prevent and end conflict; uphold the norms that safeguard humanity; leave no one behind; change people's lives—from delivering aid to ending need; and invest in humanity. According to plan, many humanitarian actors will buy into this new Agenda, which will hopefully give rise to a fourth period of management in humanitarian action, the performing phase.

The realisation of the Agenda for Humanity will pose many challenges for humanitarian actors. The need for enhanced professionalism will be greater than ever as humanitarian actors seek to transform the policies and practices to meet future demands. The following chapters in this management section offer some insight into current best practice and future challenges.

References

ALNAP (2015) State of the humanitarian system. ALNAP/ODI, London

ALNAP (2016, Feb 10th) *ALNAP - OUR ROLE*. Retrieved from ALNAP: Strengthening Humanitarian Action. http://www.alnap.org/who-we-are/our-role

Centre on Conflict, Development and Peacebuilding (2016, Feb 10th). Humanitarian Accountability Partnership International. Retrieved from Geneva Peacebuilding Platform: http://www.gpplatform.ch/pbguide/organisation/humanitarian-accountability-partnership-international-hap

CHS (2014) Core humanitarian standard on quality and accountability. Groupe URD, HAP International, People In Aid and the Sphere Project

Collins Dictionaries (2015) Collins Dictionary. Retrieved Sept 11th, 2015, from http://www.collinsdictionary.com/dictionary/english/system

GHD (2013) Good Humanitarian Donorship. Retrieved June 30, 2015, from Good Humanitarian Donorship: http://www.ghdinitiative.org/ghd/gns/resource/general-principles/core-humanitarian-principles-and-guiding-papers.html

Gibbons P (2010) Humanitarian transformation: concepts, causes and challenges. In: Moke M, Schewe C, Zwitter A (eds) Humanitarian action facing new challenges. Wissenschafts-Verlag, Berlin, pp 11–27. ISBN 978 38305-1807-5

Gibbons P, Bragg C, Roughneen D (2014) Putting Affected People at the Centre of Humanitarian Action: an argument for the Principle of Humanitarian Subsidiarity. Paper presented during the thematic consultations of the WHS process, Lausanne, Switzerland, November 30th 2014

Gillard E-C (2013) The law regulating cross-border disaster relief. Int Rev Red Cross 95 (890):351–382

Global Humanitarian Assistance Report (2015) Bristol: Development initiatives

Hilhorst D (2005) Dead letter or living document? Ten years of the code of conduct for disaster relief. Disasters 29(4):351–369

HPG Report 11 (2002) The new humanitarianisms: a review of trends in global humanitarian action. ODI, London

Humanitarian Outcomes (2015, April 20th) Aid Security Report 2015. The Aid Worker Security Database. http://www.humanitarianoutcomes.org/sites/default/files/ho_aidworkersecuritypreview2015.pdf

ICVA (2016, Feb) Global Humanitarian Platform: An Overview. Retrieved from International Council of Voluntary Agencies: http://icvanetwork.org/

IFRC (2015, Sept 11th) Code of Conduct. Retrieved from International Federation of the Red Cross and Red Crescent Societies: http://www.ifrc.org/en/publications-and-reports/code-of-conduct/

OCHA (2013) World Humanitarian Data and Trends. US: United Nations

OECD (2014) Backing recovery in fragile states. In: Development Co-operation Report 2014: Mobilising. OECD Publishing, Paris

People in Aid (2003) Code of Good Practice in in the management and support of aid personnel. Retrieved from People in Aid: www.peopleinaid.org/

Taylor G, Stoddard A, Harmer A, Harver K, Harvey P (2012) State of the humanitarian system. Overseas Development Institute, London

The Sphere Project (2011) Humanitarian charter and minimum standards in humanitarian response. Rugby: The Sphere Project. Retrieved from http://www.spherehandbook.org/en/what-is-sphere/

UN (2016, Feb 9th) AGENDA FOR HUMANITY. Retrieved from World Humanitarian Summit: http://consultations.worldhumanitariansummit.org/bitcache/5a7c81df22c7e91c35d456a1574aa6881bb044e4?vid=569102&disposition=inline&op=view

UN's High Level Panel on Humanitarian Financing (2016) Too important to fail - addressing the humanitarian financing gap. United Nations, New York

Wagner JG (2005, Dec) An IHL/ICRC perspective on 'humanitarian space'. Humanitarian Exchange Magazine, pp 24–27

Walker P, Maxwell D (2009) Shaping the humanitarian world, 1st edn. Routledge, New York
World Humanitarian Summit – Chair's Summary (2016 June 13). Standing Up For Humanity: Committing to Action, http://www.worldhumanitariansummit.org/chairs-summary-standing-humanity-committing-action-final-version
World Humanitarian Summit Secretariat (2015) Restoring humanity: synthesis of the consultation process for the world humanitarian summit. United Nations, New York

Pat Gibbons is Director of the Centre for Humanitarian Action at University College Dublin, Ireland. He served as President of NOHA between 2007 and 2014.

The Basics of Managing Emergencies

Markus Moke and Thomas Pfeiffer

1 Introduction

The current challenges in humanitarian action are diverse, plentiful and sometimes daunting in nature. In many cases, only parts of needs and their root causes can be addressed. This includes the provision of drinking water in a water-scarce area, where the team leader of a humanitarian mission tolerates water tankering as a temporary solution. A well-communicated goal and an action-oriented approach contribute to optimising the outcome (in the case above, lower mortality) of actions taken. Managing emergencies further requires special organisational arrangements. For example, in flood-prone areas where the establishment of special water-borne equipment (boats for rescue and relief purposes) is crucial, the provision of adequate staff, team composition and specially trained personnel are necessary. This, in turn, will have positive implications for aid organisations both in regard to availability of resources (time, personnel and finances) and organisational set-up.[1]

This first part of our chapter deals with the challenges and fundamentals of emergency management, as well as with the principal methodological approaches underpinning it, reflecting on how needs are to be managed and what challenges might be encountered. Management is illustrated through the needs in humanitarian aid and the goals a manager sets to respond to those needs.

[1]Carter (2008), p. 126.

M. Moke (✉)
Aktion Deutschland Hilft, e.V. (ADH), Bonn, Germany
e-mail: moke@aktion-deutschland-hilft.de

T. Pfeiffer
Technical University Berlin, Humboldt Universität zu Berlin, Berlin, Germany
e-mail: thomas.pfeiffer@mastering-aid.de

© Springer International Publishing AG 2018

H.-J. Heintze, P. Thielbörger (eds.), *International Humanitarian Action*,
DOI 10.1007/978-3-319-14454-2_20

The chapter's second part aims at showing how the project cycle management (PCM) approach may act as a universal response method to an initially unclear situation.

Supporting this method, the third part discusses the individual competencies, behaviour and role with regard to organisation, country or donor strategy. For cases where others are directed during emergencies, tools are presented such as team building and communication to help guide managers in their positions of authority, paving the way for the following sections on project design and human resource management.

The East African drought of 2011 exemplifies that natural disasters are on the rise, with a growing proportion related to climate change. Conflict-related protracted emergencies, such as those in Syria, Sudan/South Sudan and Somalia, are also occurring more frequently. During conflicts, safety and security measures require a high level of attention that does not always allow for full concentration on humanitarian needs. Besides protracted or chronic crises, a notable proportion of disasters are of a slow-onset nature, which tends to render the recognition of needs both by the broader public and institutional donors increasingly difficult. Admittedly, as challenges are growing, donors have stepped up their demands in formal aspects, namely in reporting mechanisms and accounting. Private donors have gone from a shrinking group of retired contributors to a growing pool of rich donors invested in the projects. At the same time, humanitarian aid agencies have been challenged by donor requirements vis-à-vis the need to invest in long-term organisational development, such as human resources, which may not be seen as an attractive contribution to a concrete project.

As regards humanitarian policies, the Paris-Accra-Busan process has initiated important discussions that are also relevant for humanitarian aid, such as the notion of participation. However, this policy process has not been developed further since the last high-level donor meeting in Busan in 2011. Many developing countries have become middle-income countries, and the world's population has grown to over seven billion people, creating densely inhabited cities, which are increasingly vulnerable to disasters. These contexts influence the appropriateness of responses from aid agencies and call for a change in the way programmes are developed and executed.[2] Although management expertise may seem to be of peripheral importance for an aid worker, the opposite is true as

> ... political, bureaucratic and resource constraints often characterize field missions, good management and the people involved, can sometimes mean the difference between success and failure. Sound management is essential to achieving the goals of any organization, regardless of the context, and UN field missions are no exception. Its complexity and uniqueness should not be an excuse for bad management or poor results. In fact, if managed or handled well, environmental complexity can increase the resilience of an organization and enhance its ability to adapt, learn, and thrive in changing contexts.[3]

[2]OECD (2011).

[3]International Peace Institute (2012), p. 3.

While systematic management methods offer significant potential for handling emergencies and humanitarian interventions, instinctive actions and reactions are often more appropriate and timely. The more complex a context is, the less likely comprehensive systematic decision-making processes will be feasible or efficient. High mortality rates, for example, render swift intervention an imperative. Therefore, instead of rejecting intuitive decision-making processes right away, it is recommended to explore how to appropriately make decisions while remaining flexible. Management, in its broadest sense, can be understood as the act of aiming to fulfil objectives while organising and directing a set of resources to accomplish clearly defined goals and targets.[4]

Managing emergencies involves planning, organising, leading, staffing and controlling; therefore, a wide range of leadership and management competencies are required. According to McEntire and Dawson,[5] the goal of emergency management is '...to devise policy and to implement programs that will reduce vulnerability, limit the loss of life and property, protect the environment, and improve multi-organizational coordination in disasters'.[6] Policy and implementation skills and competencies are needed to be effective, especially in times of emergencies where situations change rapidly and a high level of uncertainty is the norm. James lists four key management tasks that are essential to handling emergencies[7]:

- *Authority:* managers are accorded a certain amount of authority, as documented in organisational charts and job descriptions.
- *Responsibility*: managers have a set of tasks for which they are responsible. In addition, to achieve objectives, managers have the responsibility of coaching and supervising staff. Likewise, team members act upon their responsibility towards the project in the humanitarian situation.
- *Accountability*: managers answer to the executive and/or the board while supporting their staff. Managers are accountable for their actions and those of their organisation to different stakeholders, notably to donors and beneficiaries. This often dominates aspects of accountability of the aid organisation.
- *Delegation*: managers are responsible for organising and assigning well-distributed and sustainable workloads for their staff. When staff encounters problems with their responsibilities, managers are expected to play a supporting and advocating role.

Emergency managers are often confronted with a number of challenges that have a direct implication on decision-making processes and on how effective or ineffective their management will be. Effective management requires networking, which

[4] *Ibid.*
[5] McEntire and Dawson (2007), pp. 57–70.
[6] Demiroz and Kapucu (2012), pp. 91–101.
[7] James (2008).

helps aid workers in comprehending complex situations that they may not fully grasp on their own. According to Demiroz and Kapucu, emergency management

> …involves [a] network of organizations from various fields including public, nonprofit, and private sectors as well as organizations from different levels of government. Emergency managers must use networks and relationships to develop uniform goals and strategies. The most important tool needed for a network to work effectively in the disaster response process is communication. It is communication that fosters success in coordinating efforts that are necessary in order to achieve and maintain common goals.[8]

2 Communication as a Management Tool

Communication, or the exchange of needs, ideas and information on the basis of common values, is a necessary condition for the effective handling of any emergency.

Be it participative, in order to acquire the views of beneficiaries and colleagues, or directive, by explaining commands, communication is key to qualitative work. Precision, timeliness and efficient and effective use of time are equally important in humanitarian situations with imminent danger of loss of life. Active listening is too often not recognised as a necessary tool. Especially in team situations, such as a coordination meeting, the focus is never on one single person as the team may otherwise miss out on the opinions and resources of the other members. To achieve the necessary balance, facilitation skills are equally important.

Effective and—where necessary—assertive communication is required when humanitarian organisations take a stance with authorities, where, for example, access to beneficiaries needs to be negotiated. The way communication is used needs to be adapted to the particular context that agencies are operating in. A pertinent example would be Darfur, where after 2008, access to beneficiaries was very restricted and had to be negotiated carefully between aid agencies and national as well as local authorities. The tense situation in combination with security incidents prevented aid workers from leaving their bases and hindered effective delivery of aid. Remote management has also occurred more often, where required by the security situation. Further, communication over distances has also become the norm as NGO headquarters discuss and negotiate the state of affairs, for example concerning budgets, with their field offices. In short, effective leadership communicates vision and finds ways to inspire.

Another challenge that managers of emergency programmes are confronted with is the permanent struggle with resource constraints with regard to time and financial means, in addition to handling the dilemma of balancing feasibility, accuracy and effectiveness. Especially in crisis situations, management is facing multiple problems deriving from the heterogeneous scope of tasks that need to be addressed simultaneously. In emergency situations, managers have to cope with different

[8]Demiroz and Kapucu (2012), p. 94.

levels of experience, backgrounds and a diverse team of staff on the ground. Thus, clear rules for all team members must be in place, which can make the assignment of tasks and a clear definition of roles and responsibilities much easier.[9] Diversity within a team can enhance the process of understanding needs and contexts, yet time constraints, especially in acute emergency settings, can limit it. In a team setting, these specifics have to be communicated especially well and clearly.

The same holds true for participation. Asking target groups for advice on issues such as where to place a defecation zone to ensure safe excreta handling allows for culturally appropriate measures that are accepted by target groups and communities.[10] Yet highly participative and open attitudes may also lead to endless discussions. Finally, another aspect needs to be highlighted in the context of communication. Complex humanitarian situations, such as the 2015 Ebola outbreak in West Africa, require bold and creative decisions. Boldness is based on confidence, which a humanitarian manager needs to inspire within a given team. Team members only dare to develop initiative if they do not feel insecure. With apt communication skills, a manager therefore sets framework conditions for self-confidence and courage within his or her team. Encouraging communication styles are usually participatory in nature but also have other advantages, such as stimulating team members to be open with their ideas. Breeding an innovative atmosphere can create the necessary conditions for ingenious ideas, such as bringing food aid to malnourished people by boat in a hard-to-access territory like South Sudan during the rainy season.

3 Management Styles

Identifying the *right people* to ask is not always a trivial matter. Nevertheless, encouraging participation within a team is a question not only of directing colleagues and allocating responsibilities well but also of mobilising capacities within the team. Complementary participation and directive guidance interactions are key. For example, where a hostage situation is likely to occur, a given overheard team member with the most relevant experience may have the best ideas, offering the best chance to preserve health, safety and security to colleagues. Ensuring the effectiveness of humanitarian responses is one of the biggest challenges that aid organisations and supervisors are confronted with. Humanitarian organisations tend to have clear aims, but their set-up sometimes may be insufficiently developed to respond to acute emergencies. Without effective systems in place, management will most likely continue to remain a reaction to crisis. In addition, geographic distance between managers and staff considerably challenges how the work is carried out,

---

[9]James (2008).

[10]The Sphere Project (2011).

especially when emergencies occur in remote areas. Where access is difficult or limited, the staff is often required to work from different localities and offices, which challenges the way the overall management is implemented.[11]

4 Reacting to the Unknown

In 2010, international aid workers responded to the Haiti earthquake. Relief goods from Europe and North America were shipped in while the full extent of needs on the ground was still unknown, leaving goods stalled at airports and harbours. This experience demonstrates how important it is for the entire humanitarian community to have clarity of a humanitarian crisis individually and organisationally before initiating a response. When the Kosovar refugees returned home after the cessation of hostilities in 1999, the humanitarian community, including donors, needed to swiftly shift attention from providing refugee accommodation to rehabilitation. Needs seldom remain the same over the course of a humanitarian crisis, unless a chronic situation develops. Therefore, it is of utmost importance that humanitarian aid practices maintain flexibility.

Emergencies such as the 1994 Rwandan genocide may serve as an example. The events in Rwanda not only left hundreds of thousands of Tutsi and moderate Hutu dead but also led to the subsequent displacement of hundreds of thousands of others, mostly Hutu, to neighbouring Zaire. A complex situation ensued, where murderers who had participated in the genocide entered the camps, mixing with other refugees and received aid. The extent of misuse of aid by the perpetrators, as well as them having been hosted in refugee camps, was only researched after the emergency ended. Aid workers who were confronted with the first hints of this misuse might not have been in a position to clearly make sense of what was happening. Due to their humanitarian mandate, these aid workers helped everyone irrespective of affiliation. However, during the course of events, the situation became more obvious, prompting aid workers to change their course of action.[12]

Constantly assessing and reassessing emergency situations is therefore imperative. In this vein, a sound network between organisations and staff, as well as among colleagues, is helpful to maximise the acquisition of contextual information. Participation also plays an important role. The level of participation has to be adjusted to the necessary top-down approach, where effective, secure and swift actions are needed.

According to James, effective management in emergencies combines aspects of both management and leadership qualities, which are highlighted below[13]:

[11]James (2008).

[12]Ludlow (1999).

[13]James (2008), p. 91.

- *Knowledge*: in emergencies, stress-inducing situations can stretch people in ways that may adversely affect programmes or even an entire organisation. Leaders ought to be aware of their own personalities, approach towards others and limitations. They should also understand their organisation and its culture before an emergency intervention and how to reach its objective with little contact from supervisors.
- *Skills*: proficiency in basic skills is important. Effective managers actively seek to improve and to familiarise themselves with skills and techniques in areas under their responsibility. Where members of their staff are more experienced or qualified to conduct certain tasks, the manager may need to hand over that particular area of responsibility to such persons. As skills required may vary, verbal and written communication skills and advanced knowledge of project cycle management are essential.
- *Attitude*: managing is leading by example, which others can follow. While management tasks may change depending on the situation, managers have to fulfil additional roles, including showing empathy, concrete action and presenting a professional and positive image externally, even where their personal opinion may diverge. Preparation and training to acquire the right mix of knowledge and skills can make assuming the right attitude easier. In emergency situations, managers are responsible not only for themselves but also for their staff. They must look beyond standard work issues and consider wider concerns such as staff welfare that may affect their motivation. Hence, many aid organisations find it helpful to organise frequent staff meetings to discuss employee welfare and like-minded issues.

5 Leadership and Management

While many well-known management methods have been established for the business sector, only few of these are directly applicable to aid organisations due to the complex humanitarian contexts. Nonetheless, several management methods and tools can be useful for organisations working in emergency aid, for example project cycle management and the logical framework analysis.[14] Different emergency situations will require a set of diverse management approaches.

Managing and leading can be considered complementary in terms of overlapping activities. While managers deal with the complexity of a crisis situation and the different parts of the organisation, leaders deal with change that may challenge the status quo. In many aid organisations, the leading staff assumes the role both of manager and leader. Generally, there is no single type of effective leader, appropriate for all situations. Instead, different leadership styles need to be

[14] *Ibid.*

adapted to suit specific emergency situations and organisational set-ups.[15] The challenge for any manager is to understand which kind of leadership style is appropriate at what moment.

There are certain '[. . .] core areas where it is necessary that emergency managers be completely competent: (1) Leadership and team building, (2) networking and coordination, (3) political, bureaucratic, and social context'.[16] Above all, it is important to note that different situations require distinct approaches. Table 1 provides an overview of different leadership styles, indicating their characteristics, applicability and limitations.

Table 1 Leadership styles

Leadership styles	Characteristics	Contexts when useful	Weaknesses and limitations
Coercive/ directive	Leader gives orders and expects to be obeyed	In quick turnaround situations and crises and emergencies, security situations, dealing with insubordinate employees	Inhibits organization's flexibility, weakens employee morale, risks not utilizing available resources, makes the atmosphere suffer
Authoritative	Leader establishes overall goal/strategy and pushes people to follow	When organization is adrift or undisciplined and needs direction and supervision	Goal/strategy not informed by good ideas of staff, goal with little staff buy-in, risks of not being sustainable
Affiliative/ supportive	Leader listens, affirms and facilitates – '*people come first*' attitude	In case of a need to build team cohesion, need to raise low morale, capacity building	May cause employees not to have a clear sense of direction or purpose
Democratic/ participative	Leader gives employees role in day-to-day decision-making	To build organizational flexibility, responsiveness and responsibility (helps building capacity in the team)	May result in indecision and a sense of confusion or, at worse, long decision-making process
Pacesetting/ achievement oriented	Leader sets ambitious goals and high performance standards	With highly motivated employees who work best independently	May feel overwhelming to employees who then feel resentful or give up
Coaching	Leader directs and supports: focuses on personal development	Where employees want and receive incentive to improve professionally and for personal growth; highly sustainable with the least necessary input	Not successful when employees are resistant to change; heavy time burden on leader; convincing processes needed

Reproduced and adapted by kind permission of the publisher from Harvard Business School Press, Leading People (Boston, 2006)

[15]International Peace Institute (2012), p. 35.

[16]Patton (2007), pp. 71–84, 81; Demiroz and Kapucu (2012), p. 96.

Leadership characteristics for emergencies and disasters that are addressed by Kapucu and Van Wart[17] include the following:

- decisiveness;
- flexibility;
- informing;
- problem solving;
- managing innovation and creativity;
- planning and organising personnel;
- motivating;
- managing teams and team building;
- scanning the environment;
- strategic planning;
- networking and partnering; and
- decision-making.

6 Team Building

Team building is the selection and bringing together of different people and the development of skills within a group that aims to achieve certain goals. Team-building processes are found within many societal spheres, for example in the business and non-profit sectors, as well as in humanitarian organisations. Good team-building skills help team members focus on a common goal and to generate greater productivity. Team building can be understood as an ongoing process that contributes to forming a unified work unit. Therefore, the role of a team builder is to lead a team towards cohesiveness and productivity.[18]

According to the Tuckman model (1965), team building comprises four stages: forming, storming, norming and performing.[19]

Forming At the first stage, roles and responsibilities of team members are not yet clear. Individuals are finding their role, and strong guidance and direction from the team manager are required as team members may not always know each other. The manager's role in this phase is to explain the team's objectives, purpose and relationships among the team members.

Storming This is a critical stage as team members might encounter conflicts during decision-making processes within their group or team. Team members may adapt their positions during and after discussions with colleagues and the team manager. They might also be challenged by other team members with different agendas.

[17]Kapucu and Van Wart (2008), pp. 711–740.

[18]UCSF Human Resources (2015).

[19]Chapman (2013), James (2008).

Hence, clarity of roles and objectives are indispensable as, otherwise, uncertainties may continue to persist. At this point, it is critical that team members are clear about their purpose and stay focused on their goals in order to avoid becoming distracted by different perceptions of these aims.

Norming At this stage, roles and responsibilities are clear and accepted. Team members develop an understanding of other group members. The team reaches a level of agreement and consensus. Decisions are usually made by group agreement. Cooperation and commitment contribute to the organisations' performance. There are a number of approaches that may help foster team spirit, for example social activities. The team discusses and develops its processes and working style. There is general respect for the leader, and some level of leadership is shared among the team.

Performing At this final stage, the team is strategically settled and shares a common vision. The team is competent and begins to work together to achieve objectives. It makes the most of the decisions according to the criteria that have been agreed upon by the team leader. The team has a high degree of autonomy. Team members are taking care of each other. At this point, the team does not need to be instructed or assisted, but maintaining performance will become critical for success.

7 Needs, Goals and Effectiveness

In humanitarian action, the needs-based approach has made space for a rights-based approach as it is a necessary element of the right to life with dignity.[20] The right to health, for example, seems to be easier to turn into reality in times of natural catastrophes (for example, in the context of epidemics or when tackling high child mortality) than in other situations. In protracted crises or conflict settings, such as the Syrian civil war, a rights-based approach is often much more difficult to implement. Wounded non-combatants, for example, might have the right to be treated, but warring parties might not allow access to victims or even to treatment, although it is expressly guaranteed in international law.[21] Nevertheless, whichever approach humanitarian actors may select, humanitarian response essentially aims at lessening needs. This is why needs are seen to be at the forefront; they must be addressed in accordance with humanitarian principles while remaining realistic and meeting the expectations of the target group. It is worth mentioning that, in the context of human needs, health, food and shelter are often the focus of humanitarian aid. This is the case, for example, when addressing malnutrition of infants, maternal

[20]The Sphere Project (2011).

[21]*Id.*, p. 22.

health or the ultimate goal of health through better water supply, sanitation and hygiene (WASH), shelter or protection.

Generally, needs are defined as the difference between a given situation or the degree of self-help capacity and an accepted level of satisfaction. For example, a population with a certain under-five mortality rate (U5MR) *needs* support to reach an *accepted* or *tolerated* child mortality rate.[22] Consider that the emergency threshold for the U5MR is defined as 0.8 deaths per day and per portion of a population of 10,000 children. In other words, if a sample population of 50,000 children suffers the loss of more than four children aged below five every day, an emergency is at hand. To intervene in a way that the U5MR shrinks becomes the main objective of many interventions. Figure 1 illustrates such relations.

Humanitarian need is a recognised requirement for survival in terms of food, water, shelter, nutrition, non-food items, medical treatment and protection; while taking into account self-help capacity, interventions correspond to needs with their output and outcome, both direct and indirect.:

We will briefly discuss the aims of humanitarian intervention since they are communicated to and within the response team. Target setting and the consciousness of the effects of humanitarian interventions are an integral part of management in humanitarian aid and therefore deserve more attention. In contrast to the

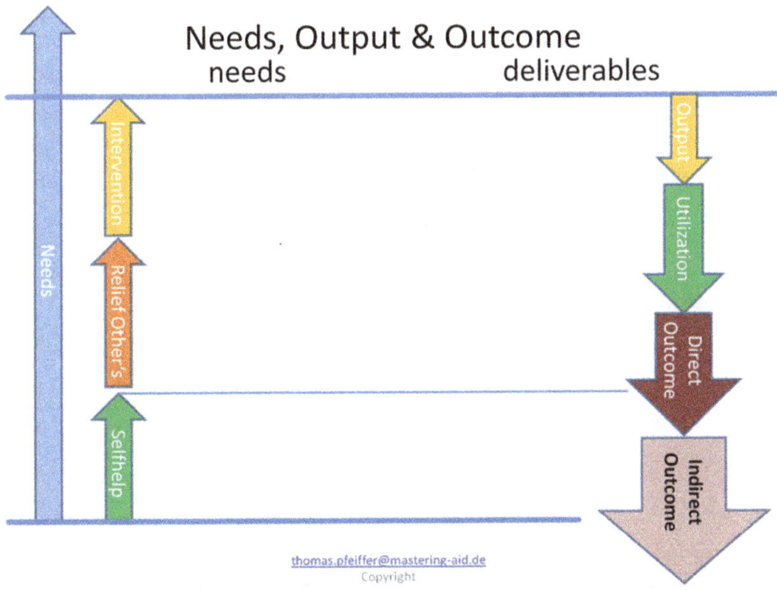

Fig. 1 Needs, output and outcome. Developed by the authors, Thomas Pfeiffer and Markus Moke, the figure expresses the degree of needs vis-à-vis the delivered performance of aid

[22] *Id.*, p. 346.

humanitarian interventions of several decades ago, recent projects contain elements of accountability in among their sets of goals. This is especially helpful where an appropriate gain is achieved by the self-controlling accountability or where ineffective decisions need to be corrected. In order to measure accountability, the situation before the intervention is compared to the one present afterward. The needs usually exceed the agencies' response capacities or funds.

Two methods to lessen this effect of overwhelming needs shall be mentioned. First, differentiating acute from chronic needs is beneficial. Not only does it help to better utilise funds from developmental donors as opposed to humanitarian donors, but acute needs usually also require an immediate response. Second, in complex situations, the division of labour is crucial whereby organisations split responsibilities between sectors so that one organisation may take the lead in a particular sector, such as health, whereas the other one focuses on an issue, such as shelter. In this way, both separately account for their work while aiming to achieve compatible goals.

7.1 Setting Objectives

Based on the above definition of needs, it is possible to formulate objectives and introduce effective aid. When winter snows were imminent after the 2006 Pakistan earthquake, the goal to protect the victims of this disaster from cold temperatures or maintain public health was evident. Humanitarians thus had to decide at the beginning of winter to what degree populations were to be put up in winter-proof shelters. Indicators based on experience serve to describe the situations ex ante and ex post and by comparison often serve to account for individual, project, as well as organisational performances and self-reflection. Indicators, however, can often only hint at the degree of success of a project. Hereby the quality of work can be assessed alongside the five OECD-DAC criteria and shall be flanked by humanitarian-aid-specific six criteria[23]:

- appropriateness/relevance;
- effectiveness;
- efficiency;
- impact;
- sustainability; and
- connectedness.

Concerning these criteria, two general points must be made.

First, sustainability is relevant not only in the context of development but also in humanitarian aid, which is visible in the example of the large-scale disasters in Pakistan. When a major earthquake struck the country in 2006, sustainable

[23]OECD (2015).

elements of humanitarian aid helped the population build resilience, which in turn had a positive impact during the responses to the 2010 floods. Fostering the resilience of populations affected by frequent disasters has gained priority in humanitarian aid and development work.

Second, impact needs to be well distinguished from effectiveness. Targeted populations need to utilise and access aid, like mothers bringing their malnourished children to feeding centres, in order for aid to accomplish a certain effect. Such a hopefully effective intervention then contributes to creating an intended impact. However, particularly after the 1994 Rwandan genocide, where *genocidaires* utilised aid to sustain their criminal agenda, possible unintended impact must also be considered, and action must be taken to prevent it. Hence, impact is an indirect consequence of the direct aid delivered to beneficiaries. Aid workers fulfil their roles best when attentively, consciously and responsibly working in often confusing humanitarian contexts. As clear-cut as it may appear here, it should be noted that these quality criteria often contradict each other and need to be balanced, or reach certain compromises depending on the context. One interesting contradiction concerns participatory approaches that lead to higher degrees of sustainability but often sacrifice time. However, in order to optimise the quality of an outcome, one must strive to find the most appropriate solution and take the most standardised approach (see Fig. 2).

When looking at the provision of humanitarian aid at the onset of the Darfur crisis in 2004, the textbook response was swift and effective. However, it was not

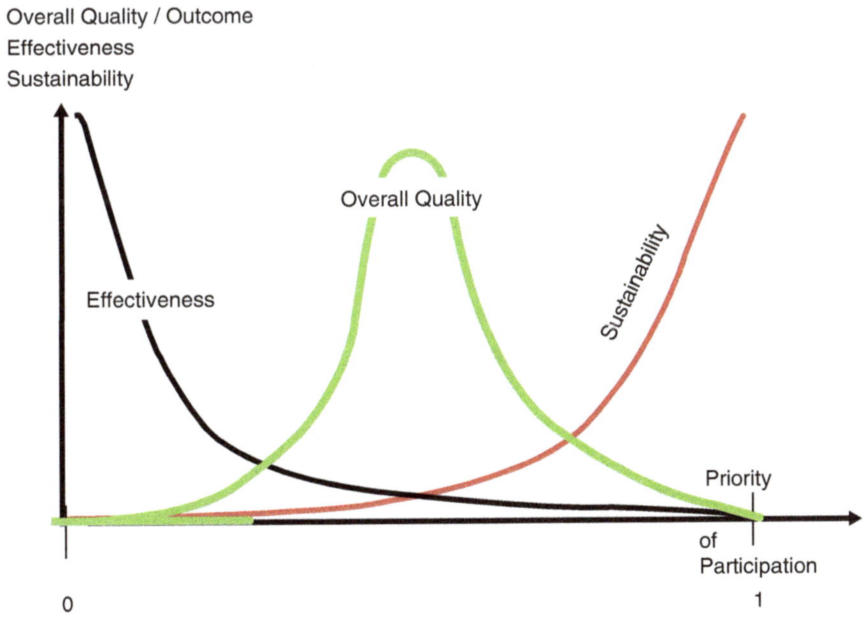

Fig. 2 Aid intensity over time. Developed by the authors, Thomas Pfeiffer and Markus Moke, the figure illustrates the intensity of aid over time after a disaster with the dominant DAC criteria

foreseeable that millions of displaced people would remain uprooted over 10 years later. The uncertainty that prevails in many humanitarian contexts requires careful consideration and a flexible approach allowing for compromises. Neither a rigid nor a dogmatic approach will enable aid workers or their organisations to respond appropriately to crises. After all, humanitarian aid deals with human beings, and it is for a good reason that humanity is one of the seven fundamental principles of the International Federation of the Red Cross and Red Crescent Societies.[24] A case-by-case approach with an activity-focused attitude that follows good quality practices in terms of principles and standards helps to enrich the management of emergencies.

7.2 *Strategic Management*

In order to capture the concept of strategic management, we must first define the term strategy. A strategy, according to the working definition used by the UN Management Handbook, is a

> …way to achieve the comprehensive long-range goals of an organization. Strategic planning is the corresponding management function, focused on developing an overall direction for an organization within the context of the challenges and opportunities of the operating environment, as well as the organization's resources.[25]

Through planning, general strategies are broken down into workable units and thus translated into specific work programmes and finally converted into individual action. As strategies can emerge unpredictably, one should strive at all times to maintain flexibility, continuously review and, if necessary, update the strategy. A clear organisational structure is critical to effective management. It is not an end in itself but rather a requirement set out by donors and governments and is helpful in communicating with stakeholders. Staff working for an aid organisation must understand the place and relationship of the emergency programme within the broader context of the organisation.

7.3 *Organisational Structure*

James distinguishes between three organisational levels (see Fig. 3): (1) headquarters, (2) country offices and (3) project sites.[26] Each level is concerned with a different view of strategy, time span, level of detail and frequency of dealing with

[24]The complete set of the seven fundamental principles can be accessed at: http://www.ifrc.org/who-we-are/vision-and-mission/the-seven-fundamental-principles/.

[25]International Peace Institute (2012), pp. 55–56.

[26]James (2008).

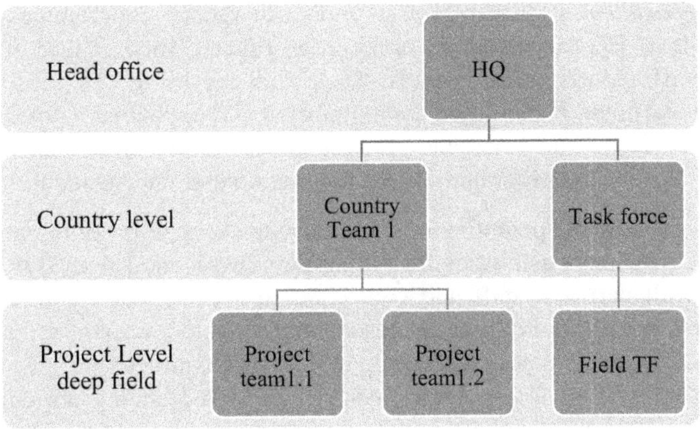

Fig. 3 Organisational levels. Reprinted by kind permission of the publisher from James, E. Managing Humanitarian Relief. An operational guide for NGOs (Practical Action Publishing Limited, Warwickshire 2008)

particular issues. When discussing the organisational design, it is useful to categorise types of staff working in an emergency, which includes programme and medical staff, trainers, community mobilisers, project managers and programme support staff, such as accountants, logisticians and drivers.

The organisational structure can be established along several lines, including by function, service users (for example, children and adults), programme (for example, shelter and water/sanitation), donor and geography. In emergencies, a pyramid structure is essential as it eases communications and assigns clear roles and responsibilities to staff. Some organisations form temporary task forces or crisis management teams. This brings together key decision-makers within an organisation and allows them to focus on a crisis.

However, no organisational structure is ideal or permanent, and so aid organisations must revisit their organisational charts periodically and make changes accordingly.[27] It is worth noting that, over the past decades, organisations have increasingly decentralised their structures, by placing operational and budgetary authority, resources and competencies closer to target areas as opposed to headquarters. As emergency programmes expand, transparency is indispensable, especially concerning the following:

- *Clarity of function* – all staff should be acquainted with their functions and roles, and those of other members, as sometimes duties that are not clearly defined can lead to misunderstandings and confusion.
- *Centralisation or decentralisation* – staff should be clear about what can and has to be managed in a decentralised way and which responsibilities are monitored and controlled from the top down.

[27] *Id.*, p. 97.

- *Cross-departmental relationships* – most emergency programmes involve a country-level HQ office and one or more sub-offices. This can lead to a situation where staff reports to two levels. Such dual reporting can cause problems between staff, and it should be communicated and explained beforehand.
- *Deputy directors* – in emergency programmes, country directors need to share the workload of the programme's administration and management.

Ways to mitigate the potential for conflict are to set up terms of reference (TOR) that set out clear responsibilities for all partners involved. These TOR should be shared with all partners, staff and colleagues to prevent confusion. In addition, information and team-building measures are important to lessen the effect of the 'us against them' thinking that may develop in dual programmes.[28]

Various approaches for strategic management and planning are employed by different organisations, depending on their needs, capacities and resources. Strategy development and planning processes typically follow a sequence of steps.[29] One useful tool to start identifying strategic alternatives based on preliminary research is a SWOT analysis, which examines the strengths and weaknesses of concerned organisation and the opportunities and threats in the environment. As such, it is a tool for generating a summary of the strategic plan of an organisation:

- Strengths are capabilities that enable your organisation or unit to perform well—capabilities that need to be leveraged.
- Weaknesses are characteristics that prohibit your organisation or unit from performing well and need to be addressed quickly.
- Opportunities are trends, forces, events and ideas that your organisation or unit can capitalise on.
- Threats are possible events outside of your control that your organisation or unit needs to plan for or decide how to mitigate.

The main purpose of a SWOT analysis is to provide an analytical basis for strategies that reflect reality by guaranteeing a maximum fit between external, environmental factors and internal factors relative to the organisation. Strategies based on this analytical model ensure that outside opportunities are exploited by inside strengths, while threats are countered and weaknesses minimised.[30]

References

Chapman A (2013) Tuckman forming storming norming performing model. http://www.businessballs.com/tuckmanformingstormingnormingperforming.htm

Carter WN (2008) Disaster management. A disaster manager's handbook. Asian Development Bank, Mandaluyong City

[28] *Id.*, pp. 99–100.

[29] International Peace Institute (2012), p. 58.

[30] *Id.*, pp. 63–64.

Demiroz F, Kapucu N (2012) The role of leadership in managing emergencies and disasters. Eur J Econ Polit Stud 5(1):91–101

Kapucu N, Van Wart M (2008) Making matters worse: an anatomy of leadership failures in managing catastrophic events. Adm Soc 40(7):711–740

International Federation of the Red Cross and Red Crescent Societies Red Cross. The seven fundamental principles. http://www.ifrc.org/who-we-are/vision-and-mission/the-seven-fundamental-principles/

International Peace Institute (2012) The management handbook. For UN field missions. United Nations, New York

James E (2008) Managing humanitarian relief: an operational guide for NGOs. Practical Action Publishing, Warwickshire

Ludlow DRL (1999) Humanitarian intervention and the Rwandan Genocide. J Conflict Stud 19 (1) http://journals.lib.unb.ca/index.php/jcs/article/view/4378/5055

McEntire D, Dawson G (2007) The intergovernmental context. In: Waugh WL Jr, Tierney K (eds) Emergency management: principles and practice for local government, 2nd edn. ICMA, Washington, pp 57–70

OECD (2011) Fourth high level forum on aid effectiveness. http://www.oecd.org/dac/effectiveness/fourthhighlevelforumonaideffectiveness.htm

OECD (2015) DAC criteria for evaluating development assistance. http://www.oecd.org/dac/evaluation/daccriteriaforevaluatingdevelopmentassistance.htm

Patton A (2007) Collaborative emergency management. In: Waugh WL Jr, Tierney K (eds) Emergency management: principles and practice for local government, vol 2007, 2nd edn. ICMA, Washington, pp 71–84

The Sphere Project (2011) Humanitarian charter and minimum standards in humanitarian response. Belmont Press Ltd, Northampton

United Nations General Assembly, Human Rights Council, Universal Periodic Review Submission for the Democratic People's Republic of Korea (North Korea), http://lib.ohchr.org/HRBodies/UPR/Documents/Session6/KP/LFNKR-HRWF_PRK_UPR_S06_2009.pdf

UCSF Human Resources (2015) Guide to Managing Human Resources. http://ucsfhr.ucsf.edu/index.php/pubs/hrguidearticle/chapter-14-team-building/

Markus Moke is Head of Quality Assurance and Training at Germany's Relief Coalition, Aktion Deutschland Hilft, e.V. (ADH). He is Senior Lecturer in the Joint European Master's Programme in International Humanitarian Action (NOHA) at Ruhr University Bochum, Germany.

Thomas Pfeiffer is a university trained Mechanical Engineer with 24 years of experience in humanitarian action around the globe.

Project Management

Sabrina Herold and Bartjan W. Pennink

1 Introduction

Projects represent the commitment of human and physical resources to produce specific outputs in a given time and budget framework.[1] Projects have five main attributes. They are as follows[2]:

- *unique* in their specific end product such that each project is of a different nature, among others, including variations of scale, scope and resource demands;
- *temporary* with a definite beginning and end;
- *iterative* and developed during their progression when details become clearer or circumstances change;
- *funded* by a primary project sponsor providing direction to the project, who gives decision-making authority to the project manager; and
- *uncertain*, due to their interplay with reality and their uniqueness, as well as no certain best plan and no guarantee for steadiness of the environment and/or stakeholders.

Project management has several stages forming a continuous process within which one builds upon the other.[3] Ideally, the five stages should be carried out in the following order: needs assessment, project design and planning, proposal writing,

[1]FA, Project Cycle Management Technical Guide, p. 11, http://www.fao.org/docrep/012/ak211e/ak211e00.pdf.

[2]Schwalbe (2009).

[3]United Nations Development Programme (2009).

S. Herold (✉) • B.W. Pennink
University of Groningen, Groningen, The Netherlands
e-mail: sabrina.herold@credit-suisse.com; b.j.w.pennink@rug.nl

© Springer International Publishing AG 2018

H.-J. Heintze, P. Thielbörger (eds.), *International Humanitarian Action*,
DOI 10.1007/978-3-319-14454-2_21

implementation, as well as monitoring and evaluation.[4] In reality, deviations are the norm, and thus over time, the subsequent stages will feed back into the former generating a feedback loop correcting for project changes.[5] The structure outlined above and applied in this chapter is also referred to as the PMC.[6] Each of its steps is discussed in more detail within this chapter.

The first stages of the PMC, i.e. from project identification up to and including proposal writing, are most crucial as only their successful completion can propel projects into the implementation phase. It is very important to note that every project exists to satisfy a certain need. Only where an assessment clearly points to the need for a specific project should subsequent PMC steps be conducted. Due to the highly dynamic environment prevailing in situations where humanitarian assistance is required, projects often fail due to incompetent needs analyses prior to implementation. An example where well-intentioned actions have had negative impacts is an NGO executing food for work programmes in Haiti with the aim of facilitating access to basic needs while unintentionally causing harm to the local economy.[7]

The latter stages of the PMC from implementation up to and including evaluation will show whether the project can achieve its milestones and develop an end product and sustainability objectives.[8]

Within the framework of project management activities, there are nine *knowledge management areas*, consisting of a set of competences and skills that must be brought to fruition during the project's life cycle and that occur during each stage of the PMC.[9] The knowledge management areas have been subdivided into four core and five facilitating knowledge management areas.

The four core knowledge management areas are as follows:

- *scope management*: entails describing the work required to complete a project successfully;
- *time management*: refers to translating the project scope into a timely schedule to guarantee on-time completion;
- *cost management*: refers to estimating costs, determining budgets and controlling costs; and
- *quality management*: refers to planning and establishing operational quality objectives and the assurance and control of their adherence throughout the project.

[4]Bishop (2001).

[5]Richardson (2015).

[6]EuropeAid Co-operation Office (2002).

[7]CARE and Save the Children (2010).

[8]Bishop (2001).

[9]Schwalbe (2009), Richardson (2015).

The five facilitating knowledge management areas are the following:

- *Project management*: refers to the project manager's overall management, comprising of one united and cohesive plan. Since key management areas are intertwined, changes within one key management area will likely affect others too; thus, sound project management becomes vital to ensure cohesion. Part of the manager's plan is defining the project team, as well as developing and guiding it throughout the project.
- *Communication management*: since communication problems were recognised as a major reason for project failure, this process has recently received more attention. It entails processes of communication planning, management and control with external and internal parties.
- *Stakeholder management*: due to the special relevance of stakeholders in humanitarian aid, their identification and management becomes vital and is directly related to communication management.
- *Risk management*: to maximise project success and minimise threats, risk management becomes crucial. Throughout each step of a project, the project manager should always keep a backup plan in mind. Being ready to take an alternative route with the same or similar desirable results can prevent lock-in effects and project failure. Also, the team's risk exposure during the project execution is assessed here.
- *Procurement management*: this term describes the acquisition management of project-related services or products from third parties. It clarifies how resource needs will be met externally and from which vendors they will be procured.

The knowledge management areas outlined above will appear again within the different PMC stages. Due to its integrative nature, the issue of project management will not be mentioned separately while explaining the PMC stages. However, readers should keep it in mind as the most prominent component of each PMC aspect. We will return to it explicitly at the last section of this chapter when talking about the relevance of human relations in advancing projects.

2 Project Identification or Needs Assessment

A project starts with identifying the main issue it seeks to address. Formulation of a specific problem usually relies on identifying an issue in which all symptoms are brought together and analysed in order to find causes and consequences as a way of structuring the problem.[10] Problems usually contain various levels from macro and

[10]Bishop (2001).

A problem is best visualized in a problem tree which can take the following form:

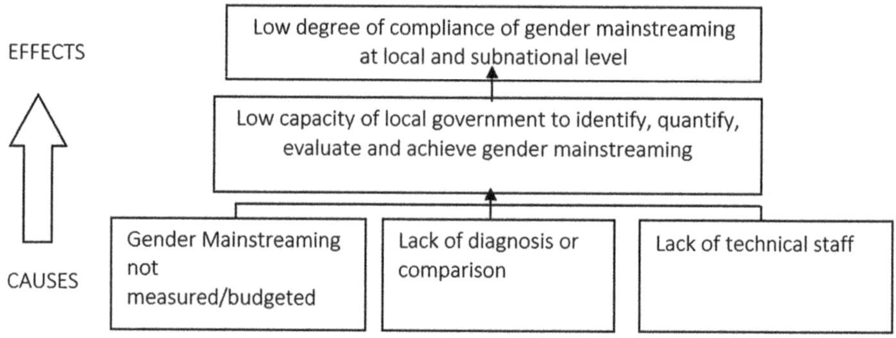

Fig. 1 Identifying problems. Developed by the authors, Sabrina Herold and Bartjan W. Pennink

very abstract to micro and less abstract. These levels are related, and it is necessary to address each one of them, as well as their interdependencies with regard to involved stakeholders.[11] Figure 1 illustrates the various elements of describing (and identifying) a problem:

2.1 *Situational Analysis*

A situational analysis comprises the active search for a problem, the uncovering of its possible causes and solutions and/or the validation of an already identified problem by other parties. Analysis needs to take into account socio-economic, political, environmental and cultural aspects.[12] These different aspects of the situational analysis can be worked out with the help of Heyse *et al.*[13]

Such an analysis ought to be conducted from two perspectives.

First, one should obtain an outsider's perspective so as to better uncover interdependencies and identify key indicators.[14] An analysis on the national level includes a review of policy objectives and current policies of the respective countries with the aid of key indicators (EuropeAid Co-operation Office 2002).[15] A more detailed explanation of indicators will be given in the section on

[11]*Ibid.*; EuropeAid Co-operation Office (2002).

[12]United Nations Development Programme (2009).

[13]Heyse et al. (2014).

[14]Bishop (2001).

[15]EuropeAid Co-operation Office (2002).

operationalisation. When selecting indicators, project management needs to bear in mind the cost and time to collect future data and the frequency of data collection necessary.

Second, an insider's perspective helps to investigate a situation from within the problem's context.[16] An example for such an inside view on a micro or community level is the execution of an activity analysis.[17] It clarifies responsibilities within a community, distinguishing between household, productive and community roles.[18]

Examples for the various facets of situational analyses include the following[19]:

- *political analysis*: investigating legal and institutional environment;
- *economic analysis*: investigating the overall (national) and specific (local) economic state;
- *sociocultural analysis*: investigating prevailing beliefs, norms, practices and attitudes; and
- *health and food analysis*: investigating the populations' access to food, (drinking) water, hygiene and overall health status.

2.2 *Stakeholder Analysis*

According to the United Nations Development Programme (UNDP), stakeholders are organisations or individuals directly or indirectly influenced by development policies and activities. These influences can have positive or negative effects on the parties concerned.[20] The latter are most commonly categorised in terms of primary or secondary stakeholders. Primary stakeholders are directly impacted by the project, while secondary stakeholders only experience an indirect effect.[21] Project managers for humanitarian aid should bear in mind that influence does not equal priority.[22]

Besides primary and secondary stakeholders, the concepts of target groups and beneficiaries also exist. The *target group* of a project is part of the set of primary stakeholders, whom the project addresses and aims to help. Beneficiaries, on the other hand, comprise all stakeholders who are positively affected by

[16]Bishop (2001).

[17]*Ibid.*

[18]*Ibid.*

[19]For details, see Heyse et al. (2014).

[20]United Nations Development Programme (2009).

[21]Bishop (2001).

[22]United Nations Development Programme (2009).

the project.[23] One may sometimes also come across the term 'direct beneficiary', which refers to the target group.

Stakeholders also vary according to the scale of the issue.[24] Its nature determines whether they are involved on the macro, intermediate or micro level.[25] By identifying the stakeholder level of involvement, one also obtains insights into the channels (for example, central government, NGO) through which the problem is best tackled.[26] Stakeholders' networks are important, too. Reach and depth of these networks can differ for each level of involvement. A stakeholder analysis thus ultimately provides answers to the following questions: which stakeholders are involved, who benefits and who is targeted?[27]

Stakeholders provide resources, represent the target group and the beneficiaries and engage in project implementation. They play a central role within project management as humanitarian aid projects would not go ahead without their time and commitment. Consequently, over the future course of project management, all relevant stakeholders should be consulted and integrated into the PMC.

Once the needs assessment is completed, it is reviewed in collaboration with stakeholders to serve the following purposes[28]:

- validation of data interpretation on the level the project ought to be carried out;
- identification of shortcomings and drawing up of new enquiry points (for example, discrepancies between situational perspectives or within);
- identification of development priorities;
- involvement of all relevant stakeholders;
- identification of any disadvantaged stakeholders and proposed actions for solutions;
- identification of conflicts between stakeholders and their remedies.

In order to investigate whether or not a project is feasible, the following questions should be considered[29]:

- What are the causes of crisis, and what will the project's effects be?
- What are the possibilities to conduct the project successfully (money, time, other resources, end product)?
- What basic assumptions are associated with the problem?
- Were there similar problems and/or projects in the past, and what is to be learned from them?

[23]European Neighbourhood and Partnership Instrument (2009).

[24]Bishop (2001).

[25]*Ibid.*

[26]*Ibid.*

[27]EuropeAid Co-operation Office (2002).

[28]Bishop (2001).

[29]EuropeAid Co-operation Office (2002), United Nations Development Programme (2009).

- Are cross-cutting issues (general criteria of equality and environment) considered?

Feasible project options remaining in the wake of the analysis are prioritised.[30] Several quality criteria help to assess the feasibility of project ideas[31]:

- Is the need assessment and problem analysis adequately comprehensive (on various levels and from different perspectives)?
- Are the project's end products in line with policy objectives for humanitarian aid?
- Are the major stakeholders clearly identified?
- Are the target group and beneficiaries clearly identified and their problems correctly described?
- Is the project's end product directly beneficial to its target group?

After finalising project ideas and selecting feasible options in collaboration with stakeholders, the possibilities of their contribution to the project are identified, an essential component of procurement management. Stakeholder contribution is vital not only from a budget perspective but also to increase their commitment and positive perception of project outcomes.[32]

2.3 Results of the Project Identification Phase

The outcome of any project selection analysis is a pre-feasibility study in consultancy with stakeholders in order to[33]

- identify the need for a project (Is there any? Has it been validated?);
- identify the end product and feasible ideas to achieve it;
- preselect best ideas for a more detailed investigation (past and comparable experiences in the region or with similar projects can be influential);
- suggest preferred option and future course of action; and
- draft a first rough cost and means estimate.

The pre-feasibility study is the first part in the process of finding a suitable project frame and thus the beginning of what is commonly known as scope management. Comparative Standards can be found in the latest publication of the Sphere Project (2015). Starting in 1997, this project has encompassed the combined

[30]Bishop (2001).

[31]EuropeAis Co-operation Office, Eur02 \I 1033, 2002.

[32]*Ibid.*

[33]EuropeAid Co-operation Office (2002).

knowledge of multiple humanitarian organisations, which define and refine standards on describing urgency. From then on till now, this project has resulted in valuable publications and work to assist the humanitarian organisations.[34]

Box 1: Insights from the Field
We have generally experienced that projects were chosen for convenience reasons and in light of resource constraints. A project to be implemented in a *favourable* location was chosen over another one in a less favourable location, whereas the needs situation on the ground was the same. Sometimes NGOs also competed within one location so that inefficiencies were inevitable.

3 Project Design and Planning

Project design and planning entail the conversion of ideas into a clear structure, including operational planning (for example, schedules), financials (budget) and the measurability of project outcomes and objectives.[35] It can therefore be directly translated into the four core knowledge management areas of scope, time, cost and quality management. The project plan should be accurate, workable and measurable.[36] It should take into account past experiences in the same geographic or thematic area in order to improve and support learning. Planning should always include efforts to maximise information sharing with relevant stakeholders.[37]

The first step within the design and planning phase is to clearly define the end product, together with its objectives. While the end product is the desired project output, it is framed around sustainability objectives to come into force after project determination. Milestones help humanitarians to work towards project goals during the operationalisation phase. All three of them need to be clearly stated. It is crucial to use the SMART formula in order to formulate specific, measurable, attainable, realistic and timely objectives.[38]

Outlining project outcomes is essential as it clarifies priorities, identifies beneficiaries and target groups and pinpoints the project focus and its borders.[39] To operationalise the end product, outcome indicators measuring short-term

[34]See also http://www.spherehandbook.org/en/.

[35]Richardson (2015).

[36]*Ibid.*

[37]EuropeAid Co-operation Office (2002).

[38]United Nations Development Programme (2009).

[39]EuropeAid Co-operation Office (2002).

consequences at the target group level are conducted at the end of each project (for example, number of patients treated or number of enrolments for school).[40]

End products can have one or multiple components and are ultimately designed to be sustainable, that is, they should further benefit the target group after project completion. Adherence to sustainable objectives is only possible through ex-post evaluation of effective goal attainment with the aid of impact indicators. The quick scan tool as introduced in Mulder and Pennink provides one such set of indicators measuring economic impact.[41]

Box 2: Insights from the Field
Completing a project with a certain set of end goals also raises questions related to the transition from emergency relief to rehabilitation and development. In this context, sustainability is crucial. All too often, NGOs do not manage to provide the necessary level of independence for vulnerable populations, creating increasing dependence on foreign aid.

Operational work plans are developed in order to achieve the end product. They provide specifications for required resource assistance (macroeconomic support, training, investment, equipment supply, etc.) and implementation ideas.[42]

Intermediate objectives or milestones track the progress towards a project's end product.[43] They are operationalised with output indicators showing the concrete and immediate impact of utilised resources during the project (for example, number of hospitals built). While output indicators measure the progress continuously, milestones warrant that progress towards a specific objective is made.[44] Figure 2 illustrates this process.

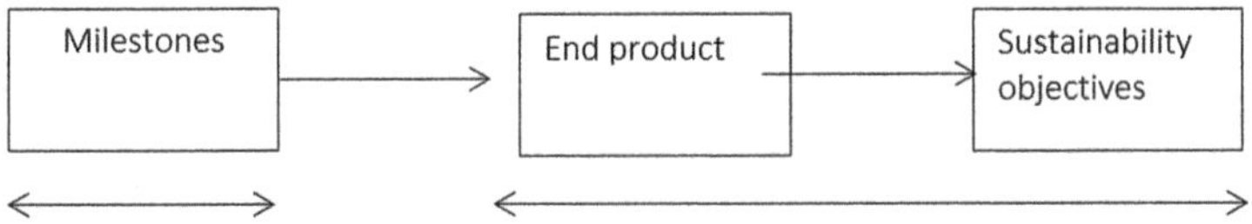

Fig. 2 A process order of sustainability objectives, end products and milestones. Developed by the authors, Sabrina Herold and Bartjan W. Pennink

[40]*Ibid.*

[41]Mulder and Pennink (2014).

[42]EuropeAid Co-operation Office (2002).

[43]*Ibid.*

[44]Bishop (2001).

3.1 Operationalisation into Indicators

The Logical Framework or Log-Framework was established as a means to introduce greater structure into project design. It is useful due to its iterative nature and the inclusion of various project cycle stages: implementation, monitoring, evaluation and overall alignment of project steps up unto the end product.[45]

Its four-by-four matrix structure covers the core parts of the original framework. Here, we describe it as a five-times-six matrix structure. With the help of this structure, one can relate each of the activities undertaken to specific indicators in order to make visible what has been achieved and what remains to be established[46]:

- SMART results and objectives guiding the project downwards and upwards from aim to operationalisation and vice versa;
- SMART indicators giving measurable answers to when, where and who;
- a baseline indicating the state of the indicator before the project start and against which to measure progress;
- a target indicating the state the indicator aims for;
- means of verification providing information about sources for utilised indicators; and
- important assumptions necessary to be in place at every stage for achieving the end product. They reflect changes in the external environment, influencing project performance beyond the control of project management.

Besides assumptions, a fifth row for preconditions may be relevant to some projects, stating what is necessary to be in place in order for the project to initially start.[47]

The structure of the Log-Framework[48] is as follows: lower columns feed into the next higher one, while each column (sustainability objectives, end product, milestones, outputs, inputs) is supported by indicators, baselines, targets, verification means and important assumptions. In formulating this matrix, an iterative approach of testing and refining or revising stages is adequate throughout project planning and implementation. Only in- and outputs, also referred to as activities and results, are under the direct control of a project and comprise the building blocks for the work plan. *Inputs* comprise the tangible and intangible means with which *outputs* in the form of products or services are developed.[49] Milestones, end product and sustainability objectives lie outside the project boundary, so that activities and results work towards them and have a combined impact on them. This Log-Framework provides the basis for work plans.

---

[45]*Ibid.*

[46]Bishop (2001).

[47]European Commission (2005).

[48]*Ibid.*

[49]*Ibid.*

The United Nations provides the following checklist of questions to ensure the smooth functioning of any Log-framework[50]:

- Is the reason why a project becomes necessary in the given situation clear?
- Is the end product identified correctly?
- Are linkages between inputs, outputs, objectives and end product logical and consistent?
- Are sufficient activities planned to obtain the end product, together with cost indications?
- Are appropriate indicators installed to assess project success?
- Did any killing factors arise in the course of project design? If so, what is the planned corrective action?

3.2 *Work Plans*

Work plans operationalise project activities and form the basis of a detailed project budget. They structure the implementation process while simultaneously providing monitoring possibilities.[51]

Work plans usually include the following three steps[52]:

- analysis of project activity and allocation of tasks in implementation schedules (identification of detailed components, duration of activities, allocation of personnel and scheduling);
- network analysis (network diagrams to represent duration of project activities sequentially and identify the critical path, that is, the timeliness of milestones in order to complete the project in a minimum of time); and
- developing a Gantt chart (in which the time frame of all activities is described in a standardised way).

3.3 *Financing Projects*

Financing should cover all aspects of the Log-Framework and set the goals for procurement management, which already begins to be enacted during the problem identification phase.

The European Commission, for instance, drafts a formal agreement with the respective project partner and sponsor (for example, government) and assesses project and financial needs through a list of criteria such as relevance, feasibility

[50]United Nations Development Programme (2009).

[51]*Ibid.*

[52]*Ibid.*

and sustainability/quality. Generally, the financing budget should provide precise answers to the question of who is funding the project and where the resources acquired through funding are utilised.[53]

3.4 *Stakeholder Consultation*

During the planning phase, project management seeks to secure and confirm the stakeholders' interests, expectations and eventual project participation. Cooperation with beneficiaries and target groups, as well as project partners as the main focus groups, is essential to ensure the desired project outcome.

Stakeholder consultation can be clearly related to stakeholder management. Strong stakeholder management describes an open and creative dialogue between the project team and stakeholders, as well as among stakeholders themselves.[54] Ownership has been determined as important for humanitarian aid projects as commitment increases efforts and motivation to achieve the envisaged end product. Giving stakeholders the opportunity to organise themselves through meetings, such as planning workshops, encourages them to work towards project goals.[55]

On the other hand, increasing stakeholder participation also heightens the complexity of project management, with the potential to prolong communication and decision-making processes. While identification of all necessary stakeholders is essential, their participation throughout the project needs to be carefully selected based on their importance, not on their influence. Nevertheless, influence in the form of increased resource commitment to the project may leverage the importance of particular stakeholders.

3.5 *Impact Analysis: Ecology, Economics and Finance*

In line with quality management and sustainability objectives, a project should aim for the smallest possible ecological footprint. Analysing the impact of a project programme is crucial during the design and planning phase.

Attention should be paid to the direct and indirect impacts from selecting suppliers to the end product (for example, care for proper waste disposal when the end product is a hospital), and project inputs and outputs need to be selected with ecological criteria in mind.

One should also take into account economic and financial impacts. Albeit less extensive than the situational analysis, it is to be assessed on a broader spectrum

[53]EuropeAid Co-operation Office (2002).

[54]United Nations Development Programme (2009).

[55]*Ibid.*

whether the planned project activities have negative impacts on any other economic or financial areas outside the project framework and, if so, how this can be prevented. Where a project has a dramatic negative effect on either one of these areas, its implementation becomes highly doubtful.

In the field and depending on the project, diverse social and cultural impacts may have to be considered besides the three impacts mentioned, for example inclusive development or gender mainstreaming.

3.6 *On Risks and Indicators*

Risk management, although already introduced as a specific knowledge management area, deserves special attention in the planning and design phase. Granted that a project team and especially the project manager should always have a plan B and a plan C in mind, balancing the risks that the project team and manager may be exposed to is most crucial for humanitarian aid projects. Thus, measures to minimise these risks need to be taken, which may, among others, include vaccination, considerations of lodging location and/or nutritional diets.

The United Nations distinguishes between quantitative and qualitative indicators, which are complementary to each other due to their differing strengths and weaknesses.[56] As it is not always possible to exactly measure each element, realistic proxies are commonly used. The data sources for indicators (especially qualitative indicators) are derived from either public databases or the field.[57] The following criteria are relevant for identification of indicators and proxies[58]:

- relevance to objectives;
- ease of collection, use and understanding;
- clarity of definition (reliable, accurate, unambiguous);
- sensitivity to changes caused by the project;
- mutual independence of indicators chosen; and
- smallest possible number of indicators.

By adhering to these criteria, the project also maintains high standards of quality management. The involvement of stakeholders in the indicator identification process is appropriate for strongly qualitative measurements and in the evaluation phase (see evaluation of strategic constituencies).

[56]Bishop (2001).

[57]*Ibid.*

[58]*Ibid.*; United Nations Development Programme (2009).

3.7 Project Review/Appraisal and Project Results

The initial planning and design phase is followed by an appraisal phase. A project is reviewed from various perspectives to decide whether to proceed with implementation or not. Assessment takes place on a technical, financial, economic, social, institutional, environmental, political, sustainability and risk level.[59] It verifies project relevance; assesses the potential future of the project after its completion, based on formerly selected sustainability objectives and quality indicators; and reviews the entire Log-Framework.[60] That includes the implementation schedule with activities and resources, responsibilities and accountable persons and bodies.[61] Although the funding party evaluates the project proposal, the executing party should consider a similar review before handing in its proposal to enhance its chances of implementing the project. After completing this stage, answers to the following questions should emerge[62]:

- How is the project funded?
- Are beneficiaries and target groups clearly defined, were they consulted and do they have a sense of ownership towards the project?
- Does the project preserve the ecological environment?
- Does it benefit the economic and financial environment?
- Are project partners identified, and have they confirmed their role in supporting the project?
- Do you have clearly defined end product and objectives in place (milestones and sustainability)?
- How feasible is the end product, and are the objectives considering the programme and available resources?
- Have you allocated the necessary resources (budget funding, personnel) appropriately?
- Do you have sufficient indicators and information sources to measure outcomes?

In sum, a project should only be implemented if it is relevant, sustainable and feasible. Also, a clear programme makes it much more likely to achieve an anticipated project outcome. Once a project proposal has been reviewed and accepted, it may be implemented. Monitoring and evaluation are the two crucial tasks during the implementation phase of a project.[63]

[59] Bishop (2001).

[60] EuropeAid Co-operation Office (2002).

[61] *Ibid.*

[62] *Ibid.*

[63] Bishop (2001).

4 Writing a Project Proposal

Proposals serve to attain the approval for a project and secure necessary funding. It thus essentially belongs to communication and stakeholder management. The views of prospective funders must be taken into account as they are likely to differ in terms of priorities and the kind of support they are likely to provide.[64] Correspondingly, proposals vary in form. No matter the format, five key points need to be addressed[65]:

- What are the project's end product and its sustainability objectives?
- What are project needs?
  - needs analysis;
  - project identification and selection process.
- What is the project about?
  - project end product and sustainability objectives;
  - stakeholders involved (target groups, beneficiaries, partners, . . .);
  - linkages between activities, results, objectives and end product;
  - procedures foreseen to monitor and evaluate project progress;
  - project in line with existing projects, the environment and/or other stakeholders.
- How is the project going to be operationalised?
  - project structure of Log-Framework;
  - work plan, including personnel and further resource requirements;
  - financing.
- What are the costs, and how is the project going to be financed?
  - financial feasibility;
  - project duration;
  - risk exposure.

Eligibility is key when writing proposals. Donors may refuse financing a project because it lies outside of their interest and/or due to specific expenditures, for example too much overhead.[66]

Besides covering the above points, proposals need to be well written and express a sense of purpose and urgency.[67] Writing a proposal is only possible once needs assessment and problem identification are completed, and with advanced projects,

[64]*Ibid.*

[65]*Ibid.*

[66]*Ibid.*

[67]*Ibid.*

design and planning. The iterative nature of projects regarding needs assessment or project design and planning may trigger alterations in proposal design.

Experience from fieldwork shows that before a proposal can be handed in, the logical framework needs to be in place and the scope of the project, the major stakeholders, the project strategy and the budget need to be well defined.

5 Implementation with a Focus on Monitoring and Evaluation

Implementation is about working the plan against the budget while considering continuous feedback from the environment and stakeholders. It essentially comes down to cost, time, quality and communication management of activities in order to reach the end product. Since a project plan is only very rarely executed as planned, adjustments become necessary when there are deviations from the plan.[68] Also, requests to change project aspects from stakeholders will demand extra time and resources as they require approval from a board or resource supplier.[69] During the implementation phase, the formerly introduced Log-Framework becomes a relevant monitoring system and a framework for evaluation.[70] Systematic attention shall be paid to cross-cutting issues, conflict management and crisis management throughout implementation.[71]

5.1 Major Tasks Within the Project Implementation Phase

The following list is based on the EuropeAid Co-operation Office[72]:

- Ensure timely execution of plans.
- Ensure budget control entailing effective and efficient allocation of means.
- Ensure project quality throughout the process with monitoring so that
  - milestones are met and processes towards attaining them run smoothly; if they are not met, corrective measures are to be suggested;
  - good external and internal communication with clear decision-making lines takes place;
  - health and life risks for the project team and managers are feasible.

[68]Richardson (2015).

[69]*Ibid.*

[70]EuropeAid Co-operation Office (2002).

[71]*Ibid.*

[72]*Ibid.*

- Ensure project effectiveness through evaluation.

Monitoring provides answers to the question 'are we doing the project correctly', while evaluation relates to 'are we doing the correct project?'[73] Therefore, the former takes place continuously during the implementation of the project; the latter is of periodical nature, mostly ex ante, mid term, final and ex post.[74]

5.2 Implementation

Implementation is to be understood as a learning process involving the following[75]:

- *Planning and re-planning*: implementation, activities, resource schedules and Log-Framework are reviewed, refined and adjusted accordingly. Any adjustments need to be justified and fed back into decision-making.
- *Monitoring*: it involves continuous and systematic collection and analysis of information for management control, feeding back into decision-making.
- *Decision-making*: the project's future course is charted by the project manager. While consulting other stakeholders and his team, he evaluates the project execution and makes decisions. The target groups influence a manager's decision heavily. If they are not willing to contribute or are resistant to the project's progression, the project fails. However, project managers do not hold absolute power as target groups and potential approval or disapproval of a project by donors inevitably influence decisions. Donors need to approve all major changes planned.
- *Reporting* is an essential part of communication and stakeholder management. It keeps responsible bodies and fund providers up to date with the progress made. Decisions about when and whom to report to are usually defined in the financial contract under which the project operates. Frequently, a quarterly time frame is employed.[76]

Box 3: Insights from the Field
Projects with intangible goals are especially complex in nature. They are even harder to manage and accomplish when the end-product definition does not account for flexibility. Defining an intangible end product very precisely diminishes flexibility within the implementation phase as investors expect compliance with proposal agreements.

---

[73]Bishop (2001).

[74]*Ibid.*

[75]EuropeAid Co-operation Office (2002).

[76]*Ibid.*

5.3 Monitoring

Monitoring of daily management activities to identify and resolve any issues arising during the implementation phase answers the following questions[77]:

- Which activities are currently undertaken, and what is their progress (weekly)?
- What is the balance between resources that have been deployed and progress achieved (monthly)?
- Have milestones been accomplished (quarterly)?
- Are the results in line with the end product and sustainability objectives (half-yearly)?
- What is the reaction of the project environment (key stakeholders, local policies and strategies)? Do assumptions hold?
- Are the risks that the project team and manager are exposed to still reasonable?

Progress is reported in a standardised format to allow for comparisons over time. Reports give updates on achievements with indicators and milestones. Data regarding intended achievements in comparison with actual achievements identifies deviations from the initial plan and highlights problems and opportunities to take corrective action.[78]

To verify whether all monitoring activities are cohesively included, one may have recourse to the following questions, elaborated by the United Nations[79]:

- Are activities executed according to schedule?
- Are outputs achieved as planned?
- If not, what are the causes for the discrepancies?
- Are original milestones and expected end product feasible?
- Were major discrepancies integrated and reworked in the Log-Framework?
- Did any assumptions arise or new risks appear that are a project kill so that an evaluation is needed?
- Were corrective measures taken in case of deviations from the plan?
- What are the responses of the stakeholders (especially target group and beneficiaries)?

5.4 Evaluation

Evaluation is a systematic quality management assessment of an ongoing or finalised project as regards design, implementation and output, performed by an external party. *An evaluation should provide information that is credible and*

[77]Richardson (2015).

[78]EuropeAid Co-operation Office (2002).

[79]United Nations Development Programme (2009).

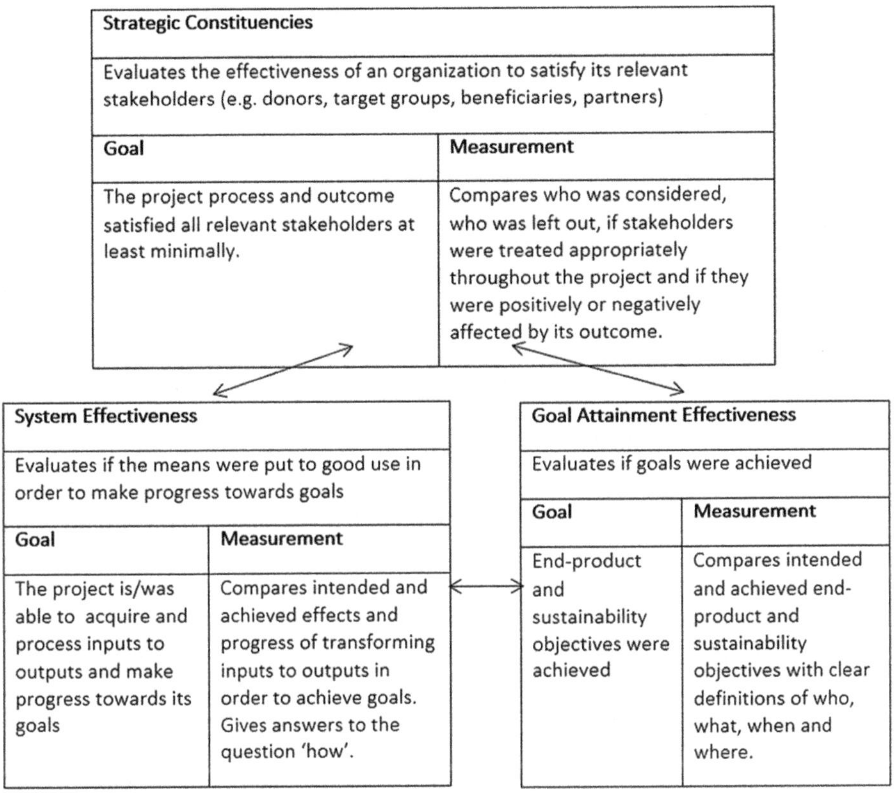

Fig. 3 Balanced evaluation card to project management evaluation. Developed by the authors, Sabrina Herold and Bartjan W. Pennink

useful, enabling the incorporation of lessons learned into the decision-making process of both recipients and donors.[80] The *big five* evaluation criteria are efficiency, effectiveness, impact, relevance and sustainability and can be described as follows[81]:

- *Efficiency* refers to the degree to which inputs were used in a productive manner to create the largest possible amount of high-quality outputs.
- *Effectiveness* describes the degree to which the project achieves its end product and sustainability objectives through its outputs. Efficiency is thus a part of effectiveness. It can be measured on various levels (see Fig. 3).
- *Impact* refers to changes that a project has made to its surroundings, either of positive or negative nature. Environmental Impact Assessment and Economic

[80] *Ibid.*; OECD/DAC (1998).

[81] European Commission (2005).

and Financial Analysis similar to the Pre-impact Analysis conducted in the planning stage are relevant here.
- *Relevance* refers to the degree to which a project is needed and thus to the very first stage of the PMC.
- *Sustainability* refers to the degree to which a project's sustainability objectives have been met from an ex-post project perspective.

Effectiveness is further described in the balanced evaluation card (Fig. 3), which unites three different approaches of project effectiveness: *goal attainment*, *system* and *strategic constituencies*. As the United Nations Development Programme states correctly, it is important to balance between what has been done, how this has been done, what were the results and who was involved in relation to each other; while for different situations and in different types of evaluations (timing) each of the three components may have a different weighting, all of them are jointly important for final and ex-post evaluation of humanitarian aid projects.[82]

Depending on the purpose and use of an evaluation, timing can be determined.[83] Three different types of timing in an evaluation can be distinguished:

- *Ex-ante* evaluation includes feasibility studies in the selection of project options and the design and planning phase. Evaluations conducted during implementation are referred to as 'mid-term'. They review progress made and, if necessary, propose major alterations of project design. While changes in monitoring refer to fine-tuning or incremental change of action, evaluation may lead to a very novel way of thinking that may drastically alter project design for the remainder of the project implementation phase.[84]
- *Mid-term* evaluation proves if the project is still feasible and needed halfway to project completion.
- *Final* evaluation takes place at the very end of the project to document inputs, outputs and achieved result, which is most favourably the end product. This evaluation serves to draw general lessons from the project to be used in future projects.[85]

Often overlooked but crucial for later projects is a formal closing process regarding administrative, team and third-party components. As regards the latter in particular, it is important to have a final meeting so that the funding partners, target groups, organisations, suppliers and others may not cause future liability problems to the project initiator. For the team, a review is essential to the impact of their actions.[86]

---

[82]United Nations Development Programme (2009).

[83]United Nations Development Programme (2009).

[84]EuropeAid Co-operation Office (2002).

[85]*Ibid.*

[86]Richardson (2015).

Lastly, *ex post* evaluation is carried out some years after project termination. It reviews the accomplishment of sustainability objectives.[87] Only after this evaluation is the Log-Framework completely filled in.

An evaluation checklist helps in carrying out assessments[88]:

- What was the project's intended achievement?
- Was the problem defined correctly?
- Is the end product still relevant for the problem?
- Was the programme appropriate to accomplish the end product?
- Are project outcomes and/or benefits sustainable?
- Who was the target group, and what were their expected benefits?
- Were there unexpected beneficiaries?
- What would have happened if the project did not exist?
- What were the anticipated links between outputs, milestones and end product?
- Were the milestones realistic?
- Were there unexpected outputs?
- Were Log-Framework assumptions relevant and did new risks appear?
- Which lessons are to be identified to learn for the future design of similar projects?

5.5 Auditing Humanitarian Projects

Auditing is meant to control whether operations and statements comply with contractual and legal obligations. An auditor is an external expert on the auditing topic. Traditionally auditing only included the oversight of financial or legal operations, for example compliance with accounting standards Auditing now also entails performance audits, which concern efficiency and effectiveness of management.

While monitoring analyses the effectiveness and efficiency by comparing targets and actual progress as an organised management activity, an evaluation analyses the effectiveness, efficiency, relevance, impact and sustainability of actions. Auditing checks the compliance with financial and legal standard and sometimes also compares to performance best practices. Since monitoring is done continuously throughout the project, the actors can take immediate action to improve performance. Because evaluating is more thorough than monitoring, takes more time and is done only once or twice during the project and mostly after the project is terminated, it has less reactive potential during an ongoing project.

Auditing is done during and/or after a project and serves as the verification of financial records or certification of good management. It is an important activity to

[87]EuropeAid Co-operation Office (2002).

[88]*Ibid*.

satisfy stakeholders but does not contribute to attaining the end product operationally.[89] Comparative Standards can be found in the latest publication of the Sphere Project.[90] The project started in 1997, bringing together a host of humanitarian organisations to create and develop minimum standards for humanitarian action processes. Sphere has resulted in many publications and generated valuable knowledge to assist humanitarian organisations in their work.[91]

6 Managing Human Relations

Successfully managing projects requires a range of soft skills.[92] These include motivation, negotiation, effective communication, a sufficient degree of influence within an organisation to complete matters, problem solving skills, along with conflict management and leadership abilities.[93]

Project managers play a crucial role in providing their teams with a vision, creating a positive and proactive work environment, delegating tasks and acting as a role model of appropriate behaviour.[94] Managers must be able to motivate different personalities and focus on team skills and their effective use. Building team spirit between the project management team and stakeholders is essential to driving the project towards its goal, while the relationship between the manager and sponsor is important for a project's overall success.[95]

Competencies and effective skills that project managers are expected to possess vary according to project situation and size. Although a theoretical distinction between managers and leaders exists, the literature agrees that project managers fulfil both roles simultaneously, balancing the need between visionary and focused action.[96] They employ a broad perspective on stakeholder needs and environmental changes while remaining focused on achieving an effective end result.

According to Cleland and King,[97] an effective project leader to a certain degree influences superiors, peers and subordinates and is able to cooperate with stakeholders and other parties involved. He needs to have conceptual, analytical and behavioural skills, which are reflected in his four major functions:

- effectively supervising resource application (human and conceptual skills);

[89] *Ibid.*

[90] The Sphere Project (2015) Sphere for Monitoring and Evaluation.

[91] See for details http://www.spherehandbook.org/en/.

[92] Schwalbe (2009).

[93] *Ibid.*

[94] *Ibid.*

[95] *Ibid.*

[96] *Ibid.*

[97] Cleland and King (1983).

- perceiving and reacting to changes in the environment (behavioural, analytical, human and conceptual skills);
- facilitating a working environment wherein everyone can attain social, economic and psychological satisfaction (behavioural, analytical and conceptual skills); and
- setting up of strategies (analytical and conceptual skills).

7 Conclusion

This chapter has provided insights into the utilisation of the Project Management Cycle and pinpointed the relevant knowledge management areas prominent within the iterative project management process. It has highlighted the importance of identifying a particular project need and explained the possible alterations throughout project planning and implementation due to dynamic environments. Stakeholder engagement was another important focus guiding this chapter throughout project identification, design, planning, implementation, monitoring and evaluation. Finally, the chapter has addressed the project manager's relevance for developing human relations.

References

Bishop C (2001) Project cycle management technical guide, socio-economic and gender analysis programme. Food and Agriculture Organizations, United Nations

CARE and Save the Children (2010) An Independent Joint Evaluation of the Haiti Earthquake Humanitarian Response

Cleland DA, King WR (1983) System analysis and project management. McGraw-Hill, New York

EuropeAid Co-operation Office (2002) Project Cycle Management Handbook

European Commission (2005) ECHO Manual Project Cycle Management

European Neighbourhood and Partnership Instrument (2009) Cross Border Corporation Programme (2007–2013). Retrieved March 23, 2015, from http://www.enpi-cbc.eu/go.php/eng/What_is_the_difference_between_target_gr/0/76/3/0)

Heyse L, Zwitter A, Wittek R, Herman J (2014) Humanitarian crises, intervention and security: a framework for evidence-based programming (Routledge Studies in Intervention and Statebuilding). Routledge, Taylor and Francis Group, London

Mulder FS, Pennink BJW (2014) The economic context. Chapter 7 of Heyse, Zwitter, Wittek & Herman

OECD/DAC (1998) Review of the DAC Principles for Evaluation of Development Assistance

Richardson G (2015) Project management theory and practice. CRC Press

Schwalbe K (2009) Introduction to project management. Course Technology Cengage Learning, Boston

The Sphere Project (2015) Sphere for Monitoring and Evaluation

United Nations Development Programme (2009) Handbook on Planning, Monitoring and Evaluating for Development Results

Further Reading

Adams D (1979) The Hitchhiker's Guide to the Galaxy
Alam MD, Guhl UF (2016) Project-Management in Practice. A Guideline and Toolbox for Successful Projects. Springer Verlag
Cleland DI, King WR (1983) Systems analysis and project management. McGraw-Hill

Sabrina Herold was a Master of Science (Honours) Student in International Business and Management at the University of Groningen at the time of writing this chapter and is now working as Project Manager Marketing for Strategic Partnerships at Credit Suisse AG.

Dr. Bartjan W. Pennink is Assistant Professor at the Faculty of Economics and Business of the University of Groningen.

Humanitarian Logistics

Gildas Vourc'h

1 Introduction

Long considered to be a peripheral activity by humanitarian stakeholders, logistics is now recognised as an essential activity that has great influence on a humanitarian operation's success or failure. Sometimes broadly defined as 'the processes and systems involved to mobilize people, resources, skills and knowledge to deliver assistance to vulnerable people',[1] it seems difficult to encounter a single and widely accepted definition of humanitarian logistics.[2] This is notably due to the great variety of actors within the humanitarian sector.

Despite its paramount importance to humanitarian action's effectiveness, logistics has long been regarded as a secondary support activity, and as a result logistics aspects were not taken into account in operational design and financial planning. Consequently, logistics needs were not sufficiently addressed. Beyond the obvious negative impacts of this situation on activities' quality and relevance,[3] it also generated tensions and a certain lack of understanding between logistics and operational teams.[4]

However, the development of professional humanitarian action and the determination to improve humanitarian action's quality and effectiveness pushed

[1] CARE International Emergency Toolkit, http://careemergencytoolkit.org/logistics/#a03.

[2] Van Wassenhove (2006), p. 476.

[3] Key logistics aspects – time, space, availability of goods, adequate freight means, etc. – and needs (equipment, assets, etc.) were not sufficiently taken into account.

[4] This is because operational teams could not understand delays, breakdowns, shortages, lack of adequate equipment, etc.

G. Vourc'h (✉)
Aix-Marseille University, Aix-en-Provence, France
e-mail: gildas.vourc-h@hotmail.com

© Springer International Publishing AG 2018

H.-J. Heintze, P. Thielbörger (eds.), *International Humanitarian Action*,
DOI 10.1007/978-3-319-14454-2_22

organisations towards recognising the essence of logistics, this horizontal activity, which is *crucial to the effectiveness and speed of response for major humanitarian programs.*[5]

1.1 The Importance of Logistics for Humanitarian Action

In the eyes of humanitarian stakeholders, logistics must now be considered an essential support function, without which relief activities' implementation would not be possible. Since *disaster relief is about 80% logistics,*[6] quality and efficient humanitarian assistance delivery requires effective logistics systems,[7] providing operational teams with the means necessary to carry out humanitarian activities (for example, goods or services to be distributed/used, transportation, structural, communication and security means, etc.). If logistics is a key element for emergency relief, it must be noted that post-emergency or even development activities require efficient and sufficient logistics support as well.[8]

1.2 The Development of Logistics Principles Within the Military, Business and Humanitarian Action

Logistics principles and systems were first developed within the military. An illustration of the importance accorded to logistics since ancient times can be found in Sun Tzu's classic treatise 'The Art of War', in which he wrote, '[t]he line between order and disorder lies in logistics'.[9] A more recent example of advanced military logistics is the Allied 'Operation Overlord' of 6 June 1944, which enabled the transport, landing and deployment of considerable human and material resources to combat the Nazi Regime.

After World War II, actors and institutions from the industrial and commercial sectors understood that improvements in their logistics systems and capacities were necessary in view of developing their activities and generating more income—notably through an enhanced and more rational supply chain management. Therefore, from a business point of view, 'logistics or supply chain management is recognized as a strategic and value-producing component in the overall operation

---

[5]Thomas (2003), p. 3.

[6]Van Wassenhove (2006), p. 475.

[7]CARE International Emergency Toolkit, at International Emergency Toolkit, http://www.careemergencytoolkit.org/logistics/#1.1.

[8]As logistics management will have impacts on the quality and durability of post emergency and development activities.

[9]Sun Tzu, The Art of War.

of commercial organizations'.[10] More recently, notably throughout the 1990s, the approach of humanitarian stakeholders towards logistics has changed: 'It is only recently that humanitarian organizations...have tried to break free of the vicious circle by pin-pointing logistics and supply chain management as key to a relief operation'.[11]

The first part of this chapter focuses on the definition of *humanitarian logistics*, its components and particularities (2). The second part introduces the humanitarian supply chain with specific attention given to some of its most central parts: needs assessment and planning, procurement, transport and warehousing (3).

2 Definition, Scope of Application and Fundamental Specificity

2.1 A Definition 'Open to Loose Interpretation'[12]

Classically, *logistics*[13] has been defined as 'the practical arrangements that are needed in order to make a plan that involves a lot of people and equipment successful'.[14] Nevertheless, it seems that there is no clear consensus on the definition of *humanitarian logistics* within the humanitarian community.

Therefore, *to many humanitarians, the definition of logistics is open to loose interpretation*,[15] and the great variety of humanitarian stakeholders contribute to a certain diversity in terms of systems and processes. In 2005, A.S. Thomas and L.R. Kopczak proposed a definition referring to

> the process of planning, implementing and controlling the efficient, cost-effective flow and storage of goods and materials, as well as related information, from the point of origin to the point of consumption for the purpose of alleviating the suffering of vulnerable people. The function encompasses a range of activities, including preparedness, planning, procurement, transport, warehousing, tracking and tracing, and customs clearance.[16]

In fact, the range of *humanitarian logistics* seems to be wider and includes additional activities,[17] without which the quality or feasibility of humanitarian operations would be questioned, such as communication and IT management, real estate management, equipment and asset management, etc.

---

[10]Thomas (2003), p. 4.

[11]Van Wassenhove (2006), p. 476.

[12]*Ibid.*

[13]From late lat. *logisticus* of calculation, computation, from Greek *logistikos*, skilled in calculation, rational.

[14]Dictionary of Contemporary English, New edition, Pearson Education Limited, 2009.

[15]Van Wassenhove (2006).

[16]Thomas and Kopczak (2005), p. 2.

[17]The definition by A.S. Thomas and L.R. Kopczak mainly refers to supply chain management.

According to the Logistics Cluster, even if 'many terms are. . .used interchangeably, in literature and in the humanitarian world', the fact that humanitarian logistics includes supply, material management and distribution is 'one quite frequently accepted view in the humanitarian sector'.[18] A transversal definition of humanitarian logistics has been given by M. Fabrice Perrot, Head of Logistics of NGO Solidarités International: '[L]ogistics is a support service that provides operational teams with appropriate material and structural resources required for humanitarian activities' implementation'.[19]

This chapter does not address the full range of humanitarian logistics components but will focus on supply chain management as this component is of critical importance for humanitarian relief activities' effectiveness.[20]

2.2 *Particularities of Humanitarian Logistics*

Aside from its obvious differences with military logistics or commercial logistics (notably, among many others, in terms of finality), humanitarian logistics has its own characteristics and particularities[21]:

- Humanitarian logistics usually operates in complex environments (due to geographic constraints, accessibility issues) and/or in volatile contexts (from the security and political point of view) and as a result requires adequate context and security follow-up, as well as adapted, specific and robust materials, assets and equipment.
- Humanitarian logistics generally operates under time pressure (as efficient and effective assistance has to be delivered in a timely manner), and therefore logistics systems must be reactive, adaptable and flexible.
- Many humanitarian stakeholders are dependent on donors' financial contribution, which can be problematic since donors tend to set up specific rules (notably for procurement) and can be perceived as reluctant to fund the entirety of stakeholders' logistics needs.[22] Humanitarian action is guided by fundamental principles (humanity, neutrality, impartiality, independence), which also have to be respected in the logistics area. In addition, humanitarian logistics has its own principles[23]: transparency (in all logistics components and phases),

[18]Logistics Cluster, http://log.logcluster.org/preparedness/logistics/index.html#introduction.

[19]Perrot (2015), p. 5.

[20]However, equipment, communication, IT, security management etc. are not to be considered secondary logistics activities.

[21]See notably Van Wassenhove (2006), pp. 477–479.

[22]Donors push stakeholders to be careful in their budget proposals with the ratio between funds allowed to direct activities implementation and funds allowed to support activities.

[23]Logistics Cluster, http://log.logcluster.org/response/procurement/index.html#procurement-in-the-humanitarian-context.

accountability (to donors and to beneficiaries) and efficiency with cost-effectiveness (assistance has to be efficient, and financial resources have to be used in a manner relevant to goals). Organisations must also keep track of ethics guidelines[24] and adhere to the 'do no harm' principle (notably through *clever* procurement, which will avoid causing disturbances in local markets).
- Humanitarian logistics operates in a crowded environment, and the great diversity of stakeholders must push them to coordinate their efforts to ensure efficient assistance delivery.

2.3 Logistics and Coordination

'Coordination saves lives.' Despite the clarity of the United Nations Office for the Coordination of Humanitarian Affairs' (OCHA) motto, humanitarian actors still have to pursue and redouble their efforts in terms of coordination, notably in order to

- enable more efficient quality assistance (as coordination allows relevant allocation, distribution and use of logistics resources); and
- respect the fundamental principles and pay attention to cost-effectiveness (coordination allows avoidance of duplication and overlaps and therefore losses of time or the misuse of resources).

The Logistics Cluster *is responsible for coordination, information management, and, where necessary, logistics service provision to ensure an effective and efficient logistics response takes place in each and every operation.*[25] It plays a key coordinating role by facilitating interagency interoperability and collaboration and, if needed, implements a set of logistics activities. Both during emergencies and post-emergency situations, it supports humanitarian organisations with (among others) coordination, information management, importation of humanitarian consignments, storage services, road and sea transport services, air transport services, purchase and distribution of fuel, cargo tracking, etc.[26] The Logistics Cluster's lead agency, the United Nations World Food Programme (WFP), developed two other logistics support network: the United Nations Humanitarian Response Depot (UNHRD) and the United Nations Humanitarian Air Service (UNHAS).

---

[24]For example, organisations avoid working with companies not respecting child labor prohibition, or buying raw materials of unclear or unknown origin.

[25]The Cluster Approach '*was designed to facilitate the formation of groups of organizations, organized by sector, which would work together to improve humanitarian response*'. It has been adopted in the framework of the Humanitarian Reform. Logistics Cluster, http://www.logcluster.org/logistics-cluster.

[26]Logistics services further include emergency response operations, service portfolio, coordination, information management, warehousing and transport, among others.

3 The Humanitarian Supply Chain

Supply chain management is a crucial component of humanitarian logistics. It refers to '…planning, implementing and controlling the efficient, cost-effective flow and storage of goods and materials, as well as related information, from the point of origin to the point of consumption for the purpose of alleviating the suffering of vulnerable people'.[27]

These networks '[consist] of suppliers, manufacturers, distributors, retailers and customers'[28] supporting three types of flows (material flows, information flows and financial flows). Due to the particularities of humanitarian logistics (which operates in complex and evolving contexts), supply chains have to work with uncertainty and risk and must be *multiple, global, dynamic and temporary*.[29] In emergencies, emphasis will be put on efficiency and time consideration, whereas organizations will focus on global quality during post-emergency phases.

This chapter focuses on the most critical steps of the humanitarian supply chain: needs assessment and planning, procurement, transport and warehousing.

3.1 Needs Assessment and Planning

Humanitarian assessments must necessarily take logistics aspects into account. Logistics assessments ensure the feasibility and effectiveness of the humanitarian response, by determining how it can be concretely implemented. *Assessing the logistics implications as early as possible in the project cycle ensures that the logistical feasibility and cost of the proposed project are fully taken into account.*[30]

A logistics assessment refers to 'the process of gathering, analysing and disseminating logistics related data and information in relation to the impact of a disaster. It determines the extent of the impact (through a situational assessment) and the logistical needs (through a capacity assessment)'.[31] All the information gathered in the logistics assessments will have direct impacts (material, financial) on the humanitarian response definition, in terms of feasibility, time efficiency and cost-effectiveness.

From the supply chain perspective, logistics assessments will notably focus on procurement, transport and warehousing (identification of needs, potential suppliers or partners, networks and infrastructures, financial aspects, etc.). Potential restrictive factors (for example, security, authorities' policies and behaviour, infrastructural condition, etc.) are also to be considered.

---

[27] Thomas and Kopczak (2005), p. 3.

[28] Van Wassenhove (2006), p. 480.

[29] *Ibid.*

[30] CARE International Emergency Toolkit, http://careemergencytoolkit.org/logistics/#4.2.

[31] *Ibid.*

Moreover, these assessments are great opportunities to receive important information about the beneficiary population's social, environmental and cultural habits, which must be taken into account to ensure an adapted response (for example, population's dietary habits, ways of using or consuming the goods, social structures, gender roles and norms, minorities' specific needs, etc.).[32]

3.2 *Procurement of Relief Goods and Services*

Procurement aims at ensuring that relief goods and services *are of the right quality, from the right source, are at the right cost and can be delivered in the right quantities, to the right place, at the right time*.[33] It plays a key role within the supply chain since poor procurement performance can delay or even jeopardise relief operations.[34] Thus, procurement needs anticipation and pushes humanitarian stakeholders to work on their emergency preparedness by taking various actions,[35] which aim at improving their capacity to mobilise quickly and efficiently.

The Logistics Cluster defines procurement as 'the process of identifying and obtaining goods and services. It includes sourcing and purchasing and covers all activities from identifying potential suppliers through to delivery to the users or beneficiaries'.[36]

The main steps of the humanitarian procurement process are sourcing, supplier selection and contracting. Humanitarian stakeholders must have clearly defined procurement rules and policies (defining how purchases, relationships with external actors or internal control has to be managed, among others) in order to ensure the delivery of the needed assistance in compliance with the six rights and with donor requirements.[37] Simplified emergency procedures should be enacted to ensure fast-enough procurement, meeting emergency needs and, in the meantime, ensuring sufficient levels of accountability.[38]

[32]CARE International Emergency Toolkit, http://careemergencytoolkit.org/logistics/#4.1.

[33]Logistics Cluster, http://log.logcluster.org/response/procurement/index.html#procurement-objectives.

[34]CARE International Emergency Toolkit, http://careemergencytoolkit.org/procurement/#a03.

[35]For example, organisations can (among many others): establish and update suppliers lists for emergency relief items; establish and update price list for '*classical*' relief items (ex. hygiene kits items—soap, water purification tablets, etc.; reinforce their knowledge of import and customs procedures; etc.

[36]Logistics Cluster, http://log.logcluster.org/response/procurement/index.html#definition.

[37]As not respecting donor requirements may generate financial liabilities for organisations (since irregular purchases may be disallowed by donors).

[38]CARE International Emergency Toolkit, http://careemergencytoolkit.org/procurement/#a08.

3.3 Transport of Humanitarian Supplies

In the humanitarian logistics scope, transport can be defined as 'the activities involved in moving supplies from point of origin to internal customers or beneficiaries'.[39] Transport planning and management can be quite complex—particularly in emergency situations or volatile contexts—as it relies on existing infrastructures, must be safe and secured, needs to be adapted to the nature of the transported goods and may have to be fast and efficient (notably in emergency situations).

Efficient humanitarian transport requires proper management of transport documents in order to ensure quality and transparent management and, ultimately, efficient and timely relief assistance delivery. Where international movements are required, organisations must pay particular attention to customs procedures and possible import restrictions.[40] Organisations must anticipate customs procedures (through an accurate knowledge and a continued follow-up of documentation, rules and procedure requirements in their potential intervention zones) in order to avoid major delays or additional and unplanned costs.[41] Transport is mainly conducted by air, road, sea and rail (Table 1).

The choice of transport modes depends on many factors, and contextual specificities[42] must absolutely be considered. As it can be difficult for one transport mode to meet all the requirements of humanitarian operations, organisations often chose multi-modal solutions (for example, consignments transported by air to main airports and by road from airports to field distribution sites).

3.4 Warehousing

Warehouses are crucial spaces in the procurement framework. Before being distributed or used, relief goods, materials and equipment must be properly stored and handled in specific and planned space. *In general, warehouses are focal points for product and information flow between sources of supply and beneficiaries. However, in humanitarian supply chains, warehouses vary greatly in terms of their role and their characteristics.*[43]

---

[39]Logistics Cluster, http://log.logcluster.org/response/transport/index.html#definition.

[40]Even if States may implement simplified customs procedures for specific items in case of emergency. These simplified procedures are notably recommended by the International Disaster Relief Law of the International Federation of Red Cross and Red Crescent (IFRC).

[41]CARE International Emergency Toolkit, http://careemergencytoolkit.org/logistics/#5.9.

[42]Time pressure, financial aspects, distance, nature of shipment, network and infrastructure, geographical, seasonal or security aspects, etc.

[43]Logistics Cluster, http://log.logcluster.org/response/warehouse-management/index.html#definition.

Table 1 Criteria of different modes of transport

Criteria	Mode: Road	Rail	Sea	Air
Relative speed	Moderate	Moderate	Slow	Very high
Reliability	Good	Good	Limited	Very good
Cost per tonne/km	Medium	Low/medium	Low/very low	High
Flexibility	High	Low	Low	Medium
Other considerations	Extensive network	Limited and fixed infrastructure	Restricted network	Limited network
	Short and medium distances e.g. Europe/Middle East. From a neighbouring country to operation site Internal transport; Short/ medium distance.	Large consignments. From port of discharge to inland operation site (warehouse). Ecological.	Large quantities; Less urgent; Pre positioning phase; Second phase; Long distance with no time constraint.	Emergency phase; Expensive goods; Fragile or perishable goods; Cold chain; No alternative option; Small shipments; e.g. diplomatic pouch; Long distance with time constraint.
Advantages	Relatively fast; No transhipment; Direct delivery; Flexible; Cost.	Economical; Large loading capacity; Range and speed (in most countries).	Economical: Large loading capacity; No restriction on loading capacity; Cheap.	Fast; Reliable; Limited losses; Direct; Easy tracking and tracing.
Disadvantages	Roads may be dangerous (land mines) or blocked (rainy season); Sometimes, driver's nationality or vehicle registration not acceptable.	Difficulty finding freight cars; Delays; Transhipment Inflexible; Tracking.	Slow: Transhipments at ports; Use as a second means of transport for large volumes; Higher theft risk in the port; Not flexible.	Expensive; Restricted to journeys between airports: Restricted loading capacity (dangerous goods, size of shipment, weight, fuel, size of packages, etc.).

Reproduced by kind permission of The Fritz Institute, Chartered Institute of Logistics and Transport (CILT) and The Certification Advisory Group (Unit 4, Transport 20/2) from Certification in Humanitarian Logistics

Global warehouses are generally facilities specifically built and designed and managed by permanent teams (pre-positioning of key relief resources might allow for more efficient and timely humanitarian response),[44] whereas field warehouses are usually temporary warehouses. The types of structures vary (tents, rub halls,

[44]Logistics Cluster, http://log.logcluster.org/response/warehouse-management/index.html#global-warehouses.

local or modern concrete buildings—adapted or, less often, built on purpose by organisations).[45]

Proper management (and therefore proper human resources training and follow-up) is required as urgent humanitarian needs cannot afford chaotic or discrepant warehousing—which may lead to losses, shortages and thus delays. Proper warehousing has to be *practical and action oriented with a focus on making the humanitarian goods available as quickly and efficiently as possible, but yet at the same time accountable.*[46]

In this respect, organisations must set up efficient, transparent and meticulous stock management rules[47] in order to ensure the timely and sufficient availability of the requested items, also with respect to transparency and accountability. Nevertheless, a certain level of flexibility needs to be maintained as logistics teams must be able to efficiently address unplanned or time-pressed demands.

Various criteria have to be taken into account for warehouse identification and selection. Generally, organisations will have a specific focus on, among others:

- *basic storage needs*: nature and volume of goods to be stored, handling equipment needed, and other services required (transit, sorting or packing zones, etc.);
- *infrastructure condition and characteristics*: accessibility, size, security, proximity from other logistics infrastructures, ventilation, security.

4 Conclusion

Growing awareness of logistics' capital importance for an operations' success within the humanitarian community has led to serious and substantial improvements of humanitarian logistics systems and processes over the last two decades. Nevertheless, due to the complexity of humanitarian contexts, logistics' quality and efficiency often remain a challenge. Therefore, organisations must pursue their work in terms of preparedness, proper processes and policy implementation and search for quality and efficiency and cost-effectiveness while continuing to respect humanitarian principles and ethics.

This persistent need for improved logistics systems has become apparent through criticisms[48] of the World Health Organization's (WHO's) response to the vertiginous Ebola outbreak in West Africa, which pushed the agency to rethink its

---

[45]Logistics Cluster, http://log.logcluster.org/response/warehouse-management/index.html#field-warehouses.

[46]*Ibid.*

[47]For inventory control, stock movements controls, etc. (waybills, stock request forms, release orders, stack cards, stock reports, etc.).

[48]WHO has been criticised for its '*late*' response by a UN-commissioned panel of outside independent experts: WHO, Ebola Interim Assessment Panel, Report by the Secretariat, A68/25, 8 May 2015.

operational and logistics capacities. Thus, WHO *is right now working with the World Food Programme to establish a common operational platform, especially for the provision of logistical support.*[49]

Coordination is one of the key challenges, but despite the Logistics Cluster and organisational efforts, its importance still has to be re-emphasised.

Fabrice Perrot has stated in his lecture that

> humanitarian actors should continue their reflection upon logistics improvements. The support given by the Logistics Cluster is highly appreciable, but NGOs need to find diverse ways of improving their capacities. Logistics pooling should be more often considered as an option in order to improve effectiveness of our humanitarian responses.[50]

In addition, collaboration and coordination with other agencies (United Nations, international or national humanitarian organisations)

> [allows] NGOs [to increase] their deployment capacity, and facilitates program funding since donors carefully watch the financial ratio between logistics and operational costs. Sharing resources or using Logistics Cluster's common services allows reducing the program budget allocated to logistics.[51]

Frédéric Urlep, WHO Senior Logistics Officer, once told me that he believes

> humanitarian stakeholders must maintain their own capacities at a sufficient level, particularly during and after post-emergency phases. Organizations (and most particularly NGOs) have to seek and find diverse partners able to bring them logistics support. UNICEF for example can be a partner of choice, by bringing substantial logistics support through the PCA[52] system.

Since adequate logistics systems and effective coordination are key elements of successful humanitarian operations, continuing improvement efforts are fundamental.

References

CARE International Emergency Toolkit. http://careemergencytoolkit.org/logistics/#5.9

Logistics Cluster, Logistics Operational Guide, http://dlca.logcluster.org/display/LOG/Logistics+Operational+Guide+(LOG)+Home

[49]Report by the Director-General to the Special Session of the Executive Board on Ebola, Special Session of the Executive Board on Ebola, Geneva, Switzerland, 25 January 2015.

[50]Perrot (2015).

[51]*Ibid.*

[52]Programme Cooperation Agreement, referring to a collaborative implementation of a jointly—developed programme or humanitarian intervention, within the framework of a UNICEF Country Programme of Cooperation. PCAs allow UNICEF to provide key logistics services (procurement, storage, etc.) to partner organisations.

Perrot F "La logistique humanitaire", teaching module of a lecture given on the 22nd of January 2015 at Institut d'Etudes Humanitaires Internationales, Aix-en-Provence, p. 5, https://facdedroit.univ-amu.fr/iehi

Sun Tzu, The Art of War

Thomas AS, Kopczak LR (2005) From logistics to supply chain management. The path forward in the humanitarian sector. Fritz Institute

Van Wassenhove LN (2006) Blackett memorial lecture - humanitarian aid logistics: supply chain management in high gear. J Oper Res Soc 57:476

Further Reading

Thomas A (2003a) Humanitarian logistics: enabling disaster response. Fritz Institute

Thomas A (2003b) Why logistics? Forced Migr Rev 18:4

Gildas Vourc'h is a Lecturer at the Institut d'Études Humanitaires Internationales of Aix-Marseille University, France. He has worked as Programme Manager, Logistician, Field Coordinator and Country Director in the humanitarian sector in many parts of the world.

Security Management in Humanitarian Organisations

Bob Ghosn

1 Introduction and Definitions

Humanitarian organisations tend to follow a rather ambiguous approach to security. On the surface, they usually recognise the value of professionally managing their security. However, security management is still too often seen as an alien concept grudgingly imported into the humanitarian world.

There is still a strong belief that good intentions, morals, international law and an often self-proclaimed humanitarian mandate are enough of a shield to ensure the security of humanitarian organisations. Facts in the field negate this belief daily, often in a sad and cruel way.[1] From Syria to Mali, it is clear today that for humanitarian organisations to remain relevant for the lives of people in need, they have to develop effective security management systems that allow them to meaningfully operate in dangerous environments. This chapter explores the main features of effective security management in humanitarian organisations, discussing concepts that are very common in the humanitarian literature. However, these concepts are often defined differently by different experts and organisations. For the purpose of this paper, we use the following definitions.

Security is achieved when the risks for an organisation, its staff and its beneficiaries in a specific geographical area of operation are identified, assessed and mitigated.

Special thanks to Sadia Bundgaard for her valuable editing of this text.

[1]According to Aid Worker Security Database, in 2014, 190 major attacks targeted humanitarian workers, http://www.aidworkersecurity.org.

B. Ghosn (✉)
Independent Humanitarian Worker, Brussels, Belgium
e-mail: solferino1859@gmail.com

© Springer International Publishing AG 2018

H.-J. Heintze, P. Thielbörger (eds.), *International Humanitarian Action*,
DOI 10.1007/978-3-319-14454-2_23

Risk is the possibility of harm or injury occurring. Each risk is a factor of a threat and a certain level of vulnerability.

A *threat* is an event that might occur and could cause harm or injury to staff members or beneficiaries, loss or damage to property or equipment, programme disruption, damage to the organisation's reputation. Threats are analysed through two criteria: the likelihood of their occurrence and their impact if they occur.

Vulnerability denotes how exposed an organisation is to each threat. It can stem from factors either at the organisational level such as identity, perception or programmes or at the individual staff level such as nationality, gender, behaviour and perception. Two examples may help to illustrate this point: in an area that poses a security threat for European staff due to kidnappings, the vulnerability of an organisation to this specific threat depends on the number of European staff deployed. On the other hand, an organisation implementing vaccination campaigns in areas were vaccination is ill-viewed by certain armed groups is vulnerable to threats by these groups because of the very nature of its programmes.

Impact is the consequence of a threat that actually occurs and may affect staff, beneficiaries, the organisation and the programmes.

A security plan contains documents that include context and risk assessments, a security strategy, as well as the procedures that staff should follow to manage security risks. A model security plan has been designed by the European Interagency Security Forum (EISF).[2]

As explained, a threat is the result of the likelihood of an unwelcome event combined with its actual impact. Consider the following example: an organisation is working on monitoring human rights violations in a certain area and collects testimonies against perpetrators. The organisation might assess the likelihood of armed actors accessing these sensitive data as very low. However, should it happen, the impact on the population would be dire as armed groups would certainly want to retaliate and silence possible witnesses. The threat for data security is thus higher than the simple likelihood of data theft because its adverse impact would be very high. Threats should therefore be assessed based on the likelihood of their occurrence and their impact. A mathematical formula allows us to illustrate how the importance of a threat is the result of a combination of its likelihood to happen and impact:

$\text{threat} = \text{likelihood} \times \text{impact}$.

A risk is the result of a combination of threat with vulnerability. We can also illustrate it by a mathematical formula:

$\text{risk} = \text{threat} \times \text{vulnerability}$.

A combination of the two formulas leads to the following equation:

$\text{risks} = \text{likelihood} \times \text{impact} \times \text{vulnerability}$.

These formulas illustrate how security management aims to keep risk as low as possible by reducing or mitigating vulnerability, likelihood and impact.

[2]See European Interagency Security Forum: Security to go: a risk management toolkit for humanitarian aid agencies, http://mhpss.net/?get=263/Security-to-go_A-Risk-Management-toolkit-for-humanitarian-Aid-Agencies3.pdf.

Thus, security management as part of humanitarian operations requires humanitarian actors to constantly heed a number of fundamental pillars:

- Recognise the different security threats.
- Assess each threat's likelihood to actually occur and its impact in case it does.
- Determine the organisation's vulnerability to each threat.

Based on these assessments, one may determine security risks and design security plans. Security plans aim to reduce risk and mitigate impact, focusing on a combination of measures to reduce

- the likelihood of a threat;
- the vulnerability of the organisation to a threat; and
- the impact of a threat when it occurs.

Consider the following example: there is an increase in night-time robbery in an unspecified context in an unspecified area. Humanitarian organisations should identify this new trend through constant monitoring of the situation and review their security plans to find ways to reduce the newly augmented threat. They could, for example, decide to set up a curfew for the staff (ban night travels) and provide safe transportation for the staff after working hours. Both measures reduce the likelihood of night robbery in the streets. Organisations could also ensure that the staff does not carry valuable or sensitive equipment or data when outside the office, thus reducing the impact of a possible incident.

Risks should be constantly monitored as they continuously vary based on political, military or social developments. This is especially relevant in volatile environments where humanitarian actors operate on a regular basis. Security measures are only useful as long as they match the actual risks. In the example at hand, the measures implemented would lose their relevance in the wake of a new threat of house robberies. Thus security management should always remain contingent to changes in the security landscape and adapt according to these.

2 Context Assessment and Stakeholder Mapping

The first cornerstone of security management is to know and understand the context an organisation operates in. Different contexts will generate different risks, thus requiring different sets of security measures and mitigation strategies. Context analysis is an essential prerequisite for comprehending the environment that organisations operate within and in understanding the dynamics at stake. Such assessment usually includes acquiring knowledge about all or part of the following issues:

- history and politics of the context;
- main religious practices and beliefs;
- different ethnic/religious/cultural groups, geographic distribution and living habits;

- interaction between said groups;
- wealth distribution, main source(s) of revenue, poverty pockets;
- technology landscape, most used communication tools, Internet penetration, cell phones, mobile Internet, most followed and used sites;
- criminality levels, most common crimes, geographical distribution, prison system;
- legal framework (both official and customary), law and order;
- law enforcement: different agencies, capacity, integrity, allegiance, agenda and focus, training;
- corruption: petty and larger, prevalence, social acceptance;
- geography, transport and commerce routes;
- main political stakeholders, the structure of their constituency, their political aim;
- main armed groups, their funding and military capacity;
- other humanitarian/development actors, their current focus and future plans.

This is a non-exhaustive list and should be adapted to each context. Wherever possible, assessing trends should be preferred to static snapshots; for example, the trends of criminality in the last six months is more telling than detailed crime statistics for the last month.

Clearly, the context assessment's value is not restricted to security assessment. It is also of great value for programming. Good programming and effective security management operate hand in hand and rely on each other at every step. Organisations should approach security management as an integral part of programming, as we discuss below.

Context assessment is time and resource intensive. It is, however, the basis of effective security management and proper humanitarian programming. The context assessment should be constantly reviewed to reflect changes in the field reality. A good context assessment should be designed to allow for updates and offer the possibility of reading trends and changes.

3 Security Stakeholder Mapping

Security stakeholders are the main actors that are influenced in the security area. They include law enforcement agencies, armed groups, private actors with security clout, etc. A list of such stakeholders should include any group capable of jeopardising the security of organisations if it decides to do so. The purpose of this mapping is so that the concerned humanitarian organisation understands the security dynamic in its area of work. Security stakeholders are usually plotted on a matrix that reflects their interest in and support to the organisation, as well as their power and influence (see Fig. 1). Based on this mapping, the organisation will decide how to interact with security stakeholders.

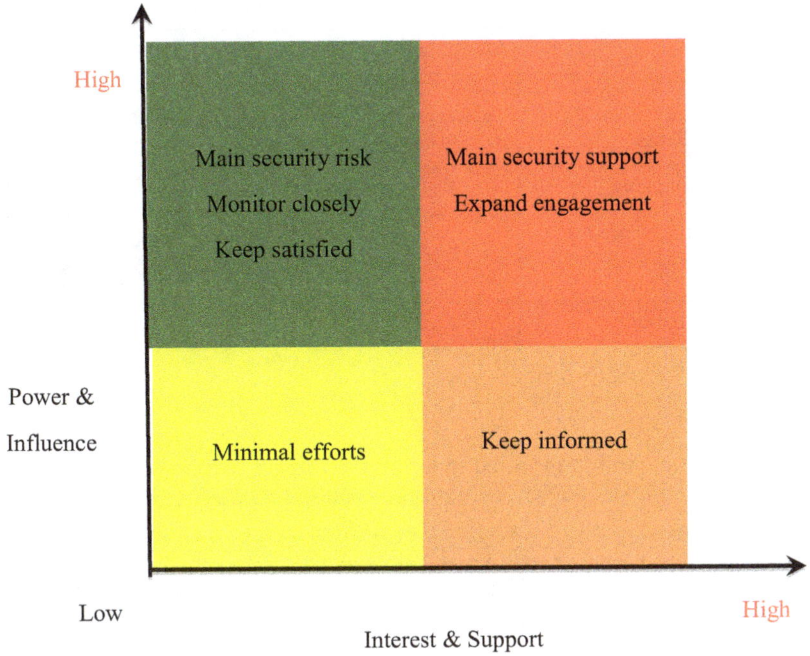

Fig. 1 Security stakeholders. Developed by the author, Bob Ghosn

4 From Context to Risk Assessment

Based on the context assessment, organisations should list all threats in the context given. For each threat, the organisation concerned should identify likelihood and impact, as well as its vulnerability to it.[3] Usually, humanitarian organisations assign figures to likelihood, impact and vulnerability in order to be able to compare risks (see Table 1).

- In this case, the likelihood of a car accident is considered high because the organisation has had several accidents over the last months. Their impact is also high because they generate high tension with the local population. Locals often block the organisations' vehicle from passing through their village, weeks after accidents. The vulnerability is also high because the organisation relies very heavily on car trips.
- Riots are very likely to happen. Tension has been simmering for weeks, and several leaders are calling for demonstrations. Last year, similar demonstrations turned into riots for days. Downtown shop owners were seen moving their valuables to other location and covering shop windows with steel curtains. If

[3]See definitions above for Impact, Threat and Vulnerability.

Table 1 Threats and risks for humanitarian organisations in dangerous areas

	Threat	Likelihood	Impact	Vulnerability	Risk level
1	Vehicle accident	3	3	3	27
2	Riots	4	3	2	24
3	Carjacking	4	4	4	64
4	Staff sexual violence/ rape	2	5	4	40
5	Kidnapping	2	5	5	50

Developed by the author, Bob Ghosn

the organisation's office is looted in a riot, the impact will be high because they store a lot of valuables, sensitive data and cash in the office. However, the office is not very vulnerable to riots since it is located in an area that is remote from downtown, where demonstrations and riots usually happen.

- There have been several carjackings in the last weeks, and the trend is increasing. Carjacking will have an important impact because it touches upon the staff's physical safety (in previous carjackings, violence was used against passengers). They are vulnerable to it because they rely very heavily on car trips on the very roads where carjacking has occurred in the past.
- Sexual violence/rape is not very likely to occur. The last case happened two years ago, and perpetrators were publicly brought to justice. Its impact would obviously be enormous as it touches upon the physical integrity of the staff. They are very vulnerable to attacks because they often have all-female teams working in the field on reproductive health with women's groups.
- Abductions are not very likely. There have not been any in the area. However, abducting humanitarian workers is now a global trend. Its impact would be obviously huge, as it threatens the life of the staff. They are very vulnerable to it because they never took any measures to mitigate this risk since no such incident ever occurred in the area.

5 From Risk Assessment to Security Planning

Based on the risk analysis, humanitarian organisations will devise or update their security plans to mitigate the risks or impact of threats. Priority should be given to the highest risks.

For instance, analysing our case above, one finds that carjacking (3) poses the highest risk for humanitarians. The organisation concerned can, for example, explore the following security measures to mitigate this problem:

- Consider alternate routes that are safer (decreases likelihood).
- Explore how to reduce car travel by setting up bases near target areas where the staff can stay overnight and reduce car travel (decreases likelihood).
- Use air travel if possible (decreases likelihood).
- Approach other organisations to organise convoys when travelling (decreases vulnerability).
- Set up a two-vehicle travel rule (decreases impact).
- Approach authorities to request more security/patrolling on the travel routes (decreases likelihood).

The second-highest risk is abduction (5). This is a risk that the organisation has never considered before. Thanks to the security assessment, it is now on the table, and security planning regarding this risk should start. The organisation can, for example, explore the following first actions:

- Check with other organisations regarding their assessment of the abduction risk and how they deal with it.
- Who should do what? How to react? Review your entire security plan in view of an abduction.
- Review passive security in the office and living quarters in view of abduction risk.
- Have discussions with your staff about kidnapping risks and listen to their concerns and suggestions.
- Ensure that some measures are taken to mitigate the abduction risk.

The third-highest risk stems from sexual violence/rape (4). The organisation can, for example, explore the following security measures to mitigate this risk:

- Change the practice of all-female teams and always have a male accompanying female teams (decreases vulnerability).
- Engage in a discussion with female staff about how they feel about this threat and what measure they suggest to mitigate it. All of their recommendations should be received with a very welcoming ear.
- Ensure that post-rape kits are readily available and psychosocial support is readily available either in-house or outside the organisation (decreases impact).

Vehicle accidents (1) cause the second-lowest security risk. The organisation can, for example, explore the following security measures to mitigate this risk:

- Explore how to reduce car travel by setting up bases near target areas where the staff can stay overnight and reduce car travel (decreases likelihood).
- Use air travel if possible (decreases likelihood).
- Set up lower speed limits (decreases both likelihood and impact).

Although riots rank lowest on the risk level scale, they still constitute a significant risk. The organisation can explore security measures to mitigate this risk. They include reviewing the relevance of holding valuables and sensitive data in the office and considering to secure cloud storage of data and the storage of valuables in different locations (reduces impact). As mentioned above, the risk assessment and the matching security plan should be constantly reviewed and adapted to ensure they reflect the reality in the field.

6 Securing People Not Career Paths

It is important that all security measures adopted by humanitarian organisations actually aim at reducing vulnerability to an actual risk, its likelihood or its impact. Security measures that do not actually make people safer should be discarded.

Security plans and rules should not include steps that aim at shielding the organisation or higher management from administrative or even legal consequences. This is a dangerous drift that is, unfortunately, very common in the current humanitarian landscape.[4]

This is counterproductive, as it adds an undue burden on security management. More importantly, such behaviour nurtures what we refer to as 'open umbrella culture', that is to say, the managers' focus shifts from safeguarding the security of people to protecting their careers and, sometimes, the organisation's liability in the aftermath of a possible security incident.[5] The priority drifts from mitigating the risk of an incident to ensuring that if an incident occurs, managers' careers will not be impacted. This is not only morally dubious but also a proliferating problem.

Once managers start acting on the premise of protecting their careers, this unwelcome trend may spread across the entire organisation like a wildfire. The entire security management system becomes paralysed by bureaucracy, disconnected from reality and completely risk-averse, making actual humanitarian action nearly impossible.

7 Security Is Everybody's Business

It is important for humanitarian organisations to nurture a culture of security amongst its entire staff. Security management should be portrayed as part of the identity and the daily work of the humanitarian organisation and not a stand-alone feature separate from programming and managed by security officers or managers.

Security management should be intertwined with programming. Planning aid activities without taking into account security parameters will invariably lead to unrealistic implementation plans. In addition to being a waste of time and resources, planning with no security inputs generates a series of missteps when

[4]As an example, in Iraq, a humanitarian organisation forced its staff to file leave requests before some field trips. In case of a security incident, the organisation could deny responsibility.

[5]The signs of such prevailing culture are the number of disclaimers staff are required to sign.

the organisation moves towards implementation; tension will rise within the team as planning collides with security constraints. Staff and management will be under undue pressure to speed up implementation or design and utilise often unsafe implementation means. Beneficiaries will see their expectations disappointed and their needs uncovered as the organisation will not be able to deliver on its commitment due to faulty planning.

Programming should incorporate security management to ensure that planning remains in the realm of reality and safety. At every stage of programming, from the initial needs assessment to the design period, security management should be incorporated in the process. Security management in humanitarian organisation is not what keeps the staff safe. It is an enabler that allows the delivery of humanitarian aid to those in need. Rather it is through the involvement of security management in the planning at every stage that the organisation will find ways of continuing to operate. It is the constant interaction between programming and security management that grounds the implementation plans in reality and allows a realistic chance of timely and effective implementation.

In order to ensure this strong link between security management and programming, it is primordial for staff to be trained in security and to imbibe that security is everyones responsibility and that part of their job is to contribute meaningfully to security management. In the field of security, availability of information is key. A security plan based on incomplete information will be faulty, and people will get hurt as a result. It is impossible to identify trends and risks without comprehensive access to updated information.

Having constant access to security information is essential for effective security management in a humanitarian organisation. Efforts should be made at all levels to facilitate the flow of security-related information towards the security management process. The constant flow of security information is the lifeline of security management; without it, security management is akin to running downstairs in darkness. A security plan based on incomplete information is by design a faulty one, which will not provide the needed security and will have adverse, sometimes lethal, consequences.

Continuous efforts should be made to ensure that security information flows freely towards and within organisations and feeds into security planning.

Several types of information sources are usually of security value. We have discussed the importance for humanitarian organisations monitoring online discussions and tapping into available information offered by private intelligence agencies. The two other sources of information we address here are other humanitarian organisations and the organisations' own staff.[6]

[6]There are obviously other sources of information ranging from open source media to confidential discussions with stakeholders.

8 Sharing Keeps Everyone Safe

Humanitarian organisations often compete for resources, field presence and programming. This is an unfortunate fact of the humanitarian landscape, and as much as we can lament it, it is reasonable to expect this situation to prevail.

However, humanitarian organisations need to understand that notwithstanding jockeying for funding and programming, in the field of security, if information is not shared, people will be harmed as a direct consequence.

It is therefore vital that humanitarian organisations set up, in every location, effective systems to facilitate and encourage the sharing of security information, such as security forums or security coordination meetings. The working arrangements should provide for real-time information sharing[7] to allow swift reactions to unwelcome and unforeseen developments.

In addition, headquarters should issue clear instructions to encourage the immediate and transparent sharing of security information. This should not be left to the chemistry amongst local heads of office or security managers. It should be a clear policy of the humanitarian organisation.

Lastly, organisations should commit to maintaining the confidentiality of security information accessed through the security coordination mechanism. This is key as organisations will be understandably reluctant to share privileged security information, unless they trust that it will remain confidential. Security forums should have effective and strict protocols for managing confidential data that all participating organisations are comfortable with. Humanitarian organisations will only share privileged information if they trust the confidentiality of the forum.

9 Let It Flow, Keep It Simple

Within organisations, there are often unintended impediments to easy and quick information sharing. Reporting, action plans and other working documents tend to continuously grow longer and heavier. This is not the place to discuss how humanitarian organisations are unduly overburdened by donors' bureaucratic requirements, but it is certainly an important question to discuss in appropriate forums.[8]

Regarding security, it is important for humanitarian organisations to realise that long security documents are seldom read, and, when they are, they hardly make a lasting impression and are quickly forgotten. When drafting security rules, drafters should put themselves in the shoes of a new staff member and draft the document in a way most conducive to helping the staff understand and remember the content.

---

[7]Arrangements can range from a WhatsApp dedicated group to a specific radio channel, depending on the context.

[8]The Good Humanitarian Donorship has contributed to this discussion.

Images, interactive scenarios, videos and other audiovisual support are always more effective than long texts.

Similarly, security updates (for example, a new development, a security incident or a near miss) should be concise and accessible. Lengthy forms, cumbersome processes and tedious reporting are counterproductive as they disincentivise the staff from properly reporting events in a timely manner, thus depriving the security monitoring system from possibly important elements regarding changes in the security landscape.

Humanitarian organisation should set up clear and simple ways for staff to report on all matters of security, be it a security incident, a near miss or a new security development.

The reporting system in place should be designed in a way that guarantees that

- the staff is able and comfortable to use it;
- it is always immediately available[9]; and
- received information will be swiftly processed.

To illustrate this, the reporting system in place should ensure that security information is

- not buried in lengthy operational reports;
- reported too late because the staff did not have immediate email access;
- not reported because the staff feared it would adversely affect the career of a colleague who breached security rules; and
- not acted upon because it slept in a mailbox until it lost its relevance.

10 Keep It Focused and Separate

Security reporting by staff often involves issues going beyond security matters. It often touches upon human resource issues, usually regarding staff behaviour and respect of security rules.

On the one hand, it is understandable that reporting staff may feel conflicted between the desire to provide accurate reporting and the desire not to harm themselves or colleagues.

On the other hand, effective security management requires knowledge of all information as accurately as possible without sugar-coating or blind spots.

The best way to avoid this dilemma is to keep security reporting separate from any other process or reporting. The staff should be able to trust that security reporting will be processed and solely used to actually improve security and not for any other operational purpose such as staff management, reward or penalty. The staff should be able to trust that information they report on security is only used to

[9] If preferred communication means are not available 24/7 alternate communication system should be set up, including emergency telephone numbers etc.

improve security management and for nothing else. Processes for assessing staff performance should be clearly separated from security incident reporting. It is important to build an effective firewall between the two to ensure that the staff feels confident enough to accurately and freely report security incidents.

Assessing compliance of individual staff members with security rules is essential. Each humanitarian organisation should have an ongoing process that serves that purpose. The point here is ensuring and monitoring compliance as an important task that is not separate from analysing security incidents. To illustrate with an example, organisations should constantly check that the staff buckle their seat belts and respect speed limits on the road, irrespective of whether a road accident has already occurred or not. Checks should be conducted on a regular basis, and faulty behaviour should entail consequences.

The objective of security incident reporting and analysis is to deal with the immediate consequences of the incident and improve security plans in light of an accident or a near miss. It is crucial to ensure that the management of security incidents remain focused on these objectives and does not drift into finger pointing. Defining individual responsibilities is important but should not be done within the security management processes. Individual responsibility is assessed through human resource mechanisms or ad hoc fact-finding task forces, which should remain separate from security management processes.

The following scenario may serve as an example: a team of a humanitarian organisation operating in a conflict area travels at night in an area that is deemed safe for day travel because the organisation enjoys high levels of acceptance by local stakeholders. The team is stopped at a checkpoint for 1 h. Team members are threatened at gunpoint, robbed of all their valuables and finally asked to be on their way.

In such a situation, a three-tier process should be triggered with three distinct points of focus:

- providing all needed support to the affected staff.
- review of security plans based on the incident; and
- individual staff accountability.

Each one of these processes should be implemented independently of the others to ensure each one's integrity.

The first process is ideally driven by a health specialist. It involves providing psychosocial support to staff and their loved ones as needed. We will not delve into the details of staff support here.

The second process is a security review of the incident. It focuses on understanding its impact on the current assessment of the area as safe for day travel. The fact that the incident occurred at night does not mean that it is of no consequence for day travel in the area. Typical questions include: who was manning the checkpoint? Why did they stop and threaten the team? In light of the incident, the team will review all elements that led them to conclude that the area was safe for day travel. Contacts with local stakeholders will be strengthened to better understand their perception of the organisation and the mission. There is also another important security component to this incident. During a security review, it is important to understand why the team decided to breach the security rules in the first place and drive at night. If the team was not safe in the location they were supposed to stay overnight or if the team felt it needed to get out during the night to fulfil expected tasks, this information is of crucial importance for the security reviews. Decisions have to be made to avoid repetition of similar situations. However, it is not relevant for the security review to understand whether Robert, Beatrix or Khadija decided to breach the security rule and drive by night. It is not for the security review to assess who is actually responsible for the breach and how to hold him or her accountable.

The third process aims at assessing the responsibilities behind the violation of the security rules. Travelling at night in an area that is deemed safe only for day travel is a clear breach of security rules. Why and how did the team decide to disregard the rule? Was this part of their prerogative, and if not, who overstepped his/her prerogative, and what measures, if any, should be taken against staff members?

It should be very clear to all staff members that the three processes are run independently. Each one should be led by a separate person, typically from the fields of health (first process), security (second process) and management (third process): the staff should be allowed to report and contribute freely to each process. If the firewall between the three processes is not trusted by the staff, it may alter their reporting, providing a partial, if not biased, picture of the situation, negatively impacting the quality of the three processes. The main objective of establishing separate processes is to create an environment conducive to accurate staff reporting.

Consider this second example on the importance of staff being able to report freely on security-related issues: a staff member knows that a driver's brother has joined an armed group. The driver feels he should just ignore the problem by not talking about it. He does not talk about it to his supervisor, fearing he might lose his job. If unreported, such a situation might expose the organisation to a new risk that is not part of its risk assessment. The fellow colleague and even the driver himself is more likely to report such a security development through a *security-only* channel, if he trusts that the information will only be used to assess and mitigate the risk. Based on this assessment, mitigation measures such as restricting field trips of this driver to certain areas can be put in place, and the situation may be monitored. The staff, including the driver himself, will only report the problem if they trust that this will make the entire organisation (including the driver) safer and not result in disciplinary proceedings questioning the driver's capacity to act impartially. Although the latter point might be an issue for discussion, the point here is that the staff feels that such information can be quickly and freely shared through *security-only* channels in order to improve the security of everyone. A human resource/management discussion of the issue will only come if the security risk is deemed too high after monitoring. In the meantime, the organisation security avoided a blind spot because the information was shared.

Within this approach of parallel processes, there is a need to set up a system that allows for key information to be shared across processes, to ensure a comprehensive view. This merging of information should take place at the senior management level, with the staff being informed about the proceedings from the beginning. This consolidation should focus on the important takeaways and not get bogged down in details. Before sharing the results of each process externally, some personal data can be anonymised,[10] and the organisation should ensure that information provided by the staff for specific purposes (for example, security) is not used in other ways (for example, disciplinary action) without his/her informed consent.

11 Security Management Strategies

Humanitarian organisations use a mix of three strategies to manage security risks: acceptance, deterrence and protection.

11.1 Acceptance: The Holy Grail?

Acceptance is a security management strategy that reduces threats by building relationships and trust. Acceptance is the favourite security strategy of humanitarian organisations. It is based on the reasonable assumption that a humanitarian organisation that is known and accepted within the local community will operate in a safer environment. If the local community understands and values the organisation's work, the former is more likely to act in ways that increase the latter's security, from warning it about threats to actually taking action to protect it. Acceptance is not a natural feature of humanitarian work. It cannot be assumed and must be nurtured.

Humanitarian organisations should not assume that local acceptance is a natural consequence of the good they are doing. This would be a false and dangerous assumption. Acceptance is highly dependent on a range of issues, including perception, transparency, daily behaviour and attitudes. Acceptance is achieved through daily engagement with communities and constant efforts. Even where local communities, overall, benefit from the humanitarian programme, acceptance should not be assumed.

Consider the following example: if an organisation is supporting a health care centre, this organisation should not assume that it is locally accepted by virtue of its support to this health care centre. Engagement with the community is very likely to show that issues such as access to services and possible unintended discrimination, payroll and recruitment matters, individual behaviour by staff, unrealistic expectations, as well as culturally sensitive topics such as reproductive health weigh heavily on the organisation's acceptance.

[10] Medical data from the support process should be managed in accordance with medical ethics.

Acceptance is an indispensable factor for any successful humanitarian operation, and it requires sustained engagement with all parties. However, humanitarian organisations tend to be overconfident about their local acceptance, assuming it on the basis of anecdotal elements such as welcoming behaviour of locals in a marketplace or friendly local staff. Therefore, organisations are often reluctant to recognise that they are not necessarily accepted in a community they are serving with dedication and commitment. This is very understandable from a human point of view. However, if, as it should be, acceptance is a key feature of security management, it must be approached in a dispassionate and professional manner. Acceptance is a security strategy that aims to specifically reduce identified threats. Thus, acceptance should be constantly monitored, and based on facts and trends the organisation should adapt both its security plans and daily practices in order to, respectively, take into account and bridge any observed acceptance gap.

Finally, humanitarian organisations should keep in mind that acceptance is not a magical wand that guarantees security. Sadly, there is no such thing. The highest level of acceptance is of no help to mitigate security risks such as being caught in a crossfire or faced with high levels of criminality following a breakdown in law and order. Such risks require different mitigation strategies that go beyond acceptance. In addition, in conflict settings, a good acceptance level by one party to the conflict often impacts negatively on acceptance by the opposing party. In addition, even where a humanitarian organisation is very well accepted by the local community, it remains exposed to the risk posed by actors from outside this community. For a mitigation strategy to be an effective risk, it must lead to acceptance by those who make up the source of the threat.[11]

11.2 Protection: Be a Harder Target

Protection is the second security management strategy. Protection reduces the vulnerability of organisations to a threat through a combination of passive measures and procedures. The objective of the security protection strategy is for any humanitarian organisation to become a hardened target, a target more difficult to attack.

Passive measures are physical features such as hardened walls, higher fences, stronger gates, safe room, bunkers, armoured vehicles, etc. A common example of a protection procedure is the decision by an organisation to always use two-vehicle convoys or to only allow daytime travel to prevent carjacking.

A protection security strategy does not reduce an identified threat. It reduces the vulnerability of the organisation and its impact when the threat materialises. The protection security strategy should be devised by taking into account two factors, in

[11] For details on acceptance, please refer to the Acceptance Toolkit: http://acceptanceresearch.files.wordpress.com/2012/01/acceptance-toolkit-final-for-print-with-notes.pdf.

addition to the risk assessment: the profile of the organisation's presence and the level of protection used by other actors in the area.

Visible protection features such as high walls, fences or 24-h external lighting in electricity-scarce areas are likely to raise organisations' profiles and might increase the security risk.

Security management should constantly seek to strike the right balance between reducing vulnerability without increasing risk. Security decisions regarding protection should also take into account the level of protection used by other actors in the area. The protection measures taken by the humanitarian organisation in question should be in line with those implemented by other actors. If a humanitarian organisation deploys lower security protection measures than other actors in the area, it will become, de facto, a soft target and is very likely to be attacked, for opportunistic reasons.

One key component of the security protection strategy is to implement measures that would lower the impact of a security incident when it happens. Measures such as back-door emergency exit, available evacuation vehicles, attack-resistant safe rooms, encryption and cloud storage of data are the type of measures that can be taken to lower the impact of security incidents.

11.3 Deterrence: The Credibility Choice

Deterrence is the third security management strategy. It reduces the likelihood of a threat through counter-threats or undesirable consequences. The rationale is to deter actors from harming organisations by showing that such act would have adverse consequences. A deterrence strategy does not have to carry a threat of violence. For example, in order to deter a risk, a humanitarian organisation can highlight that it will

- pursue legal action against any unlawful behaviour;
- suspend its programmes if the security of the organisation is threatened; and
- pull out of the area if the organisation is targeted.

Traditionally, humanitarian organisations are uncomfortable with the deterrence strategy. They incorrectly perceive it to be at odds with their humanitarian values. While it is obvious that humanitarian organisations are unable to continue operating if the security situation does not allow for it, they tend to bury this scenario under a blanket of denial.

If humanitarian organisations choose to allow local actors to think that, whatever happens, they will continue their humanitarian work at any cost, then other actors can be forgiven for thinking, for instance, that it is acceptable and of no consequences to unduly turn back the organisation's vehicles at checkpoints or even to rob the organisation's office when they are short on cash.

For a deterrence strategy to be effective, it needs to be credible. And credibility is a choice that every organisation has to make. It is an all-important choice and not an easy one. It will have consequences, also on security. One possible and highly debated deterrence strategy is the use of armed guards and/or armed escorts. Traditionally, humanitarian organisations are quite rightly reluctant to use such methods.

Humanitarian organisations have to apply the right mix of these three strategies. It is a subtle balance to strike as there always tends to be tension between the different strategies. This balancing act should be constantly reassessed based on updated security information.

11.4 The Elephant in the Room: Risk Transfer

The term risk transfer refers to cases in which a humanitarian organisation shifts the risk exposure to another organisation, usually a smaller implementing partner. The latter then bears the burden of facing what is usually a high-risk security situation.

When a humanitarian organisation, or a donor for that matter, enters into an agreement with a smaller implementing partner to operate in a dangerous setting, the bigger organisation, or the donor, is under an imperative moral and arguably legal requirement to ensure that the underlining rationale for the agreement is not to, even unwillingly, transfer the risk to an organisation that lacks either the capacity or foresight to properly assess it or the means to refuse the contract, due to precarious funding.

Hence, humanitarian organisations that delegate implementation to other organisations in high-risk areas should always assess implementation agreements from a risk standpoint. It is not enough for the contracting agency[12] to find that the implementing partner brings an added value from a risk management point of view such as higher acceptance that will lower the risk or the ability to keep a lower profile that will decrease the vulnerability to threat.

It is not about comparing access capacity between contracting agency and implementing partner. The latter usually fare better in this comparison, but this is beside the point. The issue here is to ensure that the implementing partner is effectively identifying and managing the risk in a manner that is consistent with humanitarian agencies' standard practices. Shifting risks to a smaller humanitarian organisation, or a contractor, without looking into their ability to safely operate by identifying and managing those risks is irresponsible, if not reckless.

[12] Here the contracting agency is the organisation that subcontracts the implementation to an implementation partner.

12 First, Know Thyself

An important element of the context analysis is for the humanitarian organisation to define its desired identity, in a specific setting. This identity is usually built around a mix between the organisation's mandate and mission, its principles and its programmes in the area. It should be concise and expressed in easily understandable language. The organisation should ensure that all staff know and understand this information and are able to communicate it clearly and consistently externally.

In the humanitarian field, as in other areas of life, deeds speak louder than words. It is therefore essential to enforce strict rules to ensure that staff behaviour is entirely consistent with the organisation's desired identity.

Humanitarian organisations should keep in mind that outside perception of the organisation very often differs from their own. The perception of a situation is very different from the points of view of a local standing in the dust when a humanitarian convoy passes through the village every day and of a person sitting in the said vehicle listening to music. This is a fact, and organisations should accept it as such and act accordingly. There is nothing wrong with listening to music and villages have to be crossed on the way to implementing humanitarian action to be implemented and help people. The point is to understand how people perceive the organisation, which helps anticipate how people will behave towards it.

Hence, it is vital to constantly monitor the organisation's perception amongst the population and continuously devise and implement outreach efforts to align outside perception as closely as possible with the organisation's desired identity. A damaging perception of the organisation should not be allowed to build up, as it could potentially increase security risks.

In addition to the perception of the organisation, the perception of every individual staff member is also an issue that organisations should monitor. Staff members are not only perceived as such; they are also seen through the prism of their nationality, ethnicity, gender, attitude, etc.

13 Effective Security Management: A Legal Requirement

On 25 November 2015, an Oslo District Court sentenced the Norwegian Refugee Council (NRC) to pay Steven Patrick Dennis, a former NRC staff, 5.5 million Norwegian krone (approximately 650,000 USD) for compensation and gross negligence. The case was widely covered both in mainstream media and humanitarian spheres. Steven Dennis and three other NRC staff were kidnapped in June 2012 in Dadaab refugee camp, Kenya. Dennis was wounded during the incident, and an additional NRC staff member was killed. The four kidnapped members of staff were released four days later, following a security operation. Dennis sued NRC, and the Oslo Court found NRC to be liable for compensation and gross negligence.

This landmark case established that a humanitarian organisation is legally bound by a duty of care towards its staff, even in very volatile environments. The Norwegian Court based its decision on a review of NRC security management, which it found below standards. It is remarkable to note that the Court probed the details of NRC security management and pointed out the following deficiencies:

- NRC decided not to use armed escorts against the recommendation of its own security team.
- Location and timing of the visit were maintained despite security concerns.
- The visit was a high-profile one with media coverage.
- NRC staff was not timely briefed about the security situation and so could not make informed decisions about participating in the visit, in full knowledge of the risks involved.

Impact and meaning of this landmark court decision has been widely discussed amongst aid workers and organisations.[13] In the wake of the decision, humanitarian organisations should prepare for a possible judicial review of their security management *modus operandi*. Appropriate and efficient security management of humanitarian operations has always been a moral and operational requirement. It is now, arguably, also a legal one. Although it is too early to foresee all legal ramifications and possible ripple effects of the Dennis decision, humanitarian organisations have to prepare for possible legal challenges to their security management and should ensure that they uphold their duty of care towards their staff.

14 The Cost Factor

Another challenge faced by humanitarian organisations is that proper security management is often expensive, while humanitarian budgets are restricted regarding security costs.

This, firstly, often forces humanitarian organisations to rely on ineffective half-cooked security management plans. However, the issue of available budgets is not the only challenge to effective security management by humanitarian actors.

Secondly, when budgets are available, humanitarian organisations should overcome a cultural resistance to invest sufficiently in security. There is a prevailing perception that humanitarian organisations are immune to risks as a consequence of the good they do and the purity of their commitment. This is factually incorrect, as shown by the high number of humanitarian workers targeted and sadly killed or harmed.[14]

---

[13]For a thorough analysis of the consequences of this case, see Hoppe and Williamson, ODI HPN, April 2016.

[14]According to Aid Worker Security Database, in 2014, 329 humanitarian workers were hurt in a security incident, 121 were killed, 88 injured and 120 kidnapped.

The third challenge regarding the security cost factor concerns security investments by humanitarian actors. Such investments should not be restricted to hardware, ranging from communication equipment to armoured vehicles, but also include technical means, training, staff and information access. All of these are crucial to monitoring security and effectively managing security risks. Humanitarian organisations should ensure that the technical means they use to monitor the security situation, such as software to aggregate trends, are up to current industry standards. Similarly, humanitarian organisations should have access to privileged information about specific contexts and situations, often provided by private intelligence agencies.[15]

Last but not least, security training by humanitarian actors should tap into state-of-the-art available training resources as the issue can literally become a question of life or death.

15 Security and Technology

Technology is increasingly intertwined with security. Still a relatively new but very promising field of action for humanitarian organisations, they should tap into the huge potential of digital technology to strengthen security management. Overall, there are five main areas to explore.

First, in many volatile contexts, where humanitarian needs are high, armed actors may have a strong social media presence on Twitter, Facebook, Telegram, etc. Monitoring and even reaching out to these groups online requires more than a Twitter or a Telegram account. Humanitarian organisations should be tech-savvy and acquire appropriate software and cutting-edge skilled staff to explore ways to effectively use the Internet and social media to identify trends that will meaningfully feed into their security analysis and improve their engagement with security stakeholders online.

Second, humanitarian organisations should dispose of an effective online presence to monitor the situation in their area of operation online, as well as their online reputation amongst security stakeholders. As we will see below, acceptance and perception are key to properly identifying and managing security risks. For example, if an armed group is frustrated by actions of a specific humanitarian organisation or falls victim to a rumour about this organisation, it is very likely that the group members will first vent their anger online. Provided with the proper equipment and staff, the organisation in question should be able to spot the social media chatter and the anger building up. It can then engage online, and in real life, to correct the misconception and, simultaneously, review its security plans, in view of

[15]The most renowned is the Economist Intelligence Unit that focuses on the economy. Some private intelligence agencies, such as Stratfor or Control risk, focus more on security while others such as Site Intel Group focus specifically on violent and jihadi groups.

this new development. This is not about spying or eavesdropping. Monitoring what is happening online is not any different from humanitarian staff traditionally engaging in mundane conversations in markets or around a teakettle to get a *feel* of the situation.

Third, humanitarian organisations should have the means to make their voice and their message heard online. A strong, professional online presence is essential in influencing perceptions, countering false assumptions, thus reducing the organisation's vulnerability to risks. In addition, in our digital age, security threats have become global. The days where security was a local matter are over. It is not enough for a humanitarian organisation to be accepted by local stakeholders in its area of operation or even in the entire country. News or rumours from a far-flung country travel thousands of kilometres at the speed of light and erupt on the screens of otherwise well-meaning security stakeholders. It can change their mood towards the organisation in a split second. In a real-life example, a humanitarian organisation that enjoyed broad acceptance in Southern Iraq had to scramble overnight and review its entire security management plan because certain Facebook postings in Somalia falsely claimed that the same organisation was poisoning Muslims. It is only thanks to effective online monitoring that the posts were spotted on time, thus allowing security arrangements to be immediately reviewed and an outreach effort to be launched to counter the false claims.

Fourth, there is an increasingly large digital dimension to analysing contexts and identifying risks. Humanitarian organisations should invest in areas such as big data analysis to explore ways of improving their security management. Google is exploring ways of anticipating flu epidemics in specific areas by analysing search queries. So far, this attempt has been labelled an 'epic failure'.[16] However, the potential of mining data for useful information is undeniable. Similarly, humanitarian organisations should explore ways of better understanding their working environment by analysing digital data. Fear of failure should not preclude innovative approaches. The connection between the digital and real world is a reality that creates both great opportunities and serious threats to humanitarian organisations. It is only by engaging in the field of digital data and pioneering new approaches that humanitarian organisations will learn how to harness opportunities and mitigate risks.

Fifth, the security management of humanitarian organisations can greatly benefit from an expert use of mapping and satellite imagery, as it strengthens the capacity of humanitarian organisation to identify and monitor humanitarian needs, as well as risks.

[16]What we can learn from the epic failure of Google flu trends, http://www.wired.com/2015/10/can-learn-epic-failure-google-flu-trends.

16 The Dangerous Double Fallacy of Zero Risk

Security management is about managing and mitigating risks. Properly identified and mitigated, risks do not disappear but can be lowered. However, it is important for humanitarian organisations to be transparent with their staff about security risks. Here again, denial is not a good strategy.

The staff should be made aware of the risks and the security measures in place to manage these. On this base, they should be encouraged to decide whether a security situation is above or below their personal security threshold. Being transparent about security risks is part of the relationship of trust that humanitarian organisations should build with their staff. It is also important for security management. Staff unaware of security risks will lower their guard, sloppily apply security rules and not look out for possible changes in the security landscape. Risk-aware staff is a key component of any effective security management.

In contexts where security risks are low, organisation should not fall for the fallacy of zero risk, thus ignoring security management altogether. Certain security risks always exist. Lower risk still require identification, management and, maybe more importantly, monitoring. It is only constant monitoring that will allow organisations to spot and identify a change in the security landscape or a new worrying trend to which they have to adapt.

17 Good Staff Management for Good Security

Staff is the most important asset of any humanitarian organisations. Their behaviour determines the success or failure of any programme, and the same applies to security risk management. We do not delve into good staff management here but highlight the strong link between staff and security management. The better the former, the more effective the latter will be.

A positive culture, good team spirit amongst staff, proper dispute management mechanisms in place and people who are willing to help each other enhance an organisation's security. This kind of environment leads to unobstructed information flows and the capacity to rapidly implement adjustments, when needed. A relationship of mutual trust between the staff and leadership nurtures a culture of security across the board where everyone feels part of the collective effort, including security management.

On the other hand, teams where staff members are unhappy and frustrated are prone to turf fights and silo thinking. This directly impacts security management as the staff members do not feel that they are part of the collective effort. Information is lost, and changes are cumbersome and slow to implement. The organisation loses its agility and timely adaptation to security changes. In addition, an unhappy staff is more likely to ignore security procedures, increasing security risks. Finally, a disgruntled staff often becomes a security threat.

Stress has a direct impact on security.[17] Under stress, people make poor decisions and often increase security risks. From a security management standpoint, it is essential for humanitarian organisations to manage the stress levels of its staff and to provide them with peer and professional support.

18 Conclusion

Security management is a key component of humanitarian action. Effective security management requires humanitarian organisations to grow and nurtures a culture of security within organisations. Contexts where humanitarian needs are the highest are increasingly violent, and this trend is likely to continue. In order to be able to operate in such violent contexts, humanitarian organisations have to improve and professionalise security management.

Security should not be an add-on to humanitarian programming. Effective security management is an enabler of humanitarian action and needs to be intertwined with programming. Planning humanitarian action without considering security management is a recipe for failure. Moreover, security management for humanitarian organisations cannot continue to rely on using non-humanitarian experts to transplant programming concepts developed by and for non-humanitarian actors into humanitarian settings.

If humanitarian organisations want to make a meaningful impact in dangerous settings, they must endeavour to improve both the theory and practice of security management, specifically for humanitarian contexts. They owe it to their staff and to the people in need.

References

European Interagency Security Forum: Security to go: a risk management toolkit for humanitarian aid agencies, http://mhpss.net/?get=263/Security-to-go_A-Risk-Management-toolkit-for-humanitarian-Aid-Agencies3.pdf

Hoppe K, Williamson C (2016) Dennis vs Norwegian Refugee Council: implications for duty of care. Online. ODI, http://odihpn.org/blog/dennis-vs-norwegian-refugee-council-implications-for-duty-of-care/ consulted on 24 June 2015

[17]For more on stress management in humanitarian organisations, please refer to the Antares Foundation (www.antaresfoundation.org) and the Headington Institute (www.headington-institute.org).

Further Reading

Allié M (2011) Acting at any price? Humanitarian negotiations revealed: the MSF experience. Hurst & Company, London
Behn O, Kingston M (2010) Whose risk is it anyway? Linking operational risk thresholds and organisational risk management. Humanitarian Exchange Magazine (47), June 2010
Collinson S, Duffield M (2013) Paradoxes of presence: risk management and aid culture in challenging environments. Humanitarian Policy Group, Overseas Development Institute
Egeland J, Harmer A, Stoddard A (2011) To stay and deliver: good practice for humanitarians in complex security environments. United Nations Office for the Coordination of Humanitarian Affairs (OCHA)
Fast L, O'Neill M (2010) A closer look at acceptance. Humanitarian Exchange Magazine, Issue 47, Humanitarian Practice Network
HAP International (2013) Guide to the 2010 HAP standard in accountability and quality management. HAP International, Geneva
Harmer A, Stoddard A, Toth K (2013) Aid Worker Security Report 2013: the new normal: coping with the kidnapping threat. Humanitarian Outcomes
Humanitarian Outcomes. Aid Worker Security Database. http://www.aidworkersecurity.org
Humanitarian Practice Network (2010) Operational security management in violent environments: Good Practice Review 8, revised edition. Overseas Development Institute
Kemp E, Merkelbach M (2011) Can you get sued? Legal liability of international humanitarian aid organisations towards their staff. Policy Paper, Security Management Initiative
Kingston M, Behn O (2010) Risk thresholds in humanitarian assistance. European Interagency Security Forum
Kingston M, Behn O Risk transfer through hardening mentalities? Humanitarian Practice Network. Online. http://www.odihpn.org/the-humanitarian-space/blog/risk-transfer-through-hardening-mentalities
Mission Ready. Online. Missionready.org.uk
Roberts DL (2006) Staying alive: safety and security guidelines for humanitarian volunteers in conflict areas. International Committee of the Red Cross
Stoddard A, Harmer A, Hughes M (2012) Aid Worker Security Report 2012: host states and their impact on security for humanitarian operation. Humanitarian Outcomes
Van Brabant K (2010) Managing aid agency security in an evolving world: the larger challenge. European Interagency Security Forum
Van Brabant K (2012) Incident statistics in aid worker safety and security management: using and producing them. European Interagency Security Forum
Wille C, Fast L (2013) Shifting patterns in security incidents affecting humanitarian aid workers and agencies: an analysis of fifteen years of data (1996–2010). Insecurity Insight

Bob Ghosn is an Aid and Human Rights worker. He has worked for several humanitarian agencies, including the International Committee of the Red Cross and the Belgium Red Cross. Views expressed here are personal.

Human Resource Management in the Humanitarian Sector

Sophie Borel

The humanitarian sector, like many others, relies upon professional staff and volunteers, with both international and local backgrounds. Human resources (HR) deals with individual and collective management of this diverse set of people who have different skills, abilities, knowledge, levels of commitment and motivations that may or may not be appropriate to the needs of national and international organisations.

Managing people can be a complex endeavour, especially in international settings with intertwining cultural, economic, technological, social and political differences that result in an intricate set of human relations. One may add to these points the specificities of the humanitarian sector, characterised by, amongst other factors, security risks, difficult living and working conditions, a relatively short span of action and a need to rapidly adapt to changes in terms of the nature of the work from one context to the next or within the same context (natural disasters, conflict situations, protracted crises, etc.).

This chapter is divided into three sections. The first section introduces some of the major ways of thinking about human resource management (HRM), referring to theory and practice from both the private and the humanitarian sectors. The second section presents the developments in HRM within the humanitarian sector, including the main external and internal trends that have affected the way humanitarian organisations manage people. Section 3 provides an overview of HR activities.

S. Borel (✉)
Network on Humanitarian Action (NOHA) General Secretariat, Brussels, Belgium
e-mail: s.borel@nohanet.org

© Springer International Publishing AG 2018

H.-J. Heintze, P. Thielbörger (eds.), *International Humanitarian Action*,
DOI 10.1007/978-3-319-14454-2_24

1 Introduction

The concept of HRM first appeared in the 1980s. HRM has by and large replaced what was up to this date commonly known as 'personnel management' and can be defined as 'a strategic and coherent approach to the management of an organisation's most valued assets—the people working there ... who individually and collectively contribute to the achievement of its objectives'.[1]

The Society for Human Resource Management defines HRM as 'the formal structure within an organisation responsible for all decisions, factors, principles, operations, practices, functions, activities and methods related to the management of people'.[2] HRM involves a wide array of activities ranging from, *inter alia*, recruitment and selection, learning and talent development, provision of contracts and equal opportunities, employee well-being, security and safety to ethics and knowledge management.

Many models of HRM have been developed over the years. They try to answer the fundamental questions related to the management of people and an organisation's effectiveness, taking into account factors such as the different skills, abilities and knowledge available or required within an organisation; the commitment and motivation of employees and volunteers; whether they are underutilised or overworked; and how to match actual performance with an organisation's needs.

Two models are briefly described below, the hard HRM model, typified by the Michigan School, and the soft approach, which is explained through the lens of the Harvard model. These two models are the best known of the early interpretations of HRM. They are a good basis for understanding the fundamental differences and ambiguities associated with HRM.

The Michigan model, also called the matching model or best-fit approach, posits that HR systems and an organisation's structure should be managed in a way that is consistent with its organisational strategy. Employees are considered to be resources in the same way as any other resource, and the role of human resources is limited to a reactive, organisational function. In this model, the human resource cycle consists of four generic processes or functions: selection, appraisal, rewards and development. This model has often been equated with *hard HRM*, an approach that is based on the quantitative, calculative and business-strategy aspects of HRM, the premise being that human resources are acquired, deployed and dispensed in order for organisations to gain a competitive advantage.

The Harvard model considers employees as a fundamentally different type of resource that cannot be managed in the same way as other resources. Employees are

---

[1] Armstrong (2006), p. 3.

[2] Lockwood, N.; Williams, S., Research Quarterly, third quarter 2008, Selected Cross-Cultural Factors in Human Resource Management, Society for Human Resource Management, p. 1, http://www.shrm.org/hr-today/news/hr-magazine/documents/september%202008%20research%20quarterly%20-%20selected%20cross-cultural%20factors%20in%20human%20resource%20management.pdf.

significant stakeholders in an organisation, having their own needs and concerns, just like other groups such as stakeholders and customers.[3] According to the Harvard Framework, there is a need for a longer-term perspective in managing people and considering them potential assets rather than merely a variable cost. The framework is based on the belief that 'without a central philosophy or a strategic vision – which can only be provided by general managers – HRM is likely to remain a set of independent activities'.[4] The emphasis is on the fact that HRM should be the concern of management in general rather than of a personnel function in particular. This model is in line with what has been coined 'soft HRM'. Soft HRM focuses on communication, motivation and leadership based on the notion that all potential must be nurtured and developed. The Harvard Map or model outlines four HR policy areas:

- *human resource flows*—recruitment, selection, placement, promotion, appraisal and assessment, promotion, termination, etc.;
- *reward systems*—pay systems, motivation, etc.;
- *employee influence*—delegated levels of authority, responsibility, power; and
- *work systems*—definition/design of work and alignment of people.

In recent years, greater attention has been given to issues confronting organisations operating in an international environment. The notion of International Human Resource Management (IHRM) thus emerged to respond to the specificities linked to multi-country operations.

IHRM explores the added complexity in HRM as a result of diversity in national contexts of operation, such as broader external influences, risk exposure, as well as mixed workforces of expatriates and nationals.[5] IHRM is concerned with HR policies and practices in the international sphere and the social, cultural, legal, economic, political and historical characteristics that impact human resources within and across different countries.

IHRM is of particular interest for humanitarian organisations because it addresses the weaknesses of a restrictive HRM approach, which has often been criticised for being culturally bound based on Western-centric models grounded in concepts of individualism and capitalism. IHRM thus provides analytical tools that can help organisations operating at the international level understand culture more comprehensively as a central element of human and working relations. It recognises the multicultural profile of organisations operating across borders and the fact that culture is a fundamental component of HRM.[6] International humanitarian organisations are intrinsically multicultural. An understanding of IHRM can therefore help humanitarian organisations develop strategies, processes and tools that are better adapted to the composition and background of their staff and volunteers.

---

[3]The Harvard Map of HRM, http://www.hrmguide.co.uk/introduction_to_hrm/harvard-map.htm.

[4]Armstrong (2006), p. 9.

[5]Peltonen, 2006 Dowling, P., and Welch, D., International Human Resource Management 2004.

[6]Harzing, A.-W.; Pinnington, A., International Human Resource Management, 4th edition 2015.

1.1 Comparative Human Resource Management

Organisations operating across national and cultural borders need to bridge the divide between being globally coherent and consistent in their HRM policies and practices on the one hand and the imperative of taking into account local variations in national, cultural and institutional requirements on the other.

Comparative HRM tries to make sense of these different factors and of the interrelations between national and organisational cultures and their impact on how people react. It studies what happens within organisations, that is, the internal context (for example, organisational size, structure and demography) and the external context (covering national cultures and values, as well as elements of the institutional environment such as legal regulations, the respective industry and type of economy).

In developing, implementing and evaluating HR systems, organisations operating in more than one country are confronted with an important set of questions: can HRM in different contexts be conducted in a similar fashion, or does it have to adapt to the respective circumstances? Is there one best model for HRM, or is it necessary to take into account specific contextual issues in order to achieve the best outcomes?

In an increasingly globalised world, the presumption is that HR policies and best practices are exportable and applicable to an organisation's operations worldwide. While a degree of adaptation is common and inevitable, the best practice approach, usually emanating from head offices, tends to predominate. Even when mechanisms are expressly established to ensure that HR policies and practices take into account national and local factors, in many cases country information tends to be stereotyped, inadequate or non-comparable. One may add the fact that it is often extremely difficult to be on top of the details of HRM expectations and common practices in each local context. HR managers are usually highly dependent on the information obtained from their expatriate managers and the (usually local) HRM practitioners in each country—who may have different agendas and understandings.

1.2 Culture and Cross-Cultural Management

Culture influences both who we are and how we interact with each other. The Society for Human Resource Management, going back to J.H. Bodley, refers to culture as 'a set of values and beliefs with learned behaviours shared with a particular society [that] provides a sense of identity and belonging'.[7] The literature on culture and its implications for IHRM abound. Table 1 succinctly illustrates

[7]Lockwood, N.; Williams, S., Research Quarterly, third quarter 2008, Selected Cross-Cultural Factors in Human Resource Management, Society for Human Resource Management, p. 1.

Table 1 (a) Different views on culture, (b) Sample questions for the analysis of a culturally influenced situation

Positivist views 'Culture and values'	Interpretive views 'Culture and meanings'	Critical views 'Culture and power'
(a)		
• Researchers search for laws and regularities	• Researchers search for meaning: how people make sense of their situation	• Researchers' investigation reveals silenced voices and hidden structures of inequality and domination
• Instrumental knowledge, predictions, developments and test of models	• Knowledge on sense-making and cognitive processes, as well as on social constructions	• Knowledge that questions and challenges exposing power relations and inequalities
Example: Cultural dimension constructs such as 'Power Distance' or 'Assertiveness', value-dimensions valid across many countries	Example: Meaning systems associated to notions such as 'leadership', 'job description' or 'competence'; local and specific knowledge	Example: Talks about 'cultural differences' used to masquerade another issue (of power); unveils structures of domination with local and specific examples
(b)		
How does culture influence this situation? Which are the cultural dimensions that can explain people's behavior? Which are the cultural dimensions' score differences between the countries/organisations? What are the characteristics of an environment scoring high/low on these dimensions? How does it apply here?	What does this situation mean to those involved? What do they associate with the situation/elements of the situation? What does the situation remind them of? Which terms, which metaphors do people use when talking about it? What are the arguments advanced, how do they make sense for the participants involved?	Is there a struggle between two camps? Who is in a position of power? Who is silenced? What is at stake? Are people collaborating? What are the risks for each camp? What is said to be 'normal' (status quo or stated situation)? Who decides? Is culture talked about explicitly? Which stake/camp does talking about cultural differences serve?

Reproduced by kind permission of the publisher from Harzing, A.-W.; Pinnington, A.: International Human Resource Management, p. 12, 27 (SAGE Publications, 4th edition 2015)

three of the main approaches used in cross-cultural management research. As shown, the different approaches can help to answer very specific questions. The answers to these questions can, in turn, help to define the HR policies and strategies based on a better understanding of the cultural context.

The positivist analysis helps to answer a set of essential questions: what are the value discrepancies that can be identified in a given situation? What are the external influences of culture to what is happening? The positivist approach is especially useful for identifying culture as a central consideration in any analysis of IHRM.

Culture is seen as providing answers to the basic needs that human beings have to fulfil; this is the foundation for what are known as cultural dimensions. The underlying premise is that some aspects of culture are universal, that is, they are valid and coherent across countries. This means that the influence of some dimensions on IRHM practices can be compared across countries.

Very interesting work undertaken by Hofstede and House, amongst others, has analysed the relationships between culture and various aspects of management, such as motivation, reward allocation, hierarchy, preferred forms of training and leadership. Table 2 shows a sample of the kinds of dimensions analysed.

The interpretive view is based on the premise that people act and interact in a way that makes sense to them, and it is the actor's point of view that is seen as most relevant to explain behaviour. The emphasis of this approach lies on the

Table 2 Sample of argued representative behaviour linked to hofstede's cultural dimensions and examples of country positioning

Dimension	High score	Low score
Power distance It is the extent to which the less powerful members of a society expect and accept unequal distribution of power.	• Centralised decision structure, more concentration of authority • The ideal boss is a well-meaning autocrat or good father, sees himself or herself as a benevolent decision-maker. • Subordinates expect to be guided. • Malaysia, Mexico, Singapore, France	• Decentralised decision structure, less concentration of authority • The ideal boss is a resourceful democrat, sees himself or herself as practical, orderly and relying on support. • Subordinates expect to be consulted. • Denmark, New Zealand, Sweden, Canada
Individualism Individualism pertains to societies in which the ties between the individuals are loose. Collectivism pertains to societies in which people are integrated intro strong, cohesive in-groups.	• Employees are supposed to act as 'economic men'. • Hiring and promotion decisions should be based on skills and rules only. • Employer–employee relationship is a business deal in a 'labour market'. • USA, Australia, Netherlands, South Africa	• Employees act in the interest of their in-groups, not necessarily themselves. • Hiring and promotion decisions take employees' in-group into account. • Employer–employee relationship is inherently moral, like a family link. • Ecuador, Panama, Indonesia, Pakistan, Peru
Long-term orientation Long-term orientation stands for the fostering of virtues oriented towards future rewards.	• Persistence, perseverance • Leisure time not so important • China, Hong Kong, Japan, Brazil, India	• Leisure time important • Quick results expected • Pakistan, Nigeria, Canada, USA

Reproduced by kind permission from Geert Hofstede, 'Culture's Consequences: Comparing Values, Behaviors, Institutions and Organizations Across Nations', Second Edition. Thousand Oaks, California: SAGE Publications, 2001, ISBN 0-8039-7323-3
Geert Hofstede, Gert Jan Hofstede, Michael Minkov, 'Cultures and Organizations, Software of the Mind', Third Revised Edition, McGrawHill 2010, ISBN 0-07-166418-1. ©Geert Hofstede B.V.

interpretations of individuals and the significance of the local context in the development of these meanings. While there are variations within societies between individuals, social groups or genders in the ways they make sense of situations, it is possible to identify similar national patterns of interpretation within countries. These are referred to as 'frames of meanings'. Meanings around notions of 'good work', a 'good organisation' or even a 'good boss' are very useful to know about since they influence what is perceived as desirable behaviour. Knowing what local meaning systems are associated to organisational practices is primordial. Inability to understand or take into account local meanings can lead to resistance, failures or difficulties in the transfer of HRM practices from one country to the next or from head offices to field offices.

Critical perspectives can contribute to diversity in management by encouraging questioning IHR managers regarding their views on diversity. Respecting cultural diversity for IHR managers goes beyond the consideration of *traditional* forms of diversity (such as gender, age, people with disability) to include, for example, religious belonging or professional training. Critical scholars pay attention to power imbalances between organisational members and sometimes highlight surprising results. For example, some assert that the discourse of IHR managers on diversity may reflect dominant views and reaffirm management practice and underlying inequalities. Critical perspectives can thus help IHR managers to realise they may involuntarily be reproducing the inequalities they intend to address. A critical approach to culture and power urges us to pay attention to how discourses are constructed and how *cultural difference* can be used to hide other aspects or to mask issues. Pre-expatriation training, for example, may implicitly reproduce stereotypes about non-Western cultures, thereby justifying the transfer of HRM practices from headquarters to subsidiaries in developing countries.

A concrete example of how these approaches can be used is reflected in a 2008 study on selected cross-cultural factors in human resource management; the study classifies organisations into four different ideal types of corporate culture based on their focus on tasks/relationships and the extent of hierarchy.[8] The four models depicted below are the result of an analysis of the approaches to work, authority, problem solving and relationship building (Table 3).[9]

Discussion

How can HR facilitate the maintenance of corporate culture identity while still ensuring that, on a local level, it is modified to be culturally relevant and appropriate?

[8] *Ibid.*, p.3.

[9] For a broader introduction into international human resources management, see Brewster et al. (2011), Foot and Hook (2008), and Pankhurst (2008).

Table 3 Examining cross-cultural factors in HR management

Model	Characteristics
The Family	Leaders set the tone. This model gives high priority to doing the right things rather than doing things right. Pleasing one's superior, for example, is considered a reward in itself. Some HRM policies, such as pay for performance, are viewed as threatening to family bonds. Countries that often use the family model: Japan, Italy, France, Spain
The Eiffel Tower	Roles and functions are prescribed within a rigid system. People are viewed as capital and cash resources. HRM strategies focus on workforce planning and performance appraisal. For example, Germany
The Guided Missile	It is described as egalitarian, impersonal and task oriented. Focus is on achieving the end goal – 'do whatever it takes'. The value of employees is in how they perform and to what extent they contribute to the overall outcome. Focus of HRM strategies is on management by objective and pay for performance. For example, United States, United Kingdom
The Incubator	The fulfilment of the individual is more important than the organisation. Egalitarian, personal and individualistic structure. Goal is innovative products of services. HRM strategies focus on rewards for innovation. For example Silicon Valley, Scandinavian companies.

Table developed by the author, Sophie Borel, based on information from and citing Lockwood, N.; Williams, S., Research Quarterly, third quarter 2008, Selected Cross-Cultural Factors in Human Resource Management; reproduced by kind permission of the Society for Human Resource Management, p. 3 (2008), http://www.shrm.org/hr-today/news/hr-magazine/documents/september%202008%20research%20quarterly%20-%20selected%20cross-cultural%20factors%20in%20human%20resource%20management.pdf (accessed on 14 April 2017)

2 Humanitarian Organisations and How They Manage People

'...[I]f you're not a professional in this game, you have no right to descend on someone in their moment of crisis and do on-the-job training. Saving human lives is no place for amateurs. Why is that? Because the poor, dispossessed and disaster-prone should have at least one basic right left to them: to be protected from incompetence.'[10]

External factors influence employment practices in general. One of them, culture, has already been mentioned above. It acts as the backdrop that shapes human relations within an organisation and should be taken into account at all levels of HRM. Against this backdrop, other external factors to be considered include the following:

[10]Egeland (2009).

- the political system and the dominant political tradition, notably the strength of organised labour and the nature of employment regulations; and
- the legal system, itself partly a product of the political system, which not only frames or constrains the range of options open to management when devising procedures in areas such as employee representation but also plays a part in conditioning the expectations of organisational actors.

In the humanitarian sector, additional external factors include, *inter alia*:

- situations and contexts of conflict that are increasingly politicised, constraining access and impacting the security of aid personnel;
- tensions around conflicting cultures and guiding principles, with some host governments expressing frustration about INGOs and their perceived lack of deference to national authority and sovereignty;
- increasingly assertive aid recipient governments, a new generation of aid donors and more progressively decentralised traditional donors who are setting the aid agenda at the country level, impacting the political, legal and practical landscape that shapes HR;
- donor policies characterised by restrictions on overhead costs, which has led to cuts in HRM budgets for most organisations; and
- private donors, including the general public, who are keen to see that their funds *go to field*, that is, are spent on concrete activities and projects. They do not consider overhead or administrative costs an efficient use of their money.

Internal factors also influence—and are shaped by—human resource policies and strategies (or the lack thereof). In general, HR has not been perceived as a strategic priority, nor does planning involve input from HR. Few organisations have HR specialists either at headquarters or in the field. A survey undertaken by People in Aid in 2004 found that allocating resources to HR was considered expensive and difficult to fund.[11] Very little funding was available to pay HR staff (at headquarters) a decent wage, and due to the funding situation, career planning was often not possible. The same survey found that HR staff often feels overburdened, undervalued and under-resourced. In addition, evaluating HR is not a priority in most organisations, and evaluations tend not to look at HR as a useful sector, in terms of what it can contribute to an organisation's effectiveness as a whole. There is, therefore, scant information on how and whether its HR practices are adding value to work with communities and beneficiaries.

Additional internal factors include the following:

- *Recruitment and recognition*: humanitarian organisations continue to struggle with surge capacity, an insufficient number of *surge* staff, which causes delays in programme delivery or impacts on quality. In addition, around 90 per cent of frontline aid workers are local/national staff or subcontractors, with many not recognised as humanitarian workers. National/local staff tends to find the international

[11] People In Aid (2004a, b).

humanitarian workplace disadvantageous in terms of career paths as they rarely have equal development opportunities or reward packages. Hence, most national staff feels that they are more exposed and under a greater burden of risk than their international counterparts, leaving significant room for improvement. The great majority of victims of attacks on humanitarian workers in 2012 (82%) were national staff, although the attack rate for international staff was actually more than twice as high.[12]

- *Staff turnover*: rapid turnover of expatriate staff has been cited by partners and local staff as being demotivating, having a negative impact on quality of programmes and making it difficult to cultivate a professional workforce.[13]
- *Remuneration and rewards*: applying clear, fair and consistent rewards and benefits remains difficult.
- *Motivation*: staff who enters the sector tends to be highly motivated, with strong beliefs in their organisation's values. However, keeping them engaged remains a challenge. A 2013 People in Aid study found that, in the short term, employees tend to deliver *above average* levels of performance despite (not because of) the organisation. Eventually, however, 'frustration with organisational practices, burnout and stress come to the fore'.[14]
- *Legal frameworks*: there seems to be general difficulty in reconciling the nature of humanitarian operations—that is, emergency work—with labour laws. In 2015, for example, the French Red Cross was accused of breaching labour laws by making employees work long hours. The Red Cross justified its actions by saying that it was 'dedicated to saving lives',[15] adding that 'in emergency and first-aid operations and in responding to disasters in France and internationally, our missions demand a high degree of mobilisation and availability of our employees and charity workers, regardless of the time of day or night [...] emergencies give no warning'.[16]
- *Management*: organisations (particularly major international organisations) are not good at handling poor or inadequate job performance.[17]

Despite and because of the above, HRM has been increasingly recognised as an essential component of humanitarian operations, including at the strategic level. In 1997, People in Aid developed the 'People in Aid Code of Best Practice in the management and support of aid personnel'.

In 2011, the Inter-Agency Standing Committee (IASC) endorsed five Commitments to Accountability to Affected Populations (CAAP), of which a commitment to leadership and governance includes major elements of HRM. In 2012, ALNAP

[12]Humanitarian Outcomes, Aid Worker Security Report, 2013, http://aidworkersecurity.org/sites/default/files/AidWorkerSecurityReport_2013_web.pdf.

[13]People in Aid (2013).

[14]*Id.*, p. 48.

[15]The Telegraph (31 May 2015), http://www.telegraph.co.uk/news/worldnews/europe/france/11641827/French-Red-Cross-faces-huge-fine-over-illegal-overtime.html.

[16]*Ibid.*

[17]James (2008).

identified six factors of effectiveness: timeliness, human resources, preparedness, coordination, leadership, as well as monitoring and evaluation. For OECD DAC, the major factors influencing achievement or non-achievement of objectives include aspects of human resources, such as staff competencies, management and leadership.

The work undertaken by People in Aid, IASC and ALNAP, as well as the inclusion of HRM concerns in the Sphere Standards, the Core Humanitarian Standard on Quality and Accountability and the Humanitarian Accountability Partnership (HAP), is not only symbolic of the increasing importance that HR has acquired for humanitarian organisations; it has also provided the sector with much-needed guidance and support in this area. The Code of Conduct in particular was developed with the express intention of improving agencies' support and management of their staff and volunteers. Figure 1 illustrates the main codes, standards and guidelines developed in the area of HR to date.

The push for greater professionalisation, be it through increasing the number of educational and training courses offered in humanitarian action or through other initiatives addressing the recognition and transfer of competencies, skills and knowledge in the sector, is also an explicit acknowledgment of the fact that it is humanitarian workers (national and international staff and volunteers) who make the difference. Three initiatives in particular should be highlighted.

First, in 2010, the Consortium of British Humanitarian Agencies (CBHA) renamed itself the Start Network[18] and developed the Core Humanitarian Competencies Framework. The framework provides a set of core humanitarian and leadership competencies, with the intention to improve human resource efficiencies, contribute to professionalisation in the sector, reduce the cost of staff turnover and assert an operational perspective in the design of academic and non-academic training programmes.[19] Together with the framework, CBHA developed a practical guide to support agencies in using it, based on an employee life cycle, and addressing different HR activities.[20]

Second, the European Universities on Professionalization of Humanitarian Action (EUPRHA),[21] recently renamed European Humanitarian Action Partnership (EUHAP),[22] worked extensively on a qualification framework for humanitarian

[18]The Start Network is a consortium of 24 leading NGOs working together to strengthen the humanitarian aid system. The consortium works in three areas: Start Fund (financing for emergency response); Start Build (strengthening civil society capacity); and Start Beta (creating platforms for partnerships and learning).

[19]HAP (2013), p. 39.

[20]CBHA (2011).

[21]EUPRHA is a network of 30 European universities, including 10 universities of the Network on Humanitarian Action (NOHA), two important associations—the Sphere project and the International Council of Voluntary Agencies, a global network of non-governmental organisations—and the NOHA Alumni Community, a significant body of humanitarian professionals.

[22]EUHAP is a partnership of four humanitarian sector stakeholders represented by academia (NOHA and 9 other European Universities), training providers (RedR and Bioforce), employers (Aktion Deutschland Hilft) and employees (humanitarian professionals represented by the NOHA Alumni).

IASC Commitment 1

Leadership/Governance demonstrate their commitment to accountability to affected populations by ensuring feedback and accountability mechanisms are integrated into country strategies, programme proposals, monitoring and evaluations, recruitment, staff inductions, training and performance management, partnership agreements, and highlighted in reporting.

(IASC, 2011)

IASC Commitments, Accountability to Affected Populations (2011), http://interagencystandingcommittee.org/system/files/legacy_files/IASC%20Principals%20commitments%20on%20AAP%20%2528CAAP%2529March%202013.pdf (accessed on 14 April 2017)

HAP Benchmark 2 – Staff Competency

The organisation ensures that staff have competencies that enable them to meet the organisation's requirements.

Requirements:

2.1. The organisations shall clearly define and document the knowledge, skills, behaviours and attitudes that staff need to meet its commitments.

2.2. The organisations shall have in place a staff code of conduct which refers to:

1. not exploiting and abusing people, including sexual exploitation and abuse;

2. being sensitive to local culture; and

3. the responsibility of staff to report abuses

2.3. The organisation shall ensure that staff understand the code of conduct and their responsibility under the accountability

Sphere – Code Standard 6

Humanitarian agencies provide appropriate management, supervisory and psychological support, enabling workers to have the knowledge, skills, behaviour and attitudes to plan and implement an effective humanitarian response with humanity and respect.

Key actions:

- *Provide managers with adequate leadership training, familiarity with key policies and the resources to manage effectively*
- *Establish systematic, fair and transparent recruitment procedures to attract a maximum number of appropriate candidates.*
- *Recruit teams with a balance of women and men, ethnicity, age and social background so that the team's diversity is appropriate to the local culture and context.*
- *Provide aid workers (staff, volunteers and consultants, both national and international) with adequate and timely inductions, briefings, clear reporting lines and updated job descriptions to enable them to understand their responsibilities, work objectives, organizational values, key*

Fig. 1 Examples of HR codes, standards and guidelines

framework. *2.4. The organisation shall regularly and consistently review and act on staff performance relating to knowledge, skills, behaviours and attitudes needed to meet commitments.* *2.5. The organisation shall continually develop its staff so that commitments are met more effectively.* *2.6. The organisation shall ensure that staff who interact with its partners understand the partnership agreements, the implications of the organisation's accountability framework for partners, and each partner's obligations.* *2.7. The organisations shall work with its partners to agree the knowledge, skills, behaviours and attitudes that a partner's staff need to meet agreed commitments, and to ensure these are reflected in a staff code of conduct (as in requirement 2.2).* *2.8. The organisation shall work with its partners to improve how partners implement and monitor their staff codes of conduct.* (HAP, 2010) HAP International (2013) Guide to the 2010 HAP Standard in Accountability and Quality Management. Geneva: HAP International, p. 31-32.	*policies and local context.* • *Establish security and evacuation guidelines, health and safety policies and use them to brief aid workers before they start work with the agency.* • *Ensure that aid workers have access to medical care and psychological support.* • *Establish codes of personal conduct for aid workers that protect disasters-affected people from sexual abuse, corruption, exploitation and other violations of people's human rights. Share the codes with disaster-affected people.* • *Promote a culture of respect towards the disaster-affected population.* • *Establish grievance procedures and take appropriate disciplinary action against aid workers following confirmed violation of the agency's code of conduct.* • *Carry out regular appraisal of staff and volunteers and provide feedback on performance in relation to work objectives, knowledge, skills, behaviour and attitudes.* • *Support aid workers to manage their workload and minimize stress.* • *Enable staff and managers to jointly identify opportunities fir continual learning and development.* • *Provide appropriate support to aid workers who have experienced or witnessed extremely distressing events.* (Sphere, 2011) The Sphere Project, Core Standard 6: Aid Worker Performance, http://www.spherehandbook.org/en/core-standard-6-aid-worker-performance/,

Fig. 1 (continued)

http://www.spherehandbook.org/en/core-standard-6-aid-worker-performance/ (accessed on 14 April 2017)

Core Humanitarian Standard on Quality and Accountability Commitment 8

(Additional HR components and issues are addressed in other sections of the CHS. Only the most relevant ones have been include in this table)

Communities and people affected by crisis receive the assistance they require from competent and well-managed staff and volunteers.

Quality criterion: staff are supported to do their job effectively, and treated fairly and equitably.

Key Actions

8.1 Staff work according to the mandate and values of the organisation and to agreed objectives and performance standards.

8.2 Staff adhere to the policies that are relevant to them and understand the consequences of not adhering to them.

8.3 Staff develop and use the necessary personal, technical and management competencies to fulfil their role and understand how the organisation can support them to do this.

Organisational Responsibilities

8.4 The organisation has the management and staff capacity and capability to deliver its programmes.

8.5 Staff policies and procedures are fair, transparent, non-discriminatory and compliant

Fig. 1 (continued)

with local employment law.

8.6 Job descriptions, work objectives and feedback processes are in place so that staff have a clear understanding of what is required of them.

8.7 A code of conduct is in place that establishes, at a minimum, the obligation of staff not to exploit, abuse or otherwise discriminate against people.

8.8 Policies are in place to support staff to improve their skills and competencies.

8.9 Policies are in place for the security and the wellbeing of staff.

(HAP, People in Aid, the Sphere Project, 2014)

HAP International, People In Aid and the Sphere Project, Core Humanitarian Standard on Quality and Accountability, p. 17 (2014), http://corehumanitarianstandard.org/files/files/Core%20Humanitarian%20Standard%20-%20English.pdf (accessed on 14 April 2017)

People In Aid Code of good practice in the management and support of aid personnel

Guiding Principle: People are central to the achievement of our mission.

Principle 1: Human Resources strategy: Human resources are an integral part of our strategic and operational plans.

Indicators:

1. *Our organisational strategy or business plan explicitly values staff for their contribution to organisational and operational objectives.*
2. *The organisational strategy allocates sufficient human and financial resources to achieve the objectives of the human resources strategy.*
3. *Operational plans and budgets aim to reflect fully our responsibilities for staff management, support, development and well-being. The monitoring of these plans and budgets feeds into any necessary improvements.*
4. *Our human resources strategy reflects our commitment to promote inclusiveness and diversity.*

Principle 2: Staff Policies and Practices: Our human resources policies aim to be effective, fair and transparent

1. *Policies and practices that relate to staff employment are set out in writing and are monitored and reviewed, particularly when significant changes in the legal or working environment take place.*
2. *The policies and practices we implement are consistent in their application to all staff*

Fig. 1 (continued)

except while taking into account relevant legal provisions and cultural norms.

3. *Staff are familiarised with policies and practices that affect them.*
4. *Appropriate guidance is provided to managers so that they are equipped to implement policies effectively.*
5. *The rewards and benefits for each role are clearly identified and applied in a fair and consistent manner.*
6. *Policies and practices are monitored according to how well they meet:*
   - *organisational and programme aims*
   - *reasonable considerations of effectiveness, fairness and transparency.*

Principle 3: Managing People: Good support, management and leadership of our staff is key to our effectiveness

1. *Relevant training, support and resources are provided to managers to fulfil their responsibilities. Leadership is a part of this training.*
2. *Staff have clear work objectives and performance standards, know whom they report to and what management support they will receive. A mechanism for reviewing staff performance exists and is clearly understood by all staff.*
3. *In assessing performance, managers will adhere to the organisation's procedures and values.*
4. *All staff are aware of grievance and disciplinary procedures.*

Principle 4: Consultation and Communication: Dialogue with staff on matters likely to affect their employment enhances the quality and effectiveness of our policies and practices.

1. *Staff are informed and adequately consulted when we develop or review human resources policies or practices that affect them.*
2. *Managers and staff understand the scope of consultation and how to participate, individually or collectively.*

Principle 5: Recruitment and Selection: Our policies and practices aim to attract and select a diverse workforce with the skills and capabilities to fulfil our requirements

1. *Written policies and procedures outline how staff are recruited and selected to positions in our organisation.*
2. *Recruitment methods aim to attract the widest pool of suitably qualified candidates.*

Fig. 1 (continued)

3. *Our selection process is fair, transparent and consistent to ensure the most appropriate person is appointed.*
4. *Appropriate documentation is maintained and responses are given to candidates regarding their selection/non-selection to posts. We will provide feedback if necessary.*
5. *The effectiveness and fairness of our recruitment and selection procedures are monitored.*

Principle 6: Learning, Training and Development: Learning, training and staff development are promoted throughout the organisation

1. *Adequate induction, and briefing specific to each role, is given to all staff.*
2. *Written policies outline the training, development and learning opportunities staff can expect from the organisation.*
3. *Plans and budgets are explicit about training provision. Relevant training is provided to all staff.*
4. *Managers know how to assess the learning needs of staff so they can facilitate individual development. Where appropriate training and development will be linked to external qualifications.*
5. *The methods we have in place to monitor learning and training ensure that the organisation also learns. They also monitor the effectiveness of learning and training in meeting organisational and programme aims as well as staff expectations of fairness and transparency.*

Principle 7: Health, Safety and Security: The security, good health and safety of our staff are a prime responsibility of our organisation

1. *Written policies are available to staff on security, individual health, care and support, health and safety.*
2. *Programme plans include written assessment of security, travel and health risks specific to the country or region, reviewed at appropriate intervals.*
3. *Before an international assignment all staff receive health clearance. In addition, they and accompanying dependents receive verbal and written briefing on all risks relevant to the role to be undertaken, and the measures in place to mitigate those risks, including insurance. Agency obligations and individual responsibilities in relation to possible risks are clearly communicated. Briefings are updated when new equipment, procedures or risks are identified.*
4. *Security plans, with evacuation procedures, are reviewed regularly.*

Fig. 1 (continued)

5. *Records are maintained of work-related injuries, sickness, accidents and fatalities, and are monitored to help assess and reduce future risk to staff.*
6. *Workplans do not require more hours work than are set out in individual contracts. Time off and leave periods, based on written policies, are mandatory.*
7. *All staff have a debriefing or exit interview at the end of any contract or assignment. Health checks, personal counselling and careers advice are available. Managers are trained to ensure these services are provided.*

In the case of staff on emergency rosters, managers should ensure that health clearance, immunisations and procedures for obtaining the correct prophylaxes and other essential supplies are arranged well in advance.

(People In Aid, 2003)

People in Aid, Code of Good Practice in the Management and Support of Aid Personnel, p. 7-20 (2003), http://reliefweb.int/sites/reliefweb.int/files/resources/DA4AA643ACE54425C1256C6B003B903A-pia-code.pdf (accessed on 14 April 2017)

Fig. 1 (continued)

action. The Humanitarian Action Qualifications Framework (HAQF) aims to be a neutral reference point for all types of qualification in the humanitarian sector in order to assist in the identification of potential progression routes in the context of lifelong learning and to support workers' and learners' mobility within the humanitarian sector and across sectors.

Third, in March 2010 and March 2012, Enhancing Learning and Research for Humanitarian Assistance (ELRHA) undertook two studies focusing on professionalisation.[23]

The first study informed the humanitarian sector of its uneven provision and fragmented and uncoordinated approaches to developing people and teams. It recommended, *inter alia*, the creation of professional pathways and progression routes into the humanitarian sector, formalising occupational standards for humanitarian work and quality marking of learning and development providers. It also recommended the formation of a dedicated and independent humanitarian professional association.

The second study further explored the state of professional development in the sector, looking at barriers and blockages, endorsement of core humanitarian competencies, the concept of a learning and development passport and the possible development of a professional association for humanitarian workers.

[23]Russ (2012) and Walker et al. (2010).

Discussion

Think about Egeland's statement at the beginning of this section.

In an emergency, who are the true first responders?

In the case of a lack of qualified locals, should our response be to bring in more expatriate staff or invest in equipping and empowering local potential?

How do we engage volunteers and professionalise amateurs?

How do we equip and empower?

3 Human Research Management Tasks

IHRM and HRM are not only important for HR managers. All employees are in one way or another affected by HR because HR policies, strategies and practices impact their work and lives; because they may have to manage teams; and/or because they may be involved in HR activities. This concerns line managers, in particular, because while an important part of their work may be devoted to managing people, HR is often not their primary function.

The division of HR tasks and responsibilities between HR specialists, line managers and other employees differs from one organisation to another. Smaller organisations may not have HR departments at all, with line managers taking up HR responsibilities. Even when there are fully fledged HR departments, the scope of work within these departments may vary, depending on the importance attributed to HRM, the extent to which HR specialists contribute to an organisation's overall strategy and whether their activities are restricted to an administrative function.

Table 4 shows the main activities falling under the responsibility of human resource practitioners, both specialists and line managers who are involved in one aspect or another of human resource management.

All HRM activities are generally rooted in an HRM system developed within the respective organisation. Some of these systems, or parts of them, will be explicitly laid out, especially in larger humanitarian organisations. This means that there is an established system that is translated into a set of manuals or written procedures, accessible to all staff. These include staff policies and internal regulations, as well as any other information impacting staff, taking into account both headquarter and country-level factors. Other systems, or parts of them, are implicit, stemming from the prevailing culture of the organisation and from the way it has grown and evolved. Good employment and HR management practices depend on a number of factors as discussed above, including culture, the legal systems and the political and social environment. While the private sector has witnessed a surge of very creative management and leadership practices, this development has not permeated through to humanitarian organisations. This is perhaps due to the complexity of the humanitarian field and the contexts in which humanitarian organisations operate. The sector is timidly accepting the need to invest in institutions rather than projects, especially where crises are chronic and international aid is receding. The demands of the sector, and the

Table 4 The main activities of human resource practitioners

Main areas of activity of a human resource management specialist	Examples of involvement of human resource management specialist	Examples of involvement of line manager
Recruitment and selection	Design policies and procedures for fair recruitment and selection Carry out interview or monitor and give advice on interview technique or in terms and conditions of employment	Prepare and carry out interviews Participate in selecting successful candidates
Learning and talent development	Involved in planning and learning and development opportunities for the whole organisation (for example, developing formal training courses, online materials or less formal approaches such as coaching or mentoring) Design and organise training courses Keep training records centrally and request information from line managers as part of planning exercise or for monitoring purposes	May also be involved in planning and provision of training and talent development opportunities, primarily for employees in their own department
Human resource planning	Likely to be involved to various degrees in contributing to the strategic plan Collection and analysis of data, monitoring targets Providing information to managers Conducting exit interviews and analysing reasons for leaving	Collect information on leavers and provide information on anticipated requirements for employees in their department
Provision of contracts	Provide and issue written statement of particulars for new employees Keep all employee-related records and documentation Advise on any alterations to contracts	
Provision of fair treatment	Design of policies and procedures to encourage fair treatment at work Inform and train people in these policies and procedures Monitor success of policies	Responsible for fair treatment of people in their own department Listen and respond to grievances as an initial stage of grievance procedure or informally Possibly make suggestions about design of policies
Equal opportunities	Design policies to encourage equal opportunities Inform and train managers and all employees in these policies and procedures Monitor the effectiveness of the policies	Ensure that employees under their responsibility do not suffer from any form of unfair discrimination at work

(continued)

Table 4 (continued)

Main areas of activity of a human resource management specialist	Examples of involvement of human resource management specialist	Examples of involvement of line manager
Managing diversity	Develop policies about diversity and promoting and ensuring a diverse workforce through the organisation	

Reproduced by kind permission of the publisher from Foot, M.; Hook, C., Introducing Human Resource Management, pp. 35–38 (Pearson Education Limited, 5th ed. 2008)

Table 5 Key steps in HR activities, good practices and recommendations

HR activity	Key steps	Good practices and recommendations
Recruitment and selection	Planning, issuing vacancy notices, collecting and assessing applications, conducting interviews and selecting the applicant	*Introduce use of rosters*: they are being used as a way to recruit talent fast. The START network aims to build shared surge capacity in a number of countries over the next 3 years.
		Introduce workflow forecasting: like cash flow forecasting, it encourages the HR function to gather information about future skills needs and ensure that the finances are available to support it. This gives time to upskill existing staff.
		Strengthen collaboration with other organisations: especially in terms of secondments, rosters, job training and talent exchange.
Retention and career development	Establishing management and leadership systems, including performance appraisal, staff development, staff retention, talent management	*Invest in national staff development* and consider the growing capacities of national governments to meet the needs of their own citizens in times of disaster, in advance of launching efforts.
		Invest in talent: how do humanitarian organisations deal with the talent shortage and access the right talent, and how do they unleash and leverage its human potential? This can be done through • collaborative work such as shared surge rosters; • using social media for recruitment;

(continued)

Table 5 (continued)

HR activity	Key steps	Good practices and recommendations
		• greater pay equity (especially as talent shifts from expatriates to national staff, with diaspora recruitment also being a factor); • actively seeking talent within the organisation. *Consult with staff:* also about HR activities. *Value staff engagement*: more consideration should be given to the importance of staff engagement. The aid sector benefits from more motivated staff with a stronger belief in their organisation's values than the private sector. Cerus Consulting (2013) found that many charities' approach to measuring employee engagement is flawed. The study demonstrated that, in the short term, employees often deliver 'above average' levels of performance despite (and not because of) the organisation. However, this was at a price: 'eventually frustration with organisational practices, burnout and stress come to the fore (. . .)'. Consequently, organisational performance will suffer, as well as employee well-being. *Train more and better:* MOOCs, blended learning and serious games are new forms of training. Humanitarians spend 95 per cent of their time in action and five per cent in training—the inverse of professional military forces. Many aid organisations have developed without a culture of training, rely on flawed training of trainer models, are reluctant to invest in training for fear of increasing funds spent on administration or consume too much time writing proposals and reports. Nevertheless, the effectiveness of an organisation

(continued)

Table 5 (continued)

HR activity	Key steps	Good practices and recommendations
		depends not only on its capacity to develop the skill set of its staff but also on its own ability to be a learning organisation.

Reproduced by kind permission of the publisher from Foot, M.; Hook, C., Introducing Human Resource Management, pp. 35–38 (Pearson Education Limited, 5th ed. 2008)

difficulties it faces in various aspects of HR processes, do make the case for a more creative and proactive HR management and engagement (Table 5).[24]

References

Armstrong M (2006) Human resource management practice, 10th edn

Brewster C et al (2011) International human resource management, 3rd edn. Chartered Institute of Personnel and Development, London

CBHA (2011) Core Humanitarian Competencies Guide – Humanitarian Capacity Building Throughout the Employee Life Cycle

Egeland J (2009) Saving human lives is no place for amateurs. http://reliefweb.int/report/indonesia/jan-egeland-saving-human-lives-no-place-amateurs

Foot M, Hook C (2008) Introducing human resource management, 5th edn. Prentice Hall/Financial Times, Harlow, England, New York

Gratton L (2010) Lynda Gratton investigates: the future of work. Bus Strateg Rev [Online] Q3. 16–23

Gratton L, Truss C (2003) The three-dimensional people strategy: Putting human resources policies into action. Academy of Management Executive 17(3):74–86

HAP International, People In Aid and the Sphere Project (2014) Core Humanitarian Standard on Quality and Accountability. http://corehumanitarianstandard.org/files/files/Core%20Humanitarian%20Standard%20-%20English.pdf

HAP International (2013) 2013 Humanitarian accountability report. Guide to the 2010 HAP Standard in Accountability and Quality Management. HAP International, Geneva

Inter-Agency Standing Committee (2011) IASC Commitments, Accountability to Affected Populations. http://interagencystandingcommittee.org/system/files/legacy_files/IASC%20Principals%20commitments%20on%20AAP%20%2528CAAP%2529March%202013.pdf

James E (2008) Managing humanitarian relief – an operational guide for NGOs. Practical Action Publishing, Warwickshire

Pankhurst M (2008) Building HR Capacity Handbook. People In Aid

People In Aid (2003) Code of good practice in the management and support of aid personnel

People In Aid (2004a) Enhancing quality management in the humanitarian sector – a practical guide

People In Aid (2004b) Understanding HR in the humanitarian sector – a baseline for enhancing quality in management

[24]Gratton (2010) and Gratton and Truss (2003).

People In Aid (2013) The state of HR 2013
Russ C (2012) Global Survey on Humanitarian Professionalisation. ELRHA
The Sphere Project (2013) Humanitarian charter and minimum standards in humanitarian response. Practical Action Publishing, Rugby
Walker P et al (2010) Professionalising the humanitarian sector, A scoping study. ELRHA

Sophie Borel has 19 years of field experience in the human rights and humanitarian action sectors, having managed a wide range of projects and programmes in many countries, including Cambodia, the Democratic Republic of the Congo, Jordan, Lebanon and Yemen. She currently acts as General Manager of the NOHA Network.

Financial Management

Philip Byrne

1 Introduction

The purpose of this chapter is to explore some of the key aspects of financial management that are relevant and important for non-governmental organisation (NGOs) today in managing donor-funded projects. The following four key areas of financial management are examined for the purpose of this chapter:

Area 1: Budget Management
Area 2: Financial Reporting
Area 3: Assessing an NGO partners' financial management capacity
Area 4: Audit and Control

The first part on budget management analyses some of the key criteria used by donors in appraising donor-funded projects, with a particular focus on the requirement of NGOs to link project proposals' budget components to the project plan. The chapter also examines the requirement of donors for NGOs to effectively manage and control their budgets through effective variance analysis and reporting. The human aspects of budget preparation and budgetary control are also examined.

The second part discusses where the responsibilities of NGOs lie in terms of financial reporting, including examining the key users of financial reports and the key financial reports required by donors.

The third part analyses the rationale behind NGOs assessing the financial capacity of their partners. This section of the chapter will also examine how NGOs can use a financial management health check toolkit to facilitate this task.

P. Byrne (✉)
Institute of Public Administration in Dublin, Dublin, Ireland
e-mail: pbyrne@ipa.ie

© Springer International Publishing AG 2018

H.-J. Heintze, P. Thielbörger (eds.), *International Humanitarian Action*,
DOI 10.1007/978-3-319-14454-2_25

The final part of the chapter explores a number of key aspects associated with effective audit and control, particularly the relationships between corporate governance risk management and internal controls.

2 Budget Management

According to Jacobs Alex et al., there is an increasing awareness that management techniques are crucial to project success in NGOs.[1] Generally, private NGOs have either a community or an environmental focus. They address a variety of issues such as religion, emergency aid or humanitarian affairs. They mobilise public support and voluntary contributions for aid, often have strong links with community groups in developing countries and usually work in areas where government-to-government aid is not possible. NGOs are accepted as a part of the international relations landscape, and while they influence national and multilateral policymaking, they are increasingly involved directly in local action.

All NGOs, irrespective of size, need budgets to operate, with amounts differing between organisations, as Mbugua states.[2] Unlike the budgets of smaller NGOs, those of larger NGOs may number in the hundreds of millions or billions of dollars or euros.

Keeping such large budgets afloat demands significant fundraising efforts on the part of most NGOs. Major sources of NGO funding include membership dues, the sale of goods and services, grants from international institutions or national governments, such as EU grants and private donations. Several EU grants provide funds accessible to NGOs. Although the term NGO implies independence from governments, many NGOs depend heavily on them for their funding.

2.1 *Overhead*

Overhead is the amount of money that is spent on running an NGO rather than on specific projects. It includes office expenses, salaries, banking and bookkeeping costs.

The percentage of overall budget spent on overhead is often used as a criterion to assess the soundness of an NGO's inner workings, with less than 4% viewed as very favourable.

The World Association of Non-Governmental Organisations, for its part, states that ideally more than 86% of funds should be spent on programmes (with less than

---

[1] Jacobs et al. (2004).

[2] Mbugua et al. (2008), http://www.securethefuture.com/Shared%20Documents/resource/financemng.pdf.

20% allocated to overhead). The Global Fund to Fight AIDS, Tuberculosis and Malaria has developed specific guidelines for orientation on how high the level of overhead may be in order to qualify for funding. In many cases, overhead needs to be less than 5–7%. An elevated percentage of overhead as compared to total expenditures can make it more difficult to generate funds. High overhead costs may also generate criticism with some claiming that certain NGOs with high overhead are run simply to benefit bosses and staff instead of the people working for them.

While overhead costs can be a legitimate concern, a sole focus on them can be counterproductive. Research published by the Urban Institute and the Center for Social Innovation at Stanford University has shown how rating agencies create incentives for nonprofits to lower and hide overhead costs, which may actually reduce organisational effectiveness by starving organisations of the infrastructure they need to effectively deliver services. A more meaningful rating system would provide more than financial data, a qualitative evaluation of an organisation's transparency and governance along the following lines: (1) an assessment of programme effectiveness, (2) an evaluation of feedback mechanisms designed for donors and beneficiaries and (3) opportunities for organisations to respond to evaluations by rating agencies. More generally, the popular discourse of nonprofit evaluation should move away from financial notions of organisational effectiveness and towards a more substantive understanding of programmatic impact.

2.2 Monitoring and Control

A report by former U.N. Secretary General Kofi Annan in favour of international humanitarian intervention argues that the international community has a 'right to protect citizens of the world against ethnic cleansing, genocide, and crimes against humanity'.[3] On the heels of the report, the Canadian government launched the Responsibility to Protect (R2P) project to clarify the issue of humanitarian intervention. While the R2P doctrine has been widely applied, it has also generated a considerable amount of controversy. The latter includes the Canadian government invoking the R2P to justify its intervention and support of the coup in Haiti. More recently, the World Federalist Movement, an organisation that is in favour of *the creation of democratic global structures accountable to the citizens of the world and call for the division of international authority among separate agencies*,[4] has launched Responsibility to Protect—Engaging Civil Society (R2PCS). A collaboration between the World Federalist Movement (WFM) and the Canadian government, the project aims to bring NGOs into lockstep with the principles outlined under the framework of the original R2P project.

---

[3]Previts et al. (2010).

[4]World Federalist Movement, Our Movement, http://www.wfm-igp.org/our-movement.

The governments of the countries where an NGO works or is registered in may require reporting or other monitoring and oversight. Donors generally require reporting and assessment, from the NGOs they allocate funds to, as such information is not necessarily publicly available. There may also be associations and watchdog organisations that research and publish details on the actions of NGOs working in particular geographic or programme areas.

In recent years, many large corporations have increased their corporate social responsibility departments in an attempt to pre-empt NGO campaigns against certain corporate practices. According to this reasoning, if corporations work with NGOs, NGOs will not work *against* corporations. Greater collaboration between corporations and NGOs creates inherent risks of the stronger party co-opting its weaker partner, typically the nonprofit involved.

2.3 Linking Budget and Project Plans

Most donors, when evaluating proposals, test whether the project budget is realistic and links logically to the projects' objectives, outputs and activities. The compilation of the budget is usually prescribed by the donors and broken down into categories, including personnel costs, direct programme costs, capital equipment costs and programme support/overhead costs. In order to align the budget with the plan, some unit of measure is used to derive the number of units and use them to calculate the budget by multiplying the number of units by the unit cost. In relation to personnel costs, this budget line heading usually includes all staff associated with the direct implementation of the project, and it is normally broken down to indicate costs associated with local and expatriate staff. In most large donor-funded projects, a clear justification for the use of expatriate staff should be provided.

Examples of direct programme costs could include the cost of supplies and materials for the distribution to individual or groups of beneficiaries, as well as entire project areas, such as procurement, storage and distribution costs, for example medicines, blankets, household items, seeds/tools, etc. Other examples of direct programme costs could include the costs associated with post-conflict reconstruction, including the breakdown of materials and associated labour costs. The cost of in-house training, including in-country workshops and seminars directly associated with project implementation, is seen as direct programme costs and should be appropriately budgeted for.

Under the capital equipment budget heading, the purchase of capital equipment, such as vehicles, computers, faxes, copy machines, is a regular part of the budget. However, organisations must normally justify why equipment is needed and how it is to be used/disposed of after the end of the project. Programme support costs are normally budgeted for and provided by donors particularly where justification is provided. Costs under this budget heading typically include office rent, electricity, water charges, office supplies, telephone charges, fuel and maintenance and general administration fees. The final key budget line that NGOs look for in donor funding regards management support costs. These are referred to as head office costs and normally should not exceed 6% of the total budget.

3 Budgetary Control

Budgetary control is crucially important for the survival of any organisation, whether in the private, public or not-for-profit sectors.[5] From both an applicant's and a donor's perspective, effective budgetary control ensures proper accountability, transparency and effective disbursement of donor funds. Budgetary control (often referred to as variance analysis) is a key mechanism to identify over- and underspending and to prepare appropriate action to manage the budget. Some donors (for example, Irish Aid or USAID) require NGOs to provide them with periodic budgetary control reports. These reports usually contain financial information comparing the current budget to actual expenditure for the period assessed and explains and identifies key variances.

4 The Human Dimension to Budget Preparation and Budgetary Control

In order to ensure that NGO budgets are properly prepared, sound financial practice requires guaranteeing that project staff members with the necessary expertise are allowed to participate in the preparation of organisations' budgets. In a nonprofit NGO environment, this process usually enables buy-ins from key project staff and motivates them to manage the budget effectively. Tracy posits that every organisation needs to ensure that project managers and the staff are an integral part of the budgetary process.[6] Bhimani states that proper feedback on managing budgets is essential for motivating people in organisations.[7] This can involve providing feedback to staff members verbally and in a written format. According to Reck, people within organisations are most motivated when provided with objective, democratic and participative, constructive feedback as to how they handled the budgets.[8]

[5]Drury (2015).

[6]Tracy (2013).

[7]Bhimani et al. (2013).

[8]Reck (2012).

5 Financial Reporting

The financial reports produced by NGOs provide a summary of their income and expenditure for a particular period. They allow NGOs (and other stakeholders) to monitor their financial position. For instance, they help to evaluate whether an NGO has sufficient monetary assets to pay salaries at the end of each month, complete projects or fund plans for the upcoming year. According to Walton, financial reports have to be timely, accurate and relevant.[9] They must also be easy to read. So it is always important for NGOs to talk to users about what sort of reports they find easy to use.

NGOs prepare financial reports for different audiences, including managers, trustees, beneficiaries, donors and the government, all of which may have different expectations as to what reports should comprise. Using these reports, NGO staff and donors can monitor whether activities are going ahead as planned (and whether there are enough funds to sustain projects in the future).

Beneficiaries may comment on whether funds are being spent on their real needs, whereas governments and trustees monitor the NGOs' behaviour from a legal perspective.

As financial reports are used by many different internal and external stakeholders, different kinds of reports are needed for different audiences. During the financial year, project managers summarise accounting information and compare it to the budget for internal monitoring. These reports are usually referred to as management accounts and/or variance reports.

At the end of the year, the annual accounts (or financial statements, made up of a balance sheet and income and expenditure statement) report on the outcome for the year. These reports provide information that is historic and are mainly targeted at external stakeholders. During the year, NGOs also provide donor reports to funding agencies. These usually include both financial and written progress reports. In this vein, it is important for NGOs to set up their accounting systems (especially accounting codes) to meet their various reporting needs. Reporting to donors can be complicated if NGOs have to use their own specific formats.

Assessing Financial Management Capacity of Partners Many donors require NGOs (particularly international NGOs) to use local partners to conduct their projects. Therefore, assessing the financial capacity of local partners is crucially important to identify any potential existing weaknesses or risks. The following are examples of best practice financial management areas that NGOs look for when assessing local partners:

- financial health;
- capacity of partner and its staff required to implement the project;
- internal controls and procedures in place;
- no overt reliance on a single donor;

[9]Walton and Aerts (2009).

- communication systems of the local partners;
- links and relationships with beneficiaries, that is, the local communities to whom one wants to deliver aid;
- a valid supporting document for every transaction (securely filed and stored for the minimum period required);
- a cash book for every bank account, reconciled every month;
- a Chart of Accounts—used consistently in the accounting records and budgets;
- a budget detailing costs and anticipated income for all operations;
- clear delegation of authority—from the governing body through the line management structure;
- separation of duties—sharing financial duties between at least two people; and
- annual financial statements—preferably audited by an independent person.

Audit and Control Corporate governance is concerned with managing management.[10] It denotes the system that directs and controls organisations. It is about the structures and processes that are in place at the top of an entity for organisational decision-making, accountability, controls and behaviour. It also refers to the way in which organisations manage their business, determine strategy and objectives and go about achieving them. At the heart of most organisations—private or public—lies the separation of ownership and control and the issues this creates. The Chartered Institute of Public Finance and Accountancy (CIPFA) has defined corporate governance as '[t]he arrangements put in place to ensure that the intended outcomes for stakeholders are defined and achieved'.[11]

Risk is the threat that an event or action will adversely affect an organisation's ability to achieve its objectives and to successfully execute its strategies. It has also been defined as the chance of something happening that will have an impact on business objectives.

Risk management is the process by which risks are identified, evaluated, controlled and monitored. Risks manifest themselves in two ways: as direct threats (damaging events), which may lead to failure to achieve objectives, and opportunities (constructive events), which if exploited could offer an improved way of achieving objectives but which are surrounded by threats. The essence of risk is the uncertainty of outcome (whether positive or negative). The term exposure refers to the combination of the probability of these potential risks and the magnitude of their impact.

Probability means the evaluated probability of a particular outcome actually happening (including a consideration of the frequency with which the outcome may arise). Lastly, impact is the evaluated effect or result of a particular outcome actually happening.

Table 1 offers a summary of the most common categories of risk that could apply to an NGO with examples of the nature of the source and effect issues. It does not

[10]Carlsson (2001).

[11]IFAC/CIPFA, Independent Framework: Good Governance in the Public Sector, New York/London 2014.

Table 1 Categories of risk

External	
1. Infrastructure	Relating to infrastructures such as transport systems for staff, power supply systems, suppliers, business relationships with partners, dependency on the Internet and e-mail
2. Economic	Relating to economic factors such as interest rates, exchange rates, inflation
3. Legal and regulatory	Relating to the laws and regulations that if complied with should reduce hazards (for example—Health and Safety at Work Act)
4. Environmental	Relating to issues such as fuel consumption, pollution
5. Political	Relating to possible constraints such as change of government
6. Market	Relating to issues such as competition and supply of goods
7. 'Act of God'	Relating to issues such as fire, flood, earthquake
Financial	
8. Budgetary/ financial	Relating to the availability of resources or the allocation of resources
9. Fraud or theft	Relating to the unproductive loss of resources
10. Insurable	Relating to the potential areas of loss that can be insured against
11. Capital investment	Relating to the making of appropriate investment decisions
12. Liability	Relating to the right to sue or to be sued under certain circumstances
Activity	
13. Policy	Relating to the appropriateness and quality of policy decisions
14. Operational	Relating to the procedures employed to achieve particular objectives
15. Information	Relating to the adequacy of information that is used for decision-making
16. Reputational	Relating to the public reputation of the organisation and consequent effects
17. Transferable	Relating to risks that may be transferred or to transfer of risks at inappropriate cost
18. Technological	Relating to the use of technology to achieve objectives
19. Project	Relating to project planning and management procedures
20. Innovation	Relating to the exploitation of opportunities to make gains
Human Resources	
21. Personnel	Relating to the availability and retention of suitable staff
22. Health and safety	Relating to the well-being of people
Others	
23. Inter-agency	Relating to work and activities of external bodies
24. Intra-agency	Relating to internal activities and support services

Reproduced by kind permission of the publisher from Christopher L. Culp, The Risk Management Process: Business Strategy and Tactics (Wiley, 2001)

purport to be comprehensive as some organisations may be able to identify other categories of risk applicable to their work.

Internal Control System It comprises the control environment and control procedures. It includes all policies and procedures (internal controls) adopted by management to assist in achieving their objective of ensuring, as far as practicable, the orderly and efficient conduct of the organisation's activities, including adherence to internal policies, the safeguarding of assets, the prevention and detection of fraud and error, the accuracy and completeness of the accounting records and the timely preparation of reliable financial information.[12] The board and senior management are responsible for ensuring an adequate and appropriate internal control system.

Control environment means the overall attitude, awareness and actions of the board, management and staff regarding internal controls and their importance within the organisation. It encompasses the management style, corporate culture and values shared by all employees and provides the background against which various other controls are operated. However, a strong control environment does not, by itself, ensure the effectiveness of the overall internal control system. Factors reflected in the control environment include the following:

- philosophy and operating style of the board, management and staff;
- entity's organisational structure and methods of assigning authority and responsibility; and
- mechanisms of imposing control, including the internal audit and review functions, management actions, assurance and compliance arrangements and organisational policies and procedures.

It is the responsibility of management to establish and foster a control environment which is economic, efficient and effective and which ensures that

- activities are conducted efficiently and in compliance with the organisation's objectives, policies, plans and procedures;
- assets are safeguarded and properly accounted for;
- there is reliability and integrity of financial and operational databases and controls;
- there is a provision of relevant and reliable corporate and operational management information to support tactical and strategic decision-making; and
- there is compliance with legislation, regulations, directive and directions.

Control procedures are policies and procedures complementing the control environment and that are established to achieve specific objectives.[13] They include, in particular, procedures and processes designed to prevent or to detect and correct control weaknesses, to address compliance gaps and to prevent, detect and correct errors. The primary responsibility for managing risks lies with line management. Internal audit's involvement should stop short of responsibility and accountability for risk management across the organisation and of managing risks on management's behalf. However, in order to add value, it is often beneficial for internal audit to give proactive advice or to coach management on embedding risk management

[12]Leitch (2008).

[13]American Institute of Certified Public Accountants, Internal Control over Financial Reporting, 2006.

processes into business activities. Internal audit has a vital role in challenging established risk management processes, in challenging risk identification and, more fundamentally, in providing assurance to officers and members on the effectiveness of controls. However, this is separate from the activity of establishing and operating risk management processes and control structure, which is the responsibility of management.

6 Conclusion

This chapter has examined a number of key areas that NGOs, large and small, should be aware of from a financial management perspective. In seeking donor funding, NGOs have to ensure that the project budget is intrinsic to the project plan, which means that the budget is realistic and directly relates to project activities, outputs and objectives. The chapter has also highlighted that, from a donor-funding perspective, it is crucial that NGOs effectively manage their budgets through proper and efficient budgetary control systems. The second part illustrated the importance for NGOs to produce financial reports. Some of the key reports that are statutorily required for NGOs include their annual financial statements. These are reports of the income and expenditure, assets and liabilities, and capital and reserves of an NGO for a particular period. They are normally audited by an external auditing firm and are used by many stakeholders. The third section of this chapter dealt with the need to assess the financial capacity of local partners. This is particularly important for international NGOs, which are required, from a donor-funding and capacity-building perspective, to involve local partners in their projects. The chapter presented a basic financial health checklist that may be used in assessing the financial capacity of local NGOs. The final part of this chapter looked at the area of governance and control. In particular, it examined the relationship between corporate governance, risk management and internal controls. This relationship is of paramount importance for NGOs in the management, transparency, accountability and stewardship of donor funds.

References

Bhimani A, Horngren C, Datar S, Rajan M (2013) Management and cost accounting, 5th edn. Harlow

Carlsson RH (2001) Ownership and value creation: strategic corporate governance in the new economy. New York

Drury C (2015) Management and cost accounting, 9th edn. Boston

Jacobs A, Lewis T, Manji F (2004) Practical financial management for NGOs

Leitch M (2008) Intelligent internal control and risk management: designing high-performance risk control systems

Mbugua R, Njaramba A, Young D, Mtshali P (2008) NGO financial management pocket guide, http://www.securethefuture.com/Shared%20Documents/resource/financemng.pdf
Previts G, Wolnizer P, Walton P (2010) A global history of accounting, financial reporting and public policy. Bingley
Reck JL (2012) Accounting for governmental and non-profit entities, 16th edn. New York
Tracy JA (2013) Accounting for dummies
Walton P, Aerts W (2009) Global financial accounting and reporting, principles and analysis, 2nd edn. Cengage/South-Western, London

Philip Byrne is a Senior Local Government and Finance Specialist with the Institute of Public Administration in Dublin, Ireland. He has been a Financial Management Lecturer for 25 years at a variety of institutions.

GPSR Compliance
The European Union's (EU) General Product Safety Regulation (GPSR) is a set of rules that requires consumer products to be safe and our obligations to ensure this.

If you have any concerns about our products, you can contact us on

ProductSafety@springernature.com

In case Publisher is established outside the EU, the EU authorized representative is:

Springer Nature Customer Service Center GmbH
Europaplatz 3
69115 Heidelberg, Germany

www.ingramcontent.com/pod-product-compliance
Lightning Source LLC
Chambersburg PA
CBHW070922121225
36515CB00044B/300
* 9 7 8 3 3 1 9 1 4 4 5 3 5 *